KT-153-740

Scotland

Neil Wilson
Alan Murphy

ORKNEY (p398) Remote northern islands with evocative prehistoric sites, spectacular sea cliffs and superb bird-watching

SHETLAND ISLANDS

Unst
Fetlar
Yell
Linga
Ulsta
Toft
Whalsay
Voe
Symbister
Bixter
Hillswick
South Nesting Bay
Papa Stour
Sandness
Mainland
Scalloway
Lerwick
Bressay
Quendale
Mousa
Foula

To Shetland Islands (see inset)

CAIRNGORM MOUNTAINS (p325) Subarctic plateau with unique flora and fascinating wildlife, good hiking, mountaineering and other outdoor activities

GLEN TORRIDON (p370) Perhaps the most beautiful corner of the northwest Highlands, with superb mountain and coastal scenery and excellent hill walking

ISLE OF SKYE (p373) The classic Scottish island of crofts and castles, with jagged mountain peaks, wild moors and brooding sea cliffs

ELEVATION
- 1200m
- 900m
- 600m
- 300m
- 0

LEGEND
- Motorway
- Primary
- Secondary

0 — 50 km
0 — 30 miles

ATLANTIC OCEAN

ORKNEY ISLANDS

Westray
Sanday
Eday
Rousay
Shapinsay
Stromness
Kirkwall
Stronsay
Copinsay
Mainland
Hoy
South Ronaldsay
John O'Groats

Cape Wrath
Durness
Tongue
Bettyhill
Melvich
Scrabster
Thurso
Halkirk
Castletown
Watten
Wick
Lybster
Dunbeath
Helmsdale
Brora
Golspie
Kinbrace
Kildonan

Kinlochbervie
Scourie
Handa
Point of Stoer
Lochinver
Ullapool
Ledmore
Lairg
Bonar Bridge
Ardgay
Tain
Dornoch
Portmahomack

Achiltibuie
Drumrunie
Knockan
Inverkirkaig
Dundonnell
Poolewe
Gairloch
Kinlochewe
Achnasheen
Strathpeffer
Dingwall
Evanton
Alness
Invergordon
Fortrose
Avoch
Fortrose
Culloden
North Kessock
Inverness

Lower Diabaig
Shieldaig
Torridon
Lochcarron
Achnashellach
Struy
Cannich
Drumnadrochit
Invermoriston
Foyers

Stornoway
Uig
Portree
Raasay
Sconser
Broadford
Dunvegan
Bracadale
Isle of Skye
Kyleakin
Kyle of Lochalsh
Kylerhea
Glenelg
Dornie
Five Sisters of Kintail
Fort Augustus

WESTERN ISLES
Isle of Lewis
Scalpay
Tarbert
Shiant Islands
Taransay
Pabbay
Berneray
Hermetray
North Uist
Benbecula
Lochmaddy
South Uist
Boreray

HIGHLAND

Ben Hope (927m)
Ben More Assynt (998m)
Beinn Dearg (1084m)
Beinn Eighe (1010m)
Liathach (1054m)
Sgurr na Ciche (1040m)
Monadhliath Mountains

MORAY
Cullen
Banff
Buckie
Keith
Elgin
Lossiemouth
Burghead
Findhorn
Forres
Rothes
Dufftown
Charlestown of Aberlour
Grantown-on-Spey
Nairn
Findhorn
Cawdor
Carrbridge
Aviemore
Kincraig
Kingussie
Cairngorm Mountains

ABERDEENSHINE / ABERDEENSHIRE
St Combs
Fraserburgh
Peterhead
Boddam
Strichen
Mintlaw
Ellon
Hatton
Peterculter
Oldmeldrum
Kintore
Kennay
Westhill
Aberdeen
Bartchoy
Huntly
Rhynie
Insch
Alford
Torphins
Aboyne
Ballater

Monadhliath Mountains

North Sea

THE MINCH
The Little Minch

Eddrachillis Bay
Enard Bay
Gruinard Bay
Loch Broom

EAST NEUK (p212)
Picturesque little fishing villages, sandy beaches, good coastal walking and superb seafood restaurants

EDINBURGH (p67)
One of Europe's most beautiful cities, Scotland's capital is at its most vibrant in August at the height of the festival season

BORDER ABBEYS (p147)
Magnificent Gothic architecture, fascinating history, good riverside walks, Sir Walter Scott country

ROAD TO THE ISLES (p343)
Road and rail route with superb mountain scenery and silver-sand beaches – the heart of Bonnie Prince Charlie country

ISLE OF ARRAN (p166)
Scotland in miniature – good mountain scenery, great hiking and biking, decent beaches and welcoming pubs

GLASGOW (p116)
Scotland's biggest city, famous for Victorian architecture, top shopping, great restaurants and lively pubs and clubs

Destination Scotland

Like a fine single malt, Scotland is a connoisseur's delight – an intoxicating blend of stunning scenery and sophisticated cities, of salt-tanged sea air and dark, peaty waters, of wry humour and generous hospitality.

It's a land with a rich, multilayered history that reveals its true depth and complex flavours only to those who savour it slowly, a place where every corner of the landscape is steeped in the past – a deserted croft on an island shore, a moor that was once a battlefield, a beach where Vikings hauled their boats ashore, a cave that once sheltered Bonnie Prince Charlie.

Scotland harbours some of the largest areas of wilderness left in Western Europe, a wildlife haven where you can see golden eagles soar above the mountains and lochs of the northern Highlands, spot otters frolicking along the kelp-fringed shores of the Outer Hebrides and watch minke whales breach through shoals of mackerel off the coast of Mull.

It's also an adventure playground where you can tramp the tundra plateaus of the Cairngorms, balance along tightrope ridges strung between the rocky peaks of the Cuillin, sea-kayak among the seal-haunted isles of the Inner Hebrides and take a speed-boat ride into the surging white water of the Corryvreckan whirlpool.

And it's a place that changes with the seasons, offering something new each time you visit. Spring means a lilac haze of bluebells in the woods around Loch Lomond, while in summer the Hebridean beaches flaunt their golden sands and turquoise waters like Caribbean impostors. October brings a riot of autumn colour to the Perthshire forests and in winter a fresh layer of crisp snow lends grandeur to the mountains of Glen Coe.

NEIL WILSON

Bonnie Lochs

GARETH MCCORMACK

Sheep drink from Loch Torridon (p370) beneath the misty mountains of the northern Highlands

GRAEME CORNWALLIS

Crannogs, or artificial rock islands, were built on lochs such as Loch Tay (p223) from prehistoric times to the 18th century

OTHER HIGHLIGHTS

- Majestic mountains and rolling forested hills stretch along Scotland's longest loch, the 24-mile Loch Awe (p309)
- Hauntingly beautiful Loch Shiel is home to Glenfinnan (p343), hallowed ground in Highlanders' history
- The brave can venture into the deep, dark waters of Loch Ness (p321) for a monster-hunting cruise

GARETH MCCORMACK

Loch Maree (p370) sits in the shadow of 980m-high Slioch, northern Highlands

Castles & Country Houses

JONATHAN SMITH

Craigievar Castle (p265), near Alford, is a classic example of Scottish Baronial architecture

On guard at Edinburgh Castle (p78); the castle last saw military action in 1745

NEIL SETCHFIELD

MARTIN MOOS

St Margaret's Chapel (p78), in Edinburgh Castle, is the city's oldest surviving building

OTHER HIGHLIGHTS

- The magnificent 18th-century Culzean Castle (p175), designed by Robert Adam, perches high on a cliff with views to the Isle of Arran
- Castle Stalker (p310), on a tiny island in Argyll, starred in the final scene of *Monty Python and the Holy Grail*
- Whitewashed Blair Castle (p229), near Pitlochry, is crammed with treasures collected since the 16th century

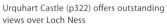
Urquhart Castle (p322) offers outstanding views over Loch Ness

DENNIS JOHNSON

JONATHAN SMITH

Hopetoun House (p112), near Queensferry, is one of Scotland's grandest stately homes

Photogenic Eilean Donan Castle (p372), on Loch Duich, graces countless postcards and calendars

GRAEME CORNWALLIS

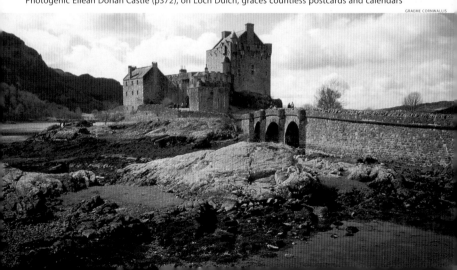

Walking Country

The mountain plateau of Cairngorms National Park (p325) is hiking heaven

DAVID TIPLING

TOM SMALLMAN

Work up an appetite with a wintry stroll along Loch Morlich (p329), near Aviemore in the Cairngorms

OTHER HIGHLIGHTS

- Beautiful Glen Affric (p321) is a walkers' wonderland of forests of native Scots pine, lochs and hills
- Hill walkers can make mountains out of molehills by climbing all 22 McPhies (90m-high 'mountains') on scenic Isle of Colonsay (p293)
- It's worth the walk up Sgurr of Eigg (p347) for the priceless views across the Highlands and chance to spot minke whales

Climbing Ben Nevis (p340), Britain's highest mountain, gives Munro baggers something to brag about

MARK DAFFEY

JONATHAN SMITH

The 78-mile Fife Coastal Path (p209) passes through the pretty fishing village of Anstruther

GRAEME CORNWALLIS

You'll feel on top of the world on 1020m-high Ladhar Bheinn (p345), on the Knoydart Peninsula

The country's most popular long-distance path, the West Highland Way (p278), traverses glorious Glen Coe

MARTIN MOOS

City Life

Try a distinctive local beer from one of Scotland's breweries (p64)

Admire the quirky, geometric lines of Glasgow's Willow Tea Rooms (p124), designed by Charles Rennie Mackintosh

MARTIN MOOS

Look down on Edinburgh from the National Monument (p87) on Calton Hill

OTHER HIGHLIGHTS

- Visit Glasgow's many pubs and clubs to discover why the city is Scotland's live-music capital (p140)
- Aberdeen's Marischal College (p254), an example of Perpendicular Gothic style, is the world's second-largest granite structure
- Dundee (p233), birthplace of comic-book hero Desperate Dan, is also home to cutting-edge art at Dundee Contemporary Arts

GARETH MCCORMACK

Edinburgh Castle is a stunning backdrop to performances in Princes Street Gardens (p85)

Sneak a peek inside Glasgow's opulent City Chambers (p123), built in the 1880s

MARTIN MOOS

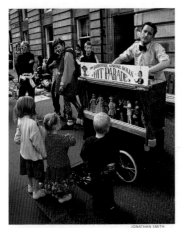

JONATHAN SMITH

Theatre aficionados of all ages enjoy the entertainment at Edinburgh International Festival (p95)

Mountains & Glens

A wee farmhouse is nestled among the mountains of Glen Coe (p333)

GRANT DIXON

GARETH MCCORMACK

Stormy skies and seas frame the Cuillin Hills on the Isle of Skye (p373)

OTHER HIGHLIGHTS

- Inverpolly Nature Reserve (p366) is a mountainous playground with three peaks perfect for sightseeing
- Caledonian pine forest and pastel-hued peaks line the drive into gorgeous Glen Lyon (p224)

Survey the northern Highlands from the sandstone pinnacles of 1062m An Teallach (p369)

GARETH MCCORMAC

Contents

Regional Map Contents

Shetland Islands p417

Orkney Islands p399

See Inset

Northern Highlands & Islands p350

Northeast Scotland p232

Central & Western Highlands p313

Central Scotland p190

Southern Highlands & Islands p274

Edinburgh p69

Glasgow p118

Southern Scotland pp148–9

The Authors

NEIL WILSON
Coordinating Author

Neil was born in Scotland and has lived there for most of his life. When he was 14 he relieved the boredom of a rainy school holiday by leafing through a book about Scottish mountains. The photographs of mist-veiled ridges, yawning cliffs and distant sea lochs opened the door to a lifelong enthusiasm for the great outdoors, and since then he has hiked, biked, climbed, sailed or snowboarded in almost every corner of the country. Neil has been a full-time writer and photographer since 1988 and has written around 40 guidebooks for various publishers, including Lonely Planet's guide to his home town of Edinburgh.

Neil wrote Destination Scotland, Getting Started, Itineraries, Snapshot, The Culture, Outdoor Activities, Food & Drink, Edinburgh, Northeast Scotland, Southern Highlands & Islands, Central & Western Highlands and Transport and cowrote the Northern Highlands & Islands.

The Coordinating Author's Favourite Trip

The highlight of this research trip was a week of glorious weather on the Isle of Skye (p373), a gift from the gods that allowed a trek through the weird landscapes of the Quiraing (p382), and a fantastic hike along the coast from Elgol via Camasunary and the Bad Step to Loch Coruisk (p375) in the heart of the Cuillin Hills (p378). But there was extravagance as well as effort – a gourmet lunch in the atmospheric Three Chimneys (p382) in Dunvegan, and a night of luxury at the Toravaig House Hotel (p377) in Sleat. There were even porpoises to watch from the rail of the Mallaig–Armadale ferry (p375).

ALAN MURPHY

Alan discovered Scotland in the mid-1990s when he lived and worked in Edinburgh for two years. Since then he has returned on many occasions and this is the second time he has coauthored Scotland. With a journalistic background, and a love for all things Scottish (except deep-fried Mars Bars), Alan considers it a privilege to write about this country. For him Scotland is inspiring, almost indescribably beautiful…almost, and, simply like coming home. Alan's favourite part of Scotland is a slice of big-tree country somewhere in Perthshire, among the glens and misty-covered peaks of the Scottish heartland.

Alan wrote the History, Environment, Glasgow, Southern Scotland, Central Scotland, Orkney & Shetland Islands and Directory chapters and cowrote the Northern Highlands & Islands chapter.

LONELY PLANET AUTHORS

Why is our travel information the best in the world? It's simple: our authors are independent, dedicated travellers. They don't research using just the Internet or phone, and they don't take freebies in exchange for positive coverage. They travel widely, to all the popular spots and off the beaten track. They personally visit thousands of hotels, restaurants, cafés, bars, galleries, palaces, museums and more – and they take pride in getting all the details right, and telling it how it is. For more, see the authors section on www.lonelyplanet.com.

Getting Started

Scotland is the sort of place you can arrive in without a plan, and have a great time just wandering around and following your whims. But planning your trip is half the fun, and essential if your time is limited or if there is something in particular that you want to see or do.

WHEN TO GO

Any time is a good time to visit Scotland, but your choice of when to go will depend on what you want to do.

The main tourist period is April to September, and the height of the season is during the school holidays in July and August when accommodation, be it camping grounds, B&Bs or luxury hotels, is at a premium. Edinburgh in particular becomes impossibly crowded during the festival period in August so book well ahead if you plan to visit then (a year ahead is not too soon to start planning!).

In winter public transport is less frequent and travel to the islands can be a problem if high winds disrupt the ferries. Outside the main cities, some tourist attractions are closed from November to March.

See Climate Charts (p433) for more information.

Considering how far north it lies – Edinburgh is on the same latitude as Labrador in Canada – you might expect Scotland to have a colder climate, but the breezes from the Atlantic are warmed by the Gulf Stream, a warm ocean current that flows from the southeast coast of the USA and bathes the western shores of the British Isles. The southern Highlands are famous for their balmy climate, and palm trees and other subtropical plants grow outdoors here.

The east coast tends to be drier than the west – rainfall averages around 650mm – and it is often warmer in summer and colder in winter. Temperatures rarely drop below 0°C on the coast, although a wind blowing off the North Sea will make you shiver any time of year. The west coast is milder and wetter, with more than 1500mm of rain and average summer highs of 19°C. The western Highlands around Fort William are the wettest place in Britain, with annual rainfall as high as 3000mm.

Statistically, your best chances of fine weather are in May, June and September; July and August are usually warm, but may be wet too. In summer daylight hours are long; the midsummer sun sets around 11pm in the Shetland Islands and even Edinburgh evenings seem to last forever in June and July. Conversely, in December the sun doesn't show its face until after 9am, and it's dark again by 4pm.

In April and May Scotland's glorious scenery is set off by snow lingering on the mountains and colourful displays of wildflowers in the bluebell woods of southern Scotland and the machair of the Western Isles. June brings a pink haze of rhododendron blossoms to the Highland

---

DON'T LEAVE HOME WITHOUT...

- a copy of your travel insurance policy details (p437)
- a pair of binoculars for whale- and dolphin-spotting
- insect repellent (p434)
- waterproofs, patience and a sense of adventure

glens, but it's not until August that the hill-sides put on their famous show of purple heather.

October sees the forests of Perthshire and the Trossachs come alight with a blaze of glorious autumn colours. Midwinter can be dreich (a wonderfully descriptive Scots word meaning 'dull and miserable'), but if you get a clear spell of hard frost and sunshine the scenery can be every bit as stunning as in summer.

The many seabird colonies around the Scottish coast are at their most spectacular during the nesting season (April to July), while coastal nature reserves see huge flocks of migrating ducks, geese and waders in spring and autumn. You can see seals, dolphins and porpoises almost all year round, but the whale-watching season peaks in July and August. One seasonal species you should definitely be aware of is the dreaded midge (p434). They are usually around from June to September, but are at their worst in July and August.

HOW MUCH?

Cappuccino £2

Restaurant meal per head £16

Glass of wine £2.75

Bottle of malt whisky £25

Car hire per day £20-30

See also Lonely Planet Index, inside front cover.

COSTS & MONEY

The strength of the pound sterling makes Scotland an expensive destination for non-Europeans. Food, accommodation and transport are all fairly pricey; the only real bargains are the many excellent museums and galleries that you can visit for free.

The price of food and fuel rises quite steeply in remote parts of the Highlands and islands where supplies depend on the ferries. Petrol can cost as much as 15% more in the Outer Hebrides than in the Central Lowlands.

Surprisingly, Scotland is one of the most expensive places to buy Scotch whisky. If your travels will be taking you to mainland Europe, you'll find you can buy whisky there for about 60% of the price charged in Scottish shops.

A realistic daily budget for two people sharing a double room, staying in B&Bs and guesthouses and eating in midrange restaurants is around £35 to £45 per person per day. Backpackers using hostels and cooking their own meals can get by on £25 a day, not including transport.

If you're travelling in your own car you'll probably average a further £10 to £15 per day on petrol and parking; rental will add a minimum of £23 a day.

If you're travelling as a family, be aware that many hotels and guesthouses have family rooms, usually with a double bed and one or two singles, plus a folding bed, which can save a fair bit of money. Most tourist attractions with admission fees also offer discounted family tickets – a major saving at places such as Edinburgh Castle, which charges £9.80 for one adult.

TRAVEL LITERATURE

Stone Voices: The Search for Scotland (2002), by respected Scots journalist Neal Ascherson, is a highly readable and very personal exploration of Scottish history and culture, filled with fascinating insights and some contentious conclusions that will provide the starting point for some lively bar-room conversations.

For a look behind the tourism gloss, *Danziger's Britain* (1997) by Nick Danziger should be required reading. The picture it paints of modern Britain is thoroughly depressing, and includes descriptions of life for the marginalised in the Highlands and Glasgow. This guy has seen the world and if this is how he says it is, then it's hard to argue with him.

TOP TENS

Favourite Festivals & Events

Scots always enjoy a good party, and will find some reason to celebrate at almost any time of the year. The following list is our Top 10, but for comprehensive listings of festivals and events see the Directory on p436.

- Up-Helly-Aa (Shetland), January (p421)
- Melrose Rugby Sevens Match (Melrose), April (p156)
- Islay Festival (Isle of Islay), May (p287)
- Burns an' a' That (Ayr), May (p172)
- Royal Highland Show (Edinburgh), June (p94)

- Jethart Callant Festival (Jedburgh), July (p158)
- Edinburgh Festival & Fringe (Edinburgh), August (p95)
- Edinburgh Military Tattoo (Edinburgh), August (p95)
- Braemar Gathering (Braemar), September (p264)
- Edinburgh's Hogmanay (Edinburgh), December (p93)

Top Reads

Scotland has produced many world-famous novelists. The following novels provide insights into Scottish culture at various periods spanning the last two centuries. See the boxed text, p44, for more Scottish reads.

- *Waverley* (1814) Sir Walter Scott
- *Kidnapped!* (1886) Robert Louis Stevenson
- *The Silver Darlings* (1941) Neil M Gunn
- *A Scot's Quair* (1946) Lewis Grassic Gibbon
- *Para Handy Tales* (1955) Neil Munro

- *The Prime of Miss Jean Brodie* (1962) Muriel Spark
- *Greenvoe* (1972) George Mackay Brown
- *Laidlaw* (1977) William McIlvanney
- *Trainspotting* (1993) Irvine Welsh
- *Black and Blue* (1997) Ian Rankin

Must-See Films

Head down to the local video store or browse www.amazon.com to pick up our choice of Scotland's 10 best films. All are set in Scotland and many were directed by Scots. See the Culture chapter, p45, for more on Scottish cinema.

- *Whisky Galore!* (1949) Director: Alexander Mackendrick
- *Tunes of Glory* (1960) Director: Ronald Neame
- *Gregory's Girl* (1981) Director: Bill Forsyth
- *Local Hero* (1983) Director: Bill Forsyth
- *Braveheart* (1995) Director: Mel Gibson

- *Rob Roy* (1995) Director: Michael Caton-Jones
- *Trainspotting* (1996) Director: Danny Boyle
- *Small Faces* (1996) Director: Gillies Mackinnon
- *Sweet Sixteen* (2002) Director: Mike Loach
- *Young Adam* (2003) Director: David McKenzie

Anyone with an interest in the Scottish hills should seek out *Always A Little Further* (1939) by Alastair Borthwick and *Mountaineering in Scotland* (1947) by WH Murray. Both are classic accounts, beautifully written, of camping, hiking and rock climbing in Scotland in the 1930s, when just getting to Glen Coe was an adventure in itself and the most advanced ice-climbing equipment was a slater's pick.

Two of the greatest Scottish travelogues date from the 18th century. *A Journey to the Western Isles of Scotland* (1759) and *Journal of a Tour to the Hebrides* (1785) by James Boswell are vivid accounts of two journeys made by the author in the company of the famous lexicographer Samuel Johnson. Boswell writes engagingly of their travails and encounters with the local people, from lairds to crofters, and paints a vivid picture of Highland life in the late 18th century.

For more information on the Gaelic language see www.savegaelic.org.

A much more recent travelogue is *Raw Spirit* (2004) by novelist Iain Banks (see the boxed text, p43), an immensely enjoyable jaunt around Scotland supposedly in search of the perfect single malt whisky. Although half the book has nothing to do with whisky, and reads more like an extended pub conversation, Banks makes an entertaining companion as he regales you with his opinions on cars (he owns several), tales of driving on Scottish roads and hilarious anecdotes from his youth.

INTERNET RESOURCES

Internet Guide to Scotland (www.scotland-info.co.uk) The best of several online tourist guides to Scotland.

Lonely Planet (www.lonelyplanet.com) Get started with summaries on Scotland, the popular Thorn Tree bulletin board and links to Scotland-related sites.

ScotchWhisky.net (www.scotchwhisky.net) Everything you wanted to know about Scotch whisky.

Scotland's People (www.scotlandspeople.gov.uk) A comprehensive online resource for exploring your Scottish ancestry.

Traveline (www.travelinescotland.com) Public transport timetables and journey planner for all of Scotland.

VisitScotland (www.visitscotland.com) The official Scottish Tourist Board site, with an online accommodation-booking service.

Itineraries

CLASSIC ROUTES

SKYE'S THE LIMIT
Two Weeks/Edinburgh to Inverness

This route is through the magnificent mountain scenery of the west Highlands. From **Edinburgh** (p67) head northwest to see Scotland's other great castle at **Stirling** (p191), then to the **Trossachs** (p197) for your first taste of Highland scenery. As you continue north, the mountain scenery becomes more impressive, culminating in the grandeur of **Glen Coe** (p333).

Keen hill walkers will pause at **Fort William** (p335) to climb **Ben Nevis** (p340), or you can view it from **Corpach** (p341) on the Road to the Isles. Head onto glorious **Glenfinnan** (p343) and the **Silver Sands of Morar** (p343), then **Mallaig** (p344); try to spend the night here and eat at one of its excellent seafood restaurants.

From Mallaig take the ferry to the **Isle of Skye** (p373); allow a day or two here to see the sights. Cross the Skye Bridge back to the mainland, and head north via the pretty village of **Plockton** (p372) to the magnificent mountain scenery of **Glen Torridon** (p370). Follow the A832 alongside lovely **Loch Maree** (p370) and continue north into the big-sky wilderness of western Sutherland, beneath the towering pinnacles of **An Teallach** (p369), before heading back east to the fleshpots of **Inverness** (p313).

In theory you could cover this spectacular 475-mile route in two days, but allowing time to stop and enjoy the scenery and the seafood makes two weeks a more realistic estimate.

CASTLES & WHISKY   Two Weeks/Edinburgh to Edinburgh

From **Edinburgh** (p67) head north across the Forth Road Bridge to Fife, stopping at Queensferry first to visit stately **Hopetoun House** (p112). Then turn east along the coastal road through the delightful fishing villages of the **East Neuk** (p212) to the home of golf, **St Andrews** (p206). Continue north across the Tay Bridge to **Dundee** (p233) and **Glamis Castle** (p247) before heading into the Grampian Mountains to reach **Braemar** (p263).

A feast of castles lies ahead as you travel east along Deeside, passing royal residence **Balmoral Castle** (p262) and fairy-tale **Crathes Castle** (p261) on your way to the granite city of **Aberdeen** (p252). Try to get a table at the Silver Darling restaurant (p257) here.

Now strike west again along the A944, making small detours to visit **Castle Fraser** (p261), **Craigievar Castle** (p265) and **Kildrummy Castle** (p265) before turning north to **Huntly** (p266) and west again to **Dufftown** (p269) in the heart of the Spey valley. Base yourself here for at least a day to explore the many whisky distilleries nearby.

Go northwest to **Elgin** (p267), then west on the A96, visiting **Brodie Castle** (p320), **Fort George** (p319), **Cawdor Castle** (p320) and **Culloden** (p319) on the way to **Inverness** (p313).

Whisky fans (see the boxed text, p65) can make the short trip north to the Glenmorangie Distillery at **Tain** (p352) before returning south to Edinburgh on the A9 and M9, stopping off at **Blair Castle** (p229), **Dunkeld** (p225) and **Scone Palace** (p217).

This journey through the heart of Scotland is a 475-mile round-trip, starting and finishing in Edinburgh, with a total driving time of around 10 to 12 hours. Tain is an extra 50-mile round-trip north of Inverness.

ROADS LESS TRAVELLED

BORDER RAID
Eight Days/Edinburgh to Glasgow

From **Edinburgh** (p67) the majority of tourists head north, which is a very good reason to head south, into the Borders…

Your first objective should be a traipse around the beautiful Border abbeys of **Melrose** (p155) and **Jedburgh** (p158). Melrose is a charming place to stay. Then head southwest to **Selkirk** (p157) and along the A708 to **Moffat** (p188). Continue to **Dumfries** (p176) and make a short side-trip to see spectacular **Caerlaverock Castle** (p178).

Push on southwest around the Galloway coast to **Newton Stewart** (p183), and detour south to visit the bookshops of **Wigtown** (p183) and the holy site of **Whithorn** (p184). From Newton Stewart head back east along the A712 to **New Galloway** (p182), via the lovely Galloway Forest Park, and then north on the A713 towards Ayr and Burns Country.

At **Alloway** (p173) allow at least a day to visit Robert Burns' birthplace and other Burns-related sites, then go on to **Ayr** (p171) and head north to **Ardrossan** (p166). Take the ferry here across to the lovely **Isle of Arran** (p166) for a spot of hill walking, fishing or relaxing at one of the island's pubs.

Back on the mainland, head north to **Wemyss Bay** (p145) and take the ferry to **Rothesay** (p280) on the Isle of Bute, where you can visit stunning Mount Stuart, one of Scotland's most impressive stately homes. Return to the mainland again and head east to **Glasgow** (p116).

You could cover this 430-mile arc through the southern uplands in two long days, or spin it out to two weeks, but eight days is comfortable.

ISLES AT THE EDGE OF THE SEA   Two Weeks/Oban to Thurso

This route can be done by car, but it also makes a brilliant cycle tour taking three to four weeks. Both start and finish are accessible by rail.

From **Oban** (p294) make the long ferry crossing to **Barra** (p396). After a look at romantic Kisimul Castle take the ferry across to **South Uist** (p395). If you've brought your fishing rod, look forward to a bit of sport on the island's many trout lochs. Keep your binoculars handy as you follow the road north through **Benbecula** (p394) and **North Uist** (p393), as this is prime bird-watching country; then take another ferry to **Harris** (p391).

Pray for sun, as the road along Harris' west coast has some of the most spectacular beaches in Scotland. The road continues north through the rugged Harris hills to **Lewis** (p386).

Turn west to make a circuit past the **Callanish Standing Stones** (p390), **Dun Carloway** (p389) and **Arnol Blackhouse Museum** (p389) – the highlights of the Western Isles – and if you have time detour west to the beautiful beaches around **Miavaig** (p391).

From bustling **Stornoway** (p386) take the ferry to **Ullapool** (p366), where you have the choice of returning direct to **Inverness** (p313), or continuing north around the mainland coast through the jaw-dropping wilderness scenery of **Inverpolly Nature Reserve** (p366), **Cape Wrath** (p364) and **Durness** (p363) to **Thurso** (p360), where the ferry to the **Orkney Islands** (p398) awaits.

CalMac's Island Hopscotch ticket No 8 (p446) includes all the ferries needed for this route.

This trip involves 290 miles between Oban and Thurso, plus 10 hours of ferry crossings. You could drive it in four days at a push, but two weeks is more enjoyable. Touring Orkney would add another 60 or 70 miles, plus four hours on the ferry.

TAILORED TRIPS

THE BONNIE PRINCE CHARLIE TRAIL

Many visitors to Scotland are captivated by the romanticised legend of Bonnie Charlie (p34), who in 1745 tried to recapture the British throne for the Stuart dynasty. The Young Pretender first set foot on Scottish soil at **Princes Strand** (p395) on the island of Eriskay, and raised his standard at **Glenfinnan** (p343) before leading his army of Highlanders south as far as Derby in England. He was harried in retreat all the way to final defeat at **Culloden** (p319) in 1746, stopping briefly at **Linlithgow Palace** (p115) on the way, after which he was on the run in the **Isle of Skye** (p378) and the **Outer Hebrides** (p394). He finally departed from Scotland for the last time from a point in Arisaig marked by the **Princes Cairn** (p343).

Museums that have exhibits relating to Bonnie Prince Charlie and other places associated with his campaign include **Ruthven Barracks** (p331), the **West Highland Museum** (p337) in Fort William, the **Seven Men of Moidart** (p342), the **Museum of the Isles** (p377) and **Dunvegan Castle** (p381) on Skye and the **Clan Cameron Museum** (p341). Sir Walter Scott's house at **Abbotsford** (p157) displays a lock of the prince's hair.

WILDLIFE-WATCHING

Begin in **Inverness** (p313) at the head of the Moray Firth, famous for its population of bottlenose dolphins. Boat trips depart from here. Head east along the southern shore of the firth to **Spey Bay** (p272), where there's an exhibit on the dolphins and the chance of seeing seals. Then follow the Spey valley southwest to the Cairngorms, where you can see nesting ospreys at **Boat of Garten** (p330) and get close to some rare species at the **Highland Wildlife Park** (p329).

Continue southwest across the country to Fort William and follow the Road to the Isles to Mallaig. Take a day trip to the **Isle of Rum** (p346), a nature reserve famed for its rare white-tailed sea eagles and Manx shearwaters. Perhaps take another trip to the **Isle of Eigg** (p346), which has fine walking and there's a good chance of spotting porpoises and whales on the crossing.

The **Isle of Skye** (p373) and the **Isle of Mull** (p300) are two of the best wildlife destinations in Scotland, and both islands have lots of boats offering whale-watching trips.

Return to Inverness via the Skye Bridge and **Loch Ness** (p322). If you don't fancy monster-spotting, make a detour west to visit the beautiful nature reserve at **Glen Affric** (p320).

Snapshot

The new Scottish parliament building (p81) was officially opened, with much royal pomp and circumstance, in October 2004. The project was dogged with controversy – it was originally scheduled to be ready in 2001 at a cost of only £40 million; it opened three years late, with the Scottish taxpayer footing a bill for £431 million, and blighted by tragedy – both the visionary Catalan architect, Enric Miralles, and the first minister of the new parliament, Donald Dewar, died during the early stages of the building's construction. And despite the official opening date in 2004, work on the building and its landscaped site was not completed until October 2005.

Reaction to the building has been mixed, to say the least. Experts have acclaimed it as a masterpiece, and it has won half a dozen major international architectural awards – in 2005 it won the Royal Institution of British Architects' annual Stirling Prize, the 'Oscars' of British architecture. But the general public has been less appreciative – in an opinion poll for a TV programme on Channel 4 the Holyrood parliament building was selected as one of the 12 buildings in the UK that people would most like to see demolished.

A public inquiry into the spiralling costs of the building laid the blame firmly on the parliament and its civil servants who, it claimed, vastly underestimated the cost of the project and then mismanaged it from start to finish. Lord Fraser of Carmyllie, who conducted the inquiry, concluded that 'not until it was too late to change was there any real appreciation of the complexity of the architect's evolving design and its inevitable cost'; and 'whenever there was a conflict between quality and cost, quality was preferred…whenever there was a conflict between early completion and cost, completion was preferred'.

One of the first laws to be passed in the new debating chamber was one that gave the Gaelic language (p452) official status. Opinion in Scotland is deeply divided, between those who believe Gaelic should receive state support in the form of bilingual signage, a dedicated Gaelic TV channel and school classes taught in Gaelic, and those who feel that Gaelic is irrelevant to modern Scotland and should be allowed to die a natural death if it cannot survive without external funding.

The Gaelic Language Act (2005) recognises Gaelic as an official language in Scotland and requires the creation of a national plan for the future development of the language. This is quite a turnaround from an attitude that began with an act passed by the old Scottish parliament in 1616 ruling that Gaelic be 'abolishit and removit' from Scotland. State persecution of Gaelic language and culture intensified following the Jacobite rebellion of 1745, and this attitude persisted well into the 20th century; indeed, there are people still alive today who can recall being beaten for speaking Gaelic in school.

If you're unfortunate enough to find yourself driving into one of Scotland's larger cities during the weekday rush hour, you'll soon find that traffic congestion is one of the country's curses. Edinburgh has led the way in trying to discourage car use with popular measures like cycle routes, dedicated bus lanes and park-and-rides schemes, and unpopular ones like increased parking charges and fines, and a small army of parking 'enforcers'. In 2005 Edinburgh citizens voted against a congestion-charging scheme, but plans are underway to reintroduce trams to the city by 2009.

One of the worst traffic bottlenecks in the country is the Forth Road Bridge and its approaches, with southbound tailbacks several miles long on weekday mornings. Ambitious – and controversial – plans have been proposed for a second road bridge across the Firth of Forth at Queensferry (p112), which would allow Edinburgh's new tram network to be extended as far as Dunfermline. Such a bridge would cost between £500 million and £1 billion and take nine years to complete. Ironically, there have also been proposals to create a modern ferry service between Fife and Edinburgh (the Forth bridges were originally built to replace ferry services), to begin operation in 2009.

Another transport issue that continues to dominate the headlines is the £130 million plan to reopen the Waverley Line, a railway link between Edinburgh and Carlisle that was closed down in the 1960s. Supporters claim that reinstating the 35-mile stretch of line between Edinburgh and Galashiels is crucial to the revival of the ailing Borders economy, but farmers and homeowners whose property lies next to – or in some cases on – the old railway line are understandably opposed to it. In September 2005 the Scottish parliament voted unanimously to support the reopening of the line; if things go smoothly, the railway could be reinstated by 2008.

The headline-grabbing clause in the Land Reform (Scotland) Act (2003) that allows crofting communities to buy out the land that they live on with the aid of taxpayers' money will probably see many more estates follow the likes of Eigg, Knoydart and North Harris into community ownership – in 2005 the crofters of South Uist voted overwhelmingly in favour of a buyout. It is hoped that developments such as these will halt or even reverse the gradual depopulation of the Highlands and islands that has been going on since the 18th century.

With Scotland's national football team having failed to qualify – yet again – for the World Cup (taking place in Germany in 2006), there will be plenty of football fans gathering in pubs across the country to watch the games on TV and support whoever happens to be playing against England. However, they will no longer be able to enjoy a cigarette with their pint – from 26 March 2006, the Scottish parliament is imposing a complete ban on smoking in public places, including pubs, clubs and restaurants. So there may be a few twitchy drinkers about – better not bring up the fact that it's the 40th anniversary of England's 1966 World Cup victory unless you want a pint of heavy emptied over your head.

History

Scottish history is a compelling, interwoven web, laced with heroic figures and defining battles. More than anything else it is the immortal figures, some heavily romanticised, who've made their mark on this extraordinary history. Although relatively recent events are well documented, the country's history stretches far back into the mists of times where myth and legend take precedence over sketchy facts and scant archaeological records.

PREHISTORIC & ROMAN TIMES

Hunters and gatherers have left remains of shells and animal bones, providing fragments of evidence of the earliest human habitation in Scotland.

A Traveller's History of Scotland by Andrew Fisher is a concise account of Scottish history that relates historical events to places you can visit.

Early Neolithic farming people moved into Scotland from mainland Europe around 4500 BC; they left behind an astonishing diary of human development including the incredibly well-preserved Neolithic village of Skara Brae (p410), dating from around 3100 BC, and extraordinary chambered cairns such as Maes Howe (p409), which indicate they had a belief in the afterlife. Today, the islands of Orkney are the best place to see such prehistoric sites, boasting Europe's greatest concentration. Kilmartin Glen (p283) also has many prehistoric sites, including extensive rock carvings.

Next came the Beaker people who were responsible for leaving behind standing stones, such as those at Callanish (p390) in Lewis; it is one of the most evocative sites in Scotland, and testament to the advanced culture that had taken root by 3000 BC.

We now leap to the Roman invasion of Britain, which began in 55 BC, when Julius Caesar's legions first crossed the English Channel. However, the Roman onslaught ground to a halt in the north, not far beyond the present-day Scottish border.

By the 2nd century Emperor Hadrian, tired of fighting the tribes in the north, decided to cut his losses and built the wall (AD 122–28) that bears his name across northern England between Carlisle and Newcastle. Two decades later Hadrian's successor, Antoninus Pius, invaded Scotland again and built a turf rampart, the Antonine Wall, between the Firth of Forth and the River Clyde. The Roman fort at Cramond (p88) marked its eastern end. In northern Britain, the Romans found they had met their match.

CHRISTIANITY, CELTS & NORSEMEN

After the disintegration of their empire, the Romans left Britain in the 5th century. At this time there were at least two indigenous peoples in the northern region of the British Isles: the Picts in the north and east, and the Celtic Britons in the south.

It is around this time that Christianity was to take root. St Ninian established the first Christian mission beyond Hadrian's Wall in Whithorn (p184) in AD 397, and conducted the first missionary work among the Picts. He remains a mysterious figure shrouded in myth, but there is little doubt that his influence was profound.

TIMELINE	4500 BC	3000 BC
	Neolithic farmers move to Scotland from mainland Europe	Beaker people create standing stones

In the early 6th century another Celtic tribe, the Scots, crossed the sea from northern Ireland and established a kingdom in Argyll called Dalriada (see Dunadd, p283).

St Columba, Scotland's most famous missionary, resumed St Ninian's work in the 6th century. After fleeing Ireland in 563 he established a monastery on Iona (p306). By the late 8th century Columba's mission was responsible for the conversion of most of pagan Scotland – Christianity was popular with pagan kings as it seemed to offer them supernatural powers.

According to legend, Columba was a scholar and a soldier-priest who went into exile after involvement in a bloody battle. After arriving on Iona he promptly set about banishing women and cows as he believed 'where there is a cow there is a woman, and where there is a woman there is mischief'. His manner of living was austere – he was said to sleep on the bare floor with a stone for a pillow. After his death he was credited with miraculous feats such as defeating what is today known as the Loch Ness monster. Today, visiting this holy island, the reconstructed 13th-century abbey and the many fine stone carvings is a highlight of the Inner Hebrides.

From the 780s onwards, Norsemen in longboats from Scandinavia began to pillage the Scottish coast and islands, eventually taking control of Orkney, Shetland and the Western Isles. The Norsemen continued to control the entire western seaboard until Alexander III broke their power at the Battle of Largs in 1263.

MACALPIN & CANMORE DYNASTIES

The Picts and Scots were drawn together by the threat of a Norse invasion and by the combination of political and spiritual power from their common Christianity. In 843 Kenneth MacAlpin, the king of Dalriada (and son of a Pictish princess), took advantage of the Picts' custom of matrilineal succession to take over the Pictish throne, thus uniting Scotland north of the Firth of Forth into a single kingdom. (One story has it that MacAlpin achieved power at a 'black dinner' by setting traps underneath the benches of Pictish nobles.) He made Scone his capital, and brought to it the sacred Stone of Destiny (see the boxed text, p79), used in the coronation of Scottish kings.

Nearly two centuries later, Kenneth MacAlpin's great-great-great-grandson, Malcolm II (r 1005–18), defeated the Northumbrian Angles led by King Canute at the Battle of Carham (1018) near Roxburgh on the River Tweed. This victory brought Edinburgh and Lothian under Scottish control and extended Scottish territory as far south as the Tweed.

With his Saxon queen, Margaret, Malcolm III Canmore (r 1058–93) – whose father Duncan was murdered by Macbeth (as described in Shakespeare's eponymous play) – founded a dynasty of able Scottish rulers. They introduced new Anglo-Norman systems of government and religious foundations.

Malcolm's son David I (r 1124–53) imported monks to found the great Border Abbeys; their fiery remains are major attractions in Melrose (p155), Jedburgh (p158) and Dryburgh (p156). He increased his power by adopting the Norman feudal system, granting land to noble Norman families in return for military service.

The enigmatic Picts (named by the Romans for their body tattoos – Picts meaning 'painted people') remain a mystery to scholars. Their carved stones, often ambiguous in meaning, are the only surviving record of their existence.

Stone of Destiny by Pat Gerber is an intriguing investigation into the history of Scotland's most famous lump of stone. Is the one in Edinburgh Castle a fake, with the real stone waiting to be rescued from its medieval hiding place?

But the Highland clans, inaccessible in their glens, remained a law unto themselves for another 600 years. The exploits of Rob Roy, especially his daring raids into the Lowlands and reputation as a champion of the poor, typified the romantic notion of these wild clans. A cultural and linguistic divide grew up between the Gaelic-speaking Highlanders and the Lowlanders who spoke the Scots tongue (p452).

ROBERT THE BRUCE & WILLIAM WALLACE

When Alexander III fell to his death over a coastal cliff in Fife in 1286, there followed a dispute over the succession to the throne. There were no less than 13 claimants, but in the end it came down to a choice of two: Robert de Brus, lord of Annandale, and John Balliol, lord of Galloway. Edward I of England, as the greatest feudal lord in Britain, was asked to arbitrate. He chose Balliol, whom he thought he could manipulate more easily.

Seeking to tighten his feudal grip on Scotland, Edward – known as the 'Hammer of the Scots' – treated the Scots king as his vassal rather than his equal. The humiliated Balliol finally turned against him and allied Scotland with France in 1295, thus beginning the enduring 'Auld Alliance' and ushering in the 'Wars of Independence'.

Edward's response was bloody. In 1296 he marched on Scotland with an army of 30,000 men, razing ports, butchering citizens, and capturing the castles of Berwick, Edinburgh, Roxburgh and Stirling. Balliol was incarcerated in the Tower of London, and, in a final blow to Scots pride, Edward I removed the Stone of Destiny from Scone and took it back to London.

Enter arguably Scotland's most tragic hero, William Wallace (see the boxed text, p193). Bands of rebels were attacking the English occupiers

---

THE CLAN WHO WOULD BE KING

In medieval times, when overland travel through the Scottish Highlands was slow, difficult and dangerous, the sea lochs, firths, kyles and sounds of the west coast were the motorways of their time. Cut off from the rest of Scotland, but united by these sea roads, the west coast and islands were a world – and a kingdom – unto themselves.

Descended from the legendary Somerled – a half-Gaelic, half-Norse warrior of the 12th century, himself descended from the Irish king Conn of the 100 Battles – the chiefs of Clan Donald claimed sovereignty over this watery kingdom. It was John Macdonald of Islay who first styled himself Dominus Insularum (Lord of the Isles) in 1353. He and his descendants ruled their vast territory from their headquarters at Finlaggan (p290) in Islay, backed up by fleets of swift *birlinns* and *nyvaigs* (Hebridean galleys), an intimate knowledge of the sea routes of the west and a network of coastal castles that included Skipness (p285), Dunstaffnage (p310), Duart (p302), Stalker (p310), Dunvegan (p381) and Kisimul (p396).

Clan Donald held sway over the isles, often in defiance of the Scottish king, from 1350 to 1493. At its greatest extent, in the second half of the 15th century, the Lordship of the Isles included all the islands on the west coast of Scotland, the west-coast mainland from Kintyre to Ross-shire, and the Antrim coast of northern Ireland. But in challenging the Scottish king for territory, and siding with the English king against him, Clan Donald finally pushed its luck too far.

Following a failed rebellion in 1493, the Lordship was forfeited to King James IV of Scotland, and the title has remained in possession of the Scottish, and later British, royal family ever since. Lord of the Isles is one of the many titles held today by Prince Charles, heir to the British throne.

5th century	6th century
Romans leave Britain	St Columba establishes Christian mission on Iona; Scotland is converted

and one such band, led by William Wallace, defeated the English army at the Battle of Stirling Bridge in 1297. Wallace was knighted and proclaimed Guardian of Scotland in 1298. However, he lost a major battle at Falkirk, resigned as guardian and went into hiding in Europe – on his return to Scotland, he was betrayed, caught and executed in 1305. This betrayal was largely put down to the fickle loyalties of the Scottish nobility who sided with Edward.

After William Wallace was executed, Robert the Bruce, grandson of the lord of Annandale, saw his chance, defied Edward (whom he had previously aligned himself with), murdered his rival John Comyn and had himself crowned king of Scotland at Scone in 1306.

Bruce mounted a campaign to drive the English out of Scotland but suffered repeated defeats. According to legend, while Bruce was on the run he was inspired to renew his efforts by a spider's persistence in spinning its web. He went on to win a famous victory over the English at the Battle of Bannockburn in 1314 – a victory which would turn the tide in favour of the Scots for the next 400 years (p193). Continued raids on northern England forced Edward II to sue for peace and, in 1328, the Treaty of Northampton gave Scotland its independence, with Robert I, the Bruce, as its king.

The film Braveheart, *starring Mel Gibson, is a romanticised Hollywood version of the life of William Wallace, though any relationship to actual historical events is pretty tenuous.*

THE STEWART DYNASTY & THE RENAISSANCE

After the death of Robert the Bruce in 1329 – he's buried at Dunfermline (see the boxed text, p205), although his heart is buried in Melrose Abbey (p155) – the country was ravaged by civil disputes and continuing wars with England. Edinburgh was occupied several times by English armies, and in 1385 the Kirk of St Giles was burned to the ground.

The last of the Bruce dynasty died in 1371 to be succeeded by the Stewards (Stewarts), who would rule Scotland and Britain for the next three centuries.

James IV (r 1488–1513) married the daughter of Henry VII of England, the first of the Tudor monarchs, thereby linking the two royal families through 'the Marriage of the Thistle and the Rose'. This didn't prevent the French from persuading James to go to war with his in-laws, and he was killed at the Battle of Flodden in 1513, along with 10,000 of his subjects.

Renaissance ideas flourished during James IV's reign. Scottish poetry thrived, created by makars (makers of verses) such as William Dunbar, the court poet of James IV, and Gavin Douglas. The intellectual climate provided fertile ground for the rise of Protestantism, a reaction against the perceived wealth and corruption of the medieval Roman Catholic Church, which would eventually lead to the Reformation.

Much graceful Scottish architecture dates from this period, and examples of the Renaissance style can be seen in alterations made to the palaces at Holyrood (p82), Stirling (p191), Linlithgow (p115) and Falkland (p206).

MARY, QUEEN OF SCOTS & THE REFORMATION

No figure in Scottish history has had a more turbulent and troublesome history than Mary, Queen of Scots (r 1542–67).

In 1542 King James V, childless, lay on his deathbed brokenhearted, it is said, after his defeat by the English at Solway Moss. On 8 December a messenger brought word that his wife had given birth to a baby girl at the

| Scotland united into one country north of Firth of Forth | King Edward 1 invades Scotland |

Palace of Linlithgow. Fearing the end of the Stewart dynasty, and recalling its origin through Robert the Bruce's daughter, James sighed, 'It cam' wi' a lass, and it will gang wi' a lass.' He died a few days later, leaving his week-old daughter, Mary, to inherit the throne as Queen of Scots.

She was sent to France at an early age, and Scotland was ruled by regents, who rejected overtures from Henry VIII of England urging them to wed the infant queen to his son. Henry was furious, and sent his armies to take vengeance on the Scots. The 'Rough Wooing', as it was called, failed to persuade the Scots of the error of their ways. In 1558, Mary was married to the French dauphin and became queen of France as well as Scotland.

While Mary was in France, being raised as a Roman Catholic, the Reformation tore through Scotland. The wealthy Catholic Church was riddled with corruption, and the preachings of John Knox, a pupil of the Swiss reformer Calvin, found sympathetic ears. To give you an idea of this influential man, Knox, concerned with the influence that political rulers wielded over the church, wrote *The First Blast of the Trumpet Against the Monstrous Regiment of Women*. It was an attack on three women rulers calling the shots in Scotland, England and France and linked his name to a hatred of women ever since

In 1560 the Scottish parliament created a Protestant Church that was independent of Rome and the monarchy. The Latin Mass was abolished and the pope's authority denied.

Following the death of her sickly husband, the 18-year-old Mary returned to Scotland in 1561. She was formally welcomed to her capital city, and held a famous audience at Holyrood Palace with John Knox. The great reformer harangued the young queen and she later agreed to protect the Protestant Church in Scotland while continuing to hear Mass in private.

She married Henry Stewart, Lord Darnley, in the Chapel Royal at Holyrood and gave birth to a son (later James VI) in Edinburgh Castle in 1565. Any domestic bliss was short-lived and, in a scarcely believable train of events, Darnley was involved in the murder of Mary's Italian secretary Rizzio (rumoured to be her lover), before he himself was murdered, probably by Mary's new lover and second-husband-to-be, the earl of Bothwell!

Mary Queen of Scots by Antonia Fraser is the classic biography of Scotland's ill-starred queen, digging deep behind the myths to discover the real woman caught up in the labyrinthine politics of the period.

THE DECLARATION OF ARBROATH

During the Wars of Independence, a group of Scottish nobles sent a letter to Pope John XXII requesting support for the cause of Scottish independence. Bearing the seals of eight earls and 31 barons, and written in Latin by the abbot of Arbroath in 1320, it is the earliest document that seeks to place limits on the power of a king.

Having railed against the tyranny of Edward I of England and having sung the praises of Robert the Bruce, the declaration famously concludes:

Yet even the same Robert, should he turn aside from the task and yield Scotland or us to the English king or people, him we should cast out as the enemy of us all, and choose another king to defend our freedom; for so long as a hundred of us remain alive, we will yield in no least way to English dominion. For we fight, not for glory nor for riches nor for honour, but only and alone for freedom, which no good man surrenders but with his life.

1314	1328
Battle of Bannockburn	Treaty of Northampton; Robert I, the Bruce, king of Scotland

The Scots had had enough – Mary's enemies finally confronted her at Carberry Hill, just east of Edinburgh, and Mary was forced to abdicate in 1567. Her son, the infant James VI (r 1567–1625), was crowned at Stirling, and a series of regents ruled in his place. When Queen Elizabeth I of England died childless in 1603 (after executing Mary), James VI of Scotland inherited the English throne in the so-called Union of the Crowns, becoming James I of Great Britain. James moved his court to London and, for the most part, the Stewarts ignored Scotland from then on. Indeed, when Charles I (r 1625–49) succeeded James, he couldn't be bothered to travel north to Edinburgh to be formally crowned as king of Scotland until 1633.

COVENANTERS & CIVIL WAR

Civil war was to strangle Scotland and England in the 17th century. The arrogant attempts by Charles I to impose episcopacy (the rule of bishops) and an English liturgy on the Presbyterian Scottish Church set off public riots in Edinburgh. The Presbyterians believed in a personal bond with God that had no need of mediation through priests, popes and kings and, on 28 February 1638, hundreds gathered in Greyfriars Kirkyard (p84) to sign a National Covenant affirming their rights and beliefs. Scotland was divided between the Covenanters and those who supported the king.

In the 1640s civil war raged in England too, where the struggle was between the Royalists and Oliver Cromwell's Parliamentarians. Although there was an alliance between the Covenanters and the English parliament against Charles I, the Scots were appalled when the Parliamentarians executed the king in 1649. They offered his son the Scottish Crown provided he signed the Covenant and renounced his father, which he did. Charles II (r 1649–85) was crowned at Scone on 1 January 1651, but was soon forced into exile by Cromwell, who invaded Scotland and captured Edinburgh.

After Charles II's restoration in 1660, he reneged on the Covenant; episcopacy was reinstated and hardline Presbyterian ministers were deprived of their churches. Charles' brother and successor, the Catholic James VII/ II (r 1685–89), made worshipping as a Covenanter a capital offence.

James' daughter, Mary, and her husband, William of Orange (1689–97) restored the Presbyterian structure in the church and kicked out the bishops, but the political and legal functions of the church were subject to parliamentary control. And so Scotland's turbulent reformation was at an end.

UNION WITH ENGLAND IN 1707

The civil wars left the country and its economy ruined. During the 1690s famine killed up to a third of the population in some areas. Anti-English feeling ran high: William was at war with France and was using Scottish soldiers and taxes – many Scots, sympathetic to the French, disapproved. This feeling was exacerbated by the failure of an investment venture in Panama (the so-called Darien Scheme, set up by the Bank of England to boost the economy), which resulted in widespread bankruptcy in Scotland.

The failure of the Darien Scheme made it clear to the wealthy Scottish merchants and stockholders that the only way they could gain access to the lucrative markets of developing colonies was through union with England. The English parliament favoured union through fear of

Scots History (www .scotshistoryonline.co.uk) gives a useful window into Scotland's past and its people going back 8000 years. It's especially good for images of historic sites.

Stewart dynasty born	Renaissance; the rise of Protestantism

Jacobite sympathies in Scotland being exploited by its enemies, the French. Despite popular opposition, the Act of Union, which brought England and Scotland under one parliament, one sovereign and one flag, took effect on 1 May 1707.

On receiving the Act of Union in Edinburgh, the chancellor of Scotland, Lord Seafield – leader of the parliament that the Act of Union abolished – is said to have murmured under his breath, 'Now there's an end to an auld sang.' Robert Burns later castigated the wealthy politicians who engineered the Union in characteristically stronger language: 'We're bought and sold for English gold – such a parcel of rogues in a nation!'

The Scottish Parliament Project provides a fascinating online history of the Scottish parliament at www.st-andrews.ac.uk /~scotparl.

THE JACOBITES

The Jacobite rebellions of the 18th century sought to displace the Hanoverian monarchy (chosen by the English parliament in 1701 to succeed the house of Orange) and restore a Catholic Stuart king to the British throne.

James Edward Stuart, known as the Old Pretender, was the son of James VII/II. With French support he arrived in the Firth of Forth with a fleet of ships in 1708, causing panic in Edinburgh, but was seen off by English men-of-war.

The Earl of Mar led another Jacobite rebellion in 1715 but proved an ineffectual leader better at propaganda than warfare. Once again the Old Pretender made his way to Scotland and Mar, who met him, demonstrated his propaganda skills by sending news to encourage his army and the people: 'Withouth any complements to him and to do him nothing but justice, set aside his being a Prince, he really is the finest gentleman I ever knew...and has the sweetest temper in the world.' His campaign fizzled out soon after the inconclusive Battle of Sheriffmuir.

In 1745 the Old Pretender's son, Charles Edward Stuart, better known as Bonnie Prince Charlie or the Young Pretender, landed in Scotland for the final uprising. He had little military experience, didn't speak Gaelic and had a shaky grasp of English. Nevertheless, supported by an army of Highlanders, he marched southwards and captured Edinburgh, except for the castle, in September 1745. He got as far south as Derby in England, but success was short-lived; a Hanoverian army led by the duke of Cumberland harried him all the way back to the Highlands, where Jacobite dreams were finally extinguished at the Battle of Culloden in 1746 (p319).

Although a heavily romanticised figure, Bonnie Prince Charlie was partly responsible for the annihilation of Highland culture, given the crackdown and subsequent clearances following his doomed attempt to recapture the crown. After returning to France he gained a reputation for mistreating his subsequent mistresses and at the age of 52 married a young princess, but she fled his drunken violence and he never got the heir he wanted.

John Prebble's wonderfully written book *The Highland Clearances* tells the terrible story of how the Highlanders were driven out of their homes and forced into emigration.

THE HIGHLAND CLEARANCES

In the aftermath of the Jacobite rebellions, Highland dress, the bearing of arms and the bagpipes were outlawed. The Highlands were effectively put under military control and private armies were banned. The relationship of Highland chief to clansman changed dramatically and land owners were tempted by the easy profits to be made from sheep farming.

1560s	1603
Reformation: Mary, Queen of Scots abdicates	Union of the Crowns

RADICALS & REDS

Scotland, and especially Glasgow, has a long history of radical politics. These were founded on the emergence of a well-educated, literate and articulate working class in the late 18th century, and the long-held belief in self-improvement.

James Keir Hardie (1856–1915) first went down the mines at the age of 10, but was an avid reader and self-improver. By the age of 22 he had become an active campaigner for better wages and working conditions, and was blacklisted by the mine owners. He founded the Scottish Labour Party in 1888 and its successor, the Independent Labour Party, in 1893, specifically to represent the interests of the working classes in parliament.

By the early years of the 20th century, Scotland had a fully fledged alternative political culture. The Independent Labour Party was joined by Marxist organisations such as the Social Democratic Federation and the Socialist Labour Party, who advocated class war and direct action. The Glasgow schoolteacher and socialist revolutionary John Maclean (1879–1923) delivered lectures on Marxist theory to audiences of thousands. Maclean was appointed 'Bolshevik consul in Scotland' by Lenin following the Russian Revolution of 1917, and was an outspoken critic of Britain's involvement in WWI; he was arrested for sedition on half a dozen occasions.

The most notorious event in the history of Scottish radicalism was the Bloody Friday Riot of 1919. Fearing mass unemployment after WWI, the Clyde Workers Committee called a strike in support of a shorter working week. Strikers demonstrating in Glasgow's George Sq began a riot and fearing a Bolshevik-style revolution, the government sent in tanks, a howitzer and machine-gunners; fortunately, no one was hurt.

Glasgow and the west of Scotland's socialist sympathies earned it the nickname of 'Red Clydeside'. Backed by the influx of Clydeside Reds at Westminster following the 1922 election, Lossiemouth-born James Ramsay Macdonald (1866–1937) was elected leader of the Labour Party and became Britain's first Labour prime minister in 1924.

Keir Hardie would barely recognise his party's present incarnation, the centre-left New Labour, which took power in Westminster in 1997.

The clansmen, no longer of any use as soldiers and uneconomical as tenants, were evicted from their homes and farms to make way for the flocks – in Easter Ross the year 1792 was known for decades afterwards as the Year of the Sheep. A few stayed to work the sheep farms; many more were forced to seek work in the cities, or to eke a living from crofts (small holdings) on poor coastal land (see the boxed text, p355). And many thousands emigrated – some willingly, some under duress – to the developing colonies of North America, Australia and New Zealand.

If you do much walking in the Highlands and islands, you are almost certain to come across a ruckle of stones among the bracken, all that remains of a house or cottage. Look around and you'll find another, and another, and soon you'll realise that this was once a crofting settlement. It's one of the saddest sights you'll see in Scotland – this emptiness, where once there was a thriving community, tears at the heart strings. The Mull of Oa on the island of Islay, for example, once supported a population of 4000, but today there are barely 40 people living there.

THE SCOTTISH ENLIGHTENMENT

Following the loss of the Scottish parliament in 1707, Edinburgh declined in political importance, but its cultural and intellectual life flourished. During the period known as the Scottish Enlightenment (roughly

1707	1745–46
Act of Union passed	Jacobite rebellion; Battle of Culloden

A well-presented
and easily absorbed
introduction to Scottish
history is at www.bbc
.co.uk/history/scottish
history.

1740–1830), Edinburgh became known as 'a hotbed of genius'. The philosophers David Hume and Adam Smith and the sociologist Adam Ferguson emerged as influential thinkers, nourished on generations of theological debate. Medic William Cullen produced the first modern pharmacopoeia, chemist Joseph Black advanced the science of thermo-dynamics and geologist James Hutton challenged long-held beliefs about the age of the Earth.

After centuries of bloodshed and religious fanaticism, people applied themselves with the same energy and piety to the making of money and the enjoyment of leisure. There was a revival of interest in Scottish history and literature. The writings of Sir Walter Scott (see the boxed text, p157) and the poetry of Robert Burns (see the boxed text, p174), a true man of the people, achieved lasting popularity.

THE INDUSTRIAL REVOLUTION

In the second half of the 18th century, the development of the steam engine ushered in the Industrial Revolution. The Carron Ironworks near Falkirk, established in 1759, became the largest ironworks and gun factory in Britain, and the growth of the textile industry saw the construction of huge weaving mills in Lanarkshire (see New Lanark, p162), Dundee, Angus and Aberdeenshire. The world's first steamboat, the *Charlotte Dundas*, sailed along the newly opened Forth and Clyde Canal in 1802, and the world's first sea-going steamship, the *Comet*, was launched on the Clyde in 1812.

Glasgow, deprived of its lucrative tobacco trade following the American War of Independence (1776–83), developed into an industrial powerhouse, the 'second city' of the British Empire (after London). Cotton mills, iron and steelworks, chemical works, shipbuilding yards and heavy-engineering works proliferated along the River Clyde in the 19th century, powered by the coal mines of Lanarkshire, Ayrshire, Fife and Midlothian.

By the start of the 20th century, Scotland was a world leader in the production of textiles, iron, steel and coal and above all in shipbuilding and marine engineering. Scottish-built ships plied the oceans the world over.

WAR & PEACE

Between 1904 and 1931
around a million people
emigrated from Scotland
to begin new lives in
North America and
Australia.

Although German bombers blitzed Clydebank in 1941, killing 1200 people, Scotland largely escaped the trauma and devastation wrought by WWII on the industrial cities of England. Indeed, the war brought a measure of renewed prosperity to Scotland as the shipyards and engineer-ing works geared up to supply the war effort. But the postwar period saw the collapse of shipbuilding and heavy industry, on which Scotland had become over-reliant.

The discovery of oil and gas in the North Sea in the 1970s brought new prosperity to Aberdeen and the surrounding area, and to the Shetland Islands. However, most of the oil revenue was siphoned off to England. This, along with takeovers of Scots companies by English ones (which then closed the Scots operation, asset-stripped and transferred jobs to England), fuelled increasing nationalist sentiment in Scotland. The Scottish Nationalist Party (SNP) developed into a third force in Scottish politics, taking 30% of the popular vote in the 1974 general election.

1740s–1830s	Late 18th century
Scottish Enlightenment	Industrial Revolution

EXPLORING YOUR SCOTTISH ROOTS

Genealogy is a hugely popular pastime, and many visitors to Scotland take the opportunity to do some detective work on their Scottish ancestry.

One of the best guides is *Tracing Your Scottish Ancestry* by Kathleen B Cory, and there are many useful websites, **GenUKI** (www.genuki.org.uk) is a good starting point.

At the **Scotland's People Website** (www.scotlandspeople.gov.uk) you can search the indexes to the Old Parish Registers and Statutory Registers up to 100 years ago (75 years ago for deaths), and the indexes to the 1881, 1891 and 1901 census returns, on a pay-per-view basis. The **International Genealogical Index** (www.familysearch.com), compiled by the Mormon Church, includes freely searchable records of Scottish baptisms and marriages from 1553 to 1875.

The following places in Edinburgh can help out:

General Register Office for Scotland (☎ 0131-314 4433; www.gro-scotland.gov.uk; New Register House, 3 West Register St, Edinburgh EH1 3YT; per full-/half-day £17/10; ☺ 9am-4.30pm Mon-Fri) The main records used in Scottish genealogical research – the Statutory Registers of births, marriages and deaths (1855 to the present), the Old Parish Registers (1533–1854) and the 10-yearly census returns from 1841 to 1901 – are held here. The registration of births, marriages and deaths became compulsory in Scotland on 1 January 1855; before that date, the ministers of the Church of Scotland kept registers of baptisms and marriages. The oldest surviving parish registers date back to 1553, but these records are far from complete, and many births and marriages before 1855 went unrecorded.

National Archives of Scotland (☎ 0131-535 1334; www.nas.gov.uk; Register House, 2 Princes St, Edinburgh EH1 3YY; admission free; ☺ 9am-4.45pm Mon-Fri) You will need to ask for a reader's ticket (free) – bring some form of ID bearing your name and signature (eg passport, driving licence, bank card). Use of the Historical Search Room is free, and is first-come, first-served.

Scottish Genealogy Society Library & Family History Centre (☎ 0131-220 3677; www.scots genealogy.com; 15 Victoria Tce, Edinburgh EH1 2JL; ☺ 10.30am-5.30pm Mon, Tue & Thu, to 8.30pm Wed, 10am-5pm Sat) Maintains the world's largest library of Scottish gravestone inscriptions. Entry is free for society members, £5 for nonmembers.

DEVOLUTION

In 1979 a referendum was held on whether to set up a directly elected Scottish Assembly. Fifty-two per cent of those who voted said 'yes' to devolution, but the Labour prime minister James Callaghan decided that everyone who didn't vote should be counted as a 'no'. By this devious reasoning, only 33% of the electorate had voted 'yes', so the Scottish Assembly was rejected.

From 1979 to 1997 Scotland was ruled by a Conservative government in London for which the majority of Scots hadn't voted. Separatist feelings, always present, grew stronger. Following the landslide victory of the Labour Party in May 1997, another referendum was held on the creation of a Scottish parliament. This time the result was overwhelmingly and unambiguously in favour.

Elections to the new parliament took place on 6 May 1999, and the Scottish parliament convened for the first time on 12 May in Edinburgh; Donald Dewar (1937–2000), formerly the Secretary of State for Scotland, was nominated as first minister (the Scottish parliament's equivalent of prime minister). After plenty of scandal and huge sums of money, a stunning new parliament building (see the boxed text, p81) was opened by the Queen in October 2004 at Holyrood in Edinburgh, with Jack McConnell presiding as the current first minister.

1970s	12 May 1999
North Sea oil and gas discovered	Scottish parliament convened for first time

The Culture

THE NATIONAL PSYCHE

Having lived next door to a large and powerful neighbour for so long, it is hardly surprising that a major part of the Scottish national identity lies in simply not being English. Throughout history England – still regularly referred to as 'the Auld Enemy' – was often seen as standing for power, greed, arrogance and oppression, and in reaction to that Scots have often seen themselves, collectively, as the plucky underdog, a freedom-loving David to England's imperialist Goliath.

Robert Louis Stevenson wrote that the mark of a Scot is that 'there burns alive in him a sense of identity with the dead even to the twentieth generation'. Scotland's unofficial anthem – *Flower of Scotland,* written by the late Roy Williamson and sung with gusto at football and rugby matches – harks back to the Battle of Bannockburn in 1314 when the Scots, outnumbered 10 to one, defeated the English; in the words of the song, they 'stood against him, proud Edward's army, and sent him homewards to think again'.

This historical baggage weighs heavily on the Scots, and has led to a long-standing resentment to English cultural and political domination. This reached a peak during the Thatcher government (1979–90), when a Conservative administration used the Scots as guinea pigs for the hugely unpopular poll tax, imposing it on Scotland a full year before it was extended to England and Wales – so much for a United Kingdom.

Although much of the resentment has dissipated since 1997, when a Labour government replaced the Conservatives, it still simmers under the surface. Just let a TV commentator once refer to a Scot as English, as occasionally happens when Scottish sportsmen and women are doing well in international competitions, and you can guarantee that a hundred hands will be reaching for the phone to complain to the BBC, while the next day's papers will be spluttering with outrage.

Today the Scotland-England rivalry is generally good-natured, and the field of conflict has long since moved from battlefield to sports stadium. A Scottish win over England at football or rugby is often seen as more important than winning an entire competition. There are few things Scots sports fans enjoy as much as an England team getting a good hiding, no matter who they are playing against. When a Scottish politician suggested that the Scots should lend their support to England during a World Cup competition that Scotland failed to qualify for, he was drowned out in a wave of ridicule. On the contrary, there was a run on football shirts and flags belonging to all of England's forthcoming opponents.

But the rivalry runs both ways. Asked whether he would support the Scottish football team if England were eliminated from the World Cup, an English fan replied: 'I have no problem at all in supporting the Scottish team. By doing so I am showing support for my fellow Britons and building on our common historical and cultural ties. Also, it really annoys them.'

LIFESTYLE

The Scottish lifestyle is pretty similar to that in any other northern European country. Unemployment is fairly low (5.7% in July 2005) and average income is reasonable (around £24,000 a year, about 92% of the UK average).

However, Scotland shares in the UK's culture of long working hours: a third of people work more than 48 hours a week, and one in six works more than 60 hours. The EU average is 40.3 hours. This encourages a work hard, play hard culture.

Just as the Eskimos are supposed to have 40 different words for snow, it seems as if the Scots have 40 different words for drunk – bevvied, blootered, hammered, guttered, fleein', fou, steamin', stotious, paralytic, plaistered and just plain pished, to name but a few.

There's no denying that, like most northern Europeans, the Scots enjoy a drink. For the vast majority that means a few pints of beer down the pub or a few glasses of wine with a meal, but for a significant minority the attitude is: if a thing's worth doing, it's worth overdoing.

Although on average Scots consume less alcohol per head than the French, much of it is in the form of binge-drinking; that is, going out to the pub on Friday and Saturday night and getting, well, blootered. Around 33% of men and 15% of women drink more than the recommended 21 units of alcohol a week (one unit equals one glass of wine). This translates into problems with drunk and disorderly behaviour on the streets, and alcohol-related health problems.

On the positive side, however, Scotland consistently rates highly in quality of life surveys. It's an attractive place to live, with excellent social, cultural and leisure amenities. There is still a strong sense of community in rural areas, and even in parts of the big cities.

From March 2006, smoking is banned in all public places in Scotland; see www .clearingtheairscotland .com.

POPULATION

The popular image of Scotland abroad is of crofts and castles and wild mountain scenery, but the country's population is in fact overwhelmingly urban, with 80% living in the cities and towns of the Central Lowlands.

The Highland region is one of Europe's most sparsely populated areas, with an average of only nine people per sq km – a mere one-thirtieth of the UK average. A major problem since WWII has been the depopulation of the rural Highlands and, especially, the Western Isles, as younger people leave to find jobs. This movement of people from rural to urban areas, which began in the 18th century, is still going on – the population of the Outer Hebrides has fallen by 10% in the last decade.

There are an estimated 60 million people around the world who claim Scottish ancestry.

Scotland's total population is decreasing (by 0.2% a year) and getting older (more than half of Scots are aged 40 or over), mainly as a result of a decreasing birth rate.

SPORT
Football
Football (soccer) in Scotland is not so much a sport as a religion, with thousands turning out to worship their local teams on Wednesdays and weekends throughout the season (August to May). Sacred rites include standing in the freezing cold of a February day, drinking hot Bovril and eating a Scotch pie as you watch your team getting gubbed.

Scotland's top 10 clubs play in the **Scottish Premier League** (www.scotprem .com), but two teams – Glasgow Rangers and Glasgow Celtic – dominate the competition. On only 18 occasions since 1890 has any team other than Rangers or Celtic won the league; the last time was when Aberdeen won in 1985. Celtic was Premier League champion in 2004, but it lost out to Rangers in 2005.

Glasgow Celtic was the first British team to win the European Cup (1967) and, so far, the only Scottish club to have done so. The team that won back then was made up entirely of Scots players from the Glasgow area. Rangers made history in 2000 by fielding a team composed entirely of non-Scottish players, and today half the players in the Premier

League are of non-Scottish origin, a situation that angers many grassroots supporters and bodes ill for the future of the national team.

If supporting local teams is like a religion, supporting the Scottish national team is more like a penance. The beginning of each European Championship and World Cup is filled with hope, but usually ends in despair.

Despite their team's often poor results, Scotland fans – known as the Tartan Army – are famed for their friendliness and good behaviour abroad, to the extent that some English and French football fans have joined them. The non-Scottish contingent has been dubbed the 'Sporran Legion'.

Rugby Union

Traditionally, football was the sport of Scotland's urban working classes, while rugby union was the preserve of agricultural workers from the Borders and middle-class university graduates. Although this distinction is breaking down – rugby's popularity soared after the 1999 World Cup was staged in the UK, and the middle classes have invaded the football terraces – it still persists to some extent.

Each year, starting in January, Scotland takes part in the Six Nations Rugby Union Championship. The most important fixture is the clash against England for the Calcutta Cup – it's always an emotive event, though Scotland has only won once in the last 12 years.

At club level, the season runs from September to May, and among the better teams are those from the Borders such as Hawick, Kelso and Melrose. At the end of the season, teams play a Rugby Sevens (seven-a-side) variation of the 15-player competition.

For more information on shinty, see www .shinty.com.

Golf

Aberdonian Paul Lawrie shot into the golfing limelight in 1999 when he came from nowhere to win the Open Championship. However, he still hasn't caught up with Colin Montgomerie, who has been Scotland's top golfer for over a decade, consistently finishing in the top five in international tournaments. In the Open at St Andrews in 2005, Montgomerie was runner-up to Tiger Woods; it was the fourth time he has come second in a major tournament, but a victory still eludes him.

Shinty

Shinty (*camanachd* in Gaelic) is a fast and physical ball-and-stick sport similar to Ireland's hurling, with more than a little resemblance to clan warfare. It's an indigenous Scottish game played mainly in the Highlands, and the most prized trophy is the Camanachd Cup. The cup final, held in September, is a great Gaelic get-together. The Kingussie team has dominated in recent times, winning the cup every year from 1997 to 2003, though Inveraray broke their winning streak in 2004 and Fort William won in 2005.

For more information on curling, see www .royalcaledoniancurling club.org.

Each year in October there's an international match between Scotland and Ireland, played under composite shinty/hurling rules, and held alternately in Ireland and Scotland.

Curling

Curling – basically lawn bowling on ice – got an enormous publicity boost when the British women's team (all Scots) won the gold medal in the 2002 Winter Olympics. The sport, which involves propelling a 42lb granite stone along the ice towards a target, was probably invented in Scotland in medieval times.

TARTANALIA TOP FIVE

Here's a quick guide to the top five icons of Scottish culture:

Bagpipes

Highland soldiers were traditionally accompanied into battle by the skirl of the pipes, and the Scottish Highland bagpipe is unique in being the only musical instrument ever to be classed as a weapon. The playing of the pipes was banned – under pain of death – by the British government in 1747 as part of a scheme to suppress Highland culture in the wake the Jacobite uprising of 1745. Officially described as a 'weapon of war', the pipes were revived when the Highland regiments were drafted into the British Army towards the end of the 18th century.

The bagpipe consists of a leather bag held under the arm, kept inflated by blowing through the blowstick; the piper forces air through the pipes by squeezing the bag with the forearm. Three of the pipes, known as drones, play a constant note (one bass, two tenor) in the background. The fourth pipe, the chanter, is the one on which the melody is played.

Ceilidh

The Gaelic word *ceilidh* (pronounced *kay*-lay) means 'visit'. A *ceilidh* was originally a social gathering in the house after the day's work was over, enlivened with storytelling, music and song. These days, a *ceilidh* means an evening of traditional Scottish entertainment including music, song and dance.

Tartan

The oldest surviving piece of tartan – a patterned woollen textile now made into everything from kilts to key rings – dates back to the Roman period. Today tartan is popular the world over, and beyond – astronaut Al Bean took his MacBean tartan to the moon and back. Particular setts (tartan patterns) didn't come to be associated with particular clans until the 17th century, although today every clan, and indeed every Scottish football team, has one or more distinctive tartans.

Kilt

The original Scottish Highland dress was not the kilt but the *plaid* – a long length of tartan cloth wrapped around the body and over the shoulder. The wearing of Highland dress was banned after the Jacobite rebellions but revived under royal patronage in the 19th century. George IV and his English courtiers donned kilts for their visit to Scotland in 1822. Sir Walter Scott, novelist, poet and dedicated patriot, did much to rekindle interest in Scottish ways. By then, however, many of the old setts had been forgotten – some tartans are actually Victorian creations. The modern kilt only appeared in the 18th century and was reputedly invented by Thomas Rawlinson, an Englishman!

Scottish Flag

Scottish football and rugby supporters can never seem to make up their minds which flag to wave – the Saltire or the Lion Rampant. The Saltire or St Andrew's Cross – a diagonal white cross on a blue ground – is one of the oldest national flags in the world, dating from at least the 12th century. Originally a religious emblem – St Andrew was crucified on a diagonal cross – it became a national emblem in the 14th century. According to legend, white clouds in the form of a saltire appeared in a blue sky during the battle of Nechtansmere between Scots and Saxons, urging the Scots to victory. It was incorporated in the Union Flag of the UK following the Act of Union in 1707.

The Lion Rampant – a red lion on a golden-yellow ground – is the Royal Banner of Scotland. It is thought to derive from the arms of King William I the Lion (r 1143–1214), and strictly speaking should be used only by a Scottish monarch. It is incorporated in the British Royal Standard, quartered with the three lions of England and the harp of Ireland.

Highland Games

You can search for your own clan tartan at www .scottish-tartans-society .co.uk.

Highland games are held in Scotland throughout the summer, and not just in the Highlands. You can find dates and details of Highland games all over the country on the **VisitScotland** (www.visitscotland.com) website – click on the About Scotland link, then Uniquely Scottish, then Highland Games by Region.

The traditional sporting events accompanied by piping and dancing competitions attract locals and tourists alike. Some events are peculiarly Scottish, particularly those that involve trials of strength: tossing the caber (heaving a tree trunk into the air), throwing the hammer and putting the stone. Major Highland games are staged at Dunoon (p279), Oban (p296) and Braemar (p264).

MEDIA

Although London dominates the UK media industry, Scotland has a flourishing media sector of its own, the legacy of a long tradition of Scottish publishing. The *Herald* (formerly the *Glasgow Herald*), established in 1783, is one of the oldest English-language newspapers in the world.

The Falkirk Tartan is a piece of cream and brown cloth that was found with a hoard of Roman coins dating from around AD 320. It is now in the Museum of Scotland in Edinburgh.

BBC Scotland is the regional arm of the UK's public service TV and radio broadcaster, producing and broadcasting programmes that reflect Scotland's distinctive cultural identity. Funded by an annual TV licence, the BBC doesn't carry advertising.

There are two Scottish-based commercial TV broadcasters. Scottish Television (STV) covers southern Scotland and some of the western Highlands, while Grampian TV transmits to the Highlands from Perth to the Western Isles and Shetland. STV, Grampian and the BBC all provide some Gaelic-language programming.

There's a healthy newspaper sector too. Sales figures for Scotland (excluding the rest of the UK) show that the three main, home-published quality newspapers – the *Scotsman, Herald* and *Press & Journal* – easily outsell all five London-produced quality dailies (*Telegraph, Times, Guardian, Independent* and *Financial Times*).

RELIGION

For news stories and information on religion in Scotland, check out the Hot Topics list on the *Scotsman* website (http://news.scotsman .com/topics.cfm), and click on Religious Issues.

Although the Christian church has played a hugely important role in Scottish history, religious observance in Scotland has been in decline for most of the 20th century. Today only 6.5% of the population regularly attend church on Sunday. Church attendance is highest in the Outer Hebrides (almost 40%) and lowest in the cities. For more on religion in the Outer Hebrides, see the boxed text, p385.

The two largest religious denominations are the Presbyterian Church of Scotland (47%) and the Roman Catholic Church (16%), with 28% claiming no religious affiliation at all. Non-Christian religions account for only 2% of the population, mostly small communities of Muslims, Hindus, Sikhs and Jews.

ARTS

Literature

Scotland's best-loved and most famous literary figure is, of course, Robert Burns (1759–96). His works have been translated into dozens of languages and are known and admired the world over (see the boxed text, p174).

In 1787 Burns was introduced to a 16-year-old boy at a social gathering in the house of an Edinburgh professor. The boy grew up to be Sir Walter Scott (1771–1832), Scotland's greatest and most prolific novelist. The son of an Edinburgh lawyer, Scott was born in Guthrie St (off Chambers St;

AUTHOR PROFILE: IAIN BANKS

One of Scotland's most successful contemporary authors, Iain Banks (1954–) is also one of its most prolific. He has published 21 novels since 1984, 10 of them science fiction written under 'the world's most penetrable pseudonym', Iain M Banks.

Hailed as one of the most imaginative writers of his generation, Banks burst on the Scottish literary scene with his dazzling debut novel *The Wasp Factory* (1984), a macabre but utterly compelling exploration of the inner world of Frank, a strange and deeply disturbed teenager. Though violent and unsettling, its dark humour and sharp dialogue keep the pages turning right to the bitter (and twisted) end.

Banks' most enjoyable books are *Complicity* (1993), a gruesome and often hilarious thriller-cum-satire on the greed and corruption of the Thatcher years, and the immensely likable *The Crow Road* (1992), a warm, witty and moving family saga based in the fictional Argyllshire town of Gallanach (a thinly disguised Oban transplanted to the shores of Loch Crinan). The latter provides one of Scottish fiction's most memorable opening sentences: 'It was the day my grandmother exploded.'

---

the house no longer exists) and lived at various New Town addresses before moving to his country house at Abbotsford (p157). Scott's early works were rhyming ballads, such as *The Lady of the Lake,* and his first historical novels – Scott effectively invented the genre – were published anonymously. He almost single-handedly revived interest in Scottish history and legend in the early 19th century, and was largely responsible for organising King George IV's visit to Scotland in 1822. Plagued by debt in later life, he wrote obsessively – to the detriment of his health – in order to make money, but will always be best remembered for classic tales such as *Waverley, The Antiquary, The Heart of Midlothian, Ivanhoe, Redgauntlet* and *Castle Dangerous.*

Along with Scott, Robert Louis Stevenson (1850–94) ranks as Scotland's best-known novelist. Born at 8 Howard Pl in Edinburgh, into a family of famous lighthouse engineers, Stevenson studied law at Edinburgh University but was always intent on pursuing the life of a writer. An inveterate traveller, but dogged by ill-health, he finally settled in Samoa in 1889, where he was revered by the natives as 'Tusitala' – the teller of tales. Stevenson is known and loved around the world for those tales: *Kidnapped, Catriona, Treasure Island, The Master of Ballantrae* and *The Strange Case of Dr Jekyll and Mr Hyde.* The Writers' Museum (p80) in Edinburgh celebrates the work of Burns, Scott and Stevenson.

Sir Arthur Conan Doyle (1859–1930), the creator of Sherlock Holmes, was born in Edinburgh and studied medicine at Edinburgh University. He based the character of Holmes on one of his lecturers, the surgeon Dr Joseph Bell, who had employed his forensic skills and powers of deduction on several murder cases in Edinburgh.

Scotland's finest modern poet was Hugh MacDiarmid (born Christopher Murray Grieve; 1892–1978). Originally from Dumfriesshire, he moved to Edinburgh in 1908, where he trained as a teacher and a journalist, but spent most of his life in Montrose, Shetland, Glasgow and Biggar. His masterpiece is *A Drunk Man Looks at the Thistle,* a 2685-line Joycean monologue.

Born in Edinburgh, Norman MacCaig (1910–96) is widely regarded as the greatest Scottish poet of his generation. A primary school teacher for almost 40 years, MacCaig wrote poetry that is witty, adventurous, moving and filled with sharp observation; poems such as *November Night, Edinburgh* vividly capture the atmosphere of his home city.

The poet and storyteller George Mackay Brown (1917–96) was born in Stromness (p407) in the Orkney Islands, and lived there almost all his life. Although his poems and novels are rooted in Orkney, his work, like that of Burns, transcends local and national boundaries. His novel *Greenvoe* is a warm, witty and poetic evocation of everyday life in an Orkney community.

Lewis Grassic Gibbon (born James Leslie Mitchell; 1901–35) is another Scots writer whose novels vividly capture a sense of place – in this case the rural northeast of Kincardineshire and Aberdeenshire. His most famous work is the trilogy of novels called *A Scot's Quair*.

Dame Muriel Spark (1918–) was born in Edinburgh and educated at James Gillespie's High School for Girls, an experience that provided material for perhaps her best-known novel, *The Prime of Miss Jean Brodie*, a shrewd portrait of 1930s Edinburgh. Dame Muriel is a prolific writer; her 22nd novel, *The Finishing School*, was published in 2004.

The most widely known Scots writers today include the award-winning James Kelman (1946–), Iain Banks (see the boxed text, p43) and Irvine Welsh (1961–). The grim realities of modern Glasgow are vividly conjured up in Kelman's short story collection *Not Not While the Giro*; his controversial novel *How Late It Was, How Late* won the 1994 Booker Prize.

ESSENTIAL SCOTTISH READS

■ *Waverley* (1814, Sir Walter Scott) English literature's first historical novel, a romantic account of a Scottish soldier caught up in the 1745 Jacobite rebellion. Hard to get into but worth the effort.

■ *Kidnapped!* (1886, Robert Louis Stevenson) A rip-roaring adventure tale for all ages, following 16-year-old Davie Balfour as he escapes through the Highlands with Jacobite rebel Allan Breck Stuart.

■ *The Silver Darlings* (1941, Neil M Gunn) A moving and mystical novel set in 19th-century Caithness, following the attempts by Highlanders dispossessed by the Clearances to wrest a living from the herring fishery.

■ *A Scot's Quair* (1946, Lewis Grassic Gibbon) A trilogy set in rural northeast Scotland that follows heroine Chris Guthrie as she tries to resolve the conflict between her love of the land and her desire to escape a constricting peasant culture.

■ *Para Handy Tales* (1955, Neil Munro) A much-loved collection of humorous stories about the crew of a steam puffer as it cruises the sea lochs of Argyllshire and the Crinan Canal.

■ *The Prime of Miss Jean Brodie* (1962, Muriel Spark) The story of a charismatic teacher in a 1930s Edinburgh girls school who leads her chosen girls – her crème de la crème – in the pursuit of truth and beauty, with devastating consequences.

■ *Greenvoe* (1972, George Mackay Brown) A vivid evocation of life in an Orkney fishing village in the 1960s; it is warm, funny, poetic and ultimately very, very moving.

■ *Laidlaw* (1977, William McIlvanney) A gritty detective story set in the mean streets of 1970s Glasgow, following in the footsteps of unorthodox policeman-cum-philosopher Jack Laidlaw.

■ *Trainspotting* (1993, Irvine Welsh) A disturbing and darkly humorous journey through Edinburgh's junkie underworld, pulling no punches as it charts hero Renton's descent into heroin addiction.

■ *Black and Blue* (1997, Ian Rankin) Stars hard-drinking detective John Rebus, Edinburgh's answer to Laidlaw, as he re-examines the notorious Bible John murders of the late 1960s. Gripping noir-style writing.

■ *The Trick Is to Keep Breathing* (1999, Janice Galloway) Follows a young drama teacher, the ironically named Joy, as she slips over the edge into depression and madness. Fluent, witty writing and comic minor characters keep the pages turning.

■ *Indelible Acts* (2003, AL Kennedy) A collection of mesmerising short stories on the theme of love and longing written by a master (or rather mistress) of the form, writing at the very top of her game.

The novels of Irvine Welsh, who grew up in Edinburgh's working-class district of Muirhouse, describe a very different world from that inhabited by Miss Jean Brodie – the modern city's underworld of drugs, drink, despair and violence. Best known for his debut novel *Trainspotting*, Welsh's best work is probably *Marabou Stork Nightmares*, in which a soccer hooligan, paralysed and in a coma, reviews his violent and brutal life.

Cinema & Television

Scotland has never really had its own film industry, but in recent years the government-funded agency **Scottish Screen** (☎ 0141-302 1730; www.scottishscreen .com) has been created to nurture native talent and promote and develop all aspects of film and TV in Scotland.

Perthshire-born John Grierson (1898–1972) is acknowledged around the world as the father of the documentary film. His legacy includes the classic *Drifters* (about the Scottish herring fishery) and *Seaward the Great Ships* (about Clyde shipbuilding). Filmmaker Bill Douglas (1934–91), the director of an award-winning trilogy of films documenting his childhood and early adult life, was born in the former mining village of Newcraighall just south of Edinburgh.

Glasgow-born writer-director Bill Forsyth (1946–) is best known for *Local Hero* (1983), a gentle comedy about an oil magnate seduced by the beauty of the Highlands, and *Gregory's Girl* (1980), about an awkward, teenage schoolboy's romantic exploits. The directing credits of Gillies MacKinnon (1948–), another Glasgow native, include *Small Faces* (1996), *Regeneration* (1997) and *Hideous Kinky* (1998). Michael Caton-Jones (1958–), director of *Memphis Belle* (1990) and *Rob Roy* (1995), was born in West Lothian and is a graduate of Edinburgh University.

For a guide to Scottish film locations check out www.scotlandthemovie .com.

In the 1990s the rise of the director-producer-writer team of Danny Boyle (English), Andrew Macdonald and John Hodge (both Scottish) – who wrote the scripts for *Shallow Grave* (1994), *Trainspotting* (1996) and *A Life Less Ordinary* (1997) – marked the beginnings of what might be described as a home-grown Scottish film industry. Other cinematic talents to emerge in this decade include actor and director Peter Mullan (*The Magdalene Sisters*, 2002) and director Lynne Ramsay (*Ratcatcher*, 1999; and *Morvern Callar*, 2002).

Writer and director David McKenzie hit the headlines in recent years with *Young Adam* (2003), starring Ewan McGregor and Tilda Swinton, which won BAFTAs for best actor, best actress, best director and best film.

Scotland's most famous actor is, of course, Sir Sean Connery (1930–), the original and best James Bond, and star of dozens of other hit films including *Highlander* (1986), *The Name of the Rose* (1986), *Indiana Jones and the Last Crusade* (1989) and *The Hunt for Red October* (1990). Connery started life as 'Big Tam' Connery, sometime milkman and brickie, born in a tenement in Fountainbridge in Edinburgh.

Despite dodgy Scottish accents from Liam Neeson and Jessica Lange, *Rob Roy* is a witty and moving cinematic version of Sir Walter Scott's tale of the outlaw MacGregor.

Other Scottish actors who have achieved international recognition include Robert Carlyle, who starred in *Trainspotting* (1996), *The Full Monty* (1997) – the UK's most commercially successful film – and *The World Is Not Enough* (1999); and Ewan McGregor, who appeared in *Trainspotting*, *Moulin Rouge* (2001) and the most recent Star Wars films.

It's less widely known that Scotland produced some of the stars of silent film, including Eric Campbell (the big, bearded villain in Charlie Chaplin's films) and Jimmy Finlayson (the cross-eyed character in Laurel and Hardy films); though born in England, Stan Laurel himself grew up and made his acting debut in Glasgow.

Music

FOLK MUSIC

Scotland has always had a strong folk tradition. In the 1960s and 1970s Robin Hall and Jimmy MacGregor, the Corries and the hugely talented Ewan McColl worked the pubs and clubs up and down the country. The Boys of the Lough, headed by Shetland fiddler Aly Bain, were one of the first professional bands to promote the traditional Celtic music of Scotland and Ireland. They have been followed by the Battlefield Band, Runrig (who write songs in Gaelic), Alba, Capercaillie and others.

The Scots folk songs that you will often hear sung in pubs and at *ceilidhs* draw on Scotland's rich history. A huge number of them relate to the Jacobite rebellions of the early 18th century and, in particular, to Bonnie Prince Charlie – *Hey Johnnie Cope*, the *Skye Boat Song* and *Will Ye No Come Back Again*, for example – while others relate to the Covenanters and the Highland Clearances.

The Living Tradition is a bimonthly magazine covering the folk and traditional music of Scotland and the British Isles, and Celtic music with features and reviews of albums and live gigs. See also www.folkmusic.net.

ROCK & POP

It would take an entire book to list all the Scottish artists and bands that have made it big in the world of rock and pop. From Glasgow-born King of Skiffle, Lonnie Donegan, in the 1950s, to the Glasgow-bred kings of guitar pop Franz Ferdinand in 2005, the roll call is long and impressive.

The 1960s saw Lulu shout her way into the charts, alongside Donovan and the Incredible String Band, while the '70s produced the Average White Band, Nazareth, the Sensational Alex Harvey Band, John Martyn and, God help us, the Bay City Rollers, a global phenomenon whose allure remains a mystery to all except those who were teenage girls in the early 1970s.

The punk era produced the short-lived but superb Rezillos, plus the more durable Big Country, followed by a long roll call of chart-toppers in the '80s – Simple Minds, The Waterboys, Primal Scream, Jesus and Mary Chain, Blue Nile, Lloyd Cole and the Commotions, Aztec Camera, The Associates, Deacon Blue, The Cocteau Twins, The Proclaimers, Wet Wet Wet, Texas, Hue and Cry, Runrig, The Bluebells – where do you stop?

The '90s saw the emergence of three bands that took the top three places in a vote for the best Scottish band of all time – melodic indie-pop songsters Belle and Sebastian, like-Oasis-only-better Brit-rock band Travis, and indie rockers Idlewild, who opened for the Rolling Stones in 2003 – as well as the Delgados, Trashcan Sinatras and Teenage Fanclub.

Scottish artists who have made an impression in the last five years include experimental rockers the Beta Band; foul-mouthed, soul-baring depressives Arab Strap; Dogs Die In Hot Cars, whose bouncy, melodic, 80s-style pop is reminiscent of XTC and Dexy's Midnight Runners; and Mylo, a DJ from the Isle of Skye. The bespectacled twin brothers Craig and Charlie Reid from Auchtermuchty in Fife, better known as The Pro-

---

TOP FIVE SCOTTISH ALBUMS OF RECENT YEARS

- *Destroy Rock and Roll* (2004) Mylo
- *Franz Ferdinand* (2004) Franz Ferdinand
- *From Heroes to Zeroes* (2004) Beta Band
- *Into the Woods* (2005) Michael Middleton
- *Weightlifting* (2004) Trashcan Sinatras

claimers, also produced a new album in 2005 *(Restless)* which is as passionate and invigorating as the songs that first made them famous back in the late 80s, 'Letter From America', and 'I'm Gonna Be (500 Miles)'.

The airwaves have been awash with female singer-songwriters in recent years, but few are as gutsy and versatile as Edinburgh-born, St Andrews–raised KT Tunstall. Although she's been writing and singing for the last 10 years, it was her 2005 debut album *Eye to the Telescope* that introduced her to a wider audience. And then there's Glasgow-born Angela McCluskey, whose husky vocals have been compared to Billie Holiday and Cerys Matthews.

For more information on Glasgow's live-music scene and current bands, see the boxed text, p140.

Architecture

There are interesting buildings all over Scotland, but Edinburgh has a particularly rich heritage of 18th- and early-19th-century architecture, and Glasgow is noted for its superb Victorian buildings.

ROMANESQUE (12TH CENTURY)

The Romanesque style – with its characteristic round arches and chevron decoration – was introduced to Scotland along with the monasteries that were founded during the reign of David I (1124–53). Good examples survive in Dunfermline Abbey (see the boxed text, p205), and St Magnus Cathedral in Kirkwall (p401).

GOTHIC (12TH TO 16TH CENTURIES)

The more elaborate Gothic style, with its tall, pointed arches, ornate window tracery and ribbed vaulting, was brought to Scotland and adapted by the monastic orders. Examples of Early Gothic architecture can be seen in the ruins of the great Border abbeys of Jedburgh (p158) and Dryburgh (p156), at Holyrood Abbey in Edinburgh (p82) and in Glasgow Cathedral (p125). The more decorative Middle and Late Gothic styles appear in Melrose Abbey (p155), the cathedrals of Dunkeld (p226) and Elgin (p268), and the parish churches of Haddington (St Mary's; p113) and Stirling (Church of the Holy Rude; p192).

POST-REFORMATION (16TH & 17TH CENTURIES)

After the Reformation many abbeys and cathedrals were damaged or destroyed, as the new religion frowned on ceremony and ornament.

During this period the old style of castle, with its central keep and curtain wall (eg Caerlaverock and Dirleton Castles), was superseded by the tower house. Good examples include Castle Campbell (p203), Loch Leven Castle (p216) and Neidpath Castle (p160). The Renaissance style was introduced in the royal palaces of Linlithgow (p115) and Falkland (p206).

Scotland's Castles by Chris Tabraham is an excellent companion for anyone touring Scottish castles – a readable, illustrated history detailing how and why they were built.

GEORGIAN (18TH & EARLY 19TH CENTURIES)

The leading Scottish architects of the 18th century were William Adam (1684–1748) and his son Robert Adam (1728–92), whose revival of classical Greek and Roman forms influenced architects throughout Europe. Among the many neoclassical buildings they designed are Hopetoun House (p112), Culzean Castle (p175) and Edinburgh's Charlotte Sq (p86), possibly the finest example of Georgian architecture anywhere.

The New Town of Edinburgh, and other planned towns such as Inveraray (Argyll) and Blair Atholl (Perthshire), are characterised by their elegant Georgian architecture.

VICTORIAN (MID- TO LATE 19TH CENTURY)

Alexander 'Greek' Thomson (1817–75) changed the face of 19th-century Glasgow with his neoclassical designs. Masterpieces such as the Egyptian Halls and Caledonia Rd Church in Glasgow combine Egyptian and Hindu motifs with Greek and Roman forms.

In Edinburgh, William Henry Playfair (1790–1857) continued the neoclassical tradition of Robert Adam in the Greek temples of the National Monument (p87) on Calton Hill, the Royal Scottish Academy (p85) and the National Gallery of Scotland (p85), before moving on to the neo-Gothic style in Edinburgh University's New College on The Mound.

The 19th-century boom in country-house building was led by architects William Burn (1789–1870) and David Bryce (1803–76). The resurgence of interest in Scottish history and identity, led by writers such as Sir Walter Scott, saw architects turn to the towers, pointed turrets and crow-stepped gables of the 16th century for inspiration. The Victorian revival of the Scottish Baronial style, which first made an appearance in 16th-century buildings such as Craigievar Castle (p265), produced many fanciful houses such as Balmoral Castle (p262), Scone Palace (p217) and Abbotsford (p157).

'Charles Rennie Mackintosh is one of the most influential exponents of the Art Nouveau style'

THE 20TH CENTURY

Scotland's most famous 20th-century architect and designer is Charles Rennie Mackintosh, one of the most influential exponents of the Art Nouveau style. The most acclaimed example of his work is Glasgow School of Art (p124), which still looks modern a century after it was built. For more on Charles Rennie Mackintosh, see the boxed text, p124. The Art Deco style of the 1930s made little impact in Scotland, with only a few examples, such as St Andrews House in Edinburgh and the beautifully restored Luma Tower in Glasgow.

During the 1960s Scotland's larger towns and cities suffered badly under the onslaught of the motor car and the unsympathetic impact of large-scale, concrete building developments. However, modern architecture discovered a new confidence in the 1980s and 1990s, exemplified by the impressive gallery housing the Burrell Collection (p127) in Glasgow and the stunning modern buildings lining the banks of Glasgow's River Clyde (p122).

Scotland's most controversial new structure is the Scottish parliament building in Edinburgh (p81).

Painting

If asked to think of a Scottish painting, most people probably picture *Monarch of the Glen,* a romanticised portrait of a magnificent Highland red deer stag by Sir Edwin Landseer (1802–73). Landseer was not a Scot but a Londoner, though he did spend a lot of time in Scotland, leasing a cottage in Glen Feshie and visiting the young Queen Victoria at Balmoral to tutor her in drawing and etching.

Perhaps the most famous Scottish painting is the portrait *Reverend Robert Walker Skating on Duddingston Loch* by Sir Henry Raeburn (1756–1823), in the National Gallery of Scotland (p85). This image of a Presbyterian minister at play beneath Arthur's Seat, with all the poise of a ballerina and the hint of a smile on his lips, is a symbol of Enlightenment Edinburgh, the triumph of reason over wild nature.

Scottish portraiture reached its peak during the Scottish Enlightenment in the second half of the 18th century with the paintings of Rae-

SCOTTISH INVENTIONS & DISCOVERIES

The Scots have made a contribution to modern civilisation that is out of all proportion to the size of their country. Although Scotland accounts for only 10% of Britain's population, it has produced more than 20% of leading British scientists, philosophers, engineers and inventors. Scots established the modern disciplines of economics, sociology, geology, electromagnetic theory, anaesthesiology and antibiotics, and pioneered the steam engine, the pneumatic tyre, the telephone and the TV.

Given the weather in Scotland perhaps it's not surprising that it was a Scot – the chemist Charles Macintosh (1766–1843) – who invented the waterproof material for the raincoat that still bears his name.

James Watt (1736–1819) didn't invent the steam engine (that was done by an Englishman, Thomas Newcomen) but it was Watt's modifications and improvements – notably the separate condenser – that led to its widespread usefulness in industry.

The chemical engineer James Young (1811–83), known as 'Paraffin' Young, developed the process of refining crude oil and established the world's first oil industry, based on extracting oil from the oil shales of West Lothian.

Not only did John Logie Baird (1888–1946) from Helensburgh invent TV, but it was his own company that produced (with the BBC) the world's first TV broadcast, the first broadcast with sound and the first outside broadcast. He also developed the concept of colour TV and took out a patent on fibre optics.

Alexander Graham Bell (1847–1922) was born in Edinburgh and emigrated to Canada and the USA, where he made a series of inventions, the most famous being the telephone in 1876.

In 1996 a team of Scottish embryologists working at the Roslin Institute near Edinburgh scored a first when they successfully cloned a sheep, Dolly, from the breast cell of an adult sheep. They added to this success when Dolly was mated naturally with a Welsh ram; in April 1998 she gave birth to a healthy lamb, Bonnie.

The list of famous Scots goes on and on: James Gregory (1638–75), inventor of the reflecting telescope; John McAdam (1756–1836), who developed road-building and surfacing techniques; Thomas Telford (1757–1834), one of the greatest civil engineers of his time; Robert William Thomson (1822–73), who patented the pneumatic tyre in 1845; John Boyd Dunlop (1840–1921), who reinvented the pneumatic tyre in 1888; Sir Alexander Fleming (1881–1955), codiscoverer of penicillin; and Sir Robert Watson-Watt (1892–1973), a direct descendant of James Watt, who developed the radar system that helped Britain to victory in WWII.

Other Scottish inventions and discoveries:

▪ antiseptic	▪ golf	▪ morphine
▪ bicycle	▪ grand piano	▪ postage stamp (adhesive)
▪ breech-loading rifle	▪ insulin	▪ refrigeration
▪ carbon dioxide	▪ iron and steel ships	▪ speedometer
▪ colour photography	▪ iron plough	▪ steam-powered ship
▪ decimal point	▪ kaleidoscope	▪ telescope
▪ electric light	▪ lawnmower	▪ ultrasound
▪ fire alarm	▪ logarithm	▪ vacuum flask
▪ gas mask	▪ marmalade	▪ water softener

Scotland has also produced a significant number of Nobel Prize winners. Sir William Ramsay (1852–1916), whose work helped in the development of the nuclear industry, received the chemistry prize in 1904. Physiologist John Macleod (1876–1935), whose work led to the discovery of insulin, received the prize for medicine in 1923. Sir Alexander Fleming (1881–1955), codiscoverer of penicillin, also received the prize for medicine (in 1945). Other prize winners include Charles Wilson, John Orr, Alexander Robertus Todd and Sir James Black.

burn and his contemporary Allan Ramsay (1713–84). You can see many fine examples of their work in the Scottish National Portrait Gallery (p86). At the same time, Alexander Nasmyth (1758–1840) emerged as an important landscape painter whose work had an immense influence on the 19th century. One of the greatest artists of the 19th century was Sir David Wilkie (1785–1841), whose genre paintings depicted rustic scenes of rural Highland life.

In the early 20th century the Scottish painters most widely acclaimed outside the country are the group known as the Scottish Colourists – SJ Peploe, Francis Cadell, Leslie Hunter and JD Fergusson – whose striking paintings drew on French postimpressionist and Fauvist influences. Peploe and Cadell, active in the 1920s and 1930s, often spent the summer painting together on the Isle of Iona, and reproductions of their beautiful landscapes and seascapes appear on many a print and postcard. Aberdeen Art Gallery (p255), Kirkcaldy Museum & Art Gallery (p205) and the JD Fergusson Gallery in Perth (p218) all have good examples of their work.

'Reproductions of Peploe and Cadell's beautiful landscapes and seascapes appear on many a print and postcard'

The painters of the so-called Edinburgh School of the 1930s were modernist landscape artists. Chief among them were William Gillies (1898–1978), Sir William MacTaggart (1903–81) and Anne Redpath (1895–1965). Following WWII, artists such as Alan Davie (1920–) and Sir Eduardo Paolozzi (1924–) gained international reputations in abstract expressionism and pop art. The Dean Gallery (p87) in Edinburgh has a large collection of Paolozzi's work.

Among contemporary Scottish artists the most famous – or rather notorious – are Peter Howson and Jack Vettriano. Howson (1958–), best known for his grim portraits of Glasgow down-and-outs and muscular workers, hit the headlines when he went to Bosnia as an official war artist in 1993 and produced some disturbing and controversial works. *Croatian and Muslim*, an uncompromising rape scene, sparked a debate about what was acceptable in a public exhibition of art. More recently his nude portraits of Madonna – the pop icon, not the religious one – garnered even more column inches in the press. His work is much sought after and collected by celebrities such as David Bowie and Madonna herself. You can see examples of Howson's work at Aberdeen Art Gallery (p255) and Glasgow's Gallery of Modern Art (p123).

Jack Vettriano (1954–) was formerly a mining engineer, but now ranks as one of Scotland's most commercially successful artists. An entirely self-taught painter, his work – realistic, voyeuristic, occasionally sinister and often carrying a powerful erotic charge – has been compared to that of the American painters Edward Hopper and Walter Sickert. You can see reproductions of his work in coffee-table books and posters, but not in any Scottish art gallery. The Scottish art establishment looks down its nose at him, despite – or perhaps because of – the enormous popularity of his work.

Environment

THE LAND

The Scottish mainland can be neatly divided into three parts – the Southern Uplands, the Central Lowlands and the Highlands.

The Southern Uplands, a range of rounded hills covered with grass and heather, bounded by fertile coastal plains, form the southern boundary to the Central Lowlands. The geological divide – the Southern Uplands Fault – runs in a line from Girvan in Ayrshire to Dunbar in East Lothian.

The Central Lowlands lie in a broad band stretching from Glasgow and Ayr in the west to Edinburgh and Dundee in the east. This area is underlaid by sedimentary rocks, including the beds of coal and oil shale that fuelled Scotland's industrial revolution. Most of the country's industry, its two largest cities and 80% of the population are concentrated here.

Another great geological divide – the Highland Boundary Fault – runs from Helensburgh in the west to Stonehaven on the east coast, and marks the southern edge of the Scottish Highlands.

These Highland hills – most of their summits reach to around the 900m to 1000m mark – were deeply dissected by glaciers during the last Ice Age, creating a series of deep, U-shaped valleys: the long, narrow sea lochs that today are such a distinctive feature of Highland scenery.

Remember that, for all their pristine beauty, the wild, empty landscapes of the western and northern Highlands are artificial wildernesses. Before the Highland Clearances (see the boxed text, p355) many of these empty corners of Scotland supported sizable populations.

WILDLIFE

Scotland's wildlife is one of its big attractions and an organised safari (p223) geared towards wildlife-watching can be the best way to see it. Many species that have disappeared from, or are rare in, the rest of Britain survive here, including red deer, golden eagles, otters, wildcats and ospreys.

Animals

Red deer are found in large numbers in Scotland, but the reindeer (apart from the herd of introduced domestic reindeer living in a semiwild state in the Cairngorms), beaver and aurochs (wild ox) are all long extinct; the last wolf was shot in Sutherland in 1700. There has been a strong push led by the Scottish Wildlife Trust to reintroduce the beaver. A small population of wildcats survives in parts of the Highlands but they are extremely shy and rarely seen in the wild.

Otters are found in most parts of Scotland, around the coast and along salmon and trout rivers. The best places to spot them are in the northwest, especially in Skye and the Outer Hebrides. The piers at Kyle of Lochalsh and Portree are otter 'hot spots', as the otters have learned to scavenge from fishing boats.

Bred for their quality beef, Highland cattle are Scotland's most distinctive bovine breed. They are fierce looking (with their horns) but docile-natured, with long reddish-brown coats.

Scotland has an immense variety of bird species and this is one of its premier wildlife attractions. For bird-watchers, the Shetland Islands (see the boxed text, p425) are paradise. Twenty-one of the British Isles' 24 seabird species are found here and being entertained by the clownish antics of the puffin is a highlight for visitors.

Scotland accounts for one third of the British mainland's surface area, but it has a massive 80% of Britain's coastline and only 10% of its population.

Contrary to the perception that the Highlands are stark naked, the northwestern Highlands have a large number of forests and woods. Grab a copy of *The Forests of the Far North* brochure, free at Tourist Information Centres (TICs).

Wild Scotland (www.wild-scotland.co.uk) has plenty of information and practical advice on wildlife-watching in Scotland.

Large numbers of grouse – a popular game bird – graze the heather on the moors. In heavily forested areas you may see a capercaillie, a black, turkey-like bird, the largest member of the grouse family. Birds of prey, such as the golden eagle, osprey, peregrine falcon and hen harrier, are protected. Millions of greylag geese winter on the Lowland stubble fields.

The ptarmigan (a relative of the grouse) is a native of the hills, seldom seen below 700m, with the unusual feature of having feathered feet. It is the only British bird that plays the Arctic trick of changing its plumage from mottled brown in summer to dazzling white in winter, the better to blend in with the snowfields. The blue mountain hare shares the ptarmigan's high mountain environment, and also its trait of swapping a grey-brown summer coat for a pure white winter one.

The waters off Scotland's west coast are rich in marine mammals, including whales. Dolphins and porpoises are fairly common, and in summer minke whales are regular visitors. Growing up to 10m long, they make an impressive sight when they breach through a shoal of herring fry. (Minke whales have also been spotted around the Isle of May in the Firth of Forth.)

Both the Atlantic grey (identified by its roman nose) and the common seal (with a face like a dog) can be seen along the coast of Scotland, including Arran's shoreline (p167).

ENDANGERED SPECIES

Scotland is home to many endangered animals and birds that are constantly threatened by the changing environment.

The habitat of the once common corncrake, for example, was almost completely wiped out by modern farming methods. Farmers now receive a subsidy for mowing in a corncrake-friendly fashion and there are good prospects for the bird's survival. Listen for their distinctive call – like a thumbnail drawn along the teeth of a comb – on the Isle of Coll (p307) and at Loch Gruinart Nature Reserve on Islay (p290).

Wildlife species that were slaughtered to the point of extermination in the 19th century – golden eagles, buzzards, pine martens, polecats and wildcats among them – are now protected by law and are slowly recovering. Both the red kite and the white-tailed sea eagle, absent from Scotland since the 19th century, have been successfully reintroduced.

The majestic osprey (absent for most of the 20th century) nests in Scotland from mid-March through to September, after migrating from West Africa. There are around 160 breeding pairs and you can see nesting sites throughout the country, including at Loch Garten (p330) and Loch of the Lowes (p226). White-tailed sea eagles, the fourth largest eagle in the world and easily distinguishable by their yellow beak and talons, are found along the west coast and in the Hebrides – visitors can see them (via closed-circuit television cameras at a secret nesting site) at the Aros Experience on Skye (p379). Galloway Forest Park (p182) is a good place to spot red kites.

INTRODUCED SPECIES

The American grey squirrel is an alien invader, introduced at the end of the 19th century and now very common. They have displaced the native red squirrel in most of England and Wales; Scotland is now home to 75% of Britain's surviving red squirrel population.

Plants

Although the thistle is commonly associated with Scotland, the national flower is the Scottish bluebell, which carpets the floor of native woodlands in spring. Heather, whose tiny pink and purple flowers emerge in

A beautifully written book about Scotland's wildlife, written by a man who lived and breathed alongside the country's critters in a remote part of the Highlands, is *A Last Wild Place* by Mike Tomkies.

Scottish Natural Heritage (www.snh.org.uk) is the government agency responsible for the conservation of Scotland's wildlife, habitats and landscapes.

August, covers much of the hills and moors. Other conspicuous flowering plants include vivid pink rhododendrons and bright yellow gorse (or whin), which both flower in May and June.

Rhododendrons – flowering shrubs with beautiful pink, purple or red flowers – were introduced in the 19th century. Planted at first in private gardens, they soon escaped the confines of estates to grow wild. Though beautiful, they grow vigorously and tend to displace native trees and shrubs.

Only 1% of Scotland's ancient woodlands survive, but regeneration forests are slowly covering more of the landscape – especially in the Highlands. Perthshire (p215) is home to many woodlands (and a 5000-year-old yew tree; p224) and forest walks.

Park	Features	Activities	Best time to visit	Page
Balranald Nature Reserve	lochan (small lochs), moor & marsh: corncrakes, red-necked phalaropes	bird-watching	Apr-Aug	p394
Caenlochan National Nature Reserve	mountain & glen: rare alpine flora	hill walking	Jul & Aug	p250
Cairngorms National Park	subarctic mountain plateau, native pine forests: ospreys, ptarmigans, pine martens	hill walking, climbing, skiing	Aug	p325
Craigellachie Nature Reserve	pine forest, crags: capercaillies, peregrine falcons	walking	May-Sep	p326
Galloway Forest Park	hills, forests, lochs: red deer, red kites	walking, mountain biking	Oct	p182
Glen Affric National Nature Reserve	mountain, loch, native pine forest: golden eagles, red deer, pine martens, wildcats	hill walking	Jul-Oct	p321
Hermaness Nature Reserve	coastal cliffs: puffins	bird-watching	Apr-Aug	p428
Inverpolly Nature Reserve	mountain, loch & moorland: red deer, wildcats, otters, golden eagles, peregrine falcons, red-throated divers	walking	Apr-Oct	p366
Isle of Rum National Nature Reserve	dramatic rocky mountains & coast: red deer, wild goats, golden eagles, white-tailed sea eagles, Manx shearwaters	walking, hill walking, bird-watching	Apr-Oct	p346
Loch Druidibeg National Nature Reserve	freshwater loch, farmland, machair: dunlins, redshanks, ringed plovers, greylag geese, corncrakes	bird-watching, walking	Apr-Oct	p395
Loch Gruinart Nature Reserve	farmland, tidal flats: corncrakes, migrating geese & waders	bird-watching	Apr-Oct	p290
Loch Lomond & the Trossachs National Park	scenic lochs, forests, hills	hill walking, angling, water sports	Sep-Nov	p274
Noss National Nature Reserve	spectacular coastal cliffs: nesting seabirds	bird-watching	May-Aug	p422
St Abb's Head National Nature Reserve	coastal cliffs: nesting seabirds	walking, bird-watching	Apr & May	p151

NATIONAL PARKS

Scotland has recently created two national parks – **Loch Lomond & the Trossachs National Park** (www.lochlomond-trossachs.org) and the **Cairngorms National Park** (www.cairngorms.co.uk).

Sites around the country are currently being considered for the country's first national marine park. The leading contender is an area off Oban which would extend to Coll and Tiree in the west and would also take in large areas of the mainland coast.

ENVIRONMENTAL ISSUES

Wind farms and the use of alternate power sources for electricity generation are hot topics on Scotland's environmental front. Essentially concentrations of giant, electricity-generating windmills, wind farms are a key element of the government's commitment to cutting greenhouse gas emissions and meeting climate-change targets (Scotland lags well behind the rest of the UK). The Scottish Executive has set a target of generating 40% of electricity in Scotland from renewable sources by 2020.

Although this will be a mix of green sources, including marine and solar power, it appears wind is top of the list. Plans to build the world's biggest wave farm on Orkney were scrapped in 2005 due to a lack of government funding, further fuelling fears of a surge in wind farm construction. The problem is, although everyone agrees that wind power is clean and economical, there's a powerful NIMBY (not in my back yard) element who don't want the windmills spoiling their view. There are also concerns that wind farms could have a detrimental effect on tourism, arguably Scotland's most important industry (who wants to go for a stroll in the Highlands to see mighty forest peaks, surging burns and…giant windmills?).

But, for better or worse, it's full steam ahead. Spurness wind farm in Orkney was opened in March 2005 and one of the biggest new wind farms is expected to come online in mid-2006: the Braes of Doune wind farm in Stirlingshire. The breezy Shetlands are fertile grounds for wind power and proposals have been put forth to develop a major wind farm there.

There's also intense debate in government circles (and the media) on whether to increase reliance on nuclear power for electricity generation. In 2005 the government named 159 sites in Scotland it had considered using to dump radioactive waste from its nuclear programmes. The Highlands and northern islands were favoured as nuclear-waste dumping grounds, with a combined total of 53 sites named in Orkney, the Shetlands and the Western Isles; and a further 45 sites in the Highlands.

In Caithness the Dounreay nuclear-waste-reprocessing plant (p362) had a poor safety record over several decades. Following a series of accidents and disclosures about errors and cover-ups – around 170kg of weapons-grade uranium remains unaccounted for – the British government decided to close it down in 1998. However cleaning up the site and storing the waste safely will take until 2036 and cost £2.7 billion; after that it'll take until 2095 to dismantle the plant safely, and encase the remains in concrete.

Since the 1980s many sea lochs and sheltered inlets on the west coast have been disfigured by salmon cages. Salmon farming is worth £300 million a year to the Scottish economy, but the industry has been blamed for spreading disease and parasites in wild fish populations, and for causing pollution and toxic algal blooms. Meanwhile, with rapidly declining fish stocks, especially cod, the future viability of the Scottish fishing industry is in doubt and strict quotas imposed by the EU in an attempt to sustain the industry are controversial, especially in the many fishing villages dotted around the Scottish coastline.

One of the best-loved pieces of Scottish wildlife writing is *Ring of Bright Water* by Gavin Maxwell, in which the author describes life on the remote Glenelg peninsula with his two pet otters in the 1950s.

Woodland Trust Scotland (www.woodland-trust .org.uk) is the Scottish arm of a UK charity dedicated to the conservation of native woodlands.

Friends of the Earth Scotland (www.foe -scotland.org.uk) is a voluntary organisation campaigning on environmental issues.

Outdoor Activities

Scotland is a brilliant place for outdoor recreation and has something to offer everyone, from those who enjoy a short stroll after breakfast to full-on adrenaline junkies. Although hiking, golf, fishing and cycling are the most popular activities, there is an astonishing variety of things to do.

Most activities are well organised and have clubs and associations that can give visitors invaluable information and, sometimes, substantial discounts. **VisitScotland** (www.visitscotland.com) and **VisitBritain** (www.visitbritain.com) have brochures on most activities.

Detailed information can be found in the regional chapters throughout this guide.

WALKING

Scotland's wild, dramatic scenery and varied landscape has made walking a hugely popular pastime for locals and tourists alike. There really is something for everyone, from after-breakfast strolls to the popular sport of Munro bagging (p60).

The best time of year for hill walking is usually May to September, although snow can fall on the highest summits even in midsummer. Winter walking on the higher hills of Scotland is for experienced mountaineers only, requiring the use of ice axe and crampons.

Highland hikers should be properly equipped, and cautious, as the weather can become vicious at any time of year. After rain, peaty soil can become boggy; always wear stout shoes or boots and carry a map and compass, waterproof clothing, a head-torch, whistle, bivouac bag, and extra food and drink – many unsuspecting walkers have had to survive an unplanned night in the open. On longer hill walks, always make sure that someone knows where you are going, and when you expect to return – don't depend on mobile phones (although carrying one with you is a good idea, and can be a life-saver if you can get a signal). If necessary, leave a note of your route and expected time of return in the windscreen of your car.

There is a tradition of relatively free access to open country in Scotland, especially on mountains and moorlands. You should, however, avoid areas where you might disrupt or disturb wildlife, lambing (generally mid-April to the end of May), grouse shooting (from 12 August to the third week in October) or deer stalking (1 July to 15 February, but the peak period is August to October). You can get up-to-date information on deer stalking in various areas through the **Hillphone** (www.hillphones.info) service.

You can buy walking maps of Scotland online from the Ordnance Survey website (www.ordnancesurvey.co.uk) – click on the Map Shop link.

ACCESS & THE LAW

Access to the countryside has been a thorny issue in Scotland for many years. In Victorian times, belligerent landowners attempted to prevent walkers from using well-established trails and moves to counter this led to successful litigation for the walkers and the formation of what later became the Scottish Rights of Way & Access Society.

In January 2003, the Scottish parliament formalised access to the countryside and passed the Land Reform (Scotland) Bill, creating statutory rights of access to land in Scotland for the first time. More information on this new legislation can be found at the **Scottish Rights of Way & Access Society** (☎ 0131-558 1222; www.scotways.com; 24 Annandale St, Edinburgh EH7 4AN).

VisitScotland's website dedicated to walking is http://walking.visitscotland.com.

Rights of way exist but local authorities aren't required to list and map them so they're not shown on Ordnance Survey (OS) maps of Scotland, as they are in England and Wales. However, the Scottish Rights of Way & Access Society (see the boxed text, p55) keeps records of these routes, provides and maintains signposting, and publicises them in its guide, *Scottish Hill Tracks*. Public access is free at all times to areas owned by the National Trust for Scotland (NTS) and to most land owned by the Forestry Commission.

Some official long-distance footpaths:

Walk	Distance	Features	Duration	Difficulty	Page
Fife Coastal Path	78 miles	Firth of Forth, undulating country	5-6 days	easy	p209
Great Glen Way	73 miles	Loch Ness, canal paths, forest tracks	4 days	easy	p322
Pilgrims Way	25 miles	Machars peninsula, standing stones, burial mounds	2-3 days	easy	p147
St Cuthbert's Way	62 miles	follows life of famous saint	6-7 days	medium	p147
Southern Upland Way	212 miles	remote hills & moorlands	9-14 days	medium-hard	p147
Speyside Way	66 miles	follows river, whisky distilleries	3-4 days	easy-medium	p58
West Highland Way	95 miles	spectacular scenery, mountains & lochs	6-8 days	medium	p278

Information

The ultimate guidebooks for Scottish hill walkers are the six district guides produced by the Scottish Mountaineering Club, which cover the Scottish hills in great detail – see www.smc.org.uk for further information.

Every Tourist Information Centre (TIC) has leaflets (free or for a nominal charge) of suggested walks that take in local points of interest. Lonely Planet's *Walking in Scotland* is a comprehensive resource, covering short walks and long-distance paths; its *Walking in Britain* guide covers Scottish walks too. For general advice, VisitScotland produces a *Walking Scotland* brochure, describing numerous routes in various parts of the country, plus safety tips and other information.

Other useful sources:

Mountaineering Council of Scotland (☎ 01738-638227; www.mountaineering-scotland.org.uk; The Old Granary, West Mill St, Perth PH1 5QP)

Ramblers' Association Scotland (☎ 01577-861222; www.ramblers.org.uk/scotland; Kingfisher House, Auld Mart Business Park, Milnathort, Kinross KY13 9DA)

GOLF

Scotland is the home of golf. The game has been played in Scotland for centuries and there are more courses per head of population here than in any other country. Most clubs are open to visitors – details can be found on the web at www.scotlands-golf-courses.com.

St Andrews is the headquarters of the game's governing body, the Royal and Ancient Golf Club, and the location of the world's most famous golf course, the Old Course (see the boxed text, p209). There are several major championship courses around the country including those at Royal Troon (p174) and Turnberry (p175).

VisitScotland publishes the *Official Guide to Golf in Scotland*, a free annual brochure listing course details, costs and clubs with information on where to stay. Some regions offer a Golf Pass, costing between £50 and £90 for five days (Monday to Friday), which allows play on a range of courses.

VisitScotland's website dedicated to golf (http://golf.visitscotland.com) has a course directory and online booking.

FISHING

Fishing – coarse, sea and game – is enormously popular in Scotland, whose waters are filled with salmon, trout (sea, brown and rainbow), pike, arctic char and many other species. Fly-fishing in particular is a joy in Scotland's many lochs and rivers – it's a tricky but very rewarding form of fishing, closer to an art form than a sport.

For wild brown trout the close season is early October to mid-March. The close season for salmon and sea trout varies between districts; it's generally from early November to early February.

Fishing rights to most waters are privately owned and you must obtain a permit – these are often readily available at the local fishing-tackle shop or hotel. Permits cost from around £15 per day but some salmon rivers – notably the Tweed, the Tay and the Spey – can be much more expensive.

There are numerous fish farms throughout Scotland with stocked ponds where you can hire equipment and have a couple of lessons; they are a particularly good option for the kids. Examples include the Drummond Trout Farm & Fishery (p222) and Inverawe Smokehouse & Fishery (p310).

The UK record for a rod-caught salmon is 29kg, caught by a Miss Ballantyne in 1922 on the River Tay in Perthshire.

The VisitScotland booklet *Fish Scotland* is a good introduction and is stocked by TICs. Other organisations that can provide information include the following:

Scottish Anglers National Association (☎ 01577-861116; www.sana.org.uk; The National Game Angling Academy, The Pier, Loch Leven, Kinross KY13 8UF)

Scottish Federation of Sea Anglers (☎ 0131-317 7192; Caledonia House, South Gyle, Edinburgh EH12 9DG)

CYCLING

Travelling by bicycle is an excellent way to explore Scotland; May to October is the best time to do so. There are forest trails and dedicated cycle routes along canal towpaths and disused railway tracks. Depending on your energy and enthusiasm you can take a leisurely trip along peaceful country lanes through idyllic farm country, stopping at the numerous pubs along the way, or thrash about all day up steep slopes, freewheeling down the other side. Cyclists in search of the wild and remote will enjoy northwestern Scotland. Its majestic Highlands and mystical islands offer quiet pedalling through breathtaking landscapes. The beautiful forests, lochs, glens and hills in the central and southern areas of Scotland are more easily accessible and have an intimate charm. The gentle undulating countryside in the beautiful Borders region is excellent cycling country.

It was a Scotsman, John Boyd Dunlop (1840–1921), who in 1888 patented the first successful pneumatic tyre for bicycles.

Hardcore mountain-bikers will also find plenty of challenges, from long off-road routes such as the Great Glen Mountain Bike Trail (p322) to world-class downhill courses such as those at Laggan Wolftrax (p332) and Nevis Range (p341). The latter hosts the **UCI Mountain Bike World Cup Finals** (www.fortwilliamworldcup.co.uk).

VisitScotland publishes a useful free booklet, *Cycle Scotland,* and has a dedicated website (www.cyclingscotland.com). Many regional TICs have information on local cycling routes and places to hire bikes. They also stock cycling guides and books.

For up-to-date, detailed information on Scotland's cycle-route network contact **Sustrans** (☎ 0845 113 0065, 0131-539 8122; www.sustrans.org.uk; 16a Randolph Cres, Edinburgh EH3 7TT).

Cyclists' Touring Club (CTC; ☎ 0870 873 0060; www.ctc.org.uk; Cotterell House, 69 Meadrow, Godalming, Surrey GU7 3HS) is a membership organisation offering comprehensive information about cycling in Britain.

BIRD-WATCHING

Scotland is a bird-watcher's paradise. There are more than 80 ornithologically important nature reserves managed by **Scottish Natural Heritage** (SNH; www.snh.org.uk), the **Royal Society for the Protection of Birds** (RSPB; www.rspb .org.uk) and the **Scottish Wildlife Trust** (SWT; www.swt.org.uk).

Scotland is the best place in the British Isles (and in some cases the only place) to spot bird species such as the golden eagle, white-tailed sea eagle, osprey, corncrake, capercaillie, crested tit and ptarmigan, and its coast and islands are some of Europe's most important seabird nesting grounds.

Further information can be obtained from the **Scottish Ornithologists Club** (☎ 01875-871330; www.the-soc.org.uk; Waterson House, Aberlady, East Lothian EH32 0PY; ⊙ 9am-5pm Mon-Fri).

HORSE RIDING & PONY TREKKING

Seeing the country from the saddle is highly recommended, even if you're not an experienced rider. There are riding schools catering to all levels of proficiency throughout the country.

For more information:

British Horse Society (☎ 08701-202244; www.bhs.org.uk; British Equestrian Centre, Stoneleigh Park, Kenilworth, Warwickshire CV8 2XZ)

Trekking & Riding Society of Scotland (☎ 01567-820909; www.ridinginscotland.com; Bruach na h'Abhainne, Maragowan, Killin, Perthshire FK21 8TN)

ROCK CLIMBING

Scotland has a long history of rock climbing and mountaineering, with many of the classic routes on Ben Nevis and Glen Coe having been pioneered in the 19th century. The country's main rock-climbing areas include Ben Nevis (p340), with routes up to 400m in length, Glen Coe (p333), the Cairngorms (p325), the Cuillin Hills of Skye (p375), Arrochar (p278) and the Isle of Arran (see p168), but there are also hundreds of smaller crags situated all over the country. One unusual feature of Scot-

---

THE SPEYSIDE WAY

This long-distance footpath follows the course of the River Spey, one of Scotland's most famous salmon-fishing rivers. It starts at Buckie and first follows the coast to Spey Bay, east of Elgin, then runs inland along the river to Aviemore in the Cairngorms (with branches to Tomintoul and Dufftown). At only 66 miles, the main walk can be done in three or four days, although including the branch trails to Dufftown and Tomintoul will push the total walking distance to 102 miles (allow seven days).

This route has also been dubbed the 'Whisky Trail' as it passes near a number of distilleries, including Glenlivet and Glenfiddich, which are open to the public. If you stop at them all, the walk may take considerably longer than the usual three or four days!

The Speyside Way guidebook by Jacquetta Megarry and Jim Strachan describes the route in detail; there's also a *Speyside Way* leaflet produced by the **Speyside Way Ranger Service** (☎ 01340-881266). Check out the route at www.speysideway.org.

land's rock-climbing scene is the sea stacks found around the coast, the most famous of these being the 140m-high Old Man of Hoy (p411).

Rock Climbing in Scotland, by Kevin Howett, and the Scottish Mountaineering Club's regional *Rock & Ice Climbs* guides are excellent references.

More information:

Mountaineering Council of Scotland (☎ 01738-638227; www.mountaineering-scotland .org.uk; The Old Granary, West Mill St, Perth PH1 5QP)

Scottish Mountaineering Club (www.smc.org.uk)

There's lots of useful information on rock climbing at www .scotclimb.org.uk.

SKIING & SNOWBOARDING

There are five ski centres in Scotland, offering downhill and cross-country skiing and snowboarding:

Cairngorm Mountain (☎ 01479-861261; www.cairngormmountain.com) 1097m; has almost 30 runs spread over an extensive area; see p327.

Glencoe (☎ 01855-851226; www.ski-glencoe.co.uk) 1108m; has only five tows and two chairlifts; see p333.

Glenshee (☎ 01339-741320; www.ski-glenshee.co.uk) 920m; situated on the A93 road between Perth and Braemar; offers the largest network of lifts and the widest range of runs in all of Scotland; see p229.

Lecht (☎ 01975-651440; www.lecht.co.uk) 793m; the smallest and most remote centre, on the A939 between Ballater and Grantown-on-Spey; p265.

Nevis Range (☎ 01397-705825; www.nevisrange.co.uk) 1221m; near Fort William; offers the highest ski runs, the grandest setting and some of the best off-piste potential in Scotland; see p341.

Each ski centre has its own website and contact number for snow reports and general information. There's an answerphone service for calls outside business hours.

The high season is from January to April but it's sometimes possible to ski from as early as November to as late as May. It's easy to turn up at the slopes, hire some kit, buy a day pass and off you go.

VisitScotland's *Ski Scotland* brochure is useful and includes a list of accommodation options. General information can be obtained from **Snowsport Scotland** (☎ 0131-445 4151; www.snsc.demon.co.uk; Hillend, Biggar Rd, Edinburgh EH10 7EF).

For weather and snow condition reports phone the **Ski Hotline** (☎ 0900 165 4654) or check the websites www.ski-scotland.com and www .winterhighland.info.

WATER SPORTS
Canoeing

Scotland, with its islands, sea lochs and indented coastline, is ideal for sea-kayaking, while its inland lochs and Highland rivers are great for both Canadian and white-water canoeing.

For information contact the **Scottish Canoe Association** (☎ 0131-317 7314; www.canoescotland.com; Caledonia House, South Gyle, Edinburgh EH12 9DQ). It publishes coastal navigation sheets as well as organising tours, including introductory ones for beginners.

Diving

It may lack coral reefs and warm, limpid waters but Scotland offers some of the most spectacular and challenging scuba diving in Europe, if not the world. The sea bed around St Abbs (p151) is Scotland's first voluntary marine nature reserve.

There are also hundreds of fascinating shipwrecks, the most famous of which are the seven remaining hulks of the WWI German High Seas Fleet, scuttled in 1919, which lie on the bed of Scapa Flow in the Orkney Islands (see the boxed text, p406).

For more information on the country's diving options contact the **Scottish Sub Aqua Club** (☎ 0141-425 1021; www.scotsac.com; The Cockburn Centre, 40 Bogmoor Place, Glasgow G51 4TQ).

Sailing

The west coast of Scotland, with its myriad islands, superb scenery and challenging winds and tides, is widely acknowledged to be one of the finest yachting areas in the world.

Experienced skippers with suitable qualifications can charter a yacht from one of dozens of agencies; prices for bareboat charter start at around £1500 a week in high season for a six-berth yacht; hiring a skipper to sail the boat for you will cost £120 a day or £700 a week. Sailing dinghies can be rented from many places for around £50 a day.

Beginners can take a Royal Yachting Association training course in yachting or dinghy sailing at many sailing schools around the coast; for details of charter agencies, sailing schools and water-sports centres, get hold of VisitScotland's *Sail Scotland* brochure, or check out the website www.sailscotland.co.uk.

Surfing

You definitely have to be hardy, even equipped with a wetsuit, to do anything more than take a quick dip around Scotland's coast. However, there is some truly magnificent coastline, beautiful sandy beaches and some of the best surfing breaks in Europe.

THE ANCIENT ART OF MUNRO BAGGING

At the end of the 19th century an eager hill walker, Sir Hugh Munro, published a list of 545 Scottish mountains measuring over 3000ft (914m) – a height at which he believed they gained a special significance. Of these summits he classified 277 as mountains in their own right (new surveys have since revised this to a total of 284), the rest being satellites of lesser consequence (known as 'tops'). Sir Hugh couldn't have realised that his name would one day be used to describe any Scottish mountain over the magical 3000ft mark. Many keen hill walkers now set themselves the target of reaching the summit of (or bagging) all 284 Munros.

The peculiar practice of Munro bagging started soon after the list was published – by 1901 the Reverend AE Robertson had bagged the lot. Between 1901 and 1981, only 250 people managed to climb all the Munros, but by 2005 the number of officially declared 'Munroists' had soared to more than 3400 (see www.smc.org.uk/munros/munros.htm). Many people have completed the round more than once; the record for single-minded Munro bagging is held by Edinburgh's Steven Fallon, who was halfway through his 13th round in 2005.

To the uninitiated it may seem odd that Munro baggers see a day (or longer) spent plodding around in mist, cloud and driving rain to the point of exhaustion as time well spent. However, for those who can add one or more ticks to their list, the vagaries of the weather are part of the enjoyment, at least in retrospect. Munro bagging is, of course, more than merely ticking names on a list – it takes you to some of the wildest, most beautiful parts of Scotland.

Once you've bagged all the Munros you can move onto the Corbetts – hills over 2500ft (700m), with a drop of at least 500ft (150m) on all sides – and the Donalds, lowland hills over 2000ft (610m). And for connoisseurs of the diminutive, there are the McPhies (see p293).

The tidal range is large, which means there is often a completely different set of breaks at low and high tides. It's the north and west coasts, particularly around Thurso (p361) and in the Outer Hebrides, which have outstanding, world-class surf. Indeed, Lewis has the best and most consistent surf in Britain, with around 120 recorded breaks and waves up to 5m. For more information contact **Hebridean Surf** (☎ 01851-705862; www .hebrideansurf.co.uk; 28 Francis St, Stornoway, Lewis HS1 2ND).

HANG GLIDING & PARAGLIDING

There's a well-established hang-gliding and paragliding scene in Scotland. The Highlands offer many impressive flying spots, complete with stunning scenery. For information and details on clubs and training schools contact the **British Hang Gliding & Paragliding Association** (www.bhpa.co.uk).

CANAL BOATING

Canal boating can be a relaxing, scenic way to travel (on a wide, lazy section of waterway) or very hard work (on a steep section of canal). Scotland's canal network is pretty limited compared with England's or Ireland's, but still offers interesting cruising opportunities.

The Millennium Link project (completed 2002) restored the 35-mile Forth and Clyde Canal (running between Grangemouth in the east and Bowling near Dumbarton in the west) and the 31-mile Union Canal (joining central Edinburgh with Falkirk) to full working order, and linked the two by means of the mighty Falkirk Wheel (see the boxed text, p203). The Linlithgow Canal Centre (p115) rents out day boats on the Union Canal. Holiday narrow boats can be hired by the week from **Capercaillie Cruisers** (☎ 0131-449 3288; www.capercailliecruisers.co.uk; 2 Lanark Rd West, Currie, Midlothian EH14 5ER).

The 60-mile Caledonian Canal, which slices through the Great Glen from Fort William to Inverness, has a mixture of canal reaches, open lochs and stunning scenery, making it fully geared to boating holidays. The main operator here is **Caley Cruisers** (☎ 01463-236328; www.caleycruisers.com; Canal Rd, Inverness IV3 8NF), which has a fleet of 40 motor cruisers ranging from two to eight berths available for hire from March to October.

Scotland's canals are owned and operated by the **British Waterways Board** (☎ 0141-332 6936; www.scottishcanals.co.uk; Canal House, 1 Applecross St, Glasgow G4 9SP), which publishes the free *Skippers' Guides* to all the canals (available online). It also publishes a list of boat-hire and canal-holiday companies.

Food & Drink

Traditional Scottish cookery is all about basic comfort food: solid, nour-
ishing fare, often high in fat, that would keep you warm on a winter's
day spent in the fields or out fishing, and sweet treats to come home to
in the evening.

STAPLES & SPECIALITIES

Haggis may be the national dish that Scotland is most famous for, but
when it comes to what Scottish people actually cook and eat most often,
the hands-down winner has to be mince and tatties (potatoes). Minced
beef, browned in the pan and then stewed slowly with onion, carrot and
gravy, is served with mashed potatoes (with a splash of milk and a knob
of butter added during the mashing) – it is tasty, warming and you don't
even have to chew.

Breakfast

Surprisingly few Scots eat porridge for breakfast – these days a café latte
and a croissant is just as likely – and even fewer eat it in the traditional
way; that is, with salt to taste, but no sugar. The breakfast offered in a B&B
or hotel usually consists of fruit juice and cereal or muesli, followed by
a choice of bacon, sausage, black pudding (a type of sausage made from
dried blood), grilled tomato, mushrooms and a fried egg or two.

Fish for breakfast may sound strange, but was not unusual in crofting
and fishing communities where seafood was a staple; many hotels still
offer grilled kippers (smoked herrings) or smoked haddock (poached in
milk and served with a poached egg) for breakfast – delicious with lots
of buttered toast.

A Caledonian Feast
by Annette Hope is a
fascinating and readable
history of Scottish cuisine,
providing a wealth of
historical and sociological
background.

Soups

Scotch broth, made with mutton stock, barley, lentils and peas, is nutri-
tious and tasty, while cock-a-leekie is a hearty soup made with chicken
and leeks. Warming vegetable soups include leek and potato soup, and
lentil soup (traditionally made using ham stock – vegetarians beware!).

Seafood soups include the delicious *Cullen skink*, made with smoked
haddock, potato, onion and milk, and *partan bree* (crab soup).

HAGGIS – SCOTLAND'S NATIONAL DISH

Scotland's national dish is often ridiculed by foreigners because of its ingredients, which admittedly don't sound promising – the finely chopped lungs, heart and liver of a sheep, mixed
with oatmeal and onion and stuffed into a sheep's stomach bag. However, it actually tastes
surprisingly good.

Haggis should be served with *champit tatties* and *bashed neeps* (mashed potatoes and turnips),
with a generous dollop of butter and a good sprinkling of black pepper.

Although it's eaten year-round, haggis is central to the celebrations of 25 January, in honour
of Scotland's national poet, Robert Burns. Scots worldwide unite on Burns Night to revel in their
Scottishness. A piper announces the arrival of the haggis and Burns' poem *Address to a Haggis* is
recited to this 'Great chieftan o' the puddin-race'. The bulging haggis is then lanced with a dirk
(dagger) to reveal the steaming offal within, 'warm, reekin, rich'.

Vegetarians (and quite a few carnivores, no doubt) will be relieved to know that veggie haggis
is available in some restaurants.

Meat & Game

Steak eaters will enjoy a thick fillet of world-famous Aberdeen Angus beef, and beef from Highland cattle is much sought after. Venison, from the red deer, is leaner and appears on many menus. Both may be served with a wine-based or creamy whisky sauce. Then there's haggis, Scotland's much-maligned national dish...

Fish & Seafood

Scottish salmon is famous worldwide, but there's a big difference between farmed salmon and the leaner, more expensive, wild fish. Smoked salmon is traditionally dressed with a squeeze of lemon juice and eaten with fresh brown bread and butter. Trout, salmon's smaller cousin – whether wild, rod-caught brown trout or farmed rainbow trout – is delicious fried in oatmeal.

> Popular Scottish TV chef Nick Nairn's book *Wild Harvest* contains over 100 recipes based on the use of fresh, seasonal Scottish produce.

SSSSSSMOKIN'!

Scotland is famous for its smoked salmon, but there are many other varieties of smoked fish – plus smoked meats and cheeses – to enjoy. Smoking food to preserve it is an ancient art that has recently undergone a revival, but this time it's more about flavour than preservation.

There are two parts to the process – first the cure, which involves covering the fish in a mixture of salt and molasses sugar, or soaking it in brine; and then the smoke, which can be either cold smoking (at less than 34°C), which results in a raw product, or hot smoking (at more than 60°C), which cooks it. Cold-smoked products include traditional smoked salmon, kippers and Finnan haddies. Hot-smoked products include *bradan rost* ('flaky' smoked salmon) and Arbroath smokies.

Arbroath smokies are haddock that have been gutted, beheaded and cleaned, then salted and dried overnight, tied together at the tail in pairs, and hot-smoked over oak or beech chippings for 45 to 90 minutes. Since 2004 the Arbroath smokie has enjoyed the 'Protected Geographical Interest' status conferred by the EU (along with the likes of Parma ham and Champagne) – only haddock smoked in the traditional manner within 5 miles of Arbroath (p247) can legally be called Arbroath smokies.

Finnan haddies (named after the fishing village of Findon in Aberdeenshire) are also haddock, but these are split down the middle like kippers, and cold-smoked. Finnan haddies, and the similar Aberdeen fillets, form the basis for delicious *Cullen skink* – a broth of smoked haddock, potato, onion and milk that you will see on many a Scottish restaurant menu.

Kippers (smoked herring) were invented in Northumberland, in northern England, in the mid-19th century, but Scotland soon picked up the technique, and both Loch Fyne and Mallaig were famous for their kippers.

There are dozens of modern smokehouses scattered all over Scotland; here are a few recommended ones:

Achiltibuie Smokehouse (☎ 01854-622353; www.summerislesfoods.com; Altandhu, Wester Ross; ⊗ 9.30am-5pm Mon-Sat Easter-Oct) Smokes everything from cheese to eels, as well as salmon and venison; see p366.

Inverawe Smokehouse & Fishery (☎ 01866-822274; www.smokedsalmon.co.uk; Inverawe; ⊗ 8am-5.30pm Mar-Oct) Delicate smoked salmon and plump, juicy kippers; see p310.

Marrbury Smokehouse (☎ 01671-840241; www.visitmarrbury.co.uk; Carsluith Castle; ⊗ 11am-4pm Thu & Fri, 10am-2pm Sat) Supplier to Gleneagles Hotel (p220) and other top restaurants; the smokehouse is located south of Creetown.

Salar Smokehouse (☎ 01870-610324; www.salar.co.uk; Lochcarnan, South Uist, Outer Hebrides; ⊗ 9am-5pm Mon-Fri) Famous for its flaky, hot-smoked salmon.

Spey Valley Smokehouse (☎ 01479-873078; www.speyvalleysmokedsalmon.com; Achnagonalin, Grantown-on-Spey; ⊗ 9am-5pm Mon-Fri, plus 10am-1pm Sat & Sun Easter-Oct) Established 1888; now owned by Ian Anderson, lead singer of rock group Jethro Tull.

As an alternative to kippers (smoked herrings) you may be offered Arbroath smokies (lightly smoked fresh haddock), traditionally eaten cold. Herring fillets fried in oatmeal are good, if you don't mind picking out a few bones. Mackerel pâté and smoked or peppered mackerel (both served cold) are also popular.

Juicy langoustines (also known as Dublin Bay prawns), crabs, lobsters, oysters, mussels and scallops are also widely available throughout Scotland.

The classic work on traditional Scottish cooking is The Scots Kitchen by F Marian McNeill, first published in 1929 but still going strong in various reprints.

Puddings

Traditional Scottish puddings are irresistibly creamy, high-calorie concoctions. *Cranachan* is whipped cream flavoured with whisky, and mixed with toasted oatmeal and raspberries. *Atholl brose* is a mixture of cream, whisky and honey, flavoured with oatmeal. *Clootie dumpling* is a rich steamed pudding filled with currants and raisins.

DRINKS

Scotland's most famous soft drink is Barr's Irn Bru: a sweet fizzy drink, radioactive orange in colour, that smells like bubble gum and almost strips the enamel from your teeth. Many Scots swear by its restorative effects as a cure for a hangover.

Scotch whisky (always spelt without an 'e' – whiskey with an 'e' is Irish or American) is Scotland's best-known product and biggest export. The spirit has been distilled in Scotland at least since the 15th century. See the boxed text, opposite.

As well as whiskies, there are whisky-based liqueurs such as Drambuie. If you must mix your whisky with anything other than water try a whisky-mac (whisky with ginger wine). After a long walk in the rain there's nothing better to put a warm glow in your belly.

At a bar, older Scots may order a 'half' or 'nip' of whisky as a chaser to a pint or half-pint of beer (a 'hauf and a hauf'). Only tourists ask for 'Scotch' – what else would you be served in Scotland? The standard measure in pubs is either 25mL or 35mL.

Scottish breweries produce a wide range of beers. The market is dominated by the big brewers – Youngers, McEwans, Scottish & Newcastle and Tennent's – but smaller local breweries generally create tastier brews, some of them very strong. The aptly named Skullsplitter from Orkney is a good example, at 8.5% alcohol by volume.

Most Scottish brews are graded in shillings so you can tell their strength; the greater the number of shillings, the stronger the beer. The usual range is 60 to 80 shillings (written 80/-). What the English call bitter, Scots call heavy – Caledonian 80/-, Maclays 80/- and Belhaven 80/- are all worth trying, but Deuchar's IPA from Edinburgh's Caledonian Brewery is our favourite.

Draught beer is served in pints (from £2 to £3) or half-pints; alcoholic content ranges from 3.2% to 8.5%.

VEGETARIANS & VEGANS

Scotland has the same proportion of vegetarians as the rest of the UK – around 8% to 10% of the population – and vegetarianism has moved away from the hippie-student image of a few decades ago and is now firmly in the mainstream. Even the most remote Highland pub usually has at least one vegetarian dish on the menu, and there are many dedicated vegetarian restaurants in the cities. If you get stuck, there's almost always an Italian or Indian restaurant where you can get meat-free

HOW TO BE A MALT WHISKY BUFF

'Love makes the world go round? Not at all! Whisky makes it go round twice as fast.'

From Whisky Galore *by Compton Mackenzie (1883–1972)*

Whisky-tasting today is almost as popular as wine-tasting was in the yuppie heyday of the late 1980s. Being able to tell your Ardbeg from your Edradour is *de rigueur* among the whisky-nosing set, so here are some pointers to help you impress your friends.

What's the difference between malt and grain whiskies?

Malts are distilled from malted barley – that is, barley that has been soaked in water, then allowed to germinate for around 10 days until the starch has turned into sugar – while grain whiskies are distilled from other cereals, usually wheat, corn or unmalted barley.

So what is a single malt?

A single malt is a whisky that has been distilled from malted barley and is the product of a single distillery. A pure (vatted) malt is a mixture of single malts from several distilleries, and a blended whisky is a mixture of various grain whiskies (about 60%) and malt whiskies (about 40%) from many different distilleries.

Why are single malts more desirable than blends?

A single malt, like a fine wine, somehow captures the essence of the place where it was made and matured – a combination of the water, the barley, the peat smoke, the oak barrels in which it was aged, and (in the case of certain coastal distilleries) the sea air and salt spray. Each distillation varies from the one before, like different vintages from the same vineyard.

How should a single malt be drunk?

Either neat, or preferably with a little water added. To appreciate the aroma and flavour to the utmost, a measure of malt whisky should be cut (diluted) with one-third to two-thirds as much spring water (still, bottled spring water will do). Ice, tap water and (God forbid) mixers are for philistines. Would you add lemonade or ice to a glass of Chablis?

Give me some tasting tips!

Go into a bar and order a Lagavulin (Islay) and a Glenfiddich (Speyside). Cut each one with half as much again of still, bottled spring water. Taking each one in turn, hold the glass up to the light to check the colour. Then stick your nose in the glass and take two or three short, sharp sniffs. By now, everyone in the pub will be giving you funny looks, but never mind.

For the Lagavulin you should be thinking: amber colour, peat smoke, iodine, seaweed. For the Glenfiddich: pale white-wine colour, malt, pear drops, acetone, citrus. Then taste them. Then try some others. Either you'll be hooked, or you'll never touch whisky again.

Where's the cheapest place to buy Scotch whisky?

A French supermarket, unfortunately. In the UK, where a bottle of single malt typically costs £25 to £35, taxes account for around 72% of the price, making Scotland one of the most expensive places in Europe to enjoy its own national drink.

Where can I learn more?

If you're serious about spirits, the **Scotch Malt Whisky Society** (☎ 0131-554 3451; www.smws .com) has branches all round the world. Membership of the society costs from £70 per year and includes use of members' rooms in Edinburgh and London.

See the boxed text, p269, for our 10 favourite single malts.

pizza, pasta or curry. Vegans, though, may find the options a bit limited outside of Edinburgh and Glasgow.

One thing to keep in mind is that lentil soup, a seemingly vegetarian staple of Scottish pub and restaurant menus, is traditionally made with ham stock.

FEEDING THE FAMILY

For a short (but growing) list of child-friendly restaurants in Scotland, see www.kids-scotland .co.uk.

Sadly, the majority of Scotland's eating places make no effort to welcome children, and many are actively hostile. In a recent survey nine out of 10 families thought the majority of UK restaurants were not family friendly. There's no way of gauging restaurant attitudes other than by asking.

This situation is changing, albeit slowly, especially in the cities and more popular tourist towns where several restaurants and pubs now have family rooms and/or play areas, but in many smaller towns and country areas kids will still get a frosty reception.

Be aware that pubs without a restaurant licence are not allowed to serve those aged under 16, even if it's just food and soft drinks.

COOKING COURSES

There are two principal places that offer courses in Scottish cookery:

Kinloch Lodge Hotel (☎ 01471-833333; www.claire-macdonald.com; Kinloch Lodge, Isle of Skye IV43 8QY) Cookery demonstrations using fresh, seasonal Scottish produce given by Lady Claire Macdonald, author of *Scottish Highland Hospitality*.

Nairns Cook School (☎ 01877-389900; www.nairnscookschool.com; Port of Menteith, Stirling FK8 3JZ) Two-day courses in modern Scottish cooking at the school owned by Scotland's top TV chef Nick Nairn, author of *Wild Harvest* and *Island Harvest*.

Edinburgh

The view as you walk out of Edinburgh's Waverley train station is probably the finest first impression of any city in the world – the castle battlements rising behind the Greek temple of the National Gallery, with the lush greenery of Princes Street Gardens in the foreground. To your left, the precipitous medieval tenements of the Old Town; to your right, the commercial bustle of Princes St. And almost all of the city's top sights – including the new and controversial Scottish parliament building – best restaurants and shopping streets are within 20 minutes' walk of where you're standing.

Not only is Edinburgh one of the most beautiful cities in Europe, it also enjoys one of Europe's most beautiful settings. There are unexpected vistas from almost every street corner – a glimpse of green sunlit hills, a blue flash of sea, silhouetted spires and rust-red crags. It's a city that begs to be explored on foot – narrow alleys, flights of stairs and hidden kirkyards tempt you off the main streets at every turn. Put the guidebook away for a bit, and just wander.

But there's more to Edinburgh than just sightseeing – there are top shops, world-class restaurants and a bacchanalia of bars to enjoy. This is a city of pub crawls and impromptu music sessions, mad-for-it clubbing and all-night parties, overindulgence, late nights and wandering home through cobbled streets at dawn.

All these superlatives come together in August at festival time, when it seems as if half the world descends on Edinburgh for one enormous party. If you can possibly manage it, join them.

HIGHLIGHTS

- Patrolling the battlements at **Edinburgh Castle** (p78)
- Taking a hike up **Calton Hill** (p87) just before sunset
- Nosing around the Queen's private quarters on the former **Royal Yacht Britannia** (p88) at Leith
- Strolling by the river in the picture-postcard village of **Cramond** (p88)
- Pondering the secrets of the Knights Templar at the mysterious **Rosslyn Chapel** (p113)

★ Cramond

★ Royal Yacht Britannia

★ Calton Hill

Edinburgh Castle

★ Rosslyn Chapel

| ■ TELEPHONE CODE: 0131 | ■ POPULATION: 430,000 | ■ AREA: 116 sq km |

HISTORY

Back in the 7th century the Castle Rock was called Dun Eiden (meaning 'Fort on the Hill Slope'). When it was captured by invaders from the kingdom of Northumbria in northeastern England in 638, they took the existing Gaelic name 'Eiden' and tacked it onto their own Old English word for fort, 'burh', to create the name Edinburgh.

Originally a purely defensive site, Edinburgh began to expand in the 12th century when King David I held court at the castle and founded the abbey at Holyrood. The royal court came to prefer Edinburgh to Dunfermline and, as parliament followed the king, Edinburgh became Scotland's capital. The city's first effective town wall was constructed around 1450, enclosing the Old Town as far east as Netherbow and south to the Grassmarket. This overcrowded area – by then the most populous town in Scotland – became a medieval Manhattan, forcing its densely packed inhabitants to build upwards instead of outwards, and creating tenements that in places soared to 12 storeys high.

The capital played an important role in the Reformation (1560–1690), led by the Calvinist firebrand John Knox. Mary, Queen of Scots held court in the Palace of Holyroodhouse for six brief years but, when her son James VI succeeded to the English throne in 1603, he moved his court to London. The Act of Union in 1707 further reduced Edinburgh's importance, but cultural and intellectual life continued to flourish.

In the second half of the 18th century a planned new town was created across the valley to the north of the Old Town. During the Scottish Enlightenment (roughly 1740–1830), Edinburgh became known as 'a hotbed of genius', inhabited by leading scientists and philosophers such as David Hume and Adam Smith.

In the 19th century the population quadrupled to 400,000, not much less today's, and the Old Town's tenements were taken over by refugees from the Irish famines. A new ring of crescents and circuses was built to the north of New Town, and grey Victorian terraces spread south of the Old Town.

Edinburgh entered a new era following the 1997 referendum vote in favour of a devolved Scottish parliament, which first convened in July 1999. The parliament is housed in a controversial new building at Holyrood at the foot of the Royal Mile – a futuristic design that went way over budget and way over schedule.

ORIENTATION

The city's most prominent landmarks are Edinburgh Castle, at the western end of the Old Town, and Arthur's Seat (251m), the rocky peak that rises above the eastern end of the Old Town. The Royal Mile (Lawnmarket, High St and Canongate) is the Old Town's main street and runs along the crest of a ridge from the castle to the Palace of Holyroodhouse at the foot of Arthur's Seat.

New Town lies to the north of the Old Town, separated by a dip containing Princes Street Gardens and Waverley train station. The city's main shopping street, Princes St, runs along the northern side of the gardens. At its eastern end rises Calton Hill, which is crowned by several monuments.

The Edinburgh & Scotland Information Centre (ESIC) lies between Waverley train station and Princes St, above Princes Mall. The bus station is nearby in New Town at the northeastern corner of St Andrew Sq, north of the eastern end of Princes St.

Long streets may be known by different names along their length. For example, the southern end of Leith Walk is variously called Union Pl and Antigua St on one side, Elm Row and Greenside Pl on the other.

Maps

Lonely Planet's fold-out *Edinburgh City Map* is handy for sightseeing. It is plastic-coated, virtually indestructible and indicates all the major landmarks, hotels, museums and shops. There's also a street index.

The Edinburgh & Scotland Information Centre (p77) issues a free pocket map of the city centre. For coverage of the whole city, the most detailed maps are Nicolson's *Edinburgh Citymap* and the Ordnance Survey's (OS) *Edinburgh Street Atlas*. You can buy these at the Edinburgh & Scotland Information Centre, bookshops and newsagents.

The OS's 1:50,000 Landranger map *Edinburgh, Penicuik & North Berwick* (Sheet No 66) covers the city and the surrounding region to the south and east at a scale of 1.25 inches to 1 mile; it's useful for walking in the Pentland Hills and exploring East Lothian.

(Continued on page 75)

INFORMATION

French Consulate	1	C2
German Consulate	2	B3
Institut Français d'Écosse	3	C2
Irish Consulate	4	C2
Japanese Consulate	5	C3
Lothian & Borders Police HQ	6	B1
Mossco Internet Café	7	B3
Napier University (Merchiston Campus)	8	C6
Royal Hospital for Sick Children	9	E5
Tarvit Launderette	10	D4
US Consulate	11	G2

SIGHTS & ACTIVITIES (pp77–94)

Burns Monument	12	G2
Caledonian Brewery	13	A6
Dean Bridge	14	C2
Dean Gallery	15	B2
Holyrood Abbey	16	G2
Holyrood Park	17	H4
Mansfield Place Church	18	E1
Our Dynamic Earth	19	G3
Palace of Holyroodhouse	20	G2
Queen's Gallery	21	G2
Royal Commonwealth Pool	22	G5
Scottish National Gallery of Modern Art	23	A3
Scottish Parliament Building	24	G2

See Central Edinburgh Map (pp72–3)

71

SLEEPING (pp94–9)
Amaryllis Guest House	25 C5
Aonach Mor Guest House	26 H6
Avondale Guest House	27 G6
Belford Hostel	28 B3
Bruntsfield Youth Hostel	29 D6
Caravel Guest House	30 E1
Dene Guest House	31 D1
Dukes of Windsor Street	32 F1
Edinburgh City B&B	33 C4
Glasshouse	34 F2
Glenallan Guest House	35 G6
Greenhouse	36 C5
Kenvie Guest House	37 H6
Menzies Guest House	38 C5
Pollock Halls of Residence	39 H5
Robertson Guest House	40 C5
Salisbury Guest House	41 G5
Sherwood Guest House	42 G6
Southside Guest House	43 F5

EATING (pp99–103)
Ann Purna	44 F4
Apartment	45 D5
Basement	46 F1
Blue Moon Café	47 F1
Favorit	48 D5
Kalpna	49 F4
Marrakech	(see 30)
Ndebele	50 D4
Peckham's	51 C5
Songkran	52 C3
Valvona & Crolla	53 F1
Valvona & Crolla Caffé-Bar	(see 53)

DRINKING (pp103–5)
Athletic Arms	54 B5
Bennet's Bar	55 D6
Cumberland Bar	56 E1
Mathers	57 F1

ENTERTAINMENT (pp105–9)
Bongo Club	58 G3
Cameo	59 D4
CC Blooms	60 F1
Edinburgh Playhouse	61 F1
Ego	62 F1
King's Theatre	63 D6
Planet Out	64 F1
Queen's Hall	65 F5
Studio 24	66 G2
UGC Fountainpark	67 B5

SHOPPING (pp109–10)
Adam Pottery	68 D1
Meadows Pottery	69 F5

TRANSPORT (pp110–12)
Biketrax	70 D4

0 ———— 100 m
0 ———— 0.05 miles

E **F** **G** **H**

York Pl

Cathedral La

Elder St East

155

Omni Centre

GREENSIDE

Greenside Row

Dublin St La

117

150

North St Andrew St

73

Little King St

St James King St

P

18

St James Centre

163

Elder St

Leith St

Calton Hill

Calton Hill

38

61

64

170

122

St Andrew Sq

161

Register St

21

New Register House

St James St

151

135

Waterloo Pl

74

69

2

Regent Rd

North St David St

9

53

3

127

126

89

68

West Register St

30

Regent Rd

Calton Rd

Rose St North

23

116

South St Andrew St

Meuse La

165

12

8

82

154

Calton Rd

New St

33

34

66

3

57

162

72

31

166

North Bridge

Waverley Train Station

Old Tolbooth Wynd

East Princes Street Gardens

Waverley Bridge

167

78

95

132

43

36

94

East Market St

Jeffrey St

Canongate

136

114

St John's St

Market St

Cockburn St

90

93

84

160

51

138

56

158

83

North Bank St

59

Giles St

37

67

17

55

52

41

97

156

Hunter Sq

40

New Skinner's Cl

South Gray's Cl

22

102

Bond's Entry

St Mary's St

Cullan's

Holyrood Rd

80

45

Bank St

157

High St

49

76

Old Fishmarket Close

101

Tron Sq

Blackfriars St

10

Dickson's

St John's Hill

128

50

Lawnmarket

OLD TOWN

High Courts

19

Cowgate

140

96

Guthrie

124

88

High School Yards

Infirmary St

Pleasance Sports Centre

125

145

Victoria St

7

Sheriff Court

148

4

Drummond St

Roxburgh St

West Adam St

East Adam St

New Arthur Pl

146

West Bow

15

85

Candlemaker Row

103

164

Chambers St

58

West College St

Edinburgh University Old College

South College St

27

118

54

Surgeons' Hall

142

The Pleasance

Oakfield Pl

Holyrood Park

47

121

Bristo Port

Brighton St

Lothian St

Potterrow

16

Richmond St

West Richmond St

Brown St

George Heriot's School

149

Forrest Hill

23

104

25

Forrest Rd

Teviot Pl

Bristo Pl

Bristo Sq

Charles St

Marshall St

107

120

Davie St

Gilmour St

Simon Sq

Hardwell Cl

Carnegie St

42

Edinburgh University

Charles Street La

George Sq

Crichton St

99

119

134

West Nicolson St

Nicolson St

West Crosscauseway

St Patrick St

East Crosscauseway

Houden Cl

Bowmont Pl

1

2

3

4

5

6

(Continued from page 68)

INFORMATION
Bookshops

Blackwell's Bookshop (Map pp72-3; ☎ 622 8222; 53-62 South Bridge; ☯ 9am-8pm Mon & Wed-Fri, 9.30am-8pm Tue, 9am-6pm Sat, noon-6pm Sun) The city's principal bookstore; big selection of academic books.

Ottakar's (Map pp72-3; ☎ 225 4495; 57 George St; ☯ 9am-7pm Mon, Wed & Fri, 9.30am-7pm Tue, 9am-8pm Thu, 9am-6pm Sat, 11.30am-5.30pm Sun) Has coffee shop.

Stationery Office Bookshop (Map pp72-3; ☎ 606 5566; 71 Lothian Rd; ☯ 9am-5pm Mon-Fri, 10am-5pm Sat) Has a good selection of books on Scottish history and travel (including Lonely Planet guides), and the widest range of OS maps in town.

Waterstone's East End (Map pp72-3; ☎ 556 3034; 13 Princes St; ☯ 9am-8pm Mon-Fri, to 7.30pm Sat, 10am-7pm Sun); George St (Map pp72-3; ☎ 225 3436; 83 George St; ☯ 9.30am-9pm Mon-Fri, to 8pm Sat, 11am-6pm Sun); West End (Map pp72-3; ☎ 226 2666; 128 Princes St; ☯ 8.30am-8pm Mon-Sat, 10.30am-7pm Sun) The West End branch has an in-store café with great views.

Cultural Centres

Institut Français d'Écosse (Map pp70-1; ☎ 225 5366; www.ifecosse.org.uk; 13 Randolph Cres; ☯ 9.30am-6.30pm Mon-Fri, to 2pm Sat) Runs courses in French and has a French language library.

Italian Cultural Institute (Map pp72-3; ☎ 668 2232; www.italcult.org.uk; 82 Nicolson St; ☯ 9am-1pm & 2-5pm Mon-Fri)

Emergency

In an emergency, dial ☎ 999 or ☎ 112 (free from public phones) and ask for police, ambulance, fire brigade or coastguard.

Edinburgh Rape Crisis Centre (☎ 556 9437; www.rapecrisisscotland.org.uk)

Lothian & Borders Police HQ (Map pp70-1; ☎ 311 3131; www.lbp.police.uk; Fettes Ave)

Lothian & Borders Police Information Centre (Map pp72-3; ☎ 226 6966; 188 High St; ☯ 10am-10pm May-Aug, to 8pm Mar, Apr, Sep & Oct, to 6pm Nov-Feb) Report a crime or make lost property inquiries here.

Internet Access

There are Internet cafés spread around the city. Some convenient ones:

connect@edinburgh (Map pp72-3; ☎ 473 3800; Princes Mall, 3 Princes St; per 15min 50p) See Edinburgh & Scotland Information Centre (p77) for hours.

easyInternetcafé (Map pp72-3; ☎ 220 3580; www.easy-everything.com; 58 Rose St; per hr £1; ☯ 7.30am-10.30pm)

e-corner (Map pp72-3; ☎ 558 7858; www.e-corner .co.uk; 55 Blackfriars St; per 20min £1; ☯ 7.30am-9pm Mon-Fri, 8am-9pm Sat & Sun)

EDINBURGH IN...

Two Days

Kick off with coffee at the **Elephant House** (see the boxed text, p105) – choose a window table with a view of the castle – then head uphill to **Edinburgh Castle** (p78) to do the touristy bit. Afterwards, begin strolling down the **Royal Mile** (p79) and think about where to have lunch; **Café Marlayne** (p100) is temptingly close by. Once you've eaten, continue to the foot of the Royal Mile to see the new **Scottish parliament building** (p81), then work up an appetite by climbing **Arthur's Seat** (p82), or ogling the designer shoes in **Harvey Nichols** (p110). Satisfy your hunger with dinner at **Oloroso** (p102), while you watch the sun set over the Firth of Forth.

On day two spend the morning soaking up some history in the **Museum of Scotland** (p84) and in the afternoon catch the bus to Leith for a visit to the **Royal Yacht Britannia** (p88). In the evening have an early dinner at **Daniel's Bistro** (see the boxed text, p100), then scare yourself silly on a guided ghost tour with **Black Hart Storytellers** (p93).

Four Days

A third day calls for a morning stroll around the **Royal Botanic Garden** (p89) then lunch at the **Old Chain Pier** (see the boxed text, p100) and a trip to the seaside village of **Cramond** (p88). Take binoculars (for bird-watching and yacht-spotting) and a book (to read in the sun). Dinner at the **Café Royal Oyster Bar** (p102) could be before or after your sunset walk to the summit of **Calton Hill** (p87).

On day four head out to the pretty harbour village of **Queensferry** (p112), nestled beneath the Forth Bridges, or take a day trip to the enigmatic and beautiful **Rosslyn Chapel** (p113).

EDINBURGH

Internet Café (Map pp72-3; ☎ 226 5400; 98 West Bow; per 30min £1; ⏰ 10am-11pm)

Mossco Internet Café (Map pp70-1; ☎ 07775 620759; mosscocafé@hotmail.com; 18 West Maitland St; per min 4p; ⏰ 8am-10pm) No minimum time required.

There are several Internet-enabled telephone boxes (10p a minute, 50p minimum) scattered around the city centre, and countless wi-fi hot spots – search on www.jiwire.com.

Internet Resources

City of Edinburgh Council (www.edinburgh.gov.uk) The city council's official site, with a useful events guide.

City of Edinburgh Museums & Galleries (www .cac.org.uk) Details of events and exhibitions in the city council's museums and galleries.

Edinburgh Architecture (www.edinburgharchitecture .co.uk) Informative site dedicated to the city's modern architecture.

Edinburgh & Lothians Tourist Board (www .edinburgh.org) Official tourist board site, with listings of accommodation, sights, activities and events.

Your Edinburgh (www.youredinburgh.info) Comprehensive directory of Edinburgh-related websites.

Laundry

Most of Edinburgh's backpacker hostels will wash and dry a load of laundry for you for around £4; some have self-service coin-operated washing machines where you do the laundry yourself. There are self-service laundries all over the city – expect to pay around £4 for a wash and dry. Check the *Yellow Pages* under Launderettes to find the nearest.

Bendix Launderette & Dry Cleaners (Map p69; ☎ 554 2180; 342 Leith Walk; ⏰ 8am-8pm Mon-Fri, to 5pm Sat, 9am-4pm Sun)

Canonmills Dry Cleaners & Launderette (Map p69; ☎ 556 3199; 7 Huntly St; ⏰ 8am-8pm Mon-Fri, to 4pm Sat, 9am-4pm Sun)

Tarvit Launderette (Map pp70-1; ☎ 229 6382; 7-9 Tarvit St; ⏰ 8am-8pm Mon-Fri, 9am-4pm Sat & Sun)

Left Luggage

Edinburgh airport left-luggage office (per item per 24hr £3; ⏰ 5am-11pm) On the ground floor between check-in and international arrivals.

St Andrew Sq bus and coach station lockers (Map pp72-3; small/medium/large locker per 24hr £3/4/5; ⏰ 6am-midnight)

Waverley train station left-luggage office (Map pp72-3; per item per 24hr £5; ⏰ 7am-11pm) Beside platform 1.

Libraries

Central Library (Map pp72-3; ☎ 242 4800; George IV Bridge; ⏰ 10am-8pm Mon-Thu, to 5pm Fri, 9am-1pm Sat) General lending library with a room devoted to Edinburgh (one floor down), another to all things Scottish (in the basement), and a reference room on the top floor.

National Library of Scotland (Map pp72-3; ☎ 226 4531; www.nls.uk; George IV Bridge; ⏰ 9.30am-8.30pm Mon, Tue, Thu & Fri, 10am-8.30pm Wed, 9.30am-1pm Sat) Copyright library with a reference-only reading room; you'll need ID (passport or driving licence) to get admission.

Media

Edinburgh's home-grown daily newspapers include the *Scotsman* (www.scotsman.com), a quality daily covering Scottish, UK and international news, sport and current affairs, and the *Edinburgh Evening News* (www.edinburghnews.com), covering news and entertainment in the city and its environs; *Scotland on Sunday* is the weekend newspaper from the same publisher.

Medical Services

Chemists (pharmacists) can advise you on minor ailments. At least one local chemist remains open round the clock – its location will be displayed in the windows of other chemists. Alternatively look in the local newspaper or in the *Yellow Pages*.

Boots (Map pp72-3; ☎ 225 6757; 48 Shandwick Pl; ⏰ 8am-9pm Mon-Fri, to 6pm Sat, 10.30am-4.30pm Sun) Chemist open longer hours than most.

Edinburgh Dental Institute (Map pp72-3; ☎ 536 4958; 3rd fl, Lauriston Bldg, Lauriston Pl; ⏰ 9am-3.30pm Mon-Fri) For urgent dental treatment, you can visit the walk-in centre here.

Royal Hospital for Sick Children (Map pp70-1; ☎ 536 0000; 9 Sciennes Rd) Casualty department for children aged under 13 years; located in Marchmont.

Royal Infirmary of Edinburgh (Map p69; ☎ 536 1000; 51 Little France Cres, Old Dalkeith Rd) Edinburgh's main general hospital; has 24-hour accident and emergency department.

Western General Hospital (Map p69; ☎ 537 1330; Crewe Rd South; ⏰ 9am-9pm) For non-life-threatening injuries and ailments, you can attend the Minor Injuries Unit without having to make an appointment.

Money

There are banks and ATMs all over the city. You can change currency and travellers cheques at bureaux de change scattered throughout the city centre, and in banks, post offices and travel agencies. Banks generally offer the best rates.

American Express (Map pp72-3; ☎ 718 2501; 69 George St; ⏲ 9am-5.30pm Mon-Fri, to 4pm Sat) Charges no commission on Amex travellers cheques, 2% on cash and generally offers a good rate of exchange.

Bank of Scotland (Map pp72-3; ☎ 465 3900; 38 St Andrew Sq; ⏲ 9am-5pm Mon, Tue, Thu, Fri, 10am-5pm Wed)

Fexco (Map pp72-3; ☎ 557 3953; Princes Mall, 3 Princes St) Convenient location inside the Edinburgh & Scotland Information Centre (below); charges no commission on cash, but has a poor exchange rate.

Royal Bank of Scotland (Map pp72-3; ☎ 556 8555; 36 St Andrew Sq; ⏲ 9.15am-4.45pm Mon, Tue, Thu & Fri, 10am-4.45pm Wed, 10am-2pm Sat)

Thomas Cook (Map pp72-3; ☎ 226 5500; 52 Hanover St; ⏲ 9am-5.30pm Mon, Tue & Thu-Sat, 10am-5.30pm Wed) Charges 2% commission (minimum £3) on both cash and travellers cheques.

Post

Frederick St post office (Map pp72-3; 40 Frederick St) In New Town.

Main post office (Map pp72-3; ☎ 0845 722 3344; St James Centre, Leith St; ⏲ 8.30am-5.30pm Mon-Fri, to 6pm Sat) Items addressed to poste restante can be picked up here.

St Mary's St post office (Map pp72-3; 46 St Mary's St) In Old Town.

Telephone

There are telephone booths scattered all over the city; see also the Directory, p440.

Tourist Information

Edinburgh & Scotland Information Centre (ESIC; Map pp72-3; ☎ 0845 225 5121; info@visitscotland .com; Princes Mall, 3 Princes St; ⏲ 9am-8pm Mon-Sat, 10am-8pm Sun Jul & Aug, 9am-7pm Mon-Sat, 10am-7pm Sun May, Jun & Sep, 9am-5pm Mon-Wed, to 6pm Thu-Sat, 10am-5pm Sun Oct-Apr) Includes an accommodation booking service, currency exchange, gift and bookshop, Internet access, and counters selling tickets for Edinburgh city tours and Scottish Citylink bus services.

Old Craighall Tourist Information Centre (TIC; ☎ 653 6172; Old Craighall Junction, A1) In a service area on the main A1 road, about 5 miles east of the city centre.

Tourist & Airport Information Desk (☎ 0845 225 5121) At Edinburgh airport.

Travel Agencies

There are hundreds of travel agencies all over the city. Two agencies that specialise in budget and student travel:

STA Travel (Map pp72-3; ☎ 226 7747; www .statravel.co.uk; 27 Forrest Rd; ⏲ 10am-6pm Mon-Wed & Fri, to 7pm Thu, to 5pm Sat)

Student Flights (Map pp72-3; ☎ 226 6868; www .studentflight.co.uk; 53 Forrest Rd; ⏲ 9.30am-6pm Mon-Fri, 11am-5pm Sat)

Universities

Edinburgh has three universities. The oldest, biggest and most prestigious is the University of Edinburgh, with more than 15,000 undergraduates.

Heriot-Watt University (☎ 449 5111; www.hw.ac .uk) The main campus is southwest of the city at Riccarton, near Currie.

Napier University (☎ 444 2266; www.napier.ac.uk) Craiglockhart campus (Map p69; 219 Colinton Rd); Merchiston campus (Map pp70-1; 10 Colinton Rd)

University of Edinburgh Information Centre (Map pp72-3; ☎ 650 1000; www.ed.ac.uk; 7-11 Nicolson St; ⏲ 9.15am-5pm Mon-Fri) Provides details of short-term courses.

DANGERS & ANNOYANCES

Edinburgh is safer than most cities of a similar size, but it has its share of crime so all of the normal big-city precautions apply here.

Lothian Rd, Dalry Rd, Rose St and the western end of Princes St, at the junction with Shandwick Pl and Queensferry and Hope Sts, can get a bit rowdy on Friday and Saturday nights after the pubs close. Calton Hill offers good views during the day but is best avoided at night. Women on their own should avoid walking across the Meadows after dark and walking in the red-light district between Salamander St and Leith Links, in Leith.

SIGHTS

Edinburgh's main attractions are concentrated in the city centre – on and around the Old Town's Royal Mile between the castle and Holyrood, and in New Town. A major exception is the Royal Yacht *Britannia*, which is in the redeveloped docklands district of Leith, 2 miles northeast of the centre.

If you tire of sightseeing, good areas for aimless wandering include the posh suburbs of Stockbridge and Morningside, the pretty riverside village of Cramond, and the winding footpaths of Calton Hill and Arthur's Seat.

Old Town

Edinburgh's Old Town stretches along a ridge to the east of the castle, and tumbles down Victoria St to the broad expanse of the Grassmarket. It's a jagged and jumbled maze of masonry riddled with closes (alleys) and wynds (narrow lanes), stairs and vaults, and cleft along its spine by the cobbled ravine of the Royal Mile.

Until the founding of New Town in the 18th century, old Edinburgh was an overcrowded and insanitary hive of humanity squeezed between the boggy ground of the Nor' Loch (North Loch, now drained and occupied by Princes Street Gardens) to the north and the city walls to the south and east. The only way for the town to expand was upwards, and the five- and six-storey tenements that were raised along the Royal Mile in the 16th and 17th centuries were the skyscrapers of their day, remarked upon with wonder by visiting writers such as Daniel Defoe. All classes of society, from beggars to magistrates, lived cheek by jowl in these urban ants' nests, the wealthy occupying the middle floors – high enough to be above the noise and stink of the streets, but not so high that climbing the stairs would be too tiring – while the poor squeezed into attics, basements, cellars and vaults amid the rats, rubbish and raw sewage.

The renovated Old Town tenements still support a thriving city-centre community, and today the street level is crammed with cafés, restaurants, bars, backpacker hostels and tacky souvenir shops. Few visitors wander beyond the main drag of the Royal Mile, but it's worth taking time to explore the countless closes that lead off the street into quiet courtyards, often with unexpected views of city, sea and hills.

EDINBURGH CASTLE

The brooding, black crags of Castle Rock rising above the western end of Princes St are the very reason for Edinburgh's existence. This rocky hill – the glacier-worn stump of an ancient volcano – was the most easily defended hill-top on the invasion route between England and central Scotland, a route followed by countless armies from the Roman legions of the 1st and 2nd centuries AD to the Jacobite troops of Bonnie Prince Charlie in 1745.

Edinburgh Castle (Map pp72-3; ☎ 225 9846; Castle Hill; adult/concession/child incl audio guide £9.80/7.50/3.50; ☉ 9.30am-6pm Apr-Sep, to 5pm Oct-Mar, last ticket sold 45min before closing) has played a pivotal role in Scottish history, both as a royal residence – King Malcolm Canmore (r 1057–93) and Queen Margaret first made their home here in the 11th century – and as a military stronghold. The castle last saw military action in 1745; from then until the 1920s it served as the British army's main base in Scotland. Today it is one of Scotland's most atmospheric, most popular – and most expensive – tourist attractions.

The **Entrance Gateway**, flanked by statues of Robert the Bruce and William Wallace, opens to a cobbled lane that leads up beneath the 16th-century **Portcullis Gate** to the cannon ranged along the Argyle and Mills Mount batteries. The battlements here have great views over New Town to the Firth of Forth.

At the far end of Mills Mount Battery is the famous **One O'Clock Gun**, where crowds gather to watch a gleaming WWII 25-pounder fire an ear-splitting time signal at exactly 1pm (every day except Sundays, Christmas Day and Good Friday).

At the western end of the castle, to the left of the castle restaurant, a road leads down to the **National War Museum of Scotland** (Map pp72-3; ☎ 225 7534; admission incl in Edinburgh Castle ticket; ☉ 9.45am-5.30pm Apr-Nov, to 4.30pm Dec-Mar), which brings Scotland's military history vividly to life. The exhibits have been personalised by telling the stories of the original owners of the objects on display, making it easier to empathise with the experiences of war than any dry display of dusty weaponry ever could.

South of Mills Mount, the road curls up leftwards through **Foog's Gate** to the highest part of Castle Rock, crowned by the tiny, Romanesque **St Margaret's Chapel**, the oldest surviving building in Edinburgh. It was probably built by David I or Alexander I in memory of their mother, Queen Margaret, sometime around 1130 (she was canonised in 1250). Beside the chapel stands **Mons Meg**, a giant 15th-century siege gun built at Mons (in what is now Belgium) in 1449.

The main group of buildings on the summit of Castle Rock are ranged around Crown Sq, dominated by the shrine of the **Scottish National War Memorial**. Opposite is

THE STONE OF DESTINY

On St Andrew's Day 1996 a block of sandstone – 26½ inches by 16½ inches by 11 inches in size, with rusted iron hoops at either end – was installed with much pomp and ceremony in Edinburgh Castle. For the previous 700 years it had lain in London, beneath the Coronation Chair in Westminster Abbey. Almost all English, and later British, monarchs from Edward II in 1307 to Elizabeth II in 1953 have parked their backsides firmly over this stone during their coronation ceremony.

The legendary Stone of Destiny – said to have originated in the Holy Land, and on which Scottish kings placed their feet during their coronation (not their bums; the English got that bit wrong) – was stolen from Scone Abbey near Perth by King Edward I of England in 1296. It was taken to London and there it remained for seven centuries – except for a brief removal to Gloucester during WWII air raids, and a three-month sojourn in Scotland after it was stolen by Scottish Nationalist students at Christmas in 1950 – an enduring symbol of Scotland's subjugation by England.

The Stone of Destiny returned to the political limelight in 1996, when the then Scottish Secretary and Conservative Party MP, Michael Forsyth, arranged for the return of the sandstone block to Scotland. A blatant attempt to boost the flagging popularity of the Conservative Party in Scotland prior to a general election, Forsyth's publicity stunt failed miserably. The Scots said thanks very much for the stone and then, in May 1997, voted every Conservative MP in Scotland into oblivion.

Many people, however, believe that Edward I was fobbed off with a shoddy imitation in 1296 and that the true Stone of Destiny remains safely hidden somewhere in Scotland. This is not impossible – some descriptions of the original state that it was made of black marble and decorated with elaborate carvings. Interested parties should read *Stone of Destiny* (1997) by Pat Gerber, which details the history of Scotland's most famous lump of rock.

the **Great Hall**, built for James IV (r 1488–1513) as a ceremonial hall and used as a meeting place for the Scottish parliament until 1639. Its most remarkable feature is the original, 16th-century hammer-beam roof.

On the eastern side of the square is the **Royal Palace**, built during the 15th and 16th centuries, where a series of historical tableaux leads to the highlight of the castle – a strongroom housing the **Honours of Scotland** (the Scottish crown jewels), the oldest surviving crown jewels in Europe. Locked away in a chest following the Act of Union in 1707, the crown (made in 1540 from the gold of Robert the Bruce's 14th-century coronet), sword and sceptre lay forgotten until they were unearthed at the instigation of the novelist Sir Walter Scott in 1818. Also on display here is the **Stone of Destiny** (see the boxed text, above).

Among the neighbouring **Royal Apartments** is the bedchamber where Mary, Queen of Scots gave birth to her son James VI, who was to unite the crowns of Scotland and England in 1603.

The **Castle Vaults** beneath the Great Hall (entered from Crown Sq via the Prisons of War exhibit) were used variously as store-rooms, bakeries and prison. The vaults have been done up to resemble 18th- and early-19th-century prisons, where graffiti carved by French and American prisoners can be seen on the ancient wooden doors.

THE ROYAL MILE

This mile-long street earned its regal nickname in the 16th century when it was used by the king to travel between the castle and the Palace of Holyroodhouse. There are four sections – Castlehill, Lawnmarket, High St and Canongate – whose names reflect their historical origins. Allow at least half a day to wander down the Mile, taking time to visit the attractions.

A short distance downhill from the Castle Esplanade, a former school houses the **Scotch Whisky Heritage Centre** (Map pp72-3; ☎ 220 0441; 354 Castlehill; adult/child incl tour & tasting £8.50/6.40; ☼ 9.30am-6.30pm May-Sep, 10am-5pm Oct-Apr; ☑). The centre explains the making of whisky from barley to bottle, in a series of exhibits that combine sight, sound and smell; look out for the distillery cat! There's also a restaurant that serves traditional Scottish dishes with, where possible, a dash of whisky thrown in.

EDINBURGH

The quaint building across the street is the **Outlook Tower & Camera Obscura** (Map pp72-3; ☎ 226 3709; Castlehill; adult/child £6.45/4.15; ☼ 9.30am-7pm Jul & Aug, to 6pm Apr-Jun, Sep & Oct, 10am-5pm Nov-Mar). The 'camera obscura' itself is a curious 19th-century device – in constant use since 1853 – that uses lenses and mirrors to throw a live image of the city onto a large horizontal screen. The accompanying commentary is entertaining and the whole experience has a quirky charm. Stairs lead up through various displays on optics to the Outlook Tower, which offers great views over the city.

With Edinburgh's tallest spire (71.7m), the **Highland Tolbooth Kirk** (Map pp72-3) is a prominent feature of the Old Town's skyline. The interior has been refurbished and it now houses the **Hub** (Map pp72-3; ☎ 473 2000; www.thehub-edinburgh.com; Castlehill; admission free; ☼ 10am-5pm Mon-Sat), the ticket office and information centre for the Edinburgh Festival. There's also a good café here.

Lawnmarket (a corruption of 'Landmarket', a market selling goods from the land outside the city) takes its name from the large cloth market that flourished here until the 18th century. This was the poshest part of the Old Town, where many of its most distinguished citizens made their homes.

One of these was the merchant Thomas Gledstanes, who in 1617 purchased the tenement later known as **Gladstone's Land** (NTS; Map pp72-3; ☎ 226 5856; 477 Lawnmarket; adult/child £5/4; ☼ 10am-7pm Jul & Aug, to 5pm Easter-Jun, Sep & Oct). It contains fine painted ceilings, walls and beams, and some splendid furniture from the 17th and 18th centuries. The volunteer guides provide a wealth of anecdotes and a detailed history.

Tucked down a close just east of Gladstone's Land you'll find the **Writers' Museum** (Map pp72-3; ☎ 529 4901; Lady Stair's Close, Lawnmarket; admission free; ☼ 10am-5pm Mon-Sat year-round, plus 2-5pm Sun during Edinburgh Festival). Located in Lady Stair's House (1622), the museum contains manuscripts and memorabilia belonging to Robert Burns, Sir Walter Scott and Robert Louis Stevenson.

High St, which stretches from George IV Bridge down to the Netherbow at St Mary's St, is the heart and soul of the Old Town, home to the city's main church, the Law Courts, the city council and – until 1707 – the Scottish parliament.

Dominating High St is the great grey bulk of **St Giles Cathedral** (Map pp72-3; ☎ 225 9442; High St; admission free but donations welcome; ☼ 9am-7pm Mon-Fri, to 5pm Sat, 1-5pm Sun May-Sep, 9am-5pm Mon-Sat, 1-5pm Sun Oct-Apr). Properly called the High Kirk of Edinburgh (it was only a true cathedral – the seat of a bishop – from 1633 to 1638 and from 1661 to 1689), St Giles was named after the patron saint of cripples and beggars. A Norman-style church was built here in 1126 but was destroyed by English invaders in 1385; the only substantial remains are the central piers that support the tower.

The present church dates largely from the 15th century – the beautiful crown spire was completed in 1495 – but much of it was restored in the 19th century. The interior lacks grandeur but is rich in history: St Giles was at the heart of the Scottish Reformation, and John Knox served as minister here from 1559 to 1572. One of the most interesting corners of the kirk is the **Thistle Chapel**, built in 1911 for the Knights of the Most Ancient & Most Noble Order of the Thistle. The elaborately carved Gothic-style stalls have canopies topped with the helms and arms of the 16 knights – look out for the bagpipe-playing angel amid the vaulting.

By the side of the street, outside the western door of St Giles, is a cobblestone **Heart of Midlothian** (Map pp72-3) set into the paving. This marks the site of the Tolbooth. Built in the 15th century and demolished in the early 19th century, the Tolbooth served variously as a meeting place for parliament, the town council and the General Assembly of the Reformed Kirk, before becoming law courts and, finally, a notorious prison and place of execution. Passers-by traditionally spit on the heart for luck (don't stand downwind!).

At the other end of St Giles is the **Mercat Cross** (Map pp72-3), a 19th-century copy of the 1365 original, where merchants and traders met to transact business and Royal Proclamations were read.

Next to the Mercat Cross is the **Loch Ness Discovery Centre** (Map pp72-3; ☎ 225 2290; 1 Parliament Sq; adult/child £5.95/4; ☼ 9am-10pm Jul & Aug, to 8pm Apr-Jun, Sep & Oct, 10am-5pm Nov-Mar), which explores the legend of the Loch Ness Monster (for more on Nessie, see the boxed text, p323) by means of various photographic displays and a 3-D movie. Plus, of course, a gift shop crammed with cheekily priced cuddly toys in the form of Nessie...

Across from the Cross is the **City Chambers** (Map pp72–3), originally built by John Adam (brother of Robert) between 1753 and 1761 to serve as the Royal Exchange – a covered meeting place for city merchants. However, the merchants preferred their old stamping grounds in the street and the building became the city council offices in 1811.

Part of the Royal Exchange was built over the sealed-off remains of Mary King's Close, and the lower levels of this medieval Old Town alley have survived almost unchanged in the foundations of the City Chambers for 250 years. Now open to the public as the **Real Mary King's Close** (Map pp72–3; ☎ 0870 243 0160; 2 Warriston's Close, Writers Ct, High St; adult/child £8/6; ☼ 9am-9pm Apr-Oct, 10am-4pm Sun-Fri, 10am-9pm Sat Nov-Mar), this spooky, subterranean labyrinth is a fascinating insight into the daily life of 16th- and 17th-century Edinburgh. Costumed characters give tours through a 16th-century town house and the plague-stricken home of a 17th-century gravedigger.

Halfway down the next block is 'the noisiest museum in the world' – the **Museum of Childhood** (Map pp72–3; ☎ 529 4142; 42 High St; admission free; ☼ 10am-5pm Mon-Sat, 2-5pm Sun). Often filled with the chatter of excited children, it covers serious issues related to childhood – health, education, upbringing and so on – but also has an enormous collection of toys, dolls, games and books.

The Royal Mile narrows at the foot of High St beside the jutting façade of **John Knox House** (Map pp72–3; ☎ 556 9579; 43-45 High St; adult/child £3/2; ☼ 10am-6pm Mon-Sat May-Jul). This is the oldest surviving tenement in Edinburgh, dating from around 1490; John Knox is thought to have lived here from 1561 to 1572. The labyrinthine interior has some beautiful painted-timber ceilings and an interesting display on Knox' life and work.

Canongate, the stretch of Royal Mile from Netherbow to Holyrood, takes its name from the Augustinian canons (monks) of Holyrood Abbey. From the 16th century it was home to aristocrats attracted to the Palace of Holyroodhouse. Originally governed by the monks, Canongate was an independent burgh separate from Edinburgh until 1856.

One of the surviving symbols of Canongate's former independence is the **Canongate Tolbooth** (Map pp72–3). Built in 1591, it served successively as a collection point for tolls (taxes), a council house, a courtroom and a jail. With its picturesque turrets and projecting clock, it's an interesting example of 16th-century architecture, and now houses a fascinating museum called the **People's Story** (Map pp72–3; ☎ 529 4057; 163 Canongate; admission free; ☼ 10am-5pm Mon-Sat year-round, plus 2-5pm Sun Aug), which covers the life, work and pastimes of ordinary Edinburgh folk from the 18th century to the present day.

Across the street from the Tolbooth is Huntly House. Built in 1570, it now houses the **Museum of Edinburgh** (Map pp72–3; ☎ 529 4143; 142 Canongate; admission free; ☼ 10am-5pm Mon-Sat year-round, plus 2-5pm Sun Aug). It covers the history of the city from prehistory to the present. Exhibits of national importance include an original copy of the National

---

SCOTTISH PARLIAMENT BUILDING

The new **Scottish parliament building** (Map pp70-1; ☎ 348 5200; www.scottish.parliament.uk; admission free; ☼ 9am-7pm Tue-Thu, 10am-6pm Mon & Fri in session, 10am-6pm Mon-Fri in recess Apr-Oct, 10am-4pm in recess Nov-Mar; ♿) was built on the site of a former brewery close to the Palace of Holyroodhouse. The competition to design the building was won by the Catalan architect Enric Miralles, who envisaged a group of lenticular buildings with curved roofs inspired by upturned boats seen on a beach in northern Scotland. The building opened in 2004, three years late and more than £300 million over budget.

The reception area has exhibits explaining the workings of the Scottish parliament, which was officially opened on 1 July 1999 – the first Scottish parliament to sit for almost 300 years – but the main attraction is the spectacular debating chamber (if you want to see the parliament in action, visit on a business day, Tuesday to Thursday). There are also 45-minute guided tours (adult/child £3.50/1.75) on offer, which let you see the floor of the debating chamber, a committee room, the office block of the Members of the Scottish Parliament (MSPs), and historic Queensberry House.

EDINBURGH

Covenant of 1638, but the big crowd-pleaser is the dog collar and feeding bowl that once belonged to Greyfriars Bobby, the city's most famous canine citizen (see p84).

Downhill on the left is the attractive curved gable of the **Canongate Kirk** (Map pp72–3), built in 1688. The kirkyard contains the graves of several famous people, including the economist Adam Smith (1723–90), author of *The Wealth of Nations*, Mrs Agnes MacLehose (the 'Clarinda' of Robert Burns' love poems), and the 18th-century poet Robert Fergusson (1750–74). Fergusson was much admired by Robert Burns, who paid for the gravestone and penned the epitaph – take a look at the inscription on the back.

HOLYROOD

The **Palace of Holyroodhouse** (Map pp70–1; ☎ 556 5100; www.royal.gov.uk; Canongate; adult/child £8.50/4.50; ☒ 9.30am-6pm Apr-Oct, to 4.30pm Nov-Mar) is the royal family's official residence in Scotland, but is most famous as the 16th-century home of the ill-fated Mary, Queen of Scots. The palace developed from a guesthouse attached to Holyrood Abbey, which was extended by King James IV in 1501. The oldest surviving part of the building, the northwestern tower, was built in 1529 as a royal apartment for James V and his wife, Mary of Guise. Mary, Queen of Scots spent six turbulent years here, during which time she debated with John Knox, married both her first and second husbands, and witnessed the murder of her secretary Rizzio. The palace is closed to the public when the royal family is visiting and during state functions (usually in mid-May, and mid-June to early July; check website for exact dates).

The guided tour leads you through a series of impressive royal apartments, ending in the **Great Gallery**. The 89 portraits of Scottish kings were commissioned by Charles II and supposedly record his unbroken lineage from Scota, the Egyptian pharaoh's daughter who discovered the infant Moses in a reed basket on the banks of the Nile.

But the highlight of the tour is **Mary, Queen of Scots' Bed Chamber**, home to the unfortunate Mary from 1561 to 1567, and connected by a secret stairway to her husband's bedchamber. It was here that her jealous first husband, Lord Darnley, restrained the pregnant queen while his henchmen murdered her secretary – and favourite – David Rizzio. A plaque in the neighbouring room marks the spot where he bled to death.

The exit from the palace leads into the ruins of **Holyrood Abbey** (Map pp70–1). King David I founded the abbey here in the shadow of Salisbury Crags in 1128. It was probably named after a fragment of the True Cross (rood is an old Scots word for cross), said to have been brought to Scotland by his mother, St Margaret. Most of the surviving ruins date from the 12th and 13th centuries, although a doorway in the far southeastern corner has survived from the original Norman church.

The **Queen's Gallery** (Map pp70–1; adult/child £5/3, joint ticket incl admission to palace £11/5.50; ☒ 9.30am-6pm Apr-Oct, to 4.30pm Nov-Mar), beside the palace ticket office, is a showcase for a range of changing exhibitions of art from the Royal Collections.

The modernistic white marquee pitched beneath Salisbury Crags marks **Our Dynamic Earth** (Map pp70–1; ☎ 550 7800; Holyrood Rd; adult/child £8.95/5.45; ☒ 10am-6pm Jul & Aug, to 5pm Apr-Jun, Sep & Oct, 10am-5pm Wed-Sun Nov-Mar, last admission 70min before closing), billed as an interactive, multimedia journey of discovery through Earth's history from the Big Bang to the present day. Hugely popular with kids of all ages, it's a slick extravaganza of whizz-bang special effects cleverly designed to fire up young minds with curiosity about all things geological and environmental. Its true purpose, of course, is to disgorge you into a gift shop where you can buy model dinosaurs and souvenir T-shirts.

In **Holyrood Park** (Map pp70–1), Edinburgh is blessed by having a little bit of wilderness in the heart of the city. The former hunting ground of Scottish monarchs, the park covers 263 hectares of varied landscape, including crags, moorland and loch. The highest point is the 251m summit of **Arthur's Seat** (Map p69), the deeply eroded remnant of a long-extinct volcano. Holyrood park can be circumnavigated by car or bike along Queen's Dr (it is closed to motorised traffic on Sunday), and you can hike from Holyrood to the summit in 45 minutes.

NORTH OF THE ROYAL MILE

Cockburn St, lined with trendy fashion, jewellery and music shops, leads down from the Royal Mile to Waverley Bridge. A right turn into Market St leads to the **Fruitmarket Gallery** (Map pp72-3; ☎ 225 2383; www.fruitmarket .co.uk; 45 Market St; admission free; ⏲ 11am-6pm Mon-Sat, noon-5pm Sun). One of Edinburgh's most innovative and popular galleries, the Fruitmarket showcases contemporary Scottish and international artists, and also has an excellent arts bookshop and café.

Across the street is the **City Art Centre** (Map pp72-3; ☎ 529 3993; 2 Market St; admission free except for temporary exhibitions; ⏲ 10am-5pm Mon-Sat, noon-5pm Sun), comprising six floors of exhibitions with a variety of themes, including an extensive collection of Scottish art.

SOUTH OF THE ROYAL MILE

The site of a cattle market from the 15th century until the start of the 20th, the **Grass-market** has always been a focal point of the Old Town. It was also the city's main place of execution, and over 100 martyred Covenanters are commemorated by a monument at the eastern end, where the gallows used to stand. The notorious murderers Burke and Hare operated from a now-vanished close off the western end. In 1827 they enticed at least 18 victims to their boarding house, suffocated them and sold the bodies to Edinburgh's medical schools.

Nowadays the broad, open square, edged by tall tenements and dominated by the looming castle, has many lively pubs and restaurants, including the **White Hart Inn** (Map pp72-3), which was once patronised by Robert Burns. **Cowgate** – the long, dark ravine leading eastwards from the Grassmarket – was once the road along

---

UNDERGROUND EDINBURGH

As Edinburgh expanded in the late 18th and early 19th centuries, many old tenements were demolished and new bridges were built to link the Old Town to the newly built areas to its north and south. South Bridge (built between 1785 and 1788) and George IV Bridge (built between 1829 and 1834) lead southwards from the Royal Mile over the deep valley of Cowgate, but so many buildings have been built closely around them that you can hardly tell they are bridges – George IV Bridge has a total of nine arches but only two are visible; South Bridge has no less than 18 hidden arches.

These subterranean vaults were originally used as storerooms, workshops and drinking dens. But as early-19th-century Edinburgh's population was swelled by an influx of penniless Highlanders cleared from their lands, and Irish refugees from the potato famine, the dark, dripping chambers were given over to slum accommodation and abandoned to poverty, filth and crime.

The vaults were eventually cleared in the late 19th century, then lay forgotten until 1994 when the South Bridge vaults were opened to guided tours (see Mercat Tours, p93). Certain chambers are said to be haunted and one particular vault was investigated by paranormal researchers in 2001.

Nevertheless, the most ghoulish aspect of Edinburgh's hidden history dates from much earlier – from the plague that struck the city in 1645. Legend has it that the disease-ridden inhabitants of Mary King's Close (a lane on the northern side of the Royal Mile on the site of the City Chambers – you can still see its blocked-off northern end from Cockburn St) were walled up in their houses and left to perish. When the lifeless bodies were eventually cleared from the houses, they were so stiff that workmen had to hack off limbs to get them through the small doorways and narrow, twisting stairs.

From that day on, the close was said to be haunted by the spirits of the plague victims. The few people who were prepared to live there reported seeing apparitions of severed heads and limbs, and the largely abandoned close fell into ruin. When the Royal Exchange (now the City Chambers) was constructed between 1753 and 1761, it was built over the lower levels of Mary King's Close, which were left intact and sealed off beneath the building.

Interest in the close revived in the 20th century when Edinburgh's city council began to allow occasional guided tours to enter. Visitors have reported many supernatural experiences – the most famous ghost is 'Sarah', a little girl whose sad tale has prompted people to leave gifts of dolls in a corner of one of the rooms. In 2003 the close was opened to the public as the Real Mary King's Close (see p81).

which cattle were driven from the pastures around Arthur's Seat to the safety of the city walls. Today it is the heart of Edinburgh's nightlife, with around two dozen clubs and bars within five minutes' walk of each other.

Candlemaker Row leads from the eastern end of the Grassmarket towards one of Edinburgh's most famous churches. **Greyfriars Kirk** (Map pp72–3) was built on the site of a Franciscan friary and opened for worship on Christmas Day 1620. In 1638 the National Covenant was signed here, rejecting Charles I's attempts to impose episcopacy and a new English prayer book, and affirming the independence of the Scottish Church. Many who signed were later executed at the Grassmarket and, in 1679, 1200 Covenanters were held prisoner in terrible conditions in the southwestern corner of the kirkyard. There's a small exhibition inside the church.

Hemmed in by high walls and overlooked by the brooding presence of the castle, **Greyfriars Kirkyard** is one of Edinburgh's most evocative cemeteries, a peaceful green oasis dotted with elaborate monuments. Many famous Edinburgh names are buried here, including the poet Allan Ramsay (1686–1758), architect William Adam (1689–1748) and William Smellie (1740–95), the editor of the first edition of the *Encyclopedia Britannica*. If you want to experience the graveyard at its scariest – inside a burial vault, in the dark, at night – go on one of Black Hart Storytellers' guided tours (see p93).

However, the memorial that draws the biggest crowds is the tiny **Greyfriars Bobby statue** (Map pp72–3), in front of the pub beside the kirkyard gate. Bobby was a Skye terrier who, from 1858 to 1872, maintained a vigil over the grave of his master, an Edinburgh police officer. The story was immortalised (and romanticised) in a novel by Eleanor Atkinson in 1912, and in 1963 was made into a movie by – who else? – Walt Disney. Bobby's own grave – marked by a small, pink granite stone – is just inside the entrance to the kirkyard. You can see his original collar and bowl in the Museum of Edinburgh (p81).

CHAMBERS STREET

The broad, elegant Chambers St stretches eastwards from Greyfriars Bobby, dominated by the long façade of the Museum of Scotland and Royal Museum. The golden stone and striking modern architecture of the **Museum of Scotland** (Map pp72–3; ☎ 247 4422; www.nms.ac.uk; Chambers St; admission free, special exhibitions extra; ☼ 10am-5pm Mon & Wed-Sat, to 8pm Tue, noon-5pm Sun) – opened in 1998 – is one of the city's most distinctive landmarks. The five floors of the museum trace the history of Scotland from geological beginnings to the 1990s, with many imaginative and stimulating exhibits – audio guides are available in several languages. Highlights include the Monymusk Reliquary, a tiny silver casket dating from AD 750, which is said to have been carried into battle with Robert the Bruce at Bannockburn in 1314, and a set of charming 12th-century chess pieces made from walrus ivory. Don't forget to take the lift to the roof terrace for a fantastic view of the castle.

The modern Museum of Scotland connects with the Victorian **Royal Museum** (Map pp72–3; ☎ 247 4422; www.nms.ac.uk; Chambers St; admission free, special exhibitions extra; ☼ 10am-5pm Mon & Wed-Sat, to 8pm Tue, noon-5pm Sun), dating from 1861, whose stolid, grey exterior gives way to a bright and airy, glass-roofed entrance hall. The museum houses an eclectic collection covering natural history, archaeology, scientific and industrial technology, and the decorative arts of ancient Egypt, Islam, China, Japan, Korea and the West.

New Town

Edinburgh's New Town lies north of the Old Town, on a ridge running parallel to the Royal Mile and separated from it by the valley of Princes Street Gardens. Its regular grid of elegant, Georgian terraces is a complete contrast to the chaotic tangle of tenements and wynds that characterise the Old Town.

Between the end of the 14th century and the start of the 18th, the population of Edinburgh – still confined within the walls of the Old Town – increased from 2000 to 50,000. The tottering tenements were unsafe and occasionally collapsed, fire was an ever-present danger, and the overcrowding and squalor became unbearable.

When the Act of Union in 1707 brought the prospect of long-term stability, the upper classes were keen to find healthier, more spacious living quarters, and in 1766 the lord provost of Edinburgh announced an architectural competition to design an extension to the city. It was won by an unknown 23-year-old, James Craig, a self-taught architect whose simple and elegant plan envisaged the main axis being George St, with grand squares at either end, and with building restricted to one side only of Princes and Queen Sts so that the houses enjoyed views over the Firth of Forth to the north and to the castle and Old Town to the south.

During the 18th and 19th centuries New Town continued to sprout squares, circuses, parks and terraces, with some of its finest neoclassical architecture designed by Robert Adam. Today Edinburgh's New Town remains the world's most complete and unspoilt example of Georgian architecture and town planning. Along with the Old Town, it was declared a Unesco World Heritage Site in 1995.

PRINCES STREET

Princes St is one of the world's most spectacular shopping streets. Built up on the north side only, it catches the sun in summer and allows expansive views across Princes Street Gardens to the castle and the crowded skyline of the Old Town.

The western end of Princes St is dominated by the red-sandstone edifice of the Caledonian Hotel, and the tower of **St John's Church** (Map pp72–3), worth visiting for its fine Gothic Revival interior. It overlooks **St Cuthbert's Parish Church** (Map pp72–3), built in the 1890s on a site of great antiquity – there has been a church here since at least the 12th century, and perhaps since the 7th century. There is a circular **watchtower** in the graveyard – a reminder of the Burke and Hare days when graves had to be guarded against robbers.

At the eastern end is the prominent clock tower – traditionally three minutes fast so that you don't miss your train – of the **Balmoral Hotel** (p99), and the beautiful 1788 **Register House** (Map pp72–3), designed by Robert Adam, with a statue of the duke of Wellington on horseback in front. It houses the National Archives of Scotland.

Princes Street Gardens (Map pp72–3) lie in a valley that was once occupied by the Nor' Loch, a boggy depression that was drained in the early 19th century. The gardens are split in the middle by **The Mound**, which was

created by around two million cart-loads of earth excavated from the foundations of New Town being dumped here to provide a road link across the valley to the Old Town. It was completed in 1830.

The eastern half of the gardens is dominated by the massive Gothic spire of the **Scott Monument** (Map pp72–3; ☎ 529 4068; East Princes Street Gardens; admission £3; ☯ 9am-6pm Mon-Sat, 10am-6pm Sun Apr-Sep, 9am-3pm Mon-Sat, 10am-3pm Sun Oct-Mar), built by public subscription in memory of the novelist Sir Walter Scott after his death in 1832. You can climb the 287 steps to the top for a superb view of the city.

ROYAL SCOTTISH ACADEMY

The distinguished Greek Doric temple at the corner of The Mound and Princes St, its northern pediment crowned by a seated figure of Queen Victoria, is the home of the **Royal Scottish Academy** (RSA; Map pp72–3; ☎ 225 6671 The Mound; admission free, special exhibitions £2-5; ☯ 10am-5pm Mon-Sat, 2-5pm Sun; �). Designed by William Playfair and built between 1823 and 1836, it was originally called the Royal Institution; the RSA took over the building in 1910. The galleries display a collection of paintings, sculptures and architectural drawings by academy members dating from 1831, and they also host temporary exhibitions throughout the year.

The RSA and the National Gallery of Scotland are linked via an underground mall – the Weston Link – which gives them twice the temporary exhibition space of the Prado in Madrid and three times that of the Royal Academy in London, as well as housing cloakrooms, a lecture theatre and a restaurant. The galleries have become famous in recent years for 'blockbuster' exhibitions such as 'Monet: The Seine and the Sea', and 'The Age of Titian'.

NATIONAL GALLERY OF SCOTLAND

Immediately south of the RSA is the **National Gallery of Scotland** (Map pp72–3; ☎ 624 6200; www.natgalscot.ac.uk; The Mound; admission free, special exhibitions extra; ☯ 10am-5pm Fri-Wed, to 7pm Thu; �). Also designed by William Playfair, this imposing classical building with its Ionic porticoes dates from the 1850s. Its octagonal rooms, lit by skylights, have been restored to their original Victorian décor of deep-green carpets and dark-red walls.

The gallery houses an important collection of European art from the Renaissance to postimpressionism, with works by Verrocchio (Leonardo da Vinci's teacher), Tintoretto, Titian, Holbein, Rubens, Van Dyck, Vermeer, El Greco, Poussin, Rembrandt, Gainsborough, Turner, Constable, Monet, Pissaro, Gauguin and Cézanne; each year in January the gallery exhibits its collection of Turner watercolours, bequeathed by Henry Vaughan in 1900.

The upstairs galleries house portraits by Sir Joshua Reynolds and Sir Henry Raeburn, and a clutch of Impressionists including Monet's luminous *Haystacks*, Van Gogh's demonic *Olive Trees* and Gauguin's hallucinatory *Vision After the Sermon*. But the painting that really catches your eye is the gorgeous portrait of *Lady Agnew of Lochnaw* by John Singer Sargent.

The basement galleries dedicated to Scottish art include glowing portraits by Allan Ramsay and Sir Henry Raeburn, rural scenes by Sir David Wilkie and impressionistic landscapes by William MacTaggart. Look out for Raeburn's iconic *Reverend Robert Walker Skating on Duddingston Loch*, and Sir George Harvey's hugely entertaining *A Schule Skailin* (A School Emptying) – a stern dominie (teacher) looks on as the boys stampede for the classroom door, one reaching for a spinning top confiscated earlier. Kids will love the fantasy paintings of Sir Joseph Noel Paton in Room B5, incredibly detailed canvases crammed with hundreds of tiny fairies, goblins and elves.

Room XII is normally graced by Antonio Canova's white marble sculpture, *The Three Graces;* it is owned jointly with London's Victoria & Albert Museum, where it was on display at the time of writing; it is due to the National Gallery of Scotland in 2007.

GEORGE STREET & CHARLOTTE SQUARE

Until the 1990s George St – the major axis of New Town – was the centre of Edinburgh's financial industry, and Scotland's equivalent of Wall St. Now many of the big financial firms have moved to premises in the Exchange office district west of Lothian Rd, and George St's former banks and offices house upmarket shops, pubs and restaurants.

At the western end of George St is **Charlotte Square** (Map pp72-3), the architectural jewel of New Town, designed by Robert Adam

shortly before his death in 1791. The northern side of the square is Adam's masterpiece and one of the finest examples of Georgian architecture anywhere. **Bute House** (Map pp72-3), in the centre at No 6, is the official residence of Scotland's first minister.

Next door is the **Georgian House** (Map pp72-3; ☎ 226 2160; 7 Charlotte Sq; adult/child £6/4; ⏱ 10am-7pm Jul & Aug, to 5pm Apr-Jun, Sep & Oct, 11am-3pm Mar & Nov), which has been beautifully restored and furnished to show how Edinburgh's wealthy elite lived at the end of the 18th century. The walls are decorated with paintings by Allan Ramsay, Sir Henry Raeburn and Sir Joshua Reynolds.

The headquarters of the **National Trust for Scotland** (NTS; Map pp72-3; ☎ 243 9300; www .nts.org.uk; 28 Charlotte Sq; admission free; ⏱ 9.30am-5pm Mon-Sat) is on the southern side of the square. As well as a shop, café and information desk, the building contains a restored 1820s **drawing room** (⏱ 11am-3pm Mon-Fri) with Regency furniture and a collection of 20th-century Scottish paintings.

ST ANDREW SQUARE

Not as architecturally distinguished as its sister at the opposite end of George St is **St Andrew Square** (Map pp72-3). Dominating the square is the fluted column of the **Melville Monument** (Map pp72-3), commemorating Henry Dundas, 1st Viscount Melville (1742–1811), who was the most powerful Scottish politician of his time, often referred to when alive as 'Harry IX, the Uncrowned King of Scotland'. The impressive Palladian mansion of **Dundas House** (Map pp72-3), built between 1772 and 1774, on the eastern side of the square, was built for Sir Laurence Dundas (1712–81) – no relation to Viscount Melville. It has been the head office of the Royal Bank of Scotland since 1825 and has a spectacular domed banking hall dating from 1857 (you can nip inside for a look).

A short distance along George St is the **Church of St Andrew** (Map pp72-3), built in 1784 with an unusual oval nave. It was the scene of the Disruption of 1843, when 451 dissenting ministers left the Church of Scotland to form the Free Church.

Just north of the square at the junction with Queen St is the Venetian Gothic palace of the **Scottish National Portrait Gallery** (Map pp72-3; ☎ 624 6200; 1 Queen St; admission free;

10am-5pm Mon-Sat, noon-5pm Sun). Its galleries illustrate Scottish history through portraits and sculptures of famous Scottish personalities, from Robert Burns and Bonnie Prince Charlie to Sean Connery and Billy Connolly. Opening hours are extended during the Edinburgh Festival.

Calton Hill

Calton Hill (100m), rising dramatically above the eastern end of Princes St, is Edinburgh's acropolis, its summit scattered with grandiose memorials mostly dating from the first half of the 19th century. It is also one of the best viewpoints in Edinburgh, with a panorama that takes in the castle, Holyrood, Arthur's Seat, the Firth of Forth, New Town and the full length of Princes St.

On the southern side of the hill, on Regent Rd, is the modernist façade of **St Andrew's House** (Map pp72–3), built between 1936 and 1939, which housed the civil servants of the Westminster government's Scottish Office until they were moved to the new Scottish Executive building in Leith in 1996.

Just beyond St Andrew's House and on the opposite side of the road is the imposing **Royal High School** (Map pp72–3) building, dating from 1829 and modelled on the Temple of Theseus in Athens. Former pupils include Robert Adam, Alexander Graham Bell and Sir Walter Scott. It now stands empty. To its east, on the other side of Regent Rd, is the 1830 **Burns Monument** (Map pp70–1), a Greek-style memorial to Robert Burns.

You can reach the summit of Calton Hill via the road beside the Royal High School or by the stairs at the eastern end of Waterloo Pl. The largest structure on the summit is the **National Monument** (Map pp72–3), an over-ambitious attempt to replicate the Parthenon and intended to honour Scotland's dead in the Napoleonic Wars. Construction – paid for by public subscription – began in 1822, but funds ran dry when only 12 columns were complete.

Looking a bit like an upturned telescope – the similarity is intentional – and offering even better views, the **Nelson Monument** (Map pp72–3; ☎ 556 2716; Calton Hill; admission £2; 1-6pm Mon, 10am-6pm Tue-Sat Apr-Sep, 10am-3pm Mon-Sat Oct-Mar) was built to commemorate Admiral Lord Nelson's victory at Trafalgar in 1805. The design of the **City Observatory** (Map pp72–3), built in 1818, was based on the

ancient Greek Temple of the Winds in Athens. Its original function was to provide a precise, astronomical time-keeping service for marine navigators, but smoke from Waverley train station forced the astronomers to move to Blackford Hill in the south of Edinburgh in 1895.

Dean Village

If you follow Queensferry St northwards from the western end of Princes St, you come to **Dean Bridge** (Map pp70–1), designed by Thomas Telford and built between 1829 and 1832. Down in the valley just west of the bridge is Dean Village (dene is a Scots word for valley). It was founded as a milling community by the canons of Holyrood Abbey in the 12th century and by 1700 there were 11 water mills here operated by the Incorporation of Baxters (the bakers' trade guild). One of the old mill buildings has been converted into flats, and the village is now an attractive residential area.

SCOTTISH NATIONAL GALLERY OF MODERN ART & DEAN GALLERY

Set in an impressive neoclassical building surrounded by a landscaped sculpture park some 500m west of Dean Village is the **Scottish National Gallery of Modern Art** (Map pp70–1; ☎ 624 6200; 75 Belford Rd; admission free, special exhibitions extra; 10am-5pm). The collection concentrates on 20th-century art, with various European movements represented by the likes of Matisse, Picasso, Kirchner, Magritte, Miró, Mondrian and Giacometti. American and English artists are also represented, but most space is given to Scottish painters – from the Scottish colourists of the early 20th century to contemporary artists such as Peter Howson and Ken Currie. There's an excellent café downstairs, and the surrounding park features sculptures by Henry Moore, Sir Eduardo Paolozzi and Barbara Hepworth among others, as well as a 'landform artwork' by Charles Jencks.

Directly across Belford Rd from the National Gallery of Modern Art, another neoclassical mansion houses its annexe, the **Dean Gallery** (Map pp70–1; ☎ 624 6200; 73 Belford Rd; admission free, special exhibitions extra; 10am-5pm Fri-Wed, to 7pm Thu). The Dean holds the Gallery of Modern Art's collection of Dada and surrealist art, including works by Dali, Giacometti and Picasso, and a large collection of sculpture and graphic art created by the Edinburgh-born sculptor Sir Eduardo Paolozzi.

Leith

Two miles northeast of the city centre, Leith (Map p69) has been Edinburgh's seaport since the 14th century and remained an independent burgh with its own town council until it was incorporated by the city in the 1920s. Like many of Britain's dockland areas, it fell into decay in the decades following WWII but has been undergoing a revival since the late 1980s. Old warehouses have been turned into luxury flats, and a lush crop of trendy bars and restaurants has sprouted along the waterfront. The area was given an additional boost in the late 1990s when the Scottish Executive (a government department) moved to a new building on Leith docks. The city council has now formulated a major redevelopment plan for the entire Edinburgh waterfront from Leith to Granton, the first phase of which is **Ocean Terminal** (Map p69), a shopping and leisure complex that includes the former Royal Yacht *Britannia* and a berth for visiting cruise liners. Parts of Leith are still a bit rough but it's a distinctive corner of the city and well worth exploring.

One of Scotland's biggest tourist attractions is the former **Royal Yacht Britannia** (Map p69; ☎ 555 5566; www.royalyachtbritannia.co.uk; Ocean Terminal, Leith; adult/child £9/5; ☼ 9.30am-6pm Apr-Sep, 10am-5pm Oct-Mar, last admission 1½hr before closing; ⓖ). She was the British royal family's floating home during their foreign travels from the time of her launch in 1953 until her decommissioning in 1997, and is now moored permanently in front of Ocean Terminal.

The tour, which you take at your own pace with an audio guide (also available in French, German, Italian and Spanish), gives an intriguing insight into the Queen's private tastes – *Britannia* was one of the few places where the royal family could enjoy true privacy. The entire ship is a monument to 1950s décor and technology, and the accommodation reveals Her Majesty's preference for simple, unfussy surroundings – the Queen's own bed is surprisingly tiny and plain.

There was nothing simple or unfussy, however, about the running of the ship. When the Queen travelled, along with her

went 45 members of the royal household, five tons of luggage and a Rolls-Royce that was carefully squeezed into a specially built garage on the deck. The ship's company consisted of an admiral, 20 officers and 220 yachtsmen. The decks (of Burmese teak) were scrubbed daily, but all work near the royal accommodation was carried out in complete silence and had to be finished by 8am. A thermometer was kept in the Queen's bathroom to make sure that the water was the correct temperature, and when in harbour one yachtsman was charged with ensuring that the angle of the gangway never exceeded 12 degrees. And note the mahogany windbreak that was added to the balcony deck in front of the bridge. It was put there to stop wayward breezes from blowing up skirts and inadvertently revealing the royal undies.

The Majestic Tour bus (see p93) runs from Waverley Bridge to *Britannia* during opening times. Alternatively, take Lothian Bus 11, 22, 34 or 35 to Ocean Terminal.

Greater Edinburgh

CRAIGMILLAR CASTLE

If you want to explore a Scottish fortress away from the crowds that throng Edinburgh Castle, try **Craigmillar Castle** (Map p69; ☎ 661 4445; Craigmillar Castle Rd; adult/child £3/1.20; ☼ 9.30am-6.30pm Apr-Sep, to 4.30pm Sat-Wed Oct-Mar). Dating from the 15th century, the tower house rises above two sets of machicolated curtain walls. Mary, Queen of Scots took refuge here after the murder of Rizzio; it was here too that plans to murder her husband Darnley were laid. Look for the prison cell complete with built-in sanitation, something some 'modern' British prisons only finally managed in 1996.

The castle is 2.5 miles southeast of the city centre. Take bus 33 eastbound from Princes St to Old Dalkeith Rd and walk 500m up Craigmillar Castle Rd.

CRAMOND

With its moored yachts, stately swans and whitewashed houses spilling down the hillside at the mouth of the River Almond, Cramond is the most picturesque corner of Edinburgh. It is also rich in history. The Romans built a fort here in the 2nd century AD (the village's name comes from Caer Amon, 'the fort on the River Almond'), but recent archaeological excavations have revealed evidence of a Bronze Age settlement dating from 8500 BC, the oldest known site in the whole of Scotland.

Cramond, which was originally a mill village, has a historic 17th-century church and a 15th-century tower house, as well as some rather unimpressive Roman remains, but most people come to enjoy the walks along the river to the ruined mills and to take the little rowing-boat ferry across the river to the Dalmeny Estate. A little downstream from the ferry landing is the **Maltings** (☎ 312 6034; Cramond Village; admission free; ☺ 2-5pm Sat & Sun Jun-Sep, daily during Edinburgh Festival), which hosts an interesting exhibition on Cramond's history.

Cramond is 5 miles northwest of the city centre; take bus 41 from The Mound, Hanover St (northbound) or Charlotte Sq to Cramond Glebe Rd, then walk north for 400m.

At the time of writing the Cramond Ferry had been closed since 2000, and was the subject of a bureaucratic wrangle. It may reopen, it may not.

EDINBURGH ZOO
Opened in 1913, **Edinburgh Zoo** (Map p69; ☎ 334 9171; www.edinburghzoo.org.uk; 134 Corstorphine Rd; adult/child £9/6; ☺ 9am-6pm Apr-Sep, to 5pm Oct & Mar, to 4.30pm Nov-Feb; ♿) is one of the world's leading conservation zoos. Edinburgh's captive breeding programme has saved many endangered species, including Siberian tigers, pygmy hippos and red pandas. The main attractions are the penguins (kept in the world's biggest penguin pool), the sea lion and red panda feeding times (check website for details), the animal-handling sessions and the Lifelinks 'hands-on' zoology centre.

The zoo is 2.5 miles west of the city centre; take Lothian Bus 12, 26 or 31, First Bus 16, 18, 80 or 86, or the Airlink Bus 100 westbound from Princes St.

ROYAL BOTANIC GARDEN
Just north of Stockbridge is the lovely **Royal Botanic Garden** (Map p69; ☎ 552 7171; www.rbge .org.uk; 20a Inverleith Row; admission free; ☺ 10am-7pm Apr-Sep, to 6pm Mar & Oct, to 4pm Nov-Feb). Twenty-eight beautifully landscaped hectares include splendid Victorian palm houses, colourful swathes of rhododendron and azalea, and a world-famous rock garden. The Terrace Café offers good views towards the city centre.

Take Lothian Bus 8, 17, 23 or 27 to the East Gate, or the Majestic Tour bus (see p93).

ACTIVITIES
Walking
Edinburgh is lucky to have several good walking areas within the city boundary, including Arthur's Seat, Calton Hill, Blackford Hill, Hermitage of Braid, Corstorphine Hill, and the coast and river at Cramond. The **Pentland Hills**, which rise to over 500m, stretch southwest from the city for 15 miles, offering excellent high- and low-level walking.

You can follow the **Water of Leith Walkway** from the city centre to Balerno (8 miles), and continue across the Pentlands to Silverburn (6.5 miles) or Carlops (8 miles), and return to Edinburgh by bus. Another good option is to walk along the towpath of the **Union Canal**, which begins in Fountainbridge and runs all the way to Falkirk (31 miles). You can return to Edinburgh by bus at Ratho (8.5 miles) or Broxburn (12 miles), and by bus or train from Linlithgow (21 miles).

Cycling
Edinburgh and its surroundings offer many excellent opportunities for cycling. The main off-road routes from the city centre out to the countryside follow the Union Canal towpath and the Water of Leith Walkway from Tollcross southwestwards to Balerno (7.5 miles) on the edge of the Pentland Hills, and the Innocent Railway Cycle Path from the southern side of Arthur's Seat eastwards to Musselburgh (5 miles) and on to Ormiston and Pencaitland. There are several routes through the Pentland Hills that are suitable for mountain bikes. For details ask at any bike shop or contact the **Pentland Hills Ranger Service** (☎ 445 3383). The *Edinburgh City Bike Map* (available from cycle shops) shows all the city's cycle routes.

The friendly and helpful folk at **Edinburgh Cycle Hire & Scottish Cycle Safaris** (Map pp72-3; ☎ 556 5560; www.cyclescotland.co.uk; 29 Blackfriars St; per day £10-15, per week £50-70; ☺ 10am-6pm Mon-Sat) rent out top-quality bikes; rates include helmet, lock and repair kit. You can hire tents and touring equipment too. The company also organises cycle tours in Edinburgh and all over Scotland – check the website for details.

Golf

There are no fewer than 19 golf courses in Edinburgh – the following are two of the best city courses.

Braid Hills Public Golf Course (☎ 447 6666; Braid Hills Approach; green fees weekday/weekend £15/17) A challenging course to the south of the city centre.

Lothianburn Golf Course (☎ 445 2206; 106a Biggar Rd, Fairmilehead; green fees weekday/weekend £18.50/24.50) Enjoys a scenic setting at the foot of the Pentland Hills, south of the city.

Swimming

The Firth of Forth is a bit on the chilly side for enjoyable swimming, but there are several indoor alternatives. The **Royal Commonwealth Pool** (Map pp70-1; ☎ 667 7211; 21 Dalkeith Rd; adult/child £3.90/1.90; ☼ 9am-9.30pm Mon, Tue, Thu & Fri, 10am-9.30pm Wed, 10am-4.30pm Sat & Sun) is Edinburgh's main facility, with a 50m pool, diving pool, children's pool, flumes and fitness centre. You'll need a 50p coin for the lockers.

Water Sports

The sheltered waters of the Firth of Forth host all kinds of water sports. **Port Edgar Marina & Sailing School** (☎ 331 3330; Shore Rd, Queensferry; ☼ boat rental 10am-noon & 2-4pm year-round, plus 7-9pm Mon-Fri Apr-Oct) rents out Topper/420/Wayfarer sailing dinghies for £11/20/27 for a two-hour session. It also offers a wide range of tuition courses in sailing, canoeing and power-boating.

Horse Riding

There are many scenic bridle paths suitable for horse riding in the countryside around Edinburgh, and a number of riding schools offer two- and three-hour treks as well as tuition:

Pentland Hills Icelandic Centre (☎ 01968-661095; www.phicelandics.co.uk; Windy Gowl Farm, Carlops, Midlothian; per 1½hr £25) South of the city.

Tower Farm Riding Stables (☎ 664 3375; 85 Liberton Dr; per hr £19) South of the city.

WALKING TOUR

Edinburgh's Old Town stretches along the Royal Mile to the east of the castle and south to the Grassmarket and Cowgate. This walk explores a few of the many interesting nooks and crannies around the upper part of the Royal Mile, and involves a fair bit of climbing up and down steep stairs and closes. Allow one to two hours.

Begin on the Castle Esplanade, which provides a grandstand view to the south over the Grassmarket. The prominent quadrangular building with all the turrets on your right is **George Heriot's School (1)**. Head towards Castlehill and the start of the Royal Mile. The 17th-century house on the right, above the steps of North Castle Wynd, is known as **Cannonball House (2)** because of the iron ball lodged in the wall (look between, and slightly below, the two largest windows). It was not fired in anger, but instead marks the gravitation height to which water would flow naturally from the city's first piped water supply.

The low, rectangular building across the street (now a touristy tartan-weaving mill) was originally the reservoir that held the Old Town's water supply. On its west wall is the **Witches Well (3)**, where a modern bronze fountain commemorates around 4000 people (mostly women) who were burned or strangled in Edinburgh between 1479 and 1722 for suspicion of witchcraft.

Go past the reservoir and turn left down Ramsay Lane, and take a look at **Ramsay Garden (4)** – one of the most desirable addresses in Edinburgh – where late-19th-century apartments were built around the nucleus of the octagonal Ramsay Lodge, once home to poet Allan Ramsay. The cobbled street continues around to the right below student residences, to the twin towers of the **New College (5)** – home to Edinburgh University's Faculty of Divinity. Nip into the courtyard to see the **statue of John Knox (6)**.

Just past New College turn right and climb up the stairs into Milne's Ct, a student residence. Exit into Lawnmarket, cross the street (bearing slightly left) and duck into **Riddell's Court (7)** at No 322–328, a typical Old Town close. You'll find yourself in a small courtyard, but the house in front of you (built in 1590) was originally the edge of the street (the building you just walked under was added in 1726). Check the doorway on the right. The arch with the inscription *Vivendo discimus* (we live and learn) leads into the original 16th-century courtyard.

Go back into the street, turn right, and then right again down Fisher's Close, which ejects you onto the delightful **Victoria Terrace**, poised above the cobbled curve of Victoria St. Wander right, enjoying the view, then

---

WALKING TOUR

Distance: 1.2km

Duration: one to two hours

descend the stairs at the foot of Upper Bow and continue downhill to the **Grassmarket**. Turn left along the gloomy defile of the Cowgate. The first bridge you come to is **George IV Bridge** (**8**; built 1829–34). Although you can see only one arch here, there are nine in total – one more is visible a block south at Merchant St, but the rest are hidden beneath and between the surrounding buildings, as are the haunted vaults of South Bridge, further west along Cowgate.

Pass under George IV Bridge. The buildings to your right are the new Law Courts, while high up to the left you can see the complex of buildings behind Parliament Sq. Past the courts and on the right is **Tailors Hall** (**9**; built 1621, extended 1757), now a hotel and bar, but formerly the meeting place of the 'Companie of Tailzeours' (Tailors' Guild).

Turn left and climb up **Old Fishmarket Close**, and perhaps stop for lunch at the brasserie **Café Marlayne** (**10**; p100). Emerge once more into the Royal Mile. Across the street and slightly downhill on the left is **Anchor Close** (**11**), named for a tavern that once stood there. It hosted the Crochallan Fencibles, an 18th-century drinking club that provided its patrons with an agreeable blend of intellectual debate and intoxicating liquor. The club was founded by William Smellie, editor of the first edition of the *Encyclopedia Britannica;* its best-known member was Robert Burns, the poet.

Should you wish to wet your own whistle, more than a dozen hostelries lie between here and Holyrood. And it's downhill all the way...

EDINBURGH FOR CHILDREN

Edinburgh has a multitude of attractions for children, and most things to see and do are child-friendly. Kids under five travel for free on Edinburgh buses, and five- to 15-year-olds pay a flat fare of 60p. However you should be aware that the majority of Scottish pubs, even those that serve bar meals, are forbidden by law to admit children under the age of 14; even in the family-friendly pubs (ie those in possession of a Children's Certificate), under-14s are only admitted between the hours of 11am and 8pm, and only when accompanied by an adult aged 18 or over.

The Edinburgh & Scotland Information Centre (p77) has lots of info on children's events, and the handy guidebook *Edinburgh for Under Fives* can be found in most bookshops. The *List* magazine (£2.20; www .list.co.uk) has a special Kids section listing children's activities and events in and around Edinburgh. The week-long **Children's International Theatre Festival** (☎ 225 8050; www .imaginate.org.uk) takes place each year in late May/early June.

There are good, safe **playgrounds** in most Edinburgh parks, including Princes Street Gardens West, Inverleith Park (opposite the Royal Botanic Garden), George V Park (New Town), the Meadows and Bruntsfield Links.

Ideas for outdoor activities include exploring the **Royal Botanic Garden** (p89), going to see the animals at **Edinburgh Zoo** (p89), visiting the statue of **Greyfriars Bobby** (p84) and feeding the swans and playing on the beach at **Cramond** (p88). During the Edinburgh and Fringe Festivals there's lots of street theatre for kids, especially on the High St and at the foot of The Mound, and in December there's an open-air ice rink and fairground rides in Princes Street Gardens.

If it's raining, you can visit the Discovery Centre, a hands-on activity zone on Level 3 of the **Museum of Scotland** (p84), play on the flumes at the **Royal Commonwealth Pool** (p90), try out the earthquake simulator at **Our Dynamic Earth** (p82), or take a tour of the haunted **Real Mary King's Close** (p81).

Childminding Services

For full listings of government-approved childminding services, check out **Childcare Link** (www.childcarelink.gov.uk), or **City of Edinburgh Childcare Information Service** (☎ 0800 032 0323). The following are reliable Edinburgh agencies that charge around £4 to £5 an hour.

Family Circle Recruitment (☎ 447 9162; www .familycircles.org; 37 Comiston Rd, Morningside)

Panda's Nanny Agency (☎ 663 3967; www .pandasnannyagency.co.uk; 22 Durham Pl, Bonnyrigg)

QUIRKY EDINBURGH

Edinburgh is full of unusual attractions and out-of-the-way corners that most visitors never see – even though they may be standing just a few metres away. Here are a few of the city's less mainstream attractions.

In complete contrast to the austerity of most of Edinburgh's religious buildings, the 19th-century, neo-Romanesque **Mansfield Place Church** (Map pp70-1; ☎ 474 8033; www.mans fieldtraquair.org.uk; Mansfield Pl; �8 1-4pm 2nd Sun of May, Jun & Sep-Dec, 10-11.45am Mon-Sat during Edinburgh Festival) at the foot of Broughton St contains a remarkable series of Renaissance-style frescoes painted in the 1890s by Irish-born artist Phoebe Anna Traquair (1852–1936). Now undergoing restoration, the murals are on view to the public at certain times (check the website for any changes).

The **Museum on the Mound** (Map pp72-3; ☎ 529 1288; The Mound; admission free; �8 10am-4.45pm Mon-Fri mid-Jun–Aug), housed in the Bank of Scotland's splendid Georgian HQ, is a treasure trove of gold coins, bullion chests, safes, banknotes, forgeries, cartoons and lots of fascinating old documents and photographs charting the history of Scotland's oldest bank. At the time of research it was due to be closed for refurbishment until mid-2006.

Musicians will enjoy the **Edinburgh University Collection of Historic Musical Instruments** (Map pp72-3; ☎ 650 2423; Reid Concert Hall, Teviot Pl; admission free; �8 3-5pm Wed, 10am-1pm Sat year-round, 2-5pm Mon-Fri during Edinburgh Festival), which contains more than 1000 instruments ranging from a 400-year-old lute to a 1959 synthesiser.

Further off the beaten track are the **Surgeons' Hall Museums** (Map pp72-3; ☎ 527 1649; Nicolson St; adult/child £5/3; �8 10am-4pm daily Aug & Sep, noon-4pm Mon-Fri Oct-Jul). The **History of Surgery** is a fascinating look at surgery in Scotland from the 15th century, when barbers supplemented their income with blood-letting, amputations and other surgical procedures, to the present day. Covering dentistry, with its wince-inducing collections of extraction tools, is the adjacent **Menzies Campbell Dental Museum**. The **Pathology Museum** houses a gruesome but compelling 19th-century collection of diseased organs, massive tumours and deformed infants pickled in formaldehyde.

While ghost tours of Edinburgh's underground vaults and haunted graveyards have become a mainstream attraction, few tourists have explored the recently opened **Gilmerton**

Cove (☎ 557 6464; www.gilmertoncove.org.uk; 16 Drum St, Gilmerton; adult/child £5/3; ⏰ tours 2pm Sat, 7pm Wed, Sat & Sun). Hidden in the southern suburbs, the mysterious Cove is a series of manmade subterranean caverns hacked out of the rock, their origin and function unknown. Book through Mercat Tours (see right).

Another refreshing alternative to the mainstream walking tours is offered by **Celtic Trails** (☎ 477 5419; www.celtictrails.co.uk; tours £22-29), whose knowledgeable owner Jackie Queally leads guided tours of Edinburgh's ancient and sacred sites, covering subjects such as Celtic mythology, geomancy, sacred geometry and the Knights Templar.

And finally, if you're in Edinburgh on the first Friday of August, head west to the village of Queensferry (p112) to see the bizarre **Burry Man**. As part of the village gala day, a local man spends nine hours roaming the streets wearing a woolly suit, which has been laboriously covered from head to toe in big, green, prickly burrs. One glance at his costume – he looks like a child's drawing of a Martian, with added prickles – would make you think he's suffering a medieval punishment, but it's actually a great honour to be selected as the Burry Man.

PARTY ON PRINCES STREET

Traditionally, the New Year has always been a more important celebration for Scots than Christmas. In towns, cities and villages all over the country, people fill the streets at midnight on 31 December to wish each other a Guid New Year and, yes, to knock back a dram or six to keep the cold at bay.

In 1993 Edinburgh's city council had the excellent idea of spicing up Hogmanay by organising some events, laying on some live music in Princes St and issuing an open invitation to the rest of the world. Most of them turned up, or so it seemed, and had such a good time that they told all their pals and came back again the next year. Now **Edinburgh's Hogmanay** (☎ 529 4454; www .edinburghshogmanay.org) is the biggest winter festival in Europe, regularly pulling in more than 250,000 partying punters. To get into the main party area in the city centre after 8pm on 31 December you'll need a ticket – book well in advance. New Year events run from 29 December to 1 January.

TOURS
Bus Tours

Open-topped buses leave from Waverley Bridge outside the main train station and offer hop-on, hop-off tours of the main sights, taking in New Town, the Grassmarket and the Royal Mile. They're a good way to get your bearings, although with a bus map and a Day Saver bus ticket (£2.30) you could do much the same thing but without the commentary. Tours run daily, year-round, except for 24 and 25 December.

Tickets for the following three tours remain valid for 24 hours.

Edinburgh Tour (☎ 555 6363; adult/child £8.50/2.50) Lothian Buses' bright red buses depart every 10 minutes from Waverley Bridge.

Mac Tours (☎ 220 0770; adult/child £8.50/2.50) Offers similar tours, but in a vintage bus.

Majestic Tour (☎ 220 0770; adult/child £8.50/2.50) Runs every 30 minutes (every 15 minutes in July and August) from Waverley Bridge to the Royal Yacht *Britannia* at Ocean Terminal via the Royal Botanic Garden and Newhaven, returning via Leith Walk, Holyrood and the Royal Mile.

Walking Tours

There are plenty of organised walks around Edinburgh, many of them related to ghosts, murders and witches. For starting times of individual walks, phone or check the following websites:

Black Hart Storytellers (☎ 225 9044; www.blackhart .uk.com; adult/concession £7/5) Not suitable for children. The 'City of the Dead' tour of Greyfriars Kirkyard is probably the best of Edinburgh's 'ghost' tours. Many people have reported encounters with the 'McKenzie Poltergeist'.

Cadies & Witchery Tours (☎ 225 6745; www .witcherytours.com; adult/child £7.50/5) The becloaked and pasty-faced Adam Lyal (deceased) leads a 'Murder & Mystery' tour of the Old Town's darker corners. These tours are famous for their 'jumper-ooters' – costumed actors who 'jump oot' when you least expect it. Ooooh, scary.

Celtic Trails (☎ 477 5419; www.celtictrails.co.uk; tours £22-29) Guided tours of the city's ancient and sacred sites (see also Quirky Edinburgh, opposite).

Edinburgh Literary Pub Tour (☎ 226 6665; www .edinburghliterarypubtour.co.uk; adult/student £8/6) An enlightening two-hour trawl through Edinburgh's literary history – and its associated howffs – in the entertaining company of Messrs Clart and McBrain. One of the best of Edinburgh's walking tours.

Mercat Tours (☎ 557 6464; www.mercattours.com; adult/ child £7.50/4) Mercat offers a wide range of fascinating tours including history walks in the Old Town and Leith, 'Ghosts & Ghouls' tours and visits to haunted underground vaults.

FESTIVALS & EVENTS

Edinburgh hosts an amazing number of festivals throughout the year, notably the Edinburgh International Festival, the Fringe Festival and the Military Tattoo, which are all held around the same time in August (see the boxed text, opposite). Hogmanay, Scottish New Year's celebrations, is also a peak party time; see the boxed text, p93.

April
Edinburgh International Science Festival
(☎ 558 7666; www.sciencefestival.co.uk) First held in 1987, it hosts a wide range of events, including talks, lectures, exhibitions, demonstrations, guided tours and interactive experiments designed to stimulate, inspire and challenge. From dinosaurs to ghosts to alien life forms, there's something to interest everyone. The festival runs over 10 days in the first two weeks of April.

May
Scottish International Children's Festival
(☎ 225 6440; www.imaginate.org.uk) This is Britain's biggest festival of performing arts for children, with events suitable for kids from three to 12. Groups from around the world perform classic tales like *Hansel and Gretel* as well as new material written specially for children. The festival takes place annually in the last week of May.

June
Caledonian Beer Festival (Map pp70-1; ☎ 228 5688; Caledonian Brewery, 42 Slateford Rd) A celebration of all things fermented and yeasty, Scotland's biggest beer-fest is hosted by Edinburgh's leading brewer of cask-conditioned ales. You can also sample a wide range of traditionally brewed beers from around the world, while enjoying live jazz and blues and snacking on pies and barbecue. Froth-topped bliss. The festival is held on the first weekend in June.

Royal Highland Show (☎ 335 6200; www.royal highlandshow.org; Royal Highland Centre, Ingliston) Scotland's hugely popular national agricultural show is a four-day feast of all things rural, with everything from show-jumping and tractor-driving to sheep-shearing and falconry. Countless pens are filled with coiffed show cattle and pedicured prize ewes. The show is held over a long weekend (Thursday to Sunday) in late June.

July
Edinburgh International Jazz & Blues Festival
(☎ 467 5200; www.edinburghjazzfestival.co.uk) Held annually since 1978, the Jazz and Blues Festival pulls in the top talent from all over the world. The Jazz Festival runs for nine days, beginning on the last Friday in July (the week before the Fringe and Tattoo begin). The first weekend

sees a Mardi Gras street parade on Saturday from the City Chambers, up the Royal Mile and down Victoria St into the Grassmarket, for an afternoon of free, open-air music. On the Sunday there's a series of free concerts at the Ross Bandstand in Princes Street Gardens.

August
See the boxed text, opposite, for details of August's festivals.

December
Edinburgh's Capital Christmas (☎ 529 4454; www.capitalchristmas.co.uk) The newest of the Scottish capital's festivals, first held in 2000, the Christmas bash includes a big street parade, a fairground and Ferris wheel, and an open-air ice rink in Princes Street Gardens. The celebrations are held over the three weeks before Christmas.

SLEEPING

A boom in hotel building has seen Edinburgh's tourist capacity swell significantly in the last decade, but you can guarantee that the city will still be packed to the gills during the festival period (August) and over Hogmanay (New Year). If you want a room during these periods, book as far in advance as possible – a year ahead if possible. In general, it's best to book ahead for accommodation at Easter and from mid-May to mid-September.

Hotels and backpacker hostels are found throughout the Old and New Towns, while midrange B&Bs and guesthouses are concentrated outside the centre in the suburbs of Tollcross, Bruntsfield, Newington and Pilrig.

If you're driving, don't even think about staying in the city centre unless your hotel has its own private car park – parking in the centre is a nightmare. Instead look for somewhere in a suburb like Newington, where there's a chance of finding free, on-street parking (even then, don't bet on getting a parking space outside the front door). Alternatively stay outside the city and travel in by bus or train.

Edinburgh accommodation is slightly more expensive than in the rest of Scotland, so the price breakdown in these listings is different from that described on p430 – budget is less than £25, midrange £25 to £50, and top end is more than £50, based on the cost per person for bed and breakfast (B&B), sharing a double room.

Accommodation Agencies

If you arrive in Edinburgh without a room, the Edinburgh & Scotland Information Centre (p77) booking service will try to find a room to suit you and will charge a £5 fee if successful. If you have the time, pick up the tourist office's accommodation brochure and ring around yourself.

You can also try VisitScotland's **Booking Hotline** (☎ 0845 225 5121), which has a £3

FESTIVAL CITY

August in Edinburgh sees a frenzy of festivals, with half a dozen world-class events running at the same time.

The month kicks off with the **Edinburgh Military Tattoo** (Map ppp72-3; ☎ 0870 755 5118; www .edintattoo.co.uk; Tattoo Office, 32 Market St), a spectacular display of military marching bands, massed pipes and drums, acrobats, cheerleaders and motorcycle display teams, all played out in front of the magnificent backdrop of the floodlit castle. Each show traditionally finishes with a lone piper, dramatically lit, playing a lament on the battlements. The Tattoo takes place over the first three weeks of August (from a Friday to a Saturday); there's one show at 9pm Monday to Friday and two (at 7.30pm and 10.30pm) on Saturday, but no performance on Sunday.

First held in 1947 to mark a return to peace after the ordeal of WWII, the **Edinburgh International Festival** (☎ 473 2000; www.eif.co.uk) is festooned with superlatives – the oldest, the most famous, the best in the world. The original was a modest affair, but today hundreds of the world's top musicians and performers congregate in Edinburgh for three weeks of diverse and inspirational music, opera, theatre and dance.

Tickets for popular events – especially music and opera – sell out quickly, so it's best to book as far in advance as possible. You can buy tickets in person at the Hub (Map pp72-3), or by phone, fax or Internet. Edinburgh's annual culture-fest takes place over the three weeks ending on the first Saturday in September; the programme is usually available from April.

When the first Edinburgh Festival was held in 1947, there were eight theatre companies who didn't make it onto the main programme. Undeterred, they grouped together and held their own mini-festival, on the fringe, and an Edinburgh institution was born. Today the **Edinburgh Festival Fringe** (Map pp72-3; ☎ 226 0026; www.edfringe.com; Edinburgh Festival Fringe Office, 180 High St) is *the* biggest festival of the performing arts anywhere in the world.

Since 1990 the Fringe has been dominated by stand-up comedy, but the sheer variety of shows on offer is staggering – everything from chain-saw juggling to performance poetry to Tibetan yak-milk gargling. So how do you decide what to see? There are daily reviews in the *Scotsman* newspaper – one good *Scotsman* review and a show sells out in hours – but the best recommendation is word of mouth. If you have the time, go to at least one unknown show – it may be crap, but at least you'll have your obligatory 'worst show I ever saw' story.

The big names play at the mega-venues like the Assembly Rooms and the Pleasance, and charge mega-prices (£8 a ticket and more), but there are plenty of good shows for under a fiver and, best of all, lots of free stuff. Fringe Sunday – usually the second Sunday – is a smorgasbord of free performances, staged in the Meadows park to the south of the city centre.

The Fringe take place over 3½ weeks in August, the last two weeks overlapping with the first two of the Edinburgh International Festival.

Held in a little village of marquees in the middle of Charlotte Sq, the **Edinburgh International Book Festival** (☎ 228 5444; www.edbookfest.co.uk) is a fun fortnight of talks, readings, debates, lectures, book signings and meet-the-author events, with a café and tented bookshop thrown in. The festival lasts for two weeks in August (usually the first two weeks of the Edinburgh International Festival).

The **Edinburgh International Film Festival** (☎ 229 2550; www.edfilmfest.org.uk) is one of the original Edinburgh Festival trinity, having first been staged in 1947 along with the International Festival and the Fringe. It is a major international event, serving as a showcase for new British and European films, and staging the European premieres of one or two Hollywood blockbusters. The festival lasts for two weeks in August (usually the first two weeks of the Edinburgh International Festival).

surcharge; or search for accommodation on the **Edinburgh & Lothians Tourist Board** (www .edinburgh.org/accommodation) website.

Budget

There's a growing number of independent backpacker hostels in Edinburgh, many of them right in the centre of town. Most have 24-hour access and no curfew.

OLD TOWN & AROUND

Brodies Hostel (☎ 556 6770; www.brodieshostels .co.uk; Brodies Hostel 1 Map pp72-3; 12 High St; dm £9-19; ☒ ⬜ ; Brodies Hostel 2 Map pp72-3; 93 High St; dm £10-22, d £35-77; ☒ ⬜) Brodies 1 is a small (50-bed), friendly place with four dorms (three mixed and one women-only) and seriously comfy hotel-quality mattresses and duvets. It has a kitchen and a cosy lounge area with a fireplace and no TV, which makes for good socialising. The newer Brodies 2, up the hill at 93 High St, offers double and family rooms too. Both have top locations in the middle of the Royal Mile, and don't accept stag-night groups.

Castle Rock Hostel (Map pp72-3; ☎ 225 9666; www.scotlands-top-hostels.com; 15 Johnston Tce; dm £12.50-14; ☒ ⬜) With its bright, spacious, single-sex dorms, superb views and friendly staff, the 200-bed Castle Rock has prompted plenty of positive feedback from travellers. It has a great location only a minute's walk from the castle (but a fair uphill trek from train and bus stations), a games room, reading lounge and big-screen video nights; the beds aren't quite as comfortable as those at Brodies.

Edinburgh Backpackers Hostel (Map pp72-3; ☎ 220 1717; www.hoppo.com; 65 Cockburn St; dm £14-18.50; ☒ ⬜) Just a short walk from the train station, Edinburgh Backpackers is clean, bright and friendly, with a lively bistro-bar on the ground floor. It's right in the heart of Edinburgh's pub culture, which makes it great for partying but not so good for a peaceful night's sleep.

St Christopher's Inn (Map pp72-3; ☎ 226 1446; www.st-christophers.co.uk; 9-13 Market St; dm £11-17, d £40-46; ⬜) The 108-bed St Christopher's is just across the street from the Market St entrance to Waverley train station, with accommodation in four- to 14-bed dorms, each with a toilet and power shower. It's a real party joint, with two bars (one chilled, one pumping) and a good-value restaurant,

and it accepts stag and hen nights, so don't expect to catch up on your beauty sleep.

Other recommendations:

Budget Backpackers Hostel (Map pp72-3; ☎ 226 6351; www.budgetbackpackers.com; 37-39 Cowgate; dm £16.50-20; ☒ ⬜) New, colourful, party place.

Royal Mile Backpackers (Map pp72-3; ☎ 557 6120; www.scotlands-top-hostels.com; 105 High St; dm £12.50-14; ☒) Small, cosy and quaint.

Central Youth Hostel (Map pp72-3; ☎ 0870 004 1115; 11/2 Robertson's Close, Cowgate; s £18-22.50; ☽ Jul & Aug) Summer only, all single rooms.

NEW TOWN & AROUND

City Centre Tourist Hostel (Map pp72-3; ☎ 441 6628; www.citycentrehostel.com; 3rd fl, 5 West Register St; dm £13-22; ☒) The City Centre is a small (around 40 beds), clean and relatively quiet hostel, with pine-wood bunks and comfy mattresses in four-, six-, eight- and 10-bed dorms. There's a small kitchen and TV lounge, and a laundry. The location is great – just two minutes' walk from train and bus stations. Don't confuse it with Princes St Backpackers, which shares the entrance.

Belford Hostel (Map pp70-1; ☎ 225 6209; www .hoppo.com; 6/8 Douglas Gardens; dm £10-18; ⬜) An unusual hostel housed in a converted church, the Belford is under the same management as Edinburgh Backpackers. Although some people have complained of noise – there are only thin partitions between dorms, and no ceilings – it's cheerful and well run with good facilities. This hostel is about 20 minutes' walk west of Waverley train station. If you're arriving by train from Glasgow or the north, get off at Haymarket station, which is much closer.

OUTSIDE THE CENTRE

Globetrotter Inn (Map p69; ☎ 336 1030; www .globetrotterinns.com; 46 Marine Dr; dm £10-20, d £30-42; ⬜) A large and comfortable hostel with luxury bunks, TV lounges, sauna and gym. Good value, but can occasionally be plagued by noisy stag-party groups. It's close to the waterfront and about 20 minutes by a free hourly shuttle bus from the city centre (pick-up from Waverley station).

Bruntsfield Youth Hostel (Map pp70-1; ☎ 0870 004 1114; 7 Bruntsfield Cres; dm £14-21; ☒ ⬜) Situated in an attractive location overlooking a tree-lined park, this hostel has spick-and-span four- to 12-bed dorms, some with castle views, a canteen-style dining room, large-screen TV and resident cat. It's about 2.5 miles from Waverley train station; take bus 11 or 16 from Princes St (gardens side) and get off at Forbes Rd.

Pollock Halls of Residence (Map pp70-1; ☎ 0800 028 7118; www.edinburghfirst.com; 18 Holyrood Park Rd; s £28-33, d £36-41; P ✗) This is a modern student complex belonging to the University of Edinburgh, with 1200 rooms (500 with en-suite bathroom). It's busy and often noisy, but close to the city centre and with Arthur's Seat as a backdrop. Available during Easter and summer vacations.

Edinburgh Caravan Club Site (Map p69; ☎ 312 6874; www.caravanclub.co.uk; Marine Dr; tent £5-7, plus per person £4) This campsite is 3 miles northwest of the city centre, overlooking the Firth of Forth. Take bus 8A from North Bridge or Broughton St. Cars with tents are not admitted during August.

Mortonhall Caravan Park (☎ 664 1533; www.meadowhead.co.uk/mortonhall; 38 Mortonhall Gate, Frogston Rd East; tent sites incl 1 car & 2 people £10-16, each extra person £1; ☼ Mar-Oct) Located in attractive parkland 5 miles southeast of the centre, Mortonhall has an onsite shop, bar and restaurant. Take bus 11 from Princes St (westbound).

Midrange

Chain hotels are the only midrange accommodation in the Old Town.

NEW TOWN

Caravel Guest House (Map pp70-1; ☎ 556 4444; caravelguest@hotmail.com; 30 London St; r per person £20-35; ✗) The friendly, family-run Caravel is handy for the New Town and for Broughton St nightlife. There's an excellent Moroccan restaurant, Marrakech, in the basement (see p101).

Castle Guest House (Map pp72-3; ☎ 225 1975; www.castleguesthouse.com; 38 North Castle St; r per person £30-40; ✗) This gorgeous Georgian house with traditional décor – deep red walls and polished wood – is centrally located; some of the seven en-suite rooms have castle views.

Dene Guest House (Map pp70-1; ☎ 556 2700; www.deneguesthouse.com; 7 Eyre Pl; r per person £20-35; ✗) The Dene is a friendly and informal guesthouse, set in a charming Georgian town house; unusually for Edinburgh B&Bs, dogs are welcome.

Stuart Guest House (Map p69; ☎ 557 9030; www.stuartguesthouse.com; 12 East Claremont St; r per person £33-50; ✗) A readers' favourite, the Stuart is a welcoming late-Georgian town house with many period features, including staircase, fireplaces and cornices.

TOLLCROSS

Tollcross is half a mile south of the western end of Princes St, along Lothian Rd.

Edinburgh City B&B (Map pp70-1; ☎ 622 0144; www.edinburghcityguesthouse.co.uk; 31 Grove St; d £50-70) This bright, cheerful B&B, with four refurbished bedrooms in a Georgian-style terrace, boasts a superb location only 10 minutes' walk from the castle, and only 400m from Haymarket train station.

Amaryllis Guest House (Map pp70-1; ☎ 229 3293; www.amaryllisguesthouse.com; 21 Upper Gilmore Pl; s £25-45, d £36-80; P) The gay-friendly Amaryllis is a cute little Georgian town house with five rooms, all except one with en-suite bathroom. Princes St is 10 minutes' walk away.

BRUNTSFIELD

Another half-mile south from Tollcross is Bruntsfield.

Greenhouse (Map pp70-1; ☎ 622 7634; www.greenhouse-edinburgh.com; 14 Hartington Gardens; s £55-80, d £60-90; ✗) The award-winning Greenhouse is a wholly vegetarian and vegan guesthouse, which uses organic and genetically modified–free foods as much as possible – the breakfast menu includes pancakes with caramel bananas and almonds – and even the soap and shampoo are free of animal products.

Robertson Guest House (Map pp70-1; ☎ 229 2652; www.robertson-guesthouse.com; 5 Hartington Gardens; r per person £28-50; ✗) Set in a homely Victorian house tucked away in a quiet backstreet, this guesthouse offers a range of healthy breakfast food, including yogurt, fruit and a cooked vegetarian breakfast.

Menzies Guest House (Map pp70-1; ☎ 229 4629; www.menzies-guesthouse.co.uk; 33 Leamington Tce; s £20-45, d £30-80; P) This is a clean, friendly and well-run place, with seven spacious, high-ceilinged Victorian rooms spread over three floors. The cheaper rooms, with shared bathroom, are small but offer excellent value.

NEWINGTON

There are lots of guesthouses on and around Minto St and Mayfield Gardens (the continuation of North Bridge and Nicolson

St) in Newington. This is the main traffic artery from the south and a main bus route into the city centre.

Aonach Mor Guest House (Map pp70-1; ☎ 667 8694; www.aonachmor.com; 14 Kilmaurs Tce; r per person £25-45; ✕ ▣) This elegant Victorian terraced house is located on a quiet back street and has seven bedrooms, beautifully decorated, with many original period features. Our favourite is the 1st-floor bedroom at the front, with bay window.

Southside Guest House (Map pp70-1; ☎ 668 4422; www.southsideguesthouse.co.uk; 8 Newington Rd; s £45-70, d £64-120; ✕) Forget traditional Edinburgh guesthouses – the eight-room Southside oozes interior design, with the clever use of bold colours and contemporary furniture.

Glenallan Guest House (Map pp70-1; ☎ 667 1667; 19 Mayfield Rd; s £45-75, d £70-110; ℗ ✕) A bit of old-fashioned luxury is on offer at the Glenallan, a Victorian terraced house with plush bedrooms, posh toiletries, and home-baked bread on the breakfast table. Set in a flower-filled garden on a main bus route into town.

Fairholme Guest House (Map p69; ☎ 667 8645; www.fairholme.co.uk; 13 Moston Tce; r per person £25-45; ✕) A pleasant, quiet Victorian villa with five rooms (four with en-suite bathroom), the gay- and vegetarian-friendly Fairholme has been recommended by several readers.

Other recommendations:

Kenvie Guest House (Map pp70-1; ☎ 668 1964; www.kenvie.co.uk; 16 Kilmaurs Rd; r per person £25-37; ✕) Situated in a quiet side street but close to a main bus route.

Salisbury Guest House (Map pp70-1; ☎ 667 1264; www.salisburyguesthouse.co.uk; 45 Salisbury Rd; r per person £24-40; ℗ ✕) Quiet, comfortable Georgian villa with large garden.

Avondale Guest House (Map pp70-1; ☎ 667 6779; avondalehouse@aol.com; 10 South Gray St; s/d £30/50; ✕)

Sherwood Guest House (Map pp70-1; ☎ 667 1200; www.sherwood-edinburgh.com; 42 Minto St; s £30-60, d £40-75; ℗ ✕)

PILRIG

Northeast of the New Town and west of Leith Walk, Pilrig St has lots of guesthouses, all within about a mile of the centre. To get there, take bus 11 from Princes St.

Ardmor House (Map p69; ☎ 554 4944; www.ardmorhouse.com; 74 Pilrig St; s £45-60, d £60-100; ✕) The gay-friendly Ardmor is a stylishly renovated Victorian house with five en-suite

bedrooms, and all those little touches that make a place special – an open fire, thick towels, crisp white bed linen and free newspapers at breakfast.

Balmoral Guest House (Map p69; ☎ 554 1857; www.balmoralguesthouse.co.uk; 32 Pilrig St; r per person £17-37; ✕) Travellers have recommended this comfortable, five-room B&B located in an elegant, flower-bedecked, Victorian terraced house with lots of period features.

Top End
OLD TOWN

Point Hotel (Map pp72-3; ☎ 221 5555; www.point-hotel.co.uk; 34 Bread St; r from £125; ✕) Housed in the beautiful former showrooms of the St Cuthbert Co-operative Association (built 1937), the Point is famous for its striking contemporary interior design. Some rooms have stunning castle views.

Apex International Hotel (Map pp72-3; ☎ 300 3456; www.apexhotels.co.uk; 31-35 Grassmarket; r £80-240; ℗ ✕) Centrally located and with good business facilities, the 175-room Apex has stylish, modern décor, large, luxurious bedrooms, a rooftop restaurant and great views of the castle.

Tailors Hall Hotel (Map pp72-3; ☎ 622 6801; www.festival-inns.co.uk; 139 Cowgate; s/d £90/120) The Tailors Hall, with bright, modern rooms decorated in blue, pink and natural pine, is located bang in the middle of Edinburgh's clubland, and has three big bars of its own downstairs. Great for partying, but not a place for the quiet life.

SOMETHING SPECIAL...

Prestonfield House Hotel (Map p69; ☎ 668 3346; www.prestonfield.com; Priestfield Rd; r £195-275; ℗ ▣) If the blonde wood, brown leather and brushed steel of modern boutique hotels leave you cold, then this is the place for you. A 17th-century mansion set in 20 acres of parkland (complete with peacocks and Highland cattle), Prestonfield House is draped in damask, packed with antiques and decorated in red, black and gold – look out for original tapestries, 17th-century embossed-leather panels, and £500-a-roll hand-painted wallpaper. The hotel's 30 rooms are supplied with all mod cons, including Internet access, Bose sound systems, DVD players and flat-screen TVs.

NEW TOWN

Balmoral Hotel (Map pp72-3; ☎ 556 2414; www
.thebalmoralhotel.com; 1 Princes St; s £210-360, d £240-
410; P ✗ ☲) The sumptuous Balmoral –
a prominent landmark at the east end of
Princes St – offers some of the best accommodation in Edinburgh, including suites
with 18th-century décor and superb views
over the city.

Glasshouse (Map pp70-1; ☎ 525 8200; www
.theetoncollection.com; 2 Greenside Pl; r £130-375;
P ✗) A palace of cutting-edge design
perched atop the Omni Centre at the foot
of Calton Hill, and entered through the preserved façade of a 19th-century church, the
Glasshouse sports luxury rooms with floor-
to-ceiling windows, leather sofas, marble
bathrooms and a rooftop garden.

Dukes of Windsor Street (Map pp70-1; ☎ 556
6046; www.dukesofwindsor.com; 17 Windsor St; s £35-80,
d £60-140; ✗) A relaxing eight-bedroom Georgian town house set on a quiet side street,
only a few paces from Princes St, Dukes
offers an appealing blend of modern sophistication and period atmosphere.

rick's (Map pp72-3; ☎ 622 7800; www.ricks
edinburgh.co.uk; 55a Frederick St; r £118) Describing
itself as a 'restaurant with rooms' (10 of
them), rick's offers sharp styling and a laid-
back atmosphere. The bedrooms boast walnut headboards and designer fabrics, with
fluffy bathrobes, well-stocked mini-bars
and Molton Brown toiletries.

Scotsman Hotel (Map pp72-3; ☎ 556 5565; www
.thescotsmanhotelgroup.co.uk; 20 North Bridge; r £250-
350; ✗ ☲ ☲) The former offices of the
Scotsman newspaper – opened in 1904 and
hailed as 'the most magnificent newspaper
building in the world' – are now home to
this luxury hotel. Rooms on the northern
side enjoy superb views over the New Town
and Calton Hill, while the Penthouse Suite
(£1200) has its own library and sauna.

EATING

The last decade has seen a boom in the
number of restaurants and cafés in Edinburgh, and there is a wide range of cuisines
to choose from. Lunch is generally served
from noon to 2.30pm and dinner from 7pm
to 10pm, but many places are open all day.

In addition to restaurants and cafés, most
pubs serve food, offering either bar meals
or more formal dining, or both; here you
generally have to order your food and drink

at the bar. Be aware that pubs without a
restaurant licence are not allowed to serve
food to those aged under 16.

Old Town & Around
BUDGET

Favorit (Teviot Pl Map pp72-3; ☎ 220 6880; 19-20
Teviot Pl; sandwiches £4-5, salads £4-6; ☼ 8am-2.30am;
Tollcross Map pp70-1; 30 Leven St) A stylish café-
bar with a retro vibe, Favorit caters for everyone – workers grabbing breakfast on the way
to the office, coffee-slurping students skiving
off afternoon lectures and late-night clubbers
with an attack of the munchies. They also do
the best bacon *butties* (sandwiches) in town.

Bar Italia (Map pp72-3; ☎ 228 6379; 100 Lothian Rd;
mains £6-9; ☼ noon-midnight Mon-Thu, noon-1am Fri &
Sat, 5pm-midnight Sun) A classic Italian restaurant
of the old school, Bar Italia comes complete
with checked tablecloths, candles in Chianti
bottles and smartly dressed, wisecracking
waiters who occasionally burst into song.
Good-value Italian nosh and a lively atmosphere make it a popular venue for birthdays
and office parties.

Khushi's (Map pp72-3; ☎ 667 0888; 26-30 Potterrow;
mains £5-9; ☼ noon-11pm Mon-Sat, 5-10pm Sun) Established in 1947, Khushi's is something of an
Edinburgh institution despite having moved
into shiny new premises. Its speciality is basic
Indian dishes cooked in the traditional way
using marinated meat, served with no frills at
very low prices. It's not licensed, but you can
bring your own booze (no corkage).

Monster Mash (Map pp72-3; ☎ 225 7069;
4a Forrest Rd; mains £5-7; ☼ 8am-10pm Mon-Fri, 9am-
10pm Sat, 10am-10pm Sun) Classic British grub
of the 1950s – bangers and mash, shepherd's pie, fish and chips – is the mainstay
of the menu at this nostalgia-fuelled café.
But there's a twist – the food is all top-
quality nosh freshly prepared from local
produce, including Crombie's gourmet
sausages. And there's even a wine list!

MIDRANGE

Apartment (Map pp70-1; ☎ 228 6456; 7-13 Barclay
Pl; mains £7-12; ☼ 5.45-11pm Mon-Fri, noon-11pm Sat
& Sun) Effortlessly cool, classy and almost
always full, the Apartment is famed for fantastic bistro food and a buzzy, busy atmosphere; book in advance – by at least three
weeks, preferably – and don't be surprised
if you still have to wait. But it's worth being
patient for treats such as lobster, salmon

and spring onion broth, or roast vegetables with *harissa* (paste of chillis and garlic), coriander and sunblush tomatoes.

Point Hotel (Map pp72-3; ☎ 221 5555; 34 Bread St; 2-course lunch £9, 3-course dinner £17; ☽ noon-2pm & 6-10pm Mon-Thu, to 11pm Fri & Sat, to 9pm Sun) The legendary lunch and dinner menus at the Point Hotel (see p98) offer exceptional value – delicious Scottish/international cuisine served in an elegant room with crisp, white linen and attentive service. Reservations are strongly recommended.

Café Marlayne (Map pp72-3; ☎ 225 3838; 7 Old Fishmarket Close, High St; mains £7-15; ☽ noon-2pm & 6-10pm Tue-Sat) The second branch of the New Town French bistro (see opposite) is a hidden gem, down a steep cobbled alley off the Royal Mile, with a changed-daily menu of fresh market produce and a lovely little lunchtime sun-trap of an outdoor terrace.

blue bar café (Map pp72-3; ☎ 221 1222; 10 Cambridge St; mains £9-15; ☽ noon-2.30pm & 5.30-10.30pm Mon-Sat) Set above the foyer of the Traverse Theatre, this cool, white space is a lighter and less formal version of the Atrium (see opposite). The food is simple but perfectly

cooked and presented, and the atmosphere loud and chatty, with all those luvvies from the theatre downstairs. There's a two-course lunch for £10.

Buffalo Grill (Map pp72-3; ☎ 667 7427; 12-14 Chapel St; mains £8-15; ☽ noon-2pm & 6-10.30pm Mon-Fri, 6-10.30pm Sat, 5-10pm Sun) The Buffalo Grill is cramped, noisy, fun and always busy, so book ahead. An American-style menu offers burgers, steaks and side orders of fries and onion rings, along with fish and chicken dishes, prawn tempura and a vegetarian burger, but steaks are the main event. You can buy booze in the restaurant, or bring your own wine (£1 corkage per bottle).

Pancho Villa's (Map pp72-3; ☎ 557 4416; 240 Canongate; mains £8-13; ☽ noon-2.30pm & 6-10pm Mon-Thu, noon-10.30pm Fri & Sat, 6-10pm Sun) With a Mexican-born owner and lots of Latin American and Spanish staff, it's not surprising that this colourful and lively restaurant is one of the most authentic-feeling Mexican places in town. The dinner menu includes delicious steak fajitas and great vegetarian spinach enchiladas. It's often busy, so book ahead.

TOP FIVE LUNCH SPOTS

Many restaurants in Edinburgh offer good-value lunches. Here are a few suggestions from various parts of the city.

Basement (Map pp70-1; ☎ 557 0097; 10a-12a Broughton St; mains £6-10; ☽ food served noon-10.30pm) The Basement is a pleasantly grungy bar with a separate restaurant area, offering a two-course lunch for only £7 (available noon to 3pm Monday to Friday). The grub is sort of international – bruschetta, nachos, chilli con carne, steak-and-red wine pie – but goes Thai on Wednesday and Mexican at the weekend.

Daniel's Bistro (Map p69; ☎ 553 5933; 88 Commercial St; mains £10-14; ☽ noon-10pm) Daniel comes from Alsace, and his all-French kitchen staff combine top Scottish and French produce with Gallic know-how to create a wide range of delicious dishes. The fish soup is excellent, and main courses range from slow-cooked knuckle of pork to Alpine *tartiflette* (French dish of cheese, potato, ham or pork, and cream). A two-course lunch is £7.65.

La P'tite Folie (Map pp72-3; ☎ 225 7983; 61 Frederick St; mains £11-15; ☽ noon-3pm & 6-11pm Mon-Sat, 6-11pm Sun) This is a delightful little restaurant with a Breton owner whose menu includes the French classics – onion soup, *moules marinières, Coquilles St Jacques* – steaks, seafood and a range of *plats du jour*. The two-/three-course lunch is a bargain at £7/8.

Old Chain Pier (Map p69; ☎ 552 1233; 1 Trinity Cres; mains £5-10; ☽ food served noon-9pm Mon-Sat, 12.30-8pm Sun) The Old Chain Pier is a lovely little pub overlooking – nay, overhanging – the Firth of Forth on the waterfront near Granton Harbour. The excellent bar menu includes soup of the day, a creamy and filling *Cullen skink*, and a succulent steak-and-onion baguette with chips. The menu of real ales is no less enticing than the food.

Petit Paris (Map pp72-3; ☎ 226 2442; 38-40 Grassmarket; mains £7-12; ☽ noon-3pm & 5.30-10pm, to 11pm Fri & Sat) Like the name says, this is a little piece of Paris, complete with checked tablecloths, friendly waiters and good-value grub – the *moules-frites* (mussels and chips) are excellent. There's a lunch deal offering the *plat du jour* and a coffee for £6 (£7 during the Edinburgh Festival).

Suruchi (Map pp72-3; ☎ 556 6583; 14a Nicolson St; mains £8-14; ◷ noon-2pm & 5.30-11pm, closed lunch Sun) A laid-back Indian eatery with handmade turquoise tiles, lazy ceiling fans and chilled-out jazz guitar, Suruchi offers a range of exotic dishes as well as the traditional tandoori standards. Try *shakuti* from Goa (lamb or chicken with coconut, poppy seeds, nutmeg and chilli), or vegetarian *kumbhi narial* (mushrooms, coconut and coriander). An amusing touch is provided by the menu descriptions – they're translated into broad Scots ('a *beezer o' a curry this...gey nippie oan the tongue*').

Amber (Map pp72-3; ☎ 477 8477; 354 Castlehill; mains £12-15; ◷ noon-4pm daily, plus 7-9pm Fri & Sat) Located in the Scotch Whisky Heritage Centre (p79), this whisky-themed restaurant manages to avoid the tourist clichés and create genuinely interesting and flavoursome dishes such as salmon cooked with pearl barley, seaweed and Islay malt whisky, or spiced apple crumble with whisky custard.

TOP END

Tower (Map pp72-3; ☎ 225 3003; Museum of Scotland, Chambers St; mains £15-21; ◷ noon-11pm) Chic and sleek, with a great view of the castle, Tower is set atop the Museum of Scotland building. It offers a menu of quality Scottish food, simply prepared – try half a dozen Loch Fyne oysters followed by a chargrilled Aberdeen Angus steak. A two-course pre-theatre menu (£12.50) is available from 5pm to 6.30pm.

Atrium (Map pp72-3; ☎ 228 8882; 10 Cambridge St; mains £17-23; ◷ noon-2pm & 6-10pm Mon-Fri, 6-10pm Sat) Elegantly draped in cream linen and candlelight, the Atrium is one of Edinburgh's most fashionable restaurants, counting Mick Jagger and Jack Nicholson among its past guests. The cuisine is modern Scottish with a Mediterranean twist, with the emphasis on the finest of fresh, seasonal produce – halibut poached in red wine, or wild mushroom risotto with truffle and tarragon.

New Town & Around
BUDGET
Blue Moon Café (Map pp70-1; ☎ 556 2788; 1 Barony St; mains £6-8; ◷ 11am-10pm Mon-Fri, 10am-10pm Sat & Sun) The Blue Moon is the focus of Broughton St's gay social life, always busy,

always friendly, and serving up delicious nachos, salads, sandwiches and baked potatoes. It's famous for its homemade hamburgers, which come plain or topped with cheese or chilli sauce, and delicious daily specials.

Marrakech (Map pp70-1; ☎ 556 4444; 30 London St; dinner £14; ◷ 6-10pm Mon-Sat) A friendly and homely little Moroccan restaurant, in the basement of the Caravel Guest House (p97), the Marrakech dishes up delicious *tajines* (a slow-cooked casserole of lamb with almonds and dried fruit, usually prunes or apricots) accompanied by home-baked, caraway-scented bread. Round off the meal with a pot of mint tea.

MIDRANGE

Café Marlayne (Map pp72-3; ☎ 226 2230; 76 Thistle St; mains £11-15; ◷ noon-2pm & 6-10pm Tue-Sat) All weathered wood and warm yellow walls, little Café Marlayne is a cosy nook offering French farmhouse cooking – *escargots* with garlic and parsley, oysters with lemon and Tabasco, *boudin noir* (black pudding) with sautéed apples, peppered duck breast with balsamic vinegar – at very reasonable prices. A new branch recently opened in the Old Town (see opposite).

Nargile (Map pp72-3; ☎ 225 5755; 73 Hanover St; mains £9-14; ◷ noon-2pm & 5.30-10.30pm Mon-Thu, noon-2pm & 5.30-11pm Fri & Sat) Throw away any preconceptions about kebabs – this glitzy Turkish restaurant is a class act. Enjoy a spread of delicious *mezeler* (think Turkish tapas) followed by meltingly sweet, marinated lamb chargrilled to crispy perfection. Finish off with *baklava* (nut-filled pastry soaked in honey) and a Turkish coffee.

Mussel Inn (Map pp72-3; ☎ 225 5979; 61-65 Rose St; mains £6-16; ◷ noon-10pm Mon-Sat, 1.30-10pm Sun) Owned by west-coast shellfish farmers, the Mussel Inn provides a direct outlet for fresh Scottish seafood. The busy restaurant, decorated with bright beech wood indoors, spills out onto the pavement in summer. A kilogram pot of mussels with a choice of sauces – try leek, bacon, white wine and cream – costs £10.

Songkran (Map pp70-1; ☎ 225 7889; 24a Stafford St; mains £8-11; ◷ noon-2.30pm & 5.30-11pm Mon-Sat) You'd better book a table – and be prepared for a squeeze – to get in to this tiny New Town basement. The reason for the crush is some of the best Thai food in Edinburgh.

Try the tender *yang* (marinated and bar-becued beef, chicken or prawn), the crisp and tart orange chicken, or the chilli-loaded warm beef salad.

VinCaffè (Map pp72-3; ☎ 557 0088; 11 Multrees Walk, St Andrew Sq; mains £8-18; ☺ 8am-late Mon-Sat, 11am-5.30pm Sun) Foodie colours dominate the décor at this delightful Italian deli-bistro –bottle-green pillars and banquettes, chocolate-and-cream coloured walls, es-presso-black tables – a perfect backdrop for VinCaffè's superb antipasto, washed down with a bottle of pink Pinot Grigio. Live jazz from 7pm on Wednesdays.

Stac Polly (Map pp72-3; ☎ 556 2231; 29-33 Dublin St; mains £12-18; ☺ noon-2.30pm Mon-Fri, 6-11pm daily) Named after a mountain in northwestern Scotland, Stac Polly's kitchen adds sophisti-cated twists to fresh Highland produce. Meals such as smoked salmon, lime and avocado mousse, followed by roast saddle of venison with a thyme and red wine reduction, keep the punters coming back for more. The res-taurant's famous baked filo pastry parcels of haggis, served with plum sauce, are so popu-lar they've almost become a national dish.

TOP END

Café Royal Oyster Bar (Map pp72-3; ☎ 556 4124; 17a West Register St; mains £16-20; ☺ noon-2pm & 7-10pm) Pass through the revolving doors on the corner of West Register St and you're trans-ported back to Victorian times – a palace of glinting mahogany, polished brass, marble floors, stained glass, Doulton tiles, gilded cornices and starched table linen so thick that it creaks when you fold it. The menu is mostly classic seafood, from oysters on ice, to *Coquilles St Jacques Parisienne* and lobster thermidor, augmented by a handful of beef and game dishes.

Oloroso (Map pp72-3; ☎ 226 7614; 33 Castle St; mains £15-22, bar snacks £5-9; ☺ restaurant noon-2.30pm & 7-10.30pm, bar 11am-1am) Oloroso is one of Ed-inburgh's most stylish restaurants, perched on a glass-encased New Town rooftop with views across a Mary Poppins' chimney-scape to the Firth of Forth and the Fife hills. Swathed in sophisticated cream linen and charcoal upholstery enlivened with splashes of deep yellow, the dining room serves top-notch Scottish produce with Asian and Mediterranean touches. On a fine afternoon

---

TOP FIVE VEGETARIAN RESTAURANTS

Many Edinburgh restaurants offer vegetarian options on the menu, some good, some bad, some indifferent. The places listed here are all 100% veggie and all fall into the 'good' category.

David Bann (Map pp72-3; ☎ 556 5888; 56-58 St Mary's St; mains £10-11; ☺ 11am-10pm) If you want to convince a carnivorous friend that cuisine á la veg can be as tasty and inventive as a meat-muncher's menu, take them to David Bann's stylish restaurant – dishes such as walnut, hazelnut and mushroom haggis are guaranteed to win converts.

Ann Purna (Map pp70-1; ☎ 662 1807; 45 St Patrick's Sq; mains £5-9; ☺ noon-2pm & 5.30-11pm Mon-Fri, 5.30-11pm Sat & Sun) This little gem of an Indian restaurant serves exclusively vegetarian dishes from southern India. If you're new to this kind of food, opt for a *thali* – a self-contained platter that contains about half a dozen different dishes, including a dessert.

Susie's Diner (Map pp72-3; ☎ 667 8729; 51-53 West Nicolson St; mains £3-6; ☺ noon-9pm Tue-Sat, to 8pm Mon) Susie's is a down-to-earth, self-service, vegetarian cafeteria with scrubbed-wood tables, rickety chairs and a friendly atmosphere. The menu changes daily but includes things such as tofu, aubergine and pepper casserole, stuffed roast tomatoes and Susie's famous falafel plates – reputedly 'the best falafel in the Western world'. BYOB, or try a bottle of organic wine.

Henderson's (Map pp72-3; ☎ 225 2131; 94 Hanover St; mains £5-7; ☺ 8am-10.45pm Mon-Sat) Estab-lished in 1962, Henderson's is the grandmother of Edinburgh's vegetarian restaurants. The food is mostly organic and guaranteed genetically modified–free, and special dietary requirements can be catered for. The self-service restaurant still has something of a 1970s cafeteria feel to it (but in a good way), and the daily salads and hot dishes are as popular as ever.

Kalpna (Map pp70-1; ☎ 667 9890; 2-3 St Patrick Sq; mains £5-7; ☺ noon-2pm & 5.30-11pm Mon-Sat, 5.30-10pm Sun) Another long-standing Edinburgh favourite, Kalpna is one of the best Indian restaurants in the country, vegetarian or otherwise. The cuisine is mostly Gujarati, with a smattering of dishes from other parts of India – try the *khoya kaju* (vegetables, cashew nuts, sultanas and pistachios in a cream sauce with coriander and nutmeg, served with coconut rice and *puri*; Indian bread).

you can savour a snack and a drink on the outdoor roof terrace while soaking up the sun and a view of the castle.

Leith

MIDRANGE

Fishers (Map p69; ☎ 554 5666; 1 The Shore; mains £12-20; ☼ noon-10.30pm) This cosy little bar-turned-restaurant, tucked beneath a 17th-century signal tower, is one of the city's best seafood places. Fishers' fish cakes are an Edinburgh institution, and the rest of the handwritten menu (you might need a calligrapher to decipher it) rarely disappoints. Booking is recommended – if you can't get a table, try the New Town branch, **Fishers in the City** (Map pp72-3; ☎ 225 5109; 58 Thistle St).

Britannia Spice (Map p69; ☎ 555 2255; 150 Commercial St; mains £8-15; ☼ noon-2.15pm & 5-11.45pm, closed lunch Sun) This award-winning curry house has ocean-liner décor, uniformed staff, and a menu that boasts a wide range of dishes from northern India, Bangladesh, Nepal, Thailand and Sri Lanka.

Raj (Map p69; ☎ 553 3980; 91 Henderson St, The Shore; mains £8-14; ☼ noon-2.30pm & 5.30-11.30pm Sun-Thu, to midnight Fri & Sat) Run by celebrity chef Tommy Miah (author of *True Taste of Asia*), the Raj is an atmospheric curry house overlooking the Water of Leith and serving Indian (including Goan) and Bangladeshi cuisine. Specialities include the tongue-tingling green Bengal chicken (marinated with lime juice, mint and chilli) and spicy Goan lamb garam fry.

TOP END

Martin Wishart (Map p69; ☎ 553 3557; 54 The Shore; mains £23-27; ☼ noon-2pm & 7-10pm Tue-Fri, 7-10pm Sat) In 2001 this restaurant became the first in Edinburgh to win a Michelin star. The eponymous chef has worked with Albert Roux, Marco Pierre White and Nick Nairn, and brings a modern French approach to the best Scottish produce, from roast fillet of John Dory to braised saddle of lamb. A set three-course lunch costs £21; book ahead as far as possible.

Self-Catering

There are grocery stores and food shops all over the city, many of them open 9am to 10pm daily. Many petrol stations also have late-opening shops that sell groceries.

There are several large supermarkets spread throughout the city such as **Sainsbury's**

(Map pp72-3; ☎ 225 8400; 9-10 St Andrew Sq; ☼ 7am-10pm Mon-Sat, 9am-8pm Sun) and **Tesco** (Map pp72-3; ☎ 456 2400; 94 Nicolson St; ☼ 7am-midnight Mon-Sat, 9am-10pm Sun). The food hall in **Marks & Spencer** (Map pp72-3; ☎ 225 2301; 54 Princes St; ☼ 9am-7pm Mon-Fri, to 8pm Thu, 8.30am-6pm Sat, 11am-5pm Sun) sells high-quality ready-cooked meals.

Good delis for buying picnic goodies include **Valvona & Crolla** (Map pp70-1; ☎ 556 6066; 19 Elm Row, Leith Walk; ☼ 8am-6.30pm Mon-Sat, 11am-5pm Sun), **Peckham's** (Map pp70-1; ☎ 229 7054; 155-159 Bruntsfield Pl; ☼ 8am-midnight Mon-Sat, 9am-11pm Sun) and the food hall in Jenners (p110).

DRINKING

Edinburgh has more than 700 bars, which are as varied as the population – everything from Victorian palaces to rough-and-ready drinking dens, and from bearded, real-ale howffs (pubs) to trendy cocktail bars.

Royal Mile & Around

Jolly Judge (Map pp72-3; ☎ 225 2669; 7a James Court) A snug little howff tucked away down a close, the Judge exudes a cosy 17th-century atmosphere (low, painted ceilings) and has the added attraction of a cheering open fire in cold weather.

Malt Shovel (Map pp72-3; ☎ 225 6843; 11-15 Cockburn St) A traditional-looking pub – all dark wood and subdued tartanry – offering a good range of real ales and more than 100 malt whiskies, the Malt Shovel has live folk music on offer on Wednesday and Thursday evenings.

Royal Mile Tavern (Map pp72-3; ☎ 557 9681; 127 High St) An elegant, traditional bar lined with polished wood, mirrors and brass, Royal Mile serves real ale, good wines and fine food – *moules marinières* (mussels) and crusty bread is a lunchtime speciality.

World's End (Map pp72-3; ☎ 556 3628; 4 High St) So named because this part of High St once lay next to the Old Town's limit – part of the 16th-century Flodden Wall can still be seen in the basement – the World's End is an old local pub, with plenty of regulars as well as tourists. They do good bar food, including excellent fish and chips.

Grassmarket & Around

The pubs in the Grassmarket have outdoor tables on sunny summer afternoons, but in the evenings are favoured by boozed-up lads on the pull, so steer clear if that's not your thing. The Cowgate – the Grassmarket's extension to the east – is Edinburgh's clubland.

Last Drop (Map pp72-3; ☎ 225 4851; 74 Grassmarket) The name commemorates the gallows that used to stand nearby, but the only swingers today are the pub's partying clientele, largely students and backpackers.

Bow Bar (Map pp72-3; ☎ 226 7667; 80 West Bow) One of the city's best traditional-style pubs (it's not as old as it looks) serving a range of excellent real ales and a vast selection of malt whiskies, the Bow Bar often has standing room only on Friday and Saturday evenings.

Three Sisters (Map pp72-3; ☎ 622 6800; 39 Cowgate) This massive pub is actually three bars – one American, one Irish and one Gothic – with a big cobbled courtyard for outdoor drinking in summer. It's a bit of a mad party place but you can come back the morning after and soothe your hangover with a big, fried breakfast – and a free Bloody Mary if you order before 11am.

Bannerman's (Map pp72-3; ☎ 556 3254; 212 Cowgate) A long-established favourite, Bannerman's straggles through a warren of old vaults and pulls in crowds of students, locals and backpackers. The beer is good but the weekend breakfasts are best avoided.

Pear Tree House (Map pp72-3; ☎ 667 7533; 38 West Nicolson St) The Pear Tree is another student favourite, with comfy sofas and board games inside, plus the city's biggest and most popular beer garden in summer.

Rose Street & Around

Rose St was once a famous pub crawl, where generations of students, sailors and rugby fans would try to visit every pub on the street (around 17 of them) and down a pint of beer in each one.

Kenilworth (Map pp72-3; ☎ 226 4385; 152-154 Rose St) A gorgeous, Edwardian drinking palace, complete with original fittings – from the tile floors, mahogany circle bar and gantry, to the ornate mirrors and gas lamps – the Kenilworth was Edinburgh's original gay bar back in the 1970s. Today it attracts a mixed crowd of all ages, and serves a good range of real ales and malt whiskies.

Robertsons 37 Bar (Map pp72-3; ☎ 225 6185; 37 Rose St) No 37 is to malt whisky connoisseurs what the Diggers (now called the Athletic Arms) once was to real-ale fans. Its long gan-

try sports a choice of more than 100 single malts and the bar provides a quiet and elegant environment in which to sample them.

Guildford Arms (Map pp72-3; ☎ 556 4312; 1 West Register St) Located next door to the Café Royal Circle Bar, the Guildford is another classic Victorian pub full of polished mahogany, brass and ornate cornices, with an unusual gallery bar from which you can look down into the main saloon.

New Town & Broughton Street

Cumberland Bar (Map pp70-1; ☎ 558 3134; 1-3 Cumberland St) Under the same management as the Bow Bar in Victoria St, the Cumberland pays similar attention to serving well-looked-after, cask-conditioned ales. The bar has an authentic, traditional wood-brass-and-mirrors look, and there's a nice little beer garden outside.

Opal Lounge (Map pp72-3; ☎ 226 2275; 51 George St; ⏰ noon-3am) The Opal Lounge is jammed at weekends with affluent twenty-somethings who've spent £200, and two hours in front of a mirror, to achieve that artlessly scruffy look. During the week, when the air-kissing, cocktail-sipping crowds thin out, it's a good place to relax with a fruit smoothie (or an expensive but excellent cocktails) and sample the tasty Asian food. Expect to queue on weekend evenings.

Kay's Bar (Map pp72-3; ☎ 225 1858; 39 Jamaica St) Housed in a former wine-merchant's office, tiny Kay's Bar is a cosy haven with a coal fire and a fine range of real ales. Good food is served in the back room at lunchtime, but you'll have to book a table – Kay's is a popular spot.

Mathers (Map pp70-1; ☎ 556 6754; 25 Broughton St) Mathers is the forty-something generation's equivalent of the twenty-somethings' the Basement (see the Top Five Lunch Spots boxed text, p100) across the street – a friendly, relaxed pub with Edwardian décor serving real ales and good pub grub.

Pivo Caffé (Map pp72-3; ☎ 557 2925; 2-6 Calton Rd) Aiming to add a little taste of Bohemia to Edinburgh's style-bar scene, Pivo (the Czech word for beer) serves goulash and dumplings, bottled and draught Czech beers, and two-pint cocktails, and has DJs on the decks from 10pm on.

Standing Order (Map pp72-3; ☎ 225 4460; 62-66 George St) One of several converted banks on George St, Standing Order is a cavernous beer hall with a fantastic vaulted ceiling and some cosy rooms off to the right – look for the one with the original 27-tonne safe. Despite its size, it can be standing-room only at weekends.

Tonic (Map pp72-3; ☎ 225 6431; 34a North Castle St) As cool and classy as a perfectly mixed martini, from the chic décor to the Phillipe Starck bar stools, Tonic prides itself on the authenticity of its cocktails, of which there are many – the menu goes on forever.

Leith & Granton
Port O'Leith (Map p69; ☎ 554 3568; 58 Constitution St) This is a good, old-fashioned, friendly local boozer. The Port is swathed with flags and cap bands left behind by visiting sailors – the harbour is just down the road. Pop in for a pint and you'll probably stay until closing time.

Starbank Inn (Map p69; ☎ 552 4141; 64 Laverockbank Rd) Along with the Old Chain Pier (see the Top Five Lunch Spots boxed text, p100), the Starbank is an oasis of fine ales and good, homemade food on Edinburgh's windswept waterfront. In summer there's a sunny conservatory, and in winter a blazing fire to toast your toes in front of.

ENTERTAINMENT
Edinburgh has a number of fine theatres and concert halls, and there are independent art-house cinemas as well as mainstream movie theatres. Many pubs offer entertainment ranging from live Scottish folk music to pop, rock and jazz as well as karaoke and quiz nights, while the new generation of style bars purvey house, dance and hip-hop to the preclubbing crowd.

The comprehensive source for what's-on info is the *List* (£3.20; www.list.co.uk), an excellent listings magazine covering both Edinburgh and Glasgow. It's available from most newsagents, and is published fortnightly on a Thursday.

Live Music
Check out the *List* and the *Gig Guide* (www.gigguide.co.uk), a free leaflet available in bars and music venues, to see who's playing where.

JAZZ, BLUES & ROCK

Henry's Jazz Cellar (Map pp72-3; ☎ 538 7385; 8a Morrison St) Edinburgh's hottest jazz joint, Henry's has something going on every night, from traditional and contemporary jazz to soul, funk, hip-hop and drum'n'bass.

Liquid Room (Map pp72-3; ☎ 225 2564; www .liquidroom.com; 9c Victoria St; tickets £9-15) One of the city's top live-music venues, the Liquid Room stages all kinds of gigs from local bands to the Average White Band. Check the programme on the website.

Whistle Binkie's (Map pp72-3; ☎ 557 5114; www .whistlebinkies.com; 4-6 South Bridge; ☻ 7pm-3am) This crowded cellar bar just off the Royal Mile has live music every night, from rock and blues to folk and jazz. Open mike night, from 10pm on Monday, showcases new talent. Check the website for what's on.

Henderson's (Map pp72-3; ☎ 225 2131; 94 Hanover St) The well-known vegetarian restaurant (see p102) has live music, mainly jazz and classical guitar, at 7.30pm most evenings.

TRADITIONAL

The capital is a great place to hear traditional Scottish (and Irish) folk music, with a mix of regular spots and impromptu sessions.

Royal Oak (Map pp72-3; ☎ 557 2976; 1 Infirmary St; admission free Mon-Sat, £3 Sun) The popular Wee Folk Club in the downstairs lounge, with a tiny bar and room for only 30 punters, is ticket-only, so get there early (9pm start) if you want to be sure of a place. Saturday night is an open-session night – bring your own instruments (or a good singing voice).

Sandy Bell's (Map pp72-3; ☎ 225 2751; 25 Forrest Rd; admission free) This unassuming bar has been a stalwart of the traditional-music scene since the Corrs were in nappies. There's music almost every evening at 9pm, and also from 2.30pm on Sunday afternoon.

Pleasance Cabaret Bar (Map pp72-3; ☎ 650 2349; 60 The Pleasance; admission £6) The Pleasance is home to the Edinburgh Folk Club, which runs a programme of visiting bands and singers at 8pm on Wednesday nights.

Clubs

Edinburgh's club scene has some fine DJ talent and is well worth exploring; there are club-night listings in the *List*. Most of the venues are concentrated in and around the twin sumps of Cowgate and Calton Rd – so it's downhill all the way…

Bongo Club (Map pp70-1; ☎ 558 7604; www.the bongoclub.co.uk; Moray House, Paterson's Land, 37 Holyrood Rd) The weird and wonderful Bongo Club is famous for its hip-hop, funk and breakbeat club night Headspin (admission £8; held second Saturday of the month from 10.30pm). Also worth checking out is the booming bass of roots and dub reggae night Messenger Sound System (admission £7; held first and third Saturday of the month from 11pm). The club is open as a café and exhibition space during the day.

Liquid Room (Map pp72-3; ☎ 225 2564; www .liquidroom.com; 9c Victoria St) Set in a subterranean vault deep beneath Victoria St, the Liquid Room is a superb club venue with a thundering sound system. There are weekly club nights Wednesday to Friday and Sunday. The long-running Evol (admission £5; Friday from 10.30pm) is an Edinburgh institution catering to the indie-kid crowd, and is regularly voted as Scotland's top club night out.

Studio 24 (Map pp70-1; ☎ 558 3758; www .studio24edinburgh.co.uk; 24 Calton Rd) The programme at Studio 24 covers all bases, from house to goth to nu metal. The Mission (admission £5; Saturday from 11pm) is the city's classic goth and metal night (with Junior Mission, for under-18s, running 7pm to 10pm the same evening), but the big session for serious clubbers is the hard house and techno of Dogma (admission £8; held on the third Friday of the month from 10.30pm).

Ego (Map pp70-1; ☎ 478 7434; 14 Picardy Pl) A glitzy two-floor venue in a former casino, with huge Renaissance-style wall paintings, gay-friendly Ego dishes up everything from the dance classics of Fever (admission £12; held third Saturday of the month from 11pm) to the hard house and trance of Nuklear Puppy (admission £8; held second Friday of the month from 10.30pm).

Venue (Map pp72-3; ☎ 557 3073; www.edin venue.com; 17-23 Calton Rd) Spread over three floors and hosting live gigs as well as club nights, the Venue is one of Edinburgh's best dark'n'dirty nightspots. Look out for Tokyo Blu (admission £5; first Saturday of month from 10.30pm), a night of laid-back Latin funk, disco and electro. Also home to top gay club night Joy (admission £10; held last Saturday of month from 11pm).

Cinema

Film buffs will find plenty to keep them happy in Edinburgh's art-house cinemas, while popcorn munchers can choose from a range of multiplexes.

Cameo (Map pp70-1; ☎ 228 4141; 38 Home St; tickets £5.90) The three-screen, independently owned Cameo is a good, old-fashioned cinema showing an imaginative mix of mainstream and art-house movies. There is a good programme of midnight movies, late-night double bills and Sunday matinees, and the seats in Screen 1 are big enough to get lost in.

Filmhouse (Map pp72-3; ☎ 228 2688; 88 Lothian Rd; tickets £5.80) The Filmhouse is the main venue for the annual International Film Festival and screens a full programme of art-house, classic, foreign and second-run films, with lots of themes, retrospectives and 70mm screenings. It has wheelchair access to all screens.

UGC Fountainpark (Map pp70-1; ☎ 0871 200 2000; Fountainpark Complex, Dundee St; tickets £5.80) The UGC is a massive 12-screen multiplex complete with café-bar, movie-poster shop and frighteningly overpriced popcorn.

VUE Cinema (Map pp72-3; ☎ 0871 224 0240; Omni Centre, Greenside Pl; tickets £6) Another 12-screen multiplex, with three 'Gold Class' screens where you can watch from a luxurious leather reclining seat complete with side table for your drink and complimentary snacks.

Classical Music, Opera & Ballet

The following are the main venues for classical music.

Edinburgh Festival Theatre (Map pp72-3; ☎ 529 6000; www.eft.co.uk; 13-29 Nicolson St; ☺ box office 10am-6pm Mon-Sat, to 8pm show nights) The modern Festival Theatre is the city's main venue for opera, dance and ballet, but also stages musicals, concerts, drama and children's shows.

Usher Hall (Map pp72-3; ☎ 228 1155; www .usherhall.co.uk; Lothian Rd; ☺ box office 10.30am-5.30pm, to 8pm show nights) The architecturally impressive Usher Hall hosts concerts by the Royal Scottish National Orchestra (RSNO) and performances of popular music.

St Giles Cathedral (Map pp72-3; ☎ 225 9442; www.stgiles.net; High St) The big kirk on the Royal Mile plays host to a regular and varied programme of classical music, including

---

TOP FIVE TRADITIONAL PUBS

Edinburgh is blessed with a large number of traditional 19th- and early-20th-century pubs, which have preserved much of their original Victorian or Edwardian decoration and serve cask-conditioned real ales and a staggering range of malt whiskies.

Athletic Arms (Diggers; Map pp70-1; ☎ 337 3822; 1-3 Angle Park Tce) Named after the cemetery across the street – the grave-diggers used to nip in and slake their thirst after a hard day's interring – the Diggers dates from the 1890s. Its heyday as a real-ale drinker's mecca is over but it's still staunchly traditional – the décor has barely changed in 100 years – and it's packed to the gills with football and rugby fans on match days.

Abbotsford (Map pp72-3; ☎ 225 5276; 3 Rose St) One of the few pubs in Rose St that has retained its Edwardian splendour, the Abbotsford has long been a hang-out for writers, actors, journalists and media people, and has many loyal regulars. Dating from 1902, and named after Sir Walter Scott's country house, the pub's centrepiece is a splendid, mahogany island bar.

Bennet's Bar (Map pp70-1; ☎ 229 5143; 8 Leven St) Situated beside the King's Theatre, Bennet's has managed to hang on to almost all of its beautiful Victorian fittings, from the leaded, stained-glass windows and ornate mirrors to the wooden gantry and the brass water taps on the bar (for your whisky – there are over 100 malts to choose from).

Café Royal Circle Bar (Map pp72-3; ☎ 556 1884; 17 West Register St) Perhaps the classic Edinburgh bar, the Café Royal's main claims to fame are its magnificent oval bar and the series of Doulton tile portraits of famous Victorian inventors. Check out the bottles on the gantry – staff line them up to look like there's a mirror there, and many a drink-befuddled customer has been seen squinting and wondering why he can't see his reflection.

Sheep Heid (Map p69; ☎ 656 6951; 43-45 The Causeway, Duddingston) Possibly the oldest inn in Edinburgh – with a licence dating back to 1360 – the Sheep Heid feels more like a country pub than an Edinburgh bar. Set in the semi-rural shadow of Arthur's Seat, it's famous for its 19th-century skittles alley and the lovely little beer garden.

popular lunchtime and evening concerts and organ recitals. The cathedral choir sings at the 10am and 11.30am Sunday services.

Queen's Hall (Map pp70-1; ☎ 668 2019; www.queenshalledinburgh.co.uk; Clerk St; ⏰ box office 10am-5.30pm, or to 15min after show begins) The home of the Scottish Chamber Orchestra also stages jazz, blues, rock and comedy.

Scottish Evenings

Thistle Hotel (Map pp72-3; ☎ 556 0111; edinburgh@thistle.co.uk; 107 Leith St; show & dinner £46.50, show only £25; ⏰ 6.45pm Apr-Oct) This hotel stages 'Jamie's Scottish Evening', a night of Scottish music, songs, dance and comedy accompanied by a four-course dinner (including the chance to try some haggis).

Sport

Edinburgh is home to two rival football teams playing in the Scottish Premier League – Heart of Midlothian (aka Hearts) and Hibernian (aka Hibs). The domestic football season lasts from August to May, and most matches are played at 3pm on Saturday or 7.30pm on Tuesday or Wednesday.

Hearts have their home ground at **Tynecastle Stadium** (Map p69; ☎ 200 7200; www.heartsfc.co.uk; Gorgie Rd), southwest of the city centre in Gorgie. Hibernian's home ground is northeast of the city centre at **Easter Road Stadium** (Map p69; ☎ 661 2159; www.hibs.co.uk; 12 Albion Pl).

Each year, from January to March, Scotland's national rugby team takes part in the Six Nations Rugby Union Championship. The most important fixture is the clash against England for the Calcutta Cup. At club level the season runs from September to May. **Murrayfield Stadium** (Map p69; ☎ 346 5000; www.scottishrugby.org; 112 Roseburn St), about 1.5 miles west of the city centre, is the venue for international matches.

Most other sporting events, including athletics and cycling, are held at **Meadowbank Sports Centre** (Map p69; ☎ 661 5351; 139 London Rd), Scotland's main sports arena.

GAY & LESBIAN EDINBURGH

Edinburgh has a small – but perfectly formed – gay and lesbian scene, centred on the area around Broughton St (known affectionately as the 'Pink Triangle') at the eastern end of New Town. Blue Moon Café (see p101) at the foot of Broughton St is a friendly G&L caff offering good food and good company. It's also a good place to pick up on what's happening on the local scene.

Scotsgay (www.scotsgay.co.uk) is the local monthly magazine covering gay and lesbian issues. Gay-friendly guesthouses in Edinburgh include the Amaryllis (p97), Ardmor House (p98) and Fairholme (p98).

Useful contacts:

Edinburgh LGBT Centre (☎ 478 7069; 58-60 Broughton St; ⏰ 11am-11pm Mon-Fri, 10am-11pm Sat & Sun)
Lothian Gay & Lesbian Switchboard (☎ 556 4049; www.lgls.co.uk; ⏰ 7.30-10pm)
Lothian Lesbian Line (☎ 557 0751; ⏰ 7.30-10pm Mon & Thu)

Pubs, Clubs & Saunas

You'll find the city's best gay club nights at Ego (p106) and the Venue (p106).

CC Blooms (Map pp70-1; ☎ 556 9331; 23 Greenside Pl, Leith Walk; ⏰ 6pm-3am Mon-Sat, 8pm-3am Sun) The raddled old queen of the Edinburgh gay scene, CC offers two floors of deafening dance and disco. It's a bit overpriced and overcrowded but worth a visit – go early, or sample the wild karaoke on Sunday nights.

Planet Out (Map pp70-1; ☎ 524 0061; 6 Baxter's Pl, Leith Walk; ⏰ 4pm-1am Mon-Fri, 2pm-1am Sat & Sun) Planet Out pulls in a younger crowd than CC, and has a better party atmosphere at weekends. It's a bit quieter during the week, when you can chill out on the sofas and chat.

Claremont Bar (Map p69; ☎ 556 5662; 133-135 East Claremont St; ⏰ 11am-midnight Mon-Thu, to 1am Fri & Sat, 12.30pm-midnight Sun) Scotland's only sci-fi theme pub (no, you have to see it), Claremont is a friendly, gay-owned bar and restaurant. Saturday nights are men-only nights, when leather, rubber, skinheads and bears are the order of the evening – the second Saturday of the month is for kilt-fanciers!

De Vils (Map p69; ☎ 657 5575; 9 Seafield Rd East; admission £5; ⏰ noon-10pm Mon-Thu, to 8pm Fri & Sat, 2-8pm Sun) Gay-owned and operated sauna.

Horse-racing enthusiasts should head 6 miles east to **Musselburgh Racecourse** (☎ 665 2859; www.musselburgh-racecourse.co.uk; Linkfield Rd, Musselburgh; admission £10-18), Scotland's oldest racecourse (founded 1816), where meetings are held throughout the year.

Theatre, Musicals & Comedy

Royal Lyceum Theatre (Map pp72-3; ☎ 248 4848; www.lyceum.org.uk; 30b Grindlay St; tickets £10-25; ☯ box office 10am-6pm Mon-Sat, to 8pm show nights) A grand Victorian theatre located beside the Usher Hall, the Lyceum stages drama, concerts, musicals and ballet.

Traverse Theatre (Map pp72-3; ☎ 228 1404; www .traverse.co.uk; 10 Cambridge St; tickets £5-12; ☯ box office 10am-6pm Mon, to 8pm Tue-Sat, 4-8pm Sun) The Traverse is the main focus for new Scottish writing and stages an adventurous programme of contemporary drama and dance. The box office is only open on Sunday when there's a performance.

King's Theatre (Map pp70-1; ☎ 220 4349; www .eft.co.uk; 2 Leven St, Bruntsfield; tickets £10-25; ☯ box office open 1hr before show) King's is a traditional theatre with a programme of musicals, drama, comedy and its famous Christmas pantomime.

Edinburgh Playhouse (Map pp70-1; ☎ 524 3301, bookings ☎ 0870 606 3424; www.edinburgh-playhouse .co.uk; 18-22 Greenside Pl; tickets £10-30; ☯ box office 10am-6pm Mon-Sat, to 8pm show nights) This restored theatre at the top of Leith Walk stages Broadway musicals, dance shows, opera and popular-music concerts.

Stand Comedy Club (Map pp72-3; ☎ 558 7272; www.thestand.co.uk; 5 York Pl; tickets £1-8) The Stand, founded in 1995, is Edinburgh's main comedy venue. It's a cabaret bar with performances every night and a free Sunday lunchtime show.

SHOPPING

Princes St is Edinburgh's principal shopping street, lined with all the big high-street stores, with many smaller shops along pedestrianised Rose St, and more expensive designer boutiques on George St. There are also two big shopping centres in the New Town – **Princes Mall** (Map pp72-3), at the eastern end of Princes St, and the nearby **St James Centre** (Map pp72-3) at the top of Leith St, next door to a new shopping complex with a flagship Harvey Nichols store on the eastern side of St Andrew Sq –

but the huge **Ocean Terminal** (Map p69) in Leith is the biggest shopping centre in the city.

For more off-beat shopping – including fashion, music, crafts, gifts and jewellery – head for the cobbled lanes of Cockburn, Victoria and St Mary's Sts, all near the Royal Mile in the Old Town, William St in the western part of New Town, and the Stockbridge district, immediately north of the New Town.

Cashmere & Wool

Woollen textiles and knitwear are one of Scotland's classic exports. Scottish cashmere – a fine, soft wool from young goats and lambs – provides the most luxurious and expensive knitwear and has been seen gracing the torsos of pop star Robbie Williams and England footballer David Beckham.

Designs On Cashmere (Map pp72-3; ☎ 556 6394; 28 High St) and the **Cashmere Store** (Map pp72-3; ☎ 226 1577; 2 St Giles St) are good places to start, with a wide range of traditional and modern knitwear, while the colourful designs at **Joyce Forsyth Designer Knitwear** (Map pp72-3; ☎ 220 4112; 42 Candlemaker Row; ☯ 11am-5.30pm Tue-Thu & Sat, to 4.45pm Fri) will drag your ideas about woollens firmly into the 21st century.

Edinburgh Woollen Mill (Map pp72-3; ☎ 226 3840; 139 Princes St) is an old stalwart of the tourist trade, with a good selection of traditional jerseys, cardigans, scarves, shawls and rugs.

Crafts & Souvenirs

Crafts Fair (cnr Princes St & Lothian Rd) During the Festival period, there's a good fair in the churchyard at St John's Church, with a wide range of jewellery, ceramics and leather goods.

Meadows Pottery (Map pp70-1; ☎ 662 4064; 11a Summerhall Pl; ☯ 10.30am-5.30pm Mon-Sat) Sells colourful stoneware, all hand-thrown on the premises.

Adam Pottery (Map pp70-1; ☎ 557 3978; 76 Henderson Row; ☯ 10am-5.30pm Mon-Sat) Produces its own ceramics, mostly decorative, or in a wider range of styles.

Flux (Map p69; ☎ 554 4075; 55 Bernard St, Leith; ☯ 9am-5pm Mon & Tue, to 7pm Wed-Fri, 11am-7pm Sat & Sun) An outlet for contemporary Scottish arts and crafts, including stained glass, metalware, jewellery and ceramics.

Department Stores

Jenners (Map pp72-3; ☎ 225 2442; 48 Princes St) Founded in 1838, this is the *grande dame* of Scottish department stores. It stocks a wide range of quality goods, both classic and contemporary.

John Lewis (Map pp72-3; ☎ 556 9121; St James Centre) The place to go for good-value clothes and household goods.

Harvey Nichols (Map pp72-3; ☎ 524 8388; 30-34 St Andrew Sq; ◷ 10am-6pm Mon-Wed, to 8pm Thu, to 7pm Fri & Sat, noon-6pm Sun) The jewel in the crown of Edinburgh's shopping scene has four floors of designer labels and eye-popping price tags.

Tartan & Highland Dress

There are dozens of shops along the Royal Mile and Princes St where you can buy kilts and tartan goods.

Kinloch Anderson (Map p69; ☎ 555 1390; 4 Dock St, Leith) One of the best, this was founded in 1868 and is still family-run. Kinloch Anderson is a supplier of kilts and Highland dress to the royal family.

Geoffrey (Tailor) Inc (Map pp72-3; ☎ 557 0256; 57-59 High St) Can fit you out in traditional Highland dress, or run up a kilt in your own clan tartan. Its offshoot, 21st Century Kilts, offers modern fashion kilts in a variety of fabrics.

GETTING THERE & AWAY

Air

Edinburgh Airport (☎ 333 1000; www.edinburghairport .com), 8 miles west of the city, has numerous flights to other parts of Scotland and the UK, Ireland and mainland Europe. See p443 for details of flights to Edinburgh from outside Scotland. **British Airways** (☎ 0845 773 3377) operates daily flights to Inverness, Orkney, Shetland and Stornoway.

Bus

Edinburgh's St Andrew Sq bus and coach station (Map pp72-3) is at the northeast corner of the square, with pedestrian entrances from the square and from Elder St. For timetable information, call **Traveline** (☎ 0870 608 2608; www.travelinescotland.com).

Scottish Citylink (☎ 0870 550 5050; www.citylink .co.uk) buses connect Edinburgh with all Scotland's cities and major towns. The following are sample one-way fares from Edinburgh.

Destination	Fare	Duration	Frequency
Aberdeen	£16	3¼hr	hourly
Dundee	£9	1¾hr	30min
Fort William	£20	4hr	3 daily
Glasgow	£4	1¼hr	20min
Inverness	£17	4hr	hourly
Portree	£27	8hr	2 daily
Stirling	£4.20	1¼hr	hourly

Stagecoach (www.stagecoachbus.com) operates competing Motorvator bus service between Edinburgh and Glasgow (£4, 1¼ hours, every 20 minutes).

It's also worth checking with **Megabus** (☎ 0900 160 0900; www.megabus.com) for cheap bus fares (from as little as £1.50) from Edinburgh to Aberdeen, Dundee, Glasgow, Inverness and Perth.

See the Transport chapter, p445, for details of buses to Edinburgh from London and the rest of the UK.

Car & Motorcycle

Arriving in or leaving Edinburgh by car during the morning and evening rush hours (7.30am to 9.30am and 4.30pm to 6.30pm Monday to Friday) is an experience you can live without. Try to time your journey to avoid these periods. In particular, there can be huge tailbacks on the A90 between Edinburgh and the Forth Rd Bridge.

Train

The main terminus in Edinburgh is Waverley train station (Map pp72-3), located in the heart of the city. Trains arriving from, and departing for, the west also stop at Haymarket station (Map pp70-1), which is more convenient for the West End. You can buy tickets, make reservations and get travel information at the **Edinburgh Rail Travel Centre** (Map pp72-3; ◷ 4.45am-12.30am Mon-Sat, 7am-12.30am Sun) in Waverley station. For fare and timetable information, phone the **National Rail Enquiry Service** (☎ 0845 748 4950; www.nationalrail .co.uk) or use the Journey Planner on the website.

First ScotRail operates a regular shuttle service between Edinburgh and Glasgow (£9.40, 50 minutes, every 15 minutes), and frequent daily services to all Scottish cities including Aberdeen (£34, 2½ hours), Dundee (£17, 1½ hours) and Inverness (£34, 3¼ hours).

See the Transport chapter, p445, for details of trains to Edinburgh from London.

GETTING AROUND
To/From the Airport

The Lothian Buses **Airlink** (www.flybybus.com) service No 100 runs from Waverley Bridge, just outside the train station, to the airport (£3/5 one-way/return, 30 minutes, every 10 to 15 minutes) via the West End and Haymarket.

An airport taxi to the city centre costs around £13 and takes about 20 minutes. Both buses and taxis depart from just outside the arrivals hall.

Bicycle

Thanks to the efforts of local cycling campaign group Spokes and a bike-friendly city council, Edinburgh is well-equipped with bike lanes and dedicated cycle tracks. You can buy a map of the city's cycle routes from most bike shops.

Biketrax (Map pp70-1; ☎ 228 6633; www.biketrax .co.uk; 11 Lochrin Pl; ⊗ 9.30am-6pm Mon-Fri, to 5.30pm Sat, noon-5pm Sun) rents out a wide range of cycles and equipment, including kids' bikes, tandems, recumbents, pannier bags, child seats – even unicycles! A mountain bike costs £16 for 24 hours, £12 for extra days, and £70 for one week. You'll need a £100 cash or credit-card deposit and some form of ID.

For more on cycling, see p57.

Car & Motorcycle

Though useful for day trips beyond the city, a car in central Edinburgh is more of a liability than a convenience. There is restricted access on Princes St, George St and Charlotte Sq, many streets are one way and finding a parking place in the city centre is like striking gold. Queen's Dr around Holyrood Park is closed to motorised traffic on Sunday.

PARKING

There's no parking on main roads into the city from 7.30am to 6.30pm Monday to Saturday. Also, parking in the city centre can be a nightmare. On-street parking is controlled by self-service ticket machines from 8.30am to 6.30pm Monday to Saturday, and costs £1.60 per hour, with a two-hour maximum. If you break the rules, you'll get a fine, often within minutes of your ticket expiring – Edinburgh's parking wardens are both nu-

merous and notorious. The fine is £60, reduced to £30 if you pay up within 14 days. Cars parked illegally will be towed away. There are large, long-stay car parks at the St James Centre, Greenside Pl, New St, Castle Tce and Morrison St. Motorcycles can be parked free at designated areas in the city centre.

CAR RENTAL

All the big, international car-rental agencies have offices in Edinburgh (see p448).

There are many smaller, local agencies that offer better rates. One of the best is **Arnold Clark** (Map p69; ☎ 228 4747; www.arnoldclarkrental .co.uk; 20 Seafield Rd East) near Portobello, which charges from £23 a day, or £110 a week for a small car, including VAT and insurance. The daily rate includes 250 miles a day; excess is charged at 4p a mile. For periods of four days and more, mileage is unlimited.

Public Transport

Edinburgh's public transport system consists entirely of buses; the main operators are **Lothian Buses** (www.lothianbuses.co.uk) and **First-Edinburgh** (www.firstedinburgh.co.uk); for timetable information contact **Traveline** (☎ 0870 608 2608; www.travelinescotland.com).

Bus timetables, route maps and fare guides are posted at all main bus stops, and you can pick up the free *Lothian Buses Route Map* from **Lothian Buses Travelshop** (Hanover St Map pp72-3; ⊗ 8.15am-6pm Mon-Sat; Shand-wick Pl Map pp72-3; ⊗ 8.15am-6pm Mon-Sat; Waverley Bridge Map pp72-3; ☎ 555 6363; ⊗ 8.15am-6pm Mon-Sat, 9.30am-5pm Sun).

Adult fares are either 80p or £1; children aged under five travel free and those aged five to 15 pay a flat fare of 60p. On Lothian Buses you must pay the driver the exact fare, but First Edinburgh buses will give change. Lothian Bus drivers also sell a Daysaver ticket (£2.30) that gives unlimited travel on Lothian Buses for a day. Night-service buses, which run hourly between midnight and 5am, charge a flat fare of £2.

You can also buy a Ridacard (from Travelshops; not available from driver) that gives unlimited travel for one week for £12.

The **Lothian Buses lost property office** (Map p69; ☎ 558 8858; lostproperty@lothianbuses.co.uk; Main Depot, Annadale St; ⊗ 9am-5pm Mon-Fri) is located north of town.

Taxi

Edinburgh's black taxis can be hailed in the street, ordered by phone (extra 60p charge), or picked up at one of the many central ranks. The minimum charge is £1.45 (£2.20 at night) for the first 340 yards, then 23p (24p at night) for every subsequent 240 yards – a typical 2-mile trip across the city centre will cost around £5. Tipping is up to you – because of the high fares local people rarely tip on short journeys, but occasionally round up to the nearest 50p on longer ones.

Capital Taxis (☎ 228 2555)
Central Radio Taxis (☎ 229 2468)
City Cabs (☎ 228 1211)
Radiocabs (☎ 225 9000)

AROUND EDINBURGH

Edinburgh is small enough that, when you need a break from the city, the beautiful surrounding countryside isn't far away and is easily accessible by public transport, or even by bike. The old counties around Edinburgh are called Midlothian, West Lothian and East Lothian, often referred to collectively as 'the Lothians'.

MIDLOTHIAN
Queensferry
☎ 0131

Queensferry is located at the narrowest part of the Firth of Forth, where ferries have sailed to Fife from the earliest times. The village takes its name from Queen Margaret (1046–93), who gave pilgrims free passage across the firth on their way to St Andrews. Ferries continued to operate until 1964 when the graceful **Forth Road Bridge** – now Europe's fifth longest – was opened.

Predating the road bridge by 74 years, the magnificent **Forth Bridge** – only outsiders ever call it the Forth Rail Bridge – is one of the finest engineering achievements of the 19th century. Completed in 1890 after seven years' work, its three huge cantilevers span 1447m and took 59,000 tonnes of steel, eight million rivets and the lives of 58 men to build.

In the pretty, terraced High St in Queensferry is the small **Queensferry Museum** (☎ 331 5545; 53 High St; admission free; ☒ 10am-1pm & 2.15-5pm Mon & Thu-Sat, noon-5pm Sun). It contains some interesting background information on the bridges, and a fascinating exhibit on

the 'Burry Man', part of the village's summer gala festivities (see p93).

There are several good pubs along High St, including the recently refurbished **Orocco Pier** (☎ 331 1298; 17 High St; mains £5-15; ☒ 9am-10pm), which has a stylish and modern dining area with a stunning view of the Forth Bridge.

The atmospheric **Hawes Inn** (☎ 331 1990; Newhalls Rd; mains £5-10; ☒ food served noon-10pm), famously mentioned in Robert Louis Stevenson's novel *Kidnapped*, serves excellent pub grub; it's opposite the Inchcolm ferry, right beside the railway bridge.

GETTING THERE & AWAY

Queensferry lies on the southern bank of the Firth of Forth, 8 miles west of Edinburgh city centre. To get there, take First Edinburgh bus 43 (£2, 30 minutes, three hourly) westbound from St Andrew Sq. It's a 10-minute walk from the bus stop to the Hawes Inn and the Inchcolm ferry.

Trains go from Edinburgh's Waverley and Haymarket stations to Dalmeny station (£3.20, 15 minutes, two to four hourly). From the station exit, the Hawes Inn is five minutes' walk along a footpath (across the road, behind the bus stop) that leads north beside the railway and then under the bridge.

Inchcolm

The island of Inchcolm lies east of the Forth bridges, less than a mile off the coast of Fife. Only 800m long, it is home to the ruins of **Inchcolm Abbey** (☎ 01383-823332; Inchcolm, Fife; adult/child £3.30/1.30; ☒ 9.30am-6pm Easter-Sep), one of Scotland's best-preserved medieval abbeys, founded by Augustinian priors in 1123.

The ferry boat **Maid of the Forth** (☎ 0131-331 4857; www.maidoftheforth.co.uk) sails to Inchcolm from Hawes Pier in Queensferry. There are two or three sailings daily in July and August, and at weekends only from April to June and in September and October. The return fare is £13/4.50 per adult/child, including admission to Inchcolm Abbey. It's a half-hour sail to Inchcolm and you get 1½ hours ashore. As well as the abbey, the trip gives you the chance to see the island's grey seals, puffins and other seabirds.

Hopetoun House
☎ 0131

Hopetoun House (☎ 331 2451; www.hopetounhouse .com; adult/child £7/4; ☒ 10am-5.30pm Easter-Sep, last admission 4.30pm) is one of Scotland's finest stately homes, with a superb location in lovely grounds beside the Firth of Forth. There are two parts – the older built to Sir William Bruce's plans between 1699 and 1702 and dominated by a splendid stairwell with (modern) trompe l'oeil paintings; and the newer designed between 1720 and 1750 by three members of the Adam family, William and sons Robert and John. The highlights are the red and yellow Adam drawing rooms, lined in silk damask, and the view from the roof terrace.

Britain's most elegant equine accommodation – where the marquis once housed his pampered racehorses – is now the stylish **Stables Tearoom** (☎ 331 3661; mains £4-8; ☻ 10am-5.30pm Easter-Sep), a delightful spot for lunch.

Hopetoun House is 2 miles west of Queensferry along the coast road. Driving from Edinburgh, turn off the A90 onto the A904 just before the Forth Bridge and follow the signs.

Rosslyn Chapel
☎ 0131

The success of Dan Brown's novel *The Da Vinci Code* has seen a flood of visitors (plus a Hollywood film crew and actor Tom Hanks working on the inevitable movie) descend on Scotland's most beautiful and enigmatic church – **Rosslyn Chapel** (Collegiate Church of St Matthew; ☎ 440 2159; www.rosslyn-chapel .com; Roslin; adult/child £6/free; ☻ 9.30am-6pm Mon-Sat, noon-4.45pm Sun). The chapel was built in the mid-15th century for William St Clair, third earl of Orkney, and the ornately carved interior – at odds with the architectural fashion of its time – is a monument to the mason's art, rich in symbolic imagery. As well as flowers, vines, angels and biblical figures, the carved stones include many examples of the pagan 'Green Man'; other figures are associated with Freemasonry and the Knights Templar. Intriguingly, there are also carvings of plants from the Americas that predate Columbus' voyage of discovery. The symbolism of these images has led some researchers to conclude that Rosslyn is some kind of secret Templar repository, and it has been claimed that hidden vaults beneath the chapel could conceal anything from the Holy Grail or the head of John the Baptist to the body of Christ himself. The chapel is owned by the Episcopal Church of

Scotland and services are still held here on Sunday mornings.

The chapel is on the eastern edge of the village of Roslin, 7 miles south of Edinburgh's centre. Lothian Bus 15A runs from St Andrew Sq in Edinburgh to Roslin (£1, 30 minutes) hourly on weekdays, every two hours on Saturday and twice a day on Sunday.

Rosslyn Tours (☎ 440 3293; www.rosslyn-tours .co.uk) offers half-day tours of the chapel and surrounding area for £25, including transport from your hotel.

Pentland Hills

Rising on the southern edge of Edinburgh, the Pentland Hills stretch 16 miles southwest to near Carnwath in Lanarkshire. The hills rise to 579m at their highest point and offer excellent, not-too-strenuous walking with great views. There are several access points along the A702 road on the southern side of the hills. MacEwan's bus 100 runs four times daily along the A702 from Princes St in Edinburgh to Biggar.

EAST LOTHIAN

Beyond the former coalfields of Dalkeith and Musselburgh, the fertile farmland of East Lothian stretches eastwards along the coast to the seaside resort of North Berwick and the fishing harbour of Dunbar. In the middle lies the prosperous market town of Haddington.

Haddington & Around
☎ 01620 / pop 8850

Haddington, straddling the River Tyne 18 miles east of Edinburgh, was made a royal burgh by David I in the 12th century. Most of the modern town, however, dates from the 17th to 19th centuries during the period of prosperity after the Agricultural Revolution. The prettiest part of town is the tree-lined Court St, with its wide pavement and grand 18th- and 19th-century buildings.

Church St leads from the eastern end of High St to **St Mary's Parish Church** (☎ 823109; Sidegate; admission free; ☻ 11am-4pm Mon-Sat, 2-4.30pm Sun Apr-Sep). Built in 1462, it's the largest parish church in Scotland and one of the finest pre-Reformation churches in the country.

A mile south of Haddington is **Lennoxlove House** (☎ 823720; Lennoxlove Estate; adult/child £4.50/2.50; ☻ guided tours 1.30-4pm Wed, Thu & Sun Easter-Oct), a hidden gem of a country house dating originally from around 1345, with major extensions and renovations from the 17th to the early 20th centuries. It contains fine furniture and paintings, and memorabilia relating to Mary, Queen of Scots. Chief among these are her death mask and a silver casket given to her by Francis II of France, her first husband. The house has been the seat of the duke of Hamilton since 1947.

With a lovely location overlooking the River Tyne, the **Waterside Bistro & Restaurant** (☎ 825764; 1-5 Waterside, Nungate, Haddington; bistro mains £7-10, restaurant mains £15-20; ☺ lunch & dinner) is a great place to have lunch on a summer's day, watching the swans and ducks go by. The bistro does good-quality light meals, while the upstairs restaurant is more formal.

First Edinburgh buses X6 and X8 run between Edinburgh and Haddington every 30 minutes. The nearest train station is at Drem, 3 miles to the north.

North Berwick
☎ 01620 / pop 6220
North Berwick is an attractive Victorian seaside resort with long sandy beaches, three golf courses and a small harbour. The **TIC** (☎ 892197; Quality St; ☺ 9am-6pm Mon-Sat, 11am-4pm Sun) is two blocks inland from the harbour.

SIGHTS & ACTIVITIES
Top marks to the bright spark who came up with the idea for the **Scottish Seabird Centre** (☎ 890202; www.seabird.org; The Harbour; adult/child £6.95/4.50; ☺ 10am-6pm Apr-Oct, to 4pm Mon-Fri, to 5.30pm Sat & Sun Nov-Mar), an ornithologist's paradise that uses remote-control video cameras sited on the Bass Rock and other islands to relay live images of nesting gannets and other seabirds – you can control the cameras yourself, and zoom in on scenes of gannet domesticity.

Off High St, a short steep path climbs up **North Berwick Law** (184m), a conical hill that dominates the town. When the weather's fine there are great views to spectacular **Bass Rock**, iced white in spring and summer with guano from thousands of nesting gannets. The **Sula II** (☎ 892838) runs boat trips (adult/child £6/4, 1¼ hours, daily April to September) around Bass Rock and Fidra Island, departing from North Berwick's harbour.

Two miles west of North Berwick is **Dirleton Castle** (☎ 850330; Dirleton; adult/child £3.30/1.30; ☺ 9.30am-6.30pm Apr-Sep, to 4pm Oct-Mar), an impressive medieval fortress with massive round towers, a drawbridge and a horrific pit dungeon, surrounded rather incongruously by beautiful, manicured gardens.

Perched on a cliff 3 miles east of North Berwick is the spectacular ruin of **Tantallon Castle** (☎ 892727; adult/child £3.30/1.30; ☺ 9.30am-6.30pm Apr-Sep, to 4pm Sat-Wed Oct-Mar). Built around 1350, it was the fortress residence of the Douglas Earls of Angus (the 'Red Douglases'), defended on one side by a series of ditches and on the other by an almost sheer drop into the sea.

SLEEPING & EATING
North Berwick has plenty of places to stay, though they can fill up quickly at weekends when golfers are in town. Recommended B&Bs include **Glebe House** (☎ 892608; Law Rd; r per person £30-45; P), a beautiful Georgian country house with three spacious bedrooms, and homely **Beach Lodge** (☎ 892257; 5 Beach Rd; r per person £27), which offers sea views and vegetarian breakfasts.

The top eating places in the area are the **Grange** (☎ 893344; 35 High St; 3-course lunch/dinner £9/18; ☺ lunch & dinner) in the centre of town, and the delightful **Deveau's Brasserie** (☎ 850241; Open Arms Hotel, Dirleton; mains £10-13; ☺ lunch & dinner) in the village of Dirleton.

GETTING THERE & AWAY
North Berwick is 24 miles east of Edinburgh. First Edinburgh bus 124 runs between Edinburgh and North Berwick (£4.60, 1¼ hours, every 20 minutes). There are frequent trains between North Berwick and Edinburgh (£4.20, 35 minutes, hourly).

Dunbar
pop 6350
Dunbar was an important Scottish fortress town in the Middle Ages, but little remains of its past save for the tottering ruins of **Dunbar Castle** overlooking the harbour. Today the town survives as a fishing port and seaside resort, famed in the USA as the birthplace of John Muir (1838–1914), pioneer conservationist and father of the US national park system.

The **TIC** (☎ 01368-863353; 143 High St; ☺ 9am-6pm Mon-Sat, 11am-4pm Sun Jun-Aug, 9am-5pm Mon-Sat Apr, May & Sep, 9am-5pm Mon-Fri Oct-Mar) is near the town hall.

The slightly down-at-heel town centre is home to **John Muir House** (☎ 01368-862595;

128 High St; admission free; 🕑 10am-5pm Mon-Sat, 1-5pm Sun Apr-Oct, 10am-5pm Wed-Sat, 1-5pm Sun Nov-Mar), the birthplace and childhood home of the great man himself. The nearby **Dunbar Town House Museum** (☎ 01368-863734; High St; admission free; 🕑 12.30-4.30pm Apr-Oct) provides an introduction to local history and archaeology.

From the castle, a scenic 2-mile cliff-top trail follows the coastline west to the sands of Belhaven Bay and **John Muir Country Park**.

Perrymans (☎ 01289-308719) bus 253 (50 minutes, every two hours) and First Edinburgh bus X6 (one hour, hourly) run between Edinburgh and Dunbar. Trains from Edinburgh's Waverley train station serve Dunbar (£7.20, 20 minutes) every hour or so.

WEST LOTHIAN

Linlithgow

☎ 01506 / pop 13,400

This ancient royal burgh is one of Scotland's oldest towns, though much of it 'only' dates from the 15th to 17th centuries. Its centre retains a certain charm, despite some ugly modern buildings and occasional traffic congestion, and the town makes an excellent day trip from Edinburgh.

The **TIC** (☎ 844600; 🕑 10am-5pm Apr-Oct) is in the Burgh Halls at the Cross.

SIGHTS & ACTIVITIES

The town's main attraction is the magnificent **Linlithgow Palace** (☎ 842896; Church Peel; adult/child £4/1.60; 🕑 9.30am-6.30pm Apr-Sep, to 4.30pm Oct-Mar), begun by James I in 1425. The building of the palace continued for over a century and it became a favourite royal residence – James V was born here in 1512, as was his daughter Mary (later Queen of Scots) in 1542, and Bonnie Prince Charlie visited briefly in 1745. The elaborately carved **King's Fountain**, the centrepiece of the palace courtyard, flowed with wine during Charlie's stay – the fountain, commissioned by James V in 1537, is the oldest in Britain, and was restored to full working order in 2005.

Beside the palace is the Gothic **St Michael's Church** (☎ 842188; Church Peel; admission free; 🕑 10am-4.30pm Mon-Sat, 12.30-4.30pm Sun May-Sep, 10am-3pm Mon-Fri Oct-Apr). Built between the 1420s and 1530s, it is topped by a controversial aluminium spire that was added in 1964. The church is said to be haunted by a ghost that foretold King James IV of his impending defeat at Flodden in 1513.

The **Linlithgow Story** (☎ 670677; Annet House, 143 High St; adult/child £1.50/1, Sun free; 🕑 10am-5pm Mon-Sat & 1-4pm Sun Easter-Oct) is a small museum that tells the story of the Stewart monarchy and the history of the town.

Just 150m south of the town centre lies the Union Canal and the pretty **Linlithgow Canal Centre** (☎ 671215; www.lucs.org.uk; Manse Rd Canal Basin; admission free; 🕑 2-5pm Sat & Sun Easter-Sep, plus 2-5pm Mon-Fri Jul & Aug), where a little museum records the history of the canal.

The centre runs three-hour **canal boat trips** (adult/child £6/3) west to the Avon Aqueduct departing at 2pm Saturday and Sunday, Easter to September, and to the **Falkirk Wheel** (see the boxed text, p203) on weekdays in July and August. Shorter 20-minute cruises (adult/child £2.50/1.50) leave every half hour during the centre's opening times.

EATING & DRINKING

Linlithgow has several good pubs and restaurants. The **Four Marys** (☎ 842171; 65-76 High St; mains £4-9; 🕑 food served noon-3pm & 5-9pm Mon-Fri, noon-9pm Sat & Sun) is an attractive traditional pub (opposite the palace entrance) that serves real ales and excellent pub grub, including haggis, neeps and tatties (haggis, mashed turnip and mashed potato). A few doors along the street is **Marynka** (☎ 840123; 57 High St; lunch mains £6-10, 2-course dinner £21.50; 🕑 noon-2pm & 6-11.30pm Tue-Sat), a pleasant little gourmet restaurant.

The rustic **Champany Inn** (☎ 834532; Champany; mains £12-22; 🕑 12.30-2pm & 7-10pm Mon-Fri, 7-10pm Sat) is a trencherman's delight, famous for its excellent Aberdeen Angus steaks and Scottish lobsters. The neighbouring **Chop and Ale House** (mains £6-14) is a less expensive alternative to the main dining room, offering delicious homemade burgers and steaks. The inn is 2 miles northeast of Linlithgow on the A803/A904 road towards Bo'ness and Queensferry.

GETTING THERE & AWAY

Linlithgow is 15 miles west of Edinburgh, and is served by frequent trains from the capital (£3.40, 20 minutes, four every hour); the train station is 250m east of the town centre.

You can also cycle from Edinburgh to Linlithgow along the Union Canal towpath (21 miles); allow 1½ to two hours.

Glasgow

Not only is a stay in Glasgow a highlight of any trip to Scotland, it's essential. Combining urban mayhem, black humour and, most of all, a delicious sense of fun, this city will entice you to linger. Where else could cutting edge–style bars and designer accommodation emerge and retain a down-to-earth character? Not only down-to-earth, but downright friendly. In fact, Glasgow is so friendly that it's sometimes unnerving – particularly if you are more used to urban living, where an untoward glance brings on hurried footsteps. Approach Glasgow with an open mind, an open heart and, most essential, a willingness to engage – if you don't have fun in this city, we'd suggest therapy.

Glasgow ain't always pretty – Victorian extravagance of the days of the Tobacco Lords lies side by side with 20th-century, overcrowded concrete monoliths, but that's Glasgow: what you see here is what you get and it wears its scars with style. The city is going through a major period of transformation, evident along the revitalised River Clyde, where visitors can explore Glasgow's maritime heritage through first-rate museums and riverfront walkways. Wandering Glasgow's hilly centre is the best way to unearth its treasures – the diversity of pubs, clubs and eateries is astounding, and easily represents the best value in the country. Try to catch a gig while here – the city is the heart of Scotland's pulsating live-music scene.

It won't be long before Glasgow's unique and most endearing aspect becomes obvious: no matter how trendy places like Bath St become, they remain Glaswegian – obstinately unpretentious and very accessible to travellers.

HIGHLIGHTS

- Exploring the **Burrell Collection** (p127), one of Britain's finest and most extraordinary museums

- Cruising along the **River Clyde** (p122), a focal point of Glasgow's regeneration and the city's compelling maritime heritage

- Discovering the architectural genius of **Charles Rennie Mackintosh** (p124), the earliest exponent of Art Nouveau in Britain

- Catching the hottest tunes from Glasgow's local artists in its seething **live-music scene** (p140)

- Sniffing out the **perfect watering hole** (p136) – from traditional pubs to the city's famed style bars

River Clyde ★
Burrell Collection ★

| ■ TELEPHONE CODE: 0141 | ■ POPULATION: 629,501 | ■ AREA: 176 sq km |

HISTORY

Glasgow grew up around the cathedral founded by St Mungo in the 6th century, and in 1451 the city became the site of the University of Glasgow, the second university to be founded in Scotland.

In the 18th century much of the tobacco trade between Europe and the USA was routed through Glasgow and provided a great source of wealth. Even after the tobacco trade declined in the 19th century, the city continued to prosper as a centre of textile manufacturing, shipbuilding, and the coal and steel industries.

The industries created a huge demand for labour, and peasants poured in from Ireland and the Highlands to crowd the tenements. The outward appearance of prosperity, however, was tempered by dire working conditions in the factories, particularly for women and children. In the second half of the 19th century life expectancy was only 30 years.

While the workers suffered, the textile barons and shipping magnates prospered, and Glasgow could justifiably call itself the second city of the empire. In the first half of the 20th century Glasgow was the centre of Britain's munitions industry, supplying arms and ships for the two world wars. After those boom years, however, the port and heavy industries began to decline, and by the early 1970s the city looked doomed. Glasgow has always been proud of its predominantly working-class nature but, unlike middle-class Edinburgh with its varied service industries, it had few alternatives when recession hit and unemployment spiralled.

In the late 20th and early 21st centuries there has been increasing confidence in the city. Glasgow won the 1990 European City of Culture award, and followed this up by serving as the UK's City of Architecture & Design in 1999. But, behind all the optimism, the general standard of living remains relatively low, and life is tough for those affected by the comparatively high unemployment and inadequate housing

GLASGOW

GLASGOW IN...

Two Days

Start your day with breakfast and a spot of people-watching in the trendy **Merchant City** (p119). Take a stroll around the leafy cathedral precinct in the **East End** (p125), popping your head into **Glasgow Cathedral** (p125) and **St Mungo's Museum of Religious Life & Art** (p125). Treat yourself to 'an ugly but good' pizza at **Brutti Ma Buoni** (p134), followed by a cask ale at **Blackfriars** (p136) and a night at **Arches** (p137), one of Glasgow's premier pubs/clubs.

A visit to the wonderful **Burrell Collection** (p127) is a must on your second day, and while in the area check out the **Scottish Football Museum** (p127). If you're here on a weekend, don't miss the **Barras** (p127), Glasgow's flea market and, some would say, its heart and soul. At night head to Bath St for unpretentious style bars and fine dining along the city centre's trendiest strip. Drop into **King Tut's Wah Wah Hut** (p141) to hear some of Glasgow's freshest live-music talent.

Four Days

Follow the two-day itinerary, then on your third day add a trip to the bohemian **West End** (p125); some of the city's best cafés and restaurants are here. Be sure to check out the **Hunterian Museum** (p126) and **Hunterian Art Gallery** (p126). On the fourth day stroll along the **Clyde Walkway** (p128) and discover the rejuvenation along Glasgow's waterfront. Learn about the city's unique heritage by taking a boat trip down the **River Clyde** (p123), visiting the **Clydebuilt** (p123) museum and **Tall Ship** (p122) en route – then catch a 3-D flick at the **Glasgow Science Centre** (p122).

One Week

Follow the four-day itinerary and then spend a day discovering what all the **Mackintoshania** (p124) fuss is about. Drop into the **Glasgow School of Art** (p124), **Willow Tea Rooms** (p124) and **Queen's Cross Church** (p128). Finish up with a couple of day trips out of the city: head to **Paisley** (p144) and marvel at its magnificent abbey, and take a wander around the revitalised waterfront at **Greenock** (p144), popping into the **HM Customs & Excise Museum** (p145).

GREATER GLASGOW

See Central Glasgow Map (p120)

ORIENTATION

The city centre is built on a grid system on the northern side of the River Clyde. The two train stations (Central and Queen St), the Buchanan bus station and the Tourist Information Centre (TIC) are all on or within a couple of blocks of George Sq, the main city square. Merchant City is the city's main commercial and entertainment district, east of George Sq.

Motorways bore through the suburbs and the M8 sweeps round the northern and western edges of the city centre, passing the airport 10 miles west.

Maps

The Automobile Association's *Glasgow Street by Street* (£5.99) is a handy, easy-to-read street guide, available in bookshops. Glasgow City Council publishes the excellent *Fit for Life* map (free from the TIC) showing cycle and walking routes around the city.

INFORMATION

The *List* (£2.20; www.list.co.uk), available from newsagents, is Glasgow and Edinburgh's invaluable fortnightly guide to films, theatre, cabaret, music, clubs – the works. The excellent *Eating & Drinking Guide* (£5.95), published by the *List* every April, covers Glasgow and Edinburgh.

Bookshops

Borders (Map p120; ☎ 222 7700; 98 Buchanan St; ☽ 8.30am-10pm Mon-Sat, 10am-8pm Sun) A browsing bonanza, also sells CDs and international newspapers and magazines.

Waterstone's (Map p120; ☎ 332 9105; 153 Sauchiehall St; ☽ 8.30am-9pm Mon, Tue, Thu & Fri, 9am-9pm Wed, 9am-8pm Sat, 10.30am-7pm Sun) A major bookshop, also sells guidebooks and street maps of Glasgow.

Emergency

Ambulance, Fire, Police, Mountain rescue or Coastguard (☎ 999, 112)

Internet Access

EasyInternet (Map p120; ☎ 222 2364; www.easy-everything.com; 57 St Vincent St; per hr £2) Consider buying a cheaper four-hour pass.

Gallery of Modern Art (Map p120; ☎ 229 1996; Royal Exchange Sq, Queen St; ☽ 10am-8pm Mon, Tue & Thu, to 5pm Wed & Sat, 11am-5pm Fri & Sun) Basement library; free Internet access. Bookings recommended. See also p123.

ICafe (Map p120; cnr Great Western Rd & Dunearn St; per hr £2; ☽ 10am-11pm) Sip a coffee and munch on a pastry while you check your emails on super-fast connections.

Mitchell Library (Map p120; ☎ 287 2999; North St; ☽ 9am-8pm Mon-Thu, to 5pm Fri & Sat) Offers free Internet access; bookings recommended.

Internet Resources

Glasgow City Council (www.glasgow.gov.uk) Has a particularly good daily 'What's On' section.

Glasgow Disability Access Guide (www.glasgowaccesspanel.org.uk) An online guide for the disabled.

Glasgow Museums (www.glasgowmuseums.com) A very useful guide to the city's superb museums.

Search Engine & Directory (www.scotfind.com) A search engine for all things Glaswegian and Scottish.

The Guide (www.glasgowlife.com) An online city guide particularly good for eating and entertainment.

GLASGOW

G L A S G O W

Left Luggage

Buchanan bus station (Map p120; ☎ 333 3708;
Killermont St; per 2 hr/day £2.10/3.15)
Central station (Map p120; ☎ 0845 748 4950;
Gordon St; small/medium/large piece of luggage per
24hr £3/4/5)

Medical Services

To see a doctor, visit the outpatients department at any general hospital. Recommended hospitals:
Glasgow Dental Hospital (Map p120; ☎ 211 9600;
378 Sauchiehall St)

Glasgow Royal Infirmary (Map p120; ☎ 211 4000;
84 Castle St)
Southern General Hospital (Map p120; ☎ 201 1100;
Govan Rd)

Money

The post office and the TIC have a bureau de change.
American Express (Amex; Map p120; ☎ 0870 600
1060; 115 Hope St; ☺ 8.30am-5.30pm Mon, Tue, Thu &
Fri, 9.30am-5.30pm Wed, 9am-noon Sat)
Clydesdale Bank (Map p120; 7 St Enoch Sq) Has four
24-hour ATMs.

Post

There are post offices in some supermarkets; the larger ones are open Sundays.

Branch post office (Map p120; 228 Hope St; ☉ 8.30am-5.30pm Mon, 9am-5.30pm Tue-Fri, 9am-1pm Sat)

Main post office (Map p120; 47 St Vincent St; ☉ 8.30am-5.45pm Mon-Fri, 9am-5.30pm Sat) Passport photos available.

Tourist Information

Glasgow TIC (Map p120; ☎ 204 4400; www.seeglas gow.com; 11 George Sq; ☉ 9am-6pm Mon-Sat Oct-May, 9am-7pm Jun & Sep, 9am-8pm Jul & Aug, 10am-6pm Sun Easter-Sep) Excellent TIC; Makes local and national accommodation bookings (£3).

St Enoch Square Travel Centre (Map p120; St Enoch Sq; ☉ 8.30am-5.30pm Mon-Sat) Travel information only.

TIC branch (☎ 848 4440; Glasgow International Airport; ☉ 7.30am-5pm Easter-Sep, 7.30am-5pm Mon-Sat, 8am-3.30pm Sun Jan-Easter & Oct-Dec)

Travel Agencies

Glasgow Flight Centre (Map p120; ☎ 353 1351; 280 Sauchiehall St)

DANGERS & ANNOYANCES

Keep clear of Orange marches, which are exhibitions of solidarity with the Protestant Northern Irish cause; violence can result when Catholics try to 'break the ranks'. These events aren't for tourists. Women should avoid walking alone at night in the red-light district situated around Anderston/Blythswood Sq. See also Dangers and Annoyances (p434) in the Directory.

SIGHTS

Glasgow's major sights are fairly evenly dispersed around the city, with the most important found along the Clyde – the focus of a major regeneration programme, the leafy cathedral precinct in the East End and the museum-rich South Side. The City Centre itself also contains a variety of attractions, particularly Mackintoshania. The trendy West End swarms with students during term time, but it's quieter during the holidays.

The Clyde

The tide is definitely turning for the Clyde. In the last decade Glasgow has been returning to its roots with a major campaign to rejuvenate the riverfront and celebrate the city's unique industrial heritage. Included in this strategy is a long-term redevelopment of Glasgow Harbour, converting former docklands into shops and public areas, and rebuilding seven Art-Nouveau Mackintosh-designed tearooms. It's also expected that access to over 3km of formerly inaccessible waterfront will be made available – to find out more about this project see www.glasgowharbour.com.

GLASGOW SCIENCE CENTRE

Scotland's flagship millennium project, the superb, ultramodern **Glasgow Science Centre** (Map p120; ☎ 420 5000; 50 Pacific Quay; Science Mall adult/child £6.95/4.95, IMAX £6.95/4.95, combined ticket £9.95/7.95; ☉ 10am-6pm, IMAX 11am-6pm Sun-Wed, 11am-8pm Thu-Sat) will keep the kids entertained for hours (that's middle-aged kids, too!). It brings science and technology alive through hundreds of interactive exhibits on four floors. Look out for the illusions (like rearranging your features through a 3-D head scan) and the cloud chamber, showing tracks of natural radiation. It consists of an egg-shaped titanium-covered **IMAX** theatre (call for current screenings) and an interactive **Science Mall** with floor-to-ceiling windows – a bounty of discovery for young, inquisitive minds. There's also a rotating **observation tower**, 127m high (closed at the time of research). Also check out the planetarium, where the **Scottish Power Space Theatre** brings the night sky to life and a **Virtual Science Theatre** treats visitors to a 3-D molecular journey. To get here take Arriva bus 24 from Renfield St or First Glasgow bus 89 or 90 from Union St.

TALL SHIP & PUMPHOUSE

Across the Clyde from the Science Centre, via Bell's Bridge, is the magnificent **Tall Ship** (Glenlee; Map p120; ☎ 222 2513; 100 Stobcross Rd, Glasgow Harbour; adult £4.95, 1 child free, then per child £2.50; ☉ 10am-5pm Mar-Oct, to 4pm Nov-Feb), one of five sailing ships built on the Clyde still afloat. The *Glenlee* was launched in December 1896. The sheer size of this three-masted ship is impressive, and there are displays about her history, restoration and life on board in the early 20th century.

Inside the nearby old **Pumphouse** (Map p120), now a visitor centre, a captivating exhibit unfurls the interwoven stories of Glasgow and the Clyde, including the amazing dredging work carried out to enable the big ships to sail into Glasgow.

Check upcoming events here, as there's often good stuff on offer for the kids over summer.

CLYDEBUILT

If immersing yourself in a city's heritage floats your boat, a visit to **Clydebuilt** (☎ 886 1013; Kings Inch Rd, Braehead; adult/child £4.25/2.50; ☻ 10am-5.30pm Mon-Sat, 11am-5pm Sun) will get you paddlin'. It's a superb collection of model ships, industrial displays and narrative, vividly painting the history of the Clyde, the fate of which has been inextricably linked with Glasgow and its people. It's a cleverly designed museum, with twists and turns that offer something new around every corner. Getting here via the Pride o' the Clyde (see the boxed text, right) is half the fun. Outside you can board *Kyles*, a typical 1872 vessel. Moored on the empty shores of the Clyde, with only the crying gulls above breaking the silence, it's a perfect place to contemplate the defunct shipyards that formed the cornerstone of Glasgow's industrial heritage.

City Centre

The grid layout of the city centre makes it easy to get around, and there are many cafés and pubs that make a good pit stop between attractions.

CITY CHAMBERS

The grand **City Chambers** (Map p120; ☎ 287 4018; George Sq; admission free), the seat of local government, were built in the 1880s at the high point of the city's wealth. Their interior is even more extravagant than their exterior, and locals highly recommend a visit. Guided tours are held at 10.30am and 2.30pm Monday to Friday.

GALLERY OF MODERN ART

Scotland's most popular contemporary **art gallery** (Map p120; ☎ 229 1996; Royal Exchange Sq, Queen St; admission free; ☻ 10am-5pm Mon-Wed & Sat, to 8pm Thu, 11am-5pm Fri & Sun) features modern works from artists worldwide in a graceful neoclassical building. The original interior is used to make a daring, inventive art display. Social issues are a focal point of the museum and if you're interested in seeing some thought-provoking artistic interpretations of the more marginalised people in today's society, you should definitely swing by this museum.

GETTING AROUND ON THE CLYDE

Pride o' the Clyde (Map p120; ☎ 07711 250 969; Central Station Bridge) is a waterbus linking Glasgow city centre with Braehead, home of the Clydebuilt museum. It's a terrific way to witness the progress of the Clyde's regeneration and to avoid city congestion. A single/return ticket costs £4/7; there are five to six sailings daily.

Seaforce (Map p120; ☎ 221 1070; Tall Ship, 100 Stobcross Rd, Glasgow Harbour) offers speedy powerboat jaunts along the Clyde. There's a variety of trips (tickets £6 to £40), including a half-hour ride around central Glasgow, an hour trip to the Erskine Bridge or four-hour rides to local wildlife hot spots.

The **Waverley** (☎ 0845 130 4647; www .waverleyexcursions.co.uk; Anderston Quay), the world's last ocean-going paddle steamer (built in 1947), cruises the Firth of Clyde from April to September (tickets £10 to £30); the website details days of departure. It serves several towns and the islands of Bute, Great Cumbrae and Arran. It departs from Glasgow Science Centre (see opposite).

McLELLAN GALLERIES

Built in 1856, the ornate **McLellan Galleries** (Map p120; ☎ 565 4137; 270 Sauchiehall St; admission free; ☻ 10am-5pm Mon-Thu & Sat, 11am-5pm Fri & Sun) has an exhibition entitled 'Art Treasures of Kelvingrove'. It's a selection of the finest treasures from Kelvingrove Museum, which is being refurbished (probably closed until mid-2006; see p126). You can view over 200 pieces from the picture galleries, including Thomas Faed's *The Last of the Clan* and Rembrandt's *A Man in Armour*. There are also displays covering Charles Rennie Mackintosh.

TENEMENT HOUSE

For an extraordinary time-capsule experience, visit the small apartment in the **Tenement House** (NTS; Map p120; ☎ 333 0183; 145 Buccleuch St; adult/child £5/4; ☻ 1-5pm Mar-Oct). It gives a vivid insight into middle-class city life at the turn of the 20th century, with box-beds, the original kitchen range, and all the fixtures and fittings of the family who lived here for more than 50 years.

It's an interesting place, but surely the Toward family wouldn't have kept it quite as squeaky clean and orderly as the National

Trust for Scotland (NTS) manages to do now. Despite the additional exhibition area in the ground-floor flat, it can get crowded.

THE ROYAL HIGHLAND FUSILIERS MUSEUM

Visitors with an interest in Scotland's proud military history should duck into the commendable **Royal Highland Fusiliers Museum** (Map p120; ☎ 332 0961; 518 Sauchiehall St; admission free; ☧ 8am-4pm Mon-Fri). It charts the history of this and previous regiments from 1678 to the present. The walls are dripping with exhibits, including uniforms, medals, pictures and other militaria. Wrought ironwork in the museum was designed by Mackintosh.

GLASGOW SCHOOL OF ART

Widely recognised as Mackintosh's greatest building, the **Glasgow School of Art** (Map p120; ☎ 353 4526; 167 Renfrew St; adult/child £6/4.80) still houses the educational institution. It's hard not to be impressed by the thoroughness of the design; the architect's pencil seems to have shaped everything inside and outside the building. The interior design is strikingly austere, with simple colour combinations (often just black and cream) and those uncomfortable-looking high-backed chairs for which Mackintosh is famous. The library, designed as an addition in 1907, is a masterpiece. To view the school, you must take a guided tour – times vary, usually six daily April to September and two daily Monday to Saturday October to March.

WILLOW TEA ROOMS

Admirers of the great Mackintosh will love the **Willow Tea Rooms** (Map p120; ☎ 332 0521; 217 Sauchiehall St; admission free; ☧ 9am-4.30pm Mon-Sat, 11-4.30pm Sun), an authentic reconstruction of the tearoom Mackintosh designed and furnished in 1904 for restaurateur Kate Cranston. Relive the original splendour of this unique tearoom and admire the architect's stroke in just about everything. He had a free rein and even the teaspoons were given his distinctive touch. Reconstruction took two years and the Willow opened as a tearoom again in 1980 (having been closed since 1926). The street name Sauchiehall means 'lane of willows', hence the choice of a stylised willow motif. See also its Eating review on p134.

THE LIGHTHOUSE

If you've been admiring Glasgow's architecture, make sure you check out the **Lighthouse** (Map p120; ☎ 221 6362; 11 Mitchell Lane; adult/child £3/1; ☧ 10.30am-5pm Mon & Wed-Sat, 11am-5pm Tue, 12-5pm Sun), one of Glasgow's hidden treasures. Tucked away in a small lane, in the former *Glasgow Herald* building, it now serves

---

THE GENIUS OF CHARLES RENNIE MACKINTOSH

Great cities have great artists and architects contributing to the cultural and historical roots of their urban environment while expressing its soul and individuality. Charles Rennie Mackintosh was all of these. The quirky, linear and geometric designs of this famous Scottish architect and designer have had almost as much influence on the city as have Gaudi's on Barcelona. Many of the buildings Mackintosh designed in Glasgow are open to the public, and you'll see his tall, thin, Art-Nouveau typeface repeatedly reproduced.

Born in 1868, Mackintosh studied at the Glasgow School of Art. In 1896, when he was aged only 27, he won a competition for his design of the School of Art's new building. The first section was opened in 1899 and is considered to be the earliest example of Art Nouveau in Britain, as well as Mackintosh's supreme architectural achievement. This building demonstrates his skill in combining function and style.

Although Mackintosh's genius was quickly recognised on the Continent, he did not receive the same encouragement in Scotland. His architectural career here lasted only until 1914, when he moved to England to concentrate on furniture design. He died in 1928, and it was only in the last decades of the 20th century that Mackintosh's genius has been widely recognised. For more about the man and his work, contact the **Charles Rennie Mackintosh Society** (☎ 946 6600; www .crmsociety.com; Queen's Cross Church, 870 Garscube Rd, Glasgow G20 7EL). From April to October the Society runs weekend tours of his buildings (once or twice a month); the cost is £300/470 for one/two people, including dinner, B&B for two nights, lunches, coach, guide and admission.

See Helensburgh (p278) for information on Hill House, perhaps Mackintosh's finest creation.

as **Scotland's Centre for Architecture & Design**, giving an insight into modern architectural feats. It was designed by Mackintosh in 1893, and also features the **Mackintosh Interpretation Centre**. Learn more about this extraordinary man, see exhibitions of avant-garde furniture and drink in great rooftop views from the former water tower. It's also worth dropping into the Doocot Cafe & Bar here for a different kind of drink – it's a good place to rest weary legs and minds.

East End

The oldest part of the city, given a facelift in the 1990s, is concentrated around Glasgow Cathedral, to the east of the modern centre. The crumbling tombs of the city's rich and famous crowd the necropolis, located behind the cathedral.

It takes 15 to 20 minutes to walk from George Sq, but numerous buses pass nearby, including buses 11, 12, 36, 37, 38 and 42.

GLASGOW CATHEDRAL

An attraction that shouldn't be missed, **Glasgow Cathedral** (HS; Map p120; ☎ 552 6891; Cathedral Sq; admission free; ☉ 9.30am-6pm Mon-Sat, 1-5pm Sun Apr-Sep, 9.30am-4pm Mon-Sat, 1-4pm Sun Oct-Mar) has a rare timelessness. The dark, imposing interior conjures up medieval might and can send a shiver down the spine. It's a shining example of pre-Reformation Gothic architecture, and the only mainland Scottish cathedral to have survived the Reformation. Most of the current building dates from the 15th century, and only the western towers were destroyed in the turmoil.

The entry is through a side door into the **nave**, which is hung with some regimental colours. The wooden roof above has been restored many times since its original construction, but some of the timber dates from the 14th century; note the impressive shields. Many of the cathedral's stunning, narrow windows of stained glass are modern and, to your left, is Francis Spear's 1958 work *The Creation*, which fills the west window.

The cathedral is divided by a late-15th-century stone choir screen, decorated with seven pairs of figures to represent the Seven Deadly Sins. Beyond is the **choir**. The four stained-glass panels of the east window, depicting the apostles and also by Francis Spear, are particularly effective. At the northeastern corner is the entrance to the 15th-century

upper chapter house, where Glasgow University was founded. It's now used as a sacristy.

The most interesting part of the cathedral, the **lower church**, is reached by a stairway. Its forest of pillars creates a powerful atmosphere around St Mungo's tomb (St Mungo founded a monastic community here in the 5th century), the focus of a famous medieval pilgrimage that was believed to be as meritorious as a visit to Rome.

Sunday services are at 11am and 6.30pm.

ST MUNGO'S MUSEUM OF RELIGIOUS LIFE & ART

A startling achievement, **St Mungo's Museum** (Map p120; ☎ 553 2557; 2 Castle St; admission free; ☉ 10am-5pm Mon-Thu & Sat, 11am-5pm Fri & Sun) is an audacious attempt to capture the world's major religions in an artistic nutshell. The result is commendable. The attraction is twofold: firstly, impressive art that blurs the lines between religion and culture; and secondly, the opportunity to delve into different faiths, an experience that can be as deep or shallow as you wish. There are three galleries, representing religion as art, religious life and, on the top floor, religion in Scotland. In the main gallery Dali's *Christ of St John of the Cross* hangs beside statues of the Buddha and Hindu deities. Britain's only Zen garden is outside.

PROVAND'S LORDSHIP

Across the road from St Mungo's Museum is **Provand's Lordship** (Map p120; ☎ 552 8819; 3 Castle St; admission free; ☉ 10am-5pm Mon-Thu & Sat, 11am-5pm Fri & Sun), the oldest house in Glasgow. A rare example of 15th-century domestic Scottish architecture, it was built in 1471 as a manse for the chaplain of St Nicholas Hospital. The ceilings and doorways are low, and the rooms are sparsely furnished with period artefacts, except for an upstairs room, which has been furnished to reflect the living space of an early-16th-century chaplain. The building's best feature is its authentic feel – if you ignore the tacky imitation-stone linoleum covering the ground floor.

West End

With its expectant buzz, trendy bars and cafés, and nonchalant swagger, the West End is probably the most engaging area of Glasgow – it's great for people-watching, and is as close as Glasgow gets to bohemian.

HUNTERIAN MUSEUM & ART GALLERY

Part of the university and housed in two separate buildings on either side of University Ave, the Hunterian contains the collection of William Hunter (1718–83), famous physician, medical teacher and one-time student of the university.

Don't forget to drag your eyes down to the exhibits in the **Hunterian Museum** (Map p120; ☎ 330 4221; University Ave; admission free; ☺ 9.30am-5pm Mon-Sat), which can be difficult as the university building itself is quite breathtaking. The museum has a disparate collection of artefacts, including a notable coin collection, fossils and minerals, dinosaur eggs, Romano-British stone slabs and carvings, and some of Captain Cook's curios from his voyages to the South Seas. The West African carvings incorporating the arrival of Europeans are fascinating.

Across the road, the Scottish Colourists (Samuel Peploe, Francis Cadell, JD Fergusson) are well represented in the **Hunterian Art Gallery** (Map p120; ☎ 330 5431; 82 Hillhead St; admission free; ☺ 9.30am-5pm Mon-Sat). There are also Sir William MacTaggart's impressionistic Scottish landscapes, and a gem by Thomas Millie Dow. There's a special collection of James McNeill Whistler's limpid prints, drawings and paintings. The **Mackintosh House** (☎ 330 5431; 82 Hillhead St; admission £2.50, after 2pm Wed free; ☺ 9.30am-12.30pm & 1.30-5pm Mon-Sat) is the final section in the gallery. Set up as a reconstruction of Charles Rennie Mackintosh's Glasgow home (which had to be demolished), the Mackintosh House is startling even today. You ascend from the gallery's sombre ground floor into the cool, white, austere drawing room. There's something otherworldly about the very mannered style of the beaten silver panels, the long-backed chairs and the surface decorations echoing Celtic manuscript illuminations. Buses 11 and 44 pass this way from the city centre (Hope St).

BOTANIC GARDENS

The best thing about walking into these beautiful **gardens** (Map p118; ☎ 334 2422; 730 Great Western Rd; ☺ daily, closes 10pm in summer, glasshouse 10am-4.45pm, visitor centre 11am-4pm) is the noise of Great Western Rd quickly receding into the background. Amazingly the lush grounds don't seem that popular with locals (except on sunny weekends) and away from the entrance you may just about have the place

to yourself. The wooded gardens follow the riverbank of the River Kelvin and there's plenty of tropical species to discover. Check out the herb garden, too, with its medicinal species. The gorgeous hilly grounds make the perfect place for a picnic lunch. There are also organised walks and concerts in summer – have a look at the noticeboard near the entrance to see what's on.

Kibble Palace, dating from 1873, is one of the largest glasshouses in Britain, but was undergoing renovation at time of research and was closed to the public. Other glasshouses remained open.

KELVINGROVE ART GALLERY & MUSEUM

In a magnificent Edwardian building this grand Victorian cathedral of culture is one of Glasgow's best, particularly its collection of Scottish and European art, and is the most visited museum in the UK outside of London. Note, however, the magnificent **Kelvingrove** (☎ 287 2699; Argyle St) was closed for a major refurbishment at time of writing, but should be open by mid-2006. Call directly for further info and opening times or call into Glasgow TIC. Until it reopens, most of the pieces are in the McLellan Galleries (p123).

MUSEUM OF TRANSPORT

Across Argyle St from the Hunterian Museum & Art Gallery is the surprisingly interesting and very comprehensive, but badly signposted, **Museum of Transport** (Map p120; ☎ 287 2720; 1 Bunhouse Rd; admission free; ☺ 10am-5pm Mon-Thu & Sat, 11am-5pm Fri & Sun). Not convinced? It's actually a very fine museum with exhibits including a reproduction of a 1938 Glasgow street scene, a display of cars made in Scotland, plus assorted railway locos, trams, bikes (including the world's first pedal-powered bicycle from 1847) and model ships. There's a room dedicated to the Clyde shipyards. It's like peeping through a porthole at the not too distant past. By train it's a 15-minute walk from Partick station. First Glasgow buses 9, 16, 18, 42, 62 and 64 all stop nearby.

FOSSIL GROVE

With sections of 350-million-year-old fossilised trees lying as they were found, **Fossil Grove** (Map p118; ☎ 287 2000; Victoria Park, Dumbarton Rd; admission free; ☺ 10am-5pm Mon-Thu & Sat, 11am-5pm Fri & Sun Apr-Sep) is an intriguing site. This Site of Special Scientific Interest (SSSI) feels quite spooky and makes you realise you're but a blip on the earth's timeline. To get here, take bus 44 from the city centre to Victoria Park Dr North, or bus 9 or 62 to Dumbarton Rd.

South Side

The south side is a tangled web of busy roads with a few oases giving relief from the urban congestion. It does, however, contain some of Glasgow's best museums.

BURRELL COLLECTION

One of Glasgow's top attractions is the **Burrell Collection** (Map p118; ☎ 287 2550; Pollok Country Park; admission free, parking £1.50; ☉ 10am-5pm Mon-Thu & Sat, 11am-5pm Fri & Sun). Amassed by wealthy industrialist Sir William Burrell before being donated to the city, it is housed in an outstanding museum, 3 miles south of the city centre. This idiosyncratic collection of treasure includes everything from Chinese porcelain and medieval furniture to paintings by Renoir and Cézanne. It's not so big as to be overwhelming, and the stamp of the collector lends an intriguing coherence.

Visitors will find their own favourite part of this museum, but the exquisite tapestry galleries are outstanding. Intricate stories capturing life in Europe are woven into staggering, wall-size pieces dating from the 13th century. The huge *Triumph of the Virgin* exemplifies the complexity in nature and theme of this medium, while posing the serious question, 'How long must this have taken?'

Within the spectacular interior, carved-stone Romanesque doorways are incorporated into the structure so you actually walk through them. Floor-to-ceiling windows admit a flood of light, and enable the surrounding landscape outside to enhance the effect of the exhibits. It feels like you're wandering in a huge tranquil greenhouse.

There are occasional guided tours. Many buses pass the park gates (including buses 45, 47, 48 and 57 from the city centre), and there's a twice-hourly bus service between the gallery and the gates (a pleasant 10-minute walk). Alternatively catch a train to Pollokshaws West from Central station (four per hour; you want the second station on the line for East Kilbride or Kilmarnock).

SCOTTISH FOOTBALL MUSEUM

Football fans will just love the **Scottish Football Museum** (Map p118; ☎ 616 6139; Hampden Park; adult/

THE GLASGOW BOYS

The great rivalry between Glasgow and Edinburgh goes back a long way. In the late 19th century a group of Glaswegian painters challenged the domineering artistic establishment in Edinburgh. Up to this point paintings were largely confined to historical scenes and sentimental visions of the Highlands. These painters – including Sir James Guthrie, EA Hornel, George Henry and Joseph Crawhall – experimented with colour and themes of rural life, shocking Edinburgh's artistic society. Like Charles Rennie Mackintosh, the Glasgow Boys achieved success on the Continent, where their work met with admiration and artistic recognition.

The Glasgow Boys had an enormous influence on the Scottish art world, inspiring the next generation of Scottish painters – the Colourists. The works of the Glasgow Boys can be seen in various Scottish collections, including the Burrell Collection (left) and Broughton House, Kirkcudbright (p180).

child £5/2.50; ☉ 10am-5pm Mon-Sat, 11am-5pm Sun), which features exhibits on the history of the game in Scotland and the influence of Scots on the world game. Football inspires an incredible passion in Scotland and the museum is crammed full of impressive memorabilia, including a cap and match ticket from the very first international football game (which took place in 1872 between Scotland and England, and ended with a score of 0-0). The museum's engrossing exhibits give insight into the players, the fans, the media and the way the game has changed over the last 130 years. The museum's location is at Hampden Park, off Aikenhead Rd. To get there, take a train to Mount Florida station or take bus 5, 31, 37 or 75 from Stockwell St.

THE BARRAS

Glasgow's flea market, the **Barras on Gallowgate** (Map p120; London Rd; ☉ 9am-5pm Sat & Sun), is the living, breathing heart of this city in many respects. It has almost a thousand stalls and people come here just for a wander as much as for shopping, which gives the place a holiday air. The Barras is notorious for designer frauds, so be cautious. Watch your wallet, too.

THE PEOPLE'S PALACE

The city's oldest park, on Glasgow Green, is the **People's Palace** (Map p120; ☎ 271 2951; Glasgow Green; admission free; ☼ 10am-5pm Mon-Thu & Sat, 11am-5pm Fri & Sun). It is an impressive museum of social history, telling the story of the city from 1750 to the present. It has creative, inventive displays, which are great for families – the kids will love the re-creation of a WWII air raid. The Palace was built in the late 19th century as a cultural centre for Glasgow's East End. Drop into the Winter Gardens next door for a coffee.

SCOTLAND STREET SCHOOL MUSEUM

An impressive Mackintosh building, the **Scotland Street School Museum** (Map p118; ☎ 287 0500; 225 Scotland St; admission free; ☼ 10am-5pm Mon-Thu & Sat, 11am-5pm Fri & Sun) is dominated by two glass towers. It's a fascinating museum of education, with reconstructions of classrooms from Victorian times and the 1940s to the 1960s. The place evokes childhood memories for just about everyone – don't be surprised if you hear a few titters from elderly visitors as they pass the headmaster's office.

HOUSE FOR AN ART LOVER

Although designed in 1901 as an entry to a competition run by a German magazine, the **House for an Art Lover** (Map p118; ☎ 353 4770; Bellahouston Park, 10 Dumbreck Rd; adult/child £3.50/2.50; ☼ 10am-4pm Mon-Wed, 10am-1pm Thu-Sun Apr-Sep, 10am-1pm Sat & Sun Oct-Mar) was not completed until 1996. Mackintosh worked closely with his wife on the design and her influence is evident, especially in the rose motif. The overall result of this brilliant architect's design is one of space and light. Buses 3, 9, 54, 55 and 56 all run here from the city centre.

HOLMWOOD HOUSE

An interesting building designed by Alexander 'Greek' Thomson, **Holmwood House** (☎ 637 2129; 61-63 Netherlee Rd, Cathcart; adult/child £5/4; ☼ noon-5pm Apr-Oct) dates from 1857. Despite ongoing renovations, it's well worth a visit. Look for sun symbols downstairs and stars upstairs in this attractive house with its adaptation of classical Greek architecture. To get to Cathcart train station, take a 'Cathcart Circle' train via Queen's Park or a train to Neilston. Otherwise, take bus 44, 44A, 44D or 66 from the city centre. Follow Rhannan Rd for about 800m to Holmwood House.

North Side

QUEEN'S CROSS CHURCH

Now the headquarters of the Charles Rennie Mackintosh Society, **Queen's Cross Church** (Map p118; ☎ 946 6600; 870 Garscube Rd; adult/child £2/free; ☼ 10am-5pm Mon-Fri Nov-Feb, 10am-5pm Mon-Fri, 2-5pm Sun Mar-Oct) is the only of Mackintosh's church designs to be built. It has excellent stained glass and relief carvings, and the wonderful simplicity and grace of the barrel-shaped design is particularly inspiring.

ACTIVITIES

There are numerous green spaces within the city. **Pollok Country Park** (Map p118) surrounds the Burrell Collection and has several woodland trails. Nearer the centre of the city, the **Kelvin Walkway** follows the River Kelvin through Kelvingrove Park (Map p118), the Botanic Gardens and on to Dawsholm Park.

The TIC has a range of maps and leaflets detailing these jaunts, and the long-distance routes described under Walking & Cycling following, most of which start from Bell's Bridge (Map p120; by the SECC). It also stocks the *Fit for Life* map detailing walking and cycling routes around the city.

Walking & Cycling

It is possible to walk 9 miles of the Clyde through Glasgow. An outstanding section lies between the Victoria Bridge and the SECC, taking in 150 years of bridge engineering and a chunk of Glasgow's shipbuilding heritage. The **Clyde Walkway** extends from Glasgow to Strathclyde Park, between Motherwell and Hamilton, and will eventually continue to the Falls of Clyde in Lanark (p161). It should be about 40 miles long when completed.

The well-trodden, long-distance footpath called the **West Highland Way** begins in Milngavie, 8 miles north of Glasgow (you can walk to Milngavie from Glasgow along the River Klein), and runs for 95 spectacular miles to Fort William.

There are several long-distance pedestrian/cycle routes that begin in Glasgow and follow off-road routes for most of the way.

The **Glasgow–Loch Lomond route** traverses residential and industrial areas, following a disused railway to Clydebank, the Forth and Clyde canal towpath to Bowling, then a disused railway to Dumbarton, reaching Loch Lomond via the towpath by the River Leven. This route continues to Inverness, from Balloch via Aberfoyle, Loch Vennachar, Callander and Strathyre to link with the Glen Ogle Trail, Killin, Pitlochry and Aviemore.

The **Glasgow–Greenock/Gourock route** runs via Paisley, the first section partly on roads. From Johnstone to Greenock the route follows a disused railway line, and the final section to Gourock has also been built. Sculpture from the Sustrans public arts project brightens parts of the way.

The **Glasgow–Irvine, Ardrossan & West Kilbride Cycle Way** runs via Paisley, then off-road to Glengarnock. From here to Kilwinning it follows minor roads, then the route is partly off-road. Ferries to the Isle of Arran, popular with cyclists, leave from Ardrossan. An extension via Ayr, Maybole and Glentrool leads to the Solway coast and Carlisle.

The **Glasgow–Edinburgh Cycle Way** partly follows the Clyde Walkway and a disused railway line. It skirts south Lanarkshire and continues through Uddingston, Airdrie, Bathgate and onto Edinburgh.

Hire a bike at **West End Cycles** (Map p118; ☎ 357 1344; 16 Chancellor St) at the southern end of Byres Rd. It hires 24-speed mountain bikes for £15/85 a day/week. You need two forms of ID, and a £100 deposit or a credit card.

WALKING TOUR

This absorbing stroll will take you from George Sq to Glasgow Cathedral through the trendy Merchant City, a planned 18th-century civic development, and home to many fine pubs and restaurants.

The TIC on **George Sq (1)** is a good starting point for exploring the city. The square is surrounded by imposing Victorian architecture, including the old post office, the Bank of Scotland and the grandiose **City Chambers** (**2**; p123). There are statues of Robert Burns, James Watt, Lord Clyde and, atop a 24m-high Doric column, Sir Walter Scott.

Once you've ogled the City Chambers, cross George Sq and walk one block south down Queen St to the **Gallery of Modern Art** (**3**; p123). This striking four-floor colonnaded building, built in 1827, was once the Royal Exchange. Pop in for a look at some of the country's best contemporary art displays.

The gallery faces Ingram St, which you should cross and then follow east for four blocks to **Hutchesons' Hall (4)**. Built in 1805 to a design by David Hamilton, this elegant building is now maintained by the NTS. On your way, duck into the former Court House cells now housing the ornate, dazzling **Corinthian** (**5**; p137) pub/club for a glimpse of the extravagant interior (and perhaps a cheeky half!). Retrace your steps one block and continue south down Glassford St past **Trades Hall (6)**, designed by Robert Adam in 1791 to house the trades guild. This is the only surviving building in Glasgow by this famous

WALKING TOUR

Distance: just over 2km
Duration: approximately 1½ hours

Scottish architect; the exterior is best viewed from Garth St. Turn right into Wilson St and first left along Virginia St, which is lined with the old warehouses of the Tobacco Lords; many of these have been converted into flats for the upwardly mobile. The **Tobacco Exchange (7)** became the Sugar Exchange in 1820, but it's now in poor condition.

Back on Wilson St, the bulky **Sheriff Court House (8)** fills a whole block. This arresting building was originally Glasgow's town hall, but is now being developed as luxury apartments. Continue east on Wilson St into Bell St and take a break at the excellent **Blackfriars pub (9**; p136), where you can people-watch while sipping a cask ale. Turn left into Albion St, then first right into Blackfriars St. Emerging onto High St, turn left and follow High St up to the **Cathedral (10**; p125). Behind the cathedral wind your way up through the noble, crumbling tombs of the **Necropolis (11)**, with great city views. On your way back you can check out the free and fabulous **St Mungo's Museum of Religious Life & Art (12**; p125) and **Provand's Lordship (13**; p125).

GLASGOW FOR CHILDREN

Although Glasgow is a bigger, busier city that Edinburgh, it's an easy city to travel around with children due to its extensive public transport system and friendly locals. The city boasts excellent family attractions, including the **Glasgow Science Centre** (p122) and **Sharmanka Kinetic Gallery & Theatre** (right), which both vie for Glasgow's top child-friendly attraction. The **People's Palace** (p128) and **Museum of Transport** (p126) are also recommended. A boat trip along the Clyde can be a lot of fun for kids. For more ideas, pick up *Glasgow Guide for Under 6's* (£5.99) from the TIC.

For suggestions of short-term child-care agencies, get in touch with the council-run **Childcare Information Service** (☎ 287 8307; www .childcarelink.org.uk/glasgowcity).

Parks in Glasgow often have playgrounds for children; call ☎ 287 5064 for information. We recommend two indoor playgrounds (far more practical). The crèche at **Buchanan Galleries** (☎ 332 4353; www.buchanangalleries.co.uk; Royal Exchange Sq) shopping centre is available for children aged two to eight and staffed by qualified nursery assistants. The **Jelly Club** (Map p120; ☎ 248 6800; www.jellyclub.com; St Enoch shopping centre; child £2.50; ☺ 10am-6pm Mon-Sat, 11am-5.30pm Sun) encourages physical activity by providing imaginative exercises to stimulate the mind and body (children under 13).

QUIRKY GLASGOW

For those up to their eyeballs in museums and galleries, check out a show at the extraordinary **Sharmanka Kinetic Gallery & Theatre** (Map p120; ☎ 552 7080; 14 King St; adult/child £4/free). Originally from St Petersburg, this mechanical theatre brings inanimate objects to life; sculptured pieces of old scrap and tiny carved figures perform humorous and tragic stories of the human spirit to haunting music. It's joyful, ironic theatre, inspirational one moment and macabre the next, but always colourful, clever and thought provoking. It's art for reflection – and lots of fun! Full performances are at 7pm Thursday and Sunday, and a matinee for families is at 3pm Sunday.

TOURS

The **Walkabout Glasgow Tours** company provides an entertaining half-hour audio commentary for a 1½- to 3½-hour walking route through the city. Headphones cost £5 per day from the TIC.

From April to October **City Sightseeing** (☎ 204 0444) runs tourist buses every 15 minutes (9.20am to 4.40pm) along the main sight seeing routes, starting at George Sq. You get on and off as you wish. A day ticket per adult/child costs £8.50/3; if you buy a day ticket you get the next day's travel for free (buy from the driver or the TIC). All buses have wheelchair access. **Guide Friday** (☎ 248 7644) runs the same route, but has live commentary (on City Sightseeing it's recorded).

FESTIVALS & EVENTS

Not to be outdone by Edinburgh, Glasgow has several festivals of its own.

Celtic Connections (☎ 353 8000; www.grch.com) Two-week music festival held in January.

City of Love (☎ 331 2668; www.cityoflove.co.uk) If you're in the city with a loved one in February, don't miss this festival celebrating St Valentine, whose partial remains lie in a city church.

Glasgow Jazz Festival (☎ 552 3552; www.jazzfest .co.uk) Excellent festival held in June; George Sq is a good place for free jazz at this time.

RSNO Proms (☎ 353 8000; www.grch.com) Classical music in June.

West End Festival (☎ 341 0844; www.westend festival.co.uk) This music and the arts event is Glasgow's biggest festival, running for two weeks in June.

World Pipe Band Championships (☎ 221 5414; tickets £6) Around 200 pipe bands; held in mid-August.

SLEEPING

Finding somewhere decent in July and August can be difficult. Finding accommodation in Glasgow on weekends can be dicey at any time of year – it's wise to book ahead.

Budget

CITY CENTRE

Euro Hostel (Map p120; ☎ 222 2828; www.euro-hostels .com; 318 Clyde St; B&B per person £12-21; 🖳) A mammoth hostel, Euro does not inspire warmth or a community feel, but it does provide high-quality budget accommodation in a central location. The dorms range in size from twin rooms through to 14 beds. Common areas are small, especially the kitchen. It's ideal for groups and has a grungy bar on-site.

Glasgow Youth Hostel (Map p120; ☎ 0870 004 1119; www.syha.org.uk; 7-8 Park Tce; dm £13-16) Completely refurbished after a blaze caused extensive damage, don't play with your cigarette lighter here. Perched on a hill overlooking Kelvingrove Park in a charming town house, this place is simply fabulous and one of Scotland's best official hostels. Dorms are mostly four to six beds and all have their own en suite – very posh. The common rooms are spacious, plush and good for lounging about.

Blue Sky Hostel (Map p120; ☎ 221 1710; www .blueskyhostel.com; 65 Berkeley St; dm £8-10, d £25-30; 🖳) Ready to party? Get in the mood because this place goes off – very grungy, a little scruffy and improvised perhaps, but with loads of personality, a friendly vibe and close to the centre. Don't come here for a cup of jasmine tea and a bubble bath, instead look forward to an education on Glasgow's nightspots.

University of Strathclyde Campus Village (Map p120; ☎ 548 4381; www.rescat.strath.ac.uk; Rottenrow East; 4-/6-bed flats weekly £330/360, B&B per person £26.50, with en suite £32.50, bed only £21.50; �险 mid-Jun–Sep) The uni opens its halls of residence to tourists over summer. The Campus Village, opposite Glasgow Cathedral, offers accommodation in shared, single-sex, self-catering flats on a weekly basis, or good-value B&B.

WEST END

Bunkum Backpackers (Map p118; ☎ /fax 581 4481; www.bunkumglasgow.co.uk; 26 Hillhead St; dm/tw £12/32) This is a backpackers with a great vibe in a terrific house with no curfew. One very big plus is the space – in an old Victorian terrace, the common rooms are large and the well-kept six-bed dorms are also a pretty good size. It's very close to Glasgow University and the hot spots on Byres Rd; most of the partying is done outside the hostel.

CAMPING

Craigendmuir Park (☎ 779 4159; www.craigendmuir .co.uk; Campsie View, Stepps; tent sites for 2 from £12.50) The nearest camping ground to town, this is about 800m from Stepps station. It has sites for caravans and tents, and a few chalets.

Midrange

CITY CENTRE

There are some fantastic options around the city centre. If you're driving, watch out for parking inspectors around here.

Old School House (Map p120; ☎ 332 7600; oschoolh@hotmail.com; 194 Renfrew St; s/d £38/56) The classiest guesthouse on this city-centre accommodation strip, The Old School House is a small exclusive detached villa with heaps of character. It was getting a major makeover when we visited; of the 17 rooms, the ones in the basement were the first to have benefited from it, exuding a modish, urban cool.

Babbity Bowster (Map p120; ☎ 552 5055; babbitybowster@gofornet.co.uk; 16-18 Blackfriars St; s/d £40/55) Smack bang in the heart of the trendy Merchant City, this lively bar has rooms with sleek furnishings and a minimalist design (No 3 is a good one). Staying here is an excellent Glaswegian experience – the building's design is attributed to Robert Adam. Unusually, room rates do not include breakfast – but that helps keep prices down.

Adelaide's (Map p120; ☎ 248 4970; www.adelaides .co.uk; 209 Bath St; s £30, s/d with en suite £43/50, family r per person £22; ♿) Eight-room Adelaide's is ideal for folk who want to stay in Glasgow's vibrant centre. It's an unusual place – a simple, friendly (and relatively cheap) guesthouse on prestigious Bath St set in an historic church conversion. Tariffs are room only and families are very welcome (there are two family rooms sleeping four or six).

Other recommendations:
Victorian House (Map p120; ☎ 332 0129; www .thevictorian.co.uk; 212 Renfrew St; s/d £32/46, with bathroom £39/60) Solid old refurbished guesthouse, offering value for money.

GLASGOW

GLASGOW

Rab Ha's (Map p120; ☎ 572 0400; www.rabhas.com; 83 Hutcheson St; r £65-75) A Merchant City favourite; atmospheric pub-restaurant with four stylish rooms.

Brunswick Merchant City Hotel (Map p120; ☎ 552 0001; www.brunswickhotel.co.uk; 106-108 Brunswick St; r £65-95) Stylish, inner-city hotel retaining its down-to-earth, friendly character.

EAST END

Craigpark Guest House (Map p118; ☎ 554 4160; www.craigparkguesthouse.com; 33 Circus Dr; s £25-30, d £36-60) Sometimes a B&B just feels good. A classy guesthouse in a top East End location, this large, airy house has modern furnishings and a rustic feel. The meticulous interior reflects the owner's quiet efficiency. Country furniture complements the radiant rooms (particularly No 3), which share bathrooms, although one double has an en-suite shower.

Cathedral House Hotel (Map p120; ☎ 552 3519; www.cathedralhouse.com; 28-32 Cathedral Sq; s £50-55, d £75-85) In the heart of the leafy, dignified East End is a very special property. A 19th-century Scottish baronial–style hotel, complete with turrets and eight individual and beautifully furnished rooms, it's hotels like this (an antithesis to chain hotels) that give Glasgow such a classy edge. Room No 4 or 7 – very spacious corner rooms that include sumptuous king-size beds – are our faves.

WEST END

Belhaven Hotel (Map p118; ☎ 339 3222; www.belhavenhotel.com; 15 Belhaven Tce; s £40-50, d £55-70) Consistently friendly and blessed with some fantastically large rooms, Belhaven has had a sympathetic makeover turning its rooms into lush little oases. A stylish Art-Nouveau red pervades with subtle lighting, a hint of decadence and, in some rooms, almost floor-to-ceiling windows. Make sure you try a pint of the delicious Kingfisher lager in the inhouse bar before you head out.

Kirklee Hotel (Map p118; ☎ 334 5555; kirklee@clara.net; 11 Kensington Gate; s/d £55/72) Want to spoil someone special? In a leafy neighbourhood, Kirklee is a quiet little gem that combines the luxury of a classy hotel with the warmth of staying in someone's home. The rooms are simply gorgeous, beautifully furnished and mostly looking onto lush gardens. For families there is an excellent downstairs room with enormous en suite.

Heritage Hotel (Map p118; ☎ 339 6955;bookings@heritagehotel.fsbusiness.co.uk; 4 Alfred Tce, Great Western Rd; s/d £35/55) A stone's throw from all the action of the West End, this hotel has a very open, airy and bright feel. Rooms are consistently good, but generally those on the 1st and 2nd floor are a bit more spacious and have a better outlook. Rooms are kitted out with pine furniture, and a speck of dirt would feel lonely in the spotless en suites.

Alamo Guest House (Map p120; ☎ 339 2395; www.alamoguesthouse.com; 46 Gray St; s/d from £28/56) The Alamo may sound forbidding, but that couldn't be further from the truth. It's a great place to stay in a leafy spot overlooking Kelvingrove Park, and oozes warmth and sumptuous living. You feel miles from the city at this strategically located place, and yet the city centre and the West End are both a walk away.

SOUTH SIDE

Holly House (Map p118; ☎ 427 5609; www.thehollyhouse.co.uk; 54 Ibrox Tce; r per person £25) If you're seeing a football game at Ibrox (Rangers home ground), this friendly place is very handy. It's an excellent, homely B&B: inside there are four rooms – one double, one family and two singles. All are a very good size and the family room, which is also let out to couples, is simply huge.

Glasgow Guest House (Map p118; ☎ 427 0129; glasgowguesthouse@hotmail.com; 56 Dumbreck Rd; s/d/f £30/48/75) The large, en-suite bedrooms are tastefully furnished with polished wood and the crisp white linen betrays the cleanliness regime. Guests may use the kitchen to prepare evening meals. There's a fair bit of noise – it's literally on a junction of the M77 motorway – although once inside this graceful property, the traffic seems to melt away.

Inn on the Green (Map p118; ☎ 554 0165; www.theinnonthegreen.co.uk; 25 Greenhead St; d £75, Gothic d £90) A charming and unique hotel in a lovely location overlooking Glasgow Green, this inn brings a rustic vibe into the heart of the city. There are two types of rooms – standard and Gothic – and they have similar handcrafted furnishings, but the Gothic are larger and overlook the Green.

Top End
THE CLYDE

City Inn (Map p120; ☎ 240 1002; glasgow.reservations@cityinn.com; Finnieston Quay; r £100; P) Popular with business travellers and ideally located for attractions along the riverfront, rooms are

SOMETHING SPECIAL

SOMETHING SPECIAL

Saint Jude's (Map p120; ☎ 352 8800; www .saintjudes.com; 190 Bath St; r/ste £95/150) This place screams style, and being in Glasgow that mean style with a smile. Just six rooms ensures that Saint Jude's pays personal attention to its guests and injects a lot of TLC into its establishment. Rooms are trendily kitted out in a chic, minimalist design and are very spacious with luxury, king-size beds. Rooms at the front generally tend to be noisier, so if that's a problem request one at the rear of the building. The suite is HUGE – about three times the size of a normal room. The restaurant on-site is the epitome of Glaswegian urban-cool, and dishes are influenced by the Mediterranean and the Far East (try the cha cha monkfish). If you really take to the food, half- and full-board deals are available.

very modern, compact and chock-a-block full of gadgetry (modern conveniences), although not all that spacious, reflecting their functional nature. The better rooms are river facing; call in advance for the best rate.

CITY CENTRE

Quality Hotel (Map p120; ☎ 221 9680; enquiries@ quality-hotels-glasgow.com; 99 Gordon St; s £105, standard/ premier d £115/130; Ⓟ) The Quality Hotel is a down-to-earth, charismatic option right on Central station. Inside everything is in huge proportion, the corridors are endless and the chandeliers baroque. Standard rooms are quite adequate, but premier rooms are only slightly more expensive and are enormous. And here's the bit for the trainspotter – you can get a room that actually overlooks the main passenger area of Central station!

Millennium Hotel (Map p120; ☎ 332 6711; www .millenniumhotels.com; George Sq; standard/club room £175/200, ste £235; Ⓟ) You want central? This is central. Overlooking George Sq, the massive Victorian building constructed for the Tobacco Lords is now a top luxury hotel blessed with helpful and attentive staff. Rooms that overlook George Sq with their floor-to-ceiling windows are best, but if you find that a bit noisy (although windows do have double glazing) rooms towards the rear of the hotel are much quieter.

Malmaison (Map p120; ☎ 572 1000; www.mal maison.com; 278 West George St; standard r Fri-Sun £99, standard r Mon-Thu £135, ste £195) Heavenly Malmaison is just so…now daaaahling. Cutting-edge urban living at its best, this sassy sister of hospitality is super slinky and a cornerstone of faith in Glaswegian accommodation. Styling rooms with their moody lighting have a dark, brooding tone, plush furnishings and a designer touch.

WEST END

One Devonshire Gardens (Map p118; ☎ 339 2001; www.onedevonshiregardens.com; 1 Devonshire Gardens; standard/superior r £135/190, mews ste £925; Ⓟ) The favoured hotel for the rich and famous and the patriarch of sophistication and comfort, this is the top place to stay in Glasgow – possibly the country. A study in elegance, it's sumptuously decorated and occupies three classical terrace houses. There are 35 rooms, all individually furnished, and two fine restaurants are on-site.

EATING

Glasgow is the best place to eat in Scotland, with an excellent range of eateries. The West End is the culinary centre of the city. Many Glasgow restaurants post offers on the Internet (changing daily) at **5pm.co.uk** (www.5pm.co.uk). Note also that pubs and bars are always a good lunchtime option.

City Centre
BUDGET

Café Lava (Map p120; ☎ 553 1123; 24 St Andrew's St; dishes £1.50-4.50; ☼ 8am-6pm Mon-Fri, 10am-5pm Sat & Sun) Everyone wants to live next door to a café like this. The understated menu here delivers delicious home cooking. Try the Stornaway black pudding and eggs Benedict. The coffee is some of the best around town, and as for the cookies and those rich, rich brownies… It's a little off the beaten track, but well worth hunting out.

Where the Monkey Sleeps (Map p120; ☎ 226 3406; 182 West Regent St; dishes £2-6; ☼ 7am-5pm Mon-Fri, 10am-6pm Sat) This funky little number in the middle of the business district is just what you need to get away from the ubiquitous coffee chains. Laid-back and a little bohemian, the bagels and *paninis*, with names like maverick or renegade, are highlights as are some very inventive dishes, such as the bacon and polish sausage chowder.

Wee Curry Shop (Map p120; ☎ 353 0777; 7 Buccleuch St; 2-course lunch £4.75, dinner mains £7; ☯ lunch Mon-Sat, dinner daily) Some of the best home-cooked curries you're likely to taste outside India can be found here. It's wise to book – it's a snug place with a big reputation, a limited menu and a sensational-value two-course lunch.

Also recommended:

Willow Tea Rooms (Map p120; ☎ 332 0521; 217 Sauchiehall St; light meals £4-6; ☯ 9am-4.30pm Mon-Sat, 11am-4.30pm Sun) Designed by Charles Rennie Mackintosh in 1904; at lunch and tea-time the queues can extend into the shop downstairs. There's a second **branch** (Map p120; ☎ 204 5242; 97 Buchanan St).

Noodle Bar (Map p120; ☎ 333 1883; 482 Sauchiehall St; dishes £3.50-6; ☯ noon-4am) For large doses of late-night noodles with oodles of different combinations.

MIDRANGE

Bar 91 (Map p120; ☎ 552 5211; 91 Candleriggs; mains £5-7; ☯ noon-9pm Mon-Thu, to 6pm Fri-Sun, bar until midnight daily) By day this happy, buzzy bar serves excellent meals, far better than average pub food. Tortillas, salads, pasta and fish cakes are among the many tasty offerings, and in summer tables spill out onto the sidewalk – ideal for some people-watching of the bold and the beautiful.

Italian Kitchen (Map p120; ☎ 572 1472; 64 Ingram St; mains £8; ☯ lunch & dinner) If you ever needed proof that simplicity and fresh ingredients are the key to Italian cooking – here it is. Dishing out pasta, pizza and salads, the meals are fresh, vibrant and a taste sensation. Chrome fittings, large windows and exposed stone make for a modern, airy dining experience, while wall friezes of tomatoes, peppers and figs point to the secret of its success.

Centre for Contemporary Arts Café (Map p120; ☎ 332 7959; 350 Sauchiehall St; light meals £4-10; ☯ 9am-9pm Tue-Thu, to 10pm Fri & Sat) This lovely, minimalist-style open café is a trendy dining experience and a popular meeting spot. The skylight-roof makes you feel as though you're dining outdoors. Food highlights include the soups, pasta dishes, and fish cakes with avocado and dill relish.

West Regent St Bistro (Map p120; ☎ 331 0303; 48 West Regent St; starters £4, mains £9; ☯ noon-10pm) Chic, stylishly laid-back and sleek in design, this bistro serves big wholesome portions of food at very reasonable prices. Popular with the after-work crowd between 4pm and 7pm sipping cocktails before dinner, avoid this time and come later to indulge in some seriously fine food. During lunch pick up a gourmet *panini* or sandwich for £6.

Café Gandolfi (Map p120; ☎ 552 6813; 64 Albion St; mains £7-12; ☯ 9am-11.30pm Mon-Sat, noon-11.30pm Sun) In the fashionable Merchant City, this café was once part of the old cheese market. It's been pulling in the punters for over 20 years, and packs an interesting clientele: die-hard Gandolfers, the upwardly mobile and tourists. It's an excellent, friendly bistro and upmarket coffee shop – very much the place to be seen. Book a Tim Stead–designed, medieval-looking table in advance for well-prepared Scottish and Continental food.

Artà (Map p120; ☎ 552 2101; 13 Walls St; tapas £4-6, mains £10-14; ☯ closed Mon & Tue) If only every city had an Artà. Very much a favourite, this extraordinary hacienda-style place has to be seen to be believed. Eat on the mock-baroque, Spanish-style ground floor among the drinking crowd, or the elegant upstairs restaurant while kicking back to R & B or soul tunes. The Mediterranean-inspired menu has vegetarian options. All dishes are half-price Sunday to Thursday evening.

Arisaig (Map p120; ☎ 204 5399; 140 St Vincent St; starters £5-8, mains £11-17; ☯ lunch & dinner) Candle-light, crisp linen, an open kitchen and calming landscape pictures on the walls combine to create a soothing, relaxed dining atmos-

---

SOMETHING SPECIAL

Brutti Ma Buoni (Map p120; ☎ 552 0001; 106 Brunswick St; mains £5-9; ☯ noon-9pm Mon-Sat, to 8pm Sun) If you like dining in a place that has a sense of fun, Brutti delivers – it's the antithesis of some of the pretentious places around the Merchant City. With dishes such as 'ugly but good' pizza and 'angry or peaceful' prawns, Brutti's menu draws a smile for its quirkiness and its prices. The Italian and Spanish influences give rise to tapas-like servings or full-blown meals, which are imaginative, fresh and frankly delicious. The 'brutti' is a misshapen version of a thin-bread Italian pizza, or try the bruschetta (especially with spicy chorizo, feta and rocket). Baguettes, pasta, fish and prawn dishes also feature on the menu. The funky surrounds are laid-back and friendly, while service is efficient. One of our favourite venues in Glasgow, it's great for a bite or just a drink.

phere in this classy, airy restaurant. Dishes are divided into The Sea and The Land and are sourced from around the country, like grilled Shetland monkfish or Ayrshire lamb cutlets. This place is also highly regarded for its inventive vegetarian dishes that include deep-fried beetroot and nettle cake.

Also recommended:

Paperino's (Map p120; ☎ 332 3800; 283 Sauchiehall St; pizza & pasta dishes £8; ☺ lunch & dinner) Great little Italian diner, with booth seating ideal for couples; early evening three-course meal £10.

Loon Fung (Map p120; ☎ 332 1240; 417 Sauchiehall St; mains £8.50-12.50; ☺ lunch & dinner) One of the best Chinese restaurants in town; pre-theatre 2-course meal is £8.

Red Onion (Map p120; ☎ 221 6000; 257 West Campbell St; starters £6, mains £8-12; ☺ 9am-11pm) An eclectic, Asian-influenced menu drives the dining at this impressive restaurant.

West End

Just off Byres Rd, on the east side, Ashton Lane is packed with places to eat, including some of Glasgow's best restaurants.

BUDGET

Moka (Map p118; ☎ 337 1642; 219 Byres Rd; lunch £2.50-4.50; ☺ 7.15am-9pm Mon-Sat, 9am-9pm Sun) If you're looking for lunch in the West End, drop into Moka where you can sit in or take away (to the nearby Botanic Gardens, for example). Sarnies, *paninis*, baguettes and salads are all on offer, and fillings are fresh and inventive. Try the Atomic – spicy pepperoni, onion, cheddar and a splash of Tabasco on a mini pizza. It's also good for vegetarians, and there are freshly squeezed juices available.

Monster Mash (Map p118; ☎ 339 3666; 41 Byres Rd; mains £5-6.50; ☺ breakfast, lunch & dinner) A greasy spoon, but not as you know it! An upmarket, cheery, retro café, Monster Mash deals out delicious Crombie sausages, massive proportions of mash and your choice of gravy. Wash it all down with a Newcastle Brown Ale (remember those?). With shepherd's pie and haggis, neeps and tatties (haggis, mashed turnip and mashed potato) also featuring, this is comfort food at its very best.

MIDRANGE

On the west side of Byres Rd, directly across from Ashton Lane, is Ruthven Lane. Here and nearby are a number of fine places to eat. Those staying in the vicinity of Kel-

vingrove Park will find a scattering of good restaurants on or around Gibson St and Great Western Rd.

Oran Mor Brasserie & Conservatory (Map p118; ☎ 357 6200; cnr Byres & Great Western Rds; brasserie mains £15-22, conservatory mains £7-13; ☺ lunch & dinner) This temple to Scottish dining and drinking is a superb new venue in an old church. Giving new meaning to the word 'conversion', the brasserie pumps out ambitious and high-quality meals in a dark, Mackintosh-inspired space. There are also cheaper bistro-style meals, such as *Cullen skink* (soup made with smoked haddock, potato, onion and milk) or steak and gravy pie, and more relaxed dining in the conservatory, adjoining the main bar (see p138).

Wee Curry Shop (Map p118; ☎ 357 5280; 29 Ashton Lane; dinner mains £9; ☺ lunch & dinner) A bit classier and more pricey than its city-centre cousin, Wee Curry, upstairs at Jinty McGuintys, is very big on quality home-cooked Indian food. The curries are exceptional and a window seat gives people-watching potential over Ashton Lane. Indian tapas-style dishes (£3) are available at lunchtime.

Stravaigin II (Map p118; ☎ 334 7165; 8 Ruthven Lane; starters £5.50, mains £9-18; ☺ lunch & dinner) Clinking wine glasses and cracking mussel shells greet patrons at this classy eatery. It boasts the best scotch beef burgers (it also does ostrich burgers) on a chargrilled menu that also features roast shark gumbo and a range of inventive taste trips, such as lime and chilli'd lamb *empanadas*. Two-course, pre-theatre meals are great value at £12.

Bay Tree Café (Map p120; ☎ 334 5898; 403 Great Western Rd; mains £6-9; ☺ 9.30am-10pm Mon-Sat, to 9pm Sun) This mostly vegetarian café is excellent value. It has smiling staff, filling mains (mostly Middle Eastern and Greek), generous salads and a good range of hot drinks. The café is famous for its all-day Sunday brunch, including vegetarian burger, tattie scone, mushrooms, beans and tomato. It also serves a vegan breakfast. Good people-watching potential, too.

Bothy (Map p118; ☎ 334 4040; 11 Ruthven Lane; lunch/dinner mains £7/10, 3-courses £13.50; ☺ noon-10pm) A bothy is not normally the most comfortable of abodes, but this West End newbie pays little heed to this tradition boasting a combo of modern design and comfy retro furnishings. It also blows apart the myth that Scottish food is stodgy and uninteresting. The Bothy dishes out traditional, home-style fare – such as stovies, pot roast and steak pie – that will tempt most palates with fresh wholesome dishes delivering a uniquely Scottish flavour.

Loft (Map p118; ☎ 341 1234; Ashton Lane; mains £7; ⊗ noon–10pm) The Loft is a huge retro space with an Art-Deco bar plonked in the centre. With heaps of room – furnishings are generously spread out (loads of chunky leather couches and right angles) – it's popular with families, and offers pizza and pasta dishes for £5 from 4pm to 6.30pm Monday to Thursday. If you're catching a film at the cinema downstairs, it's the ideal spot for a pre-show bite or drink.

TOP END

Ubiquitous Chip (Map p118; ☎ 334 5007; 12 Ashton Lane; 2-/3-course dinner £34/39; ⊗ lunch & dinner) The original champion of Scottish produce, this restaurant has won lots of awards for its excellent Scottish cuisine, seafood and game dishes, and for its lengthy wine list. Set among potted plants of arboreal proportions, this is an excellent place for a night out and an ideal place to treat that someone special. There's a cheaper restaurant here, **Upstairs at the Chip** (mains £10), where the menu follows in the tradition of creativity and top-notch ingredients.

Buttery (Map p120; ☎ 221 8188; 652 Argyle St; 2-/3-course dinner £34/38; ⊗ lunch Tue-Fri, dinner Tue-Sat) This well-respected, elegant restaurant is just west of the M8. Although it's surrounded by grim, grey, tower-block flats (get a taxi here or drive), it's a top, Victorian-era restaurant offering fine dining among crisp tablecloths and oak panelling, with a classy clientele to match. The menu is a combination of seasonal Scottish and British organic produce.

Stravaigin (Map p120; ☎ 334 2665; 28 Gibson St; 2-course dinner £23; ⊗ lunch Fri-Sun, dinner Tue-Sun) Stravaigin is a serious foodie's delight, with a menu constantly pushing the boundaries of originality and offering creative culinary excellence. There's a buzzing bar upstairs (open daily and offering simpler food) and a cool contemporary dining space in the basement with booth seating, and helpful, laid-back waiting-staff to assist in deciphering the audacious menu.

DRINKING

Some of Scotland's best nightlife is found in the din and sometimes roar of Glasgow's pubs and bars. There are as many different styles of bar as there are punters to guzzle in them; a month of solid drinking wouldn't get you past the halfway mark.

City Centre
TRADITIONAL PUBS

Glasgow is simply laden with traditional pubs exuding an old-world character.

Drum & Monkey (Map p120; ☎ 221 6636; 93-95 St Vincent St) Jazz fans can get their fix on Sunday afternoon; the rest of the week jazz records accompany the dark wood and marble columns of this attractive drinking emporium, peppered with church pews and leather lounge chairs. Its cosy and relaxing vibe makes you want to curl up in an armchair with a pint for the afternoon.

Horse Shoe (Map p120; ☎ 221 3051; 17 Drury St) This legendary city pub and popular meeting place dates from the late 19th century and is largely unchanged. It has the longest continuous bar in the UK, but its main attraction is what's served over it – real ale and good food. Upstairs in the lounge are the best-value three-course lunches (£3.20) in town.

Scotia (Map p120; ☎ 552 8681; 112 Stockwell St) Drinks have been poured down throats at Scotia, Glasgow's oldest pub, since 1792. And while the last good airing feels like it happened back in the mid-1850s, Scotia's cheery charm outweighs the grungy atmosphere. There's an open session on Saturday – musos welcome.

Blackfriars (Map p120; ☎ 552 5924; 36 Bell St) Merchant City's most relaxed and atmospheric pub, Blackfriars' friendly staff and chilled-out house make it special. Importantly, you don't have to ask – it's a cask. There's a seating area with large windows that are great for people-watching. Saturday night is a comedy fest.

Babbity Bowster (Map p120; ☎ 552 5055; 16-18 Blackfriars St) Babbity Bowster has a Continental feel and is perfect for a quiet daytime drink, particularly in the adjoining beer garden. There's also accommodation here (see p131). The interior has a classy vibe, with a suit crowd to match on weekday evenings. There's music on Saturday night, usually of the folky-fiddler variety.

BARS

Artà (Map p120; ☎ 552 2101; 13-19 Walls St; ⊗ until 3am) As its door slides open, Artà's opulent, cavernous candle-lit interior is exposed. Floor-to-ceiling velvet, red curtains reveal a staircase to the tapas bar and restaurant above (p134) in a show of decadence that the Romans would have appreciated. This mock baroque-cum-Mediterranean showpiece is a must-see, but stay for at least one drink as it's a relaxed, chilled place with a mixed crowd. There's live music on weekends. Aimed at the pre-clubbing crowd, entry may set you back £7 after 10pm on weekends.

Corinthian (Map p120; ☎ 552 1101; 191 Ingram St) A breathtaking domed ceiling and majestic chandeliers make Corinthian an awesome venue, and it's recently been refurbished giving it a very square countenance in a very circular interior. Originally a bank and later Glasgow's High Court, this regal building also houses a plush club, downstairs in old court cells, which pumps out funk, and club classics on Fridays and Saturdays. There's a strict dress code. Don't miss the half-price cocktails on Friday and Saturday in the cocktail lounge. It also has Glasgow's only latenight piano bar, open until 3am nightly.

Bloc (Map p120; ☎ 574 6066; 117 Bath St) A top basement bar, Bloc is a great spot to drink with friends. A happy, buzzing little place, it's attitude-free and welcomes everyone. There's plenty of wood, retro furnishings and cushioned ledges. Sitting at the bar is a good option and there are excellent nibbles – try the chilli beef nachos. There are regular bands and DJs, and live jazz on Saturday – the cool beats round off the drinking experience.

Bar 10 (Map p120; ☎ 572 1448; 10 Mitchell Lane) A tiny city treasure that will cause the canny

Glasgow drinker to give you a knowing glance if you mention its name. As laidback as you could ask in a hip city bar, the friendly, tuned-in staff complete the happy picture. It transforms from a quiet daytime bar to a happening weekend pub on Friday and Saturday nights.

Nice 'n' Sleazy (Map p120; ☎ 333 9637; 421 Sauchiehall St) Close to the Glasgow School of Art, students come here to discuss primers, Duchamp and Nietzsche over some of Glasgow's cheapest drinks. With 1970s retro décor, relaxed atmosphere and great menu for under a fiver, it's a top spot to kick back and relish the tunes of the city's freshest live music.

Pivo Pivo (Map p120; ☎ 564 8100; 15 Waterloo St) A cavernous downstairs beer hall with a chilled atmosphere and beers aplenty – 100 from 32 different countries to be exact. Add to that an impressive array of vodka and schnapps, and it may be a while before you see daylight. Monday night is quiz night.

Arches (Map p120; ☎ 565 1035; 253 Argyle St) A one-stop culture/entertainment fix, this place doubles as a theatre showing contemporary, avant-garde productions and there's also a club (p139). The hotel-like entrance belies the deep interior, which make you feel as though you've discovered Hades' bohemian underworld. The crowd is mixed – hiking boots are as welcome as Versace.

Waxy O'Connors (Map p120; ☎ 354 5154; 46 West George St) If you've been trying to avoid those acid flashbacks, steer clear of Waxy

---

THE GLESCA PATOIS John McKenna

Glasgow enjoys a rich local dialect (read: bloody hard to understand) and a knowledge of the vernacular will help you know when to stand and chat and when to run.

Unusually, for Scotland, the pub is the focal point of social life and there may be some football supporters in the crowd. The 'Bhoys' (Celtic football club) wear green colours and are traditionally supported by the 'Tims' (Catholics). The 'Gers' (Rangers football club) wear blue and are the 'Huns' (Protestant) team. Football can be a touchy subject in Glasgow. Tell anyone who asks that you're a 'Jags' (Partick Thistle) supporter and you're on neutral ground. The comedian Billy Connolly, who grew up in Partick, claims that he always thought the full team name was 'Partick Thistle Nil'.

When males spot a *wee stoater* (good-looking young woman) in the bar, they might be inclined to try their 'patter' (witty chat) on her. Should her boyfriend, 'the Big Yin', arrive unexpectedly, and offer to *mollocate, wanner* or *stiffen* the would-be Lothario, or alternatively to give him his *heid in your hauns* (head in your hands), then violence is probably imminent.

At that point it's best to *shoot the crow* (go) before a *stooshie* (brawl) develops and, in future, to give that particular pub the *body swerve* (a wide berth).

However, Glaswegians are very friendly to travellers. If you refer to their city as *Glesca,* and never *Glasgie,* they may even mistake you for a local.

O'Connors. This labyrinthine maze of six bars on three levels (you may not emerge for days), including the inspiringly named Murphy's Bar, is an Escher drawing brought to life. Sadly, it's also an Irish-themed bar, but even that doesn't ruin the surreal fun.

Moskito (Map p120; ☎ 331 1777; 200 Bath St) A classic Bath St basement bar, Moskito is just the place to kick back and get boozed up. Let the inhouse DJs mellow you out with their deep beats and electronica. Grab the pool table if all this lying about drinking is getting too much.

Mojama (Map p120; ☎ 332 4760; Sauchiehall St) Very retro and very futuristic at the same time, it's worth popping your head into this *Jetsons*-like place to curl up nursing a drink in the blood-red interior. And take advantage of its incredible food offers – everything under £2 before 7pm. On Monday it's wannabee DJs who spin their own tracks.

Edge (Map p120; ☎ 552 1740; 57 Cochrane St) With its brilliant location right on the edge of George Sq and its up-tempo beat, this place is the perfect pre-clubbing venue. It combines exposed stone walls with polished wood and funky, chunky furniture. Ideal for groups and a great spot to get the evening started.

West End
TRADITIONAL PUBS
Uisge Beatha (Map p120; ☎ 564 1596; 232-246 Woodlands Rd) If you enjoy a drink among dead things, you'll love Uisge Beatha (Gaelic for whisky, literally 'water of life'). This mishmash of church pews, stuffed animal heads and portraits of depressed nobility (the Maggie mannequin is our favourite) is patrolled by Andy Capp–like characters during the day and students at night. With 100 whiskies and four quirky rooms to choose from, this unique pub is one of Glasgow's best – an antidote to style bars.

Aragon Bar (Map p118; 131 Byers Rd) A traditional bar located in this trendy part of town, with changing guest ales and board games behind the bar for those lazy afternoons. There's also a decent wine selection.

BARS
Oran Mor Brasserie & Conservatory (Map p118; ☎ 357 6200; cnr Byres & Great Western Rds) Now some may be a little uncomfortable with the thought of drinking in a church. But we say – the lord giveth. Praise be and let's give thanks – a converted church and an almighty one

at that is now a new bar, eating venue (see p135) and club/venue. The bar feels like it's been here for years – all wood and thick, exposed stone giving it warmth and a celestial air. There's an excellent array of whiskies and Arran Blond ale on tap. The only thing missing is holy water on your way in.

Jinty McGuinty's (Map p118; ☎ 339 0747; 23-29 Ashton Lane) This is a popular Irish theme pub with unusual booth seating and a literary hall of fame, with a spacious and popular beer garden that often spills into secluded Ashton Lane in summer.

Brel (Map p118; ☎ 342 4966; 39 Ashton Lane) A popular watering hole on Ashton Lane, the name may be pretentious (it's named after a famous – famous in Belgium – musician), as are the Belgian beers, but fortunately Brel's clientele – mainly students – keeps it down to earth and informal. There's a conservatory out the back so you can pretend you're sitting outside when its raining, and when the sun does peek through there's a beer garden, and tables on the lane out the front for some top people-perving.

Vodka Wodka (Map p118; ☎ 341 0669; 31 Ashton Lane; cocktails £3.50) This watering hole is every vodka drinker's dream, with more varieties of the stealthy poison than you could possibly conquer in one sitting. It attracts the type of crowd trying to do just that.

ENTERTAINMENT
Glasgow is Scotland's entertainment city, from classical music, fine theatres and ballet, to cracking nightclubs pumping out cheesy chart tunes or the latest dance-music phenomenon, and contemporary Scottish bands at the cutting edge of modern music.

To tap into your scene, check out the *List* (www.list.co.uk), an invaluable fortnightly events guide available at newsagents and bookshops. If you plan to spend any time in the city, pick up a copy of *Itchy* (£3.50), a handy pocket-sized entertainment guide, available at bookshops. The *Herald* and the *Evening Times* newspapers list events happening around the city. Pick up a copy of the *Gig Guide* (www.gigguide.co.uk), published monthly and available free in most pubs and venues for the latest on music gigs.

For theatre tickets book directly with the venue. For concerts, a useful booking centre is **Tickets Scotland** (☎ 204 5151, 0870 220 1116; www.tickets-scotland.com; 239 Argyle St).

Clubs

Glasgow has one of Britain's biggest clubbing scenes attracting style-cats from afar. Glaswegians usually hit clubs after the pubs have closed, so many clubs offer discounted admission and cheaper drinks if you go before 11pm. Entry costs £3 to £7 (up to £10 for bigger venues), although bars often hand out free passes. Most clubs close around 3am.

Arches (Map p120; ☎ 565 1023; Argyle St) With a capacity of 2000 people and a design based around hundreds of arches slammed together, this venue is a must for funk and hip-hop freaks. It is one of the city's biggest clubs pulling top DJs, and you'll also hear some of the UK's up-and-coming turntable spinners. It's located off Jamaica St.

Cathouse (Map p120; ☎ 248 6606; 15 Union St; ☉ Thu-Sun) Don the ghostly war paint, dust off the steel caps and rejoin your Goth brethren at the three-level Cathouse, Glasgow's top indie and alternative venue. It has two dance floors: upstairs is pretty intense with lots of metal and hard rock, downstairs is a little less scary if you're not keen on moshing.

MAS (Map p120; ☎ 221 6381; 29 Royal Exchange Sq; ☉ Thu-Tue) Run by the same folk as the achingly cool **Republic Biere Halle** (☎ 204 0706; 9 Gordon St), with its long room, mood lighting and mirrors, MAS is less style obsessed and instead puts on Glasgow's best hard house (Thursday's 'Mirrorbraw' is huge). It has a party vibe, quality DJs and thumping weekends with plenty of beautiful people.

GAY & LESBIAN GLASGOW

Glasgow has a vibrant gay scene, with the gay quarter found in and around the Merchant City (particularly Virginia, Wilson and Glassford Sts). The city's gay community has a reputation for being very friendly.

To get the lowdown, the best contact for gay and lesbian travellers is the **Glasgow LGBT Centre** (Map p120; ☎ 221 7203; www.glgbt.org.uk; 11 Dixon St; ☉ 10am-midnight) at the back of St Enoch Sq. It has a bulletin board with information about activities and events, as well as personal ads; there's also a bar here. For confidential advice or help try the **Gay & Lesbian switchboard** (☎ 332 8372). See also the Gay & Lesbian section (p437) in the Directory.

Spa 19 (Map p120; ☎ 572 0347; 2nd fl, 19 Dixon St; admission £9; ☉ noon-10pm Sun-Fri, to 4am Sat) is an excellent gay health centre, with a small gym, sauna and Jacuzzi, TV lounge, café and cyber centre for firing off emails.

To tap into the scene, check out the *List*, the free *Scots Gay* magazine and the **GayScotland .com website** (www.gayscotland.com/glasgow/glasgow_index.htm).

Many straight clubs and bars have gay and lesbian nights, such as the cheesy **Allure@The Tunnel** (Map p120; ☎ 204 1000; 84 Mitchell St; admission £3; ☉ 11pm-3am) on Wednesday.

The following are just a selection of gay and lesbian pubs and clubs in the city.

Waterloo Bar (Map p120; ☎ 229 5891; 306 Argyle St) This is a traditional place and Scotland's oldest gay bar. It attracts punters of all ages. It's very friendly and, with a large group of regulars, a good place to meet people.

Polo Lounge (Map p120; ☎ 553 1221; 84 Wilson St; ☉ 5pm-1am Mon-Thu, to 3am Fri-Sun) Staff claim 'the city's best talent' is found here; a quick glance at the many glamour pusses – male and female – proves their claim. The downstairs club is packed on weekends; just the main bars open on other nights.

Moda (Map p120; ☎ 553 2553; cnr Virginia & Wilson Sts; ☉ 5pm-late) Blonde wood and fake tan are the chief attributes of Moda, a place where beautiful folk strike a pose over daytime drinks, or recuperate before returning to the Polo Lounge next door or going downmarket at Delmonica's.

Delmonica's (Map p120; ☎ 552 4803; 68 Virginia St) Metres from the Polo Lounge, Delmonica's is a world away, with its predatorial feeling of people on the pull. It's packed on weekday evenings. Friday night is glam night with chart tunes and Sunday is a karaoke free-for-all.

Revolver (Map p120; ☎ 553 2456; 6a John St) Hip little Revolver, downstairs on cosmopolitan John St, sports a relaxed crowd and, crucially, a free jukebox.

Bennet's (Map p120; ☎ 552 5761; www.bennets.co.uk; 90 Glassford St) Glasgow's longest-running gay club, has three bars over two levels and cranks out tunes from hard house to cheesy chart faves from Wednesday to Sunday.

If you're in Glasgow in autumn check out **Glasgay** (☎ 334 7126; www.glasgay.co.uk), a gay performing arts festival, held around October/November each year.

Tunnel (Map p120; ☎ 204 1000; 84 Mitchell St) This is a good venue to hear big-name DJs, such as Paul Oakenfold and Judge Jules; Wednesday night is the city's biggest gay night, 'Allure' (see the boxed text, p139), Friday is for house, hip-hop and soul rock worshippers, while Saturday is devoted to funky tunes and disco – something for everyone.

Sub Club (☎ 248 4600; 22 Jamaica St) Offering up hardcore beats (not for those with sensi-

tive hearing) to a student crowd, Sub Club, with its claustrophobic, last-one-in vibe, is not for those faint of heart. This is serious clubbing, and Sunday night is becoming a favourite on the clubbing scene.

Cleopatra's (Map p118; ☎ 334 0560; cnr Great Western Rd & Bank St; ◷ Wed-Sun) Clatty Pats in the West End gets packed; it's pretty grungy, but a lot of fun, and best enjoyed in a crowd. And no, that's not chewing gum making your shoes stick to the floor.

SCOTLAND'S LIVE-MUSIC CAPITAL Bryan McRitchie (Edinburgh songwriter)

Year after year, touring musicians, artists and travellers alike name Glasgow as one of their favourite cities in the world to enjoy live music. See opposite for a list of venues around the city.

As much of Glasgow's character is encapsulated within the soul and humour of its inhabitants, the main reason for the city's musical success lies within its audience and the musical community it has bred and nurtured for years. Glaswegians laugh together, cry together and sing together, and it is their passion and intensity, coupled with an almost intrinsic understanding and love of music, that makes the live-music experience in Glasgow unique.

The growing popularity of Scottish bands and artists, like Travis, Idlewild, Franz Ferdinand, Teenage Fanclub, Mogwai, Texas, KT Tunstall, Belle and Sebastian, Mylo and the adopted Snow Patrol (to name but a few), make it very difficult to see any of these acts without prebooking tickets, usually several months in advance. However, with such a strong musical heritage, it is inevitable that Glasgow and its surrounding communities consistently produce new, potent acts to an enthusiastic audience.

Odeon Beat Club, the latest pretenders to Glasgow's live-music crown, are currently cresting on their wave of guitar-propelled melodic snapshots on modern-day life. In the process they are building a persuasive live reputation and a considerable fan base, as are Sneak Attack Tigers, who adopt a heavier assault on their own battered prose. Biffy Clyro, Aereogramme and Terra Diablo all serve up interestingly distinct slices of Glaswegian rock. Sons and Daughters blend blues, country and folk with intense passion and anger, while Viva Stereo dabble in electro guitar noise beat confusion. My Latest Novel are, by contrast, buoyant and weightless, floating on distinctive melodies and pop aesthetics.

Of course, not all of the bands that haunt the venues of Glasgow originate from the west coast. Edinburgh continues to produce a very high quality of local artists, musicians and acts. Ballboy are plying a fine line in intelligently crafted paeans wrapped in a strong pop sensibility, while X-Tigers take a harder, more jagged approach, combining melody with a surging intensity and charisma. Degrassi leak angularity and melody with a hard-core subtlety that comes enjoyably close to implosion, while the combination of break beats, dirty blues and traditional folk combine to make Mystery Juice an exceptional and original live experience. Further down the coast from the capital, Hobotalk have found an idyllic country inflection that tiptoes sensitively through lost love's last whispers.

From across the Firth of Forth in Fife, James Yorkston and the Athletes peddle a beautifully restrained nu-folk vibe, which is both consuming and hypnotic. In a similar aesthetic but with a more psychedelic trajectory, Lone Pigeon treads a delicate path through his fragile tales of life and loss.

On any given night you may find your breath taken by a wave of voices as the audience spontaneously harmonises with an artist on a chorus, a song or even, on special nights, an entire show. Maybe it's the spine-tingling, hear-a-pin-drop silence that the audience respectfully affords an artist as they perform a quiet, acoustic or delicate piece. Whatever the occasion, the band or the venue, Glasgow is, by proxy of its inhabitants, a music city, an intricate web of emotions and poetry, passion and melody, and most of all honesty and soul.

Live Music

Glasgow has long been regarded as the centre of Scotland's live-music scene (see opposite).

King Tut's Wah Wah Hut (Map p120; ☎ 221 5279; www.kingtuts.co.uk; 272a St Vincent St) One of the city's premier live-music pub venues, the excellent King Tut's hosts bands every night of the week. Oasis were signed after playing here.

Two bars to see the best, and worst, of Glasgow's newest bands are **Brunswick Cellars** (Map p120; ☎ 332 9329; 239 Sauchiehall St) and the **Halt Bar** (Map p120; ☎ 352 9996; 160 Woodlands Rd), which is a popular university pub that hasn't been tarted up.

Other recommendations:

13th Note Cafe (Map p120; ☎ 553 1638; 50-60 King St)

ABC (Map p120; ☎ 0870 903 3444; www.abcglasgow .com; 300 Sauchiehall St) Former cinema, new venue; medium- to large-size acts.

Barfly (Map p120; ☎ 0870 907 0999; www.barflyclub .com; 260 Clyde St)

Barrowland (Map p120; ☎ 552 4601; www.glasgow -barrowland.com; 244 Gallowgate) An exceptional old dancehall catering for some of the larger acts that visit the city.

Clyde Auditorium (Map p120; ☎ 0870 040 4000; www.secc.co.uk) Also known as the Armadillo because of its bizarre shape, adjoins SECC, and caters for big national and international acts.

Glasgow Academy (Map p120; ☎ 418 3000; www .glasgow-academy.co.uk; 121 Eglinton St)

Mono (Map p120; ☎ 553 2400; www.stereomono.info; 12 Kings Crt, King St) Stereo's sister venue: small- to medium-size acts.

Nice 'n' Sleazy (Map p120; ☎ 333 0900; 421 Sauchiehall St) Nurturing much of Glasgow's alternative music scene.

SECC (Map p120; ☎ 0870 040 4000; www.secc.co.uk; Finnieston Quay) Adjoins Clyde Auditorium, and hosts major national and international acts.

Stereo (Map p120; ☎ 576 5018; www.stereomono.info; 12-14 Kelvinhaugh St)

Cinemas

Glasgow Film Theatre (Map p120; ☎ 332 8128; www.gft.org.uk; 12 Rose St; adult/concession £4.50/3.50) The two-screen Glasgow Film Theatre, off Sauchiehall St, screens arthouse cinema and classics.

Odeon Renfield Street (Map p120; ☎ 0870 505 0007; 56 Renfield St; adult/concession £5.50/3.50) The nine-screen Odeon Renfield Street shows mainstream films.

Theatres & Concert Halls

Theatre Royal (Map p120; ☎ 332 3321; www.theatre royalglasgow.com; 282 Hope St) This is the home of Scottish Opera, and the Scottish Ballet often has performances here. Ask about standby tickets if you'll be in town for a few days.

Glasgow Royal Concert Hall (Map p120; ☎ 353 8080; www.grch.com; 2 Sauchiehall St) A feast of classical music is showcased at this concert hall, the modern home of the Royal Scottish National Orchestra.

King's Theatre (Map p120; ☎ 240 1300; www .kings-glasgow.co.uk; 297 Bath St) This theatre hosts mainly musicals; on rare occasions there are variety shows, pantomimes and comedies.

Citizens' Theatre (Map p120; ☎ 429 0022; www .citz.co.uk; 119 Gorbals St) This is one of the top theatres in Scotland and it's well worth trying to catch a performance here.

Tron Theatre (Map p120; ☎ 552 4267; www.tron .co.uk; 63 Trongate; ticket sales 10am-6pm Mon-Sat) Tron Theatre stages contemporary Scottish and international performances. There's also a good café.

Centre for Contemporary Arts (Map p120; ☎ 352 4900; www.cca-glasgow.com; 350 Sauchiehall St) After a £10-million facelift, this is a shmick venue making terrific use of space and light. It showcases the visual and performing arts, including movies, talks and galleries.

Tramway (Map p118; ☎ 422 2023; 25 Albert Dr) This theatre and exhibition space attracts cutting-edge theatrical groups, the visual and performing arts, and a varied range of artistic exhibitions.

Sport

Two football clubs dominate the sporting scene in Scotland, having vastly more resources than other clubs and a long history (and rivalry). This rivalry is also along partisan lines, with Rangers representing Protestant supporters, and Celtic, of course, Catholic.

Celtic Football Club (☎ 0845 671 1888; www.celticfc .co.uk; Celtic Park, Parkhead; tickets £15-24) Has a 60,832-seat stadium.

Rangers Football Club (☎ 0870 600 1972; www .rangers.co.uk; Ibrox Stadium, 150 Edmiston Dr; tickets £10-£22) Tours of the stadium and trophy room run three times daily Monday and Friday, once on Saturday (tours £6/5 per adult/child). Rangers' stadium holds 50,500 seats.

GLASGOW

SHOPPING

Boasting the UK's largest retail contingency outside London, Glasgow is a shopaholic's paradise.

Fashion junkies can procure relief at **Versace** (☎ 552 6510) and **Armani** (☎ 552 2277) in the stylish **Italian Centre** (Map p120; John St). Alternatively, **Designer Exchange** (☎ 221 6898; 3 Royal Exchange Ct) stocks cheaper samples and re-sale designer labels. Trendy traders litter the pedestrian malls of Sauchiehall and Buchanan Sts. Try **Buchanan Galleries** (☎ 332 4353; www .buchanangalleries.co.uk; Royal Exchange Sq) and the exquisite **Princes Sq** (Map p120), which is set in a magnificent 1841 renovated square.

Munro baggers and other outdoor enthusiasts can go berserk at **Tiso's** (Map p120; ☎ 248 4877; 129 Buchanan St; ⏰ 9.30am-5.30pm Mon-Wed, Fri & Sat, to 7pm Thu, noon-5pm Sun) and **Adventure 1** (Map p120; ☎ 353 3788; 38 Dundas St), which is an excellent place to buy hiking boots.

Institutions include Buchanan St's splendid, jewellery-laden **Argyll Arcade** (Map p120), where you'll find **Catherine Shaw** (Map p120; ☎ 221 9038; www.carrick-jewellery.co.uk) for distinct pieces transcending mass production, and the **Barras** (Map p120; ☎ 552 4601; London Rd), a burgeoning flea market open every weekend.

GETTING THERE & AWAY

Glasgow is 42 miles from Edinburgh and 166 miles from Inverness.

Air

Ten miles west of the city, **Glasgow International Airport** (☎ 887 1111; www.baa.co.uk/glasgow) handles domestic traffic and international flights. Glasgow Prestwick airport, 30 miles southwest of Glasgow, handles some of the cheap, no-frills airlines. There are direct flights from many European cities, including Amsterdam, Brussels, Prague and Dublin. **Ryanair** (☎ 0871 246 0000; www.ryanair .com) flies to Glasgow Prestwick airport from London Stansted airport (1¼ hours, frequent) for around £30 plus taxes, but check its website for ridiculously cheap specials.

Bus

All long-distance buses arrive and depart from **Buchanan bus station** (Map p120; ☎ 333 3708; Killermont St).

Buses from London are very competitive. **Megabus** (☎ 0900 160 0900; www.megabus.com) should be your first port of call if you're looking for the cheapest fare. It has one-way fares for around £10; check the website for your date of departure.

Silver Choice (☎ 01355-230403; www.silver choicetravel.co.uk) also has great deals (advance-purchase return ticket £24, 8½ hours). It departs at 10pm daily from both London Victoria coach station and Buchanan bus station in Glasgow. The service is very popular, so you'll need to book well in advance.

SHIPBUILDING ON THE CLYDE

One of the earliest permanent Lower Clyde shipyards was established in 1711 by John Scott at Greenock. Initial construction was for small-scale local trade but, by the end of the 18th century, large ocean-going vessels were being built. As the market expanded, shipyards also opened at Dumbarton and Port Glasgow.

The *Comet*, Europe's first steamship, was launched at Port Glasgow in 1812. By the 1830s and 1840s the Clyde had secured its position as the world leader in shipbuilding. Steel hulls came into use by the 1880s, allowing construction of larger ships with the latest and best engines.

In 1899 John Brown & Co, a Sheffield steelmaker, took over a Clydebank yard and by 1907 had become part of the world's largest shipbuilding conglomerate, producing ocean-going liners. Output from the Clyde shipyards steadily increased up to WWI and, with the advent of the war, there was huge demand for new shipping from both the Royal Navy and Merchant Navy.

During and after the war many small companies disappeared and shipbuilding giants, such as Lithgows Ltd, took their place. The depression years of the 1920s and 1930s saw many yards mothballed or closed. Another boom followed during WWII but these were to be the twilight years.

Many yards went into liquidation in the 1960s, and in 1972 Upper Clyde Shipbuilders was liquidated, causing complete chaos, a sit-in and a bad headache for Ted Heath's government.

Now the great shipyards of the Clyde are mostly derelict and empty. The remains of a once-mighty industry include just a handful of companies still operating along the Clyde.

National Express (☎ 0870 580 8080; www.national express.com) leaves from the same bus stations (single £30, nine hours, at least four daily). There's a daily direct overnight bus from Heathrow Airport, usually departing at 11.05pm.

National Express also has numerous links with other English cities. Services and single tickets include: up to five daily buses from Birmingham (£40.50, six hours); one from Cambridge (£46, 10¼ hours); at least nine from Carlisle (£16, two hours); one from Newcastle (£25.50, four hours); and one from York (£29.50, seven hours).

Scottish Citylink (☎ 0870 550 5050; www.city link.co.uk) has buses to most major towns in Scotland. There are very frequent services to Edinburgh (£4, 1¼ hours), every 20 minutes during the day. Frequent buses also run to Stirling (£4.20, 45 minutes), Inverness (£16.70, four hours) and Aberdeen (£17.20, 3¼ to four hours). Regular long-distance services to/from Glasgow include Oban (£13.10, three hours, three direct daily), Fort William (£14, three hours, four daily) and Portree on Skye (£25, 6¼ to seven hours, three daily).

There's a twice-daily service via Stranraer, connecting with the ferry, to Belfast in Northern Ireland (single/return £20/35, six hours).

Stagecoach Express (☎ 01592-261461; www .stagecoachbus.com) runs services to Anstruther (three hours, hourly) and St Andrews (2¼ hours, hourly); the return fare to both destinations costs £10.

Walkers should check out **First Glasgow** (☎ 423 6600), which runs buses every hour or two to Milngavie (30 minutes), the start of the West Highland Way.

Car & Motorcycle

There are numerous car-rental companies; the big names have offices at Glasgow International Airport. Companies include the following:

Arnold Clark (☎ 339 9886; www.arnoldclark.co.uk; 118 Castlebank St) Rates per day/week from £19/100.

Avis (☎ 0870 606 0100, 221 2827; www.avis.co.uk; 70 Lancefield St)

Train

As a general rule, Glasgow Central station serves southern Scotland, England and Wales, and Queen St station serves

the north and east. There are buses every 10 minutes between them. There are direct trains from London's King's Cross and Euston stations; they're much quicker (from £25, five hours, 10 direct daily) and more comfortable than the bus.

First ScotRail (☎ 0845 755 0033; www.firstgroup .com/scotrail/index.php) runs the West Highland line heading north to Oban and Fort William, and other direct links to Dundee (£22.50), Aberdeen (£34) and Inverness (£34). There are trains every 15 to 30 minutes to/from Edinburgh (£8.60, 50 minutes).

GETTING AROUND
To/From the Airport

There are buses every 10 or 15 minutes from Glasgow International Airport to Buchanan bus station (single/return £3.30/5). A taxi costs about £20.

Car & Motorcycle

The most difficult thing about driving in Glasgow, as with most Scottish urban centres, is the confusing one-way system. If you miss a turn-off, you can end up a long way from your destination, particularly if you get spat out on the motorway encircling the CBD – likely. For short-term parking (30 minutes to two hours) you've a decent chance of finding something on the street, especially away from the city centre (around the city centre it's very expensive – 30p for 10 minutes). Otherwise multistorey car parks are probably your best bet – the St Enoch Centre in the city has free parking. Note that the West End generally, and Great Western Rd in particular, are very busy during the day and bumper to bumper during peak hour (8am to 9.30am and 4pm to 6pm).

Public Transport

Glasgow has an excellent public transport system, especially the rail network. The Roundabout Glasgow ticket (adult/child £4.50/2.25) covers all underground and train transport in the city for a day.

First Glasgow (☎ 423 6600; www.firstglasgow.com) has a FirstDay ticket that allows hop-on/off travel on all its buses; it can be bought from drivers for £2.65/2.35 before/after 9am and is valid until midnight. It also covers unlimited travel in the Greater Glasgow area as far as East Kilbride or Paisley.

GLASGOW

WORTH THE TRIP

Effectively a suburb about 5 miles west of Glasgow, the reason for visiting **Paisley** is to see its timeless abbey – one of the finest in southern Scotland. Overlooking the river like a giant sentinel, **Paisley Abbey** (☎ 0141-889 7654; www.paisleyabbey.org.uk; Abbey Close; admission free; ☙ 10am-3.30pm Mon-Sat) is an awesome sight. Inside, the stonework gives a chilly embrace and you feel as though you've passed through a portal to another age – the scruffy town outside seems a world away.

The abbey was founded in 1163 by Walter Fitzallan, the first high steward of Scotland and ancestor of the Stuart dynasty. It was damaged by fire during the Wars of Independence in 1306, but rebuilt soon after. Most of the nave is 14th or 15th century. The building was a ruin from the 16th century until the 19th-century restoration, not completed until 1928. There are two royal tombs in the abbey, excellent stained-glass windows and the 10th-century Celtic **Barochan Cross**.

If you've time, at the western end of the High St, there's the **University of Paisley** and the **Museum and Art Gallery** (☎ 0141-889 3151; High St; admission free; ☙ 10am-5pm Tue-Sat, 2-5pm Sun), which features Paisley psychedelia! There are some marvellous exhibits, including contemporary displays of children in the modern world – it's worth at least a couple of hours. It also has collections of local and natural history, ceramics and 19th-century Scottish art.

There are frequent buses from Central Rd. Trains leave Glasgow's Central station for Paisley's Gilmour St Station (off-peak/day return £3/4, 15 minutes, eight per hour).

BUS

City bus services are frequent. You can buy tickets when you board buses, but on most you must have the exact change. First Glasgow publishes the complicated but useful *Glasgow Mapmate* (£1), which shows all local First Glasgow bus routes. Trips around the city cost on average £1. Pick up a copy of the First Glasgow *Night Network* brochure to find out about services running through until the wee hours.

TAXI

There's no shortage of taxis, and if you want to know anything about Glasgow, striking up a conversation with a cabbie is a good place to start.

You can pay by credit card with **Glasgow Taxis** (☎ 429 2900) if you order by phone; most of its taxis are wheelchair accessible.

TRAIN & SUBWAY

There's an extensive suburban network of trains in and around Glasgow; tickets should be bought before travel if the station is staffed, or from the conductor if it isn't.

There's also an underground line that serves 15 stations in the centre, west and south of the city (single £1). The rail network connects with the Underground at Buchanan St station. The Discovery Ticket (£1.70) gives unlimited travel after 9.30am on the Underground system for a day.

AROUND GLASGOW

There are some wonderful sights in the urban centres around Glasgow, although it's best to visit this grim hinterland of postindustrial communities via a day trip. It's like finding diamonds in a coal mine – well worth looking, but you wouldn't want to spend the night there. Paisley's abbey should head your itinerary – it's a stupendous sight and a marvellous architectural achievement. If you're interested in Clyde shipbuilding and its spectacular fall from economic grace, Greenock is a must.

INVERCLYDE

The ghostly remains of once-great shipyards still line the banks of the Clyde west of Glasgow.

The only place worth stopping along the coast west of the city is Greenock, although there are a couple of items of interest in the otherwise unprepossessing town of **Port Glasgow**, including the fine 16th-century **Newark Castle** (HS; ☎ 01475-741858; adult/child £2.50/1; ☙ 9.30am-6.30pm Apr-Sep), which is still largely intact.

Greenock

☎ 01475 / pop 45,467

Greenock has a lovely, revitalised waterfront area by the James Watt College, which is very pleasant to wander around. Other parts of town are a little scrappy and can be confusing to navigate.

An enjoyable walk up to Lyle Hill, above Gourock Bay, leads to the Free French memorial, commemorating sailors who lost their lives in the Battle of the Atlantic during WWII, and a great view over the Firth of Clyde.

SIGHTS

McLean Museum and Art Gallery (☎ 715624; 15 Kelly St; admission free; ☑ 10am-5pm Mon-Sat) is well worth checking out. It's quite an extensive collection, with displays charting the history of steam power and Clyde shipping. There's also a pictorial history of Greenock through the ages, while upstairs there are very good temporary exhibitions and small displays from China, Japan and Egypt. The natural history section highlights the sad reality of species extinction in the modern world.

HM Customs & Excise Museum (☎ 881300; Custom House Quay; admission free; ☑ 10am-4pm Mon-Fri) is intriguing in parts, and good for killing an hour or so. You can also learn a thing or two about searches and smuggling techniques. You have to feel sorry for the customs officers who searched an Airbus from the West Indies and found more than 5kg of marijuana in the aircraft toilet tanks! The search took 4½ hours.

SLEEPING & EATING

James Watt College (☎ 731360; enquiries@jameswatt .ac.uk; Halls of Residence, Custom House Way; r per person from £20; ☒) Fairly central and down on the waterfront, this residence hall has 164 single rooms, many with en suite. It's good value, and the management only ask that you leave the place as you found it. Fair enough.

Tontine Hotel (☎ /fax 723316; www.tontinehotel .co.uk; 6 Ardgowan Sq; s £60-75, d £80-95) This grand hotel with well-appointed rooms, each with en suite, is genteel and well worth the pounds. The premier rooms in the old wing are more luxurious and spacious. Book early for stays over summer – ask about room-only rates, too.

Port & Harbour (☎ 730370; Custom House Pl; mains £10-16; ☑ lunch & dinner) On the waterfront next to the HM Customs & Excise Museum, this fine restaurant offers candle-lit dining, specialising in local seafood, lamb and venison dishes. The surroundings are suitably dark and cosy, perfect for blustery nights.

GETTING THERE & AWAY

Greenock is 27 miles west of Glasgow. The Glasgow–Greenock/Gourock pedestrian/cycle route (p129) follows an old railway track for 10 miles. There are trains from Glasgow Central station (£5.10 off-peak return, 45 minutes, three per hour) and hourly buses.

Gourock

☎ 01475 / pop 11,511

Gourock is a seaside resort situated 3 miles west of Greenock. Although the small central area is run-down, the town's location is wonderful and it is an important hub for transport.

For accommodation, you'd best head for Glasgow or Dunoon, though there are options in Gourock.

Spinnaker Hotel (☎ 633107; www.spinnakerhotel .co.uk; 121 Albert Rd; s/d from £27.50/55, mains £7) is an excellent pub. Rooms (with either en suite or shared bathroom) have country-pine décor, are clean and spacious, and have large screen TVs. Downstairs the comfy bar is laid-back and has guest ales on tap. Pretty basic pub grub is also on offer.

CalMac (☎ 650100) ferries leave daily for Dunoon (passenger/car £3.10/7.65, 20 minutes, hourly) on Argyll's Cowal peninsula. CalMac also runs a passenger-only service to Kilcreggan (£1.90, 12 minutes, 12 daily Monday to Saturday, three Sunday) and Helensburgh (£1.90, 40 minutes, three or four daily).

Western Ferries (☎ 01369-704452) has a service to Dunoon (passenger/car £3.20/9, 20 minutes, two to three hourly) from McInroy's Point, 2 miles from the train station; Scottish Citylink buses run to here.

Gourock train station is next to the CalMac terminal; there are trains to/from Glasgow Central station (£4.50, 45 minutes, three per hour).

Wemyss Bay

☎ 01475 / pop 2466

Eight miles south of Gourock is Wemyss Bay (pronounced weemz), where you can jump off a train and onto a ferry for Rothesay on the Isle of Bute (p280). There are trains from Glasgow (£5, 50 minutes, hourly). **CalMac** (☎ 520521) ferries to Rothesay connect with most trains and cost £3.65/15 per passenger/car.

GLASGOW

Southern Scotland

Enchanting southern Scotland lures with a mystique born from its relative obscurity. Surprisingly undiscovered by international tourists, this magical corner of the country has been a favourite with locals for years. Traditionally pulling in visitors north and south of the border, southern Scotland is home to stately mansions and picture-perfect countryside encapsulating the turmoil of centuries of conflict with England. The landscape is dominated by lush valleys and undulating hills, and the bellow of the red deer reverberates in its remote forests.

One of the delights of travel here is stumbling across a pocket of country you'll have all to yourself. And that's one of southern Scotland's most alluring aspects – crowd-free castles to ramble around, miles of open countryside and small traffic-free roads along which to explore it all. Walking and cycling are popular ways to discover the region, whose gentle slopes encourage people to get around under their own steam.

Southern Scotland consists of four distinct areas: the Borders, an area that was once the front line for battle between the old arch foes, as evidenced by the fiery remnants of the great Border abbeys; South Lanarkshire, where New Lanark captivates with its preserved 19th-century portal to the past; Ayrshire, with its retro seaside towns, magnificent Isle of Arran and Burns-mania; and Dumfries & Galloway – the jewel in the crown and particularly good for families, walkers and cyclists, with the exhilarating, remote Galloway forest.

This is an area that ignites the imagination – Sir Walter Scott and Robert Burns, Scotland's two great literary sons, romanticised the region. After a short time here it's easy to see why.

HIGHLIGHTS

- Touring the lush Border region and discovering the fiery remnants of the **great Border abbeys** (opposite)

- Nursing a local brew in a beer garden overlooking the Holy Isle on the **Isle of Arran** (p166), a walking and cycling paradise

- Hiking the challenging **Southern Upland Way** (opposite), a unique way to experience the beauty of the countryside

- Contemplating the force of nature from stunning **Culzean Castle** (p175), perched on wild sea cliffs

- Coming face to face with red deer in the vast wilderness of **Galloway Forest Park** (p182)

Isle of Arran ★

★ Great Border Abbeys

Culzean Castle ★

Galloway ★ Southern Upland Way
Forest Park

- POPULATION: 1,245,911

- AREA: 16,769 sq km

History

Historically, southern Scotland was the buffer between the rambunctious, imperialist English and the equally unruly Scots.

The wars of Scottish independence, fought at the end of the 13th century and the beginning of the 14th, took a terrible toll on southern Scotland. The Debatable Lands, as they were known, were virtually ungoverned and ungovernable from the late 13th to the mid-17th centuries. It's been argued that this continuous state of guerrilla warfare had an indelible effect on the region and its people.

Following the 1707 union, peace allowed a new surge of development, and during the 19th century the knitting and weaving industries that survive today were created.

Getting Around

Call **Traveline** (☎ 0870 608 2608) for public transport information. Bus transport is excellent around Ayrshire (p164), the Borders (p148) and Lothians, and reasonable on the main north–south routes and the A75 to Stranraer, but limited elsewhere in Dumfries & Galloway. Various explorer tickets, which can be bought from bus drivers or at bus stations, are usually your best-value option.

Train services are limited. There are stations at Berwick-upon-Tweed (in Northumberland on the English side of the border, but the jumping-off point for the Tweed Valley) on the main east-coast line; at Dumfries on the main west-coast line; and at Stranraer and Ayr, which are linked to Glasgow. For timetables and fares, call the **National Rail Enquiry Service** (☎ 0845 748 4950; www.railtrack.co.uk).

BORDERS REGION

The Borders teems with domestic tourists in summer, eager to explore links to the country's medieval past. It's a distinctive region – centuries of war and plunder have left an indelible impression on the landscape, represented by their modern-day ambassadors, the scorched remnants of the great Border abbeys. From the 12th century small burghs supported large, wealthy monastic communities. They were an irresistible magnet during the Border wars, and were destroyed and rebuilt numerous times. The monasteries met their fiery end in the 16th century and were never rebuilt. Today these massive stone shells are the region's finest attraction.

But there's much more to this captivating region – welcoming villages with ancient traditions pepper the countryside, one of the best cold-water diving sites in Europe is off the coast, and grandiose mansions all await exploration. It's fine walking and cycling country, lush with an artist's palette of innumerable shades of green. And whatever you do, don't miss Hermitage Castle; nothing encapsulates the region's turbulent history like this spooky stronghold.

SOUTHERN SCOTLAND

WALKING & CYCLING

The region's most famous walk is the challenging 212-mile **Southern Upland Way**. If you want a sample, one of the best bits is the two-day section from St John's Town of Dalry to Beattock. Another long-distance walk is the 62-mile **St Cuthbert's Way**, inspired by the travels of St Cuthbert (a 7th-century saint who worked in Melrose Abbey), which crosses some superb scenery between Melrose and Lindisfarne (in England). In Galloway the **Pilgrims Way** follows a 25-mile trail from Glenluce Abbey to the Isle of Whithorn.

The recently created **Borders Abbeys Way** will eventually link all the great Border abbeys in a 65-mile circuit. For shorter walks and especially circular loops in the hills, the towns of Melrose, Jedburgh and Kelso all make ideal bases.

With the exception of the main north–south A roads and the A75 to Stranraer, traffic is sparse, which, along with the beauty of the countryside, makes this ideal cycling country.

The **Tweed Cycle Way** is a waymarked route running 62 miles along the beautiful Tweed Valley following minor roads from Biggar to Peebles (13 miles), Melrose (16 miles), Coldstream (19 miles) and Berwick-upon-Tweed (14 miles). Jedburgh Tourist Information Centre (TIC) has details (see p158).

For an island tour, the **Isle of Arran** offers excellent cycling opportunities. The 50-mile coast-road circuit is stunning and is worth splitting into two or three days.

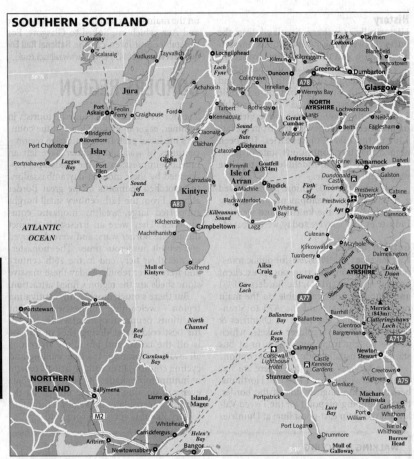

SOUTHERN SCOTLAND

Getting Around

There's a good network of local buses. **First** (☎ 0870 872 7271) operates between most of the border towns and connects the larger towns with Edinburgh. Local bus companies serving border towns also include **Munro's of Jedburgh** (☎ 01835-862253) and **Buskers** (☎ 01896-755808). The TICs stock excellent public-transport booklets to local areas.

COLDSTREAM
☎ 01890 / pop 1813

On a sweeping bend of the River Tweed, which forms the border with England, Coldstream is small and relatively hidden from the well-trodden Borders tourist beat. It can be a handy base when nearby Kelso is

overflowing with visitors and accommodation options are sparse.

The proud history of the Coldstream Guards is covered in the **Coldstream Museum** (☎ 882630; 12 Market Sq; admission free; ⊗ 10am-4pm Mon-Sat, 2-4pm Sun Apr-Sep, 1-4pm Mon-Sat Oct), including recent missions in the 1990s. The Coldstream Guards were formed in 1650 in Berwick-upon-Tweed for duty in Scotland as part of Oliver Cromwell's New Model Army. The regiment took its present name from the town where it was stationed in 1659. The regiment played a significant part in the restoration of the monarchy in 1660. It saw service at Waterloo against Napoleon, at Sebastopol during the Crimean War, in the Boer War, at the Somme and Ypres in WWI, and at Dun-

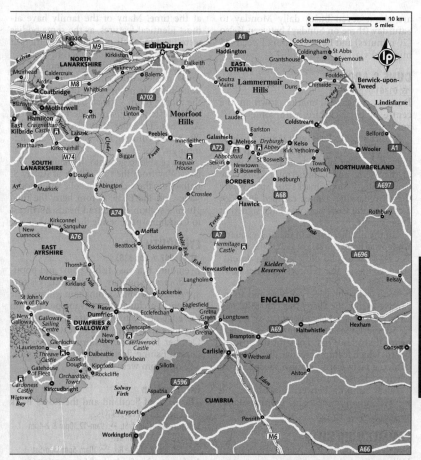

kirk and Tobruk in WWII. It remains the oldest regiment in continuous existence in the British army and is the only one directly descended from the New Model Army.

Sleeping & Eating

Eastbraes B&B (☎ 883949; godfrey.bryson@talk21 .com; 100C High St; d £55) Eastbraes is full of personality and good vibes. A double and twin share a bathroom and there's one en-suite double, which is enormous – most rooms have stupendous views. This is a terrific family-run place in a gorgeous building with plenty of walking opportunities literally on the doorstep.

Calico House (☎ 885870; www.calicohouse.net; 44 High St; r 1/2 nights £60/50) Set behind a shop that

churns out high-quality interior designs, this is a superb B&B with sumptuous rooms blessed with great views and attention to detail. Privacy from your hosts and value for money are two very strong points in this excellent accommodation option.

Castle Hotel (☎/fax 882830; 11 High St; r per person £27; lunch mains £6-9) Castle Hotel has good en-suite rooms and also does delicious bar meals (roast lunch on Sunday). There's a restaurant serving decent kids' meals. This is a real local drinking hole good for a yak.

Getting There & Away

Coldstream is on the busy A697 road that links Newcastle upon Tyne in Northumberland, England, with Edinburgh. There are about seven buses daily Monday to Saturday (three on Sunday) between Kelso (20 minutes) and Berwick-upon-Tweed (45 minutes) via Coldstream.

DUNS & AROUND
☎ 01361 / pop 2308

Duns is a peaceful market town in the centre of Berwickshire, with some pleasant walks.

You can get to **Duns Law** (218m) in Duns Castle Estate by following Castle St up from the square. The summit offers great views of the Merse and Lammermuir Hills. The Covenanter's Stone marks the spot where the Covenanting armies camped in 1639; a copy of the Covenant was later signed at Duns Castle.

On the northern side of the main square, **White Swan Hotel** (☎ 883338; 31-32 Market Sq; s £25-35, d £40-60) is a solid old place with decent-sized rooms – the refurbished ones have en suites.

With its bright, cheery service and an inventive menu, the **Cherry Tree** (☎ 883100; Market Sq; mains £3.50-5, 3-course dinner £16; ☺ breakfast Tue-Sat, lunch Tue-Sun, dinner Thu, Fri & Sat) is a village bistro that stands out. Look for the specials board, which features creative dishes – it included a tasty warm Spanish sausage salad when we passed through.

Buses running between Galashiels and Berwick-upon-Tweed (six to nine daily) stop at Duns.

LAMMERMUIR HILLS

North of Duns, the low-lying Lammermuir Hills, with their extensive grouse moors, rolling farmland and wooded valleys, run east–west along the border with East Lothian. The hills are popular with walkers and there are numerous trails, including a section of the **Southern Upland Way**.

To the west the Way can be accessed at **Lauder**, where it passes through the grounds of **Thirlestane Castle** (☎ 01578-722430; castle & grounds adult/child £5.50/3, grounds only £2/1; ☺ 10.30am-3.30pm Wed, Thu, Fri & Sun May–mid-Sep, plus Mon & Tue Jul & Aug). The narcissism and folly of the aristocracy is evident here perhaps more than in most 'great homes'. Notice how many of the family portraits adorning the walls look similar. The extensive assemblage here is the result of the common practice of mass production used

at the time. Many of the family have almost identical features, as the same bodies were used for their portraits with different clothes, faces and hands superimposed.

Thirlestane is also home to some of the finest plasterwork ceilings in Europe, and don't miss Henry the Ram (a snuff box) in the dining room – kitsch beyond kitsch!

Thirlestane is just outside town, off the A68, beside Leader Water. Munro's buses 29 and 30, running between Kelso and Edinburgh, pass by.

You're able to get onto the Southern Upland Way from the tiny village of Abbey St Bathan's in the secluded, bucolic Whiteadder Valley, off the B6355. From here, the final 10-mile section of the trail heads northeast to Cockburnspath beside the coast.

EYEMOUTH
☎ 018907 / pop 3383

Eyemouth is a busy fishing port and popular domestic holiday destination. Visitors approaching from Coldingham will spot the evidence: a clutch of caravans perched on the edge of the town's cliffs. The community here suffered its greatest catastrophe in October 1881, when a storm destroyed the coastal fishing fleet, killing 189 fishermen, 129 of whom were locals.

Information

The Bank of Scotland and the Royal Bank of Scotland have ATMs.
Laundrette (Church St; ☺ 9am-12.30pm & 2-4pm Mon-Fri, 9am-12.30pm Sat)
TIC (☎ 50678; Manse Rd; ☺ 10am-5pm Mon-Sat Apr-Sep, noon-3pm Sun Apr-Jun & Sep, noon-4pm Sun Jul & Aug, 10am-4pm Mon-Sat Oct) Very helpful; it's in Eyemouth Museum near the harbour.

Sights & Activities

Captivating **Eyemouth Museum** (☎ 50678; Auld Kirk, Manse Rd; adult/child £2.50/free; ☺ 10am-5pm Mon-Sat Apr-Sep, noon-3pm Sun Apr-Jun & Sep, noon-4pm Sun Jul & Aug, 10am-4pm Mon-Sat Oct) has local-history displays, particularly relating to the town's fishing heritage. Its centrepiece is the tapestry commemorating the 1881 fishing disaster.

If you feel like clearing the lungs, get a copy of the brochure *Walks In & Around Eyemouth* (30p), available from the TIC, which describes a number of short walks. One of the most scenic is the 4-mile cliff-top path south to Burnmouth.

Sleeping & Eating

Bantry (Mackays; ☎ 51900; 20 High St; r per person £25)
Plonked on top of the restaurant of the same
name on the main drag, this place has good
clean rooms right on the waterfront. Bathrooms are shared (and downstairs) and it's
a bit pricey, but the location is spot on. Try
to get room No 3, if you're after a double, as
it's the only one with sea-facing views.

Hillcrest (☎ 50463; Coldingham Rd; r per person £20)
The central Hillcrest is a traditional family home and has three rooms with shared
bathroom. There's also a shared sitting
room with hot drinks ready for guests. It's
very handy for the harbour.

Obló (☎ 52527; 20 Harbour St; mains £12; ☒ breakfast, lunch & dinner) For the best shot of caffeine
in town and one of the few places open for
chow on weekends, find your way upstairs
into this modern bar-bistro with its comfy
seating and modish interior. It's urban, it's
trendy, it's just down from the TIC. In the
evening you'll find local produce, including
lobster (£13 for half), on the menu.

The pubs along the quay have suitably nautical names – the **Contented Sole**
(☎ 50268; 3 Old Quay, Harbour Rd) and the **Ship
Hotel** (☎ 50224; Harbour Rd) – and serve freshly
caught seafood.

Getting There & Away

Eyemouth is 5 miles north of the Scotland–
England border. Bus C4 runs to/from Kelso
via Duns (1½ hours, once daily Monday
to Friday); buses 34, 235, 236 and 253 go
south to Berwick-upon-Tweed (15 minutes,
every 30 minutes), which has the nearest
train station. Bus 253 from Berwick to Edinburgh (£4.25, 1¾ hours, six daily Monday
to Saturday, three Sunday) passes through
Eyemouth.

SOUTH OF EYEMOUTH

Further south, beyond the village of Foulden
and about 3 miles west of the A1 along the
B6461, is **Paxton House** (☎ 01289-386291; adult/
child £6/3; ☒ 11am-5pm Apr-Oct, grounds 10am-sunset
Apr-Oct). It's beside the River Tweed and surrounded by over 32 hectares of parkland
and gardens. It was built in 1758 by Patrick
Home for his intended wife, the daughter
of Prussia's Frederick the Great. Unfortunately, she stood him up, but it was her loss;
designed by the Adam family – brothers
John, James and Robert – it's acknowledged

as one of the finest 18th-century Palladian
houses in Britain. It contains a large collection of Chippendale and Regency furniture,
and its picture gallery houses paintings
from the national galleries of Scotland.

In the grounds are walking trails and a
riverside museum on salmon fishing.

COLDINGHAM BAY & ST ABB'S HEAD

About 3 miles north of Eyemouth, this picturesque area is fantastic for those who love
the great outdoors – there's loads to do,
as evidenced by the anglers, scuba divers,
bird-watchers and walkers who flock here.

From the village of Coldingham, with its
twisting, winding streets, take the B6438
downhill to the small fishing village of St
Abbs, a gorgeous, peaceful little community with a picture-perfect harbour nestled
below the cliffs. St Abbs is a great place
for walking – head for the car park at the
harbour and have a stroll over the rocky sea
walls to get a feel of this fabulous location.

The clear, clean waters around St Abbs
form part of **St Abbs & Eyemouth Voluntary Marine
Reserve** (☎ 018907-71443; www.marine-reserve.org.uk;
Rangers Cottage, Northfield, St Abbs), one of the best
cold-water diving sites in Europe. The reserve
is home to a variety of marine life, including
grey seals and porpoises. Visibility is about
7m to 8m but has been recorded at 24m.

Drop by the **St Abbs Dive Centre** (☎ 018907-
71237; www.stabbs.org; ☒ 8am-4pm Mon, 8am-4.30pm
Tue, Thu & Fri, 8am-1pm Wed, 8.30am-3.30pm Sat,
8.30am-3pm Sun) at the post office; these folk
provide plenty of advice on diving in the
area, and also sell and repair equipment.
Divers can charter boats from **Paul Crowe**
(☎ 018907-71945).

In Coldingham you could try **Sub Aqua
Divers** (☎ 018907-71669; www.scoutscroft.co.uk; Scoutscroft Holiday Centre, St Abbs Rd, Coldingham) for pointers on the best places to dive in the area
and what you'll likely see. You can also hire
equipment here (£40) and organise a boat
dive (£20: note that combined equipment
hire and dive is cheaper.)

Back in Coldingham, a signposted turnoff to the east leads 0.75 miles down to
quiet, away-from-it-all Coldingham Bay,
which has a sandy beach and a cliff-top
walking trail to Eyemouth (3 miles).

North of St Abbs, the 78-hectare **St Abb's
Head National Nature Reserve** (NTS; ☎ 018907-
71443; Rangers Cottage, Northfield St, St Abbs) is an

ornithologist's wonderland, with large colonies of guillemots, kittiwakes, herring gulls, fulmars, razorbills and some puffins. You get to the reserve by following the trail that begins beside the Northfield Farm car park (£2/4 for two/three or more passengers) and Smiddy café, on the road just west of St Abbs. Note that the cliff-top walks here are spectacular, especially on sunny days.

Sleeping

Mrs Wilson (☎ 018907-71468; 7 Murrayfield St, St Abbs; r per person £18-22) If you're staying in town, Mrs Wilson's provides homely accommodation in clean and tidy facilities. It's popular with divers who are tuckered out after a day's exploration of the marine reserve's underwater treasures.

Castle Rock Guest House (☎ 018907-71715; www .castlerockbandb.co.uk; Murrayfield St, St Abbs; s/d £29/58) If you want to stay at the place with the best views and a prime cliff-top location close to the town centre – look no further – here it is. There are sea views from all rooms, which have en suite and satellite TV.

Old Smiddy (☎ 018907-71707; St Abbs Rd; lunch £5; ⊙ lunch daily, dinner Fri & Sat) Highly recommended on a sunny day when you can stretch out on its bench seating on luxuriant lawns, seafood dominates the menu here (try the smoked fish chowder or a St Abbs crab baguette). There are also artistic endeavours to explore while you wait for your meal and a children's play area.

Coldingham Sands Youth Hostel (SYHA; ☎ 0870 004 1111; The Mount; dm s/d £12.50/9; ⊙ Apr-Sep) This hostel is on the cliff above the southern side of the bay and is a grand old property with a slightly school-holiday-camp feel. But you can't fault the excellent location set amid lush greenery with sweeping sea views. Facilities include a small kitchen and a pool table.

St Veda's Hotel (☎ 018907-71679; www.stvedas .co.uk; Coldingham Bay; s/d £30/70; mains £5-8) Just opposite the path down to the beach, St Veda's is a cheery, British beach resort–style hotel. Make sure you get a sea-facing room, as the views can be magnificent. It's well kept, with a touch of faded grandeur, and is very popular at weekends over summer.

Getting There & Away

Bus 253 between Edinburgh and Berwick-upon-Tweed (six daily Monday to Saturday, three Sunday) stops in Coldingham and St Abbs, as does bus 235, which runs at least hourly from Eyemouth.

COCKBURNSPATH

The 16th-century Mercat Cross in Cockburnspath village square, about a mile inland from the coast, is the official eastern-end start of the Southern Upland Way.

KELSO

☎ 01573 / pop 5116

Kelso, a prosperous market town with a broad, cobbled square, flanked by Georgian buildings, has a French feel to it. During the day it's a busy little place, but after 8pm you'll have the streets to yourself. Kelso has a lovely site at the junction of the Rivers Tweed and Teviot, and is one of the most enjoyable towns in the Borders.

Information

Border Books (☎ 225861; Horsemarket; ⊙ 10.30am-4pm Mon, Tue & Thu-Sat) Great range of books, especially out of date and antiquarian.

Kelso Library (☎ 223171; Bowmont St; ⊙ 10am-1pm & 2-5pm Mon, Tue, Thu & Fri, plus 5.30-7pm Tue & Thu, 10am-1pm Wed, 9.30am-12.30pm Sat; ⌨) Free Internet access.

TIC (☎ 0870 608 0404; www.visitscottishborders.com; Town House, The Square; ⊙ daily Apr-Oct, Mon-Sat Nov-Mar)

Sights & Activities
KELSO ABBEY

Once one of the richest abbeys in southern Scotland, **Kelso Abbey** (HS; admission free; Bridge St; ⊙ 9.30am-6.30pm Mon-Sat, 2-6pm Sun Apr-Dec) was built by the Tironensians, an order founded at Tiron in Picardy and brought to the Borders around 1113 by David I. English raids in the 16th century reduced it to ruins, though what remains today is some of the finest surviving Romanesque architecture in Scotland.

Nearby, the rare, octagonal **Kelso Old Parish Church** (⊙ 10am-4pm Mon-Fri, May-Sep), built in 1773, is intriguing.

FLOORS CASTLE

Grandiose **Floors Castle** (☎ 223333; adult/child £6/3.25; ⊙ 10am-4.30pm Easter-Oct) is Scotland's largest inhabited mansion and overlooks the Tweed about a mile west of Kelso. Built by William Adam in the 1720s, the original

Georgian simplicity was 'improved' in the 1840s with the addition of rather ridiculous battlements and turrets. Inside, view the vivid colours of the 17th-century Brussels tapestries in the drawing room and the intricate oak carvings in the ornate ballroom. Palatial windows reveal a ribbon of green countryside extending well beyond the estate. Unfortunately, there's also a rather questionable collection of stuffed birds, easily interpreted as bad taste. Floors is unashamedly in the tourism business – you walk past the restaurant to enter and past the gift shop to leave.

WALKING

The **Pennine Way**, which starts its long journey at Edale in the Peak district, ends at Kirk Yetholm Youth Hostel, about 7 miles southeast of Kelso on the B6352.

The new **Borders Abbeys Way** walk will eventually link the great abbeys of Kelso, Jedburgh, Melrose and Dryburgh to create a 65-mile circuit. At the time of writing the Kelso–Jedburgh, Hawick–Selkirk and Selkirk–Melrose links were open (the final link, Melrose–Kelso, should be open by the

time you read this); the Kelso–Jedburgh section (12 miles) is a fairly easy walk, largely following the River Teviot between the towns. The TIC has a free leaflet with a map and description of the route.

Less ambitious walkers should leave the Square by Roxburgh St and take the signposted alley to **Cobby Riverside Walk**, a pleasant ramble along the river to Floors Castle (although you have to rejoin Roxburgh St to gain admission to the castle).

Sleeping

Accommodation can be difficult to find during local festivals and over summer.

Dispensary House (☎ 228738; 106 Roxburgh St; r per person £30) A guesthouse with wonderful views, sumptuous rooms (one with a four-poster bed) and clipped accents, it's a very refined place. The doubles (grab the four-poster) have huge bathrooms and the single comes with a shared bathroom that has an enormous Victorian bathtub.

Duncan House (☎ 225682; Chalkheugh Tce; s/d £40/60) This elderly resident in the hospitality industry has finally had the refurbishment it's

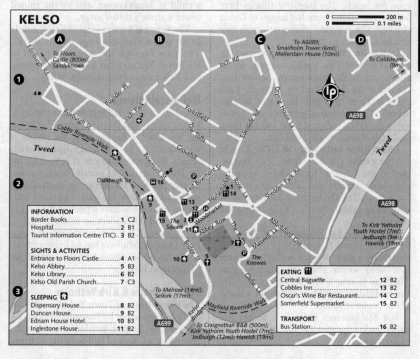

KELSO

To Floors Castle (800m); Sandyknowe
To A6089; Smailholm Tower (6mi); Mellerstain House (10mi)
To Coldstream (9mi)
To Kirk Yetholm Youth Hostel (7mi); Jedburgh (9mi); Hawick (19mi)
To Melrose (14mi); Selkirk (17mi)
To Craignethan B&B (500m); Kirk Yetholm Youth Hostel (7mi); Jedburgh (12mi); Hawick (19mi)

Edinburgh Rd · Poynder Pl · Roxburgh St · Cobby Riverside Walk · Tweed · Inch Park · Inch Rd · Forestfield · The Tofts · Bowmont St · Grovehill · Chalkheugh Tce · East Bowmont St · Horsemarket · Rose La · Woodmarket · The Square · Abbey Row · Bridge St · Glebe La · The Knowes · Maxwell La · Shedden Park Rd · Abbotsford Gve · DryING House La · Edenside Rd · The Butts · Mayfield Riverside Walk · Kelso Bridge · A698 · A699 · Tweed

INFORMATION
Border Books	1	C2
Hospital	2	B1
Tourist Information Centre (TIC)	3	B2

SIGHTS & ACTIVITIES
Entrance to Floors Castle	4	A1
Kelso Abbey	5	B3
Kelso Library	6	B2
Kelso Old Parish Church	7	C3

SLEEPING
Dispensary House	8	B2
Duncan House	9	B2
Ednam House Hotel	10	B3
Inglestone House	11	B2

EATING
Central Baguette	12	B2
Cobbles Inn	13	B2
Oscar's Wine Bar Restaurant	14	C2
Somerfield Supermarket	15	B2

TRANSPORT
Bus Station	16	B2

0   200 m
0   0.1 miles

SOUTHERN SCOTLAND

long been crying out for. It's a lovely Georgian house with views over the Rivers Tweed and Teviot, and now has elegantly kitted-out rooms with Victorian furnishings, freestanding bathtubs and a whole lotta TLC.

Ednam House Hotel (☎ 224168; www.ednamhouse .com; Bridge St; s/d from £65/95; ⚹) The genteel, Georgian Ednam House, touched with a quiet dignity, contains many of its original features and is the top place in town, with fine gardens overlooking the river and the excellent Ednam House Restaurant. It organises salmon fishing on the River Tweed (£30 a day) and golfing breaks.

Also recommended:

Craignethan B&B (☎ 224818; Jedburgh Rd; s/d £25/44) Welcoming, laid-back family home with stupendous views.

Inglestone House (☎ 225800; www.inglestonehouse .co.uk; Abbey Row; s/d £40/55; ⚹) Wedged between the Square and abbey; well-run guesthouse great for families or couples.

Eating

Central Baguette (☎ 228853; 52 The Square; large baguette £2; ☽ breakfast & lunch Mon-Sat) A great spot for lunch. The baguette fillings here feature everything from hot haggis to Cajun chicken. On a sunny afternoon, grab one and head down to the river.

Cobbles Inn (☎ 223548; 7 Bowmont St; mains £12; ☽ lunch & dinner) This traditional pub, up an alley north of the main square, serves delicious bar meals, including Mothers Ruin (king prawns in a gin, lime and tomato sauce). The generous portions are better value than those of most other pubs in town and veggie options are available.

Ednam House Restaurant (☎ 224168; Bridge St; 2-/3-course dinner £18/24; ☽ dinner) The restaurant at the Ednam House Hotel turns out delectable dinners and is the perfect place for a treat. Try the barbary duck breast or haunch of rabbit; there's a daily vegetarian option, too.

Oscar's Wine Bar Restaurant (☎ 224008; 33 Horsemarket; starters £5, mains £10-13; ☽ dinner) If you enjoy a glass of wine with your dinner in a classy setting, this is the place for you. The food is simple and well prepared – try the chargrilled monkfish and salmon skewers in coconut sauce.

For self-caterers there is a Somerfield supermarket located on the corner of the main square.

Getting There & Away

See Coldstream (p148) for details on the bus service to Berwick-upon-Tweed. Munro's bus 20 runs to/from Jedburgh (25 minutes, up to 11 daily Monday to Saturday, five Sunday) and Hawick (one hour, seven daily Monday to Saturday, four Sunday). There are also frequent services to Galashiels (55 minutes), and from there to Edinburgh.

AROUND KELSO
Smailholm Tower

Perched on a rocky knoll above a small lake, the narrow, stone **Smailholm Tower** (HS; ☎ 01573-460365; Sandyknowe Farm, Smailholm; adult/ child £2.50/1; ☽ 9.30am-6.30pm Apr-Sep, 9.30am-4.30pm Sat-Wed Oct, 9.30am-4.30pm Sat & Sun Nov-Mar) provides one of the most evocative sights in the Borders and keeps the bloody uncertainties of its history alive. Although the displays inside are sparse, the panoramic view from the top is worth the climb.

The nearby farm, **Sandyknowe**, was owned by Sir Walter Scott's grandfather. As Scott himself recognised, his imagination was fired by the ballads and stories he heard as a child at Sandyknowe, and by the ruined tower a stone's throw away.

The tower is 6 miles west of Kelso, a mile south of Smailholm village on the B6397. You pass through the farmyard to get to the tower. Munro's bus 65 between Melrose and Kelso stops in Smailholm village.

Mellerstain House

Finished in 1778, **Mellerstain House** (☎ 01573-410225; Gordon; adult/child £5.50/free; ☽ 12.30-5pm Sun, Mon & Wed-Fri May-Sep, Easter, plus Sun Oct) is considered to be Scotland's finest Robert Adam–designed mansion. It is famous for its classic elegance, ornate interiors and plaster ceilings; the library in particular is outstanding. Give the garish upstairs bedrooms a miss, but have a peek at the bizarre puppet and doll collection in the gallery.

It's about 10 miles northwest of Kelso near Gordon. Munro's bus 65 between Melrose and Kelso passes about a mile from Mellerstain House.

Town Yetholm & Kirk Yetholm

The twin villages of Town Yetholm and Kirk Yetholm, separated by Bowmont Water, are close to the English border, about 6 miles southeast of Kelso. Hill-walking centres, they lie at the northern end of the **Pennine Way** and on **St Cuthbert's Way** between Melrose and Lindisfarne (Holy Island) in Northumberland.

As the last stop on the Pennine Way, **Kirk Yetholm Youth Hostel** (SYHA; ☎ 0870 004 1132; Kirk Yetholm, Kelso; dm adult/child £12/9; 🕑 Apr-Sep) is often busy – there's a twin room and two dorms (six and eight beds); book well in advance. Bus 81 from Kelso runs up to seven times a day Monday to Saturday (three times on Sunday).

MELROSE
☎ 01896 / pop 1656

Tiny, charming Melrose is a polished village running on the well-greased wheels of tourism. This little enclave is a complete contrast with overbearing Galashiels, whose urban sprawl laps at its western edges. Sitting at the feet of the three heather-covered Eildon Hills, Melrose entices walkers and cyclists. It has a classic market square and some attractive parks, and its most famous resident is one of the great abbey ruins.

Information
Melrose Library (☎ 823052; 18 Market Sq; 🕑 10am-1pm & 2.30-5pm Mon & Wed, 2.30-5pm & 5.30-7pm Fri; 🖳) Free Internet access.
Post office (Buccleuch St)
TIC (☎ 0870 608 0404; Abbey House, Abbey St; 🕑 10am-5pm Mon-Sat, 10am-2pm Sun Apr & May, 9.30am-5pm Mon-Sat, 10am-2pm Sun Jun & Sep, 9.30am-5.30pm Mon-Sat, 10am-2pm Sun Jul & Aug, 10am-4pm Mon-Sat, 10am-1pm Sun Oct, 10am-2pm Mon-Sat Nov-Mar)

Sights
MELROSE ABBEY
Perhaps the most interesting of all the great Border abbeys, the red-sandstone **Melrose Abbey** (HS; ☎ 822562; adult/child £4/1.60; 🕑 9.30am-6.30pm Apr-Sep, 9.30am-4.30pm Oct-Mar) was repeatedly destroyed by the English in the 14th century. The remaining broken shell is pure Gothic and the ruins are famous for their decorative stonework – see if you can glimpse the pig gargoyle playing the bagpipes on the roof. You can climb to the top for tremendous views. The abbey was founded by David I in 1136 for Cistercian monks from Rievaulx in Yorkshire. It was rebuilt by Robert the Bruce, whose heart is buried here. The ruins date from the 14th

and 15th centuries, and were repaired by Sir Walter Scott in the 19th century.

The adjoining **museum** (free for abbey ticket holders) has many fine examples of 12th- to 15th-century stonework and pottery found in the area. Note the impressive remains of the 'great drain' outside – a medieval sewerage system.

TRIMONTIUM EXHIBITION
The small but absorbing **Trimontium Exhibition** (☎ 822651; The Ormiston, Market Sq; adult/child £1.50/1; 🕑 10.30am-4pm Apr-Oct) tells the story of the Roman fort of Trimontium (literally 'three hills') at nearby Newstead, and of life on the Scottish-Roman frontier. You can also join a 3½-hour guided Trimontium Walk to the Roman sites around Melrose; walks start at 1.30pm Thursday (and Tuesday July and August) and cost £3.

MELROSE RUGBY HERITAGE CENTRE
This **centre** (☎ 822993; The Greenyards; admission free; 🕑 11am-3pm Mon, Wed & Fri), Melrose's latest

---

SOMETHING FOR THE WEEKEND
Start your weekend by checking into **Glenfriars Guest House** (p158) in Jedburgh; when you've finished admiring the magnificent view, have a stroll around town and explore **Jedburgh Abbey** (p158) in the late-afternoon sun. A pint and a quality bar meal await at the **Carters Rest** (p159). On Saturday morning check out the Border towns of **Kelso** (p152), with its cobbled square and grand **castle** (p152), and **Melrose** (left), with its fiery **abbey** (left) remnants. Treat yourself to a gourmet focaccia for lunch at **Marmion's Brasserie** (p156). In the afternoon pull on the hiking boots and head for the **Eildon Hills** (p156), or make a beeline to **Peebles** (p160) for an easy riverside stroll to **Neidpath Castle** (p160) and check into historical **Cross Keys Hotel** (p160). That evening tuck into some wild-boar sausages at the cheery **Sunflower Restaurant** (p160). On Sunday take a leisurely drive through gorgeous countryside to magical **Hermitage Castle** (p160). Finish the weekend with a picnic lunch in the grounds of **Dryburgh Abbey** (p156) and admire the pink-hued stones of the greatest Border abbey.

attraction, will appeal to rugby fans – it offers an insight into Rugby Sevens, which was founded here in the late 19th century.

Activities

There are many attractive walks in the **Eildon Hills**, accessible via a footpath off Dingleton Rd (the B6359) south of the town, or via the trail along the River Tweed. Grab a copy of the *Walks Around Melrose* booklet (£1) for local guidance.

The **St Cuthbert's Way** long-distance path starts in Melrose, while the coast-to-coast **Southern Upland Way** passes through town. You can do a day's walk along St Cuthbert's Way as far as Harestanes (16 miles), on the A68 near Jedburgh, and return to Melrose on the hourly Jedburgh–Galashiels bus. The **Tweed Cycle Way** also passes through Melrose.

Festivals & Events

In mid-April rugby followers fill the town to see the week-long **Melrose Rugby Sevens** competition. The latest event on the festivals calendar is the **Borders Book Festival** (www.bordersbookfestival.org), stretching over four days in late June.

Sleeping

Melrose B&Bs and hotels aren't cheap by Scottish standards, but they are of a high standard; this would make a great place to treat yourself.

Melrose Youth Hostel (SYHA; ☎ 0870 004 1141; Priorwood; dm adult/child £13.50/10.50; ☼ Mar-Oct; 🖳) Housed in a large Georgian mansion on the edge of town, these spick-and-span dorms are complemented by a big garden and barbecue area. Not a party house, this hostel is mainly used by walkers looking to turn in early. From Market Sq, follow the signposts to the A68.

Braidwood (☎ 822488; www.braidwoodmelrose .co.uk; Buccleuch St; r per person £25-28) Mr Graham's popular town house near the abbey is an excellent place, with high-quality facilities and a warm welcome. The small sparkling rooms are finely decorated, and there's home baking, too.

Townhouse (☎ 822645; www.thetownhousemelrose .co.uk; Market Sq; s/d £54/90, superior r £110) The classy Townhouse, exuding warmth and professionalism, has some of the best rooms in town – tastefully furnished with attention

to detail. There are two superior rooms that are enormous in size with lavish furnishings; the one on the ground floor in particular has an excellent en suite, which includes a Jacuzzi. It's well worth the price.

Burts Hotel (☎ 822285; www.burtshotel.co.uk; Market Sq; s/d £54/100) Set in an early-18th-century house, and with an enviable reputation, Burts retains much of its period charm and has been run by the same couple for over 30 years. It would suit older visitors or families. Room No 5 is the best.

Eating

Marmion's Brasserie (☎ 822245; Buccleuch St; starters £6, mains £16; ☼ lunch & dinner Mon-Sat) This atmospheric, oak-panelled niche serves snacks all day, but the lunch and dinner menus include gastronomic delights, such as roast quail, braised lamb, and salmon with mango, prawn and chilli salsa. For lunch the focaccias with creative fillings are a good choice.

Townhouse (☎ 822645; Market Sq; mains £12, 3-course dinner £23; ☼ lunch & dinner) The gourmet cuisine here is the best in town, as evidenced by its 'Best Eating Place in the Borders' award in 2004/05. Dishes are exquisitely prepared, and your stomach will thank you for weeks should you treat yourself to a three-course dinner.

Russell's Restaurant (☎ 822335; Market Sq; dishes £4-7; ☼ 9.30am-4.30pm Mon-Thu, 9.30am-5pm Fri, noon-5pm Sun) Russell's is a stylish little tearoom/ restaurant with a large range of snacks and more substantial offerings, such as a ploughman's lunch. It also brews an excellent mug of coffee.

Getting There & Away

There are First buses to/from Galashiels (20 minutes, frequent), Jedburgh (30 minutes, at least hourly Monday to Saturday), Peebles (1¼ hours, eight daily Monday to Saturday) and Edinburgh (£5, 2¼ hours, eight daily Monday to Saturday).

AROUND MELROSE
Dryburgh Abbey

The most beautiful, complete Border abbey is **Dryburgh Abbey** (HS; ☎ 01835-822381; adult/ child £3.30/1.30; ☼ 9.30am-6.30pm Apr-Sep, 9.30am-4.30pm Oct-Mar), partly because the neighbouring town of Dryburgh no longer exists (another victim of the wars) and partly because it has a lovely site in a sheltered valley by the River Tweed, accompanied only by a symphony of birds. The abbey conjures up images of 12th-century monastic life more successfully than its counterparts in nearby towns. Dating from about 1150, it belonged to the Premonstratensians, a religious order founded in France. The pink-hued stone ruins were chosen as the burial place for Sir Walter Scott.

The abbey is 5 miles southeast of Melrose on the B6404, which passes famous **Scott's View** overlooking the valley. You can hike there along the southern bank of the River Tweed, or take a bus to the nearby village of Newtown St Boswells.

Abbotsford

Fans of Sir Walter Scott should visit his former residence, **Abbotsford** (☎ 01896-752043; adult/child £4.75/2.40; 9.30am-5pm Mon-Sat late Mar-Oct, 2-5pm Sun Mar-May & Oct, 9.30am-5pm Sun Jun-Sep).

SIR WALTER SCOTT (1771–1832)

Sir Walter Scott is one of Scotland's greatest literary figures. It was here, rambling around the Borders countryside as a child, that he developed a passion for historical ballads and Scottish heroes.

Scott wrote a number of successful ballads. *The Lay of the Last Minstrel* (1805) was an early critical success; further works earning him an international reputation included *The Lady of the Lake* (1810), set around Loch Katrine and the Trossachs. He later turned his hand to novels and virtually invented the historical genre. *Waverley* (1814), which dealt with the 1745 Jacobite rebellion, set the classical pattern of the historical novel. Other works included *Guy Mannering* (1815) and *Rob Roy* (1817). In *Guy Mannering* he wrote about Border farmer Dandie Dinmont and his pack of dogs, which became so popular that they became known as Dandie Dinmont Terriers, the only breed of dog named after a literary character.

Later in life Scott wrote obsessively to stave off bankruptcy. His works virtually single-handedly revived interest in Scottish history and legend in the early 19th century. TICs stock a *Sir Walter Scott Trail* booklet, guiding you to many places associated with his life in the Borders.

Probably drawing inspiration from the surrounding 'wild' countryside, he created an extraordinary collection of works. These are on display, as are many other personal possessions.

The mansion is about 2 miles west of Melrose between the River Tweed and the B6360. Frequent buses run between Galashiels and Melrose; alight at the Tweed bank roundabout and follow the signposts (it's a 15-minute walk). You can also walk from Melrose to Abbotsford in an hour along the southern bank of the Tweed.

GALASHIELS

☎ 01896 / pop 14,361

Galashiels has little to recommend it – during the day it's uninviting and in the evening it carries an air of menace, but it's an important transport hub for the Scottish Borders. Fortunately, the charming town of Melrose is just 3 miles east.

The unmanned TIC is in the **Lochcarron Cashmere & Wool Centre** (☎ 751100; Waverley Mill, Huddersfield St; Mon-Sat year-round, plus Sun Jun-Sep), which also houses a museum on Galashiels history. Tours are available (adult/child £2.50/free).

There are frequent buses to/from Edinburgh, Melrose, Hawick, Kelso and Peebles.

SELKIRK

☎ 01750 / pop 5742

Selkirk is a serene little town that climbs a steep ridge above the Ettrick Water, a tributary of the Tweed. Mills came to the area in the early 1800s, but today it's a quiet place with a couple of great attractions.

The helpful **TIC** (☎ 20054; Halliwell's Close; Apr-Oct) is tucked away off Market Sq. Inside is **Halliwell's House Museum** (☎ 20096; Halliwell's Close; admission free; 10am-5pm Mon-Sat, to noon Sun late Mar-Sep, except 10am-1pm Sun Jul & Aug, 10am-4pm Mon-Sat, to noon Sun Oct), the oldest building in Selkirk (1712). The museum charts local history with an engrossing exhibition. Drop into **Sir Walter Scott's Court Room** (☎ 20096; Market Sq; admission free; 10am-4pm Mon-Fri, to 2pm Sat Apr-Sep, plus 10am-2pm Sun May-Aug, 1-4pm Mon-Sat Oct), where the great man served as sheriff of Selkirk County. It houses an exhibition on his life and writings. There is also a fascinating account of the courageous explorer Mungo Park (born near Selkirk) and his search for the River Niger.

SOUTHERN SCOTLAND

You're better off staying overnight in Melrose or Jedburgh, or try the **County Hotel** (☎ 21233; www.countyhotelselkirk.co.uk; Market Sq; s/d £35/60; bar meals £7), which has comfortable rooms with small couches and is popular with golfers. It also serves good bar meals.

First bus 95 and express bus X95 run hourly between Hawick, Selkirk, Galashiels and Edinburgh. From Selkirk to Edinburgh costs £4.50 (two hours).

JEDBURGH
☎ 01835 / pop 4090

The most popular of the Border towns, attractive Jedburgh is a lush, compact oasis, where many old buildings and wynds (narrow alleys) have been intelligently restored, inviting exploration by foot. It's constantly busy with domestic tourists, but wander into some of the pretty side streets and you won't hear a pin drop.

Information
Library (Castlegate; �Y☏ 10am-1pm & 2-5pm Mon-Fri, 5.30-7pm Mon & Fri; ☐) Free Internet access.
Post office (High St)
TIC (☎ 863170; Murray's Green; �Y☏ 9.15am-5pm Mon-Sat, 10am-5pm Sun Apr, May & Oct, 9am-6pm Mon-Sat, 10am-5pm Sun Jun & Sep, 9am-7pm Mon-Sat, 10am-6pm Sun Jul & Aug, 9.30am-4.30pm Mon-Sat Nov-Mar) Best TIC in the Borders.

Sights
JEDBURGH ABBEY
Dominating the town skyline, **Jedburgh Abbey** (HS; ☎ 863925; Abbey Bridge End; adult/child £4/1.60; �Y☏ 9.30am-6.30pm Apr-Sep, 9.30am-4.30pm Mon-Sat, 2-4.30pm Sun Oct-Mar) was the first great Border abbey to be passed into state care, and it shows – audio and visual presentations telling the abbey's story are scattered throughout the carefully preserved ruins (good for the kids or if it's raining). The red-sandstone ruins are roofless but relatively intact, and the ingenuity of the master mason can be seen in some of the rich (if somewhat faded) stone carvings in the nave (be careful of the staircase in the nave – it's slippery when wet). The abbey was founded in 1138 by David I as a priory for Augustinian canons.

MARY QUEEN OF SCOTS HOUSE
Mary stayed at this beautiful 16th-century **tower house** (☎ 863331; Queen St; adult/child £3/free; �Y☏ 10am-4.30pm Mon-Sat, 11am-4.30pm Sun Mar-Nov)

RIDING OF THE MARCHES

The Riding of the Marches, or Common Riding, takes place in early summer in the major Border towns. Like many Scottish festivals it has ancient traditions, dating back to the Middle Ages, when riders would be sent to the town boundary to check on the common lands. The colourful event normally involves extravagant convoys of horse riders following the town flag or standard as it's taken on a well-worn route. Festivities vary between towns but usually involve lots of singing, sport, pageants, concerts and a screaming good time! If you want to zero in on the oldest and largest of the Ridings, head to Selkirk.

---

in 1566 after her famous ride to visit the injured earl of Bothwell, her future husband, at Hermitage Castle (p160). The interesting displays evoke the sad saga of Mary's life.

Activities
The TIC sells some handy walking booklets, including *Walks around Jedburgh* (£1), which has 1.5-mile to 5.5-mile walks, good route descriptions and small maps. Those looking to really stretch the legs can take on small sections of the Southern Upland Way – grab a copy of *Short Walks* (£2.50). For information about the **Borders Abbeys Way**, see Kelso (p153).

Festivals & Events
For two weeks in late June/early July the **Jethart Callant Festival** marks the perilous time when people rode out on horseback checking for English incursions (above).

Sleeping
Reiver's Rest (☎ 864977; relax@reiversrest.co.uk; 91 Bongate St; r £48) This place should be the first port of call in town for couples. The sole room is more like a small luxury apartment, and it's at the rear of the property, making it very private. There's a huge double bed, a small sitting room, a sauna and a TV/video player (with a selection of movies). It's extremely friendly to boot! It's on the main A68 road about 800m north of the town centre.

Glenfriars Guest House (☎ 862000; glenfriars@edenroad.demon.co.uk; Friarsgate; s/d £30/55) Glenfriars is classy in a run-down kind of way.

It was being redecorated when we passed through, and room Nos 4 and 6 both look excellent, especially the old drawing room (No 4), which has stupendous views. Four-poster beds, laid-back hosts and plenty of space make this stylish, ramshackle hotel a favourite.

Froylehurst (☎ 862477; Friars; r per person from £20) Walkers seem to like the elevated position of this excellent B&B. They probably enjoy the friendly hospitality as well. It's a very comfortable option at a very affordable price (it has shared bathrooms). There's no surcharge for singles, and it's recommended for women travellers.

Jedburgh Camping & Caravanning Club Site (☎ 863393; Elliot Park, A68; tent sites £8.30) About a mile north of the town centre, opposite Jedburgh Woollen Mill, this site is set on the banks of Jed Water and is quiet and convenient, particularly if you're interested in fishing.

Also recommended:

Craigowen (☎ 862604; duggleby21@hotmail.com; 30 High St; s/d £25/40) B&B with terrific, central location and huge rooms.

Mrs Elliot (Akaso Uram; ☎ 862482; 7 Queen St; s/d £18/32) Musty and fusty, sure, but the cheapest digs in town.

Eating

Cookie Jar (37 High St; breakfast £5, dishes £2-4.50; ☽ breakfast & lunch) This is a top café, with a bright little dining area just perfect for coffee and a snack. The freshly prepared sandwiches, rolls and sweet treats are too tempting for most mortals. Grab a window seat for a bout of people-watching.

Nightjar (☎ 862552; 1 Abbey Close; mains £8-13; ☽ dinner Tue-Sat) A classy restaurant dishing out a mix of well-constructed meals, including seafood and Thai cuisine. The real highlight, if you're lucky enough to be here on the last Tuesday of the month, is when a special Thai menu is revealed; locals rave about this night.

Carters Rest (☎ 864745; Abbey Place; mains £7-13; ☽ lunch & dinner) Upmarket pub dining that would suit families or older couples. The dinner menu is much better than lunch, featuring dishes such as seared fillets of sea bass on basil-scented ratatouille. It also makes a good pit stop for a cold drink after an exploration of the abbey – it's practically on its doorstep.

Getting There & Away

Jedburgh has good bus connections to Hawick (25 minutes, roughly hourly), Melrose (30 minutes, at least hourly Monday to Saturday) and Kelso (25 minutes, up to 11 daily Monday to Saturday, four Sunday). Munro's bus 29 runs from Edinburgh to Jedburgh (£5.60, two hours, up to 10 daily Monday to Saturday, five Sunday).

HAWICK

☎ 01450 / pop 14,573

Straddling the River Teviot, Hawick is the largest town in the Borders and has long been a major production centre for knit-wear. Most people come to Hawick to shop: it's a bargain hunter's paradise with numerous factory outlets, including **Pringle** (☎ 377644; Commercial Rd); a full list is available from the TIC.

The **TIC** (☎ 372547; 1 Tower Knowe; ☽ 10am-5pm Sat, noon-3pm Sun Mar, 10am-5pm Mon-Sat, noon-3pm Sun Apr-Sep, 10am-5pm Mon-Sat Oct) is at the western end of High St. In the same building is **Drumlanrig's Tower Visitor Centre** (☎ 377615; 1 Tower Knowe; adult/child £2.50/free; ☽ 10am-5pm Sat, noon-3pm Sun Mar, 10am-5pm Mon-Sat, noon-3pm Sun Apr-Sep, 10am-5pm Mon-Sat Oct), which tells the story of cross-border warfare from the 16th century.

Across the river, **Hawick Museum & Scott Art Gallery** (☎ 373457; Wilton Lodge Park; admission free; ☽ 10am-noon & 1-5pm Mon-Fri, 2-5pm Sat & Sun Apr-Sep, 1-4pm Mon-Fri, 2-4pm Sun Oct-Mar) has an interesting collection of mostly 19th-century manufacturing and domestic memorabilia.

You'll be met with a cheery welcome at the amiable **Bridgehouse B&B** (☎ 370701; sergioshawick@aol.com; Sandbed; s/d £30/44). Functional rooms, in a former stables dating back to 1760, are brightly decorated and as neat as a pin, and there's a café, a bar and a great courtyard. If you feel like something more substantial, pop into **Sergio's** (☎ 370094; mains £7; ☽ lunch & dinner) next door for pizza and pasta dishes.

For a bit of R&R and great Turkish coffee or a herbal tea, grab a newspaper and head for snug little **Damascus Drum Café-Bookshop** (2 Silver St; snacks £2-5). Look for the signs near the TIC car park.

The hourly First buses 95 and X95 connect Hawick with Galashiels, Selkirk and Edinburgh (£4.50, two hours).

HERMITAGE CASTLE

A massive collection of stone, with a heavy cubist beauty, **Hermitage Castle** (HS; ☎ 01387-376222; adult/child £2.50/1; ☉ 9.30am-6.30pm Apr-Sep) sits isolated beside a rushing stream surrounded by bleak, empty moorland. Dating from the 13th century, but substantially rebuilt in the 15th, it embodies the brutal history of the Borders; the stones themselves almost speak of the past. Sir Walter Scott's favourite castle, it is probably best known as the home of the earl of Bothwell and the place to which Mary, Queen of Scots, rode in 1566 to see him after he had been wounded in a border raid.

It's also where, in 1338, Sir William Douglas imprisoned his enemy Sir Alexander Ramsay in a pit and deliberately starved him to death. Ramsay survived for 17 days by eating grain that trickled into his pit (which can still be seen) from the granary above. The castle is said to be haunted and it certainly has a slightly spooky feel, especially when dark clouds gather. If you have the place to yourself, a visit can be quite magical – it's one of the best castles to visit in southern Scotland.

The castle is about 12 miles south of Hawick on the B6357.

PEEBLES

☎ 01721 / pop 8065

Prosperous Peebles sits smugly on the banks of the River Tweed, content in the knowledge that it has a prime Borders location, set among rolling, wooded hills. Its agreeable and picturesque ambience will happily entice you to linger for a couple of days. The helpful **TIC** (☎ 720138; High St; ☉ daily Apr-Dec, Mon-Sat Jan-Mar) will chase down accommodation for you.

Sights & Activities

Have a quick look at **Tweedale Museum & Gallery** (☎ 724820; High St; admission free; ☉ 10am-noon & 2-5pm Mon-Fri year-round, plus 10am-1pm & 2-4pm Sat Easter-Oct) in the Chambers Institute. It's mainly given over to famous Border sons, such as Sir Walter Scott, and there are often temporary exhibitions celebrating local artists. There's also a 'museum' of a Victorian museum.

If it's sunny, the **riverside walk** along the River Tweed has plenty of grassed areas ideal for a picnic, and there's a children's play-

ground (near the main road bridge). You could even walk to **Neidpath Castle** (☎ 720333; adult/child £3/1; ☉ 10.30am-5pm Wed-Sat, 12.30-5pm Sun May-Sep), a tower house perched on a bluff above the River Tweed. It's in a lovely spot, a mile west of the town centre, with good views from the parapets.

Sleeping & Eating

Rowanbrae (☎ 721630; john@rowanbrae.freeserve .co.uk, 103 Northgate; r per person £22) This is a classy B&B in a quiet cul-de-sac, a short walk from the town centre. The rooms are beautifully furnished and the lovely doubles come with en suite. The breakfasts are huge.

Cross Keys Hotel (☎ 724222; fax 724333; Northgate; s/d/f £32/56/65) The Cross Keys is a renovated 17th-century coaching inn, and the current owners have maintained the tradition of fine hospitality. Some rooms are very large, though all are neat and well presented. Kings Orchard Brasserie here knocks together good pub grub (mains £6), and there's a bar with real ales and live music at weekends.

Cringletie House Hotel & Restaurant (☎ 725750; www.cringletie.com; s/d from £120/160; 3-course dinner £37; ☒) This elegant baronial mansion, 2 miles north of Peebles on the A703, calls itself a house, but that's being coy – it's a mansion. A very luxurious, baronial mansion, in fact, set in lush, wooded grounds with an excellent restaurant. If you enjoy pampering, genteel elegance and linen so soft you could wrap a newborn in it, this is the place for you.

Rosetta Caravan & Camping Park (☎ 720770; www.rosettacaravanpark.com; Rosetta Rd; tent site & 2 people £12; ☉ Apr-Oct) This award-winning camping ground, about 800m north of the town centre, has an exquisite green setting just minutes' drive from town. There are plenty of amusements for the kids, such as a bowling green and a games room.

Sunflower Restaurant (☎ 722420; 4 Bridgegate; starters £7, mains £12; ☉ lunch Mon-Sat, dinner Thu-Sat) The Sunflower, with its warm yellow dining room, is in a quiet spot off the main drag. It serves good salads for lunch and has an admirable menu in the evenings, with dishes such as wild-boar sausages or pasta with crab, chilli, garlic and lemon.

Central Baguette (High St; baguettes £2; ☉ breakfast & lunch Mon-Sat) For baguettes bursting with fresh fillings head here – it also churns out filled rolls in the morning and stovies and *paninis* any time.

Getting There & Away

The bus stop is beside the post office on Eastgate. First bus 62 runs hourly to Edinburgh (£4, 1¼ hours), Galashiels (45 minutes) and Melrose (1¼ hours).

AROUND PEEBLES
Traquair House

One of Scotland's great country houses, **Traquair House** (☎ 01896-830323; www.traquair.co .uk; Innerleithen; adult/child £5.80/3.25; ☺ 10.30am–5pm Jun-Aug, noon–5pm Apr-May & Sep, 11am–4pm Oct; ♿) has a powerful ethereal beauty, and an exploration here is like time travel. Odd, sloping floors and a musty odour bestow a genuine feel, and parts of the building are believed to have been constructed long before the first official record of its existence in 1107. The massive tower house was gradually expanded over the next 500 years but has remained virtually unchanged since 1642.

Since the 15th century the house has belonged to various branches of the Stuart family, and the family's unwavering Catholicism and loyalty to the Stuart cause are largely why development ceased when it did. The family's estate, wealth and influence were gradually whittled down after the Reformation, and there was neither the opportunity nor, one suspects, the will to make any changes.

One of its most interesting places is the concealed room where priests secretly lived and performed Mass – up until 1829 when the Catholic Emancipation Act was finally passed. Other beautiful, time-worn rooms hold fascinating relics, including the cradle used by Mary for her son, James VI of Scotland (who also became James I of England), and many letters written by the Stuart pretenders to their supporters.

In addition to the house, there's a **garden maze**, an **art gallery**, a small **brewery** producing the tasty Bear Ale, and an active craft community. The **Scottish Beer Festival** takes place here in late May and there's the **Traquair Fair** in early August.

Traquair is 1.5 miles south of Innerleithen, about 6 miles southeast of Peebles. Bus C1 departs from Peebles at 10.15am for Traquair daily and returns at 3.05pm.

SOUTH LANARKSHIRE

South Lanarkshire is an area of contrasts. It combines a highly urbanised area south of Glasgow with scenically gorgeous country around the Falls of Clyde and the World Heritage–listed area of New Lanark, by far the biggest drawcard of the region. If you're roaring up to Scotland on the M74, there are some fine places to break your journey.

South and east of Glasgow are the large satellite towns of **East Kilbride, Hamilton, Motherwell** and **Coatbridge**. These are, for the most part, urban nightmares, and day trips only from Glasgow are recommended. Note also that you're far better off on public transport, given the plethora of roundabouts and one-way streets in these towns.

BLANTYRE
☎ 01698

Blantyre's most famous son is David Livingstone, epitome of the Victorian missionary-explorer, who opened up central Africa to European religion. Visitors with an interest in Africa shouldn't miss the absorbing **David Livingstone Centre** (NTS; ☎ 823140; 165 Station Rd; adult/child £5/4; ☺ 10am–5pm Mon-Sat, 12.30–5pm Sun Easter-Dec), which tells the story of his life. In 30 years it's estimated he travelled 29,000 miles, mostly on foot – the sheer tenacity of the man was incredible. The centre is just downhill from Blantyre train station.

It's a 30-minute walk along the river to **Bothwell Castle** (HS; ☎ 816894; adult/child £2.50/1; ☺ 9.30am–6.30pm Apr-Sep, 9.30am–4.30pm Sat-Wed Oct-Mar), regarded as the finest 13th-century castle in Scotland. The stark, roofless, red-sandstone ruins are substantial and, largely due to their beautiful green setting, romantic. The castle is very popular with wedding parties.

Trains run from Glasgow Central station to Blantyre (£3.95/3 peak/off-peak return, 20 minutes, three hourly).

LANARK & NEW LANARK
☎ 01555 / pop 8253

Below the market town of Lanark, in an attractive gorge by the River Clyde, is the World Heritage site of **New Lanark** – an intriguing collection of restored mill buildings and warehouses.

Once the largest cotton-spinning complex in Britain, it was better known for the pioneering social experiments of Robert Owen, who managed the mill from 1800. New Lanark is really a memorial to this enlightened capitalist. He provided his workers with housing, a cooperative store (the inspiration for the modern cooperative movement), the world's first nursery school for children, a school with adult-education classes, a sickpay fund for workers and a social centre he called the New Institute for the Formation of Character. You'll need at least half a day to explore this site, as there's plenty to see.

Information

There are two banks with ATMs on High St.

Lanark Health Centre (☎ 665522)

Post office (St Leonards St)

TIC (☎ 661661; Horsemarket, Ladyacre Rd, Lanark; ☽ 10am-5pm Easter-Oct, 10am-Sat Nov-Easter) Close to the bus and train stations.

Sights & Activities

NEW LANARK

The best way to get the feel of New Lanark is to wander round the outside of this impressive place. What must once have been a thriving, noisy, grimy industrial village, pumping out enough cotton to wrap the planet, is now a peaceful oasis with only the swishing of trees and the rushing of the River Clyde to be heard.

At the **New Lanark Visitor Centre** (☎ 661345; www.newlanark.org; New Lanark Mills; adult/child/family £5.95/3.95/16.95; ☽ 11am-5pm Sep-May, 10.30am-5pm Jun-Aug) you need to buy a ticket to enter the main attractions. These include the **Historic Schoolhouse**, which contains an innovative, hi-tech journey to New Lanark's past via a 3-D hologram of the spirit of Annie McLeod, a 10-year-old mill girl who describes life here in 1820. The kids will love it as it's very realistic, although the 'do good for all mankind' theme is a little overbearing.

Also included in your admission is a **millworker's house**, Robert Owen's **home** and exhibitions on 'saving New Lanark'. There's also a 1920s-style **village store**.

FALLS OF CLYDE

After you have viewed New Lanark you can then walk up to the **Falls of Clyde** (one hour) through the beautiful nature reserve managed by the Scottish Wildlife Trust. But before you go, drop into the **Falls of Clyde Wildlife Centre** (☎ 665262; admission free; ☽ 11am-5pm Mar-Dec, noon-4pm Jan & Feb) by the river in New Lanark. There are exhibits on peregrine falcons, woodlands and peatland conservation. Note that this place was undergoing refurbishment at the time of writing. An admission fee is likely to be charged upon opening (probably a couple of pounds).

WALKING

You can organise bat walks (£4) or badgerwatching (£6) at the Falls of Clyde Wildlife Centre (left). There's also a walk for 2.5 miles to the beautiful **Cora Linn** (waterfalls that inspired both Turner and Wordsworth) and beyond them to **Bonnington Linn**.

CRAIGNETHAN CASTLE

This **castle** (HS; ☎ 860364; Tillietudlem; adult/child £2.50/1; ☽ 9.30am-6.30pm Apr-Sep, 9.30am-4.30pm Sat-Wed Oct, 9.30am-4.30pm Sat & Sun Nov-Mar) has a very authentic feel – it hasn't been restored beyond recognition – and is in a stunning, tranquil spot, too. You'll feel miles from anywhere, so bring a picnic and make a day of it.

With a commanding position above the River Nethan, this extensive ruin includes a virtually intact tower house and a **caponier** (unique in the UK) – a small gun emplacement with holes in the wall so men with handguns could pick off attackers. The chilly chambers under the tower house are quite eerie.

Craignethan is 5 miles northwest of Lanark. If you don't have your own transport, take an hourly Lanark–Hamilton bus to Crossford, then follow the footpath along the northern bank of the River Nethan (20 minutes).

Sleeping

New Lanark Youth Hostel (SYHA; ☎ 0870 004 1143; Wee Row, Rosedale St, New Lanark; dm adult/child £14/10, tw £28; ☽ Mar-Oct; 🖳) This hostel has a great location in an old mill building by the River Clyde. There are four-bed dorms with attached bathroom and one twin room. It makes a great base for exploring this fascinating World Heritage site.

Summerlea (☎ 664889; 32 Hyndford Rd; s/d £25/48) Just up from the TIC, this modern guesthouse is one of the more central choices available. It has all the comforts of home and mainly twin rooms. The huge single is a great choice as long as you don't mind the colour lavender.

Mrs Berkley (☎ 665487; mary@martinberkley.com; 159 Hyndford Rd; r per person £20-28) A green oasis next to the thumping A73, Mrs Berkley provides simple, traditional accommodation on a lovely property.

Clarkston Farmhouse (☎ 663751; www.clarks tonfarm.com; B7018, Kirkfieldbank; s/d £26/46) If you fancy a stay on a farm with panoramic views of the countryside and a generous breakfast, this is a good choice. There are two twins and one double room. You'll receive a hearty welcome. It's off the A72 to Hamilton.

New Lanark Mill Hotel (☎ 667200; hotel@new lanark.org; Mill One, New Lanark; s/d from £65/100, cottages per week from £265) Cleverly converted from an 18th-century mill, this hotel is full of character and is a stone's throw from the major attractions. It has luxury rooms or self-catering accommodation in cottages. The hotel also serves meals.

Eating

Cafe Espresso (Bannatyne St; light meals under £4; ☺ 8am-4pm Mon-Sat) For a decent coffee after tramping around New Lanark all morning, drop into this café, pull up a pew by the window and watch Lanark life tick by.

Prego (☎ 666300; 3 High St; mains £7-12; ☺ lunch & dinner) This perpetually busy Italian restaurant manages to create a modern ambience in a traditional setting. It dishes up excellent pasta, pizza and fillet steak at very reasonable prices, and the service matches the cuisine. There's a bargain two-course dinner for £10 from 5pm to 7pm on Tuesday, Wednesday and Thursday.

Crown Tavern (☎ 664639; 17 Hope St; lunch £6, dinner mains £9-12; ☺ lunch & dinner) Off the main street, the Crowny is a local favourite. It's a highly regarded place that does good bar meals and even better food (pasta, seafood and vegetarian dishes) in the evenings in its restaurant. Try the local trout or the Highlander chicken.

Also recommended:

Mill Pantry (snacks £2-5; ☺ 10am-5pm) In the New Lanark Visitor Centre.

New Lanark Mill Hotel (☎ 667200; hotel@newlanark .org; Mill One, New Lanark; bar meals £8, 2-course dinner £17) Creative and tasty bar meals.

Getting There & Around

Lanark is 25 miles southeast of Glasgow. Express buses from Glasgow, run by Irvine's Coaches, make the hourly run from Monday to Saturday (£4.50, one hour).

Trains also run daily between Glasgow Central station and Lanark (£4.60, 55 minutes, every 30 minutes).

There's a half-hourly bus service from the train station (daily) to/from New Lanark. If you need a taxi, call **Clydewide** (☎ 663221).

BIGGAR

☎ 01899 / pop 2098

Biggar is a pleasant town in a rural setting dominated by Tinto Hill (712m). The town is well worth a visit – it probably has more museums and attractions per inhabitant than anywhere else its size.

Information

Health Centre (☎ 220383; South Croft Rd)
Post office (High St)
Royal Bank ATM (High St)
TIC (☎ 221066; 155 High St; ☺ 10am-5pm Mon-Sat, noon-5pm Sun Easter-Sep)

Sights

The **Biggar Museums Trust** (☎ 221050) looks after four major museums in the town.

Moat Park Heritage Centre (☎ 221050; Kirkstyle; adult/child £2/1; ☺ 10.30am-5pm Mon-Sat, 2-5pm Sun Easter–mid-Oct), in a renovated church, covers the history of the area with geological and archaeological displays.

Greenhill Covenanter's House (☎ 221050; Burnbrae; adult/child £1/50p; ☺ 2-5pm May-Sep) is an intelligently reconstructed farmhouse, with 17th-century furnishings and artefacts relating to the fascinating story of the local Covenanters, who valiantly defied their king to protect their religious beliefs.

Gladstone Court (☎ 221050; North Back Rd; adult/child £2/1; ☺ 10.30am-5pm Mon-Sat, 2-5pm Sun Easter–mid-Oct) is an indoor street museum with historic nook-and-cranny shops that you can pop into to steal a glimpse of the past. Don't miss the old printing press and the Albion A2 Dogcart, one of the oldest British cars still around.

Biggar Puppet Theatre (☎ 220631; Broughton Rd; all seats £6; ☺ 10am-4.30pm Tue-Sat) has miniature Victorian puppets and bizarre modern ones over 1m high that glow in the dark. There are several ultraviolet displays, but you

SOUTHERN SCOTLAND

shouldn't need your sunglasses. Different shows are suitable for varying age groups, so inquire before you take along the kids. Guided tours cost £2.50/2 per adult/child.

Tinto Hill dominates the town. The hill is a straightforward 4.5-mile ascent by its northern ridge from the car park just off the A73 by Thankerton Crossroads. Look out for the Stone Age fort on your way up.

Sleeping & Eating

School Green Cottage (☎ 220388; isobel.burness@ virgin.net; 1 Kirkstyle; r per person £23) There's a double and a twin available in this conveniently located cottage. The neat rooms are well kitted out with New Zealand oak furnishings. Expect homespun hospitality, but be warned – there's no puffin' on the premises.

Cornhill House (☎ 220001; www.cornhillhouse hotel.com; Coulter; s/d £58/80; mains £15) This is a well-appointed place, complete with turrets, and is situated in a peaceful setting 2 miles southwest of Biggar. The rooms are good value, particularly those that have been refurbished, and a three-course breakfast is included. Its excellent restaurant serves local produce.

La Capannina Restaurant (☎ 221032; 55 High St) This intimate Italian restaurant, around the corner from School Green Cottage, was

---

WORTH THE TRIP

The excellent **St Bride's Church** (☎ 01555-851657; Main St; admission free) in Douglas brings to life this shabby town's links with Scottish history. The 14th-century choir stalls and nave contain three Douglas family wall-tombs, including one for the Good Sir James, who was killed in Spain in 1330 while taking Robert the Bruce's heart to the Holy Land. Look out for the lead-encased hearts of James and Archibald, 5th earl of Angus (also known as 'Bell-the-Cat', one of the most colourful figures in Scottish history), on the floor of the chapel. The superb 16th-century clock tower has the oldest working clock in Scotland (1565). **Mrs Cowan** (☎ 851657; 2 Clyde Rd), behind the Crosskeys Inn, holds the key for the church.

Douglas is about 7 miles northwest of Abington.

---

closed for refurbishment – it should be open by the time you read this, and hopefully the pasta will be just as good.

Getting There & Away

Biggar is 33 miles southeast of Glasgow. McEwan's bus 100 runs to/from Edinburgh (£2.70, 1¼ hours, nine Monday to Saturday, three Sunday). HAD Coaches bus 191 runs hourly to/from Lanark (30 minutes).

ABINGTON
☎ 01864

Abington, 35 miles south of Glasgow, has a 24-hour motorway service station with a **TIC** (☎ 502436; 10am-5pm). In Abington village you'll find a general store, post office, tearoom and Royal Bank. If you need to stay overnight, try the peaceful **Holmlands Country House** (☎ 502753; www.holmlandscotland.co.uk; 22 Carlisle Rd, Crawford; s/d £25/50), which is in a pleasant spot, sheltered from the motorway.

AYRSHIRE

This region's main drawcard is the irresistible Isle of Arran. With fine local produce infused into the culinary scene, atmospheric watering holes (with some of the best beer gardens in the country), and the most varied and scenic countryside of the southern Hebridean islands, this easily accessible island shouldn't be missed.

On the mainland, retro holiday towns by the seaside, such as Largs, give Ayrshire a unique flavour, while towns such as Irvine provide a link to the region's maritime heritage. There's also spectacular coastal scenery, best admired at Culzean Castle, one of the finest stately homes in the country.

It's the birthplace of that famous poet Robert Burns, and there's enough Burns memorabilia to satisfy his most fanatic admirers.

Getting There & Around

Call **Traveline** (☎ 0870 606 2608) for public-transport information. **Stagecoach Western** (☎ 01292-613500) is the main bus operator on the mainland. On Arran, **Western** (☎ 01770-302000) and **Royal Mail** (☎ 01463-256200) buses whiz you around the island, while **CalMac** (☎ 01770-302166) ferries will get you there from the mainland.

SOUTHERN SCOTLAND

NORTH AYRSHIRE

Largs

☎ 01475 / pop 11,241

Largs has a kitsch, yesteryear, resort-style waterfront that is loads of fun. You need to approach the amusements, old-fashioned eateries and bouncing castle with the right attitude – on a sunny day buy an ice cream and go for a stroll to check out this slice of retro Scotland.

There's a **TIC** (☎ 689962; ☺ 9am-5pm Mon-Sat Easter-Oct) at the train station. The **post office** (Aitken St) is just off Main St.

The main attraction in Largs is the award-winning **Vikingar!** (☎ 689777; Greenock Rd; adult/child £4/3; ☺ 10.30am-5.30pm Apr-Sep, 10.30am-3.30pm Oct & Mar, 10.30am-3.30pm Sat & Sun Nov & Feb). This multimedia exhibition describes Viking influence in Scotland until its demise at the Battle of Largs in 1263. Tours with staff in Viking outfits run every half-hour. There's also a theatre, cinema, café, shop, swimming pool and leisure centre. To get here, follow the A78 coast road north from the TIC. You can't miss it, as it's the only place with a longship outside.

FESTIVALS & EVENTS

Largs hosts a **Viking festival** during the first week in September. The festival celebrates the Battle of Largs (1263) and the end of Viking political domination in Scotland. In early June the **Largs Jazz Festival** (www .largsjazzfestival.org.uk) gets cranked up.

SLEEPING & EATING

Glendarroch (☎ 676305; 24 Irvine Rd; r per person £22) This B&B typifies Scottish hospitality – the rooms are well kept and the owner is friendly without being intrusive. If it's full, staff will probably ring around to try and find you something else.

Brisbane House Hotel (☎ 687200; www.brisbane househotel.com; 14 Greenock Rd, Esplanade; s/d from £70/85; ☺) A genteel place standing proudly on the foreshore, the refined Brisbane House is set in lovely gardens and has luxury rooms, some with spas and sea views. Children under five stay for free and cots are available.

Two solid guesthouses in a street full of 'em are **Glenroy Guest House** (☎ 674220; 3 Charles St; r per person £18), which doesn't bother locking the doors – always a good sign, and **Haven House** (☎ 676389; 18 Charles St; r per person

£18), where you'll be greeted with a smile. They're typical of the friendliness of this town and are a short walk to the ferry. Rooms share a bathroom, but are comfortable, clean and a good size.

Townhouse (☎ 675767; Gallowgate Sq; mains £7.50-10; ☺ lunch & dinner) Here you'll find bistro-style dining in swankier surrounds than the town's pubs. The lunch deal is great value (two/three courses £5.95/7.95). Tuck into dishes such as pink peppercorn–crusted salmon on a potato rosti or goats cheese, spinach and roasted-tomato tartlet.

Chippies rule this town, but self-caterers need not despair: there's a large Morrisons supermarket beyond the southern end of Main St.

GETTING THERE & AWAY

Largs is 32 miles west of Glasgow by road. Buses run to Greenock (45 minutes, half-hourly), and at least half-hourly to Ardrossan (30 minutes), Irvine (50 minutes) and Ayr (1¼ hours). There are trains to Largs from Glasgow Central station (£5.50, one hour, hourly).

Isle of Great Cumbrae

☎ 01475 / pop 1200

Walking or cycling is the best way to explore this accessible, hilly island (it's only 4 miles long), ideal for a day trip from Largs. **Millport** is the only town, strung out a long way around the bay overlooking neighbouring Little Cumbrae. With the frequent ferry service, the place buzzes with day-trippers and families (there's heaps of stuff for kids to do, such as crazy golf and a funfair). Walking around the bay admiring the views is one of the most pleasurable things to do in town, where you'll find a post office, supermarket, bank (with ATM) and your choice of chippies.

The town boasts Europe's smallest cathedral, the lovely **Cathedral of the Isles** (☎ 530353; College St; admission free; ☺ daylight hours), which was completed in 1851. Inside it's quite ornate with a lattice woodwork ceiling and fragments of early Christian carved stones.

Just east of town is the interesting **Robertson Museum & Aquarium** (☎ 530581; adult/child £1.50/1; ☺ 10am-12.45pm & 2-4.45pm Mon-Fri year-round, plus Sat Jun-Sep). A short way along the coast from the aquarium is a remarkable rock feature, the **Lion**.

Rural parts of the island are pleasant for **cycling**; the narrow Inner Circle Rd is a particularly good cycle route. There are several bike-hire places in Millport, including **Mapes** (☎ 530444; 3-5 Guildford St; per 1/6 hr £1.90/4.20).

If you're staying overnight on the island, try the unusual **College of the Holy Spirit** (☎ 530353; tccumbrae@argyll.anglican.org; College St; s £20-25, d £40-52), next to the cathedral; there's a refectory-style dining room and a library.

The **Dancing Midgie** (24 Glasgow St; snacks £2-4; ◷ 9am-4pm) is a cheerful café on the seafront providing some healthy, tasty alternatives to the chippies in town, as well as an ideal spot for a read of the newspaper. Food is freshly prepared (sandwiches, salads, soups) and the coffee freshly brewed.

A very frequent 15-minute CalMac ferry ride links Largs with Great Cumbrae (passenger/car £3.50/15.50) daily. Buses meet the ferries for the 3.5-mile journey to Millport (£2.20 return).

Ardrossan
☎ 01294 / pop 11,000
The main reason – OK the *only* reason – for coming here is to catch a CalMac ferry to

Arran. Trains leave Glasgow Central station (£5, one hour, half-hourly) to connect with ferries.

Ardrossan is very run down, and if you're hungry you're better off saving your appetite for more palatable surrounds, which beckon just across the bay.

If you need a B&B, **Edenmore Guest House** (☎ 462306; fax 604016; 47 Parkhouse Rd; s/d £25/44) is the saving grace of this ramshackle town. It's very friendly, and offers small, spotless rooms and a hearty welcome – nothing seems too much trouble for the owner. Room No 4 is the best double. The guesthouse is just off the main A78 and offers evening meals (thank goodness!).

ISLE OF ARRAN
☎ 01770 / pop 4800
Enchanting Arran is a jewel in Scotland's tourism crown. Strangely undiscovered by foreign tourists, the island is a visual feast, and boasts culinary delights, cosy pubs (including its own brewery) and stacks of accommodation. The variations in Scotland's dramatic landscape can all be experienced on this one small island, best experienced by pulling on the hiking boots or jumping on a bicycle. Arran offers some challenging walks in the mountainous north, often compared to the Highlands, while the island's circular road is very popular with cyclists.

Arran's many watering holes are legendary, and over summer most have regular live-music sessions.

Orientation & Information
The ferry from Ardrossan docks at Brodick, the island's main town. To the south, Lamlash is actually the capital and, like nearby Whiting Bay, a popular seaside resort. From the village of Lochranza in the north there's a ferry link to Claonaig on the Kintyre peninsula.

In Brodick there are banks with ATMs.

Arran Library (☎ 302835; Brodick Hall; ◷ 10am-5pm Tue, 10am-7.30pm Thu & Fri, 10am-1pm Sat; 🖳) Free Internet access.

Hospital (☎ 600777; Lamlash)

Internet resources (www.ayrshire-arran.com, www.arrantourism.com)

Kildonan Hotel (☎ 820207; Kildonan; 🖳) Free Internet access.

Laundrette (☎ 600886; Brodick; per load £2.55;

<hr />

WORTH THE TRIP

Boat lovers should check out the **Scottish Maritime Museum** (☎ 278283; Gottries Rd, Harbourside; family/adult/child £7/3/2; ◷ 10am-5pm Apr-Oct) in Irvine. In the massive Linthouse Engine Shop – an old hangar with a cast-iron framework – is an absorbing collection of boats and machinery. A ticket also gives admission to the boat shop, with its wonderful works of art and huge kids activity area. Free guided tours leave from the boat shop – guides will take you down to the pontoons where you can clamber over various ships and visitors can also see a shipyard worker's restored flat.

If you're feeling peckish, drop into the wonderful **Ship Inn** (☎ 279722; 120 Harbour St; mains £7-9; ◷ lunch & dinner). It's the oldest pub in Irvine (1597), serves tasty bar meals and has bucket loads of character.

Irvine is 26 miles from Glasgow. There are frequent buses from Ayr (30 minutes) and Largs (45 minutes). Trains run to/from Glasgow Central station (£5, 35 minutes, half-hourly); the other way they go to Ayr.

ISLE OF ARRAN

SOUTHERN SCOTLAND

(🌙 9am-5pm Mon-Sat) Located by Collins Good Food Shop.

TIC (☎ 303774/6; arran@visitscotland.com; 🌙 9am-7.30pm Mon-Sat, 10am-5pm Sun Jun-Sep, 9am-5pm Mon-Sat, 10am-5pm Sun Oct-May) Efficient; near Brodick pier.

Sights
BRODICK
Most visitors arrive in Brodick, the heartbeat of the island, and congregate along the coastal road to admire the town's long curving bay.

Brodick Castle & Park (NTS; ☎ 302202; adult/child castle & park £10/7, park only £5/4; 🌙 castle 11am-4pm Apr-Oct, park 9.30am-sunset) is 2.5 miles north of Brodick. The first impression is that of an animal morgue as you enter via the hunting gallery, wallpapered with prized deer heads. On your way to the formal dining room (with its peculiar table furnishings), note the intricacy of the fireplace in the library. The castle has more of a lived-in feel than some NTS properties. Only a small portion is open to visitors. The extensive grounds, now a country park with various trails among the rhododendrons, justify the steep entry fee.

As you follow the coast along Brodick Bay, look out for **seals**, often seen on the rocks around Merkland Point. Two types live in these waters, the Atlantic grey seal and the common seal. They're actually quite easy to tell apart – the common seal has a face like a dog; the Atlantic grey seal has a Roman nose.

CORRIE TO LOCHRANZA
The coast road continues north to the small, pretty village of Corrie, where there's a shop and hotel, and one of the tracks up **Goatfell** (the island's tallest peak) starts here. Corrie Village Shop sells wonderful sculptures by local artist Marvin Elliot. After **Sannox**, with a sandy beach and great views of the mountains, the road cuts inland. Heading to the very north, on the island's main road, visitors weave through lush glens flanked by Arran's towering mountain splendour.

LOCHRANZA
The village of Lochranza is in a stunning location in a small bay at the north of the island. On a promontory stand the ruins of the 13th-century **Lochranza Castle** (HS; admission free; 🌙 always open), said to be the inspiration for the castle in *The Black Island*, Hergé's Tintin adventure. It's basically a draughty shell inside, with interpretive signs to help you decipher the layout.

Also in Lochranza is **Isle of Arran Distillers** (☎ 830264; 🌙 10am-6pm mid-Mar–Oct), which has innovative tours (adult/child £3.50/free), including an obligatory dram.

WEST COAST
On the western side of the island, reached by String Rd across the centre (or the coast road), is the **Machrie Moor Stone Circle**, upright sandstone slabs erected around 6000 years ago. It's an eerie place, and these are the most impressive of the six stone circles on the island. There's another group at nearby **Auchagallon**, surrounding a Bronze Age burial cairn.

Blackwaterfoot is the largest village on the west coast; it has a shop/post office and two hotels. You can walk to **King's Cave** from here, via Drumadoon Farm – Arran is one of several islands that lay claim to a cave where Robert the Bruce had his famous arachnid encounter (p31). This walk could be combined with a visit to the Machrie stones.

SOUTH COAST

The landscape in the southern part of the island is much gentler; the road drops into little wooded valleys, and it's particularly lovely around **Lagg**. There's a 10-minute walk from Lagg post office to **Torrylin Cairn**, a chambered tomb over 4000 years old where at least eight bodies were found. **Kildonan** has pleasant sandy beaches, a gorgeous water outlook, two hotels, a campground and an ivy-clad ruined castle.

In **Whiting Bay** you'll find small sandy beaches, a village shop, a post office and craft shops.

LAMLASH

Lamlash is an upmarket town (even the streets feel wider here) in a dazzling setting, strung along the beachfront. The bay was used as a safe anchorage by the Navy during WWI and WWII.

Just off the coast is **Holy Island**, owned by the Samye Ling Tibetan Centre and used as a retreat, but day visits are allowed. The **ferry** (☎ 600998) makes eight trips a day (£9, 15 minutes) from Lamlash and runs between May and September. No dogs, alcohol or fires are allowed on the island. There's a good walk to the top of the hill (314m), taking two or three hours return.

Activities

Drop into the TIC for plenty of walking and cycling suggestions around the island. The handy *18 Walks on Arran* leaflet (£2.50) has details of treks ranging from 2 to 8 miles. There are also plenty of maps available.

The walk up and down **Goatfell** takes up to eight hours return, starting in Brodick and finishing in the grounds of Brodick Castle. If the weather's fine, there are superb views to Ben Lomond and the coast of Northern Ireland. It can, however, be very cold and windy up there; take the appropriate maps (available at the TIC), waterproof gear and a compass.

More moderate walks here include the trail through Glen Sannox, which goes from the village of Sannox up the burn, a two-hour return trip. From Whiting Bay Youth Hostel there are easy one-hour walks through the forest to the **Giant's Graves** and **Glenashdale Falls**, and back – keep an eye out for golden eagles and other birds of prey.

The 50-mile circuit on the coastal road is popular with cyclists and has few serious hills – more in the south than the north.

The **Arran Adventure Company** (☎ 302244; www.arranadventure.com; Shore Rd, Brodick) has loads of activities on offer and runs a different one each day (such as gorge walking, kayaking, abseiling, power kiting and mountain biking). All activities run for about three hours and cost £35/15 for adults/kids. Drop in to see what's available while you're around.

Festivals & Events

The week-long **Arran Folk Festival** (☎ 302623; www.arranfolkfestival.org) takes place in early June. There are also local village festivals from June to September.

Sleeping

If you're after a self-catering option, **Arran Hideaways** (☎ 302303; www.arran-hideaways.co.uk; Brodick) has properties all over the island. They cost about £250 to £850 per week. Check out the website for details.

BUDGET

Camping isn't allowed without permission from the landowner, but there are several camping grounds (open April to October).

Lochranza Youth Hostel (SYHA; ☎ 0870 004 1140; Lochranza; dm adult/child £12.50/9.50; ☺ Mar-Oct) In the north of the island, this hostel has clean, spacious dorms, helpful owners and buckets of information about Arran.

Whiting Bay Youth Hostel (SYHA; ☎ 0870 004 1158; Shore Rd, Whiting Bay; dm adult/child £11.50/9.75; ☺ Apr-Oct) In a rather austere building, this is plainer and smaller than its cousin in the north. Dorms range from three to eight beds, and it's popular with cyclists and walkers.

Glen Rosa Farm (☎ 302380; camp sites per person £3.50) In a lush glen by a river, 2 miles from Brodick, this large place has plenty of nooks and crannies to pitch a tent. It's remote camping with cold water and toilets only. To get there from Brodick head north, take String Rd, then turn right almost immediately on the road signed to Glen Rosa. After 400m, on the left is a white house where you book in; the campground is further down the road.

Seal Shore Camping Site (☎ 820320; Kildonan; camp sites per person/tent £5/50p) This campground is by the sea, and the breeze keeps the midges away. It has a manicured grassed area and is right next to the Kildonan Hotel.

MIDRANGE

Brodick

Glenfloral (☎ /fax 302707; Shore Rd; s £18-19, d £20-22)
This B&B claims a prime spot overlooking the bay, so you'll need to book early to claim a space. The spacious double upstairs with a bay view is recommended, although unlike its counterpart at the rear of the house it doesn't have an attached bathroom.

McAlpine Hotel (☎ 302155; mcalpine@arran-hotels.co.uk; Shore Rd; s/d £35/70) An enormous, ageing hotel, just up from the pier, McAlpine is the epitome of faded glory – in its heyday it must have been a stunner. It has undergone extensive internal redevelopment in the last couple of years. The results are gloriously large, simply furnished rooms, many with sweeping views. It's great value.

Rosaburn Lodge (☎ /fax 302383; d £54; 🔊) By the River Rosa, 800m from the centre of Brodick, this very friendly lodge gets heaps of natural light. The Rosa suite overlooks the river via its bay window and is closer to an apartment than a bedroom. Note that there are no singles.

Corrie

Corrie Hotel (☎ 810273; corriehotel@btinternet.com; r per person £21, with en suite £26) The traditional stone Corrie Hotel offers quaint, slightly ramshackle but comfy, loft-style rooms – No 6 is a good option for three people. Singles are very small and plain, although some have good views of the Holy Isle. Its wonderful beer garden scrapes the water's edge.

SOMETHING SPECIAL

Argentine House (☎ 700662; Shore Rd, Whiting Bay; s/d from £45/63; 🔲) Swiss hospitality in very modish, minimalist rooms is what you can expect at this small hotel. Of the five stylish rooms, the 'Firth of Clyde' is by far the best with smashing views and heaps of space. The owners speak French, German, Italian and Spanish. There's an extensive book and CD collection that guests can use, and evening dinners can be arranged. Breakfast in the morning is a highlight – if you don't enjoy your stay here you really *are* fussy. Note that prices increase for a sea-facing room but decrease with multiple-night stays.

Lochranza

Castlekirk (☎ 830202; www.castlekirkarran.co.uk; r per person £23-25) In a converted 19th-century church (a little creepy), Castlekirk has congenial staff and comfortable rooms, and a fine collection of local Scottish art in its in-house art gallery.

Lochranza Hotel (☎ /fax 830223; hotel@lochranza.co.uk; s/d £45/72) The Lochranza, a bastion of Arran hospitality, has some rooms with outrageous pink floral décor, but they're a good size, sort of homely, and the double and twin at the front (room Nos 1 and 10) have views you can't buy.

Apple Lodge (☎ /fax 830229; Lochranza; d £68-74) Lavish Apple Lodge, the finest place to stay in Lochranza, has beautifully, individually furnished rooms, one with a four-poster bed, and a guest lounge perfect for curling up with a good book. It makes all the difference when your hosts love their job.

Whiting Bay

Viewbank House (☎ 700326; www.viewbank-arran.co.uk; s £22-27, d £56) Appropriately named, it does indeed have tremendous views from its vantage point above Whiting Bay. Rooms are tastefully furnished and well kept. The real pull of this wonderful B&B, however, is its friendly hosts – expect a good dose of Arran hospitality. There's also a great lawn at the front to stretch out on those shimmering sunny Arran days.

Royal Hotel (☎ 700286; www.royalarran.co.uk; r per person £33; dinner £18; 🔊) Each room is unique at this excellent, homely hotel with an elegant interior, amicable staff and a faithful clientele; there's no surcharge for single travellers either. Room No 1 downstairs is a great size and has a private patio.

Lamlash

Brudair (☎ 600570; Shore Rd; s/d £30/50) On the south side of Lamlash, you'll find good clean rooms with en suite in this beautiful old house. There's also a guests' lounge with satellite TV and a fridge to keep your beers cold. If the rain is lashing outside, stock up the fridge and get cosy.

TOP END

Kilmichael Country House Hotel (☎ 302219; www.kilmichael.com; Glen Cloy; s/d from £100/150) The island's best hotel, the Kilmichael is also the oldest building – it has a glass window dating from 1650. The hotel is a luxurious, tastefully decorated hideaway, a mile outside Brodick, with eight rooms and an excellent restaurant.

Lagg Inn (☎ 870255; www.lagghotel.com; Lagg; r per person £42-95) An 18th-century coach house, this inn has a beautiful location and is the perfect place for a romantic weekend. Grab a superior room with garden views. The package deals (from £170 per person, including ferry tickets, car, dinner and B&B for three nights) are terrific value. There's also a cracking beer garden and a fine restaurant.

Kildonan Hotel (☎ 820207; www.kildonanhotel.com; Kildonan; r per person £75; ☐) The Kildonan offers stylish, upmarket B&B in light and airy rooms with a minimalist bent. The grassed area in the front of this classy hotel is being landscaped into a beautiful garden providing a fantastic seating area overlooking the water – perfect on a sunny day. Bar meals are available all day and the restaurant specialises in fresh, local seafood – the menu changes daily depending on the catch.

Eating & Drinking

Creelers Seafood Restaurant (☎ 302810; Duchess Ct; lunch £8, dinner mains £14-17; ☣ closed all Mon & Thu lunch) This award-winning restaurant, 1.5 miles north of Brodick, is religious about seafood and sources all of its delicacies from Arran and the Western Isles. It's a bistro-style place with some outside seating. The Smokehouse next door sells seafood over the counter.

Island Cheese Co (Home Farm, Duchess Ct) Anyone with a fetish for cheese should stop by this place, where you can stock up on the famed local cheeses and watch the masters at work.

Home Farm Kitchen (☎ 302731; Duchess Ct; light meals £2.50-5; ☣ breakfast & lunch) Opposite the Island Cheese Co, you can have a snack in this pleasant eatery, where you'll find tasty baguettes, *paninis*, fresh coffee and an all-day brekky.

Brodick Bar & Brasserie (☎ 302169; Alma Rd, Brodick; mains £10-16; ☣ lunch Mon-Sat, dinner daily; ☣) By the post office, this is a good choice for an upmarket bar meal – fresh fish is the speciality, as well as game dishes such as pheasant. It's popular with families (high chairs are available) and the older crowd.

Ormidale Hotel (☎ 302293; Glen Cloy; mains £6-9; ☣ lunch & dinner) This hotel has decent bar

food. Vegetarians should try the chickpea chilli, while carnivores can dig into smoked pork chops in a cider sauce or a cold Kintyre salmon salad. Arran beers are on tap. Live music cranks out on some nights, creating a good atmosphere.

Eagle's Nest (☎ 830264; Lochranza; starters £5, mains £7-10; ☣ 10am-5pm) Arran's specialities, including salmon, game and cheese, are used in inventive and elegant ways at this fine restaurant in the Isle of Arran Distillers. The dining area is modern and sunny. Skip the baguettes and go straight to dishes like oak-smoked salmon with a whisky and Arran mustard dressing.

Catacol Bay Hotel (☎ 830231; Catacol; bar mains £5-8; ☣ lunch & dinner) Two miles from Lochranza, this bar does great food. The Sunday buffet for £9.50 (over 60s – £6) is famous, and the cheery service makes you feel like a local. With its snug bar, sunny beer garden, frequent live music and great beers on tap, its the best pub on the island.

Breadalbane Hotel (☎ 820284; Kildonan; mains £7-12; ☣ lunch & dinner) Good home-cooked food is served here, and you can dine by the fire on blustery nights or on the decking overlooking the water if the sun is shining. If you want to drown out the sound of your chomping, give the jukebox a whirl.

Joshua's (☎ 700308; Shore Rd, Whiting Bay; starters £4, mains £8.50-12; ☣ 9am-9pm Mon-Sat, 10am-5pm Sun) This funky new place decked out in suave red tones and with a sun-drenched conservatory on the water's edge serves grills, seafood and salads in the evening, with lighter offerings during the day.

Drift Inn (☎ 600656; Shore Rd, Lamlash; mains £5-7.50; ☣ lunch & dinner; ☣) There are few better places to be on the island on a sunny day than the beer garden at this child-friendly hotel ploughing your way through an excellent bar meal while gazing over to the Holy Isle. There are pub faves and genuine Angus beef burgers, with generous portions all round.

Lighthouse Tearoom & Bunkhouse (☎ 850240; Pirnmill; mains £5-9; ☣ lunch & dinner) Calling itself a tearoom is being coy! The restaurant here has an extensive menu, great desserts and outdoor seating, all in a very, very blue lighthouse theme.

Other recommendations:
Corrie Hotel (☎ 810273; Corrie; mains £7-9; ☣ lunch & dinner) Substantial bar meals; delicious Banoffee pie.

Pantry (☎ 700489; Shore Rd, Whiting Bay; mains £7-10; ☺ closed dinner Sun) Fantastic views, friendly service; bistro-style food and takeaway pizza (£8).

Glenisle Hotel (☎ 600559; Shore Rd, Lamlash; starters £5, mains £8-12; ☺ lunch & dinner) Excellent pub food; Wednesday is Italian night. Good wine list.

Getting There & Away

CalMac runs a car ferry between Ardrossan and Brodick (passenger/car £8.40/51 return, 55 minutes, four to six daily), and from late March to late October runs services between Claonaig and Lochranza (passenger/car £7.55/34 return, 30 minutes, seven to nine daily).

Getting Around

BICYCLE

Several places hire out bicycles in Brodick, including **Arran Adventure Company** (☎ 302244; Shore Rd; day/week £12/45) and the **Boathouse** (☎ 302868; Brodick Beach; day/week from £7/25). Other bike-hire places around the island include **Blackwaterfoot Garage** (☎ 860277; Blackwaterfoot; day/week £8/20).

CAR & MOTORCYCLE

At the service station near the ferry pier, **Arran Transport** (☎ 302121; Brodick) hires cars from around £26 per day. Note that it also hires cars for part days at a pro-rata rate. Child seats are available.

PUBLIC TRANSPORT

There are frequent bus services on the island. Five or six buses daily go from Brodick pier to Lochranza (45 minutes, Monday to Saturday), and three to 10 daily go from Brodick to Lamlash and Whiting Bay (30 minutes). Pick up a timetable from the TIC. An Arran Rural Rover ticket costs £4 and permits travel anywhere on the island for a day (buy it from the driver).

For a taxi, call ☎ 302274 in Brodick or ☎ 600903 in Lamlash.

EAST AYRSHIRE

In **Kilmarnock**, where Johnnie Walker whisky has been blended since 1820, is **Dean Castle** (☎ 01563-522702; www.deancastle.com; Dean Rd; admission free; ☺ 11-5pm Apr-Oct, 11-4pm Nov-Mar), a 15-minute walk from the bus and train stations. The castle, restored in the first half of the 20th century, has a virtually windowless keep (dating from 1350) and an adjacent palace (1468), with a superb collection of medieval arms, armour, tapestries and musical instruments. The grounds, an 81-hectare park, are a good place for a picnic, or you can eat at the visitor centre's tearoom, where snacks and light meals cost under £4. Free guided tours are available. From Ayr there are frequent buses throughout the day.

SOUTH AYRSHIRE
Ayr
☎ 01292 / pop 46,431

Ayr is a large, bustling town and a convenient base for a tour of Burns territory. The town's long sandy beach has made it a popular family seaside resort since Victorian times. There are many fine Georgian and Victorian buildings, although some areas of town are showing signs of neglect.

INFORMATION

Banks with ATMs are on High St and Sandgate. The post office is also on Sandgate.

Ayr Hospital (☎ 610555) South of town, by the Dalmellington road.

Carnegie Library (☎ 286385; 12 Main St; ☺ 10am-7.30pm Mon, Tue, Thu & Fri, 10am-5pm Wed & Sat; ☐) Offers fast, free Internet access.

TIC (☎ 0845 225 5121; 22 Sandgate; ☺ 9am-5pm Mon-Sat Apr-Jun & Sep-Mar, 9am-6pm Mon-Sat, 10am-5pm Sun Jul & Aug)

SIGHTS

Most things to see in Ayr are Burns-related. The bard was baptised in the **Auld Kirk** (Old Church; ☎ 262938) off High St; Sunday Mass is at 11am. Several of his poems are set here in Ayr; in *Twa Brigs* Ayr's old and new bridges argue with one another. The **Auld Brig** (Old Bridge) was built in 1491 and spans the river just north of the church. In Burns' poem *Tam o'Shanter*, Tam spends a boozy evening in the pub that now bears his name, at 230 High St.

St John's Tower (☎ 286385; Eglinton Tce; admission free; ☺ by arrangement) is the only remnant of a church where a parliament was held in 1315, the year after the celebrated victory at Bannockburn. John Knox's son-in-law was the minister here, and Mary, Queen of Scots, stayed overnight in 1563.

ACTIVITIES

With only a few steep hills, the area is well suited to cyclists. From Ayr, you could cycle

AYR

INFORMATION
Carnegie Library..........................1 B1
Royal Bank of Scotland............(see 3)
Royal Bank of Scotland ATM..2 B3
Tourist Information Centre
(TIC)..3 B2

SIGHTS & ACTIVITIES
AMG Cycles..................................4 B3
Auld Brig......................................5 B2
Auld Kirk.....................................6 C2
St John's Tower............................7 A2

SLEEPING
Belmont Guest House...............8 B3
Crescent.......................................9 B4
Eglinton Guest House..............10 A2
Lochinver Guest House............11 B3

EATING
Caprice..12 B2
Fouter's Bistro...........................13 B2
Pancake Place............................14 C2
Pumpernickel.............................15 B2

DRINKING
Tam o'Shanter Pub....................16 C3

TRANSPORT
Bus Station.................................17 B2

to Alloway and spend a couple of hours seeing the Burns sights before continuing to Culzean via Maybole. You could either camp here, after seeing Culzean Castle, or cycle back along the coast road to Ayr, a return trip of about 22 miles.

In Ayr **AMG Cycles** (☎ 287580; 55 Dalblair Rd; day/weekend/week £12.50/15/35) hires out bikes.

FESTIVALS & EVENTS
The **Burns an' a' That** festival, held in Ayr in May, has been running for only four years, but looks set to become one of Scotland's biggest cultural events. In 2005 it was huge and included Pete Doherty from Babyshambles reciting the spoken word in honour of the bard.

SLEEPING
A selection of Ayr's B&Bs and small hotels is within a 10-minute walk of the bus station. Several are huddled in a quiet crescent.

Eglinton Guest House (☎ /fax 264623; 23 Eglinton Tce; r per person £22; ⊕) A short walk west of the bus station, this family-run Georgian property is in a lovely cul-de-sac and has a range of traditional, tidy rooms. The location is brilliant – between the beach and the town.

Belmont Guest House (☎ 265588; www.belmont guesthouse.co.uk; 15 Park Circus; s/d £28/52) There's a relaxing lounge and library for guests in this comfortable Victorian town house. It's a little deceptive inside, with the '70s décor punctuated by pictures of wildlife staring hungrily down at diners, but the rooms with

Victorian furnishings are clean and mostly of a good size. Note that over busy periods it doesn't accommodate singles.

Lochinver Guest House (☎ /fax 265086; 32 Park Circus; s/d £24/46) Though a little faded, Lochinver is a very welcoming, solid old guesthouse that is particularly good value for singles. Most rooms are well sized in this towering old Victorian terrace house.

Crescent (☎ 287329; www.26crescent.freeserve.co.uk; 26 Bellevue Cres; s £40, d £56-70) If you want to move up a couple of rungs on the luxury and comfort scale, consider this outstanding small hotel. There are five opulent, individually furnished rooms, including a four-poster suite fit for royalty and a room with French doors opening onto the garden.

Heads of Ayr Caravan Park (☎ 442269; tent site & 2 people £12; ☽ Mar-Oct) This caravan park is in a lovely, quiet location. From Ayr take the A719 south for about 5 miles.

EATING & DRINKING

Pumpernickel (Newmarket St; snacks £3.50-6; ☽ breakfast & lunch Mon-Sat) Continental-style toasties and other delicious snacks are dished out at this deli-café, among the cheeses, meats and preserves inside or at outdoor tables on the pedestrianised street. It's a good spot for a glass of wine in the afternoon, too. If the weather's right, go for a gelato (£6).

Fouter's Bistro (☎ 261391; 2a Academy St; lunch mains £8.50-12; dinner starters/mains £6/16; ☽ lunch & dinner Tue-Sat) The best place to eat in town, in a former bank vault opposite the town hall, Fouter's is a class act. It's an ideal place to splash out on a top-class dinner without breaking the budget. It specialises in Ayrshire produce and Mediterranean-style seafood.

Caprice (☎ 610916; 48 Newmarket St; mains £8-12; ☽ lunch & dinner daily, breakfast Mon-Fri) This upmarket French bistro-style bar-café provides dining among imported beers and well-to-do locals. The food, such as mussels, is very reasonably priced. Look out for the 'early' drink promos, too.

If you're after a supermarket for self-catering, there's a huge **Tesco** (Whitletts Rd) by Ayr Racecourse, and there's an **Asda** (Wallace St) near the river.

Also recommended:

Pancake Place (☎ 288666; 231 High St; mains £4-7; ☽ 9.30am-6pm Mon-Sat, 11am-5pm Sun) Serves sweet and savoury pancakes (with fillings such as Mexican chilli or toffee apple) and all-day breakfasts.

Tam 'o' Shanter (☎ 611684; 230 High St; mains £6.50; ☽ lunch & dinner) Atmospheric old pub with traditional pub grub.

GETTING THERE & AROUND

Ayr is 33 miles from Glasgow and is Ayrshire's major transport hub. The main bus operator in the area is **Stagecoach Western** (☎ 613500) – its hourly X77 service (Monday to Saturday) from Glasgow to Ayr costs £4.30 (one hour). It also runs buses from Ayr to Stranraer (£6.30, two hours, four to eight daily), Greenock (£6.20, 1¾ hours, half-hourly Monday to Saturday, every two hours Sunday), Largs (£4.50, 1¼ hours, half-hourly Monday to Saturday, every two hours Sunday) and Dumfries (£5, 2¼ hours, five to seven daily).

The Ayr Dayrider (£3) allows one day's unlimited travel in and around Ayr, including Alloway, from 9am.

There are at least two trains an hour from Glasgow Central station to Ayr (£5.70, 50 minutes), and some trains continue south from Ayr to Stranraer (£11, 1½ hours).

For a taxi, call **Central Taxis** (☎ 267655).

Alloway
☎ 01292

The pretty, lush town of Alloway (3 miles south of Ayr) should be on the itinerary of every Robert Burns fan – he was born here on 25 January 1759. Even if you haven't been seduced by Burns mania, it's still well worth a visit since the Burns-related exhibitions give a good impression of life in Ayrshire in the late 18th century. The sights are within easy walking distance of each other and come under the umbrella title **Burns National Heritage Park** (www.burnsheritagepark.com).

The **Burns Cottage & Museum** (☎ 441215; adult/child £3/2; ☽ 9.30am-5.30pm Apr-Sep, 10am-5pm Oct-Mar) stands by the main road from Ayr. A 10-minute video introduces you to Burns, his family and the cottage. Born in the little box bed in this cramped thatched dwelling, the poet spent the first seven years of his life here. A fascinating museum of Burnsiana next to the cottage exhibits some fabulous artwork, and many of his songs and letters.

From here, you can visit the ruins of **Alloway Auld Kirk**, the setting for part of *Tam o'Shanter*. Burns' father, William Burnes (his son dropped the 'e' from his name), is buried in the kirkyard.

The **Burns Monument & Gardens** (🕙 9am-5pm) are nearby. The monument was built in 1823 and affords a view of the 13th-century **Brig o'Doon** (see below). There are also statues of Burns' drinking cronies in the gardens.

GETTING THERE & AWAY

Stagecoach Western bus 57 operates hourly between Alloway and Ayr from 8.45am to 3.45pm Monday to Saturday (10 minutes). Otherwise, rent a bike and cycle here.

Troon

☎ 01292 / pop 14,766

Troon, a major sailing centre on the coast 7 miles north of Ayr, has excellent sandy beaches and six golf courses. The demanding championship course **Royal Troon** (☎ 311555; www.royaltroon.co.uk; Craigend Rd) offers two rounds of golf for £200, including lunch in the clubhouse (caddie hire is £35 extra).

Dundonald Castle (☎ 01563-851489; Dundonald; adult/child £2.50/1.50; 🕙 10am-5pm Apr-Oct) commands impressive views and has one of the finest barrel-vaulted ceilings in Scotland. The compulsory guided tour can be tiresome, but inside you can still see the original mason's signature on the stones. It was the first home of the Stuart kings, built by Robert II in 1371, and reckoned to be the third most important castle in Scotland, after Edinburgh and Stirling. The visitor centre has a useful time line of settlements here starting from 1500 BC. There are also models of the castle's development starting with a Dark Age fort from about 500AD.

GETTING THERE & AWAY

Dundonald Castle is 4 miles northeast of Troon. Stagecoach Western runs hourly buses (Monday to Saturday) between Troon and Kilmarnock, via Dundonald village.

There are half-hourly trains to Ayr (£2, 11 minutes) and Glasgow (£5.20, 45 minutes).

P&O (☎ 0870 242 4777; www.poirishsea.com) sails twice daily to Larne in Northern Ireland (£16 to £24 for passengers, £98 to £145 for a car and driver, two hours).

ROBERT BURNS (1759–96)

Best remembered for penning the words of *Auld Lang Syne*, Robert Burns is Scotland's most famous poet and a popular hero whose birthday (25 January) is celebrated as Burns Night by Scots around the world. The Scottish executive hopes to turn Burns Night into a national celebration to rival Ireland's St Patrick's Day.

Burns was born in 1759 in Alloway. At school he soon showed an aptitude for literature and a fondness for the folk song. He later began to write his own songs and satires. When the problems of his arduous farming life were compounded by the threat of prosecution from the father of Jean Armour, with whom he'd had an affair, he decided to emigrate to Jamaica. He gave up his share of the family farm and published his poems to raise money for the journey.

The poems were so well reviewed in Edinburgh that Burns decided to remain in Scotland and devote himself to writing. He went to Edinburgh in 1787 to publish a second edition, but the financial rewards were not enough to live on and he had to take a job as a customs officer in Dumfriesshire. He contributed many songs to collections published by Johnson and Thomson in Edinburgh, and a 3rd edition of his poems was published in 1793. To give an idea of the prodigious writings of the man, Robert Burns composed more than 28,000 lines of verse over 22 years. Burns died of rheumatic fever in Dumfries in 1796, aged 37.

Burns wrote in Lallans, the Scottish Lowland dialect of English that is not very accessible to the Sassenach (Englishman), or foreigner; perhaps this is part of his appeal. He was also very much a man of the people, satirising the upper classes and the church for their hypocrisy.

Many of the local landmarks mentioned in the verse-tale *Tam o'Shanter* can still be visited. Farmer Tam, riding home after a hard night's drinking in a pub in Ayr, sees witches dancing in Alloway churchyard. He calls out to the one pretty witch, but is pursued by them all and has to reach the other side of the River Doon to be safe. He just manages to cross the Brig o'Doon, but his mare loses her tail to the witches.

The Burns connection in southern Scotland is milked for all it's worth and TICs have a *Burns Heritage Trail* leaflet leading you to every place that can claim some link with the bard. Burns fans should have a look at www.robertburns.org.

Culzean Castle & Country Park

The Scottish National Trust's flagship property, magnificent **Culzean** (NTS; cull-ane; ☎ 01655-884400; adult/child/family £12/8/30, park only adult/child £6/4; ☺ castle 10.30am-5pm Apr-Oct, 11am-4pm Sat & Sun Nov-Mar, park 9.30am-sunset) is one of the most impressive of Scotland's great stately homes. The entrance to Culzean is a converted viaduct, and on approach the castle appears like a mirage, floating into view. Designed by Robert Adam, who was encouraged to exercise his romantic genius in its design, this 18th-century mansion is perched dramatically on the edge of the cliffs. Robert Adam was the most influential architect of his time, renowned for his meticulous attention to detail and the elegant classical embellishments with which he decorated his ceilings and fireplaces.

The beautiful oval staircase here is regarded as one of his finest achievements. On the 1st floor, the opulence of the circular saloon contrasts violently with the views of the wild sea below. Lord Cassillis' bedroom is said to be haunted by a lady in green, mourning for a lost baby. Even the bathrooms are palatial, the dressing room beside the state bedroom being equipped with a Victorian state-of-the-art shower.

There are also two ice houses, a swan pond, a pagoda, a re-creation of a Victorian vinery, an orangery, a deer park and an aviary. Wildlife in the area includes otters.

If you really want to experience the magic of this place, it's possible to stay in the **castle** (culzean@nts.org.uk; s/d from £140/225, Eisenhower ste £250/375) from April to October. If you're not in that league there's a **Camping & Caravanning Club** (☎ 01655-760627; tent sites members/nonmembers £7/12) with good facilities in the park.

GETTING THERE & AWAY

Culzean is 12 miles south of Ayr; Maybole is the nearest train station, but since it's 4 miles away it's best to come by bus from Ayr (30 minutes, 11 daily, Monday to Saturday). Buses pass the park gates, from where it's a 20-minute walk through the grounds to the castle.

Turnberry

☎ 01655 / pop 192

Visitors playing the world-famous golf course here usually stay at the luxurious **Westin Turnberry Resort** (☎ 331000; turnberry @westin.com; s/d from £135/160), where they're able to land their private aircraft or helicopter. If you can afford the price of accommodation, a four-course dinner in the award-winning restaurant is a snip at £55.

Kirkoswald

☎ 01655 / pop 500

Just 2 miles east of Kirkoswald, by the A77, **Crossraguel Abbey** (HS; ☎ 883113; adult/child £2.50/1; ☺ 9.30am-6.30pm Apr-Sep) is a substantial ruin dating back to the 13th century that's good fun to explore. The recently renovated 16th-century gatehouse is the best part of the ruin – you'll find decorative stonework and superb views from the top. Inside, if you have the place to yourself, you'll hear only the whistling wind – an apt reflection of the abbey's long-deceased monastic tradition. Don't miss the echo in the chilly sacristy.

Stagecoach Western runs Ayr to Girvan buses via Crossraguel Abbey and Kirkoswald (35 minutes, hourly Monday to Saturday, every two hours Sunday).

Ailsa Craig

Curiously shaped Ailsa Craig can be seen from much of southern Ayrshire. While its unusual blue-tinted granite has been used by geologists to trace the movements of the great Ice Age ice sheet, bird-watchers know Ailsa Craig as the world's second-largest gannet colony – around 10,000 pairs breed annually on the island's sheer cliffs.

To see the island close up you can take a cruise from Girvan on the **MV Glorious** (☎ 01465-713219; bookings at 7 Harbour St). It's possible to land if the sea is reasonably calm; a four-hour trip costs £15/10 per adult/child (an extra £5 if you want to do a spot of fishing). A minimum of eight people and one week's notice are required.

Trains going to Girvan run approximately hourly (with only three trains Sunday) from Ayr (£3.70, 30 minutes).

DUMFRIES & GALLOWAY

Dumfries & Galloway is an ideal travel destination for families. A traditional domestic holiday hot spot, it is largely outside the radar of foreign tourists. That's one of the reasons it's so good to explore. More elbow room, plenty on offer for the kids and, happily, restaurants and B&Bs/guesthouses that are very used to children.

Adding to the appeal of this enticing region is a string of southern Scotland's most idyllic towns and remote forests, where red deer, kites, majestic ospreys and other wildlife can be readily seen. Although the towns are devoid of the tourist crush, domestic daytrippers flood ones like pretty Castle Douglas when the sun shines. And shine it does. Warmed by the Gulf Stream, this is the mildest region in Scotland, a phenomenon that has allowed the development of some famous gardens. Off the major routes, public transport seems to have passed the region by, so it's better to explore the mountains, forests, castles and dramatic coastline with your own wheels – motorised or pedal powered.

Getting There & Around

Buses between London and Belfast, via Birmingham, Manchester, Carlisle, the towns along the A75 (including Dumfries and Newton Stewart) and Stranraer are available with **Eurolines/National Express** (☎ 0870 514 3219).

Local bus operators frequently change, although routes (and bus numbers) rarely alter. The main operators are **Stagecoach Western** (☎ 01387-260383, 01776-704484) and **MacEwan's** (☎ 01387-256533). The Day Discoverer (adult/child £5/2) is a useful day ticket valid on most buses in the region and on Stagecoach Cumberland in Cumbria.

Two train lines from Carlisle to Glasgow cross the region, via Dumfries and Moffat respectively. The line from Glasgow to Stranraer runs via Ayr.

DUMFRIES

☎ 01387 / pop 31,146

Despite having several important Burns-related museums, Dumfries has escaped mass tourism. Lovely, red-hued sandstone bridges connect the sprawling town, which is bisected by the wide River Nith, and there are pleasant grassed areas along the river bank.

Historically, Dumfries held a strategic position in the path of vengeful English armies. Consequently, although it has existed since Roman times, the oldest standing building dates from the 17th century.

Information

There is a Royal Bank of Scotland with ATMs near the TIC.

Ewart library (☎ 253820; Catherine St; ⏲ 9.15am-7.30pm Mon-Wed & Fri, 9.15am-5pm Thu & Sat; 🖳) Free Internet access at this excellent cyber centre.

Laundrette (☎ 252295; 26 Annan Rd; ⏲ 9am-5pm Mon-Fri, 9am-4pm Sat) Wash and dry from £7.50.

TIC (☎ 253862; info@dgtb.visitscotland.com; 64 Whitesands; ⏲ 9.30am-5pm Mon-Sat Apr-Jun, 9am-6pm Mon-Sat, 11am-4.30pm Sun Jul & Aug, 9am-5.30pm Mon-Sat, 11am-4.30pm Sun Sep, 9.30am-5pm Mon-Sat, 11am-4pm Sun Oct, 9am-5pm Mon-Sat Nov-Mar) A very good TIC with plenty of information on the region. You can book Eurolines and Scottish Citylink buses here. Pick up a copy of the town's *Pub Guide* if you're planning a boozy stay.

Sights

The red-sandstone bridges arching over the River Nith are the most attractive features of the town, and Devorgilla Bridge (1431) is one of the oldest bridges in Scotland.

Burns House (☎ 255297; Burns St; admission free; ⏲ 10am-5pm Mon-Sat, 2-5pm Sun Apr-Sep, 10am-1pm & 2-5pm Tue-Sat Oct-Mar) is a place of pilgrimage for Burns enthusiasts; it's here that the poet spent the last years of his life, and there are some interesting relics, original letters and manuscripts.

Robert Burns Centre (☎ 264808; Mill Rd; admission free, audiovisual presentation £1.60/80p; ⏲ 10am-8pm Mon-Sat, 2-5pm Sun Apr-Sep, 10am-1pm & 2-5pm Tue-Sat Oct-Mar) is an award-winning museum in an old mill on the banks of the River Nith. It tells the story of Burns and Dumfries in the 1790s. The audiovisual presentation explains the exhibition's content, and there are original Burns manuscripts. There's also a restaurant, Hullabaloo.

Burns' **mausoleum** is in the graveyard at **St Michael's Kirk**. At the top of High St is a **statue** of the bard; take a close look at the sheepdog at his feet.

Sleeping

Haven (☎ 251281; www.thehavenbandb.co.uk; 1 Kenmure Tce; r per person £25) A brilliantly located B&B with twin rooms and a single, but no doubles (no cuddle tonight). This shortfall is well and truly compensated for by its spot right on the river bank and next to a pedestrian bridge. The B&B has the best location in Dumfries. Rooms are well-cared for (as are guests); No 2 and the single have the best views.

Torbay Lodge (☎ 253922; www.torbaylodge.co.uk; 31 Lovers Walk; r per person £25-30) This place offers fine hospitality and has those extra little touches (such as lollies in the foyer) that set it apart from the rest. Impeccable hosts, an immaculate house (actually two houses, as the guesthouse extends to the property next door) and 10 elegant, well-appointed rooms make this an impressive operation. Expect to find crisp sheets, heaps of windows, a top brekkie and off-street parking.

Ferintosh Hotel (☎ 252262; www.ferintoshhotel .co.uk; 30 Lovers Walk; s/d £35/54) A Victorian villa, opposite the train station, Ferintosh has sumptuous rooms done in individual themes. The whisky room is our fave and the owners are mad keen on the stuff – there'll probably be a free dram awaiting you on arrival. Great local hospitality.

Two B&Bs, opposite each other, that excel in the B&B trade are **Glencairn Villa** (☎ /fax 262467; info@glencairnvilla.co.uk; 45 Rae St; s/d from £20/44) – room No 3 is a great double – and efficiently run **Lindean Guest House** (☎ 251888; 50 Rae St; s/d £20/46).

Eating

Coffee House (☎ 251771; 148 High St; snacks £2.50-3.50; ⏰ 8am-6pm Mon-Wed, Fri & Sat, 8am-8pm Thu, 11am-4.30pm Sun) For a relaxing pit stop smack bang in the middle of the High St, check out this cheeky little number bringing a bit of caffeine snobbery to Dumfries. Grab the paper, your favourite tea or coffee and watch the world tick by.

Hullabaloo (☎ 259679; Mill Rd; lunch mains £3.50-5.50, dinner mains £9-14; ⏰ lunch daily, dinner Tue-Sat) Locals flock to this contemporary restaurant, at the Robert Burns Centre, at weekends. At lunch you'll get wraps, melts and ciabattas, but for dinner it's inventive angles on traditional creations – try the monkfish, pancetta and rosemary kebab.

Globe Inn (☎ 252335; 56 High St; bar mains £5.50; ⏰ lunch & dinner) A traditional, rickety old nook-and-cranny pub, said to be Burns' favourite watering hole, serving great home-cooked bar meals. The Globe is atmospheric, warm and welcoming. You'll experience the best food on Friday and Saturday nights when the kitchen really gets revved up.

SOUTHERN SCOTLAND

DUMFRIES

0 _____ 200 m
0 _____ 0.1 miles

INFORMATION
Ewart Library Cyber Centre................1 C1
Police Station.......................................2 C2
Post Office...3 C2
Royal Bank of Scotland........................4 B3
Tourist Information Centre (TIC)........5 B2

SIGHTS & ACTIVITIES
Burns House...6 C3
Robert Burns Centre.............................7 B3
St Michael's Kirk & Burns'
  Mausoleum..8 C3
Statue of Burns....................................9 B2

SLEEPING 🏠
Ferintosh Hotel..................................10 D1
Glencairn Villa...................................11 C1
Haven...12 B3
Lindean Guest House.........................13 C1
Torbay Lodge.....................................14 C1

EATING 🍴
Coffee House......................................15 B2
Globe Inn...16 C3
Hullabaloo...................................(see 7)
Morrisons Supermarket......................17 C3
Rose of India.....................................18 B2

TRANSPORT
Buses to Moffat, Carlisle & Towns
  on the A74......................................19 A2
Grierson & Graham Cycle Centre......20 B1

To Glasgow (75mi);
Edinburgh (80mi)

Dumfries
Train
Station

To A709;
Lockerbie (13mi)

To
Laundrette
(250m)

To Dalbeattie
(13mi)

To New
Abbey (7mi);
Solway Coast

TOP FIVE DISTRACTIONS FOR KIDS IN DUMFRIES & GALLOWAY

Mabie Farm Park (right)
Galloway Wildlife Conservation Park (p181)
Cream o' Galloway (p182)
Galloway Forest Park (p182)
Caerlaverock Castle (right)

Rose of India (☎ 248555; 46 Buccleuch St; mains £5-9; ⌚ lunch & dinner) Scotland has many good curry houses, but not many better than this one. The traditional, freshly prepared dishes may come as a surprise if you're expecting the usual tandoori or tikka masala. Fragrant, tasty meals are very good value, and there's an all-you-can-eat buffet nightly. This is one curry house not to be missed.

For self-caterers looking for a supermarket, you can buy all you need at the huge **Morrisons** (Brooms Rd).

Getting There & Away

Dumfries is 80 miles southwest of Edinburgh on the A76. Stranraer is 68 miles west on the A75, via Castle Douglas and Newton Stewart.

BUS

Eurolines and National Express run buses 920 and 921 twice daily between London and Belfast, via Carlisle, Dumfries, towns along the A75 and Stranraer; London to Dumfries is £29.

Local buses run regularly to Kirkcudbright (1¼ hours, at least hourly Monday to Saturday, six on Sunday) and towns along the A75 to Stranraer (£6, 2¼ hours, eight daily Monday to Saturday, three on Sunday).

Bus 100 runs to/from Edinburgh (£5.50, 2¾ hours, five daily Monday to Saturday, three on Sunday), via Moffat and Biggar.

TRAIN

There are trains between Carlisle and Dumfries (£7.10, 35 minutes, every hour or two Monday to Saturday), and direct trains between Dumfries and Glasgow (£10.70, 1¾ hours, eight daily Monday to Saturday); there's a reduced service on Sunday.

Getting Around

Bikes are available for hire from **Grierson & Graham** (☎ 259483; 10 Academy St; per 24hr from £15;

⌚ 9am-5pm Mon-Sat), but don't forget to bring photo ID and cash for your deposit. For a taxi call **Dixon's Taxis** (☎ 720900).

SOUTH OF DUMFRIES

Caerlaverock

The ruins of **Caerlaverock Castle** (HS; ☎ 01387-770244; adult/child £4/1.60; ⌚ 9.30am-6.30pm Apr-Sep, 9.30am-4.30pm Oct-Mar), by Glencaple on a beautiful stretch of the Solway coast, are among the loveliest in Britain. Surrounded by a moat, lawns and stands of trees, the unusual pink-stoned triangular castle looks impregnable – in fact, it fell several times. The current castle dates from the late 13th century. Inside, there's an extraordinary Scottish Renaissance façade to apartments that were built in 1634. With nooks and crannies to explore, passageways and remnants of fireplaces, this castle is great for the whole family.

It's worth combining a visit to the castle with a visit to **Caerlaverock Wildlife & Wetlands Centre** (☎ 01387-770200; adult/child £4.40/2.70; ⌚ 10am-5pm), a mile east. It protects 546 hectares of salt marsh and mud flats, the habitat for numerous birds, including barnacle geese. There's free, daily wildlife safaris with experienced rangers and a coffee shop that serves organic food.

New Abbey

The small, picturesque village of New Abbey lies 7 miles south of Dumfries and contains the remains of the 13th-century Cistercian **Sweetheart Abbey** (HS; ☎ 01387-850397; adult/child £2/80p; ⌚ 9.30am-6.30pm Apr-Sep, 9.30am-4.30pm Sat-Wed Oct-Mar). The shattered, red sandstone remnants of the abbey are impressive and stand in stark contrast to the manicured lawns surrounding them. The abbey was founded by Devorgilla de Balliol in honour of her dead husband (with whom she had founded Balliol College, Oxford). On his death, she had his heart embalmed and carried it with her until she died 22 years later. She and the heart are buried in the presbytery – hence the name.

Mabie Farm Park (☎ 01387-259666; www.mabie farm.co.uk; family/adult/child £16/4.50/4; ⌚ 10am-5pm Mar-Nov) Kids complaining? Has your trip been all castles, historic sights, the odd pub and Robert Burns? Pack up the clan and get down to this park, 4 miles north of New Abbey off the A710. There's plenty of animals and activities for kids, including petting and feeding sessions, donkey rides, quad biking, go-karting, slides, a soft play area, picnic areas... the list goes on – put a full day aside.

Dalbeattie

Off the B794, 2 miles north of Dalbeattie, the **Motte of Urr** (admission free) is one of Scotland's largest 12th-century Norman motte-and-bailey castles. About 4 miles south is the 15th-century **Orchardton Tower** (HS; Palnackie; admission free; ⊗ 9.30am-6.30pm Apr-Sep, 9.30am-4.30pm Mon-Sat, 2-4.30pm Sun Oct-Mar), the only circular tower house in Scotland; the keyholder lives in the nearby cottage.

From Dalbeattie, you can either follow the scenic coast road to Kirkcudbright or head inland on the A745 to Castle Douglas.

Getting There & Away

From Dumfries, Stagecoach Western bus 371 runs nine times a day Monday to Saturday (twice Sunday) to Caerlaverock Castle. By car take the B725 south.

McEwan's bus 372 from Dumfries stops in New Abbey, Kirkbean, Rockcliffe, Kippford and Dalbeattie; from there bus 505 continues to Kirkcudbright (but not on Sunday).

CASTLE DOUGLAS & AROUND
☎ 01556 / pop 3671

Castle Douglas attracts a lot of day-trippers but hasn't been 'spruced up' for tourism. It's an open, attractive, well-cared-for town. There are some remarkably beautiful areas close to the centre, such as the small **Carlingwark Loch**. The town was laid out in the 18th century by Sir William Douglas, who had made a fortune in the Americas.

The **TIC** (☎ 502611; Market Hill, King St; ⊗ Mon-Sat Oct, daily Easter-Sep) is in a small park on King St. The **library** (☎ 502643; Market Hill, King St; ⊗ 10am-7.30pm Mon-Wed & Fri, 10am-5pm Thu & Sat; 🖳) has free Internet access.

Sights & Activities
SULWATH BREWERY

You can see traditional brewing processes at **Sulwath Brewery** (☎ 504525; 209 King St; adult/child £3.50/free; ⊗ 10am-4pm Mon-Sat). Admission includes a half-pint of Galloway real ale (tea or coffee is also available). Recommended is the Criffel, an original pale ale, and Knockendoch, a dark brew with a delicious taste of roasted malt.

THREAVE GARDEN

A mile west off the A75, **Threave Garden** (NTS; ☎ 502575; Threave House; adult/child £5/3.75; ⊗ visitor centre 9.30am-5.30pm Apr-Oct, 10am-4pm Feb, Mar & Nov-23 Dec, garden 9.30am-sunset year-round) houses the National Trust for Scotland (NTS) horticultural school, and is noted for its spectacular spring daffodil display from mid-March to mid-May.

THREAVE CASTLE

Two miles further west, **Threave Castle** (HS; ☎ 07711-223101; adult/child incl ferry £2.50/75p; ⊗ 9.30am-6.30pm Apr-Sep) is an impressive tower on a small island in the River Dee. Built in the late 14th century, it became a principal stronghold of the Black Douglases. It's now basically a shell, having been badly damaged by the Covenanters in the 1640s, but it's a romantic ruin nonetheless.

It's a 10-minute walk from the car park to the ferry landing, where you ring a bell for the custodian to take you across to the island in a small boat.

LOCH KEN

Stretching for 9 miles northwest of Castle Douglas beside the A713, Loch Ken is a popular outdoor recreational area. The range of water sports includes windsurfing (£35 per day), sailing, canoeing (£18 per half-day), power-boating and fishing. **Galloway Sailing**

WORTH THE TRIP

About a mile southeast of Kirkbean, there's a cottage on a hill-side overlooking the Solway Firth that was the birthplace of John Paul Jones (1747–92), a former pirate who became father of the US navy. **John Paul Jones Cottage** (☎ 01387-880613; adult/child £2/1; ⊗ 10am-5pm Tue-Sun Apr-Sep, daily Jul & Aug) is a museum that provides a glimpse of this man's remarkable life. An audiovisual presentation gives an overview, explaining that it took over 100 years for his feats to be recognised – he's famous for his naval fights against the British as part of the US Independence movement. There is also an interpretive display filling in the parts of his life the video skims over. Next door is the cottage he was born in (small but authentic) and a less-interesting commentary on life in the 18th century.

SOUTHERN SCOTLAND

Centre (☎ 01644-420626; www.lochken.co.uk; ☉ 9am-7pm Apr-Oct), on the eastern bank north of Parton village, provides equipment, training and accommodation. There are also walking trails and a rich variety of bird life. The Royal Society for the Protection of Birds (RSPB) has a **nature reserve** (☎ 01671-402861) on the western bank, north of Glenlochar.

Sleeping & Eating

Woodlea (Kings B&B; ☎ 502247; 37 Ernespie Rd; r per person £21) Woodlea is a welcoming stone-built villa, and a warm reception is guaranteed. The spacious rooms are tastefully furnished and share a huge bathroom. The family room is particularly good. You feel as though you're a guest sharing your host's house.

Douglas House (☎ 503262; www.douglas-house .com; Queen St; s £30-50, d £60-80; ☐ ☒) In this delightful guesthouse just behind the town centre, lacy rooms are chock-a-block with soft furnishings and some of the en suites are enormous. It's a little over the top, but you'll be well rested and extremely well fed in the morning. Vegetarians are catered for.

Douglas Arms Hotel (☎ 502231; www.douglasarms hotel.co.uk; King St; s/d £45/70; bar meals £8-15) Smack bang in the middle of town, Douglas Arms was originally a coaching inn, but these days all the mod cons comfort the weary traveller. There's a range of decent rooms, some with large-screen TVs (good if the football is on). The lively bar serves scrummy food.

Lochside Caravan & Camping Site (☎ /fax 502949; Lochside Park; tent sites £9.30-11.10; ☉ Easter-Oct) This is an attractive spot beside Carling-wark Loch; there's plenty of grass and fine trees providing shade. With over 50 pitches available, booking isn't necessary.

Kings Arms Hotel (☎ 502626; cnr Queen & St Andrew Sts; mains £6.50-12; ☉ lunch & dinner) This traditional pub sells very traditional pub meals – and it does them pretty well. It's recommended by locals, and there's plenty of them in here scoffing the tempting morsels. If you arrive for dinner and you're not dining in the restaurant, make sure you ask for the a la carte menu, as the waiting staff will assume you only want to see the bar meals menu.

Also recommended:

Galloway Sailing Centre (☎ /fax 01644-420626; Loch Ken; dm £12.50) Year-round backpacker accommodation 6 miles north of Castle Douglas.

Simply Delicious (134 King St; mains £2-6; ☉ lunch Mon-Sat) Great café serving all-day brekky £5, luxury melts and freshly ground coffee.

Getting There & Away

McEwan's buses 501 and 502 pass through Castle Douglas roughly hourly Monday to Saturday (eight times Sunday) en route to Dumfries (45 minutes) and Kirkcudbright (20 minutes). Buses 520 and S2 along the A713 connect Castle Douglas with New Galloway (30 minutes, six daily Monday to Saturday, one Sunday) and Ayr (£5.50, 2¼ hours, two or three daily Monday to Saturday, one Sunday).

KIRKCUDBRIGHT

☎ 01557 / pop 3447

Kirkcudbright (kirk-*coo*-bree), with its dignified streets of 17th- and 18th-century merchants' houses and its appealing harbour, is the ideal base from which to explore the south coast. This delightful town has one of the most beautifully restored high streets in Dumfries & Galloway. Look out for the nook-and-cranny wynds in the elbow of the High St. With its architecture and setting, it's easy to see why Kirkcudbright has been an artists' colony since the late 19th century.

Information

There's a handy **TIC** (☎ 330494; kirkcudbrighttic@ visitscotland.com; Harbour Sq; ☉ daily mid-Feb–Nov) with useful brochures detailing walks and road tours in the surrounding district. You'll find a bank with an ATM on St Mary St. Check out www.kirkcudbright.co.uk and www.kirkcudbrightartiststown.co.uk for heaps of information on the town.

Sights & Activities

Kirkcudbright is a great town for a wander and it won't be long before you stumble across its charming sights.

MacLellan's Castle (HS; ☎ 331856; Castle St; adult/child £2.50/1; ☉ 9.30am-6.30pm Apr-Sep), near the harbour, is a large, atmospheric ruin built in 1577 by Thomas MacLellan, then provost of Kirkcudbright, as his town residence. Inside look for the 'lairds' lug', a 16th-century hidey hole designed for the laird to eavesdrop on his guests.

Tolbooth Arts Centre (☎ 331556; High St; admission free; ☉ 11am-5pm Mon-Sat May, 11am-5pm Mon-Sat, 2-5pm Sun Jun & Sep, 10am-6pm Mon-Sat, 2-5pm

Sun Jul & Aug, 11am-4pm Mon-Sat Oct-Apr), as well as catering for today's local artists, has an exhibition on the history of the town's artistic development. The place is as interesting for the building itself as for the artistic works on display. It's one of the oldest and best-preserved tolbooths in Scotland and interpretive signboards reveal its past.

Nearby, the 18th-century **Broughton House** (NTS; ☎ 330437; 12 High St; adult/child £8/5; ☒ noon-5pm Apr-Oct) displays paintings by EA Hornel (he lived and worked here), one of the Glasgow Boys group of painters (p127). Behind the house is a lovely Japanese-style garden. The library with its wood panelling and stone carvings is probably the most impressive room. You need to be very interested in this style of art to justify the hefty entry fee.

Stewartry Museum (☎ 331643; St Mary St; admission free; ☒ 11am-5pm Mon-Sat, 2-5pm Sun May, Jun & Sep, 10am-5pm Mon-Sat, 2-5pm Sun Jul & Aug, 11am-4pm Mon-Sat Nov-Apr) is definitely worth nosing around. It's an interesting local museum in a beautiful old building, and has an eclectic collection of exhibits reflecting the history of the town and the Solway region.

Galloway Wildlife Conservation Park (☎ 331645; Lochfergus Plantation; adult/child £5/3.50; ☒ 10am-6pm Mar-Oct, 10am-4pm Fri-Sun Nov-Feb), a mile from Kirkcudbright on the B727, makes an easy walk from town, and you'll see red pandas, wolves, monkeys, kangaroos, Scottish wildcats and many more creatures in a beautiful setting. An important role of the park is the conservation of rare and threatened species.

Sleeping & Eating

Toadhall (☎ 330204; toadh16@aol.com; 16 Castle St; d £40) This is a wonderfully eccentric house with artefacts from the owners' travels and general bric-a-brac dripping from the walls. It's very friendly, and rooms are terrific value and an excellent size (the upstairs double has a four-poster bed). It's possibly the best option in town, considering its central location, welcoming hosts and stonking breakfasts.

Parkview (☎ 330056; kathmac@talk21.com; 22 Millburn St; s/d £20/36) A small blue-painted, traditional guesthouse off St Cuthbert St, Parkview is a great choice. Rooms are tidy and well kept. Be careful if you scale the steep staircase under the influence.

Gordon House Hotel (☎ /fax 330670; 116 High St; s/ d £40/70; mains £7-10) The small, laid-back hotel rooms are in good shape, but they vary a

bit, so have a look at a few. No 2 is probably the best of the doubles. You can dine in the restaurant or the lounge bar (which really does feel like a lounge!), and there's a beer garden for sunny afternoons. Traditional Sunday roast lunch costs £10.

Silvercraigs Caravan & Camping Site (☎ /fax 330123; Silvercraigs Rd; car & tent £9.30-11.10) There are brilliant views from this campground; you feel like you're sleeping on top of the town. Great stargazing on clear nights. The campground has good facilities, too, including a laundry.

Auld Alliance (☎ 330569; 5 Castle St; starters £5-7, mains £12-16; ☒ dinner, plus Sun lunch) The Auld Alliance is the best place to eat in town. The name refers to the former political alliance between Scotland and France, but here it also means a combination of local fresh Scottish produce (such as small scallops known as queenies), with French cooking and wine. Booking is advised.

Kirkpatricks (☎ 330888; cnr St Mary & St Cuthbert Sts; mains £12-15; ☒ lunch Tue-Sun, dinner Tue-Sat Apr-Sep) A small but fine restaurant upstairs from the street, Kirkpatricks makes excellent use of local produce in traditional Scottish dishes. Lunch is much cheaper, with open sandwiches for under £5. It's popular with locals.

Also recommended:

Selkirk Arms Hotel (☎ 330402; www.selkirkarms hotel.co.uk; High St; s/d £70/100; mains £7-14; ☒) Rooms in the nearby cottage are more spacious and have king-size beds.

Mrs McGeoch (☎ 331885; 109 St Mary St; s £21) Homely B&B with small rooms, including a single, and immaculate shared bathroom.

Getting There & Away

Kirkcudbright is 28 miles west of Dumfries. Buses 501 and 505 run hourly to Dumfries (one hour) via Castle Douglas and Dalbeattie respectively. To get to Stranraer (about £5.50), take bus 501 to Gatehouse of Fleet (two to five daily) and change to bus 500 or X75.

GATEHOUSE OF FLEET

☎ 01557 / pop 892

Gatehouse of Fleet is an attractive little town stretched along a sloping main street, in the middle of which sits an unusual castellated clock tower. The town lies on the banks of the Water of Fleet, completely off the beaten track, and is surrounded by partly wooded hills. There's a TIC (☎ 814212; High St; ☺ Mon-Sat Easter-Jun & Oct, daily Jul-Sep).

One mile southwest on the A75, the well-preserved **Cardoness Castle** (HS; ☎ 814427; adult/child £2.50/75p; ☺ 9.30am-6.30pm Apr-Sep, to 4.30pm Sat & Sun Oct-Mar) was the home of the McCulloch clan. It's a classic 15th-century tower house with great views from the top. **Mill on the Fleet Museum** (☎ 814099; High St; admission free; ☺ 10.30am-5pm Apr-Oct), in a converted 18th-century cotton mill, traces the history of the local industry. The town was originally planned as workers' accommodation. Check out the magnificent *View over Gatehouse* painting, and the fantastic jumbled bookshop and small gallery in the loft.

Bobbin Guest House (☎ 814229; 36 High St; s/d £35/50; ♿), situated right in the middle of town, is a homely, child-friendly place with well-appointed rooms.

The friendly family-run **Bank of Fleet Hotel** (☎ 814302; www.bankoffleet.co.uk; 47 High St; s/d from £25/56; mains £7-9) has bright rooms with a blue décor that gives them a cool, contemporary feel. Live entertainment and good bar meals (try the grilled Galloway trout) are on offer.

Buses X75 and 500 between Dumfries (one hour) and Stranraer (1¼ hours) stop here eight times daily (three on Sunday). Bus 501 from Dumfries (one hour, eight daily), via Castle Douglas, terminates in the village.

AROUND GATEHOUSE

Ideal for families, **Cream o' Galloway** (☎ 814 040; Rainton; adult/child £1.50/3; ☺ 10am-4pm Feb & Mar, 10am-6pm Easter-Aug, 10am-5pm Sep & Oct, 10am-4pm Sat & Sun Nov; ♿) has taken off big time. It offers a plethora of activities and events at the home of that delicious ice cream you'll see around the region. There are 4 miles of nature trails, an adventure playground for all ages, a 3-D maze, wildlife-watching, a farm to explore and plenty of ice cream to taste. Try the daily Ready, Steady, Freeze event (£5), when you get ingredients to create your own ice cream (the kids will love it!). It's about 4 miles from Gatehouse off the A75 – signposted all the way. You can also hire bikes from here.

NEW GALLOWAY & AROUND

☎ 01644 / pop 290
New Galloway lies in the Glenkens district, north of Loch Ken. The unremarkable village is surrounded by some magnificent country-side in which you feel as if you're on a high plateau, surrounded by tumbling, short-pitched hills. This great swath of wooded landscape is unique in southern Scotland.

Galloway Forest Park

South and northwest of town is the 300-sq-mile Galloway Forest Park, with numerous lochs and great whale-backed, heather- and pine-covered mountains. The highest point is **Merrick** (843m). The park is crisscrossed by some superb signposted walking trails, from gentle strolls to long-distance paths, including the **Southern Upland Way** (p147).

The 19-mile A712 (Queen's Way) between New Galloway and Newton Stewart slices through the southern section of the park.

On the shore of Clatteringshaws Loch, 6 miles west of New Galloway, is **Clatteringshaws Visitor Centre** (☎ 420285; admission free, car-park fee £1; ☺ 10.30am-5pm Apr-Sep, 10.30am-4.30pm Oct), with an exhibition on the area's flora and fauna. Pick up a copy of the *Galloway Kite Trail* leaflet here, which details a circular route through impressive scenery that offers a good chance to spot one of the majestic birds. From the visitor centre you can walk to a replica of a Romano-British homestead, and to Bruce's Stone, where Robert the Bruce is said to have rested after defeating the English at the Battle of Rapploch Moss (1307).

Near the loch there are ranger-guided walks of the **Galloway Red Deer Range** (☎ 07771-748400; adult/child £3.50/1.25). During rutting season in autumn it's a bit like watching a bullfight as snorting, charging stags compete for the harem. Walks take place at 11am and 2pm Tuesday and Thursday, and at 2.30pm Sunday from mid-June to mid-September.

Walkers and cyclists head for **Glentrool** in the park's west, accessed by the forest road east from Bargrennan off the A714, north of Newton Stewart. Located just over a mile from Bargrennan is the **Glentrool Visitor Centre** (☎ 01671-402420; admission free; ☺ 10.30am-5pm Apr-Sep, to 4.30pm Oct), which stocks information on activities in the area. There is a coffee shop with snacks to replenish those weary legs. The road then winds and climbs up to Loch Trool, where there are magnificent views.

St John's Town of Dalry

St John's Town of Dalry is a charming village, distinctly more pleasant than New

Galloway, hugging the hill-side about 3 miles north on the A713. It's on the Water of Ken and gives access to the Southern Upland Way.

Sleeping

Kendoon Youth Hostel (SYHA; ☎ 0870 004 1130; St John's Town of Dalry; dm adult/child £12/9; ☯ Apr-Sep) This hostel, popular with walkers, is about 5 miles north of St John's on the B7000. Bus 520 stops about a mile away.

Lochinvar Hotel (☎ 430210; www.lochinvarhotel .com; St John's Town of Dalry; s/d from £35/50) The vine-engulfed Lochinvar, an old coaching inn with a stately interior, is a fine place to stay. Front rooms have the best views and all rooms have high ceilings. It was in the process of being renovated when we dropped by.

Leamington House Hotel (☎ 420327; www.leam ington-hotel.com; High St, New Galloway; s/d from £28/50; ♿) The Leamington has a range of rooms, with and without bathroom. The congenial owner prides herself on guest comfort and wouldn't let a fly in the bedrooms. The split-level family room would suit three people.

Newfield B&B (☎ 430227; Newfield Farm, St John's Town of Dalry; r per person £20) This comfortable B&B has a gorgeous landscaped garden and neat rooms.

Getting There & Away

Bus 521 runs once or twice daily (except Sunday) to Dumfries (55 minutes). Bus 520/S2 connects New Galloway with Castle Douglas (30 minutes, six daily Monday to Saturday, one Sunday); one to three continue north to Ayr (1¼ to 1¾ hours).

NEWTON STEWART

☎ 01671 / pop 3573
On the banks of the sparkling River Cree, Newton Stewart is at the heart of some beautiful countryside, and is popular with hikers and anglers. On the eastern bank, across the bridge, is the older and smaller settlement of Minnigaff. It's worth dropping into the **TIC** (☎ 402431; Dashwood Sq; ☯ 10am-4.30pm Mon-Sat Easter-Jun & Oct, 10am-5pm Mon-Sat, 11am-4pm Sun Jul-Sep).

Sleeping & Eating

Minnigaff Youth Hostel (SYHA; ☎ 0870 004 1142; Minnigaff; dm adult/child £12/9; ☯ Apr-Sep) This converted school is a well-equipped hostel in a tranquil spot 800m north of the bridge

on the eastern bank. Although it's popular with outdoor enthusiasts, you may just about have the place to yourself.

Flowerbank Guest House (☎ 402629; www.flower bankgh.com; Millcroft Rd, Minnigaff; s/d from £25/54) This dignified 18th-century house is set in a magnificent landscaped garden on the banks of the River Cree. The two elegantly furnished rooms at the front of the house are slightly more expensive, but are spacious and have lovely garden views.

Creebridge House Hotel (☎ 402121; www .creebridge.co.uk; Minnigaff; s/d £50/100) This is a magnificent refurbished 18th-century mansion built for the earl of Galloway. A maze inside, the tastefully decorated rooms have modern furnishings and loads of character. Try to get a room overlooking the garden (No 7 is a good one).

Kilwarlin (☎ 403047; hazelkilwarlin@bushInternet .com; 4 Corvisel Rd; r per person £20) Just uphill from the TIC, this friendly B&B has good, solid rooms with shared bathrooms. The double room is the best.

Bruce Hotel (☎ 402294; 88 Queen St; mains £7.50-10) Situated in the quieter part of town, the filling bar meals here include local seafood, venison, salmon and lamb. Its a good place to try Galloway beef (steaks £17).

Getting There & Away

Buses stop in Newton Stewart (Dashwood Sq) on their way to Stranraer (45 minutes) and Dumfries (1½ hours), including buses 920 and 921 (Eurolines/National Express) and buses X75 and 500 (various operators, three to eight daily).

Frequent buses also run south to the Isle of Whithorn.

THE MACHARS

South of Newton Stewart, the Galloway Hills give way to the softly rolling pastures of the triangular peninsula known as The Machars. The south has many early Christian sites and the loping 25-mile **Pilgrims Way**.

Bus 415 runs every hour or two between Newton Stewart and the Isle of Whithorn (one hour) via Wigtown (15 minutes).

Wigtown

☎ 01988 / pop 987
Wigtown is a huge success story. Economically run down for many years, the town's revival began in 1998 when it became

Scotland's National Book Town. Today 24 bookshops offer the widest selection of books in Scotland and give book enthusiasts the opportunity to get lost here for days (check out www.wigtown-booktown.co.uk).

The **Book Shop** (☎ 402499; 17 North Main St; ◷ 9am-5pm Mon-Sat) claims to be Scotland's largest secondhand bookshop, and has a great collection of Scottish and regional titles. **Readingglasses Bookshop Café** (☎ 403266; 17 South Main St; ◷ 10am-5pm Mon-Sat, noon-5pm Sun) sells caffeine to prolong your reading time. There are sometimes local musicians here to keep your ears as well as your eyes entertained.

Folk in this town love their resident ospreys. It's a good conversation starter and if you'd like to learn a bit more about the majestic birds and see a live CCTV link to a nearby nest, drop by the **Wigtown County Buildings** (Market Sq; admission free; ◷ 10am-5pm Mon, Thu & Sat, 10am-7.30pm Tue, Wed & Fri, 2-5pm Sun) for its osprey exhibition.

Four miles west of Wigtown, off the B733, the well-preserved recumbent **Torhouse Stone Circle** dates from the 2nd millennium BC.

Wow! That's what we said when we saw the rooms in **Hillcrest House** (☎ 402018; www.hillcrest-wigtown.co.uk; Maidland Pl, Station Rd; s £25, d £50-60). Spend the extra and get a Superior room, which have stupendous views. The colour schemes are…well, questionable, but who cares when you stay in huge, airy rooms overlooking rolling green hills and the sea beyond. This is all complemented by a ripper breakfast involving fresh local produce.

Pop into the bright dining room at **Café Rendezvous** (☎ 402074; 2 Agnew Cres; dishes £3-5; ◷ breakfast & lunch Mon-Sat) for fresh, home-cooked *paninis* and filled crepes. There's also decent coffee, gooey treats and outdoor seating.

Garlieston

You can't get more off the beaten track than Garlieston, which has a neat little harbour with a ring of 18th-century cottages behind a bowling green. A coastal path leads south to the ruins of **Cruggleton Castle**.

Drop into the **Harbour Inn** (☎ 01988-600685; 18 South Cres; mains £5-10) for great views and tasty pub grub.

Whithorn

☎ 01988 / pop 867

Whithorn has a broad, attractive High St virtually closed at both ends – designed to enclose a medieval market. There are few facilities in town, but it's worth visiting because of its fascinating history.

In 397, while the Romans were still in Britain, St Ninian established the first Christian mission beyond Hadrian's Wall in Whithorn (predating St Columba on Iona by 166 years). After his death, Whithorn Priory, the earliest recorded church in Scotland, was built to house his remains, and Whithorn became the focus of an important medieval pilgrimage.

Today the priory's substantial ruins are the centre point of the **Whithorn Trust Discovery Centre** (☎ 500508; 45 George St; adult/child £2.70/1.50; ◷ 10.30am-5pm Apr-Oct), with absorbing exhibitions and an audiovisual display. The considerable remains of the old monastic settlement are being excavated and you'll see some important finds. There's also a museum with some fascinating early Christian stone sculptures, including the Latinus Stone (c 450), reputedly Scotland's oldest Christian artefact. Learn about the influences their carvers drew from around the British Isles and beyond.

Isle of Whithorn

☎ 01988 / pop 400

The Isle of Whithorn, once an island but now linked to the mainland by a causeway, is a curious place with an attractive natural harbour and colourful houses. The roofless 13th-century **St Ninian's Chapel**, probably built for pilgrims who landed nearby, is on the windswept, evocative rocky headland. Around Burrow Head, to the southwest but accessed from a path off the A747 before you enter the Isle of Whithorn, is **St Ninian's Cave**, where the saint went to pray.

The 300-year-old **Dunbar House** (☎ 500336; pompeylewis@aol.com; Tonderghie Rd; s/d £20/34) overlooking the harbour has large, bright rooms. You can admire the view while you tuck into your breakfast in the dining room.

The quayside **Steam Packet Inn** (☎ 500334; www.steampacketinn.com; Harbour Row; r per person £30-35, mains £5-8) is a popular pub with real ales, scrumptious bar meals, a snug bar and comfy lodgings. Try to get a room to the front of the building as they have lovely views over the little harbour (No 2 is a good one).

STRANRAER

☎ 01776 / pop 10,851

Though a little ramshackle, Stranraer is more pleasant than the average ferry port. There's no reason to stay unless you're catching or coming off a ferry, or you need a base to explore some of the beautiful Galloway peninsula.

Orientation & Information

The bus stops, train station, accommodation and TIC are close to the Stena Sealink terminal.

Clydesdale Bank (Bridge St) Has ATM.

Stranraer library (☎ 707400; North Strand St; ⏰ 9.15am-7.30pm Mon-Wed & Fri, 9.15am-5pm Thu & Sat; 🖥) Free Internet access.

TIC (☎ 888143; stranraertic@visitscotland.com; 28 Harbour St; ⏰ Mon-Sat Sep–mid-Jun, daily mid-Jun–Aug) Organises day trips to Ireland for £20/27 per child/adult.

Sights

Worth a quick visit, **St John's Castle** (☎ 705544; George St; admission free; ⏰ 10am-1pm & 2-5pm Mon-Sat Easter–mid-Sep) was built in 1510 by the Adairs of Kihilt, a powerful local family. The old stone cells carry a distinctly musty smell. There are displays and a couple of videos that trace its history and, from the top of the castle, superb views of Loch Ryan and the ferries chugging out to Ireland.

Stranraer Museum (☎ 705088; 55 George St; admission free; ⏰ 10am-5pm Mon-Fri, 10am-1pm & 2-5pm Sat) houses exhibits on local history. The highlight is the carved stone pipe from Madagascar.

Sleeping

Balyett Farm Hostel & B&B (☎ /fax 703395; www .balyettbb.co.uk; Cairnryan Rd; dm/s/d £12/25/40; 🚲) A mile north of town on the A77, Balyett provides tranquil accommodation in its tidy hostel section, which accommodates six people and has a kitchen/living area. The relaxed B&B at the nearby ivy-covered farmhouse could be the best deal in town. The rooms are light, bright and clean as a whistle.

Ivy House (☎ 704176; www.ivyplace.worldonline .co.uk; 3 Ivy Pl; r per person £20-25) This is a great guesthouse and does Scottish hospitality proud, with excellent facilities, personable hosts, tidy rooms and a smashing breakfast. Nothing is too much trouble for the hosts, who always have a smile for their guests.

INFORMATION	
Clydesdale Bank ATM	1 B2
Police	2 A2
Post Office	3 B2
Stranraer Library	4 A2
Tourist Information Centre (TIC)	5 A2

SIGHTS & ACTIVITIES	
St John's Castle	6 A2
Stranraer Museum	7 A2

SLEEPING	
Harbour Guest House	8 A2
Ivy House	9 B3
North West Castle Hotel	10 B2

EATING	
Arches Restaurant	11 B2
L'Aperitif	12 B3
Tesco	13 B2
Waterline	14 B2

TRANSPORT	
Buses for Towns on the A75 & Whithorn	15 B2
Long-Distance Buses	16 B2
Portpatrick and Town Buses	17 B2
Stena Sealink Terminal	18 B1

North West Castle Hotel (☎ 704413; www.north westcastle.co.uk; Port Rodie; s/d from £75/120) Elegant and old-fashioned, this is the most luxurious hotel in Stranraer and was formerly the home of Arctic explorer Sir John Ross. Its a little fussy and, although an interior designer would tut over the busy designs and clash of colours, the rooms are sumptuous indeed. But here's the real puller: it was the first hotel in the world to have an indoor curling rink!

Aird Donald Caravan Park (☎ 702025; aird@mimmanu-net.com; London Rd; tent sites for 2 £10) The nearest tent-friendly campground is 1 mile east of the town centre. It has manicured lawns, plenty of trees and countless bunnies.

Also recommended:

Harbour Guest House (☎ 704626; www.harbourguesthouse.com; 11 Market St; B&B per person £25) On the harbour front, near the town centre.

Corsewall Lighthouse Hotel (☎ 853220; www.lighthousehotel.co.uk; Kirkcolm; r per person £75-135; ♿) Thirteen miles northwest of Stranraer at Corsewall Point. Single occupancy is the same rate minus £20.

Eating

L'Aperitif (☎ 702991; London Rd; mains £10-13, set 3-course dinner £13.50 available 5-7pm; ☺ lunch & dinner Mon-Sat) With its extensive menu, fine wines and delectable food, this is the best restaurant in town by a long shot. The service is also excellent.

Waterline (☎ 889727; North Strand St; mains £5.50; ☺ lunch & dinner Mon-Sat) This chain pub across from the TIC is soulless, but it's family-friendly, a short walk to/from the ferry, and for Stranraer is a decent option for a meal or quiet drink. Good-value burgers, baguettes, pasta dishes, curries and pub faves are dished out all day.

Arches Restaurant (☎ 702196; 77 Hanover St; mains £4-6; ☺ breakfast & lunch Mon-Sat) Arches is a bright, perpetually busy café with huge windows – great for people-watching.

If you're after a supermarket for self-catering, there's a **Tesco** (Charlotte St) in town.

Getting There & Away

BOAT

See the Transport chapter (p445) for full details on services to Northern Ireland. From Stranraer there are two alternatives: **P&O** (☎ 0870 242 4777; www.poirishsea.com) ferries from Cairnryan to Larne, and **Stena Line** (☎ 0870 570 7070; www.stenaline.co.uk) HSS and Superferries from Stranraer to Belfast.

The Cairnryan to Larne service is used mainly by motorists and hauliers. Cairnryan is 5 miles north of Stranraer on the eastern side of Loch Ryan. Bus 358 runs frequently to Cairnryan (terminating at the post office). For a taxi to Cairnryan (around £6), contact **McLean's Taxis** (☎ 703343; 21 North Strand St; ☺ 24hr), just up from the TIC. Stena Line ferries for Belfast connect directly with rail and bus services. The train station is on the ferry pier.

BUS

Eurolines and National Express buses 920 and 921 run twice daily between London and Belfast, via the towns along the A75 and Stranraer.

Scottish Citylink buses run to Glasgow (£10, 2½ hours, twice daily) and Edinburgh (£12, 3¾ hours, twice daily).

There are also several daily local buses to Kirkcudbright and the towns along the A75, such as Newton Stewart (45 minutes, three to eight daily) and Dumfries (£5.50, 2¼ hours, eight daily Monday to Saturday, three on Sunday).

TRAIN

First Scotrail runs to/from Glasgow (£16.50, 2½ hours, two to seven trains daily); it may be necessary to change at Ayr.

AROUND STRANRAER

Magnificent **Castle Kennedy Gardens** (☎ 01776-702024; www.castlekennedygardens.co.uk; Rephad; adult/child £4/1; ☺ 10am-5pm Apr-Sep), 3 miles east of Stranraer, are among the most famous in Scotland. They cover 30 hectares and are set on an isthmus between two lochs and two castles (Castle Kennedy, burnt in 1716, and Lochinch Castle, built in 1864). The landscaping was undertaken in 1730 by the earl of Stair, who used unoccupied soldiers to do the work. Bus 430 (hourly) and 500 from Stranraer stop here.

PORTPATRICK

☎ 01776 / pop 585

Portpatrick is a charming port on the rugged west coast of the Rhinns (or Rhins) of the Galloway peninsula. Until the mid-19th century it was the main port for Northern Ireland, so it's quite substantial. It's now a coastguard station and a quiet holiday resort.

It is also a good base from which to explore the south of the peninsula, and it's the starting point for the Southern Upland Way. You can follow part of the Way to Stranraer (9 miles). It's a cliff-top walk, followed by sections of farmland and heather moor. Start at the Way's information shelter at the northern end of the harbour. The walk is waymarked until 800m south of Stranraer, where you get the first good views of the village.

Harbour House Hotel (☎ 810456; www.harbour house.co.uk; 53 Main St; s/d from £30/60, bar meals from £6.50-9) was formerly the customs house but is now a popular, solid old pub. Some of the tastefully furnished rooms have brilliant views over the harbour. The tariff is an extra £5 if you bring your pooch. The hotel is also a warm nook for a traditional bar meal. You may have trouble dragging yourself outside again given the delicious real ales on tap, including Kilkellan.

For total luxury, check out the **Portpatrick Hotel** (☎ 810333; www.shearingsholidays.com; Heugh Rd; r from £60) perched high above the town and gazing imperiously over the harbour and out to sea. It's part of a chain, but the location is unrivalled in town.

Buses 358 and 367 run to Stranraer (20 minutes, roughly hourly, three Sunday).

SOUTH OF PORTPATRICK

From Portpatrick, the road south to the Mull of Galloway passes coastal scenery that includes rugged cliffs, tiny harbours and sandy beaches. The warm waters of the Gulf Stream give the peninsula the mildest climate in Scotland.

This mildness is demonstrated at **Logan Botanic Garden** (☎ 01776-860231; adult/child £3.50/1; ◷ 10am-5pm Mar & Oct, 10am-6pm Apr-Sep), a mile north of Port Logan, where an array of subtropical flora includes tree ferns and cabbage palms. The garden is an outpost of the Royal Botanic Garden in Edinburgh.

Further south, **Drummore** is a fishing village on the east coast. From here it's another 5 miles to the **Mull of Galloway**, Scotland's most southerly point. It's a rocky, bleak and windy headland. The 26m-high lighthouse here was built by Robert Stevenson in 1826. The Mull of Galloway RSPB nature reserve, home to thousands of sea birds, has a **visitor centre** (☎ 01776-830682; admission free; ◷ 10am-4pm Apr-Sep).

ANNANDALE & ESKDALE

These valleys, in Dumfries & Galloway's east, form part of two major routes that cut across Scotland's south. Away from the

highways, the roads are quiet and there are some interesting places to visit, especially if you're looking to break a road trip.

Gretna & Gretna Green
☎ 01461 / pop 2705

This is one eccentric place, and it's worth dropping by just to experience the tourist hordes. Many people are drawn to Gretna and Gretna Green by its romantic associations (see the boxed text, below). Today's Gretna Green, on the northwestern edge of Gretna, is very touristy and very tacky – but the place has a real buzz. Such is the power of the name that about 5000 weddings are performed here annually.

The very helpful **TIC** (☎ 337834; gretnatic@vis itscotland.com; Gretna Gateway village, Gretna; ◷ 10am-6pm mid-Mar–Oct, 10am-4.30pm Mon-Sat, 10am-4pm Sun Nov–mid-Mar) is able to assist with most inquiries.

The commercialised **Old Blacksmith's Shop** (☎ 338441; Gretna Green; adult/child £2.50/2; ◷ 9am-5pm Nov-Mar, 9am-6pm Apr, May & Oct, 9am-7pm Jun & Sep, 9am-8pm Jul & Aug) has an exhibition on Gretna Green's history, a sculpture park and a coach museum (there's even an anvil marriage room!).

Hazeldene Hotel (☎ 338292; www.hotels-gretna green.co.uk; Gretna Green; s/d from £40/60, honeymoon

---

TYING THE KNOT IN GRETNA GREEN

From the mid-18th century, eloping couples south of the border realised that under Scottish law people could (and still can) tie the knot at the age of 16 without parental consent (in England and Wales the legal age was 21). Gretna Green's location close to the border made it the most popular venue.

At one time anyone could perform a legal marriage ceremony, but in Gretna Green it was usually the local blacksmith, who became known as the 'Anvil Priest'. In 1940 the 'anvil weddings' were outlawed, but eloping couples still got married in the church or registry office.

Today many people make or reaffirm their marriage vows in the village. If you want to get married over the famous anvil in the Old Blacksmith's Shop at Gretna Green, check out the **Gretna Green Weddings website** (www.gretnaweddings.com).

ste £120), a small hotel near the Old Black-smith's Shop, has eight modern, comfort-able rooms. The honeymoon suite has a four-poster bed, a sauna and a complimen-tary bottle of champagne.

Bus 79 runs between Gretna and Dumfries (one hour, hourly Monday to Saturday, every two hours Sunday). Trains run from Gretna Green to Dumfries (£5.70, 25 minutes, every hour or two, five Sunday) and Carlisle (£3.50, 11 minutes).

Lockerbie
☎ 01576 / pop 4009

Red-sandstone buildings line the main street of this small country town. Its peace was shattered in 1988 when pieces from a Pan-Am passenger jet fell on the town after a bomb blew up the aircraft; 207 people were killed, including 11 townsfolk. In 2001 a Libyan intelligence agent was convicted of the bombing and sentenced to life impris-onment. A second Libyan was acquitted. In 2003 Libya agreed to set up a $2.7 billion fund for the families of people killed in the bombing, admitting 'civil responsibility' for the tragedy. In early 2005 Libya withdrew $500 million from this fund in protest at the US government's refusal to remove it from a list of countries considered to sup-port terrorism.

Little evidence of the event remains, but the townspeople have created a small gar-den of remembrance in **Dryfesdale Cemetery**, about a mile west on the Dumfries road. Bus 382 runs to/from Moffat (30 minutes, hourly).

Moffat
☎ 01683 / pop 2135

Moffat lies in wild, hilly country near the upper reaches of Annandale. The former spa town is now a centre for the local wool industry, symbolised by the bronze ram statue on High St. The **TIC** (☎ 220620; Ladyknowe; ⏰ 10am-5pm Mon-Sat late Mar-late Jun, 9.30am-5.30pm Mon-Sat, 11am-5pm Sun late Jun-late Sep, 10am-4.30pm Mon-Sat, 11am-4pm Sun late Sep-Oct) is well organised.

At **Moffat Woollen Mill** (☎ 220134; Ladyknowe; admission free; ⏰ 9am-5pm), near the TIC, you can see a working weaving exhibition, and trace your Scottish ancestry. The flower-decked **Buchan Guest House** (☎ 220378; www .buchanguesthouse.co.uk; Beechgrove; s/d £27/50) is in

a quiet street just a short walk north of the town centre. Room No 5 is a good choice, as it has a lovely outlook over nearby fields.

There are several daily buses to Edinburgh (buses 100 and X100), Glasgow (Scottish Citylink bus 974) and Dumfries (buses 100 and 114). Bus 382 runs regularly to Gretna Green and Carlisle, via Lockerbie.

Langholm
☎ 013873 / pop 2311

The waters of three rivers – the Esk, Ewes and Wauchope – meet at Langholm, a gra-cious old town at the centre of Scotland's tweed industry. Most people come for **fish-ing** and **walking** in the surrounding moors and woodlands; check out the **Langholm Walks website** (www.langholmwalks.co.uk) for details.

There's a useful **local information point** (☎ 80914; www.langholm-online.co.uk; High St; ⏰ 10am-4pm Mon-Fri, 10am-noon Sat May-Sep) that also has a small historical display about the town and a range of leaflets detailing local drives.

Well-sized rooms (the downstairs double in particular), a lovely hostess and big sink-in-and-smile beds makes **Border House** (☎ 803 76; High St; r per person £25) an excellent central option. Or try **Whitecroft Hotel** (☎ 81343; www .whitecroft-hotel.co.uk; 81 High St; s/d £40/70), with its medieval vibe and very classy range of rooms (Nos 2 and 3 are our faves). Bus 124/112 has up to five daily connections with Eskdalemuir (no Sunday service).

Eskdalemuir

Surrounded by wooded hills, Eskdalemuir is a remote settlement 13 miles northwest of Langholm. About 1.5 miles further north is the **Samye Ling Tibetan Centre** (☎ 013873-73232), the first Tibetan Buddhist monastery built in the West (1968). The colourful prayer flags and the red and gold of the temple itself are a striking contrast to the stark grey and green landscape. The centre of-fers meditation courses, including weekend workshops (£50) for which basic food and board is available (dorm beds £17, breakfast £2 and lunch £4).

Those staying here are asked to give two hours a day to help in the kitchen, garden and farm. The temple opens to casual visi-tors (9am to 5pm), for whom there's also a small café.

Buses A1 and 112 from Langholm/Lockerbie stop at the centre.

Central Scotland

The country's extraordinary diversity really starts to blossom when you reach central Scotland. Delightful towns and significant ruins chronicle the region's charismatic history, and it's also home to big-tree country, with pockets of ancient forests – a refreshing change from the naked landscape that dominates a lot of Scotland.

It's accessible too, with most major centres within easy reach, and yet it feels miles away from the rat race, offering a quick and convenient option for washing away urban grit. Dine in a stylish café or nurse a pint of real ale in a historic pub in Stirling, Perth or St Andrews, and then spend the late afternoon clambering around the wild, soaring peaks of the Highlands and the wooded glens in this big-sky country for which Scotland is famous.

An area of enormous beauty and variation, it's easy to fall in love with and difficult to leave. With possibly the most scenically diverse territory in Britain, it could literally take weeks to explore. The Highland line, a massive geological fault, snakes across part of the region. West Perthshire is one of the country's hidden gems, offering an opportunity to explore some of Scotland's most beautiful and remote countryside – and when you see villages such as Kenmore, teetering on the shores of Loch Tay, you'll understand the expression 'picture-perfect'. The 'kingdom' of Fife is another area in this diverse package that has no parallel, holding onto a unique Lowland identity that differentiates it from the rest of the country. An exploration of East Neuk and its fishing villages, along with medieval St Andrews, peels away yet another thickness of central Scotland's multilayered skin.

HIGHLIGHTS

- Exploring the atmospheric old town of **Stirling** (p191), culminating in the imperious castle lording it over the city

- Belting a golf ball down the hallowed fairways of **St Andrews Old Course** (p209), the home of golf

- Discovering Perthshire's scenic magic, including ancient woodlands, and wildlife around **Glen Lyon** (p224) and **Loch Rannoch** (p224)

- Munching on seafood in the fishing villages dotted along the **East Neuk** (p212) coast

- Wandering around decadent Scone Palace in **Perth** (p217), a site dripping with historical importance

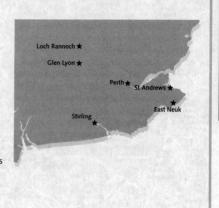

Loch Rannoch ★
Glen Lyon ★
Perth ★   St Andrews ★
East Neuk ★
Stirling ★

- POPULATION: 764,000
- AREA: 9254 sq km

Getting Around

For public-transport info, call **Traveline** (☎ 0870 608 2608). **Scottish Citylink** (☎ 0870 550 5050) connects the main towns in the area, and Perth is a major hub for its services. **Royal Mail postbuses** (☎ 01246-546329) serve many remote communities, such as those in West Perthshire, charging on average £2 to £5 for single journeys.

The Central Scotland Rover rail ticket (£30), valid for three days out of seven, allows train travel between Edinburgh, Glasgow, Falkirk and Stirling.

STIRLING REGION

Playing a pivotal role in Scotland's historical development for aeons, the Stirling region is peppered with landmark battlegrounds and tales of legendary figures.

A compact area providing a mesmerising snapshot of central Scotland, its historical importance is immense and its natural attractions impressive. The capital, also named Stirling, controlled the main route

into the Highlands and its strategic location meant it was the stage for some of Scotland's crucial battles of independence against the repressive English. It has one of the finest castles in Scotland and a wonderfully atmospheric old town. Nearby are many historic battlegrounds, including the most famous of all – Bannockburn. The Stirling region was also home to Rob Roy, and the legendary exploits of this champion of the poor still echo around the southern border of the Highlands.

The region has lured walkers and climbers since Victorian times, and the forests and wildlife in this unique environment are protected as part of the Loch Lomond & the Trossachs National Park (p274).

Getting Around

For local transport information in the Stirling region, phone ☎ 01786-442707. The main bus operator is **First** (☎ 0870 872 7271). Its FirstDay ticket (£4.80) gives one day's travel on all its services in the central Scotland region and through to Edinburgh or Glasgow.

From late May to early October the vintage **Trossachs Trundler** (☎ 01786-442707) is a useful bus service circling Aberfoyle, Callander and Trossachs Pier on Loch Katrine. A day ticket per adult/child is £8/2.50. The bus is wheelchair accessible and can carry two bikes. It runs daily except Wednesday. Call for details of its reduced winter timetable. Stirling town is the rail hub, but the lines only skirt the rest of the region.

STIRLING

☎ 01786 / pop 45,115

Recently declared a city, Stirling lies at one of Scotland's most strategic sites and has been at the heart of many conflicts. Its vibrant streets, mainly due to a healthy student population and constant influx of enthusiastic tourists, make Stirling one of the country's most appealing urban areas. For visitors the city rivals Edinburgh (but on a smaller scale) for historical attractions and the atmosphere of its old town.

Replete with winding cobblestone streets, the old town clings to the slopes beneath the castle and the fascinating remnants divulge tales of Stirling's historical development, stretching over a 500-year period. Another parallel with Edinburgh is the magnificent castle, perched high on a rocky outcrop gazing over the city. The old town slopes up from the train and bus stations to the castle, which sits 75m above the plain atop the plug of an extinct volcano.

Information

Post office (Barnton St)

Royal Bank of Scotland (Barnton St) Has ATM.

Stirling Library (Corn Exchange Rd; ☿ 9.30am-5.30pm Mon, Wed & Fri, to 7pm Tue & Thu, to 5pm Sat; 🖳) Free Internet access.

Stirling Royal Infirmary (☎ 434000; Livilands Rd) South of the town centre.

Tourist Information Centre (TIC; ☎ 475019; stirling@visitscotland.com; 41 Dumbarton Rd; ☿ Mon-Sat year-round, plus Sun Jun–mid-Sep; 🖳) Plenty of brochures about Stirling's attractions and the region, but staff can be uninterested and unhelpful.

Sights

STIRLING CASTLE & ARGYLL'S LODGING

Hold Stirling and you control the country. This simple strategy has ensured that a **castle** (HS; ☎ 450000; adult/child incl Argyll's Lodging £8/3; ☿ 9.30am-6pm Apr-Sep, to 5pm Oct-Mar) has existed

here since prehistoric times. The superb views it commands mean you cannot help drawing parallels with Edinburgh Castle – but Stirling is better. Location, architecture and historical significance combine to make it one of the grandest of all Scottish castles.

There has been a fortress of some kind here for several thousand years, but the current building dates from the late 14th to the 16th century, when it was a residence of the Stuart monarchs. The Great Hall and Gatehouse were built by James IV; observe the hammer-beam roof and huge fireplaces in the largest medieval hall in Scotland and the result of 35 years' worth of restoration.

The spectacular palace was constructed in the reign of James V (1540–42), however it was closed at the time of writing for extensive restorations, which will hopefully restore it to its former glory. Work is due to finish in 2008; until then there may be limited access when you visit. Meanwhile, drop into the Tapestry Studio, where you can watch weavers creating seven exquisite tapestries using traditional methods for the Queen's Apartments in the palace.

James VI remodelled the Chapel Royal and was the last king of Scots to live here.

In the King's Old Building is the museum of the **Argyll & Sutherland Highlanders** (admission free, donations encouraged), which traces the history of this famous regiment from 1794 to the present day. It has a great collection of ornately decorated dirks (daggers).

The **Royal Burgh of Stirling Visitor Centre** (☎ 479901; Castle Esplanade; admission free; ☿ 9.30am-6pm Apr-Oct, to 5pm Nov-Mar) has an audiovisual presentation and exhibition about Stirling, including the history and architecture of the castle.

There's a car park next to the castle (£2 for two hours). Visitors in wheelchairs should contact **Historic Scotland** (HS; ☎ 0131-668 8600; www.historic-scotland.gov.uk; Longmore House, Salisbury Pl, Edinburgh) for a courtesy vehicle to assist their entry into the castle.

Complete with turrets, spectacular **Argyll's Lodging** is the most impressive 17th-century town house in Scotland and you'll find it by the castle, at the top of Castle Wynd. It's the former home of William Alexander, an earl of Stirling and noted literary figure. It has been tastefully restored and gives an insight into lavish, 17th-century aristocratic life.

STIRLING

0 — 400 m
0 — 0.2 miles

To Dunblane (5mi); Doune (8mi)
To Callander (14mi); Glasgow (26mi)
To Wallace Monument (2.5mi); Bridge of Allan (2.5mi); Witches Craig Caravan Park (3mi)
To Wallace Monument (2.5mi)
Forth
Forth
Stirling Train Station
Stirling Royal Infirmary (500m); Bannockburn (2mi); Edinburgh (35mi)

INFORMATION	
Post Office	1 C3
Royal Bank of Scotland	2 C3
Stirling Library	3 C3
Tourist Information Centre (TIC)	4 C3

SIGHTS & ACTIVITIES	
Argyll's Lodging	5 B2
Church of the Holy Rude	6 B3
Cowane's Hospital	7 B3
Mar's Wark	8 B3
Royal Burgh of Stirling Visitor Centre	9 B2
Stirling Castle	10 B2
Tolbooth	11 B3

SLEEPING	
Burnsview Guest House	12 C3
Cairns	(see 17)
Castlecroft Guest House	13 A2
Garfield Guesthouse	14 B3
Linden Guest House	15 D4
Mrs MacGregor's	16 C3
Munro Guest House	17 C3
Neidpath	(see 15)
Stirling Highland Hotel	18 C3
Stirling SYHA Hostel	19 B3
Willy Wallace Backpackers Hostel	20 C3

EATING	
Aura	(see 22)
Barnton Bar & Bistro	21 C3
Cambio	22 C3
Darnley's Coffee House	23 C3
Italia Nostra	24 C3
Mr Singh's	25 C3

Papa Joe's	26 C4
Scala D'Oro	(see 11)

DRINKING	
Portcullis	27 B2
Settle Inn	28 C2

TRANSPORT	
Arnold Clark	29 D4
Bus Station	30 D3

OLD TOWN

Below the castle, the old town has a remarkably different feel to modern Stirling, its cobblestone streets packed with fine examples of 15th- to 17th-century architectural gems. Its growth began when Stirling became a royal burgh, about 1124, and in the 15th and 16th centuries rich merchants built their houses here. The steep slopes ensure visitors will enjoy recuperation in a nearby coffee shop or pub after exploring for a couple of hours.

Stirling has the best surviving town wall in Scotland. It was built around 1547 when Henry VIII of England began the 'Rough Wooing' – attacking the town in order to force Mary, Queen of Scots to marry his son so that the two kingdoms could be united. The walk can be followed on the **Back Walk**, which follows the line of the wall from Dumbarton Rd (near the TIC) to the castle, continuing around Castle Rock and back to the old town.

Mar's Wark, on Castle Wynd at the head of the old town, is the ornate façade of what was once a Renaissance-style town house commissioned in 1569 by the wealthy earl of Mar, regent of Scotland during James VI's minority.

The **Church of the Holy Rude** (St John St; admission free; 11am-4pm May-Sep) has been the town's parish church for 500 years and James VI was crowned here in 1567. The nave and tower date from 1456, and the church features one of the few surviving medieval open-timber roofs. Behind the church is **Cowane's hospital** (☎ 472247; 49 St John St; admission free, donations welcome; ☽ 10am-5pm). Built as an almshouse in 1637 by the merchant John Cowane, its medicinal methods now include hosting *ceilidhs* (evenings of traditional Scottish entertainment including music, song and dance), banquets and concerts. There's a family-tree database where you can search for your ancestry.

The **Mercat Cross**, in Broad St, is topped with a unicorn and was once surrounded by a bustling market. Nearby is the **Tolbooth**, built in 1705 as the town's administrative centre. A courthouse and jail were added in the following century and it was renovated in 2001 as a performing arts centre.

BANNOCKBURN
On 24 June 1314, the greatest victory in the history of Scotland's struggle to remain independent took place at the Battle of Bannockburn. Robert the Bruce overcame superior numbers and sent Edward II's English force running for their lives. In the long and bitter struggle against the threat of English domination, this victory turned the tide of fortune sufficiently in favour of the Scots for the following 400 years.

Bannockburn Heritage Centre (NTS; ☎ 812664; Glasgow Rd; adult/child £5/4; ☽ 10am-5.30pm Apr-Oct, 10.30am-4pm Feb, Mar, Nov & Dec) tells the story of the battle in a simple and eloquent exhibition, including a 12-minute audiovisual display that stirs the imagination, helping to bring the historic battle to life. There are also interesting dioramas about medieval Scotland and the Battle of Stirling Bridge. Outside is the eerie Borestone site, said to have been Robert the Bruce's command post before the battle. Check out his grim-looking statue, dressed in full battle gear and mounted on a charger. The battle site itself never closes. Bannockburn is located 2 miles south of Stirling.

WALLACE MONUMENT
Two miles north of Stirling is Scotland's impressive Victorian **monument** (☎ 472140; Abbey Craig, Causewayhead; adult/child/family £6/4/15; ☽ 10am-5pm Mar-May & Oct, to 6pm Jun, 9.30am-6pm Jul & Aug, 9.30am-5pm Sep, 10.30am-4pm Nov-Feb) to Sir William Wallace, who was hung, drawn and quartered by the English in 1305. The view from the top, of no less than seven battlegrounds, is as breathtaking as the 67m climb up to it. The monument contains interesting displays, including a parade of other Scottish heroes and Wallace's mighty two-handed sword. Clearly, the man was no weakling.

Tours
From April to October, **City Sightseeing** (www .citysightseeing.co.uk) runs an open-top, hop-on, hop-off bus tour daily every 30 minutes (hourly November to March) between the castle and the Wallace Monument via Bridge of Allan. A day ticket costs £7/3 per adult/child.

Sleeping
BUDGET
Stirling Hostel (SYHA; ☎ 0870 004 1149; St John St; dm adult/child £14/13.50; ☐) The façade of an 18th-century church conceals this place, which is in a perfect location in the old part of town. It's a superb, modern hostel with 126 beds in four- to six-bed dorms. A less attractive annexe in Union St opens in summer only.

WILLIAM WALLACE, SCOTTISH PATRIOT

William Wallace is one of Scotland's most endearing heroes and a patriot whose exploits helped revive interest in Scottish history. Born in 1270, he was catapulted into fame and a place in history as a highly successful guerrilla commander who harassed the English invaders for many years.

Wallace was knighted by Robert the Bruce and proclaimed Guardian of Scotland in March 1298. However, it was only a matter of time before English military superiority and the fickle nature of the nobility's loyalties would turn the tide against the defender of Scottish independence.

Disaster struck in July of that year when Edward's force defeated the Scots at the Battle of Falkirk. Wallace resigned as guardian, went into hiding, and travelled throughout Europe to drum up support for the Scottish cause. Many of the Scots nobility were prepared to side with Edward, and Wallace was betrayed after his return to Scotland in 1305.

Sir William Wallace was tried for treason at Westminster, and he was hanged, beheaded and disembowelled at Smithfield, London.

CENTRAL SCOTLAND

Willy Wallace Backpackers Hostel (☎ 446773; manager@willywallacehostel.com; 77 Murray Pl; dm £9-14) This is an excellent, clean and friendly hostel in the middle of town. There are mixed, male and female dorms generally accommodating six to eight beds. The lounge area has comfy chairs and great views.

Witches Craig Caravan Park (☎ 474947; www .witchescraig.co.uk; Blairlogie; tent sites £11-12; ☺ Apr-Oct) In a brilliant spot right at the foot of the Ochil Hills, which are begging to be walked, Witches Craig is 3 miles east of Stirling by the A91. It's a former 'national loo of the year' winner.

MIDRANGE

Mrs MacGregor's (☎ /fax 471082; jennifer@sruighlea .com; 27 King St; d £40) This place feels like a secret hideaway, but it's conveniently located smack bang in the centre of town. You'll feel like a local staying here, and there are eating and drinking places practically on the doorstep. It's a B&B that welcomes guests with the kind of warmth that keeps them returning.

Burnsview Guest House (☎ 451002; m.watt@ totalise.co.uk; 1 Albert Pl; d per person £21-23) Burnsview has four renovated rooms, two with en-suite facilities, and is monastic in its sobriety. It's not for party animals – the thoughtful owners enjoy hosting discerning guests.

Two high-quality guesthouses sit side by side in a great central location about 10 minutes from the castle. **Munro Guest House** (☎ 472685; www.munroguesthouse.co.uk; 14 Princes St; s £27-32, d £40-50) is a family-run place with five en-suite rooms all bordering on luxurious, and friendly **Cairns** (☎ 479228; 12 Princes St; s £25, d & tw £50) next door has a double and a twin, both with en suite, and two single rooms.

Other recommendations:

Castlecroft Guest House (☎ 474933; www .castlecroft-uk.com; Ballengeich Rd; s/d £44/52) Brilliant location, nestled just under the castle and blessed with panoramic views of the countryside.

Linden Guest House (☎ /fax 448850; www.linden guesthouse.co.uk; 22 Linden Ave; d & tw per person £20-25) No singles, but three well-furnished rooms.

Neidpath (☎ 469017; 24 Linden Ave; s/d £35/46) Spotless rooms and a filling breakfast.

TOP END

Stirling Highland Hotel (☎ 272727; stirling@paramount -hotels.co.uk; Spittal St; r per person £49-59; ☒) The smartest hotel in town, Stirling Highland

---

Hotel is a sympathetic refurbishment of the old high school. It's very convenient for the castle and old town and the rooms are deluxe, although staying in an old school may not generate good memories for everyone!

Eating

Cambio (☎ 461041; 1 Corn Exchange Rd; mains £4-7; ☺ lunch & dinner) Attracting the town's style-cats, this trendy, nouveau bar-restaurant serves amazingly cheap food. The décor and furnishings are minimalist. Melts and wraps feature for lunch, while mains such as pesto-stuffed chicken or mushroom and nut linguine tickle the taste buds in the evening.

Darnley Coffee House (☎ 474468; 18 Bow St; snacks £3.50-5; ☺ breakfast & lunch) Just down the hill from the castle, beyond the end of Broad St, Darnley Coffee House is a good pit stop for home baking and speciality coffees on a walk around the old town.

Barnton Bar & Bistro (☎ 461698; 312 Barnton St; mains £3.50-5; ☺ daily until late) Opposite the post office, this is a very popular, grungy hangout serving excellent all-day breakfasts, chilli, homemade lasagne and burgers. It is a great place to eat or drink, and there's something on most weeknights from tarot reading to the Friday night indie-punk music fest.

Italia Nostra (☎ 473208; 25 Baker St; antipasto £6, pizza & pasta £8-10; ☺ lunch & dinner; ☒) The Nostra is a busy Italian place popular with families. It has a warm, friendly atmosphere and is also good for women or solo travellers. There's a large menu, including delicious *gelato*, and it does takeaways.

Scala D'Oro (☎ 274010; Tolbooth; 2/3 courses £19.50/23.50; ☺ lunch & dinner Tue-Sun) Claiming to be the only Scottish-Italian fusion restaurant in central Scotland (they may just be right), this place has upmarket dining with crisp linen and clinking wine glasses in a historic building. Scala is the place to spoil that someone special and tuck into some delicious original cuisine.

Also recommended:

Papa Joe's (☎ 446414; 21 Dumbarton Rd; lunch mains £5.50, dinner mains £7-14; ☺ lunch Sat, dinner daily) Dine on excellent pizzas and seafood, vegetarian, pasta and some Tex-Mex dishes among an eclectic collection of antiques, musical instruments and sporting paraphernalia.

Mr Singh's (☎ 472137; 16-18 Barnton St; starters £4, mains £6-8; ☺ lunch & dinner Mon-Sat, dinner Sun) Fine curry house with a terrific-value buffet lunch (£6).

Drinking

Portcullis (☎ 472290; Castle Wynd) With a friendly atmosphere and a great location just below the castle, this is the best pub in Stirling. Excellent bar meals are served all day and there's a large range of malt whiskies, too.

Settle Inn (☎ 474609; 91 St Mary's Wynd) Established in 1733, the Settle Inn is the oldest pub in Stirling and is a good place to rest weary legs and enjoy a cosy drink, especially when the rain is lashing outside.

Barnton Bar & Bistro (opposite) is another popular place for a drink.

Getting There & Away
BUS

Scottish Citylink runs frequent buses to/from Glasgow (£4.20, 45 minutes). Some buses continue to Aberdeen (£16.70, 3½ hours) via Perth (£4.90) and Dundee (£8); others go to Inverness. For buses to Inverness (£14, 3½ hours) you'll usually have to

change at Perth. A four-times-daily service from Edinburgh to Fort William goes via Stirling once a day (with connections to Oban or Skye); fares to Edinburgh, Oban, Fort Williams and Portree are £4.20, £14.70, £15.30 and £26, respectively. All buses go from the bus station on Goosecroft Rd.

First runs local buses (to Callander, Aberfoyle and so on) and operates an express service to Edinburgh (one hour, hourly Monday to Saturday).

TRAIN

First ScotRail has services to/from Edinburgh (£5.70, 55 minutes, at least twice hourly Monday to Saturday, hourly Sunday). Services run at least twice an hour from Glasgow (£5.90, 40 minutes, every two hours or so on Sunday), and there are regular services to Perth (£8.60, 35 minutes), Dundee (£13.20, 55 minutes) and Aberdeen (£32, 2¼ hours).

Getting Around

It's easy enough to walk around the central part of the town.

If you want wheels, you can hire a car from **Arnold Clark** (☎ 478686; www.arnoldclark.com; Kerse Rd). The cheapest deal is for an economy car at £19 per day (or £95 for a week).

AROUND STIRLING
Bridge of Allan

☎ 01786 / pop 4607

This upbeat former spa town, just 2.5 miles north of Stirling, has an open street plan, giving it a laid-back sense of space. It's quite upmarket, with few sleeping options but plenty of excellent places to eat, and is well worth a visit.

At the **Bridge of Allan Brewery** (☎ 834555; Queen's Lane; admission free; ☺ noon-5pm Apr-Sep, noon-5pm Sat & Sun Oct-Mar), just off Henderson St, you can learn about the microbrewing techniques behind traditional Scottish ales. This is a great spot for a taste of local beers – it's very friendly and the genuine quality microbrews are recommended, particularly the Wallace Monument (tastings are free).

SLEEPING & EATING

Inverallan Lodge (☎ 832791; david.thursby@tesco.net; 116 Henderson St; s/d/f £25/45/60; 🖫) This is the best guesthouse in town and a travellers' favourite. Down to earth, perpetually friendly (but not overbearing) and good value, the lodge has fantastic good-sized rooms, some with huge bay windows drawing in lots of light.

Queen's Hotel (☎ 833268; www.queenshotel scotland.com; 24 Henderson St; s/d £85/130, bar mains £6-8; ✷ lunch & dinner) Gorgeous, modern, plush rooms here have a dark and fuzzy décor that makes you want to get naked and have a good roll around. All rooms have showers, but only some come with bath. The rooms are different sizes, so ask to see a few. Even if you're not staying, drop in and taste the contemporary cooking in the bar.

Jekyll's Restaurant (2/3 courses £26/30; ✷ dinner) If you're a serious foodie, try this restaurant attached to the Queen's Hotel. The menu does delightful and imaginative things with Scottish produce including salmon sausages and Skye scallops – most dishes are drizzled with a superb sauce designed to bring out the full flavour of the dish.

Clive Ramsay Café (☎ 831616; Henderson St; mains £8-12; ✷ breakfast, lunch & dinner) With a claim to 'sexy food', this little show pony also has a wonderful deli next door selling fresh local produce. The café has a very trendy vibe and somehow seems the centre of the town's universe.

GETTING THERE & AWAY

You can walk to Bridge of Allan from Stirling in just over an hour. Frequent local buses from Stirling stop in Henderson St. Trains to Dunblane, Stirling, Glasgow and Edinburgh depart frequently from the station at the western end of Henderson St.

Dunblane

☎ 01786 / pop 7911

Dunblane is a very enjoyable town to wander, although the name will always be associated with the horrific massacre that took place in the primary school in March 1996.

There's a friendly, seasonal **TIC** (☎ 0870 720 0613; Stirling Rd; ✷ 10am-5pm Mon-Sat May, Jun & Sep, 10am-5pm Mon-Sat & 11am-4pm Sun Jul & Aug).

The main attraction is the fabulous **Dunblane Cathedral** (HS; ☎ 823388; Cathedral Sq; admission free; ✷ 9.30am-6.30pm Mon-Sat, 1.30-6.30pm Sun Apr-Sep, 9.30am-4.30pm Mon-Wed & Sat, 9.30am-12.30pm Thu, 2-4.30pm Sun Oct-Mar), which is well worth a detour. It's a superb, elegant sandstone building – a fine example of Gothic style. The lower parts of the walls date from Norman times, the rest is mainly 13th to 15th century. There is a sculpted Pictish stone

on display (found on the site), suggesting that it was used as a centre of worship well before the current structure existed.

The musty old **Leighton Library** (☎ 822296; 61 High St; admission free; ✷ 10am-12.30pm & 2-4.30pm Wed-Fri May-Oct), dating from 1684, is the oldest private library in Scotland. There are 4500 books in 90 languages.

Rooms at the **Stirling Arms** (☎ 822156; Stirling Rd; s from £45, d & tw from £70, mains £12) vary a lot, so ask to see a few – some doubles are huge, while twins tend to be more cramped, especially the bathrooms. Its excellent oak-panelled restaurant has a Scottish and international menu and serves the best food in town.

You can walk to Bridge of Allan from Dunblane along Darn Rd, an ancient path used by monks, in about an hour. Alternatively, Scottish Citylink buses run to Stirling, Glasgow and Perth once every hour or two. Trains to Stirling and Glasgow or Edinburgh are more frequent – roughly three per hour, fewer on Sunday.

THE CAMPSIES & STRATHBLANE

The beautiful Campsie Fells, commonly called the Campsies, reach nearly 600m and lie 10 miles north of Glasgow. The plain of the River Forth lies to the north; Strathblane and Loch Lomond lie to the west.

One of several villages around the Campsies, attractive **Killearn** is known for its 31m-high obelisk, raised in honour of George Buchanan, James VI's tutor. Eight miles to the east, **Fintry** has carved itself a gorgeous spot deep in the Campsies on the banks of Endrick Water, which has an impressive 28m waterfall, the **Loup of Fintry**. Six miles north of Fintry, **Kippen** has a very attractive **parish church** (admission free; ✷ 9.30am-5pm). In the west (on the West Highland Way) is **Drymen**, a pretty village with lots of character, which is popular due to its close proximity to Loch Lomond. There's a **TIC** (☎ 01360-660068; The Square; ✷ 9.30am-5pm Mon & Fri, to 7pm Tue & Thu, 9am-1pm Sat; 🖳) in Drymen Library.

Activities

One of the best walks in the area is the ascent of spectacular Dumgoyne hill (427m) from Glengoyne distillery, about 2 miles south of Killearn. Allow at least one hour for the ascent of Dumgoyne. It will take another hour to Earl's Seat, and 1½ hours to return from there to the distillery. The

---

WORTH THE TRIP

Doune Castle (HS; ☎ 01786-841742; Castle Rd, Doune; adult/child £3/1.20; ☯ 9.30am-6.30pm Apr-Sep, to 4.30pm Sat-Wed Oct-Mar) is one of the best-preserved 14th-century castles in Scotland, having remained largely unchanged since it was built for the duke of Albany. It was a favourite royal hunting lodge, but was also of great strategic importance because it controlled the route between the Lowlands and Highlands, and Mary, Queen of Scots stayed here. The inner hall was restored in 1883. There are great views from the castle walls, and the lofty gatehouse is very impressive, rising nearly 30m. If you're a Monty Python fan you may recognise the castle from the *Holy Grail*.

Doune is 7 miles northwest of Stirling. First buses run every hour or two to Doune from Stirling (30 minutes), less frequently on Sunday.

TIC in Drymen and other local TIC offices have detailed route information.

Sleeping & Eating

Elmbank B&B (☎ 01360-661016; Stirling Rd, Drymen; s £28, d £22-26) Just off the square, this property has recently expanded and the friendly owner now offers a variety of rooms. She offers to undercut any other price in town so get ready to bargain. The recommended rooms include the large double with en suite downstairs and the smallish double upstairs with king-size bed.

Culcreuch Castle (☎ 01360-860555; Fintry; r per person £65-85) Fancy a night in a 700-year-old castle? Culcreuch dates to 1296 and has 14 individually styled rooms in a remarkably well-preserved historic building. The rooms are all different with individual Victorian décor, but most are sumptuous and look out onto the collage of greenery engulfing the surrounding estate. A little dowdy perhaps, but popular with groups, but this place, with its period furnishings, has real character. The castle is signposted from the village and is 600m off the B822 coming into Fintry.

Black Bull Hotel (☎ 01360-550215; www.blackbull hotel.com; 2 The Square, Killearn; s/d £48/70; ♿) The 15 rooms at this stylish, modern hotel are in a historic shell with plenty of character. The

excellent service and top-notch facilities ensure most visitors are repeat clientele.

Clachan Inn (☎ 01360-660824; The Square, Drymen; mains £6-16; ☯ lunch & dinner) The best place to eat in the area is the cosy Clachan Inn, (opened in 1734). The extensive menu includes steaks, burgers, salads and vegetarian dishes. Try the smoked salmon, herring and prawn salad for lunch, washed down beautifully with a pint of St Andrews Ale.

Also recommended:

Fintry Inn (☎ 01360-860224; rrr.fintryinn@barbox.net; 23 Main St, Fintry; r per person £25) Above the inn is a self-catering flat sleeping up to six.

Lander B&B (☎ 01360-660273; davidlander@drymen .com; 17 Stirling Rd, Drymen; s/d £23/40) Simple B&B lodgings, private access to guest rooms – very homely.

Getting There & Away

First bus 10 runs from Glasgow to Killearn and Balfron every hour or two; change at Balfron for Aberfoyle (£4 from Glasgow). There are six services daily (except Sunday) between Balfron and Drymen. A Royal Mail postbus runs twice on weekdays between Balfron and Fintry, once on Saturday.

THE TROSSACHS

The Trossachs has been a major tourist draw since the early 19th century when Sir Walter Scott's historical novel *Rob Roy* brought eager visitors to the region. In the 21st century its natural beauty, variety of wildlife and fragile environment have been recognised with the establishment of the Loch Lomond & the Trossachs National Park (p274).

The narrow glen between Loch Katrine and Loch Achray is actually named the Trossachs, but the term is now used to describe a wider scenic area around the southern border of the Highlands.

Aberfoyle & Around

☎ 01877

Crawling with visitors most weekends and dominated by a huge car park, Aberfoyle (population 576) is a hit with domestic tourists and best avoided by everyone else, unless you're using it as a base to explore the beautiful Trossachs.

The **TIC** (☎ 0870 720 0604, 382352; Main St; ☯ daily mid-Mar–Oct, Sat & Sun Nov–mid-Mar; 🖳 ♿) is in the Trossachs Discovery Centre, which details a history of the Trossachs and provides a soft play area for kids.

CENTRAL SCOTLAND

Three miles east is the Lake of Menteith. A ferry takes visitors from Port of Menteith village (on the lake) to the substantial ruins of **Inchmahome Priory** (HS; ☎ 385294; Inchmahome Island; adult/child incl ferry ride £3.50/1.30; ☢ 9.30am-6.30pm Apr-Sep). Mary, Queen of Scots was kept safe here as a child during Henry VIII's 'Rough Wooing' (p31).

Half a mile north of Aberfoyle, on the A821, is the **David Marshall Lodge Visitor Centre** (☎ 382258; admission free, car-park fee £1; ☢ 10am-6pm Mar-Dec, Sat & Sun Jan & Feb; ⚘) in the **Queen Elizabeth Forest Park**, which has info about the many walks and cycle routes in and around the park (many departing from the visitor centre). The Royal Society for the Protection of Birds (RSPB) has a display here on local bird life, the highlight being a live video link to the resident osprey family. There's plenty of info about other birds in the area, such as the peregrine falcon and red kite. The centre is worth visiting solely for the views.

ACTIVITIES
Waymarked walking trails start from the David Marshall Lodge Visitor Centre on the hills above the town; the TIC has a booklet for £1.

There's an excellent 20-mile circular cycle route that links up with the **Sir Walter Scott Steamship** (☎ 376316) along Loch Katrine. Following the southern shore of Loch Achray, you reach the pier on Loch Katrine; departures are at 11am daily May to October. The ferry should drop you at Stronachlachar (adult/child one way £5/3.50) at the western end (note that there are also afternoon departures but they do not stop here). From Stronachlachar, follow the B829 via Loch Ard to Aberfoyle.

SLEEPING & EATING
Crannaig House (☎ 382276; crannaighouse@aol.com; s/d from £35/64; ⚘ ⚘) An opulent Victorian house, Crannaig provides excellent B&B in four family rooms, a single and a twin room. Being a grandiose Victorian affair, all the rooms are a good size. The upstairs family room, with bay window and couch, is the pick of the bunch. There's a cot for youngsters and there are discounts for kids.

Mayfield Guest House (☎ 382962; randmhooks@btopenworld.com; Main St; s/d £28/46) Nothing is too much trouble for the friendly hosts at this guesthouse.

Forth Inn (☎ 382372; www.forthinn.com; Main St; s/d £40/56, bar meals £6, dinner mains £13; ☢ lunch & dinner; ⚘) In the middle of the village, the solid Forth Inn seems to be the lifeblood of the town, with locals and visitors alike queuing up for good honest pub fare. The tasty bar meals are the best in town – try the minted lamb casserole. It also provides shelter and beer, with drinkers spilling outside into the sunny courtyard.

GETTING THERE & AWAY
First has up to four daily buses from Stirling (£4.70) and connecting services from Glasgow (£4) via Balfron.

A postbus does a return trip, Monday to Saturday, from Aberfoyle to Inversnaid Hotel on Loch Lomond, giving access to the West Highland Way.

The Trossachs Trundler does a circuit starting from Stirling that includes Aberfoyle, Port of Menteith, Trossachs Pier on Loch Katrine and Callander; a day ticket per adult/child is £8/2.50. It's wheelchair accessible and can carry two bikes. The bus runs from late May to early October daily except Wednesday.

GETTING AROUND
Bicycles can be hired from **Trossachs Cycle Hire** (☎ 382614; Trossachs Holiday Park; half-/full day £9/16).

Callander
☎ 01877 / pop 3000
Callander has been pulling in the tourists for over 150 years, especially domestic day-trippers from Glasgow and Stirling who flock to the town on weekends. It's a far better place than Aberfoyle to spend time in, quickly lulling visitors into lazy pottering. There's also an excellent array of accommodation options.

INFORMATION
Bank of Scotland (Main St) Has ATM.
Health Clinic (Main St)
Post office (Main St)
Rob Roy & Trossachs Visitor Centre (☎ 0870 720 0628; Ancaster Sq; audiovisual Rob Roy show adult/child £3.60/2.40; ☢ 10am-5pm Mar-May & Oct, 10am-6pm Jun-Sep, 11am-4pm Nov-Feb) This helpful centre has heaps of info on the area and runs an audiovisual show about the great man.
Royal Bank of Scotland (Main St) Has ATM.

CALLANDER

0 ──────── 400 m
0 ──────── 0.2 miles

To Bracklinn Falls (1.5mi);
Callander Crags (2mi)

Leny Rd [A84]
To Loch
Achray (10mi);
Balquhidder (13mi);
Killin (22mi);
Crianlarich (31mi)

Ancaster Rd
Glenartney Rd
Cross St
Bridge St
Nith Church Rd
Craigard Rd
Main St
Pearl St
Church St
Teith
Manse Ln
Invertrossachs Rd [A81]
To Trossachs
Backpackers
(1mi)

Muirdston Ave
Stirling Rd
Menteith Cres
Bracklinn Rd
Station Rd

To Loch Katrine (10mi);
Aberfoyle (11mi);
Glasgow (35mi)

To Doune (7mi);
Stirling (14mi) [A84]

INFORMATION
Bank of Scotland..............................1 A1
Health Clinic.....................................2 C2
Post Office..3 C2
Rob Roy & Trossachs Visitor Centre
  (TIC)...4 B1
Royal Bank of Scotland...................5 B1

SLEEPING
Arden House......................................6 C1
Bridgend House Hotel.......................7 A2
Callander Meadows...........................8 A1
Linley Guest House............................9 B1
Roman Camp Hotel.........................10 C2

EATING
Co-op Supermarket..........................11 B1

ACTIVITIES

The impressive Bracklinn Falls are reached by track and footpath from Bracklinn Rd (30 minutes each way from the car park). Also off Bracklinn Rd, a woodland trail leads up to Callander Crags, with great views over the surroundings; a return trip is about 4 miles from the car park. Note that at the time of research the bridge at the falls was out of use, due to flooding.

SLEEPING & EATING

Trossachs Backpackers (☎ /fax 331200; info@scottish-hostel.co.uk; Invertrossachs Rd; dm/tw £13.50/37) This backpackers is in a beautifully isolated spot; take Bridge St off Main St, then turn right onto Invertrossachs Rd and follow the road, which runs on the southern side of the river draining Loch Vennachar, for a mile. The excellent dorms are very spacious with four or six beds and their own bathroom. Rates include sheets and breakfast.

Callander Meadows (☎ 330181; meadows@callanderinn.fsnet.co.uk; 24 Main St; r per person £23-27, mains £12-14; ☾ lunch & dinner) Rooms have been tastefully redecorated here and have the best of modern convenience in Victorian elegance. Room No 1 has a great view of the River Teith, while No 2 is a grandiose four-poster-bed affair. The restaurant here is small and personal, providing sophisticated dining, beautifully presented food and faultless service.

Roman Camp Hotel (☎ 330003; www.roman-camp-hotel.co.uk; s/d from £75/125, 4-course dinner £39, á la carte

mains £23) Indulgent Roman Camp is the spot to spoil yourself. It's magnificently located by the River Teith and dates from 1625. There is complimentary sherry upon arrival, a first-class restaurant (reservations required) and even a tiny chapel for weddings.

Bridgend House Hotel (☎ 330130; www.bridgendhotel.co.uk; Bridgend; r from £55, mains £6-10; ☾ lunch & dinner; ⓕ) Mock-Tudor Bridgend House Hotel, across the river and by the A81, serves good Scottish-style meals in the bar and restaurant and has four comfortable en-suite rooms. It's a snug place inside, and there's also a beer garden for those days when the sun is peeping through the clouds.

Along Main St you'll find a Co-op supermarket and lots of places offering meals and snacks for under £5.

Also recommended:

Linley Guest House (☎ 330087; www.linleyguesthouse.co.uk; 139 Main St; r per person £18-21) A spick-and-span B&B with light and bright rooms and helpful owners.

Arden House (☎ /fax 330235; www.ardenhouse.org.uk; Bracklinn Rd; r per person £30-36) A wonderful place for grown-ups (no kids allowed). Guests are well looked after in luxury rooms.

GETTING THERE & AWAY

First operates buses from Stirling (45 minutes, hourly Monday to Saturday) and Killin (45 minutes, three to six daily Monday to Saturday). There's also a daily Scottish Citylink bus from Callander to Edinburgh (£9.60, 1¾ hours) and Fort William (£13.50,

CENTRAL SCOTLAND

2½ hours) via Crianlarich, with connections to Oban and Skye.

Royal Mail runs a postbus from Callander to Trossachs Pier linking with the sailing of the SS *Sir Walter Scott* on Loch Katrine (see below).

The Trossachs Trundler calls at Callander (p198) and reaches the pier on Loch Katrine 26 minutes later four times daily, except Wednesday. A trip covering just the Trossachs area is £5/1.75 per adult/child.

Loch Katrine & Loch Achray

This rugged area, 6 miles north of Aberfoyle and 10 miles west of Callander, is the heart of the Trossachs. From April to October the **SS Sir Walter Scott** (☎ 01877-376316; www.loch katrine.com; adult/child return from £5.80/4.30) chugs along Loch Katrine from Trossachs Pier at the eastern tip of the loch.

There are two good **walks** starting from Loch Achray. The path to the rocky cone called **Ben A'an** (460m) begins at a car park near the old Trossachs Hotel. It's easy to follow, and the return trip is just under 4 miles.

On the other side of the Trossachs lies rugged **Ben Venue** (727m) – there's a path all the way to the summit. Start walking from Loch Achray Hotel, follow the Achray Water westwards to Loch Katrine, then turn left and ascend the steep flanks of Ben Venue. There are great views of the Highlands and the Lowlands from the top. The return trip is about 5.5 miles – allow four to five hours.

BALQUHIDDER & AROUND

Steeped in clan history, this mountainous and sparsely populated area is in the northern part of the Stirling administrative region. There are a few villages and lots of good hill walks.

Balquhidder

☎ 01567 / pop 50

In this small village (pronounced 'balwhidder'), 2 miles off the A84, there's a churchyard with **Rob Roy's grave** (which has the words 'Despite Them' defiantly etched onto the headstone) – it's an appropriately beautiful spot in a deep, winding glen in big-sky country. There are some other interesting headstones in the graveyard, and a plaque on the old kirk wall helps unravel their origins. His wife and two of his sons are also interred

> ### ROB ROY
>
> As all the tourist literature repeatedly informs you, this is Rob Roy country. Rob Roy Macgregor (1671–1734) was the wild leader of one of the wildest of Scotland's clans, Clan Gregor. Although he claimed direct descent from a 10th-century king of Scots and rights to the lands the clan occupied, these Macgregor lands stood between powerful neighbours. Rob Roy became notorious for his daring raids into the Lowlands to carry off cattle and sheep – hence the clan's sobriquet, 'Children of the Mist' – and led to the outlawing of the clan. He also achieved a reputation as a champion of the poor. Rob Roy is buried in the churchyard at Balquhidder, by Loch Voil.

here. In the church are the 8th-century **St Angus' stone**, a 17th-century church bell and a free leaflet giving details on notable gravestones, artefacts and people of the area.

The minor road continues along pretty **Loch Voil** to Inverlochlarig, where you can climb **Stob Binnein** (1165m) by its southern ridge. Stob Binnein is one of the highest mountains in the area, and it has a most unusual shape, like a cone with its top chopped off.

GETTING THERE & AWAY

Buses between Callander and Killin stop at the Kings House Hotel. On weekdays a postbus operates from Killin to Callander; it also stops at the Kings House Hotel. The daily Scottish Citylink bus from Edinburgh to Fort William stops here at 11.04am.

Crianlarich & Tyndrum

☎ 01838 / combined pop 350

In good tramping country, and on the West Highland Way, these villages are little more than service junctions on the main A82 road, just north of the Loch Lomond & the Trossachs National Park. There's a train station at Crianlarich. Tiny Tyndrum, just 5 miles along the road, is blessed with two stations and a very flash **TIC** (☎ 400246; info@tyndrum .visitscotland.co.uk; ☒ 10am-5pm Apr, May, Sep & Oct, to 6pm Jun, 9.30am-6pm Jul & Aug), which has piles of information and a bureau de change. Ask here about day walks along the West Highland Way and ascents of popular An Caisteal

(995m), Ben More (1174m) and magnificent Ben Lui (1130m). The TIC stocks OS maps and has detailed route information.

The **Green Welly Stop** (☎ 400271; www.the greenwellystop.co.uk; Tyndrum; hot meals £6.50) is a shrine to tourism. This little shopping complex has a very good (if slightly pricey) outdoor store, ideal if you're looking for supplies before you grapple with your Munro. It's also a good fuel stop, with hot meals served all day.

SLEEPING & EATING

Crianlarich Youth Hostel (SYHA; ☎ 0870 004 1112; Station Rd; dm adult/child £12.50/9.50; ☐) This hostel is a modern bungalow with six-bed dorms. It has a good Highland setup – large kitchen, clean dining area and warm, comfy lounge. There's bike hire (£12 per day) and it's the best budget option (B&Bs tend to be expensive in Crianlarich).

Auchtertyre Farm (Strathfillan Wigwams; ☎ 400 251; www.sac.ac.uk/wigwams; Tyndrum; wigwam per adult/child £11/6.50, camp sites per person £6, lodge d £50-60) This charismatic place, 3 miles from Crianlarich (and 2 miles from Tyndrum), is off the A82 and has 16 heated wigwams – essentially wooden A-frame cabins. They're a little squashy (each has five beds) but great value. Auchtertyre Farm also has camping with access to all facilities and a self-contained lodge, ideal for families.

Invervey Hotel (☎ 400219; Tyndrum; s £23-27, d/f £54/£80, bar meals £5; 🛇) In Tyndrum you'll get fairly basic accommodation and good cheer in this well-run hotel. Walkers should head for room Nos 1 to 12, which are towards the back and a bit quieter, ensuring a decent night's shuteye. It was undergoing refurbishment at the time of writing.

GETTING THERE & AWAY

Scottish Citylink runs several buses daily to Glasgow, Oban and Skye from both villages. A postbus service links Crianlarich, Tyndrum and Killin twice on each weekday (with connections to Callander) and once on Saturday.

First ScotRail runs train services from Tyndrum and Crianlarich to Fort William (£13.50, 1¾ hours, four daily Monday to Saturday, two on Sunday), Oban (£8, one hour, three daily Monday to Saturday) and Glasgow (£12.50, 1¾ hours, three or four daily).

Killin

☎ 01567 / pop 700

Tumbling through the centre of this charming little village are the frothy **Falls of Dochart**. The canny locals have made the best of their unusual water feature, pulling in many a passing tourist coach. Killin is in the northeastern corner of the Stirling region and is a handy base for exploring the mighty mountains and glens that surround it.

INFORMATION

The village has a post office and a Bank of Scotland ATM, both on Main St.

Outdoor Centre (☎ 820652; Main St) Hires out all sorts of equipment, including canoes (£40 per day) and mountain bikes (£11/15 per half-/full day). Note that a child's seat is complimentary when two bikes are hired.

TIC (☎ 0870 720 0627; 🕙 Mar-Oct) In the Breadalbane Folklore Centre, by the River Dochart.

SIGHTS

Bringing ancient magic and miracles to life is the **Breadalbane Folklore Centre** (☎ 820254; adult/child £2.50/1.65; 🕙 10am-5pm Mar-May & Oct, to 6pm Jun & Sep, 9.30am-6.30pm Jul & Aug), in an old water mill overlooking the falls. There is an audiovisual presentation about St Fillan, a local saint whose religious teachings are said to have helped unite the ancient kingdoms of the

---

SOMETHING SPECIAL

At the junction with the A84, **Kings House Hotel** (☎ 01877-384646; www.kingshouse-scotland .co.uk; Balquhidder; s/d £33/55, self-catering cottage per wk from £180; 🛇) is a classic inn built in 1779 for £40, at the request of the drovers. Nowadays it offers B&B in more salubrious surroundings; the upstairs rooms are lovely, with fine views. There's a narrow, sloping passageway reminding visitors that they're treading in the 200-year-old-plus footsteps of many a passing traveller. There are also six excellent self-catering cottages set in the national park – cots and children's beds are available here. The **Rob Roy Bar** (mains £3-7) at the hotel is a tiny, rickety wood-and-stone affair providing food and shelter from the elements. There's everything from sandwiches to a rollmop and smoked trout Highland platter to local venison sausages. It also serves an outstanding pint of Guinness, best drunk by the open fire.

Scots and the Picts in the 8th century. Robert the Bruce carried a relic of the saint into battle at Bannockburn some 600 years later, which he used to inspire his followers. There are displays about local and clan history, including the Macgregors and MacNabs.

The **Clan MacNab burial ground** lies on an island in the river, crossed by the main road and just downstream from the falls; ask at the TIC for the gate key.

ACTIVITIES

Killin is at the northern end of the **Lochs and Glens cycle route** from Glasgow, which follows forest trails, small roads and disused rail routes via the Trossachs – the TIC has detailed information.

Seven miles northeast of Killin, **Ben Lawers** (1214m) rises above Loch Tay. There's an NTS visitor centre here and trails lead to the summit (see p223).

Glen Lochay runs westwards from Killin into the hills of Mamlorn. You can take a **mountain bike** for about 11 miles up the glen to just beyond Batavaime. The scenery is impressive and the hills aren't too difficult to climb. It's possible, on a nice summer day, to climb over the top of **Ben Challum** (1025m) and descend to Crianlarich, but it's hard work.

For more information, pick up a copy of the *Walks Around Killin* leaflet (30p) from the TIC.

SLEEPING & EATING

Drumfin Guest House (☎ 820900; drumfinn@aol.com; Manse Rd; r per person £26-30) This top guesthouse has had an extensive refit and now boasts pristine facilities. Two rooms share a bathroom while three have en suites. Have a look at a couple of rooms, as the view varies, although all are light and bright. But it's the friendly, enthusiastic owners who set this place apart. Besides, anyone who has frog musicians in the garden gets our vote – the garden gnome has met its match.

Falls of Dochart Inn (☎ 820270; Falls of Dochart; s/d £40/60, mains £9-14) Overlooking the falls, the Dochart Inn has smallish, pristine upstairs rooms – try to request one with a view of the falls (eg No 2). Rooms at the back are quiet but have no real view. Downstairs is a very snug, atmospheric space with a roaring fire, a good beer and wine selection and creative takes on traditional Scottish dishes. The impressive service is friendly and efficient.

WORTH THE TRIP

Alloa Tower (NTS; ☎ 211701; Alloa Park; adult/child £5/4; ☙ 1-5pm Apr-Oct) is a short, clearly signposted walk from the centre of Alloa and set in a lovely grassed area. The 24m-high tower dates from before 1497 and it's one of the most interesting NTS properties in the region. The Italianate staircase and dome are superb. There are also a well, a pit dungeon, and furnishings and paintings belonging to the Mar family. Views from the parapet walk are spectacular.

Many people incorporate a visit to Castle Campbell in Dollar in the morning and Alloa Tower in the afternoon.

Alloa is 6 miles east of Stirling. First runs buses to Clackmannan, Dollar, Stirling (30 minutes, frequent) and Glasgow.

Killin Youth Hostel (SYHA; ☎ 0870 004 1131; dm adult/child from £13/9; ☙ Mar-Oct) At the northern end of the village, this lovely Victorian mansion has one family room and well-kept four- to 12-bed dorms. Dorms are an excellent size and most (such as No 3) have bay windows drawing in plenty of light. Common areas, including the kitchen, are very clean.

High Creagan (☎ 820449; Aberfeldy Rd; camp sites per person £4) This place has a well-kept, sheltered camping site with plenty of grass set high on the slopes overlooking sparkling Loch Tay, just outside Killin.

You'll find supermarkets along Main St, including Costcutter and Co-op.

GETTING THERE & AWAY

First runs a service from Stirling (£5, 1¾ hours, once or twice daily Monday to Friday, once on Saturday) via Callander. There's a postbus to Crianlarich and Tyndrum twice on weekdays and once on Saturday. There's a postbus service between Aberfeldy and Killin (1¾ hours to Aberfeldy) Monday to Saturday. A Scottish Citylink bus leaves for Oban twice a day (Friday to Monday, 1½ hours).

CLACKMANNANSHIRE

Inviting Clackmannanshire has some great attractions that are worth a detour if you're in the Stirling region. The tiny district is a top spot for day trips from the city of Stirling.

DOLLAR

☎ 01259 / pop 2877

About 11 miles east of Stirling, in the lower Ochil Hills, is the charming town of Dollar. **Castle Campbell** (HS; ☎ 742408; Dollar Glen; adult/child £3.30/1.30; ☐ 9.30am-6.30pm Apr-Sep, to 4.30pm Sat-Wed Oct-Mar) is a 20-minute walk up **Dollar Glen**, into the wooded hills above the town. It's a spooky old stronghold of the dukes of Argyll and stands between two ravines; you can clearly see why it was known as Castle Gloom. There's been a fortress of some kind on this site from the 11th century, but the present structure dates from the 15th century. The castle was sacked by Cromwell in 1654, but the tower is well preserved. There's a great ramble with sweeping views over Castle Campbell and the surrounding country from the little car park near the castle. Note that it can get boggy if it's been raining.

There are regular First buses to Dollar from Stirling; other services run from Alloa (every two hours Monday to Friday).

CLACKMANNAN

☎ 01259 / pop 3450

This quiet village (you really could hear a pin drop) lies 2 miles southeast of Alloa and has several interesting sights. **Clackmannan Stone** (Main St) sits on top of a large shaft – it's sacred to the pagan deity Mannan and predates Christian times.

The adjacent 17th-century **Cross** is engraved with the Bruce coat of arms; the lower part is heavily worn, due to prisoners' chains. Also adjacent is the striking **Tolbooth**, built in 1592 for £284, which served as court and prison. **Clackmannan Tower**, uphill from the church and about 450m from Main St, was a residence of the Bruce family from 1365 to 1772. The widow of the last laird knighted Robert Burns in the tower, with the sword of Robert the Bruce, in 1787. The five-storey tower has structural problems due to subsidence and it isn't open to the public, but the exterior is well worth a look. The idyllic views aren't bad either.

First buses run to/from Stirling (40 minutes, every 20 minutes) and frequently to Alloa.

FALKIRK REGION

The little administrative district of Falkirk contains one of Scotland's modern marvels of engineering – the Falkirk Wheel, which, more than anything else in the district, is encouraging a new wave of tourism. The region also covers some interesting areas to the east, including Bo'ness.

FALKIRK

☎ 01324 / pop 32,379

Falkirk, a large town about 10 miles southeast of Stirling, is home to the famous Falkirk Wheel – an astounding achievement of modern engineering. Watching it spin its boat-bound occupants around is becoming a major tourist attraction. Drop into the **TIC**

MODERN MARVELS

A £78-million Millennium Link Project has restored the Forth and Clyde, and Union Canals to full working order, linking Edinburgh with west and central Scotland. The expansion of the railways in the mid-19th century rendered the canals, built in 1822, obsolete and they had fallen into disuse.

The centrepiece is the Falkirk Wheel, a unique engineering structure designed to replace the flight of locks that once linked the two canals at Falkirk. It is the world's first rotating boat lift, raising vessels (plus almost 300 tonnes of water) 35m in one steel caisson, while descending boats are carried down in the second caisson on the opposite side of the wheel.

Visitors can take boat trips on the **Falkirk Wheel** (☎ 0870 050 0208; www.thefalkirkwheel.co.uk; adult/child/family £8/4/21, car-park fee £2; ☐ 9am-5pm Nov-Mar, to 6pm Apr-Oct), spinning around on its giant gondolas. Boats leave every half-hour (hourly in winter) and travel from the visitor centre into the wheel, getting delivered to the Union Canal, high above. Boats then go through Roughcastle Tunnel before the descent on the wheel and return trip to the visitor centre. Anyone with an interest in engineering marvels should not miss this boat ride – it's great for kids, too. The nearby visitor centre explains the workings of the mighty wheel – it only takes the power of about eight toasters for a full rotation!

(☎ 0870 720 0614; 2 Glebe St) for more information, and see the boxed text, p203.

First runs regular buses to Stirling and Edinburgh. Trains go to Stirling, Dunblane, Perth, Glasgow (£5) and Edinburgh (£4.20) from Falkirk Grahamston station. Glasgow–Edinburgh express trains stop at Falkirk High station every 15 to 30 minutes.

BO'NESS & KINNEIL RAILWAY

The town of Bo'ness on the Firth of Forth is best known for the steam train that shuttles to and fro on the **Bo'ness & Kinneil Railway** (☎ 01506-822298; Bo'ness Station, Union St; adult/child return £4.50/2). The train runs from April to October, with four departures each weekend. In July and August the train runs from Tuesday to Friday as well. Tickets costing £7.50/4 per adult/child include admission to the **Birkhill Fireclay Mine**, 130 steps down in the Avon gorge; guided tours run in conjunction with train arrivals. There's also a free **railway exhibition** at the station in Bo'ness.

Direct buses to Bo'ness from Glasgow, Edinburgh, Falkirk and Stirling are run by First.

FIFE

A chubby finger of land jutting out into the icy North Sea, Fife, or 'the kingdom of Fife', as it likes to be known – it was home to the early Scottish faith and to Scottish kings for 500 years – is a treasure-trove of attractions. Highlights include a string of delightful fishing villages perched on the East Neuk coast, and, further north, one of the most appealing towns in the country: St Andrews. Despite integration with the rest of Scotland, Fife has held onto its unique Lowland identity. Many people enter 'the kingdom' via the Forth Road or Tay Bridges – perhaps traversing these enormous gateways adds to the sense of entering a new realm. The Fife Coastal Path now links these two bridges along 80 miles of glorious coastal scenery, and the laid-back, serene countryside with its rolling, lush farmland invites exploration.

Getting Around

Fife Council produces a useful transport map, *Getting Around Fife*, available from TICs – good links for public-transport in-

formation can be found at www.fifedirect .org.uk. The main bus operator is **Stagecoach Fife** (☎ 01334-474238). For £5 you can buy a Fifedayrider ticket, which gives unlimited travel around Fife on Stagecoach buses.

If you are driving from the Forth Road Bridge to St Andrews, a slower but much more scenic route than the M90/A91 is along the signposted **Fife Coastal Tourist Route**.

CULROSS

☎ 01383 / pop 460

A thicket of forest above the town wedges Culross (pronounced coo-*ross*) between the firth and wooded slopes. An enchanting little town, it's Scotland's best-preserved example of a 17th-century Scottish burgh, and the NTS owns 20 of the buildings, including the palace. Small, red-tiled, whitewashed buildings line the cobbled streets, and the winding Back Causeway to the abbey is embellished with whimsical stone cottages.

Sights

You can visit **Culross Palace** (NTS; ☎ 880359; admission to palace, town house & study adult/child £8/5; ☾ noon-5pm Easter-Sep), more a large house than a palace, which features extraordinary decorative painted woodwork, barrel-vaulted ceilings and an interior largely unchanged since the early 17th century. It's dark and spooky inside on an overcast day. The **town house** (visitor centre downstairs) and the **study**, also completed in the early 17th century, are open to the public, but the other NTS properties can only be viewed from the outside.

Ruined **Culross Abbey** (admission free; ☾ 9am-7pm Easter-Aug, other times by arrangement), founded by the Cistercians in 1217, is on the hill in a lovely peaceful spot with vistas of the firth; the choir of the abbey church is now the parish church. In the northeastern corner of the north transept there's an unusual sight – statues of eight children kneeling in front of their parents' memorial.

Sleeping

Burnbank Cottage (☎ 880240; Blairburn, Low Causeway; r per person £20) This cottage has one double and one twin, both with shared bathroom. It's home-grown Scottish hospitality at its best, and the cosy private living room for guests is great for an evening snuggle.

Getting There & Away

Culross is 12 miles west of the Forth Road Bridge. Stagecoach Fife buses 14 and 14A run roughly hourly between Stirling (one hour) and Dunfermline (20 minutes), less often on weekends, via Culross.

ABERDOUR

☎ 01383 / pop 1690

It's worth stopping in this popular seaside town to ramble around impressive **Aberdour Castle** (HS; ☎ 860519; adult/child £3/1.25; ✵ 9.30am-6.30pm Apr-Sep, 9.30am-4.30pm Sat-Wed Oct-Mar, closed Thu & Fri). The castle was built by the Douglas family in 1342, but by the 18th century it was partly in ruins and abandoned by its owners. There's an interesting account of James Douglas, 4th earl of Morton, giving an insight into treachery among the nobility. An impressive feature of the castle is its attractive walled garden (good for quiet contemplation), and evidence of 16th-century terraced gardens can also be seen. There's a fine circular dovecote (called a *doocot* in Scotland), shaped like a beehive, dating from the 16th century – it was a giant medieval larder. **St Fillan's Church**, by the castle, was founded in 1123, but the current building is mostly 17th century. It's believed to have been visited by Robert the Bruce and there's certainly a sense of the ancient inside, where harsh grey stone walls contrast vividly with stunning stained-glass windows.

With real ales and good vegetarian choices on the menu, the family-run **Aberdour Hotel** (☎ 860325; www.aberdourhotel.co.uk; 38 High St; s/d £50/70, mains from £6) is not only a good place to stay but also the best place to eat in town. Old-fashioned rooms have poky en suites in this lovable old hotel, and it's very friendly – ask about the package deals.

There are trains to Edinburgh (£3.90, one hour, at least hourly daily, every two hours on Sunday).

KIRKCALDY

☎ 01592 / pop 46,912

Kirkcaldy (kir-kod-ay) sprawls along the edge of the sea for several miles and has a rather shabby promenade with spectacular pounding surf on windy days. It's worth stopping in town to visit the excellent museum.

The **TIC** (☎ 267775; Merchant House, 339 High St; ✵ 9.30am-5.30pm Mon-Sat, 11am-4pm Sun) is at the eastern end of High St. The pedestrianised part of High St has the Mercat Cross shopping centre and banks with ATMs.

Just a short walk east from the train and bus stations, in the War Memorial Gardens, you'll find the **Kirkcaldy Museum & Art Gallery** (☎ 412860; admission free; ✵ 10.30am-5pm Mon-Sat, 2-5pm Sun), which combines historical accounts with contemporary exhibits. The kids will have a ball as there are plenty of hands-on attractions. The museum has very good temporary exhibitions – when we popped in there was a display on the impact of debris, especially plastic, on the Fife shoreline. There's also an impressive collection of Scottish paintings from the 18th to the 20th century, including the Scottish Colourists and the Glasgow Boys.

You're better off staying in Edinburgh, East Neuk or St Andrews, but you could try **Cherrydene** (☎ 202147; www.cherrydene.co.uk; 44 Bennochy Rd; s/d £25/45), which has large, tastefully furnished rooms and is close to the bus and train stations.

Frequent buses (usually hourly) run from Hill St bus station, two blocks inland from the Esplanade. Destinations include St Andrews (one hour), Anstruther (one hour 15 minutes) and Edinburgh (one hour). Kirkcaldy is on the main railway line between Edinburgh (£5.20, 45 minutes) and Dundee (£9, 40 minutes); there are two to four trains an hour.

FALKLAND
☎ 01337 / pop 1183

Below the soft ridges of the Lomond Hills in the centre of Fife is the charming village of Falkland. This is one of the most captivating inland towns in the region and there are many heritage-listed conservation buildings here. It's a top spot to soak up central Scotland's historical roots.

Sights

Rising majestically out of the town centre and dominating the skyline is the outstanding 16th-century **Falkland Palace** (NTS; ☎ 857397; adult/child £8/5; ☼ 10am-6pm Mon-Sat, 1-5.30pm Sun Mar-Oct), a country residence of the Stuart monarchs. Mary, Queen of Scots is said to have spent the happiest days of her life 'playing the country girl in the woods and parks' at Falkland. The palace was built between 1501 and 1541 to replace a castle dating from the 12th century; French and Scottish craftspeople were employed to create a masterpiece of Scottish Gothic architecture. The king's bedchamber and the chapel, with its beautiful painted ceiling, have both been restored. Don't miss the prodigious 17th-century Flemish hunting tapestries in the hall. One feature of the royal leisure centre still exists: the oldest royal tennis court in Britain, built in 1539 for James V. It's in the grounds and still in use.

If you're curious about the town's history, drop into the **Royal Burgh of Falkland Exhibition** (Old Town Hall, Back Wynd; admission free; ☼ 11am-5pm Mon-Sat, 2-5pm Sun Apr-Oct). It's a small, growing museum that has fascinating displays on Falkland's historical development. Better yet is the curator, a very knowledgeable guide and storyteller who's happy to impart some of his extensive archival knowledge to visitors.

Sleeping & Eating

Burgh Lodge (☎ 857710; www.burghlodge.co.uk; Back Wynd; dm £12, f from £44; ☐ � �(♣)) This is one of the best budget accommodation options in Fife. It's good for backpackers or families and the facilities are very well kept. The dorms range in size from two to eight modern bunks and there are two family rooms. It's luxury budget accommodation, extremely friendly and would make a great base for exploring the area.

Hunting Lodge (☎ 857226; timlees@huntinglodge .fsbusiness.co.uk; High St; s/d from £25/40) Opposite the palace, this very cosy little inn dates back to 1607. The homely rooms, exuding warmth and character, are upstairs, while pints and chattering locals furnish the downstairs area.

Covenanter Hotel (☎ 857224; www.covenanter hotel.com; The Square; s/d/ste £45/58/65, mains £8-16) This 18th-century coaching inn, on the square opposite the palace, is a snug, classy little abode with fine rooms that are often discounted when things are quiet (it's worth asking!). The three-person suite is the best. The bistro meals here are inventive to say the least (try the Arran cheddar, beer and walnut cheesecake with warm potato and asparagus salad) and the hotel specialises in succulent cuts of Angus beef.

Getting There & Away

Falkland is 11 miles north of Kirkcaldy. There are Stagecoach Fife buses roughly every two hours Monday to Saturday to/from Perth (one hour) and Cupar (30 minutes).

ST ANDREWS
☎ 01334 / pop 14,209

Nestled into a wide, sweeping bay, St Andrews combines an international student population with a nostalgia for Pringle sweaters and a reverence for golf; it's probably the only place in Scotland you'll see the plummy Pimms advertised. Touched with a gentle dignity, the town also has a surprisingly intact medieval layout and dramatic ruins that evoke a sense of just how deeply its historical roots are embedded in Fife's sandy soils. When the sun tears a hole through the clouds this is one of Scotland's most fascinating and enjoyable towns to explore. Its multicultural appeal ensures a thriving pub and café scene, and the dining is second to none in this part of the country.

You'll hear just as many English accents around town as you will Scottish; it's home to an ancient university where wealthy English undergraduates rub shoulders with Scottish theology students.

History

St Andrews is said to have been founded by St Regulus, who arrived from Greece in the 4th century bringing the bones of St Andrew – Scotland's patron saint. The town soon grew into a major pilgrimage centre and St Andrews developed into the ecclesiastical capital of the country. The university was founded in 1410, the first in Scotland. By the mid-16th century there were three colleges, St Salvator's, St Leonard's and St Mary's.

St Andrews is the headquarters of golf's governing body, the Royal & Ancient Golf Club. It's also the location of the world's most famous golf course, the Old Course. The British Open Championship has taken place regularly at St Andrews since 1873.

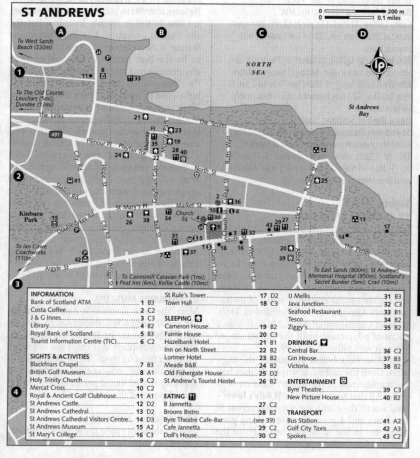

ST ANDREWS

INFORMATION		
Bank of Scotland ATM	1	B3
Costa Coffee	2	C2
J & G Innes	3	C3
Library	4	B2
Royal Bank of Scotland	5	D3
Tourist Information Centre (TIC)	6	C2

SIGHTS & ACTIVITIES		
Blackfriars Chapel	7	B3
British Golf Museum	8	A1
Holy Trinity Church	9	C2
Mercat Cross	10	C2
Royal & Ancient Golf Clubhouse	11	A1
St Andrews Castle	12	D2
St Andrews Cathedral	13	D2
St Andrews Cathedral Visitors Centre	14	D2
St Andrews Museum	15	A2
St Mary's College	16	C3

St Rule's Tower	17	D2
Town Hall	18	C3

SLEEPING		
Cameron House	19	B2
Fairnie House	20	C3
Hazelbank Hotel	21	B1
Inn on North Street	22	B2
Lorimer Hotel	23	B2
Meade B&B	24	B2
Old Fishergate House	25	D2
St Andrew's Tourist Hostel	26	B2

EATING		
B Jannetta	27	C2
Broons Bistro	28	B2
Byre Theatre Cafe-Bar	(see 39)	
Cafe Jannetta	29	C2
Doll's House	30	C2

IJ Mellis	31	B3
Java Junction	32	C3
Seafood Restaurant	33	B1
Tesco	34	B2
Ziggy's	35	B2

DRINKING		
Central Bar	36	C2
Gin House	37	B3
Victoria	38	B2

ENTERTAINMENT		
Byre Theatre	39	C3
New Picture House	40	B2

TRANSPORT		
Bus Station	41	A2
Golf City Taxis	42	A3
Spokes	43	C2

CENTRAL SCOTLAND

Orientation

St Andrews preserves its medieval plan of parallel streets with small closes (alleys) leading off them. The most important parts of the old town, lying to the east of the bus station, are easily explored on foot. Like Cambridge and Oxford, St Andrews has no campus – most university buildings are integrated into the central part of the town. There's a small harbour near the cathedral, and two sandy beaches: East Sands extends south from the harbour and the wider West Sands is north of the town.

Information

Parking in the central area requires a voucher (60p per hour), which is on sale in many shops and at the TIC.

Bank of Scotland (South St) Has ATM.

Costa Coffee (81 Market St; per hr £3; 🕑 8am-6pm Mon-Sat, 10am-1pm Sun; 🖳) A few terminals with Internet access.

J&G Innes (☎ 472174; 107 South St) Plenty of local-interest books, such as Fife's history of burning witches.

Library (Church Sq; 🕑 9.30am-5pm Mon, Fri & Sat, to 7pm Tue-Thu; 🖳) Free Internet access – drop-in only; no bookings.

Royal Bank of Scotland (South St)

St Andrews Memorial Hospital (☎ 472327; Abbey Walk) Minor injuries only; located south of Abbey St.

TIC (☎ 472021; www.visit-standrews.co.uk; 70 Market St; 🕑 Mon-Sat Nov-Mar, daily Apr-Oct) Helpful staff with good knowledge of St Andrews and Fife.

Sights

ST ANDREWS CATHEDRAL

Situated at the eastern end of North St is the ruined western end of **St Andrews Cathedral** (HS; ☎ 472563; The Pends; adult/child £3/1.20, incl St Andrews Castle £5/2; 🕑 9.30am-6.30pm Apr-Sep, to 4.30pm Oct-Mar; 🚻), once the largest and one of the most magnificent cathedrals in Britain; the striking ruins convey a sense of its immensity. Although it was founded in 1160, it wasn't consecrated until 1318. It was a focus of pilgrimage until the Reformation, when it was pillaged in 1559.

St Andrew's bones lay under the high altar. Until the cathedral was built, they had been enshrined in the nearby Church of St Rule. All that remains is the **St Rule's Tower** – well worth the climb for the view across St Andrews and a great place for taking photographs. In the same area are parts of the ruined 13th-century priory.

The **St Andrews Cathedral Visitors Centre** includes the **calefactory**, the only room where the monks could warm themselves by a fire; masons' marks on the red sandstone blocks, identifying who shaped each block, can still be clearly seen. There's also a collection of Celtic crosses and gravestones that were found on the site. The highlight is the carved stone **sarcophagus**. It was carved in the 8th century and the detail is simply amazing. What survives is mainly a woodland hunting scene with the animals seemingly about to leap off the stone. Although it's Pictish it shows definite Mediterranean influence.

ST ANDREWS CASTLE

Not far from the cathedral and with dramatic coastline views, **St Andrews Castle** (HS; ☎ 477196; The Scores; adult/child £4/1.60; 🕑 9.30am-6.30pm Apr-Sep, to 4.30pm Oct-Mar) is mainly in ruins, but the site itself is evocative. The most intriguing feature is the complex of siege tunnels, said to be the best surviving example of siege engineering in Europe. You can walk along the damp, mossy tunnels, now lit by electric light – but be warned, it helps if you're short. The castle was founded around 1200 as the fortified home of the bishop. A visitor centre gives a good audiovisual introduction and also has a small collection of Pictish stones.

In 1654, part of the castle was pulled down to provide materials for rebuilding the harbour wall and pier. Enough survives to give an idea of what each chamber was used for. After the execution of Protestant reformers in 1545, other reformers retaliated by murdering Cardinal Beaton and taking over the castle. The cardinal's body was hung from a window in the Fore Tower before being tossed into the dungeon. The reformers then spent almost a year besieged in the castle.

ST ANDREWS MUSEUM

Near the bus station, **St Andrews Museum** (☎ 412690; Kinburn Park, Doubledykes Rd; admission free; 🕑 10am-5pm Apr-Sep, 10.30am-4pm Oct-Mar) has interesting displays that chart the history of the town from its founding by St Regulus to its growth as an ecclesiastical, academic and sporting centre. Local preservation work is a focal point of the museum.

BRITISH GOLF MUSEUM

Golfers shouldn't miss the **British Golf Museum** (☎ 460046; Bruce Embankment; adult/child £5/2.75;

9.30am-5.30pm Mon-Sat, 10am-5pm Sun Easter-Oct, 10am-4pm Mon-Sun Nov-Mar), an interesting (even for nongolfers), modern museum charting the history of the game and its intimate association with St Andrews. It's equipped with audiovisual displays and touch screens, as well as golf memorabilia.

Opposite the museum is the clubhouse of the **Royal & Ancient Golf Club**. Outside the club is the **Old Course** (see the boxed text, below), and beside it stretch the West Sands, the beach made famous by *Chariots of Fire*.

Activities

The TIC has a list of local walks and also sells OS maps. The **Fife Coastal Path** (www .fifecoastalpath.com), stretching from the Forth Road Bridge to the Tay Bridge (Dundee) – a distance of 78 miles – was recently completed, but the section between St Andrews and just north of Crail is recommended for experienced walkers only (particularly the section between St Andrews and Boarhills), as the path is not as clearly defined and includes tidal and rough terrain. The TIC has a detailed map.

Kellie Castle (p214) is within easy cycling distance. You can also cycle north to the forest, beach and nature trail at Tentsmuirs Sands (8 miles).

Walking Tour

The best place to start is **St Andrews Museum** (opposite). Turn left out of the museum driveway and follow Doubledykes Rd back to the roundabout on City Rd. Turn right, then left onto South St. You'll pass through **West Port**, formerly Southgait Port, the main entrance to the old town. Built in 1589, it was based on Netherbow Port in Edinburgh. Walking east along South St, you pass **Louden's Close** on the right, a good example of the closes built according to the city's medieval street plan. Continue along South St to see the apse of the 16th-century **Blackfriars Chapel**, which stands in front of Madras College.

Opposite the Victorian **town hall** is **Holy Trinity Church**, the town's parish church, built in 1410. On the same side of the street as the town hall is **St Mary's College**, founded in 1537; beside it is the university library. The oak tree in the courtyard is over 250 years old.

Go left along Church St to cobbled Market St. Street markets are held around the **Mercat Cross**, although the cross is now a fountain. The TIC is nearby, at No 70.

Tours

St Andrews Walkabout Tours (☎ 472021; audio tours £5) Self-guided audio tours of the town, which relate stories of historical St Andrews. There's an option to hire overnight and tours last for one to three hours. Tours include discounted entry to other attractions. Collect the audio guide from the TIC.

Witches Tour (☎ 655057; adult/child £7/5) Recounts the history and folklore of the town in an unusual fashion, with tales of ghosts and witches enlivened by theatrical stunts. It starts at 8pm (7.30pm October to March) on Friday (and Sunday in June, July and August and Thursday in July and August). Meet outside the Tudor Inn on North St.

PLAY THE OLD COURSE

Golf has been played at St Andrews since the 15th century, and by 1457 it was apparently so popular that James II had to ban it because it was interfering with his troops' archery practice. Few people realise that anyone can play the Old Course, the world's most famous golf course. Although it lies beside the exclusive, all-male Royal & Ancient Golf Club, the Old Course is a public course and is not owned by the club.

Getting a tee-off time is – literally – something of a lottery. Unless you book months in advance, the only chance you have of playing here is by entering a ballot before 2pm on the day before you wish to play. Be warned that applications by ballot are normally heavily oversubscribed, and green fees are a mere £115. There's no play on Sunday.

If your number doesn't come up, there are five other public courses in the area, none with quite the cachet of the Old Course but all significantly cheaper. Their fees are: New £55, Jubilee £55, Eden £33, Strathyrum £22 and Balgove £10. See the TIC for more information on playing these courses.

Bookings for the Old Course can be made on line or by letter, fax or email to the **Reservations Office, St Andrews Links Trust** (☎ 466666; fax 479555; reservations@standrews.org.uk; www.standrews .org.uk; Pilmour House, St Andrews, Fife KY16 9SF). A booking form is on the website.

Festivals & Events

The Royal & Ancient Golf Club is the body that organises the annual **Open Golf Championship**, which takes place in July. However, the tournament venue changes from year to year, and the Open only comes to St Andrews itself every five or six years – the venue for future championships can be found on the Open's official website (www .opengolf.com).

St Andrews Highland Games (☎ 476305) are held on the North Haugh on the last Sunday in July.

During the **Lammas Fair**, held over four days preceding the second Tuesday in August, South St and part of Market St are taken over by carnival rides, craft stalls and street theatre.

St Andrews Week is five days of festivities held around St Andrews Day (30 November), the feast day of Scotland's patron saint. The celebrations include a festival of Scottish food and drink, and various arts events.

Sleeping

Bear in mind that St Andrews accommodation is often heavily booked year round (especially in summer), so you're well advised to book in advance.

BUDGET

St Andrews Tourist Hostel (☎ 479911; www .standrewhostel.com; Inchcape House, St Mary's Pl; dm £12) Not the best-run show in the country, admittedly, but the staff do try to keep the place clean and tidy. It's not overly cheery either, but it's the only year-round hostel in town and has a good, modern kitchen and a large lounge ideal for flopping around in. The male and female dorms (six or eight beds) are clean and a little austere.

St Andrews Summer Hostel (SYHA; ☎ 0870 155 3255; reservations@syha.org.uk; David Russell Apartments, Buchanan Gardens; s/d £25/38) This very good hostel is unfortunately only open in July and August. It provides accommodation in shared apartments, each with five en-suite double rooms, lounge and kitchen.

Cairnsmill Caravan Park (☎ 473604; cairnsmill@aol .com; Largo Rd; tent sites for 2 from £12; ☼ Apr-Oct) About a mile west of St Andrews on the A915, this camping ground is on a crest with brilliant views over the town. There's not much space between sites – they pack 'em in.

MIDRANGE

Note that single rooms are extremely hard to come by and should be booked in advance. Almost every house on Murray Park and Murray Pl is a guesthouse. The area couldn't be more convenient, but prices are on the high side.

Meade B&B (☎ 477350; annmeade@hotmail.com; 5 Albany Pl; r per person £20-23; ⚿) This family home has three rooms on offer, and it's an absolute bargain. The congenial owner will happily let to singles without charging a supplement – a rarity in St Andrews (and in Fife for that matter). The red room is the best – large and airy. All rooms share a bathroom. It's in a great location and has free parking just across the road. Children are very welcome – under 16s are charged £17.50; under fours are free.

Fairnie House (☎ 474094; www.fairniehouse.free serve.co.uk; 10 Abbey St; r per person £22-28) A relaxed and friendly B&B in a Georgian town house near the Byre Theatre, Fairnie House has one double and two twin rooms. There's a very homely feel to this place, and the communal dining room encourages conversation.

Old Fishergate House (☎ 470874; www.oldfisher gatehouse.co.uk; North Castle St; d £90) This historic 17th-century town house, furnished with period pieces, is in a great location – the oldest part of town – close to cathedral and castle. The two twin rooms are very spacious and even have their own sitting room and cushioned ledges on their window sills. On a scale of one to 10 for quaintness we'd rate it about a 9½.

Lorimer House (☎ /fax 476599; www.lorimer house.com; 19 Murray Park; r per person £25-34) This well-run, cheerful, spick-and-span place has cosy, well-furnished rooms, most admitting a flood of natural light. There are two larger doubles (see if one of those is available first), spacious family rooms, and single rooms.

Cameron House (☎ 472306; www.cameronhouse-sta .co.uk; 11 Murray Park; r per person £34) Cameron House is a soft and cuddly place (with a cheery owner) that makes you feel right at home, especially with the teddy bears hanging off the bedposts. Single rooms are available.

TOP END

Hazelbank Hotel (☎ /fax 472466; www.hazelbank .com; 28 The Scores; s £80, d £90-120) The elegant Hazelbank is a small (10 rooms) but comfy

SOMETHING SPECIAL

Inn on North Street (☎ 473387; relax@ theinnonnorthstreet.com; 127 North St; s/d £70/100) If you want to eat, drink and sleep in the same stylish place then this classy inn could be for you. Effortlessly dashing with a Gaelic twist, rooms are all the same price, but some are much better than others. Room Nos 1 to 3 come with Jacuzzi and more space, while all rooms have DVD player, crisp, white linen and large windows giving them an airy feel. The Oak room is the place for breakfast and a read of the paper, the bar (p212) is perfect for a snug tipple, and the Lizard Lounge in the basement is a late-night bar that gets cranked with live gigs and regular DJs.

family-run hotel in a fine 1898 Victorian town house. Every room is different at this affable place – No 7 has stupendous views while No 3 also has fine views and is huge. Book ahead, as it's very popular.

Eating

BUDGET

Café Jannetta (☎ 473285; 33 South St; dishes £4-5; breakfast & lunch) This buzzing place has outdoor seating, an impressive array of salads, baguettes and *paninis*, and terrific smoothies made with the ice cream from next door. They'll whisk your meal under your nose before you can blink and if you like coronation chicken, order it here.

B Jannetta (☎ 473285; 31 South St; 1-4 dip cone £0.90-3) This is a St Andrews institution. On a hot weekend there's a constant stream of people outside the place feverishly licking a delicious cone before it becomes a puddle. You can choose from 52 varieties of ice cream. The most popular flavour? Vanilla. The weirdest? Irn Bru!

Java Junction (97 South St; dishes £2-4; breakfast & lunch) Serving toasties, *paninis* and filled rolls along with a good coffee selection, this slick place is popular with students. The French doors opening onto the street make it a great spot for people-watching on a breezy summer day.

Some self-catering options:

Tesco (138 Market St) A good centrally located supermarket.

IJ Mellis (149 South St) Traditional cheesemonger.

MIDRANGE

Byre Theatre Cafe-Bar (☎ 468720; Abbey St; lunch mains £5, dinner mains £11; breakfast, lunch & dinner) A happy, buzzy spot with comfy couches, works of art on the wall and a well-developed menu that encompasses some delicious fusion cooking. Sandwiches at lunch come with interesting fillings such as chargrilled spicy Merguez sausage with Harissa mayo dip. Dinner gets more sophisticated, featuring dishes such as vegetable jambalaya and plenty of seafood and Scottish sirloin. Try the sweet-and-sour pickled figs if you dare!

Broons Bistro (☎ 478479; 117 North St; mains £6-12; lunch & dinner) Broons is a friendly, humming bar-bistro with a cosy, intimate and cheerful atmosphere and, importantly, kicking cocktails. It does a little bit of everything with a token veggie dish or two. Ideal spot for a meal before migrating to the cinema next door.

Ziggy's (☎ 473686; 6 Murray Pl; mains £6-12; lunch & dinner) This small, darkened restaurant has an offbeat recording-studio theme. There's an open kitchen and a menu that does a bit of everything, including pizza, burgers, a range of steaks, and Mexican, seafood and veggie dishes.

Doll's House (☎ 477422; 3 Church Sq; mains £10-13; lunch & dinner) With its high-backed chairs, bright colours and creaky wooden floor, the Doll's House tries to be rustic and modern at the same time. The result is a surprising warmth and no pretensions. The menu makes the most of local fish and other Scottish produce. The two-course lunch for £6.95 is unbeatable value, and the early-evening two-course deal for £12.95 isn't bad either.

TOP END

Peat Inn (☎ 840206; 3-course lunch/dinner £21/32; lunch & dinner Tue-Sat) Run by master chef and wine expert David Wilson, the Peat Inn is one of the best restaurants in Scotland. Housed in a rustic country inn about 6 miles west of St Andrews, its Michelin rosette–winning menu is culinary heaven. To get there, head west on the A915 then turn right on the B940.

Seafood Restaurant (☎ 479475; The Scores; 3-course dinner £35; lunch & dinner) The Seafood Restaurant occupies a stylish glass-walled room, built out over the sea, with plush navy carpet, crisp white linen, an open kitchen and panoramic views of St Andrews Bay. It offers top seafood and an excellent wine list, and its clutch of awards, including AA Restaurant of the Year 2004–05, means it has taken over the mantle of St Andrews' finest restaurant.

Drinking

Central Bar (Market St) The Central Bar is all polished brass and polished accents, full of students from south of the border, tourists and locals. This is the best pub in town with an impressive array of real ales.

Victoria (☎ 476964; 1 St Mary's Pl) Upstairs at the Victoria is popular with all types of students and serves good bar meals. There's a grungy café-bar with plenty of natural light or a classier lounge bar where you can sink into a sofa.

Inn on North Street (127 North St) The cosy bar at this stylish sleeping choice (see the boxed text, p211) has a medieval, Gaelic vibe, large bay window, lots of unpolished wood and some excellent beers (such as Little Creatures). Perfect on a rainy, windswept St Andrews afternoon.

Gin House (☎ 473473; 116 South St) A slightly dark, retro feel is exuded here, in what is a very modern bar by Scottish standards. It's popular with students, and DJs regularly pump out the tunes. There's plenty of space, a good Oz and French wine list and fine beers on tap. Avoid during big football games unless you're a fan.

Entertainment

Check the local *What's On* guide, published weekly and available from the TIC or its website (www.visit-standrews.co.uk).

Byre Theatre (☎ 475000; www.byretheatre.com; Abbey St) This theatre company started life in a converted cow byre in the 1930s, and is now in a flashy premises making clever use of light and space. Contact the TIC or check the website for details of performances.

New Picture House (☎ 473509; North St; tickets £4) This two-screen cinema shows current films.

Getting There & Away

St Andrews is 55 miles north of Edinburgh and 13 miles south of Dundee.

BUS

Stagecoach Fife operates a bus service from Edinburgh to St Andrews via Kirkcaldy

(£6.50, two hours, hourly). Buses to Dundee (30 minutes, three hourly) and Cupar (20 minutes, at least hourly) also run frequently. Bus 23 runs to Stirling (£5.50, two hours, six daily Monday to Saturday). Frequent services to East Neuk destinations include Crail (30 minutes) and Anstruther (40 minutes). All buses leave from the bus station on Station Rd.

TRAIN

There is no train station in St Andrews itself, but you can take a train from Edinburgh (try to get a seat on the right-hand side of the carriage for great firth views) to Leuchars, 5 miles to the northwest (£9.30, one hour, hourly), and then a bus (£1.85) or taxi into town.

From Leuchars, buses 94, 96 and 99 leave every 20 minutes during the day (hourly in the evening) for St Andrews.

Getting Around

Ian Cowe Coachworks (ICC Rentals; ☎ 472543; carhire@iccrentals.com; 76 Argyle St) hires out small cars for £25 per day with unlimited mileage.

There are taxi ranks at the bus station and at Holy Trinity Church on South St. To order a cab, call **Golf City Taxis** (☎ 477788; Argyle St). **Town & Country** (☎ 840444) has taxis with wheelchair access. A taxi between Leuchars train station and the town centre costs around £9.

Spokes (☎ 477835; 37 South St) hires out mountain bikes for £6.50/10.50 per half/full day.

EAST NEUK

The section of the southern Fife coast that stretches from Crail westwards to Largo Bay is known as East Neuk (neuk means 'corner' in Scots). There are several picturesque fishing villages and some good coastal walks in the area. Pick up a copy of the *East Neuk* bus-timetable booklet from TICs.

Crail

☎ 01333 / pop 1695
One of the prettiest East Neuk villages and a favourite with artists, Crail has a much-photographed and painted harbour ringed by stone cottages with red pantiled roofs.

The helpful **TIC** (☎ 450869; 62 Marketgate; ⏲ 10am-1pm & 2-5pm Mon-Sat, noon-5pm Sun Easter-early Oct) is at the museum. The nearby **Royal Bank** (cnr St Andrews Rd & Marketgate) has an ATM.

There are far fewer fishing boats here now than there once were, but you can still buy fresh lobster (£20 per kilogram) and crab (£2.50 per serving) from a **kiosk** (🕑 usually noon-4pm) at the harbour. Just to the east is a large grassed area with seating, the perfect place to munch on your shellfish while admiring the view across to the Isle of May. The village's history and involvement with the fishing industry is outlined in the **Crail Museum** (☎ 450869; 62 Marketgate; admission free; 🕑 10am-1pm & 2-5pm Mon-Sat & 2-5pm Sun Jun-Oct, 2-5pm Sat & Sun Apr & May).

Crail Gallery (☎ 450316; 22 High St; 🕑 10.30am-5pm) is a local gallery with some terrific artists' impressions of Crail and East Neuk. There are also framed prints of St Andrews.

The 18th-century **Selcraig House** (☎ 450697; www.selcraighouse.co.uk; 47 Nethergate; s/d £30/60) is a gold mine for antiquaries and very friendly. Some of the rooms are just fantastic, especially on the 1st floor, where you get a four-poster, bucket-loads of space and beautiful furnishings. You can even listen to records spun on a Victorian-era gramophone in the conservatory.

Honeypot Tearoom (☎ 450935; 6 High St; snacks under £3; 🕑 10.30am-5pm Wed-Mon Mar-Oct) doesn't look much from the outside, but this excellent place serves delicious, fresh home baking and has cheery, efficient service. Try the brie and bacon toastie.

Crail is 10 miles southeast of St Andrews. Stagecoach Fife bus 95 between Leven, Anstruther, Crail and St Andrews passes through Crail hourly every day (30 minutes to St Andrews).

Anstruther

☎ 01333 / pop 3442

Anstruther is a vivacious former fishing village with lots of twisting streets, interesting wynds (lanes) and knick-knack shops lining Rodger and High Sts. The waterfront is popular in summer with tourists and locals chomping down on fish and chips while enjoying the sunshine. It's getting quite trendy, too, with alfresco dining at nearby café-restaurants. Anstruther (often pronounced en-ster) has grown to become the main tourist centre of East Neuk.

The **TIC** (☎ 311073; Fisheries Museum, St Ayles, Harbourhead; 🕑 10am-5pm Mon-Sat, 11am-4pm Sun Easter-Oct) is the best in East Neuk. There are banks with ATMs in the town centre.

SIGHTS

The displays at the excellent **Scottish Fisheries Museum** (☎ 310628; www.scotfishmuseum.org; St Ayles, Harbourhead; adult/child £4.50/free; 🕑 10am-5.30pm Mon-Sat, 11am-5pm Apr-Sep, 10am-4.30pm Mon-Sat, noon-4.30pm Sun Oct-Mar) include the Zulu Gallery, which houses the huge, partly restored hull of a traditional Zulu-class fishing boat, redolent with the scent of tar and timber. Afloat in the harbour outside the museum lies the *Reaper*, a fully restored Fifie-class fishing boat, built in 1902.

The mile-long **Isle of May**, 6 miles southeast of Anstruther, is a stunning nature reserve. Between April and July the intimidating cliffs are packed with breeding kittiwakes, razorbills, guillemots, shags and around 40,000 puffins. Minke whales have also been spotted around the island in early summer. Inland are the remains of the 12th-century **St Adrian's Chapel**, dedicated to a monk who was murdered on the island by the Danes in 875.

The five-hour trip to the island on the **May Princess** (☎ 310103; www.isleofmayferry.com; adult/child £15/7), including two to three hours ashore, sails Saturday to Thursday (weather permitting) from May to October. You can make reservations and buy tickets at the harbour kiosk near the museum at least an hour before departure. Departure times vary depending on the tide – check times for the next week or so by calling, or checking the website.

SLEEPING & EATING

Finding reasonably priced B&B accommodation in Anstruther is difficult – for solo travellers almost impossible. Try the following, which have only a couple of rooms each and don't take singles in summer, but are very comfortable and well located: the **Sheiling** (☎ 310697; 32 Glenogil Gardens; r per person from £20); and **Mrs Watson** (☎ 310453; tomwatson@beeb.net; 8 Melville Tce, Crail Rd; r per person £20-25; 🕑 Apr-Oct).

Spindrift (☎ /fax 310573; info@thespindrift.co.uk; Pittenweem Rd; r per person £27-32) This is a top place to spoil yourself – it's a luxury, licensed small hotel in a 19th-century sea-captain's house. The hosts ensure you'll enjoy their sumptuous accommodation, which is a cut above the other guesthouses on this street.

Dreel Tavern (☎ 310727; 16 High St West; mains £8; ☺ lunch & dinner) This charming old pub on the banks of the Dreel Burn has bucket-loads of character and serves excellent bar meals (try the smoked-fish pie); chow down in the outdoor beer garden in summer. There are also some top-quality cask ales here.

Cellar Restaurant (☎ 310378; 24 East Green; 3-course set dinner £33; ☺ lunch & dinner Tue-Sun) Tucked away in an alley behind the museum, the Cellar is famous for its seafood – try the seared, peppered rare tuna – and fine wines. Inside it's elegant and upmarket. Advance bookings are essential.

There's a fresh-seafood kiosk situated on the waterfront selling dressed crab (£2.50 per serving), mussels and jellied eel.

GETTING THERE & AWAY

Anstruther is located 9 miles south of St Andrews. Stagecoach Fife bus 95 runs daily from Leven (more departures from St Monans) to Anstruther and on to St Andrews (40 minutes, hourly) via Crail.

Around Anstruther

A magnificent example of Lowland Scottish domestic architecture, **Kellie Castle** (NTS; ☎ 01333-720271; adult/child £8/5; ☺ castle 1-5pm Easter & May-Sep, garden 9.30am-sunset May-Sep) has creaky floors, crooked little doorways and some remarkable works of art, giving it an air of authenticity. It's set in a beautiful garden, and many rooms contain superb plasterwork, the Vine room being the most exquisite. The original part of the building dates from 1360; it was enlarged to its present dimensions around 1606.

The castle is 3 miles west of Anstruther on the B9171. Stagecoach bus 95A runs from Anstruther to Grangemuir (two daily Monday to Saturday); from here it's about a 1.5 mile walk to the castle.

Three miles north of Anstruther, off the B9131 to St Andrews, is **Scotland's Secret Bunker** (☎ 01333-310301; www.secretbunker.co.uk; Troy Wood; adult/child £7.50/4.60; ☺ 10am-6pm Apr-Oct). This fascinating Cold War relic was to be one of Britain's underground command centres and a home for Scots leaders in the event of nuclear war. Hidden 30m underground and surrounded by nearly 5m of reinforced concrete are the austere operation rooms, communication centre and dormitories. It's very authentic and uses artefacts of the period,

which make for an absorbing exploration. The Scottish CND (Campaign for Nuclear Disarmament) have an exhibit, bringing home the realities of Britain's current nuclear Trident policy. The bunker is a gripping experience and highly recommended.

Take Stagecoach bus X26, which goes from Anstruther to St Andrews, jump off at the Drumrack crossroads and walk east for about 1.5 miles along the B940 to reach the bunker.

Pittenweem
☎ 01333 / pop 1640

This is now the main fishing port on the East Neuk coast, and there are lively fish sales at the harbour from 8am. On a sunny day, buy an ice cream and stroll the short, breezy promenade, admiring the picturesque waterfront. The village name means 'place of the cave', referring to **St Fillan's cave** in Cove Wynd, which was used as a chapel by a 7th-century missionary. The saint reputedly possessed miraculous powers – apparently, when he wrote his sermons in the dark cave, his arm would illuminate his work by emitting a luminous glow. The cave is protected by a locked gate, but a key is available from the **Gingerbread Horse Café** (☎ 311495; 9 High St; ☺ 10am to 5pm Sat, noon-5pm Sun) for £1.

Harbour Guest House (☎ 311273, 312937; 14 Mid Shore; s/d £30/60) has en-suite rooms overlooking the harbour. Prices depend on time of year and how many nights you stay.

Drop into **Heron Gallery & Bistro** (☎ 311014; 15a High St; mains £7; ☺ 11am-4pm) for a snack or meal. It's also open for dinner some Saturday nights. Dressed crab features on the menu, and you dine amongst local works of art that inject some real colour into this pretty harbour town – it's good for a browse and everything is for sale.

Bus details are as for Anstruther.

St Monans
☎ 01333 / pop 1435

This ancient fishing village is just over a mile west of Pittenweem and is named after a local cave-dwelling saint who was probably killed by pirates.

The **parish church**, at the western end of the village, was built in 1362 on the orders of a grateful King David II, who was rescued by villagers from a shipwreck in the Firth of

Forth. A model of a full-rigged ship, dating from 1800, hangs above the altar. The church commands sweeping views of the firth, and the past echoes inside its cold, whitewashed walls.

St Monans Heritage Collection (5 West Shore; admission free; ⊙ 11am-1pm & 2-4pm Tue, Thu, Sat & Sun Easter-Oct), on the harbour, is a wonderful small gallery devoted to the history of the St Monans' fishing industry through a collection of 20th-century B&W photos and several artefacts. Most of the photos were taken by a local photographer and the collection changes monthly.

You're better off staying in Anstruther as there is little accommodation in St Monans.

Green Door Café (☎ 739066; 6 Station Rd; light meals £3; ⊙ 10am-4pm Mon, Tue, Thu & Fri, 11am-4pm Sat & Sun; ⊒) is a community-run café promoting healthy eating and serving excellent sandwiches and fresh cakes. It has changing photographic exhibitions. The **Seafood Restaurant** (☎ 730327; 16 West End; 3-course dinner £35; ⊙ lunch & dinner, winter closed Mon & Tue) is an outstanding restaurant just west of the harbour and within salt-spray distance of the sea. It commands sweeping harbour views and has been highly commended for its delectable seafood. In summer cheaper bar food is also on offer.

Stagecoach Fife bus 95 runs daily from St Monans to St Andrews (50 minutes, at least hourly), via Anstruther.

Elie & Earlsferry

☎ 01333 / pop 1500

These two attractive villages mark the southwestern end of East Neuk. There are great sandy beaches and good walks along the coast.

Elie Watersports (☎ 330962; www.eliewatersports .com), on the harbour at Elie, hires out windsurfers (£28 for two hours), sailing dinghies (Lasers £14 per hour, Wayfarers £18 per hour), canoes (£8 an hour) and mountain bikes (£10 a day) and provides instruction as well.

Ship Inn (☎ 330246; The Toft, Elie; mains £8-12; ⊙ lunch & dinner; ⚓), down by Elie harbour, is a pleasant and popular place for a bar lunch. Seafood and Asian dishes feature on the menu and, on a sunny day, you can tuck in at an outside table overlooking the wide sweep of the bay. Try the king-prawn skewers or Cajun salmon.

PERTHSHIRE & KINROSS

Perthshire and Kinross is the living, breathing heart of Scotland in more ways than one: the region is the former home of the Stone of Destiny, Aberfeldy is the geographical centre of the country and Perth is the former capital of Scotland.

It's the most dynamic part of the country, with new attractions popping up all the time. This, coupled with its outstanding natural beauty and accessibility, makes it one of Scotland's best areas for tourists.

The region is a joy to explore with its hulking castles, historic roots, medieval cathedrals and, perhaps its greatest drawcard, its stunning countryside: from rolling, verdant lowlands to the spectacular summits of the Highlands. In an area of high winds and a thriving logging industry, Perthshire is home to big-tree country, where ancient woodlands survive among younger, prosperous regeneration forests.

Scenically, Perthshire and Kinross contain, in miniature, as many variations in terrain as Scotland itself. Loch Tay in western Perthshire is a highlight with picture-perfect Kenmore at its eastern head, Ben Lawers (1214m) standing guard over its northern bank and remote, magical Glen Lyon on the other side of the strapping Ben Lawers.

Getting Around

Perth and Kinross Council produces a useful public-transport map showing all services in the region; it's available at TICs. The major bus operators in the region:

Aberfeldy postbus (☎ 01887-820400) Serves remote west Perthshire.

Scottish Citylink (☎ 0870 550 5050)

Stagecoach Fife (☎ 01592-261461)

Stagecoach Perth (☎ 01738-629339)

Strathtay Scottish (☎ 01382-228345)

Trains run alongside the A9, destined for Aviemore and Inverness. The other main line connects Perth with Stirling (in the south) and Dundee and Arbroath (in the east).

KINROSS & LOCH LEVEN

☎ 01577 / pop 4681

Kinross is best known as the access point for Loch Leven Castle, a quintessential Scottish treasure – a castle that sits on a

CENTRAL SCOTLAND

small island. The loch itself is the largest in the Lowlands and is known for its extensive bird life.

The helpful **Heart of Scotland TIC** (☎ 863680; kinrosstic@visitscotland.com; 🕙 10am-5pm Mon-Sat year-round, 10am-5pm daily Jul & Aug), by junction 6 of the M90, has an exhibition on the area.

Sights

Evocative **Loch Leven Castle** (HS; ☎ 0777 804 0483; adult/child incl Kinross ferry £3.50/1.30; 🕙 9.30am-6.30pm, last sailing 5.15pm Apr-Sep) served as a fortress and prison from the late 14th century. Its most famous captive was Mary, Queen of Scots, who spent almost a year incarcerated here from 1567. Her infamous charms bewitched Willie Douglas, who managed to get hold of the cell keys to release her, then rowed her across to the shore. The castle is now roofless but basically intact.

Sleeping & Eating

Turfhills House B&B (☎ 863881; turfhills@hotmail .com; s/d £40/60) Turfhills is a sumptuous, genteel, musty old Georgian house with grand Victorian furnishings, set in some lush gardens. It's next to the tourist office and makes an excellent overnight stop if you're whizzing up the M90 motorway. It also makes a great base for exploring some of Perthshire's charms. Note that no singles are available in July and August.

Roxburghe Guest House (☎ 862498; www .roxburgheguesthouse.co.uk; 126 High St, Kinross; s/d/tr £30/50/60) A lovely guesthouse with cool, tastefully furnished rooms in a rickety old property, Roxburghe feels like a home away from home. Prices may be up for negotiation for small groups.

Carlin Maggie's (☎ 863652; 191 High St, Kinross; lunch mains £5-8, dinner mains £12-18; 🕙 lunch Tue-Sun, dinner Tue-Sat) This is a highly recommended restaurant specialising in seafood and vegetarian dishes. Carnivores will delight in the roast trio of Angus game (beef, pigeon and duck), while seafood lovers should tuck into the monkfish tail roasted in five Chinese spices. Delectable open sarnies and salads are available at lunch.

Getting There & Away

Scottish Citylink and Stagecoach Fife have bus services between Perth (30 minutes, hourly) and Kinross. In the other direction buses go to Edinburgh (1½ hours, hourly).

PERTH
☎ 01738 / pop 43,450

Lodged snugly in a lush valley alongside the M90, Perth's biggest draw card is historical Scone Palace, but the city's grand Georgian buildings by the banks of the River Tay possess their own splendour. This market town was once a weaving, dyeing and glove-making centre and Scotland's capital. Today it exudes a demure pride, suggesting the town walls have not forgotten their past significance. Perth is not simply quaint, though; embedded in the centuries-old architecture skirting the cobblestone streets is a cosmopolitan vibe, reflected in imaginative cuisine, welcoming pubs, historical sites and a gallery or two.

History

Perth's rise in importance derives from Scone (pronounced scoon), 2 miles north of the town. In 838, Kenneth MacAlpin became the first king of a united Scotland and brought the Stone of Destiny to Scone. An important abbey was built on the site. From this time on, all Scottish kings were invested here, even after Edward I of England stole the sacred talisman, carting it off to London's Westminster Abbey in 1296. In 1996 Prime Minister John Major persuaded the Queen to promise to return it to Scotland, but it went to Edinburgh Castle rather than Scone. There's actually some doubt about whether Edward I stole the real stone – he might have stolen a fake!

From the 12th century, Perth was Scotland's capital, and in 1437 James I was murdered here. There were four important monasteries in the area and the town was a target for the Reformation movement in Scotland.

BATTLE OF THE CLANS

In 1396 the Chattan and Mackay clans faced off on North Inch to settle a long-running feud. A fight to the death ensued between 30 warriors from either clan. The Mackays were wiped out, the only survivor jumping in the River Tay to escape. Only 10 Chattans perished, and local legend has it that the Chattans were short a soldier so a saddler was paid to take up arms – he survived, having joined the right side!

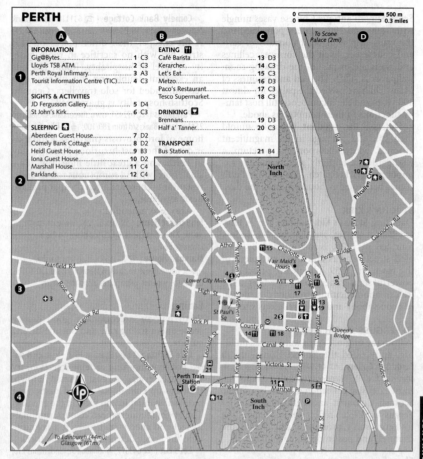

PERTH

INFORMATION		EATING	
Gig@Bytes	1 C3	Café Barista	13 D3
Lloyds TSB ATM	2 C3	Kerarcher	14 C3
Perth Royal Infirmary	3 A3	Let's Eat	15 C3
Tourist Information Centre (TIC)	4 C3	Metzo	16 D3
		Paco's Restaurant	17 C3
SIGHTS & ACTIVITIES		Tesco Supermarket	18 C3
JD Fergusson Gallery	5 D4		
St John's Kirk	6 C3	DRINKING	
		Brennans	19 D3
SLEEPING		Half a' Tanner	20 C3
Aberdeen Guest House	7 D2		
Comely Bank Cottage	8 D2	TRANSPORT	
Heidl Guest House	9 B3	Bus Station	21 B4
Iona Guest House	10 D2		
Marshall House	11 C4		
Parklands	12 C4		

Orientation

Most of the town lies on the western bank of the Tay River; Scone Palace and some of the B&Bs are on the eastern bank. There are two large parks: North Inch, the scene of the infamous Battle of the Clans in 1396, and South Inch. The bus and train stations are close to each other, near the northwestern corner of South Inch.

Information

Gig@Bytes (☎ 451580; 5 St Paul's Sq; per hr £5; ⏰ 10am-6.30pm Mon-Sat; 💻) Internet access.
Lloyds TSB (King Edward St) Has an ATM.
Perth Royal Infirmary (☎ 623311; Taymount Tce) West of the town centre.

TIC (☎ 450600; Lower City Mills, West Mill St; ⏰ daily Apr-Oct, Mon-Sat Nov-Mar) An efficient place that can assist with tracking down accommodation.

Sights
SCONE PALACE

Decadent **Scone Palace** (☎ 552300; adult/child £6.95/3.80; ⏰ 9.30am-5.30pm Apr-Oct), 2 miles north of Perth and just off the A93 near Old Scone, was built in 1580 on a site intrinsic to Scottish history. It's one of Perthshire's premier tourist attractions.

The interior is a gallery of fine French furniture, including Marie Antoinette's writing table and a 16th-century needlework hanging, worked by Mary, Queen of

CENTRAL SCOTLAND

Scots. Superb antique Chinese vases mingle with 18th- and 19th-century porcelain, and the walls drip with regal portraits of earls and countesses. Even the cornices, ceilings and walls are exquisite (the drawing-room wallpaper is silk!). The earl and countess of Mansfield have owned the palace for almost 400 years and the incumbents still host family functions in their sumptuous abode.

Outside, the resident peacocks unfold their splendid plumage in the magnificent grounds, which incorporate a pinetum, a wild garden, a butterfly garden and the all-important cricket pitch. Bus 3 from Perth comes here roughly hourly most of the day.

ST JOHN'S KIRK

Daunting **St John's Kirk** (admission free; 10am-4pm Mon-Sat May-Sep, plus 10am-1pm Sun Jun-Sep), founded in 1126, is surrounded by cobbled streets and is still the centrepiece of the town. In 1559 John Knox preached a powerful sermon here that helped begin the Reformation, inciting a frenzied destruction of Scone abbey and other religious sites.

JD FERGUSSON GALLERY

Within the original Perth waterworks building, aptly titled the Round House, the **JD Fergusson Gallery** (441944; cnr Marshall Pl & Tay St; admission free; 10am-5pm Mon-Sat) contains the most extensive collection of work by notable Scottish Colourist and Perthshire local JD Fergusson. Pieces reflect heavy French (due to Fergusson's prolonged stay across the channel) and postimpressionist influences.

Sleeping

Heidl Guest House (635031; www.heidl.co.uk; 43 York Pl; s/d from £23/40) A solid old favourite, close to the centre, the Heidl has raised the bar on accommodation standards, offering an excellent range of rooms and serving up a decent brekky, too. Ask for room No 3 or 4 in the 'tower' at the top of the building; they share a bathroom and have lots of space, and a recent makeover has made them top notch.

Aberdeen Guest House (/fax 633183; buchan@aberdeenguesthouse.fsnet.co.uk; 13 Pitcullen Cres; d £50) A cheery place with terrific, spacious rooms and thoughtful hosts – if you find a friendlier guesthouse than this, take it. Rooms are well furnished and homely, and have that extra touch that comes from people who enjoy their work. French and German spoken.

Comely Bank Cottage (631118; comelybankcott@hotmail.com; 19 Pitcullen Cres; r per person £22-24) A bit cheaper than other places on this strip, but with no sacrifice in room quality or level of hospitality. Room No 1 is an excellent double and this place is also recommended for solo travellers. Genuine Scottish hospitality is guaranteed.

Parklands (622451; www.theparklandshotel.com; 2 St Leonard's Bank; s/d from £80/100;) The former home of lord provosts (mayors), Parklands is one of the most luxurious places to stay in Perth, and a great little hideaway. It's a small hotel with 14 sumptuous rooms and a restaurant. There are often cheaper package deals available.

Also recommended:

Iona Guest House (/fax 627261; www.ionaperth.co.uk; 2 Pitcullen Cres; s/d £25/50) Room No 2 is a favourite here.

Marshall House (442886; gallagher@marshall-guest-house.freeserve.co.uk; 6 Marshall Pl; s/d £30/40) One of the superior-value places along this stretch.

Eating

Perth has an exceptionally good dining scene and a strong café and outside-dining culture.

Café Barista (28 High St; mains £5-8; lunch & dinner) For that morning caffeine injection, try this place, serving the best espresso in town. It dishes up *paninis*, salads and pasta, with more substantial Italian food in the evening. The bright Mediterranean colours, minimalist feel and cheery staff make it a favourite (and the gooey desserts aren't bad either).

Let's Eat (643377; 77 Kinnoull St; lunch mains £10, dinner mains £14; lunch & dinner) Noted for its excellent service, this award-winning bistro is the best place in town for splashing out on a special meal. Outstanding cuisine comes in the form of creative dishes with a slight Italian bent (Scottish pastrami aside). Enjoy an apéritif on the comfy couches before indulging your palate.

Metzo (626016; 33 George St; lunch mains £8, dinner mains £12; lunch & dinner) Metzo is proving popular with diners – service is excellent and it's noted as being great value for money. The cool, clean interior is ambient and relaxed. Highlights include the seafood and the desserts, and there's plenty for carnivores, too, such as a grilled, peppered gigot of lamb.

Kerarcher (449777; 168 South St; starters £5-8, mains £12-15; lunch Fri & Sat, dinner Tue-Sat) This classic seafood restaurant keeps things simple. Fresh seafood and fresh ingredients adding hints of flavour, complementing but not overpowering the dishes, are a recipe for success. If you want to have a go yourself, fresh seafood is sold downstairs.

Also in town:

Paco's Restaurant (☎ 622290; 3 Mill St; mains £7-15; ☼ lunch Sat, dinner daily) Recommended. Huge selection of meals (steaks, burgers, pizza, pasta, seafood) and veggie options.

Tesco supermarket (South St)

Drinking

Perth has a healthy pubs-per-capita ratio and in the courtyard situated around St John's Kirk you won't have to stray far to change draughts.

Half a' Tanner (St John's Pl) A warm, popular and hospitable place, on fine days the crowd spills into the courtyard.

Brennans (St John's St) This pub is small in size but big on personality – there's live music on weekends and a happy buzz every night. It's a bit of a warren inside, with a low ceiling, but it's very friendly and there are good ales on tap.

Getting There & Away

BUS

Scottish Citylink operates regular buses from Perth to Glasgow (£6.50, 1½ hours), Edinburgh (£6.20, 1½ hours), Dundee (£4.20, 35 minutes), Aberdeen (£13, 2¼ hours) and Inverness (£11.60, 2¾ hours).

Stagecoach buses serve Dunkeld (40 minutes, roughly hourly Monday to Saturday), Pitlochry (1¼ hours, roughly hourly Monday to Saturday) and Aberfeldy (1¼ hours, roughly hourly Monday to Saturday). Stagecoach also serves Crieff (45 minutes, at least hourly), St Fillans (1¼ hours, five daily Monday to Saturday – some services change in Crieff) via Crieff and Comrie, and Dunning (40 minutes, eight daily Monday to Saturday) via Fortevito.

Strathtay Scottish buses travel from Perth to Blairgowrie (45 minutes, hourly Monday to Saturday) and Dundee (£3, 1¾ hours, hourly).

TRAIN

There's a train service from Glasgow's Queen St (£10.70, one hour, at least hourly Monday to Saturday, every two hours Sunday),

and a rather erratic service from Edinburgh (£10.70, 1½ hours). Other rail destinations include Stirling (£8.60, 30 minutes, one or two per hour) and Pitlochry (£9, 30 minutes, nine daily, fewer on Sunday).

STRATHEARN

West of Perth, the wide strath (valley) of the River Earn was once a great forest where medieval kings hunted. The whole area is known as Strathearn, a very attractive region of undulating farmland, hills and lochs. The Highlands begin in the western section of Strathearn.

Dunning

☎ 01764 / pop 900

If you think you've entered spooky country around here, you may just be right. On the way into Dunning, about a mile west of the town by the B8062, there's a strange **cross** on a pile of stones with the words 'Maggiewall burnt here 1657 as a witch'. We'd recommend keeping away from bonfires.

The village is dominated by the 12th-century Norman tower of **St Serfs church**, but most of the building dates from 1810. The magnificent 9th-century **Dupplin Cross**, one of the earliest Christian stone crosses in Scotland, was originally near Fortevito (3 miles from Dunning). It's now the regal centrepiece of St Serfs Church. Historic Scotland provides a guided talk on the mysterious monolith.

A wonderful, eccentric little nook-and-cranny pub, **Kirkstyle Inn** (☎ 684248; Kirkstyle Sq; mains £6-15; ☼ lunch & dinner) is an atmospheric inn with a warm glow and a local touch – the food's not half bad either. Try the Spitfire brew. Book ahead at weekends as it's very popular.

Historic Dunning is about 8 miles southwest of Perth. Stagecoach bus 17 runs from Perth to Fortevito and Dunning (40 minutes, eight daily, Monday to Saturday). Docherty's Midland Coaches runs between Dunning and Auchterarder (15 minutes, three daily Monday to Friday, two Saturday).

Auchterarder

☎ 01764 / pop 3945

Four miles west of Dunning, the small, neat town of Auchterarder meanders along a winding High St. There's a **TIC** (☎ 663450; 90 High St; ☼ 10am-5pm Mon-Sat Apr-Jun, 9.30am-5.30pm

CENTRAL SCOTLAND

Mon-Sat, 11am-4pm Sun Jul-Sep) with a **heritage centre** (admission free) detailing wide-ranging aspects of local history. There are absorbing B&W pictures of the town and nearby Dunning.

Just up the road, 3 miles from Auchterarder on the A9, you'll find **Tullibardine** (☎ 682252; Blackford; tours £3; ✈ 9am-6pm Mon-Sat, 10am-6pm Sun), Scotland's newest distillery. It's just off the A9 and recently reopened after being closed for 10 years. Tours are short and sweet, which means 'tasting time' comes around nice and quick.

The highly rated **Gleneagles Hotel** (☎ 662231; www.gleneagles.com; Auchterarder; r from £355; ⚐ ⚑), just over 2 miles west of Auchterarder, is a splendid place with three championship golf courses. Room charges include full use of the extensive leisure facilities. The priciest room is the £1800 Royal Lochnagar Suite, complete with antiques, silk-lined walls and hand-woven carpets. The hotel even has its own train station, 50 minutes (£10.50) from Glasgow, and there's free transport between the station and the hotel. However, if you can afford to stay here, you can afford the limousine from Glasgow airport (£150). Gleneagles has also earned a reputation as a very child-friendly hotel, making it ideal for families. There's plenty here to keep kids entertained, including a nursery with all the latest gizmos. Check the website for special deals.

Large upstairs rooms in the basic but comfortable **Thistledhu** (☎ 662154; 39 Townhead; r per person £18) share a bathroom. There is one family room, and the friendly host is happy to rent out to singles.

Docherty's Midland Coaches runs buses from Auchterarder to Dunning (eight minutes, three daily Monday to Friday, two Saturday), Stirling (40 minutes, four daily Monday to Friday) and Perth (40 minutes, at least hourly).

Crieff & Around
☎ 01764

Scraping the edge of the Highlands, elegant Crieff (population 6579) is an old, resort-style town, as popular with tourists today as it was in Victorian times.

INFORMATION
Bank of Scotland (Lodge St) Has ATM.
Library (☎ 653418; 6 Comrie St; ✈ 10am-1pm & 2-7.30pm Mon, Wed & Fri, 10am-1pm & 2-5pm Tue, 10am-1pm Thu, 10am-12.30pm Sat; ▯) Free Internet access.

Police Station (King St)
Post office (High St)
Royal Bank of Scotland (West High St) Has ATM.
TIC (☎ 652578; criefftic@visitscotland.com; Town Hall, High St; ✈ 9.30am-5.30pm Mon-Sat, 11am-3pm Sun Apr-Jun & Oct, 9.30am-6.30pm Mon-Sat, 10am-4pm Sun Jul-Sep) In the clock tower.

SIGHTS
In the basement at the TIC, **Stones, Stocks & Stories** (☎ 652578; High St; admission free) is a small but interesting exhibition of the town stocks (leg clamps used as a form of punishment), the Drummond Cross (1400–1600) and a formidable 9th-century Pictish cross slab.

The highly rated **Famous Grouse Experience** (☎ 656565; The Hosh; tours £6; ✈ 9am-6pm), at the Glenturret Distillery, 1 mile north of town, has a range of tours of the traditional malting process. Visitors are also treated to a hi-tech interactive display.

Innerpeffray Library (☎ 652819; Innerpeffray; adult/child incl tour £2.50/50p; ✈ 10am-12.45pm & 2-4.45pm Mon-Wed, Fri & Sat, 2-4pm Sun Mar-Oct, by appointment only Nov-Feb), about 4 miles southeast of Crieff on the B8062, is Scotland's first lending library (founded in 1680). There's a huge collection of rare, interesting and ancient books, some of them 500 years old.

SLEEPING & EATING
Comely Bank Guest House (☎ 653409; www.comely bank.demon.co.uk; 32 Burrell St; r per person £19-22; ⚑) This is a top Scottish guesthouse, welcoming, homely and neat as a pin. The downstairs double is huge, frilly and velvety, while upstairs rooms have a more modern décor and are still a good size. All rooms are en suite except for one double.

Leven House Hotel (☎ 652529; Comrie Rd; r per person £20-25) Probably trading since Victorian times, the best way to describe Leven House is floral, floral, floral. The décor may not win any design awards, but this 1970s-era hotel offers good-value rooms and the friendly hosts make you feel right at home.

Red Onion Bistro (☎ 654407; 1 West High St; ✈ lunch mains £5-8, dinner mains £15; ✈ lunch & dinner Tue-Sat) This place had just opened its doors when we passed through town, and the signs were very good. A simple, pleasing dining room complements a good cross-section of dishes from burgers to chargrilled ostrich fillet. Vegetarian dishes are also available.

Bank (☎ 656575; 32 High St; mains £15; ♥ lunch & dinner Tue-Sun). This place has won plenty of foodie awards for its quality meals and use of local produce. What you'll get is creative cooking with flair and you'll dine in a wood-panelled room that exudes both space and intimacy.

For self-catering, there's a **Somerfield supermarket** (Union Tce).

Also recommended:

Crieff Hydro (☎ 655555; www.crieffhydro.com; Ferntower Rd; dinner, B&B per person £35-185; ♿ 👶) An upmarket, classy hotel that's refreshingly unpretentious. The Children's Club will keep the kids happy for hours.

Baan Thai Restaurant (☎ 652652; Waverley Hotel, 7 James Sq; starters £4.50, mains £6.50-10; ♥ lunch & dinner) Locals rave about the Thai food at this simple eatery.

GETTING THERE & AWAY

Hourly Stagecoach buses link Crieff with Perth (45 minutes), less frequently on Sunday. Other buses run to Comrie (20 minutes, roughly hourly Monday to Saturday, every two hours Sunday), St Fillans (35 minutes, five daily Monday to Saturday) and Stirling (50 minutes, four to nine daily).

Upper Strathearn
☎ 01764

The two Highland villages of **Comrie** (population 1839) and **St Fillans** (population 350), in upper Strathearn, are surrounded by forests and craggy, bare mountain tops where deer and mountain hares both live in abundance.

CRIEFF

0 ——————— 200 m
0 ——————— 0.1 miles

To Famous Grouse Experience (1mi); Comrie (7mi)

To Perth (17mi)

CENTRAL SCOTLAND

INFORMATION
Bank of Scotland.............................1 B3
Library..2 B3
Police Station..................................3 B3
Post Office.......................................4 C3
Royal Bank of Scotland...................5 B3
Tourist Information Centre (TIC).....6 B3

SIGHTS & ACTIVITIES
Stones, Stocks & Stories................(see 6)

SLEEPING 🛏
Comely Bank Guest House................7 A3
Crieff Hydro....................................8 C1
Leven House Hotel..........................9 A2

EATING 🍴
Baan Thai Restaurant.....................10 B3
Bank...11 B3
Red Onion Bistro............................12 B3
Somerfield Supermarket................13 A4

Comrie has a rather tattered elegance hinting at its previous heyday. If you fancy trying to hook a big one, visit the **Drummond Trout Farm & Fishery** (☎ 670500; Comrie; 2hr session adult/child £3.50/3; ☒ 10am-5pm Sep-May, to 10pm Jun-Aug), just outside town. It's a great place to take the kids, who can fumble around in the pool while you get serious in the specimen pond. You can hire all the gear you need (rods £3).

St Fillans enjoys an excellent location at the eastern end of **Loch Earn**, which reflects the silhouettes of distant, towering peaks in its glittering waters.

Comrie is 24 miles west of Perth, and St Fillans is about 5 miles further west. Stagecoach operates daily buses from Perth, via Crieff, to Comrie and St Fillans (see p221).

WEST PERTHSHIRE

This remote area of Perthshire is a jewel in central Scotland's crown. It's difficult to reach via public transport – buses are usually once-a-day postal services; however, these fabulous hills and lochs are well worth making an effort to see.

Aberfeldy

☎ 01887 / pop 1895

So it's not a Scottish sex symbol, fair enough, but Aberfeldy tends to get a bad rap and we can't figure out why. Slightly shabby and rough around the edges it may be, but with some great attractions nearby and a spot deep in forest country, Aberfeldy will entice you to linger.

The helpful, knowledgeable **TIC** (☎ 820276; The Square; ☒ 9.30am-5pm Easter-Oct, 9.30am-5pm Mon-Sat Nov-Easter), in an old church, is an exceptionally efficient and friendly place. The **Royal Bank of Scotland** (8 The Square) has an ATM.

SIGHTS

The **Watermill** (☎ 822896; www.aberfeldywatermill .com; Mill St; admission free; ☒ 9am-5pm Mon-Sat, noon-5pm Sun; ☒) is an unusual and much-needed attraction in the centre of town. Incorporating a bookshop (the largest in the Highlands) with a great Scottish collection, gallery with contemporary works of art and a coffee shop, you could while away several hours in this old mill. Bucket-loads of character is thrown in for good measure and the highlight is perhaps the working mill machinery, giving the gallery a unique space to exhibit its works of art.

SLEEPING & EATING

Tigh'n Eilean Guest House (☎ /fax 820109; www .tighneilean.com; Taybridge Dr; s/d £35/55) Everything about this property screams comfort – it's a gorgeous place overlooking the Tay. Individually designed rooms all have a unique sense of space. For couples our fave is the Jacuzzi room (it's huge!) and for solo travellers the wood-lined twin with private bath is very snug.

Novar (☎ 820335; hardie@novaraberfeldy.fsnet.co .uk; Home St; r per person £20) Just off the main drag, Novar epitomises the old-fashioned, well-maintained B&B and has a couple of great rooms; the front bedroom overlooks the street, has a very comfy bed and gets plenty of light. Breakfast is filling and your host discerning.

Kiwis (☎ 829229; The Square; lunch mains £5, dinner mains £10-12; ☒ lunch daily, dinner Thu-Mon) Located in a modern room with subtle lighting and efficient service, Kiwis is a little ray of sunshine in the town's dining scene, bringing everything good about antipodean dining to Aberfeldy. Fresh ingredients and a simple style delivers a range of filling and tasty dishes.

Also recommended:

Balnearn House (☎ 820431; www.balnearnhouse .com; Crieff Rd; s/d from £40/49) A sedate, refined and quite luxurious option close to the town centre.

Black Watch Inn (☎ 820699; Bank St; mains £5-10; ☒ lunch & dinner) Good range of pub food dabbling in Thai and Scottish dishes.

SOMETHING SPECIAL

Guinach House (☎ 820251; www.guinach house.co.uk; Urlar Rd; r £95-105) Have we got a treat for you! More like a boutique hotel, Guinach has modish rooms and a casual, laid-back ambience – if you can't relax here we suggest therapy. Rooms have private access from the rest of the house and are individually styled – our fave is the zebra room, although the red room with free-standing bathtub runs a close second. Breakfast is served at a small dining table in your room and the whole place is set on a large estate, so there's plenty of rambling options just beyond the front doorstep. The ruins of an Iron Age fort are nearby. Guinach House is easy to fall in love with and difficult to leave.

GETTING THERE & AWAY

Stagecoach runs buses from Aberfeldy to Pitlochry (45 minutes, six Monday to Saturday, three Sunday), Blairgowrie (1¼ hours, two daily Monday to Friday) and Perth (1¼ hours, 10 daily Monday to Saturday).

Local bus operators run between Aberfeldy and Kenmore about seven times daily from Monday to Saturday (no service on Sunday); two of these continue on to Fortingall, at the head of Glen Lyon, on Monday, Thursday and Friday.

A postbus service goes to Killin (three hours) via Kenmore, and another goes to the top of Glen Lyon, at Lubreoch, via Fortingall (both once daily Monday to Saturday).

Around Aberfeldy

Castle Menzies (☎ 01887-820982; Weem; adult/child £3.50/2; ☼ 10.30am-5pm Mon-Sat, 2-5pm Sun Apr–mid Oct), 1.5 miles west of town by the B846, is the impressive restored 16th-century seat of the chief of the clan Menzies. The Z-plan tower house is magnificently located against a backdrop of Scottish forest. And inside it doesn't disappoint. The place smells just like a castle should – musty and lived in. It reeks of authenticity despite extensive restoration work and is a highly recommended ramble. Check out the fireplace in the dungeon-like kitchens and the gaudy great hall upstairs, with windows unfurling a ribbon of lush, green countryside extending into wooded hills beyond the estate.

Glenlyon Gallery (☎ 01887-820202; www.glen lyongallery.com; Boltachan; ☼ 10am-6pm), near Aberfeldy, brings the wildlife and startling natural beauty of Perthshire to life with vivid paintings and sketches by a talented local artist. Some of Scotland's most priceless treasures are captured on canvas and, if you're interested, can be shipped anywhere in the world. The gallery is signposted off the B846.

Highland Adventure Safaris (☎ 01887-820071; www.highlandadventuresafaris.co.uk; B846; ⚐) is ideal for those wanting to spot some wildlife or simply enjoy Perthshire's magnificent countryside. The operator is very environmentally conscious and will tailor trips to your wishes. Standard trips include the two-hour Adventure Safari for £32.50/12.50 per adult/child, which includes a dram in the wilderness, and the Safari Hike for £55, which

CRANNOGS

Usually built in a loch for defensive purposes, a crannog (from the Gaelic word *crann*, meaning 'tree') consists of an artificial rock island with timber posts and struts supporting a hut above high-water level. Crannogs were used on many lochs, including Lochs Awe, Earn and Tay, from prehistoric times up to the 18th century. Some crannogs had curious underwater causeways that could zigzag or had traps, making night-time assaults without a boat extremely difficult

includes a walk in the mountains and a picnic. Wildlife you may spot includes golden eagles, osprey and red deer. There's also gold-panning for kids at the visitor centre. It's on the B846, just past Castle Menzies.

Loch Tay

The greater part of mighty Ben Lawers (1214m), Scotland's ninth-tallest peak, looms over Loch Tay. Drop into the **visitor centre** (NTS; ☎ 01567-820397; adult/child £1/60p, parking donation £2; ☼ 10.30am-5pm May-Sep) high on the slopes of the mountain; the access road is off the A827, on the northern shore of the loch and continues over a wild pass to Glen Lyon. A trail leads to the summit from the centre, but you should take a good map (OS map No 51). There is also a much easier nature trail from the visitor centre and ranger-guided walks in summer. Call by for the jaw-dropping views if nothing else.

A stout little water-bus, **MV Glen Lyon** (☎ 01567-820111) takes passengers on one-hour cruises of Loch Tay. The departure point is the Tay Forest Park car park at the eastern end of the loch, near Kenmore. Cruises depart hourly, weather permitting, and cost £6.50/4.50 per adult/child.

KENMORE

The wealthy village of Kenmore, at the eastern end of Loch Tay, is about 6 miles west of Aberfeldy. It's a small but pretty place dominated by a church and clock tower. Don't forget the camera, as it's the perfect place for some happy snaps. Just a quarter of a mile along the south Loch Tay road from the village, the **Scottish Crannog Centre** (☎ 01887-830583; adult/child £4.75/3; ☼ 10am-4.30pm mid-Mar–Oct, 10am-4.30pm Sat & Sun Nov) has a fascinating reconstruction of an artificial, Iron Age island-house. There are exhibits from archaeological dives of crannogs (see the boxed text, p223) and artistic impressions of what they may have looked like. Tours run hourly.

Kenmore Hotel (☎ 01887-830205; www.kenmore hotel.com; The Square; s/d £65/100), touched with a quiet sense of dignity, claims to be Scotland's oldest inn and dates from 1572. Its quaint, spacious rooms are generously furnished and full of character. On the chimneypiece in the bar look out for the romantic description of the countryside written by Robert Burns in 1787. After a few drinks in the bar, watch out for the low doorways on your way upstairs. The **Taymouth Restaurant** (starters £5, mains £10-15; ☒ dinner) overlooks Loch Tay and the mouthwatering menu uses Scottish produce in simple but tasty combinations (some, admittedly, like blackfaced lamb, are a bit disturbing!); the service is first class.

See Aberfeldy (p223) for your public-transport options.

Fortingall & Glen Lyon

Fortingall is one of the prettiest villages in Scotland, with 19th-century thatched cottages in a very tranquil setting. The **church** (admission free; ☒ 10am-4pm Apr-Oct) has impressive wooden beams and a 7th-century **monk's bell**. In the churchyard, there's a 5000-year-old **yew**, probably the oldest tree in Europe. This tree was already ancient when the Romans camped on the meadows by the River Lyon. It's also famous as the reputed birthplace of Pontius Pilate. Today it's a shell of its former self – at its zenith it had a girth of over 17m! But souvenir hunters have reduced it to two much smaller trunks.

Rickety Roman bridges, Victorian lodges, a Caledonian pine forest and sheer peaks (splashed with pink and purple heather)

poking through swirling clouds mark the drive along the tiny road into the wonderful **Glen Lyon**. The longest enclosed glen in Scotland, it becomes wilder and more uninhabited as it snakes its way west toward Loch Lyon – few visitors penetrate its remote upper reaches, where capercaillie live in patches of pine forest. You'll need wheels, preferably the motorised kind, but if you're keen and you've the time, cycling through Glen Lyon would be a great way to experience this special place. Stop at the **Glenlyon Post Office, Shop & Tearoom** (Bridge of Balgie; dishes £2-5; ☒ lunch Fri-Tue) for sandwiches, soup, homemade savoury tarts and sweetie-treaties, all served with a smile.

Invervar Lodge (☎ 01887-877206; invervar .lodge@btinternet.com; r per person from £33) is an old Victorian hunting lodge, and its isolation makes it the perfect country hideaway. Five miles from Fortingall, the Swedish hosts offer massages and reflexology after a hard day's tramping. The food here is also very good.

See the Aberfeldy section for public-transport options (p223).

Lochs Tummel & Rannoch

The route along Lochs Tummel and Rannoch is worth doing any way you can – by foot, bicycle or car – just don't miss it! Hills of ancient birch and forests of spruce, pine and larch make up the Tay Forest Park – the king of Scotland's forests. These wooded hills roll into the glittering waters of the lochs, and while tracking along the southern side of Loch Tummel you'll be greeted by Highland cattle, grand houses and startling views – a reminder of the undeniable raw beauty of Perthshire. A visit in autumn is recommended, when the birch trees are at their finest.

Queen's View Visitor Centre (☎ 01796-473123; Strathtummel; car-park fee £1; ☒ 10am-6pm late Mar–mid-Nov), at the eastern end of Loch Tummel, has a magnificent outlook towards Schiehallion (1083m). There are displays and audiovisual programmes about the area, while picnic tables make an outdoor lunch an inviting option.

Kinloch Rannoch is a great base for local walks (you can walk up Schiehallion from Braes of Foss – see www.jmt.org for more information) or cycle around **Loch Rannoch**. There are a supermarket with a few

CENTRAL SCOTLAND

local-information leaflets and a post office next door. If you're up for an easy stroll, try the **clan trail** around the loch, which has roadside notice boards about local clans. Beyond the western end of the loch you enter bleak Rannoch Moor, which extends all the way to Glen Coe. The rivers and lochs on the moor are good for fishing.

SLEEPING & EATING

Bunrannoch House (☎ /fax 01882-632407; www .bunrannoch.co.uk; Kinloch Rannoch; s/d £30/50, dinner, B&B per person £44) Grand Bunrannoch House is a former shooting lodge, set back from the edge of town. It has a distinctly worn and warm design that makes you feel at home straight away. Rooms have great views and some have four-poster beds.

Moor of Rannoch Hotel (☎ /fax 01882-633238; r per person £40, mains from £7; ☺ lunch & dinner) If you get as far as Rannoch Station (16 miles west of Kinloch Rannoch) you'll be rewarded with the excellent food and lodging.

SOMETHING FOR THE WEEKEND

Start your weekend by checking into **Kenmore Hotel** (opposite) – Scotland's oldest inn – and squeeze in a cruise on steely blue **Loch Tay** (p223), admiring the dramatic splendour of Ben Lawers. In the evening nurse a pint in the inviting bar before migrating to **Taymouth Restaurant** (opposite) for some fine cuisine using local produce. Saturday morning drop into the **Scottish Crannog Centre** (p223) and learn about these intriguing loch-based dwellings. Head to Fortingall with its 5000-year-old **yew tree** (opposite) and then plunge the depths of **Glen Lyon** (opposite) – Scotland's longest enclosed valley. Have a ramble around authentic **Castle Menzies** (p223) on your way to Aberfeldy and check into the stylish **Guinach House** (see the boxed text, p222). Fine cuisine awaits at **Kiwis** (p222) that evening. In the morning chill out with a coffee in the **Watermill** (p222) and have a browse through its excellent Scottish book collection. Drop by the **Glenlyon Gallery** (p223) and capture some local landscape memories on canvas. Finish off the weekend with a fine lunch in one of Perthshire's best rural pubs – the **Moulin Inn** (see the boxed text, p228), just outside Pitlochry.

Loch Tummel Inn (☎ 01882-634272; Strathtummel; bar suppers £6, restaurant mains £9-12; ☺ lunch & dinner) This old coaching inn is a snug spot for a decent feed from a menu featuring seafood. The bar is open all day for a leisurely pint in the beer garden overlooking Loch Tummel. The inn is about 3 miles from Queen's View.

Kilvrecht (☎ 01350-727284; Kinloch Rannoch; tent sites £6; ☺ Apr-Oct) This simple, basic camping ground (no electricity or showers) has terrific grassy areas for camping, picnic tables and clean toilets. If you enjoy space and your own company, head here – it's 3.5 miles from Kinloch Rannoch on the south Loch Rannoch road.

GETTING THERE & AWAY

Elizabeth Yule Transport (☎ 01796-472290) operates a service between Kinloch Rannoch and Pitlochry (50 minutes, up to five Monday to Saturday) via Queen's View and Loch Tummel Inn. The Pitlochry–Rannoch Station postbus has a once-daily service (Monday to Saturday) via Kinloch Rannoch and both sides of the loch.

First ScotRail runs two to four trains daily from Rannoch Station north to Fort William (£7, one hour) and Mallaig, and south to Glasgow (£16.50, 2¾ hours).

PERTH TO AVIEMORE

There are a number of major sights strung along the A9 – which becomes a scenic treat after Pitlochry. It's the main route north to Aviemore and Inverness in the Highlands.

Dunkeld & Birnam
☎ 01350 / pop 1005
Ever been to a feel-good town? Well, Dunkeld and Birnam, with their enviable location nestled in the heart of Perthshire's big-tree country, await. The towns happily throb with tourists, and so they should – there are architectural delights to enjoy here, including a magnificent cathedral. It is walkers in the surrounding area, though, who really grease the wheels of tourism, even through the winter months. Dunkeld's **TIC** (☎ 727688; dunkeldtic@visitscotland .co.uk; The Cross; ☺ Mon, Tue, Fri & Sat Nov-Mar, daily Apr-Oct) has to be one of the friendliest in all of the country. Pick up its leaflet on local walks.

SIGHTS & ACTIVITIES

Situated between open grassland between the River Tay on one side and rolling hills on the other, **Dunkeld Cathedral** (HS; ☎ 727601; High St; admission free; ⏰ 9.30am-6.30pm May-Sep, to 4.30pm Oct-Apr) is one of the most beautifully sited cathedrals in Scotland. Don't miss it on a sunny day, as there are few more lovely places to be. Half the cathedral is still in use as a church, the rest is in ruins, and you can explore it all. The oldest part of the original church is the choir, completed in 1350. The 15th-century tower is still standing. The cathedral was damaged during the Reformation and burnt during the Battle of Dunkeld in 1689.

If you're looking to entertain the kids for a few hours, drop by **Going Pottie** (☎ 728044; www.goingpottie.com; Cathedral St; activities from £5; ♿) where kids can get a paintbrush in their hand and create colourful ceramics…and mayhem.

Across the bridge is Birnam, made famous by *Macbeth*. There's not much left of Birnam Wood, but there is a small, leafy **Beatrix Potter Park** (the author spent childhood holidays in the area). In the park you'll find some local history on the life of the author who wrote the evergreen story of Peter Rabbit.

Loch of the Lowes Wildlife Centre (☎ 727337; Loch of the Lowes; admission £2; ⏰ 10am-5pm Apr-Sep), 2 miles east of Dunkeld off the A923, has wildlife displays mostly devoted to the majestic osprey. There's also an excellent birdwatching hide with binoculars provided, where you can see the birds nesting during breeding season.

SLEEPING & EATING

Taybank (☎ 727340; admin@thetaybank.com; Tay Tce, Dunkeld; s/d £22.50/45, mains £4.50-7) The Taybank is a live-music bar fielding musos from around the area who specialise in late-night jamming. There are great, simple rooms upstairs with shared bathroom. Traditional Scottish food includes the beloved stovie. It's very friendly and once you gaze out over the Tay from the breakfast room nursing your hangover, you may not want to leave at all.

Birnam House Hotel (☎ 727462; www.birnam househotel.co.uk; Perth Rd, Birnam; r per person from £38; ♿) At the time of research, this grand-looking place with crow-stepped gables was undergoing renovation (damn, we liked it the way it was – unrenovated and proud of it). Tastefully fitted rooms differ in size and quality of furnishings, so have a look at a few. Most, fortunately, retain the character of the building. Dishes at the adjoining **Tap Inn** (mains £6-8) display a distinctive creative flair.

GETTING THERE & AWAY

Dunkeld is 15 miles north of Perth. Scottish Citylink buses between Glasgow/Edinburgh (£9.30, two hours, at least three daily) and Inverness stop at Birnam House Hotel. Birnam to Perth (£5) or Pitlochry (£5) takes 20 minutes.

Strathtay Scottish has a bus between Blairgowrie (30 minutes) and Aberfeldy (40 minutes), via Dunkeld, twice daily Monday to Friday; there's no bus to Aberfeldy during school holidays.

Trains run to Glasgow (£11, 1½ hours, nine daily Monday to Saturday, four on Sunday) and to Inverness (£18, two hours, eight daily Monday to Saturday, five on Sunday).

Pitlochry
☎ 01796 / pop 2564

Teeming with tourists, Pitlochry manages to absorb its annual influx of visitors and retain the charm of a Highland town. Clever trick. The main drag is always busy, but with all the wonderful sights nearby you won't need to spend long on it anyway. It's an excellent place to base yourself if you want to explore the region, and it has good transport connections if you're long on time and short on wheels.

INFORMATION

Computer Services Centre (☎ 473711; 67 Atholl Rd; per min 5p; ⏰ 9.30am-5.30pm Mon-Fri, 12.30-5.30pm Sat; 🖥) Internet access; opposite the Royal Bank.
Police Station (Atholl Rd)
Post office (Atholl Rd)
Royal Bank of Scotland (Atholl Rd) Has ATM.
TIC (☎ 472215; pitlochrytic@visitscotland.com; 22 Atholl Rd; ⏰ daily Apr-Oct, Mon-Sat Nov-Mar) Inconsistent service – some staff helpful, others uninterested; sells the useful publication *Pitlochry Walks* (50p), which lists four short and four long local walks.

SIGHTS

If you fancy a tour of a whisky distillery, Pitlochry has two. **Bell's Blair Athol Distillery**

(☎ 482003; Atholl Rd; tour incl voucher redeemable against purchases £4; ☉ 11am-3pm Mon-Fri Jan-Easter, Nov & Dec, 9.30am-5pm Mon-Sat Easter-May, 9.30am-5pm Mon-Sat & noon-5pm Sun Jun-Sep, 10am-4pm Mon-Fri Oct) is at the southern end of town. The **Edradour Distillery** (☎ 472095; admission free; ☉ 9.30am-6pm Mon-Sat, 11.30am-5pm Sun Mar-Oct; call to confirm winter hr) is proudly Scotland's smallest distillery, 2.5 miles east of Pitlochry on the A924.

At the Pitlochry Festival Theatre, the excellent **Explorers: The Scottish Plant Hunters Garden** (☎ 484600; adult/child £3/1; Foss Rd; ☉ 10am-5pm Mon-Sat, 11am-5pm Sun Apr–late Oct) commemorates 300 years of plant collecting and those who hunted down 'new' species. Opened in 2003, the new-age landscaping in the 2.5-hectare garden includes a couple

of pavilions built from Scottish timber and an amphitheatre. The whole collection is based on plants brought back to Scotland by Scottish explorers. In their words: 'These men would put Indiana Jones to shame'. There is plenty of seating to drink in the views over town.

SLEEPING

Pitlochry is packed with places to stay, but anything central tends to be a bit pricey.

Tir Aluinn Guest House (☎ 473811; www.tiraluinn .co.uk; 10 Higher Oakfield; s/d £25/50; ☖) This place is a real find – there are three extremely well-kept, bright rooms and the hosts *sooo* have the right attitude. Apart from being thoughtful and charming, they don't levy a

PITLOCHRY

INFORMATION		
Computer Services Centre	1	B2
Police Station	2	C3
Post Office	3	B2
Royal Bank of Scotland	4	B2
Tourist Information Centre (TIC)	5	C3
SIGHTS & ACTIVITIES		
Bell's Blair Athol Distillery	6	D4
Explorers: The Scottish Plant Hunters Garden	7	B4
SLEEPING 🛏		
Knockendarroch Hotel	8	C2
Pitlochry Backpackers	9	B2
Strath Garry	10	B2
Sunnybank	11	C3
Tir Aluinn Guest House	12	C2
EATING 🍴		
Co-op Supermarket	13	B2
Festival Restaurant	(see 15)	
McKay's Hotel	14	B2
ENTERTAINMENT 🎭		
Pitlochry Festival Theatre	15	B4
TRANSPORT		
Buses to Perth & Edinburgh	16	B2
Escape Route Bike Repairs & Hire	17	C3

0 — 200 m
0 — 0.1 miles

To Moulin Inn (1mi);
Edradour Distillery (2.5mi)

To Pass of Killiecrankie (3.5mi); Blair Atholl (7mi); Blair Castle (7mi); Inverness (86mi)

Atholl Rd

Rie-Achan Rd

Station Rd

Pitlochry Train Station

Loch Faskally

To Aviemore (58mi); Inverness (86mi)

Dam; Fish Ladder

Port na Craig Rd

Greenside Rd

A924

Bonnethill Rd

Well Brae

Higher Oakfield Rd

Lower Oakfield Rd

West Moulin Rd

Knockard Rd

Tomnacroich Rd

East Moulin Rd

Finlay Tce

Tomcroy Tce

Ferry Rd

Bruach La

Tummel

Foss Rd

Bridge Rd

Perth Rd

To A9 South (1mi)

A9

To Perth (26mi)

CENTRAL SCOTLAND

surcharge at solo travellers because in their words 'we've too many single friends and it's not their fault'. Right on. Highly recommended and good value for Pitlochry.

Strath Garry (☎ 472469; www.strathgarryhotel .co.uk; 113 Atholl Rd; d £60) Recently refurbished and with a top location, Strath Garry makes you never want to leave. Why? Well, it's a (small) hotel-bar-café-restaurant – you'll never want for anything, and they do it all pretty well. En-suite rooms are very snug and have some luxurious touches – we lost a researcher who sunk into one of the beds and was never seen again.

Pitlochry Backpackers (☎ 470044; www.scotlands tophostels.com; 134 Atholl Rd; dm/tw/d £12/£28/£32) This is a cracking hostel smack-bang in the middle of town with three- to eight-bed dorms that are in mint condition, and there's no extra charge for linen (towel 20p). Couples should grab the excellent en-suite double, a real bargain. Friendly, laid-back and very comfortable.

Knockendarroch Hotel (☎ 473473; www.knocken darroch.co.uk; Higher Oakfield Rd; dinner, B&B per person £48-76) Geez we like this place. Location, location, location…oh and character…and comfort. This hotel lures visitors with its grace, ornate grandeur and old-world charisma. Sumptuous rooms vary – No 3 is the largest and has gorgeous views, although rooms on the top floor have the real stunners. Take your partner here – they won't forget it. To cap it off the restaurant here is outstanding.

Sunnybank (☎ 473014; ellson@onetel.net.uk; 19 Lower Oakfield Rd; r per person £20-26) Austrian-run Sunnybank certainly has a sunny aspect and offers fresh, good-value rooms in a large modern house. Some rooms have that alpine thing going on.

EATING

Strath Garry (mains £4-12; ☺ breakfast, lunch & dinner) The bright, slick eating area at this hotel is complimented by delicious dishes, from tasty sandwiches at lunch time to locally sourced ingredients for more sophisticated dining (such as grilled Shetland salmon) in the evening. Highland lamb also features and the sweets are very tempting.

Festival Restaurant (☎ 484626; Foss Rd; lunch £4.50-6.50, 2-/3- course set dinner £18.50/21.50; ☺ lunch & dinner) Admire views from floor to ceiling windows and watercolour paintings of Highland scenes in this elegant restaurant at the Pitlochry Festival Theatre. Dishes such as the bonnet of Highland wild game casserole, followed by Scottish cheeses and oatcakes, go down a treat.

McKay's Hotel (☎ 473885; 138 Atholl Rd; mains £4-7; ☺ lunch & dinner) This place is one big pub-restaurant serving basic, filling Scottish pub fare – it'll stick to ya ribs. There's a huge open fireplace, perfect for toasting the tush in winter. The boisterous barn of a bar in the rear serves the same food with more atmosphere and live bands.

There's a **Co-op supermarket** (West Moulin Rd) if you're self-catering.

DRINKING & ENTERTAINMENT

See the boxed text, below, for details on the Moulin Inn, one of the best pubs in Scotland, and some of the best microbrewed beers you'll taste in the country.

Pitlochry Festival Theatre (☎ 484626; Foss Rd; tickets £5-30; ♿) This well-known theatre stages a different play for six nights out of seven during its season from May to mid-October.

GETTING THERE & AWAY

Scottish Citylink runs approximately hourly buses between Inverness and Glasgow/Edinburgh via Pitlochry. Prices and journey times to destinations from Pitlochry are: Inverness (£9.50, two hours), Aviemore

---

SOMETHING SPECIAL

Moulin Inn (☎ 01796-472196; Moulin; starters £3-6, mains £6-9; ☺ lunch & dinner) Just a mile north of Pitlochry, the Moulin is a gem with plenty of great nooks and is one of our fave pubs in the country. Fireplaces, a low roof, stained glass, lots of unpolished wood – it's an atmospheric little inn that was trading here long before visitors arrived in nearby Pitlochry. It makes a great spot to escape the crowds for a meal or an afternoon drink – you could walk here from town. There's a reasonably priced menu with simple, home-cooked food served in generous portions and a specials board that changes regularly; try the seafood pancake. The hotel brews its own ales – the smooth, ruby-coloured Atholl Ale is particularly good.

(1¼ hours), Perth (45 minutes), Edinburgh (£9.40, two hours) and Glasgow (£9.40, 2¼ hours).

Stagecoach runs buses to Aberfeldy (30 minutes, up to eight Monday to Saturday, three Sunday), Dunkeld (25 minutes, up to 10 daily Monday to Saturday) and Perth (one hour, up to 10 daily Monday to Saturday).

Pitlochry is on the main rail line from Perth to Inverness. There are nine trains a day from Perth (£9, 30 minutes), fewer on Sunday.

GETTING AROUND
Escape Route Bike Repairs & Hire (☎ 473859; 3 Atholl Rd; half-/full day £9/15; ☺ 9am-5.30pm Mon-Sat, 10am-5pm Sun) rents out bikes. For a taxi, call **Elizabeth Yule Transport** (☎ 472290); a taxi to Blair Castle will cost you £10.

Pass of Killiecrankie
Drop into the **Killiecrankie Visitors Centre** (NTS; ☎ 01796-473233; Killiecrankie; admission free, car-park fee £2; ☺ 10am-5.30pm Apr-Jun, Sep & Oct, 9.30am-6pm Jul & Aug) in this beautiful, rugged gorge, 3.5 miles north of Pitlochry. It has great inter-active displays on the Jacobite rebellion, and local flora and fauna. There's plenty to touch, pull and open – great for kids. There are some stunning walks into the wooded gorge; keep an eye out for red squirrels.

Local buses run between Pitlochry and Blair Atholl via Killiecrankie (10 minutes, three to six daily).

Blair Castle & Blair Atholl
☎ 01796
One of the most popular tourist attractions in Scotland, magnificent **Blair Castle** (☎ 481207; Blair Atholl; castle & grounds adult/child/family £6.90/4.30/17.50; ☺ 9.30am-5.30pm Easter-Oct, call Pitlochry TIC for winter hr) is the seat of the duke of Atholl. Set beneath forested slopes above the River Garry, this impressive whitewashed castle plays host (in May) to the parade of the Atholl Highlanders – the only private army in Europe.

Thirty rooms are open to the public, and they're packed with paintings, arms and armour, china, lace, and embroidery, pre-senting a near-complete picture of upper-class life in the Highlands from the 16th century to the present. One of the most impressive rooms is the ballroom. The 11th (and current) duke was a distant relative

(in every sense of the word – he lives in South Africa) to the 10th duke, who died a bachelor in 1996. The duke returns to his inheritance every May to review the Atholl Highlanders.

Blair Castle is 7 miles north of Pitlochry, and a mile from Blair Atholl village. For a great cycle, walk or drive, take the stunning road to **Glenfender** from Blair Atholl village. It's about 3 miles on a long, windy uphill track to a farmhouse; the views of snow-capped peaks along the way are spectacular.

The gothic **Atholl Arms Hotel** (☎ 481205; Blair Atholl; s/d from £40/50), a pub near the train sta-tion, is convenient for the castle and some-times does special deals.

Local buses run a service between Pit-lochry and Blair Atholl (25 minutes, three to six daily). Two buses a day (Monday to Saturday) go directly to the castle. There's a train station in the village, but not all trains stop here.

For a continuation of this route, see the Cairngorms section, p325.

BLAIRGOWRIE & GLENSHEE
The route along the A93 through Glenshee is one of the most spectacular drives in the country. The meandering burns and soaring peaks, splotched with glaring snow, tend to dwarf open-mouthed drivers – it's surpris-ing there aren't more accidents along this road! Blairgowrie (population 8500) and Braemar (see p263) are the main accommo-dation centres for the Glenshee ski resort, although there's a small settlement 5 miles south of the ski runs at **Spittal of Glenshee**.

There's a helpful **TIC** (☎ 01250-872960; blairgowrietic@visitscotland.com; 26 Wellmeadow; ☺ daily Apr-Oct, Mon-Sat Nov-Mar) with plenty of walk-ing information. You'll find two banks with ATMs on High St, just behind the TIC.

Skiing
Glenshee ski resort (☎ 01339-741320; www.ski-glenshee.co.uk), on the border of Perthshire and Aberdeenshire, has 38 pistes and is one of Scotland's largest skiing areas. After a good fall of snow and when the sun burns through the clouds, you'll be in a unique position to drink in the beauty of this country; the ski-ing isn't half bad either. The chairlift can whisk you up to 910m, near the top of the **Cairnwell** (933m). Whenever there's enough snow in winter it opens daily (it's usually

closed in summer, but check with the TIC). A one-day lift pass and ski hire costs from £38, although it's cheaper for beginners and if you're hiring over two or more days.

Sleeping & Eating

Ben Blair (☎ 01250-872393; Balmoral Rd, Blairgowrie; r per person £18) At this well-kept family home you'll receive old-fashioned hospitality in cosy surrounds and be sent on your way with a smile and a hearty breakfast. There are two rooms with shared bathroom upstairs: a triple and a twin, both a good size.

Rosebank House (☎ 01250-872912; colhotel@ rosebank35.fsnet.co.uk; Balmoral Rd, Blairgowrie; s/d £25/50) This fine Georgian property is a great deal. Good-sized rooms upstairs are well kept and have small but clean en suites, and there's a large front garden. The friendly owners take good care of guests, and no surcharge is levied on solo travellers. Try to get a room overlooking the garden. Note that rooms do not have TVs as the owners like to encourage communal conversation.

Spittal of Glenshee Hotel (☎ 01250-885215; www.spittalofglenshee.co.uk; Spittal of Glenshee; dm £14-15.50, r per person from £22, with en suite from £32) This hotel is a very 'Scottish experience' – it's a great old country lodge that has burnt down numerous times, but don't worry; the insurers have calculated that the next likely fire won't be until 2029. There's a good bar and a bunkhouse (without cooking facilities).

Rendez-vous (☎ 01250-870088; Boat Brae, Blairgowrie; mains £5-9; ☽ lunch & dinner) Bright and modern, this café-bar-bistro serves a little of everything, with pasta dishes featuring. It's simple, wholesome food, convenient to the town centre.

Getting There & Away

Strathtay Scottish operates a service from Perth to Blairgowrie (50 minutes, three to seven daily). There's also a bus from Blairgowrie to Dundee (50 minutes, hourly, less frequent on Sunday).

The only service from Blairgowrie to the Glenshee area, about 30 miles away, is the postbus to Spittal of Glenshee (no Sunday service).

AROUND BLAIRGOWRIE

Alyth is a charming little village with a small canal and some exquisite stone bridges about 5 miles east of Blairgowrie. Ask at Blairgowrie's TIC for the *Walk Old Alyth* leaflet; there are lots of historical buildings, including church ruins dating from 1296. If you're looking to escape the rain, perusing the displays on local history at **Alyth Museum** (☎ 01738-632488; Commercial St; admission free; ☽ 1-5pm Wed-Sun May-Sep) is a fine way to pass an hour or so.

Alyth Hotel (☎ 01828-632447; Commercial St, Alyth) is a classic town pub under new management that was being renovated when we passed through town. The signs are very good and it would be worth inquiring after both food and lodging here.

Off the A94 and 8 miles east of Blairgowrie, **Meigle** is worth the trip for those with a fascination for Pictish stones. The tiny **Meigle Museum** (HS; ☎ 01828-640612; adult/child £2.20/80p; ☽ 9.30am-12.30pm & 1.30-6.30pm Apr-Sep) has 26 such carved stones from the 7th to the 10th century, all found in the local area. The pieces range from the Nordic to the exotic – they include a Viking headstone and, bizarrely, a carving of a camel.

Northeast Scotland

The great elbow of land that juts into the North Sea between the Firth of Tay and the Moray Firth comprises a broad mantle of fertile lowlands fringed with forests, draped around the barren shoulders of the Grampian Mountains. Around its edge, the varied coastline is hemmed with long, sandy beaches and rugged, bird-haunted cliffs, bejewelled here and there with picturesque little fishing villages.

Within its bounds you will find two of Scotland's four largest cities – Dundee, the city of jute, jam and journalism, the cradle of some of Britain's favourite comic characters, and home to Captain Scott's Antarctic research ship, the *Discovery*; and Aberdeen, the granite city, an economic powerhouse fuelled by the riches of North Sea oil.

The countryside is home to a thriving indigenous culture, where the old Scottish dialect known as the Doric still survives, and boasts the greatest concentration of Scottish Baronial castles anywhere in the country. Royalty watchers come to nose around the Queen's summer pad at Balmoral and the late Princess Margaret's birthplace at Glamis Castle.

It was in the northeast, in the 19th century, that the Aberdeen Angus breed of beef cattle was perfected, and where the barley for Speyside malt whiskies was first grown. It's home to a rich array of local produce, such as the Arbroath smokie and Finnan haddie, the Forfar bridie and Aberdeen rowie, and the delicious fish soup known as *Cullen skink*. There are distillery tours, Highland games, heritage railways, Pictish relics and the only bronze statue of a comic-book character anywhere in Scotland.

HIGHLIGHTS

- Soaking up the views from the hills around beautiful **Glen Clova** (p250)
- Meditating on the meaning of the mysterious **Pictish stones** (p249) of Angus
- Relishing the royal heritage of fairytale **Glamis Castle** (p247)
- Exploring the hills, forests, castles and pretty villages of **Royal Deeside** (p261)
- Being initiated into the mysteries of malt whisky on a Speyside **distillery tour** (p269)

★ Speyside

Royal ★ Deeside

Glen Clova ★

★ Angus

Glamis ★ Castle

- POPULATION: 780,000
- AREA: 10,979 SQ KM

NORTHEAST SCOTLAND

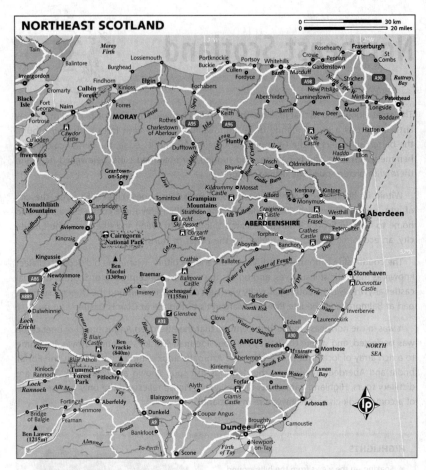

NORTHEAST SCOTLAND

Getting Around

The Dundee to Aberdeen route is served by **Scottish Citylink** (☎ 0870 550 5050; www.citylink .co.uk) buses. **Strathtay Scottish** (☎ 01382-227201) in Dundee and Angus and **Stagecoach Bluebird** (☎ 01224-212266; www.stagecoachbus.com/bluebird) in Aberdeenshire and Moray are the main regional bus operators, with services linking all the main towns and cities. Stagecoach Bluebird offers a Bluebird Explorer ticket (adult/child £11/5.50) that allows unlimited travel on all its services for one day.

From mid-May to September, Stagecoach Bluebird operates the Speyside Stroller bus service (500), which runs from Cullen, on the Banffshire coast, to the Cairngorm Mountain Railway via Buckie, Spey Bay, Fochabers,

Elgin, Dufftown, Tomintoul, Grantown-on-Spey and Aviemore (£5, 3¾ hours, once daily, Saturday and Sunday only).

Royal Mail postbuses (☎ 0845 774 0740; www.post bus.royalmail.com) run to remote communities in the Angus Glens and Deeside, charging on average £2 to £5 for single journeys.

The Dundee–Inverness railway line passes through Arbroath, Montrose, Stonehaven, Aberdeen, Huntly and Elgin.

DUNDEE & ANGUS

Angus is a region of fertile farmland stretching north from Dundee – Scotland's fourth-largest city – to the Highland border. It's an attractive area of broad straths (valleys) and low, green hills contrasting with the rich, red-brown soil of freshly ploughed fields. Romantic glens finger their way into the foothills of the Grampian Mountains, while the scenic coastline ranges from the red-sandstone cliffs of Arbroath to the long, sandy beaches around Montrose. This was the Pictish heartland of the 7th and 8th centuries, and many interesting Pictish symbol stones (see the boxed text, p249) survive here.

Apart from the crowds visiting Discovery Point in newly confident Dundee and the coach parties shuffling through Glamis Castle, Angus is a bit of a tourism backwater and a good place to escape the hordes.

DUNDEE

☎ 01382 / pop 144,000

London's Trafalgar Sq has Nelson on his column, Edinburgh's Princes St has its monument to Sir Walter Scott and Belfast has a statue of Queen Victoria outside City Hall. Dundee's City Sq, on the other hand, is graced – rather endearingly – by the bronze figure of Desperate Dan. Familiar to generations of British school children, Dan is one of the best-loved cartoon characters from the children's comic *The Dandy*, published by Dundee firm DC Thomson since 1937.

Dundee enjoys perhaps the finest location of any Scottish city, spreading along the northern shore of the Firth of Tay, and can boast tourist attractions of national importance in Discovery Point and the Verdant Works museum. Add in the attractive seaside suburb of Broughty Ferry, some lively nightlife and the Dundonians themselves – among the friendliest, most welcoming and most entertaining people you'll meet – and Dundee is definitely worth a stopover.

History

During the 19th century Dundee grew from its trading port origins to become a major player in the shipbuilding, whaling, textile and railway engineering industries. Dundonian firms owned and operated most of the jute mills in India, and the city's textile industry employed as many as 43,000 people – little wonder Dundee earned the nickname 'Juteopolis' (jute is a natural fibre used in making ropes and sacking).

Dundee is often called the city of the 'Three Js' – jute, jam and journalism. Ac-cording to legend, it was a Dundee woman Janet Keillor who invented marmalade in the late 18th century; her son founded the city's famous Keillor jam factory. Jute is no longer produced, and when the Keillor factory was taken over in 1988 production was transferred to England. Journalism still thrives, however, led by the family firm of DC Thomson. Best known for children's comics, such as *The Beano*, Thomson is now the city's largest employer.

In the late 19th and early 20th centuries Dundee was one of the richest cities in the country – there were more millionaires per head of population here than anywhere else in Britain – but the textile and engineering industries declined in the second half of the 20th century, leading to high unemployment and urban decay.

In the 1960s and '70s Dundee's cityscape was scarred by ugly blocks of flats, office buildings and shopping centres linked by unsightly concrete walkways – the view as you approach across the Tay Road Bridge does not look promising – and most visitors passed it by. Since the mid-1990s, however, Dundee has reinvented itself as a tourist destination, and a centre for banking, insurance and new industries, such as biotechnology. It also has more university students – one in seven of the population – than any other town in Europe, except Heidelberg.

Orientation

The compact city centre is focussed on City Sq, just 400m from the northern end of the Tay Road Bridge. The train station and Discovery Point are 300m south of City Sq; the bus station is 400m to the northeast along Seagate. Immediately north of the city centre is the prominent hill of Dundee Law (174m), and 4 miles to the east is Broughty Ferry, Dundee's seaside resort.

Information

You'll find banks with ATMs on High St and Murraygate.

Intercafé (per 10min 50p; ⏱ 9.30am-5.30pm Mon-Wed & Fri, to 7pm Thu, 9.15am-5.30pm Sat, 11am-4.30pm Sun; 🖥) On the 1st floor of Debenhams department store in the Overgate Shopping Centre.

Main post office (☎ 0845 722 3344; 4 Meadowside) A block north of the Overgate Shopping Centre.

Ninewells Hospital (☎ 660111; ⏱ casualty 24hr) At Menzieshill, west of the city centre.

DUNDEE

INFORMATION	Apex City Quay Hotel............ **13** D3	**ENTERTAINMENT**
Intercafe..................................**1** B3	Number 25.............................**14** A4	Caird Hall...............................**24** C3
Main Post Office.....................**2** B3	Queen's Hotel.......................**15** A4	Dundee Jazz Club............(see 25)
Tourist Information Centre		Dundee Rep Theatre...........**25** A4
(TIC)......................................**3** C3	**EATING**	Fat Sams................................**26** A3
Waterstones............................**4** B3	André's..............................(see 22)	Reading Rooms.....................**27** D2
	Deep Sea...............................**16** B4	
SIGHTS & ACTIVITIES	Fisher & Donaldson............**17** B3	**TRANSPORT**
Desperate Dan Statue...........**5** C3	Het Theatercafé................(see 25)	Arnold Clark..........................**28** D2
Discovery Point......................**6** C4	Jahangir.................................**18** A3	Bus Station............................**29** C2
Dundee Contemporary Arts....**7** B4	Jute Café-Bar.......................(see 7)	National Car Rental..............**30** C3
HM Frigate Unicorn...............**8** D3	Number 25.........................(see 14)	Travel Dundee.......................**31** B3
McManus Galleries.................**9** B2	Tesco Metro...........................**19** C2	
Old Steeple......................(see 10)	Twin City Café.....................**20** C3	
St Mary's Church.................**10** B3		
	DRINKING	
SLEEPING	Globe....................................**21** A3	
Aauld Steeple Guest House...**11** B4	Nether Inn............................**22** B4	
Abalree..................................**12** B3	Social....................................**23** A4	

Tourist Information Centre (TIC; ☎ 527527; www
.angusanddundee.co.uk; 21 Castle St; ☑ 9am-6pm Mon-
Sat, noon-4pm Sun Jun-Sep, 9am-5pm Mon-Sat Oct-May)
Just east of City Sq; sells CalMac ferry tickets, and Scottish
Citylink and National Express bus tickets.
Waterstones (☎ 200322; 35 Commercial St; ☑ 9am-
6pm Mon-Wed, Fri & Sat, to 7pm Thu, 11am-5pm Sun)
Dundee's biggest bookshop.

Sights
CITY CENTRE
The heart of Dundee is **City Sq**, flanked to the
south by the 1930s façade of **Caird Hall** (p245),
gifted to the city by a textile magnate and
now home to the City Chambers. A more
recent addition to the square, unveiled in
2001, is a bronze statue of **Desperate Dan**, the

lantern-jawed hero of the children's comic
The Dandy (he's clutching a copy in his
right hand), which has been published in
Dundee since 1937.

Pedestrianised High St leads west into
Nethergate, flanked to the north by **St Mary's
Church**. Most of the church dates from the
19th century, but the **Old Steeple** was built
around 1460.

The focus for the city's emerging Cultural
Quarter – the city council's new name for
the West End – is **Dundee Contemporary Arts**
(☎ 606220; www.dca.org.uk; Nethergate; admission free;
☑ galleries & shop 10.30am-5.30pm Tue, Wed, Sat & Sun,
to 8pm Thu & Fri, print studio 11am-9pm Tue-Thu, to 6pm
Fri & Sat), a centre for modern art, design and
cinema. The galleries here exhibit work by

contemporary UK and international artists, and there are printmakers' studios where you can watch artists at work, or even take part in craft demonstrations and workshops. There's also the Jute Café-Bar (p236).

DISCOVERY POINT

The three masts of Captain Robert Falcon Scott's famous polar expedition vessel the **RRS Discovery** (☎ 201245; www.rrsdiscovery.com; Discovery Quay; adult/child £6.45/3.85; ⏰ 10am-6pm Mon-Sat, 11am-6pm Sun Apr-Oct, 10am-5pm Mon-Sat, 11am-5pm Sun Nov-Mar) dominate the riverside to the south of the city centre. The ship was built in Dundee in 1900, with a wooden hull at least half a metre thick to survive the pack ice, and sailed for the Antarctic in 1901, where she spent two winters trapped in the ice. From 1931 on she was laid up in London where her condition steadily deteriorated, until she was rescued by the efforts of Peter Scott (son of Robert) and the Maritime Trust, and restored to her 1925 condition. In 1986 she was given a berth in her home port of Dundee, where she became a symbol of the city's regeneration.

Exhibitions and audiovisual displays in the main building provide a fascinating history of both the ship and Antarctic exploration, but *Discovery* herself – afloat in a protected dock – is the star attraction. You can visit the bridge, the galley and the mahogany-panelled officers' wardroom, and poke your nose into the cabins used by Scott and his crew.

A joint ticket that gives entry to both Discovery Point and the Verdant Works costs £10.95/7 per adult/child.

HM FRIGATE UNICORN

Unlike the polished and much-restored *Discovery*, Dundee's other floating tourist attraction retains the authentic atmosphere of a salty old sailing ship. Built in 1824, the 46-gun **HM Frigate Unicorn** (☎ 200893; Victoria Dock; adult/child £4/3; ⏰ 10am-5pm Apr-Sep, noon-4pm Wed-Fri, 10am-4pm Sat & Sun Oct-Mar) is the oldest British-built ship still afloat – perhaps because it never saw action. By the mid-19th century sailing ships were outclassed by steam and the *Unicorn* served as a gunpowder store, then later as a training vessel. When it was proposed to break up the ship for scrap in the 1960s, a preservation society was formed.

Wandering around the four decks gives you an excellent impression of what it must have been like for the crew forced to live in such cramped conditions. The *Unicorn* is berthed in Victoria Dock, just northeast of the Tay Road Bridge. The entry price includes a guided tour (also available in French and German).

VERDANT WORKS

One of the finest industrial museums in Europe, the **Verdant Works** (☎ 225282; www.verdant works.com; West Henderson's Wynd; adult/child £5.95/3.85; ⏰ 10am-6pm Mon-Sat, 11am-6pm Sun Apr-Oct, 10.30am-4.30pm Wed-Sat, 11am-4.30pm Sun Nov-Mar) explores the history of Dundee's jute industry. Housed in a restored jute mill complete with original machinery still in working condition, the museum's interactive exhibits and computer displays follow the raw material from its origins in India through to the manufacture of a wide range of finished products, from sacking to rope to wagon covers for the pioneers of the American West.

MCMANUS GALLERIES

Housed in a solid Victorian Gothic building designed by Gilbert Scott in 1867, **McManus Galleries** (☎ 432084; www.mcmanus.co.uk; Albert Sq; admission free; ⏰ 10.30am-5pm Mon-Sat, 12.30-4pm Sun) contains the city's museum and art collection. The exhibits cover the history of the city from the Iron Age to the present day, plus an impressive display of Scottish Victorian paintings, furniture and silver. Look out for the display on William McGonagall, Scotland's worst poet, whose lines commemorating the Tay Rail Bridge disaster of 1879 are truly awful.

DUNDEE LAW

It's worth making the climb up **Dundee Law** (174m) for great views of the city, the two Tay bridges, and across to Fife. The **Tay Rail Bridge** – at just over 2 miles long, it was the world's longest when it was built – was completed in 1887, replacing an earlier bridge whose stumps can be seen alongside. The original bridge collapsed during a storm in 1879, less than two years after it was built, taking a train and 75 lives along with it. The 1.5-mile **Tay Road Bridge** was opened in 1966.

Dundee Law is a short walk northwest of the city centre, along Constitution Rd.

NORTHEAST SCOTLAND

Festivals & Events

If you're around in early July, look out for the **Dundee Blues Bonanza** (www.dundeebluesbonan za.co.uk), a two-day festival of free blues and rock (second weekend in July).

Sleeping

Most of Dundee's city-centre hotels are business-oriented, and offer lower rates on weekends. The main concentrations of B&Bs are along Broughty Ferry Rd and Arborath Rd east of the city centre, and on Perth Rd to the west. If you don't fancy a night in the city, consider staying at nearby Broughty Ferry (p246).

BUDGET

Abalree (☎ 223867; 20 Union St; s/d £20/34) This is a basic B&B – there are no rooms with en suites, though all have TV – but it couldn't be more central, close to both train and bus stations. This makes it very popular, so book ahead.

University of Abertay (☎ 308059; accommo@aber tay.ac.uk; Bell St; apt per person per night £15; ☼ Jun-Aug; P) During the summer holidays the university offers self-catering apartments for two to eight people in various parts of the city.

Riverview Caravan Park (☎ 535471; riverviewcara van@btInternet.com; Marine Dr, Monifieth; tent or camper-van sites £10-12; ☼ Apr-Oct) The nearest camping ground to the city is attractively sited near the beach, 5 miles east of the city centre.

MIDRANGE

Aauld Steeple Guest House (☎ 200302; 94 Nethergate; s/d £23/40; ✗) Just as central as the Abalree, but a bit more upmarket, the Aauld Steeple has spacious double and family rooms, some with views of St Mary's Church.

Number 25 (☎ 200399; www.g1group.co.uk; 25 South Tay St; r £60) The fashionable Number 25 restaurant, set in an elegant Georgian town house in the heart of the city's cultural quarter, has four luxurious en-suite bedrooms upstairs.

Shaftesbury Hotel (☎ 669216; www.shaftesbury -hotel.co.uk; 1 Hyndford St; s/d £66/80; ✗) The family-run, 12-room Shaftesbury is a Victorian mansion built for a jute baron and has many authentic period features, including a fine marble fireplace in the dining room. It's 1.5 miles west of the city centre, just off Perth Rd.

Grampian Hotel (☎ 667785; www.grampianhotel .com; 295 Perth Rd; s/d £45/70; P) The Grampian is

a small and welcoming hotel set in a restored Victorian town house with six spacious bedrooms (all en suite), just five minutes' walk from the West End.

Errolbank Guest House (☎ 462118; 9 Dalgleish Rd; s/d £32/50; P ✗) A mile east of the city centre, just north of the road to Broughty Ferry, Errolbank is a lovely Victorian house, with small, tastefully furnished en-suite rooms.

Queen's Hotel (☎ 322515; www.queenshotel-dundee .com; 160 Nethergate; s/d £72/92; P ✗) Despite having been Best Westernised, this grand Victorian hotel in the heart of lively West End retains some period charm, and is only a few minutes' walk from the city centre.

TOP END

Apex City Quay Hotel (☎ 202404; www.apexhotels .co.uk; 1 West Victoria Dock Rd; s/d from £70/80; P ✗ 🖭) Though it looks pretty bleak from the outside, the Apex overlooks the city's redeveloped waterfront and sports the sort of stylish, spacious, sofa-equipped rooms that make you want to lounge around all evening munching chocolate in front of the TV. If you can drag yourself away from your room, there are spa treatments, saunas and Japanese hot tubs to enjoy.

Eating

Jute Café-Bar (☎ 909246; Dundee Contemporary Arts, 152 Nethergate; mains £9-13; ☼ food served noon-4pm & 5-9.30pm) The industrial-chic café-bar in the Dundee Contemporary Arts centre (p234) serves excellent pasta dishes and salads, as well as more adventurous fusion cuisine; shame that the picture-window view over the Tay is blocked by a few ugly buildings.

André's (☎ 224455; 134a Nethergate; 2-course lunch £7, mains £7-11; ☼ noon-3pm & 5-11pm Tue-Sat, 1-11pm Sun) A quaint little corner that appears to have been fashioned out of someone's attic bedroom, André's nevertheless offers an authentic taste of France with a small, ever-changing menu of French classics ranging from onion soup to *boeuf bourguignon*.

Number 25 (☎ 200399; 25 South Tay St; mains £5-9; ☼ food served noon-9pm Sun-Thu, noon-7pm Fri & Sat) Formerly Howie's, this elegant style bar set in a Georgian town house offers a mellow, candle-lit dining room serving good-value bistro cuisine, including Caesar salad, gourmet burgers and smoked salmon fish cakes.

(Continued on page 245)

MARTIN MOOS

Greyfriars Bobby statue (p84), Edinburgh

Edinburgh's Old Town (p78) from Arthur's Seat

JONATHAN SMITH

JONATHAN SMITH

Calton Hill (p87), Edinburgh

Posters for Edinburgh International Festival (p95)

GARETH MCCORMACK

Horse Shoe pub (p136), Glasgow

Quirkily attired Wellington Monument, Gallery of Modern Art (p123), Glasgow

Glasgow Science Centre (p122)

Glasgow Cathedral (p125)

St Abbs (p151), Borders region

NICHOLAS REUSS

Kelso Abbey (p152), southern Scotland

PAUL BIGLAND

Glen Rosa, Isle of Arran (p166)

GRAEME CORNWALLIS

Crail harbour (p212), East Neuk, Fife

GLENN BEANLAND

Old Course (p209), St Andrews

MARTIN MOOS

Forth Bridge (p112), Queensferry

NEIL WILSON

Water wheel, Glen Clova Hotel (p250),
Angus Glens

Glamis Castle (p247), Angus

Old fishing village near Aberdeen harbour (p254)

Malt whisky trail (p269), northeast Scotland

Tobermory harbour (p302), Isle of Mull

Kildalton Chapel (p288), Isle of Islay

GRAEME CORNWALLIS

Highland cattle, Isle of Mull (p300)

MARTIN MOOS

DENNIS JOHNSON

Loch Ness monster (p323)

Steall waterfall (p340), Glen Nevis

MARTIN MOOS

ANN CECIL

Downtown Inverness (p313), the
Highlands capital

Glencoe Lochan (p333), west Highlands

GARETH MCCORMACK

Skara Brae (p410), Orkney Islands

Eshaness (p427), Shetland Islands

Ardvreck Castle (p365) on Loch Assynt,
northern Highlands

Callanish Standing Stones (p390), Lewis, Outer Hebrides

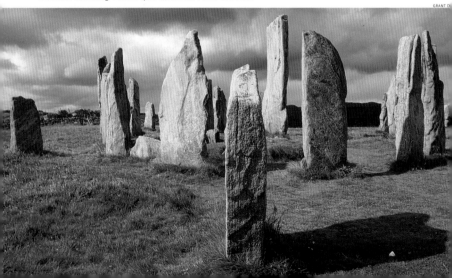

(Continued from page 236)

Het Theatercafé (☎ 206699; Tay Sq; mains £5-11; ✆ café 10am-late, restaurant noon-3pm & 5-10pm Mon-Sat) The city's arty types hang out in this Continental-style café-bar and restaurant in the foyer at the Dundee Rep Theatre. Great sandwiches and pizza, as well as tasty steaks, fish cakes and veggie dishes.

Twin City Café (☎ 223662; 4 City Sq; mains £5-7.50; ✆ 7.30am-6pm Mon-Sat, 10.30am-5pm Sun) A pleasant café on the main square with outdoor tables in summer, Twin City has good salads and sandwiches, including tasty veggie stuff like stuffed vine leaves and hummus wraps.

Jahangir (☎ 202022; 1 Session St; mains £7-10; ✆ 5pm-midnight) It's worth going to this curry house for the décor alone – pure Hollywood Moghul, with an over-the-top tent and a tinkling fountain inhabited by live goldfish and carp (no, they're not on the menu).

Fisher & Donaldson (12 Whitehall St; ✆ 6.30am-5pm Mon-Sat) There's an excellent tearoom in this upmarket bakery and patisserie.

Deep Sea (81 Nethergate; ✆ 9.30am-6.30pm Mon-Sat) Dundee's best fish and chips can be found here.

Tesco Metro (Murraygate; ✆ 7am-midnight Mon-Fri, to 10pm Sat, 10am-7pm Sun) Self-caterers should head to this supermarket.

Drinking

There are many lively pubs, especially in the West End and along West Port.

Nether Inn (☎ 349970; 134 Nethergate) This large, stylish inn, with its comfy couches, pool table and drinks promos, is popular with students.

Social (☎ 202070; 10 South Tay St) A lively style bar with a separate dining area.

Globe (☎ 224712; 53-57 West Port) Serves good bar meals from noon to 7.30pm (6pm Sunday) and often has live music.

Entertainment

Dundee's nightlife may not be as hot as Glasgow's, but there are lots of places to go – pick up a copy of the free *Accent* what's-on guide from the TIC, or check out the Events and Entertainment section of www.dundee.com. Tickets for most events are on sale at the Dundee Contemporary Arts centre (p234).

Caird Hall (☎ 434940; www.cairdhall.co.uk; 6 City Sq; ✆ box office 9am-4.30pm Mon-Fri, 9.30am-1.30pm Sat) The Caird Hall hosts regular concerts of classical music, as well as organ recitals, rock bands, dances, fetes and fairs. Check its website for details of coming events.

Dundee Rep Theatre (☎ 223530; www.dundee reptheatre.co.uk; Tay Sq; ✆ box office 10am-6pm or start of performance) Dundee's main venue for the performing arts, the Rep is home to Scotland's only full-time repertory company and to the Scottish Dance Theatre.

Fat Sams (☎ 228181; www.fatsams.co.uk; 31 South Ward Rd; admission £4-7; ✆ 10.30pm-2.30am Tue-Sun) Fat Sams has been around for more than 20 years, but has recently had a facelift and is again one of the city's most popular clubs, with nights of '80s and '90s dance hits pulling in a young crowd (including lots of students from St Andrews University).

Reading Rooms (☎ 07905 353301; www.thereading rooms.co.uk; 57 Blackscroft; admission £3-8; ✆ 8.30pm or 10.30pm-2.30am Wed-Sat) Dundee's hippest venue is the place to be for some of Scotland's best club nights, as well as being the best place in the city for live music.

Dundee Jazz Club (☎ 206699; Het Theatercafé, Dundee Rep Theatre, Tay Sq; admission £4.50; ✆ 10.30pm-late Fri) The Jazz Club brings the top names in Scottish jazz to the foyer of the Dundee Rep Theatre on Friday nights.

Getting There & Away

The Tay Road Bridge linking Dundee and Fife costs 80p per car southbound, but is toll-free for northbound traffic.

AIR

Two and a half miles west of the city centre, **Dundee Airport** (☎ 662200; Riverside Dr) has daily scheduled services to London City airport with ScotAirways. A taxi to the airport takes five minutes and costs £2.50.

BUS

The bus company **National Express** (☎ 0870 580 8080; www.nationalexpress.com) operates two direct services a day from London to Dundee (£34, 10½ hours).

Scottish Citylink (☎ 0870 550 5050; www.citylink.co .uk) has hourly buses from Dundee to Edinburgh (£9, 1¾ hours), Glasgow (£9.40, 2¼ hours), Perth (£4.20, 35 minutes) and Aberdeen (£9, two hours). Some Aberdeen buses travel via Arbroath, others via Forfar. Change at Perth for buses to Oban (£17, 6¾ hours).

Strathtay Scottish (☎ 227201) operates buses to Perth (one hour, hourly), Blairgowrie (one hour, hourly), Forfar (40 minutes, once or twice an hour), Kirriemuir (one hour, half-hourly), Brechin (1¼ hours, 10 daily, change at Forfar) and Arbroath (one hour, half-hourly). It sells a Day Rover ticket (adult/child £5.60/3.60) that allows unlimited travel on its buses for one day.

Stagecoach Fife (☎ 01334-474328) bus 99 runs to St Andrews (40 minutes, every 20 minutes Monday to Saturday, hourly on Sunday).

TRAIN

Trains run to Dundee from Edinburgh (£17, 1¼ hours) and Glasgow (£22, 1½ hours) at least once an hour, Monday to Saturday; hourly on Sunday from Edinburgh, every two hours on Sunday from Glasgow.

Trains from Dundee to Aberdeen (£20, 1¼ hours) travel via Arbroath and Stonehaven. There are around two trains an hour, fewer on Sunday.

Getting Around

The city centre is compact, and is easy to get around on foot. For information on local public transport, call **Travel Dundee** (☎ 201121; www.traveldundee.co.uk; Forum Shopping Centre, 92 Commercial St; ◷ 9.15am-4.55pm Mon-Fri, 10am-3.55pm Sat). City bus fares cost 45p to £1.10 depending on distance; buy your ticket from the driver (exact fare only – no change given).

Phone **Discovery Taxis** (☎ 732111) if you need a taxi. If you'd like to drive yourself, rental companies in Dundee include **Arnold Clark** (☎ 225382; East Dock St) and **National Car Rental** (☎ 224037; 45-53 Gellatly St).

BROUGHTY FERRY

☎ 01382

This attractive seaside suburb, known locally as 'The Ferry', lies 4 miles east of Dundee city centre. It has a castle, a long, sandy beach, and a number of good places to eat and drink, and is handy for the golf courses at nearby Carnoustie.

Sights

Broughty Castle Museum (☎ 436916; Castle Green; admission free; ◷ 10am-4pm Mon-Sat, 12.30-4pm Sun Apr-Sep, 10am-4pm Tue-Sat, 12.30-4pm Sun Oct-Mar) occupies a 16th-century tower house that looms imposingly over the harbour, guarding the entrance to the Firth of Tay, and includes a fascinating exhibit on Dundee's whaling industry.

Sleeping

Fisherman's Tavern (☎ 775941; www.fishermans -tavern-hotel.co.uk; 10-16 Fort St; s/d £39/62; ✕) A delightful 17th-century terraced cottage just a few paces from the seafront, the Fisherman's was converted to a pub in 1827. It now has 11 stylishly modern rooms, most with en suite, and an atmospheric pub-restaurant (see Eating & Drinking).

Brook House (☎ 779166; www.brookhouseguest house.co.uk; 86 Brook St; s/d £30/50; P ✕) Set in a spacious Edwardian villa that was once the village doctor's house, this cosy family B&B offers four comfortable en-suite rooms just a few blocks west of Broughty Ferry train station.

Invermark House (☎ 739430; enquiries@invermark hotel.com; 23 Monifieth Rd; s/d £30/45; P ✕) Invermark is a grand Victorian villa set in its own grounds, built for a jute baron in the mid-19th century, with five large en-suite bedrooms and an elegant dining room with a view of the gardens.

Hotel Broughty Ferry (☎ 480027; www.hotel broughtyferry.com; 16 W Queen St; s/d £60/80; P ✕ ☎) Doesn't look like much from the outside, but this is the Ferry's swankiest place to stay, with 16 beautifully decorated bedrooms, a sauna and solarium, and a small, heated pool. It's only a five-minute stroll from the waterfront.

Eating & Drinking

Fisherman's Tavern (☎ 775941; 10-16 Fort St; mains £6-9; ◷ lunch & dinner) The Fisherman's – a maze of cosy nooks and open fireplaces situated in a 17th-century cottage – is a lively little pub where you can wash down fresh local seafood with a choice of Scottish real ales.

Ship Inn (☎ 779176; 121 Fisher St; mains £9-14; ◷ food served noon-2pm & 5-10.30pm Mon-Fri, noon-10.30pm Sat & Sun) Overlooking the seafront around the corner from the Fisherman's is the snug, wood-panelled, 19th-century Ship Inn, which serves top-notch dishes ranging from gourmet haddock and chips to venison steaks.

Visocchi's (☎ 779297; 40 Gray St; mains £5-7; ◷ 9.30am-7.30pm Mon-Thu, to 9.30pm Fri & Sat, to 5.30pm Sun) Visocchi's – a 70-year-old institution – is a traditional, family-run Italian café that sells delicious homemade ice cream, good coffee, and a range of pasta dishes and pizza.

Getting There & Away

Travel Dundee buses 7 to 12 run from Dundee High St to Broughty Ferry (20 minutes) several times an hour from Monday to Saturday, and hourly on Sunday. There is also an infrequent train service between Dundee and Broughty Ferry (seven minutes, four or five daily Monday to Saturday), with two early morning and two evening services timed to suit commuters.

GLAMIS CASTLE & VILLAGE

Looking every inch the Scottish Baronial castle, with its roofline sprouting a forest of pointed turrets and battlements, **Glamis Castle** (☎ 01307-840393; adult/child £7/3.80; ◷ 10am-6pm mid-Mar–Oct, noon-4pm Nov & Dec, closed 22 Dec–mid-Mar) was the legendary setting for Shakespeare's *Macbeth*. A royal residence since 1372, it is the family home of the earls of Strathmore and Kinghorne – the Queen Mother (born Elizabeth Bowes-Lyon; 1900–2002) spent her childhood at Glamis (pronounced 'glams') and Princess Margaret (the Queen's sister; 1930–2002) was born here.

The five-storey, L-shaped castle was given to the Lyon family in 1372, but was significantly altered in the 17th century. Inside, the most impressive room is the drawing room, with its vaulted plasterwork ceiling. There's a display of armour and weaponry in the haunted crypt and frescoes in the chapel (also haunted). Duncan's Hall is where King Duncan was murdered in *Macbeth*. You can also look around the royal apartments, including the Queen Mother's bedroom. The one-hour guided tours depart every 15 minutes (last tour at 4.30pm).

The **Angus Folk Museum** (NTS; ☎ 01307-840288; Kirkwynd, Glamis; adult/child £5/4; ◷ 11am-5pm Mon-Sat, 1-5pm Sun Jul & Aug, noon-5pm Fri-Tue Easter-Jun & Sep), in a row of 18th-century cottages just off the flower-bedecked square in Glamis village, houses a fine collection of domestic and agricultural relics.

Glamis Castle is 12 miles north of Dundee. There are two to four buses a day from Dundee (35 minutes) to Glamis, run by Strathtay Buses; some continue to Kirriemuir.

ARBROATH

☎ 01241 / pop 22,800

Arbroath is an old-fashioned seaside resort and fishing harbour, home of the famous Arbroath smokie (a form of smoked haddock) – no visit is complete without buying a pair of smokies from one of the many fish shops and eating them with your fingers while sitting beside the harbour. Yum.

The town has its own **TIC** (☎ 872609; Market Pl; ◷ 9.30am-5.30pm Mon-Sat, 10am-3pm Sun Jun-Aug, 9am-5pm Mon-Fri, 10am-5pm Sat Apr, May & Sep, 9am-5pm Mon-Fri, 10am-3pm Sat Oct-Mar), supermarket, post office and several banks with ATMs.

Sights & Activities

The magnificent, red-sandstone ruins of **Arbroath Abbey** (HS; ☎ 878756; Abbey St; adult/child £3.30/1.30; ◷ 9.30am-6.30pm Apr-Sep, to 4.30pm Oct-Mar), founded in 1178 by King William the Lion, dominate the town centre. It is thought that Bernard of Linton, the abbot here in the early 14th century, wrote the famous Declaration of Arbroath in 1320 asserting Scotland's right to independence from England (see the boxed text, p32).

The **Arbroath Museum** (☎ 875598; Ladyloan; admission free; ◷ 10am-5pm Mon-Sat Sep-Jun, 10am-5pm Mon-Sat, 2-5pm Sun Jul & Aug), housed in the elegant Signal Tower, covers local history, including the textile and fishing industries. The tower was originally used to communicate with the construction team working on the Bell Rock Lighthouse 12 miles offshore, which was built between 1807 and 1811 by the famous engineer Robert Stevenson (grandfather of writer Robert Louis Stevenson).

At St Vigeans, about a mile north of the town centre, is the excellent **St Vigeans Museum** (HS; ☎ 878756; admission free; ◷ key available 9.30am-6.30pm Apr-Sep, to 4.30pm Mon-Sat Oct-Mar). Its collection of Pictish and medieval sculptured stones includes crosses, and human and animal carvings. The museum is unstaffed – call Arbroath Abbey to arrange access; the key is kept at cottage No 7.

If you fancy catching your own fish, the **Marie Dawn** (☎ 873957) and **Girl Katherine II** (☎ 874510) offer three-hour sea-angling trips (usually from 2pm to 5pm) out of Arbroath harbour for £14 per person, including tackle and bait.

The coast northeast of Arbroath consists of dramatic red-sandstone cliffs riven by inlets, caves and natural arches. An excellent walk follows a path along the top of the cliffs for 3 miles to the quaint fishing village of **Auchmithie**.

Sleeping & Eating

Harbour Nights Guest House (☎ 434343; www.har
bournights-scotland.com; 4 Shore; s/d from £40/50; ✗)
With a superb location overlooking the harbour, five stylishly decorated bedrooms and
a gourmet breakfast menu, Harbour Nights
is our favourite place to stay in Arbroath.
Rooms 2 and 3, with harbour views, are a
bit more expensive (doubles £55 to £65),
but well worth asking for when booking.

Scurdy House (☎ 872417; 33 Marketgate; s/d £25/40)
Colourful flower baskets and a pastel blue
façade single out this spick-and-span B&B,
set in a listed fisherman's cottage halfway
between harbour and abbey.

Old Vicarage (☎ 430475; www.theoldvicaragebandb
.co.uk; 2 Seaton Rd; s/d £28/45; P ✗) The three en-
suite bedrooms in this attractive Victorian
villa have a pleasantly old-fashioned atmosphere, and the extensive breakfast menu includes Arbroath smokies. The house is on a
quiet street close to the start of the cliff-top
walk to Auchmithie.

Sugar & Spice Tearoom (☎ 437500; 9-13 High
St; mains £4-6; ☽ 10am-4pm Mon-Sat, noon-4pm Sun)
With its flounces, frills and black-and-white
uniformed waitresses, this chintzy tearoom
verges on the twee. However, the place is
child-friendly – there's an indoor play area
and a Wendy house out the back – and the
tea and scones are sublime. You can even
try an Arbroath smokie, grilled with lemon
butter.

But'n'Ben Restaurant (☎ 877223; 1 Auchmithie;
mains £6-10; ☽ noon-3pm, 4-5.30pm & 7-10pm Mon
& Wed-Sat, noon-5.30pm Sun) Set above the harbour in Auchmithie, this cosy, tartan-clad
cottage restaurant serves the best of local
seafood – the Arbroath smokie pancakes
are recommended.

Gordon's Restaurant (☎ 830364; Main St, Inverkeillor; 3-course lunch/dinner £21/33; ☽ noon-1.45pm Wed-
Sun, 7-9pm Tue-Sun) Six miles north of Arbroath,
in the tiny and unpromising-looking village of Inverkeillor, is this hidden gem – an
intimate and rustic eatery serving gourmet-
quality Scottish cuisine.

Getting There & Away

There are frequent buses from Dundee to
Arbroath (see p245), but the scenic train
journey along the coast (£4, 20 minutes,
half-hourly) is the better option. Trains continue from Arbroath to Aberdeen (£16, 50
minutes) via Montrose and Stonehaven.

GN Wishart (☎ 828747) bus 140 runs from
Arbroath to Auchmithie (15 minutes, six
daily Monday to Friday, three daily on Saturday and Sunday).

MONTROSE
☎ 01674 / pop 11,800
Despite its attractive seaside setting, broad
main street of Victorian buildings, and
reputation as a golfing and seaside resort,
Montrose exudes an austere and slightly
down-at-heel atmosphere. It sits at the mouth
of the River South Esk, where its industrial
harbour serves the North Sea oil industry,
and is backed by the broad, tidal mud flats
of Montrose Basin, a rich feeding ground
for thousands of resident and migrant birds.

Montrose Basin Wildlife Centre (☎ 676336; Rossie
Braes; adult/child £3/2; ☽ 10.30am-5pm Apr-Oct, to 4pm
Nov-Mar) at the southern edge of town has indoor and outdoor hides, and viewing platforms with high-powered binoculars and
remote-controlled TV cameras where you
can zoom in on the local wildlife. In summer
you can see curlews, oystercatchers and eider
ducks – and perhaps an otter if you're lucky –
and in autumn the basin is invaded by huge
flocks of pink-footed and greylag geese.

Prettier than Montrose's town beach is the
2-mile strand of **Lunan Bay** to the south, overlooked by the dramatic ruin of **Red Castle**.

Montrose lies on the Dundee to Aberdeen
railway line.

FORFAR
☎ 01307 / pop 13,200
Forfar, the county town of Angus, is the
home of Scotland's answer to the Cornish
pasty: the Forfar bridie. A shortcrust pastry turnover filled with cooked minced beef,
onion and gravy, it was invented in Forfar
in the early 19th century. If you fancy trying
one, head for **James McLaren & Son** (☎ 462762; 8
The Cross; ☽ 8am-4.30pm Mon-Wed, Fri & Sat, to 1pm Thu),
a family bakery bang in the centre of town,
which has been selling tasty, home-baked
bridies since 1893.

Strathtay Scottish buses from Dundee to
Kirriemuir travel via Forfar. See p245 for
details.

ABERLEMNO
Five miles northeast of Forfar, on the B9134,
are the mysterious **Aberlemno Pictish stones**,
some of Scotland's finest sculptured stones.

PICTISH SYMBOL STONES

The mysterious carved stones that dot the landscape of eastern Scotland are the legacy of the warrior tribes who inhabited these lands 2000 years ago. The Romans occupied the southern half of Britain from 55 BC to AD 410, but the region to the north of the firths of Forth and Clyde – known as Caledonia – was abandoned as being too dangerous, sealed off behind the ramparts of the Antonine Wall and Hadrian's Wall.

Caledonia was the homeland of the Picts, a collection of tribes named by the Romans for their habit of painting or tattooing their bodies. In the 9th century they were culturally absorbed by the Scots, leaving behind only a few archaeological remains, a scattering of Pictish place names beginning with 'Pit', and hundreds of mysterious carved stones decorated with intricate symbols, mainly in northeast Scotland. The capital of the ancient Southern Pictish kingdom is said to have been at Forteviot in Strathearn, and Pictish symbol stones are to be found throughout this area and all the way up the eastern coast of Scotland into Sutherland and Caithness.

It is thought that the stones were set up to record Pictish lineages and alliances, but no-one is sure exactly how the system worked. They are decorated with unusual symbols, including z-rods (lightning bolt?), circles (the sun?), double discs (hand mirror?) and fantastical creatures, as well as figures of warriors on horseback, hunting scenes and (on the later stones) Christian symbols.

Local tourist offices provide a free leaflet titled the *Angus Pictish Trail*, which will guide you to the main Pictish sites in the area. The finest assemblage of stones in their natural outdoor setting is at **Aberlemno** (opposite), and there are excellent indoor collections at **St Vigeans Museum** (p247) and the **Meigle Museum** (p230). The **Pictavia** interpretive centre at Brechin (p252) provides a good introduction to the Picts, and is worth a look before you visit the stones.

The Pictish Trail by Anthony Jackson lists 11 driving tours, while *The Symbol Stones of Scotland* by the same author provides more detail on the history and meaning of the Pictish stones.

By the roadside there are three 7th- to 9th-century slabs with various symbols, including the z-rod and double disc, and in the churchyard at the bottom of the hill there's a magnificent 8th-century stone displaying a Celtic cross, interlace decoration, entwined beasts and, on the reverse, scenes of the Battle of Nechtansmere (see the boxed text, above). The stones are covered up from November to March; otherwise there's free access at all times.

KIRRIEMUIR

☎ 01575 / pop 6000

Known as the Wee Red Town because of its close-packed, red-sandstone houses, Kirriemuir is famed as the birthplace of JM Barrie (1860–1937), writer and creator of the much-loved *Peter Pan*. A willowy bronze statue of the 'boy who wouldn't grow up' graces the intersection of Bank and High Sts.

The town has a **TIC** (☎ 574097; Cumberland Close; ☻ 10am-5pm Mon-Sat Apr-Sep), banks, ATMs and a post office.

Sights

JM Barrie's Birthplace (NTS; ☎ 572646; 9 Brechin Rd; adult/child £5/4; ☻ 11am-5pm Mon-Sat, 1-5pm Sun Jul & Aug, noon-5pm Sat-Wed Easter-Jun & Sep) is the town's big attraction, a place of pilgrimage for *Peter Pan* fans from all over the world. The two-storey house where Barrie was born has been furnished in period style, and preserves Barrie's writing desk and the wash house at the back that served as his first 'theatre'. The ticket also gives admission to the **Camera Obscura** (adult/child £3/2; ☻ 11am-5pm Mon-Sat, 1-5pm Sun Jul & Aug, noon-5pm Sat-Wed Easter-Jun & Sep) on the hill-top northeast of the town centre, gifted to the town by Barrie himself.

The old Town House opposite the *Peter Pan* statue dates from 1604 and houses the **Gateway to the Glens Museum** (☎ 575479; admission free; ☻ 10am-5pm Mon-Wed, Fri & Sat, 1-5pm Thu), a useful introduction to local history, geology and wildlife for those planning to explore the Angus Glens.

Sleeping & Eating

Airlie Arms Hotel (☎ 572847; www.airliearms-hotel .co.uk; St Malcolm's Wynd; s/d £35/60; ℗ ✗) This attractive old coaching inn, just a few minutes' walk from the TIC, has luxurious en-suite rooms and a stylish, candle-lit café-bar called the **Wynd** (mains £6-7; ☻ 8am-9.30pm).

NORTHEAST SCOTLAND

Crepto B&B (☎ 572746; Kinnordy Pl; s/d £25/44; P ☒) You'll get a warm welcome at this modern B&B, tucked away in a quiet cul-de-sac 10 minutes' walk from the town centre (head along Glengate and Kinnordy Rd).

Visocchi's (☎ 572115; 37 High St) A proudly old-fashioned family café that serves good coffee and great homemade ice cream.

Getting There & Away

Strathtay Scottish operates bus services from Dundee to Kirriemuir (£5, 1¼ hours, hourly Monday to Saturday, every two hours Sunday) via Glamis (20 minutes, two daily Monday to Saturday) and Forfar (25 minutes).

ANGUS GLENS

The northern part of Angus is bounded by the Grampian Mountains, where five scenic valleys – Glens Isla, Prosen, Clova, Lethnot and Esk – cut into the hills along the southern edge of the Cairngorms National Park (see p325). All have attractive scenery, though each glen has its own distinct personality: Glen Clova and Glen Esk are the most beautiful, while Glen Lethnot is the least frequented. You can get detailed information on walks in the Angus Glens from the TIC in Kirriemuir (p249) and from the Glen Clova Hotel in Glen Clova (right).

Glen Isla

At Bridge of Craigisla at the foot of the glen, 3 miles north of Alyth (p230) is a spectacular, 24m waterfall called **Reekie Linn**; the name Reekie (Scottish for 'smoky') comes from the billowing spray that rises from the falls.

A 5-mile hike beyond the road-end at Auchavan leads into the wild and mountainous upper reaches of the glen, where **Caenlochan National Nature Reserve** protects rare alpine flora on the high plateau.

A **Royal Mail postbus** (☎ 0845 774 0740) runs from Blairgowrie to Auchavan via Alyth (once daily, except Sunday).

Glen Prosen

Near the foot of Glen Prosen, 6 miles north of Kirriemuir, there's a good forest walk up to the **Airlie monument** on Tulloch Hill (380m); start from the eastern road, about a mile beyond Dykehead.

From Glenprosen Lodge, at the head of the glen, a five-hour (9 miles) hike along the

Kilbo Path leads over a pass between Mayar (928m) and Driesh (947m), and descends to Glendoll Lodge at the head of Glen Clova.

Glen Clova

The longest and loveliest of the Angus Glens stretches north from Kirriemuir for 20 miles, broad and pastoral in its lower reaches but growing narrower and craggier as the steep, heather-clad Highland hills close in around its head.

The minor road beyond the Glen Clova Hotel ends at a Forestry Commission car park (£1.50 per car) with toilets and a picnic area, which is the trailhead for a number of strenuous hikes through the hills to the north.

Jock's Road is an ancient footpath that was much used by cattle drovers, soldiers, smugglers and shepherds in the 18th and 19th centuries; 700 Jacobite soldiers passed this way on their retreat in 1746, en route to final defeat at Culloden. From the car park the path strikes west along Glen Doll, then north across a high plateau (900m) before descending steeply into Glen Callater and on to Braemar (15 miles, allow five to seven hours). The route is hard going and should not be attempted in winter; you'll need OS 1:50,000 maps Nos 43 and 44.

An easier, but still strenuous, circular hike starts from the Glen Clova Hotel, making a circuit of the scenic corrie (glacial hollow) that encloses **Loch Brandy** (6 miles, four hours).

The **Glen Clova Hotel** (☎ 01575-550350; www .clova.com; Glen Clova; s/d £40/70, mains £6-8; ☺ food served noon-8.15pm Sun-Thu, to 8.45pm Fri & Sat; P) is a lovely old drover's inn near the head of the glen, and a great place to get away from it all. As well as 10 comfortable, country-style, en-suite rooms (one with a four-poster bed), it has a more basic bunkhouse out the back (£11 per person), a climbers' bar with a roaring log fire, a restaurant and a lovely conservatory with views across the glen.

Just 50m beyond the hotel, **Brandy Burn House** (☎ 01575-550231; www.glenclova.co.uk; Glen Clova; per weekend/week from £300/450) offers excellent self-catering accommodation in a five-bedroom former manse.

A **Royal Mail postbus** (☎ 0845 774 0740) to Glen Clova departs from Kirriemuir post office at 8.30am and 3.10pm Monday to Friday, 8.30am only on Saturday. The morning run goes all the way to the head of the glen (2½ hours), the afternoon one only as far as Glen Clova Hotel.

Glen Lethnot

This glen is noted for the **Brown and White Caterthuns** – two extraordinary Iron Age hill forts, defended by ramparts and ditches, perched on twin hill-tops at its southern end. A minor road crosses the pass between the two summits, and it's an easy walk to either fort from the parking area in the pass; both are superb viewpoints. If you don't have a car, you can walk from Brechin (6 miles) or from Edzell (5 miles).

Glen Esk

The most easterly of the Angus Glens, Glen Esk, runs for 15 miles from Edzell to lovely **Loch Lee**, surrounded by beetling cliffs and waterfalls. Ten miles up the glen from Edzell is **Glenesk Folk Museum** (☎ 01356-670254; The Retreat; adult/child £2/1; ☼ noon–6pm Jun–mid-Oct, to 6pm Sat & Sun Easter-May), an old shooting lodge that houses a fascinating collection of antiques and artefacts documenting the local culture of the 17th, 18th and 19th centuries. It also has an excellent tearoom and gift shop.

Five miles further on the public road ends at **Invermark Castle**, an impressive ruined tower guarding the southern approach to the Mounth, a hill track to Deeside.

EDZELL

☎ 01356 / pop 785

The picturesque village of Edzell, with its broad main street and grandiose monumental arch, dates from the early 19th century when Lord Panmure decided that the original medieval village, a mile to the west, spoiled the view from Edzell Castle. The old village was razed and the villagers moved to this pretty, planned settlement.

Lord Panmure's predecessors as owners of **Edzell Castle** (HS; ☎ 648631; adult/child £3.30/1.30; ☼ 9.30am-6.30pm Apr-Sep, to 4.30pm Sat-Wed Oct-Mar; ♿) were the Lindsay earls of Crawford, who built this 16th-century L-plan tower house. Sir David Lindsay, a cultured and well-travelled man, laid out the castle's beautiful **Pleasance** in 1604 as a place of contemplation and learning. Unique in all of Scotland, this Renaissance walled garden is lined with niches for nesting birds, and sculptured plaques illustrat-

ing the cardinal virtues, the arts and the planetary deities.

Two miles north of Edzell, the B966 to Fettercairn crosses the River North Esk at Gannochy Bridge. From the lay-by just over the bridge, a blue-painted wooden door in the stone wall gives access to a delightful footpath that leads along the wooded river gorge for 1.5 miles to a scenic spot known as the **Rocks of Solitude**.

Inchcape (☎ 647266; alison.mcm@btInternet.com; High St; r per person £20; ℗ ✗) is an attractive Edwardian villa with comfortable rooms (all en suite), while the **Panmure Arms Hotel** (☎ 648950; www.panmurearmshotel.co.uk; 52 High St; s/d £48/70; bar meals £7-8; ☼ meals served noon-2pm Mon-Fri, noon-9pm Sat & Sun; ℗ ✗) is a pretty, mock-Tudor place serving excellent bar meals.

Strathtay Scottish bus 29A or 29C from Brechin to Laurencekirk stop at Edzell (15 minutes, two to four a day Monday to Friday, one on Saturday).

BRECHIN

☎ 01356 / pop 7200

The name of the local football team, Brechin City, proclaims this diminutive town's main claim to fame – as the seat of **Brechin Cathedral** (now demoted to a parish church) it has the right to call itself a city, albeit the smallest one in Scotland. Adjacent to the cathedral is a 32m-high **round tower** built around 1000 as part of a Celtic monastery. It is of a type often seen in Ireland, but one of only three that survive in Scotland. Its elevated doorway, 2m above the ground, has carvings of animals, saints and a crucifix.

Housed nearby in the 18th-century former town hall, court room and prison, **Brechin Museum** (☎ 622687; St Ninian's Sq; admission free; ☼ 9am-5pm Mon-Fri, 10am-noon Sat) records the history of the round tower, cathedral and town.

The town's (OK, city's) picturesque Victorian train station dates from 1897, and is now the terminus of the restored **Caledonian Railway** (☎ 377760; www.caledonianrailway.co.uk; 2 Park Rd), which runs steam trains (adult/child £5/3 return) along a 3.5-mile stretch of track to Bridge of Dun. Trains run on Sunday from late May to mid-September, on Saturday in July and August, and at Easter and Christmas. From Bridge of Dun it's a 15-minute walk to the **House of Dun** (NTS; ☎ 810264; adult/child £8/5; ☼ 11.30am-5.30pm Jul &

Aug, 12.30-5.30pm Wed-Sun Easter-Jun & Sep), a beautiful Georgian country house built in 1730.

Adjoining Brechin Castle Centre (a gardening and horse-riding centre on the A90 just west of Brechin), is **Pictavia** (☎ 626241; www.pictavia.org.uk; adult/child £3.25/2.25; ☑ 9.30am-5.30pm Mon-Sat, 10.30am-5.30pm Sun Apr-Sep, 9am-5pm Mon-Sat, 10am-5pm Sun Oct-Mar), an interpretive centre telling the story of the Picts, and explaining current theories about the mysterious carved symbol stones they left behind. It's worth making a trip before going to see the Pictish stones at Aberlemno (p248).

Getting There & Away

Scottish Citylink buses between Dundee and Aberdeen stop at Clerk St in Brechin (see p245). Strathtay Scottish buses depart from South Esk St to Forfar (30 minutes, hourly), Aberlemno (15 minutes, six a day) and Edzell.

MW Nicoll (☎ 01561-377262) buses link Brechin and Stonehaven (55 minutes, six daily Monday to Saturday, three on Sunday).

ABERDEENSHIRE & MORAY

Since medieval times Aberdeenshire and its northwestern neighbour Moray have been the richest and most fertile regions of the Highlands. Aberdeenshire is famed for its Aberdeen Angus beef cattle, its many fine castles and the prosperous 'granite city' of Aberdeen. Moray's main attractions are the Speyside whisky distilleries that line the valley of the River Spey and its tributaries.

ABERDEEN

☎ 01224 / pop 197,300

Aberdeen is the powerhouse of the northeast, fuelled by the North Sea petroleum industry. Oil money has made the city as expensive as London and Edinburgh, and there are hotels, restaurants and clubs with prices to match the depth of petroleum industry pockets. Fortunately, most of the cultural attractions, such as the excellent Maritime Museum and the Aberdeen Art Gallery, are free.

Known throughout Scotland as the granite city, much of the town was constructed using silvery grey granite hewn from the now abandoned Rubislaw Quarry, at one time the biggest artificial hole in the ground in Europe. On a sunny day the granite lends an attractive glitter to the city, but when low, grey rain clouds scud in off the North Sea it can be hard to tell where the buildings stop and the sky begins.

The city is a good base for exploring northeastern Scotland, with Royal Deeside easily accessible to the west, Dunnottar Castle to the south, sandy beaches to the north and whisky country to the northwest.

History

Aberdeen was a prosperous trading and fishing port centuries before oil became a valuable commodity. After the townspeople supported Robert the Bruce against the English at the Battle of Bannockburn in 1314, the king rewarded the town with land for which he had previously received rent. The money was diverted into the Common Good Fund, to be spent on town amenities, as it still is today: it finances the colourful floral displays that have won the city numerous awards.

The name Aberdeen is a combination of two Pictish-Gaelic words, *aber* and *devana*, meaning 'the meeting of two waters'. The area was known to the Romans, and was raided by the Vikings when it was already an important port trading in wool, fish, hides and fur. By the 18th century paper- and rope-making, whaling and textile manufacture were the main industries, and in the 19th century it became a major herring-fishing centre.

Since the 1970s Aberdeen has been the main focus of the UK's offshore oil industry, home to oil company offices, engineering yards, a bustling harbour filled with supply ships, and the world's busiest civilian heliport. Unemployment rates, once among the highest in the country, are now among the lowest.

Orientation

Central Aberdeen is built on an east–west ridge to the north of the River Dee. Union St, the main shopping street, runs along the crest of this ridge between Holburn Junction in the west and Castlegate in the east. The bus and train stations are next to each other, between Union St and the river. Aberdeen Beach is 800m east of the city centre. Old Aberdeen is just over a mile to the north of the city centre along King St.

ABERDEEN

INFORMATION
Central Library	1 B2
Costa Coffee	2 C1
Main Post Office	3 D2
Ottakar's	4 C3
Tourist Information Centre (TIC)	5 D2
Union St Post Office	6 A4
Waterstone's	7 B3

SIGHTS & ACTIVITIES
Aberdeen Art Gallery	8 C2
Fish Market	9 E3
Marischal College	(see 10)
Marischal Museum	10 D1
Maritime Museum	11 D2
Mercat Cross	12 E1
Provost Ross's House	(see 11)
Provost Skene's House	13 D2
Salvation Army Citadel	14 E1
St Nicholas Church	15 D2

SLEEPING
Brentwood Hotel	16 C4
Butler's Guest House	17 C4
Robert Gordon University	18 C1
Royal Crown Guest House	19 C4
Thistle Aberdeen Caledonian Hotel	20 C2

EATING
Café 52	21 D2
Carmine's	22 B2
Howie's	23 B3
Nargile Meze Bar Café	24 A3
Poldino's	25 C2
Somerfield	26 B3
Victoria Restaurant	27 C2

DRINKING
Beautiful Mountain	28 C2
Cameron's Inn	29 C2
Globe Inn	30 B2
Lemon Tree Cafe	(see 41)
Old Blackfriars	31 E2
Prince of Wales	32 D2

ENTERTAINMENT
Aberdeen Arts Centre	33 E1
Bar Indigo	34 D2
Belmont Cinema	35 C2
Box Office	(see 42)
Correction Records	36 C3
Drum	37 C3
Forum	38 B2
His Majesty's	39 B2
Kef	40 C2
Lemon Tree Theatre & Cafe	41 E1
Music Hall	42 C3
O'Neill's	43 C2
One Up Records	(see 40)
Vue Cinema	44 E2

TRANSPORT
Alpine Bikes	45 A4
Bus Station	46 D3
Ferry Terminal (Northlink Ferries)	47 E3
First Travel Centre	48 D2

NORTHEAST SCOTLAND

Information

BOOKSHOPS

Ottakar's (☎ 592440; 3-7 Union Bridge; ⏰ 9am-6pm Mon & Wed-Sat, 10am-6pm Tue, 11am-5pm Sun)
Waterstone's (☎ 210161; 269 Union St; ⏰ 9am-8pm Mon-Thu, to 6pm Fri & Sat, 11am-6pm Sun)

INTERNET ACCESS

Central Library (☎ 652500; Rosemount Viaduct; ⏰ 9am-8pm Mon-Thu, to 5pm Fri & Sat) In the Reference department; sessions limited to 30 minutes. Free access.
Costa Coffee (☎ 645504; 31-33 Loch St; per 15min £1.80; ⏰ 8am-6pm Mon-Wed, Fri & Sat, to 7.30pm Thu, 10am-5pm Sun) On the north side of the Bon Accord Shopping Centre.
TIC (☎ 288828; www.agtb.org; 23 Union St; per 10min 50p; ⏰ 9am-7pm Mon-Sat, 10am-4pm Sun Jul & Aug, 9am-5pm Mon-Sat, 10am-4pm Sun Jun & Sep, 9am-5pm Mon-Sat Oct-May) On the corner of Union St and Shiprow.

MEDICAL SERVICES

Aberdeen Royal Infirmary (☎ 681818; Foresterhill) About a mile northwest of the western end of Union St.

MONEY

There are banks with ATMs all over the city centre.

POST

Main post office (☎ 0845 722 3344; St Nicholas Shopping Centre, Upperkirkgate; ⏰ 9am-5.30pm Mon-Sat)
Union St post office (☎ 0845 722 3344; 489 Union St)

TOURIST INFORMATION

TIC (☎ 288828; www.agtb.org; 23 Union St; ⏰ 9am-7pm Mon-Sat, 10am-4pm Sun Jul & Aug, 9am-5pm Mon-Sat, 10am-4pm Sun Jun & Sep, 9am-5pm Mon-Sat Oct-May) On the corner of Union St and Shiprow.

Sights

ABERDEEN HARBOUR

Aberdeen has a busy, working harbour crowded with survey vessels and supply ships servicing the offshore oil installations, and car ferries bound for Orkney and Shetland. From dawn until about 8am the colourful **fish market** on Albert Basin operates as it has done for centuries.

Overlooking all this nautical bustle is the **Maritime Museum** (☎ 337700; www.aagm.co.uk; Shiprow; admission free; ⏰ 10am-5pm Mon-Sat, noon-3pm Sun), centred on a three-storey replica of a North Sea oil production platform, with exhibits explaining all you ever wanted to know about the petroleum industry. Other

galleries, some situated in **Provost Ross's House**, the oldest building in the city, cover the shipbuilding, whaling and fishing industries. Sleek and speedy Aberdeen clippers were a 19th-century shipyard speciality, used by British merchants for the importation of tea, wool and exotic goods (opium, for instance) to Britain, and, on the return journey, the transportation of emigrants to Australia.

UNION ST

Union St is the city's main thoroughfare, lined with solid, Victorian granite buildings. The oldest area is **Castlegate**, at the eastern end, where the castle once stood. When it was captured from the English for Robert the Bruce, the password used by the townspeople was 'Bon Accord', which is now the city's motto.

In the centre of Castle St stands the 17th-century **Mercat Cross**, bearing a sculpted frieze of portraits of Stuart monarchs. The Baronial heap towering over the eastern end of Castle St is the **Salvation Army Citadel**, which was modelled on Balmoral Castle.

On the northern side of Union St, 300m west of Castlegate, is **St Nicholas Church**, the so-called 'Mither Kirk' (Mother Church) of Aberdeen. The granite spire dates from the 19th century, but there has been a church on this site since the 12th century; the early 15th-century **St Mary's Chapel** survives in the eastern part of the church.

Surrounded by concrete and glass office blocks in what was once the worst slum in Aberdeen is **Provost Skene's House** (☎ 641086; Guestrow; admission free; ⏰ 10am-5pm Mon-Sat, 1-4pm Sun), a late-medieval, turreted town house occupied in the 17th century by the provost (the Scottish equivalent of a mayor) Sir George Skene. It was also occupied for six weeks by the duke of Cumberland on his way to Culloden in 1746. The tempera-painted ceiling with its religious symbolism, dating from 1622, is unusual for having survived the depredations of the Reformation. It's a period gem featuring earnest-looking angels, soldiers and St Peter with crowing cockerels.

MARISCHAL COLLEGE

Across Broad St from Provost Skene's House is **Marischal College**, founded in 1593 by the 5th Earl Marischal, and merged with King's College (founded 1495) in 1860 to create the modern University of Aberdeen. The huge and impressive façade in Perpendicular Gothic style – unusual in having such elaborate masonry hewn from notoriously hard-to-work granite – dates from 1906 and is the world's second-largest granite structure (after L'Escorial near Madrid). It now houses the university's science faculty.

Founded in 1786, the **Marischal Museum** (☎ 274301; Marischal College, Broad St; admission free; ☽ 10am-5pm Mon-Fri, 2-5pm Sun) houses a fascinating collection of material donated by graduates and friends of the university over the centuries. In one room, the history of northeastern Scotland is depicted through its myths, customs, famous people, architecture and trade. The other gallery gives an anthropological overview of the world, incorporating objects from vastly different cultures, arranged thematically (Polynesian wooden masks alongside gas masks and so on). There are the usual Victorian curios, an Inuit kayak found in the local river estuary in the 18th century and Inuit objects collected by whalers. Go through the arch from Broad St, straight across the quadrangle and up the stairs; the museum is on the 1st floor.

ABERDEEN ART GALLERY

Behind the grand façade of **Aberdeen Art Gallery** (☎ 523700; www.aagm.co.uk; Schoolhill; admission free; ☽ 10am-5pm Mon-Sat, 2-5pm Sun) is a cool, marble-lined space exhibiting the work of contemporary Scottish and English painters, such as Gwen Hardie, Stephen Conroy, Trevor Sutton and Tim Ollivier. There are also several landscapes by Joan Eardley, who lived in a cottage on the cliffs near Stonehaven in the 1950s and '60s, and painted tempestuous oils of the North Sea and poignant portraits of slum children. Among the Pre-Raphaelite works upstairs, look out for the paintings of Aberdeen artist William Dyce (1806–64), ranging from religious works to rural scenes.

Downstairs is a large, empty, circular, white room, with fish-scaled balustrades evoking the briny origins of Aberdeen's wealth, commemorating the 165 people who lost their lives in the Piper Alpha oil rig disaster in 1988.

ABERDEEN BEACH

Just 800m east of Castlegate is a spectacular 2-mile sweep of clean, golden sand stretching between the mouths of the Rivers Dee and Don. At one time Aberdeen Beach was a good, old-fashioned British seaside resort, but the availability of cheap package holidays has lured Scottish holidaymakers away from its somewhat chilly delights. On a warm summer's day, though, it's still an excellent beach.

The Esplanade sports several traditional seaside attractions, including **Codona's Amusement Park** (☎ 595910; Beach Blvd; admission free, pay per ride; ☽ 1pm-late Jun-Aug, 1pm-late Fri-Sun Mar-May & Sep-Nov), complete with stomach-churning waltzers, dodgems, a roller coaster, log flume and haunted house. The adjacent **Sunset Boulevard** (☎ 595910; admission free, pay per game; ☽ 10am-midnight) is the indoor alternative, with tenpin bowling, Dodgems, arcade games and pool tables.

Halfway between the beach and the city centre is **Satrosphere** (☎ 640340; www.satrosphere .net; 179 Constitution St; adult/child £5.50/4; ☽ 10am-5pm), a hands-on, interactive science centre.

You can get away from the fun fair atmosphere by walking north towards the more secluded part of the beach. There's a **birdwatching hide** on the south bank of the River Don, between the beach and King St, which leads back south towards Old Aberdeen.

Buses 14 and 15 (eastbound) from Union St go to the beach; or you can walk from Castlegate in 10 minutes.

OLD ABERDEEN

Just over a mile north of the city centre is the district called Old Aberdeen. The name is misleading – although Old Aberdeen is certainly old, the area around Castlegate is older. It was originally called Aulton, from the Gaelic for 'village by the pool', and this was anglicised in the 17th century to Old Town.

It was here that Bishop Elphinstone established King's College, Aberdeen's first university, in 1495. The 16th-century **King's College Chapel** (☎ 272137; College Bounds; admission free; ☽ 9am-4.30pm Mon-Fri) is easily recognised by its crown spire; the interior is largely unchanged since it was first built, with impressive stained-glass windows and choir stalls. The nearby **King's College Visitor Centre** (☎ 273702; College Bounds; admission free; ☽ 10am-5pm Mon-Sat, 2-5pm Sun) houses a multimedia display on the university's history and a pleasant coffee shop.

The 15th-century **St Machar's Cathedral** (☎ 485988; The Chanonry; admission free; ☺ 9am-5pm), with its massive twin towers, is a rare example of a fortified cathedral. According to legend, St Machar was ordered to establish a church where the river takes the shape of a bishop's crook, which it does just here. The cathedral is best known for its impressive heraldic ceiling, dating from 1520, which has 48 shields of kings, nobles, archbishops and bishops. Sunday services are held at 11am and 6pm.

Bus 20 from Littlejohn St (just north of Marischal College) runs to Old Aberdeen every 15 to 20 minutes.

GORDON HIGHLANDERS MUSEUM

The excellent **Gordon Highlanders Museum** (☎ 311200; St Lukes, Viewfield Rd; adult/child £2.50/1.50; ☺ 10.30am-4.30pm Tue-Sat, 1.30-4.30pm Sun Apr-Oct) records the history of one of the British Army's most famous fighting units, described by Winston Churchill as 'the finest regiment in the world'. Originally raised in the northeast of Scotland by the 4th duke of Gordon in 1794, the regiment was amalgamated with the Seaforths and Camerons to form the Highlanders regiment in 1994. The museum is about a mile west of the western end of Union St – take bus 14 or 15 from Union St.

Sleeping

There are clusters of B&Bs on Bon Accord St and Springbank Tce (both 400m southwest of the train station), and along Great Western Rd (the A93, a 25-minute walk southwest of the city centre). They're usually more expensive than the Scottish average and, with all the oil industry workers here, single rooms are at a premium. Prices tend to be lower on weekends.

BUDGET

Aberdeen Youth Hostel (SYHA; ☎ 0870 004 1100; 8 Queen's Rd; dm £12-15) This hostel, set in a granite Victorian villa, is a mile west of the train station. Walk west along Union St and take the right fork along Albyn Pl until you reach a roundabout; Queen's Rd continues on the western side of the roundabout.

Dunrovin Guest House (☎ 586081; www.dunrovin guesthouse.co.uk; 168 Bon Accord St; s/d £25/40, with bathroom £30/50; P ✗) Dunrovin is a typical, granite Victorian house with eight bedrooms; the upstairs rooms are bright and airy, and the friendly owners will provide a veggie breakfast if you wish.

During the university summer holidays some colleges let rooms to visitors:

Robert Gordon University (☎ 262134; www.scotland 2000.com/rgu; Business & Vacation Accommodation Service, Schoolhill, Aberdeen AB10 1FR; 2 people for 2 nights from £115; ☺ mid-Jun–mid-Aug; ✗) Flats comprise six to eight single rooms with shared bathroom, lounge and kitchen, close to the city centre.

University of Aberdeen (☎ 272664; www.abdn.ac.uk /catering; Conference Office, King's College, Old Aberdeen AB24 3FX; s/d £39/52; ☺ mid-Jun–mid-Aug; ✗) The single and twin rooms at Kings Hall, in the heart of Old Aberdeen, are available year-round.

MIDRANGE

Royal Crown Guest House (☎ 586461; www.royal crown.co.uk; 111 Crown St; s £23-36, d £36-50; ✗) The Royal Crown has eight small but nicely furnished bedrooms, and is only five minutes' walk from the train station (though up a steep flight of stairs).

Butler's Guest House (☎ 212411; www.butlersguest house.com; 122 Crown St; s £28-45, d £44-50; ✗ 🖳) Just across the street from the Royal Crown, Butler's is a cosy place with a big breakfast menu that includes fresh fruit salad, kippers and kedgeree as alternatives to the traditional fry-up.

Brentwood Hotel (☎ 595440; www.brentwood-hotel .co.uk; 101 Crown St; s £38-78, d £56-88; P ✗ 🖳) The friendly and flower-bedecked Brentwood, set in a granite town house, is one of the most attractive hotels in the area, comfortable and conveniently located, but often busy during the week – weekend rates are much cheaper.

Strathisla Guest House (☎ 321026; elza@strathisla -guesthouse.co.uk; 408 Great Western Rd; s/d £32/44; P ✗) The child-friendly Strathisla is a spacious, granite, terraced house with five warm and welcoming en-suite rooms, plus a free slice of cake with your cup of tea. It's 1.5 miles southwest of Union St.

Other recommendations:

Crynoch Guest House (☎ 582743; www.crynoch-guest house.co.uk; 164 Bon Accord St; s/d £32/50; P)

Penny Meadow Private Hotel (☎ 588037; penny meadow@amserve.com; 189 Great Western Rd; s/d £46/70; P ✗) Southwest of centre.

Kildonan Guest House (☎ 316115; dey@kildonan .fsbusiness.co.uk; 410 Great Western Rd; s/d £35/50; ✗) Southwest of the centre.

TOP END

Thistle Aberdeen Caledonian Hotel (☎ 0870 333 9151; www.thistlehotels.com/aberdeencaledonian; 10-14 Union Tce; s £39-130, d £60-300; P ✕) This is a fine old Victorian hotel with bags of character, bang in the city centre. The hotel's Terrace Restaurant, and a good number of its rooms, overlook Union Terrace Gardens.

Simpson's Hotel (☎ 327777; www.simpsonshotel.co .uk; 59 Queen's Rd; s £75-135, d £85-150; P ✕) Simpson's, a mile west of Union St, is a stylish boutique hotel decorated with a Mediterranean theme in shades of terracotta and aqua. It's aimed at both business and private guests, and is totally wheelchair-accessible. Cheaper rates on weekends.

Patio Hotel (☎ 633339; www.patiohotels.com; Beach Blvd; s £45-162, d £63-165; P ✕ ⚘) Part of a Norwegian hotel chain, the attractively modern Patio is a 10-minute walk northeast of Castlegate, and only a few minutes' stroll from the beach. It has a pool, sauna, gym and solarium.

Eating

BUDGET

Self-caterers will find large supermarkets at Bridge of Dee and Bridge of Don.

Nargile Meze Bar Café (☎ 454203; 3-5 Rose St; mains £3-6; ☺ noon-3pm & 5.30-10.30pm Mon-Thu, noon-3pm & 5.30-11pm Fri & Sat) If you don't want the full, sit-down, linen-tablecloth treatment at Rendezvous (see Midrange, right), you can sample the delights of Turkish and Middle Eastern cuisine at its BYOB café and takeaway outlet, just off Union St.

Ashvale Fish Restaurant (☎ 596581; 42-48 Great Western Rd; takeaways £2-4, sit-in mains £6-9; ☺ 11.45am-11pm) The Ashvale, an upmarket fish and chip shop, is well known outside the city, having won several awards. Try some mushy peas with your haddock and chips – they taste much better than they sound.

Somerfield (Union St; ☺ 8am-8pm Mon-Wed & Sat, to 9pm Thu & Fri, 10am-7pm Sun) This convenient supermarket is near the Music Hall.

MIDRANGE

Café 52 (☎ 590094; 52 The Green; mains £12-15; ☺ noon-9.30pm) This little haven of laid-back industrial chic, a high, narrow space lined with bare stonework, rough plaster and exposed ventilation ducts painted bronze and black, serves some of the finest and most inventive cuisine in the northeast – try the

cassoulet of duck and rabbit cooked in Pernod and chilli with butter beans and caramelised vegetables, or vegetarian dishes, such as aubergine, mint and ginger crepe with tzatziki and mixed salad leaves.

Rendezvous @ Nargile (☎ 323700; 106-108 Forest Rd; mains £8-13; ☺ noon-3pm & 5.30-10.30pm Mon-Thu, noon-3pm & 5.30-11pm Fri & Sat) An Aberdeen institution for more than a decade, and probably the best Turkish restaurant in Scotland, Nargile recently opened this modern, romantically styled venue in the West End, serving tasty spreads of *mezes* (starters) followed by delicious, melt-in-the-mouth kebabs and marinated meats.

Sand Dollar Café (☎ 572288; 2 Beach Esplanade; mains £6-7; ☺ 9am-6pm Sun-Tue, to 8pm Wed-Sat) This place is a cut above your usual seaside café – on sunny days you can sit at the wooden tables outside and share a bottle of chilled white wine – there's a tempting menu that includes pancakes with maple syrup, homemade burgers and lasagne, Caesar salads and Orkney ice cream. It stays open later on Friday and Saturday evenings in summer, with live music on Friday night.

Carmine's (☎ 624145; 32 Union Tce; 3-course lunch £5, pizza £5-8; ☺ noon-7.30pm Tue-Sat) Carmine's is famed for good, inexpensive Italian food, including the best pizza in town; the lunch deal is available noon to 2pm Monday to Friday. No licence, so BYOB.

Howie's (☎ 639500; 50 Chapel St; 2-course lunch/dinner £9/16; ☺ noon-2.30pm & 6-10.30pm) The Aberdeen branch of the well-known Edinburgh chain of restaurants is a chic bistro dishing up great value 'modern Scottish' cuisine and very reasonably priced house wine.

Poldino's (☎ 647777; 7 Little Belmont St; lunch mains £9-16; ☺ noon-2.30pm & 6-10.45pm Mon-Sat) Poldino's is a long-established Aberdeen eatery, an upmarket, Italian family restaurant that never fails to impress with the quality of its food and service.

Victoria Restaurant (☎ 621381; 140 Union St; sandwiches £4-5, mains £6-8; ☺ 9am-5pm Fri-Wed, to 6.30pm Thu) The Victoria, above the Jamieson & Carry jewellery shop, is a traditional, posh Scottish tearoom, with delicious fresh soups, salads and sandwiches.

TOP END

Silver Darling (☎ 576229; Pocra Quay, North Pier; lunch mains £11-14, dinner mains £19-23; ☺ noon-1.45pm Mon-Fri & 7-9.30pm Mon-Sat) The Silver Darling (an old Scottish nickname for herring) is housed in the former Customs office, with picture windows overlooking the sea at the entrance to Aberdeen harbour. Here you can enjoy fresh Scottish seafood prepared by a top French chef while you watch the porpoises playing in the harbour mouth. The lunch menu offers good-value gourmet delights, such as pan-fried sea bream with caramelised carrots, chicory and a veal and orange jus; bookings are recommended.

Drinking

Aberdeen is a great city for a pub crawl – it's more a question of knowing when to stop than where to start. There are lots of pre-club bars in and around Belmont St, with more traditional pubs scattered throughout the city centre. There are also lots of good cafés.

Beautiful Mountain (☎ 645353; 11-13 Belmont St; mains £5; ☒ 8am-5pm Mon-Fri, 9am-5pm Sat) This cosy café is squeezed into a couple of tiny rooms (seating upstairs), but serves exquisite espresso and consummate cappuccino, along with all-day breakfasts and tasty sandwiches (smoked salmon, Thai chicken, pastrami) on sourdough, bagels, ciabatta and lots of other breads.

Lemon Tree Café (☎ 621610; 5 West North St; mains £5-7; ☒ lunch Thu-Sun) The lively café-bar at the theatre does excellent coffee, cakes and light meals, ciabatta sandwiches, baked potatoes and veggie dishes, and delicious homemade puddings. There's free live music on Friday, Saturday and Sunday.

Globe Inn (☎ 624258; 13-15 North Silver St; ☒ noon-3pm & 5-11pm Mon-Wed, noon-midnight Thu-Sat, 12.30pm-midnight Sun) This lovely Edwardian-style pub with wood panelling and white marble-topped tables, decked out with old musical instruments, is a great place for a quiet lunchtime or afternoon drink. It serves good coffee as well as real ales and malt whiskies, and has live music Thursday to Sunday. Plus probably the poshest pub toilets in the country.

Prince of Wales (☎ 640597; 7 St Nicholas Lane) Tucked down an alley off Union St, Aberdeen's best-known pub boasts the longest bar in the city, and a great range of real ales and good-value pub grub. Quiet in the afternoons, but standing-room only in the evenings.

Cameron's Inn (☎ 644487; 6 Little Belmont St) Known as Ma Cameron's, this is Aberdeen's oldest pub, established in 1789. It has a

pleasantly old-fashioned atmosphere, with lots of wood, brick and stone, and a range of excellent real ales and malt whiskies.

Old Blackfriars (☎ 581922; 52 Castlegate) This is one of the most attractive traditional pubs in the city, with a lovely stone and timber interior and a relaxed atmosphere – a great place for an afternoon pint.

Blue Lamp (☎ 647472; 121 Gallowgate) A long-standing feature of the Aberdeen pub scene, the Blue Lamp is a favourite student hangout – a dark, but not dingy, drinking den with good beer, good *craic* and a jukebox selection that has barely changed since Elvis died.

Entertainment
CINEMAS

Vue Cinema (☎ 0871 224 0240; 10 Shiprow; adult/child £6.30/4) This is a seven-screen multiplex that shows mainstream, first-run films, conveniently located just off Union St.

Belmont Cinema (☎ listings 343534, bookings ☎ 343536; 49 Belmont St; adult/child £6.10/3.70) The Belmont is a great little arthouse cinema, with a lively programme of cult classics, director's seasons, foreign films and mainstream movies. There's also a Saturday morning kids club, with a children's movie screened at 11.30am.

NIGHTCLUBS

Check out what's happening in the club and live-music scene at a local record shop, such as **Correction Records** (13 Correction Wynd) or **One Up Records** (17 Belmont St).

Kef (☎ 648000; 9 Belmont St; admission free-£5; ☒ 11pm-2am Sun-Thu, to 3am Fri & Sat) Decked out with a Turkish theme – there are booths with lots of rugs and comfy cushions to lie around on – this is Aberdeen's coolest venue, with club nights seven days a week, regular big-name DJs and live bands. On Thursday night Precipeace delivers four hours of live jazz, while Friday usually sees resident DJs playing hip-hop, acid house and soul.

Drum (☎ 210174; www.drum-aberdeen.co.uk; 40-42 Windmill Brae; admission £3-5; ☒ 10.30pm-3am Fri & Sat) Lots of young, hardcore clubbers rave about Drum, saying it has the best atmosphere in town (despite the somewhat shabby décor), with DJs – notably resident Tommy Fraser– pumping out hard house, trance and techno on Friday and Saturday nights.

Bar Indigo (☎ 586949; 20 Adelphi; after midnight Fri & Sat admission £2; ☺ 8pm-2am Mon-Thu, to 3am Fri & Sat) Hidden away on an alley just off Union St (there's a separate entrance next to Hotel Metro on Market St – the sign still says Oh Henry's, the bar's former name), Bar Indigo is the city's most popular gay nightclub, with a big lounge overlooking the harbour, and a crowded dance floor playing pop, dance and retro tunes.

O'Neill's (☎ 621456; 9 Back Wynd; admission £2-4; ☺ to 2am Sun-Thu, 3am Fri & Sat) Upstairs at O'Neill's you're guaranteed a wild night of pounding, hardcore Irish rock, indie and alternative tunes; downstairs is a quieter bar, with live music and soothing pints of Murphy's stout.

Forum (☎ 633336; 3 Skene Tce; admission £6; ☺ 10pm-3am first Sat of month) One of the city's best club nights, the once-a-month **Vegas** (www.vegasscotland.co.uk) is located here.

THEATRE & CONCERTS

His Majesty's (☎ 637788; Rosemount Viaduct) The main theatre in Aberdeen hosts everything from ballet and opera to pantomimes and musicals.

Aberdeen Arts Centre (☎ 635208; King St) The Arts Centre stages regular drama productions in its theatre, and changing exhibitions in its gallery.

Lemon Tree Theatre (☎ 642230; www.lemontree .org; 5 West North St) The Lemon Tree theatre has an interesting programme of dance, music and drama, and often has rock, jazz and folk bands playing. It also has an excellent café (see Drinking, opposite).

You can book tickets for most concerts and other events at the **Box Office** (☎ 641122; ☺ 9.30am-6pm Mon-Sat) next to the **Music Hall** (☎ 632080; Union St), the main venue for classical music concerts.

Getting There & Away

AIR

The **Aberdeen Airport** (☎ 722331) is at Dyce, 6 miles northwest of the city centre. The presence of the oil industry ensures there are regular flights to numerous Scottish and UK destinations, including Orkney and Shetland, and international flights to the Netherlands, Norway and Denmark.

Bus 27 runs regularly from Union St to the airport (£1.40, 35 minutes). A taxi from the airport costs £10 to £12.

BOAT

Car ferries from Aberdeen to Orkney and Shetland are run by **Northlink Ferries** (☎ 0845 6000 449; www.northlinkferries.co.uk). For more details, see p398. The ferry terminal is a short walk east of the train and bus stations.

BUS

The **bus station** (Guild St) is next to the train station.

National Express runs direct buses from London (£39, 12 hours) twice daily, one of them overnight. Scottish Citylink runs direct services to Dundee (£9.40, two hours), Perth (£13, 2½ hours), Edinburgh (£16, 3¼ hours) and Glasgow (£18, 4¼ hours).

Stagecoach Bluebird (☎ 212266) is the main local bus operator. Bus 10 runs hourly to Inverness (£11, 3¾ hours) via Huntly, Keith, Fochabers, Elgin (£9, two hours) and Nairn. Service 201 runs every half-hour (hourly on Sunday) to Crathes Castle gate (45 minutes), continuing once an hour (less frequently on Sunday) to Ballater (1¾ hours) and every two hours to Crathie (for Balmoral Castle) and Braemar (£7.40, 2¼ hours).

Other local buses serve Stonehaven, Fraserburgh, Peterhead, Banff and Buckie.

TRAIN

There are several trains a day from London's King's Cross to Aberdeen (£109, 7½ hours); most services involve a change of train at Edinburgh.

Other destinations served from Aberdeen by rail include Edinburgh (£34, 2½ hours), Glasgow (£34, 2¾ hours), Dundee (£20, 1¼ hours) and Inverness (£21, 2¼ hours).

Getting Around

BICYCLE

Mountain bikes can be rented from **Alpine Bikes** (☎ 211455; 64 Holburn St; ☺ 9am-6pm Mon-Sat, to 8pm Thu, 11am-5pm Sun), which charges £15 a day during the week and £30 for a weekend (Friday evening to Monday morning).

BUS

The main city bus operator is **First Aberdeen** (☎ 650065; www.firstaberdeen.com). Fares cost 70p to £1.40; pay the driver as you board the bus. A FirstDay ticket (adult/child £2.70/1.70) allows unlimited travel from time of purchase until midnight on all First Aberdeen buses. Information, route maps and tickets

NORTHEAST SCOTLAND

are available from the **First Travel Centre** (47 Union St; ✆ 8.45am-5.30pm Mon-Sat).

The most useful services for visitors are buses 18, 19 and 24 from Union St to Great Western Rd (for B&Bs), bus 27 from the bus station to the Aberdeen Youth Hostel and the airport, and bus 20 from Marischal College to Old Aberdeen.

CAR

For rental cars try **Arnold Clark** (✆ 249159; www .arnoldclarkrental.com; Girdleness Rd) or **1car1 Car Hire** (✆ 594248; www.1car1.com; 16 South College St).

TAXI

The main city-centre taxi ranks are at the train station and on Back Wynd, off Union St. To order a taxi, phone **ComCab** (✆ 353535) or **Rainbow Cabs** (✆ 878787).

AROUND ABERDEEN
Stonehaven
✆ 01569 / pop 9600
Originally a small fishing village, Stonehaven has been the county town of Kincardineshire since 1600 and is now a thriving, child-friendly seaside resort. There's a **TIC** (✆ 762806; 66 Allardice St; ✆ 10am- 7pm Mon-Sat, 1-6pm Sun Apr-Oct) near Market Sq in the town centre.

From the lane beside the TIC, a boardwalk leads south along the shoreline to the picturesque cliff-bound **harbour**, where you'll find a couple of appealing pubs and the town's oldest building, the **Tolbooth**, built about 1600 by the Earl Marischal. It now houses a small **museum** (admission free; ✆ 10am-noon & 2-5pm Mon & Thu-Sat, 2-5pm Wed & Sun) and a restaurant.

At the northern end of town is the **Open-Air Swimming Pool** (✆ 762134; adult/child £3/1.80; ✆ 10am-7.30pm Mon-Fri, to 6pm Sat & Sun Jul & Aug, 1-7.30pm Mon-Fri, 10am-6pm Sat & Sun Jun), an Olympic-size 50m pool in Art Deco style, dating from 1934. The pool is also open for 'midnight swims' from 10pm to midnight on Wednesday from the end of June to mid-August.

A pleasant, 15-minute walk along the cliff tops south of the harbour leads to the spectacular ruins of **Dunnottar Castle** (✆ 762173; adult/child £4/1; ✆ 9am-6pm Mon-Sat, 2-5pm Sun Easter-Oct, 9am-dusk Mon-Fri Nov-Mar, last admission 30min before closing), spread out across a grassy promontory rising 50m above the sea. As dramatic a film set as any director could wish for, it was used for Franco Zeffirelli's *Hamlet*, starring Mel Gibson. The original fortress was built in the

9th century; the keep is the most substantial remnant, but the drawing room (restored in 1926) is more interesting.

The town hosts several special events, including the famous **Fireball Ceremony** (www .stonehavenfireballs.co.uk) during New Year, when people parade along the High St swinging blazing fireballs around their heads, and the three-day **Stonehaven Folk Festival** (www.stone havenfolkfestival.co.uk) in mid-July.

SLEEPING & EATING
24 Shorehead (✆ 767750; 24 Shorehead; s/d £30/50; ✖) Location makes all the difference, and the location of this former cooperage offering peaceful B&B accommodation can't be beat – last house at the end of the road, overlooking the harbour, with lovely sea views.

Beachgate House (✆ 763155; www.beachgate.co .uk; Beachgate Lane; s/d £35/50; P ✖) This luxurious modern bungalow is right on the seafront, just a few paces from the TIC; two of its five rooms have sea views, as does the lounge/dining room.

Marine Hotel (✆ 762155; 9-10 The Shore; mains £7-11; ✆ food served noon-2pm & 5-9pm) This harbourside hotel is an excellent real-ale pub, with a great 1970s jukebox and good bar meals, including fresh seafood specials.

Tolbooth Restaurant (✆ 762287; Old Pier; mains £14-17; ✆ noon-2pm & 6-11pm Wed-Sun) Set in a 17th-century house overlooking the harbour, this is one of the best seafood restaurants in the region – reservations are recommended. From Tuesday to Friday you can get a three-course lunch for £15.

Carron Restaurant (✆ 760460; 20 Cameron St; mains £10-13; ✆ noon-10.30pm Tue-Sun) This beautiful Art-Deco restaurant is a remarkable survival from the 1930s, complete with bow-fronted terrace, iron fanlights, Deco mirrors, player piano and original tiled toilets. Just the place for high tea on a summer afternoon.

Boathouse Café (✆ 764666; Old Pier; ✆ 9am-4.30pm Tue & Wed, to 10pm Thu-Sat, to 6.30pm Sun) You can enjoy excellent coffee and cakes with a view of the harbour here.

Bervie Chipper (✆ 762658; 12 David St; ✆ noon-9pm) This place serves the best fish and chips in town, and is a branch of the Inverbervie chip shop that lay claims to inventing the notorious deep-fried Mars Bar – and yes, it's still on the menu!

GETTING THERE & AWAY

Stonehaven is 15 miles south of Aberdeen, and is served by the frequent buses travelling between Aberdeen (£3.30, 45 minutes, hourly) and Dundee (£7.50, 1½ hours). Trains to Dundee are faster (£11, 55 minutes, hourly) and offer a more scenic journey.

Castle Fraser

The impressive 16th- to 17th-century **Castle Fraser** (NTS; ☎ 01330-833463; adult/child £8/5; ☺ 11am-5pm Jul & Aug, noon-5pm Tue-Thu, Sat & Sun Easter-Jun & Sep) is the ancestral home of the Fraser family. The largely Victorian interior includes the great hall (with a hidden opening where the laird could eavesdrop on his guests), the library, various bedrooms and an ancient kitchen, plus a secret room for storing valuables; Fraser family relics on display include needlework hangings and a 19th-century artificial leg. The 'Woodland Secrets' area in the castle grounds is designed as an adventure playground for kids.

The castle is 16 miles west of Aberdeen, and 3 miles south of Kemnay. Stagecoach Bluebird buses from Aberdeen to Alford stop at Kemnay.

Haddo House

Designed in Georgian style by William Adam in 1732, **Haddo House** (NTS; ☎ 01651-851440; Tarves; adult/child £8/5; ☺ 11am-4.30pm Jul & Aug, 11am-4.30pm Sat & Sun Easter weekend, May, Jun & Sep) is best described as a classic English stately home transplanted to Scotland. Home to the Gordon family, it has sumptuous Victorian interiors with wood-panelled walls, Persian rug–scattered floors and a wealth of period antiques.

Haddo is 19 miles north of Aberdeen, near Ellon. Stagecoach Bluebird buses run hourly Monday to Saturday from Aberdeen to Tarves/Methlick, stopping at the end of the Haddo House driveway; it's a mile-long walk from bus stop to house.

Fyvie Castle

Though a magnificent example of Scottish Baronial architecture, **Fyvie Castle** (NTS; ☎ 01651-891266; adult/child £8/5; ☺ 11am-5pm Jul & Aug, noon-5pm Fri-Tue Easter-Jun & Sep) is probably more famous for its ghosts, which include a phantom trumpeter and the mysterious Green Lady. The castle's art collection includes portraits by Gainsborough and Raeburn.

The castle is 25 miles north of Aberdeen, on the A947 towards Turriff. A Stagecoach Bluebird bus runs hourly every day from Aberdeen to Banff and Elgin via Fyvie village, a mile from the castle.

DEESIDE

The valley of the River Dee – often called Royal Deeside because of the royal family's long association with the area – stretches west from Aberdeen to Braemar, closely paralleled by the A93 road. From Deeside north to Strathdon is serious castle country – there are more examples of fanciful Scottish Baronial architecture here than anywhere else in Scotland.

The Dee, world-famous for its **salmon fishing**, has its source in the Cairngorm Mountains west of Braemar, the starting point for long hikes into the hills. The **FishDee website** (www.fishdee.co.uk) has all you need to know about fishing on the river.

Crathes Castle

The atmospheric, 16th-century **Crathes Castle** (NTS; ☎ 01330-844525; adult/child £8/5; ☺ 10am-5.30pm Easter-Sep, to 4.30pm Oct, last admission 45min before closing) is famous for its Jacobean painted ceilings, magnificently carved canopied beds, and the 'Horn of Leys', presented to the Burnett family by Robert the Bruce in the 14th century. The beautiful formal **gardens** include 300-year-old yew hedges and colourful herbaceous borders. From November to Easter only guided tours are available (10am to 3.45pm Thursday to Sunday).

The castle is on the A93, 16 miles west of Aberdeen, on the main Aberdeen to Ballater bus route.

Ballater

☎ 01339 / pop 1450

Ballater is an attractive little village that owes its 18th-century origins to the curative waters of nearby Pannanich Springs (now bottled commercially as Deeside Natural Mineral Water), and its prosperity to nearby Balmoral Castle. Note the crests on the shop fronts proclaiming 'By Royal Appointment' – the village is a major supplier of provisions for Balmoral. When Queen Victoria travelled to Balmoral she would alight from the royal train at Ballater's **Old Royal Station** (☎ 755306; Station Sq; admission free; ☺ 9am-6pm Jun-Sep, 10am-5pm Oct-Mar). The station has been beautifully restored, and now houses a museum, a restaurant and a **TIC** (☎ 755306; ☻ 9am-6pm Jun-Sep, 10am-5pm Oct-May). At the time of research an extension was being built to house a Victorian royal coach.

Nearby is **Dee Valley Confectioners** (☎ 755499; Station Sq; admission free; ☻ 9am-noon & 2-4.30pm Mon-Thu Apr-Oct), where you can drool over the manufacture of traditional Scottish sweeties, and **Cabin Fever** (☎ 754004; Station Sq), where you can rent mountain bikes (£9/15 per half/ full day), or arrange to go pony-trekking, quad-biking, clay-pigeon shooting or off-road 4WD-ing.

As you approach Ballater from the east the hills start to close in, and there are many pleasant **walks** in the surrounding area. The steep woodland walk up **Craigendarroch** (400m) takes just over one hour. **Morven** (871m) is a more serious prospect, taking about six hours, but offers good views from the top; ask at the TIC for more info.

SLEEPING & EATING

Accommodation here is fairly expensive and budget travellers usually continue to Braemar.

Celicall (☎ 755699; celicall@euphony.net; 3 Braemar Rd; s/d £30/44; ℗ ✗) Celicall is a friendly, family-run B&B in a modern cottage located right across the street from Station Sq, in easy walking distance from all attractions.

Auld Kirk Hotel (☎ 755762; www.auldkirkhotel.com; Braemar Rd; s/d from £52/75; ✗) Here's something a little out of the ordinary – a small, six-bedroom hotel housed in a converted 19th-century church. Original features include the bell tower, the wooden front doors, and the stained-glass window that hangs on the main staircase. There's also a good restaurant, and a Whisky Lounge with a range of single malts.

Green Inn (☎ 755701; www.green-inn.com; s/d £40/60, 2/3-course dinner £29/34; ☻ dinner 7-9pm Mon-Sat; ℗ ✗) A lovely old house dotted with plush armchairs and sofas, this 'restaurant with rooms' (two comfortable en-suite bedrooms) is famed for its fine dining – the signature dish is roast fillet of Aberdeen Angus beef with Loch Fyne scallops and crayfish, puréed parsnips, pancetta and truffle-infused *beurre blanc.*

Old Royal Station (☎ 755050; Station Sq; mains £6-8; ☻ 9am-6pm) The former waiting room at Queen Victoria's train station is now an attractive dining area with black-and-white floor tiles, basketwork chairs, and marble fireplace and table tops. Daily specials make good use of local produce, from salmon to venison, and good coffee and home-baking are available all day.

GETTING THERE & AWAY

Stagecoach Bluebird bus 201 runs from Aberdeen to Ballater (£6, 1¾ hours, hourly Monday to Saturday, six on Sunday) via Crathes Castle, and continues to Braemar (30 minutes).

Balmoral Castle

Eight miles west of Ballater lies **Balmoral Castle** (☎ 01339-742334; www.balmoralcastle.com; adult/child £6/1; ☻ 10am-5pm Apr-Jul, last admission 4pm), the Queen's Highland holiday home, screened from the road by a thick curtain of trees. Built for Queen Victoria in 1855 as a private residence for the royal family (and designed by William Smith, the city architect of Aberdeen), it kicked off the revival of the Scottish Baronial style of architecture that characterises so many of Scotland's 19th-century country houses.

Dedicated royal-watchers will love the place; otherwise it's hard to justify braving the crowds and the admission fee just for a lot of photographs of smiling royals, a few pieces of art, some stuffed animals and the odd regimental memento. Only a small part of the castle is open to the public; don't expect to see the Queen's private quarters!

The massive, pointy-topped mountain that looms to the south of Balmoral is **Lochnagar** (1155m), immortalised in verse by Lord Byron, who spent his childhood years in Aberdeenshire:

England, thy beauties are tame and domestic
To one who has roamed o'er the mountains afar.
O! for the crags that are wild and majestic:
The steep frowning glories of dark Lochnagar.

Balmoral is beside the A93 at Crathie and can be reached on the Aberdeen to Braemar bus (see p264).

Braemar

☎ 01339 / pop 400

Braemar is a pretty little village with a grand location, on a broad plain ringed by mountains where the Dee valley and Glen Clunie meet. In winter this is one of the coldest places in the country – temperatures as low as minus 29°C have been recorded – and during spells of severe cold hungry deer wander the streets looking for a bite to eat. Braemar is an excellent base for hill walking, and there's skiing at nearby Glenshee (p229).

The **TIC** (☎ 741600; The Mews, Mar Rd; ☼ 9am-6pm Jul & Aug, 9am-5.30pm Jun & Sep, 10am-1.30pm & 2-5pm Mon-Sat, noon-5pm Sun Oct-May), opposite the Fife Arms Hotel, has lots of useful info on walks in the area. There's a bank with an ATM in the village centre, a couple of outdoor equipment shops and an **Alldays** (☼ 7.30am-7pm Mon-Sat, 9am-6pm Sun) grocery store.

SIGHTS & ACTIVITIES

The **Braemar Highland Heritage Centre** (☎ 741944; Mar Rd; admission free; ☼ 9am-6.30pm Jul & Aug, 10am-6pm Jun & Sep, 10am-5.30pm Mon-Sat, noon-5pm Sun May, call for winter hr), beside the TIC, tells the story of the area with displays and videos.

Just north of the village, turreted **Braemar Castle** (☎ 741219; adult/child £3.50/1.50; ☼ 10am-6pm Jul & Aug, 10am-6pm Sat-Thu Easter-Oct) dates from 1628 and served as a government garrison after the 1745 Jacobite rebellion.

An easy walk from Braemar is up **Creag Choinnich** (538m), a hill to the east of the village above the A93. The route is waymarked and takes about 1½ hours. For a longer walk (three hours) and superb views of the Cairngorms, head for the summit of **Morrone** (859m), southwest of Braemar. Ask at the TIC for details of these and other walks.

FESTIVALS & EVENTS

More than 20,000 people, including the royal family, descend on Braemar on the first Saturday in September for the annual **Braemar Gathering** (☎ 755377; www.braemargathering .org; adult/child £7/2), the most famous Highland games in the country. Bookings for ringside and grandstand seats (£13 to £22) are essential. See the boxed text, p264, for more information.

SLEEPING

Braemar Youth Hostel (SYHA; ☎ 0870 004 1105; 21 Glenshee Rd; dm £10.50-14; ☼ late Dec-Oct) This hostel is housed in a grand former shooting lodge just south of the village centre on the A93 to Perth, and has a comfy lounge with pool table, and a barbecue in the garden.

Rucksacks Bunkhouse (☎ 741517; 15 Mar Rd; dm £7-10; P ☒) An excellent bunkhouse comprising a cottage dorm with comfy beds, an alpine-style hut (sleeps 10), a drying room, a laundry and even a sauna, Rucksacks is understandably popular with walkers and climbers. Nonguests are welcome to use the laundry (£2) and even the showers (£1), and the friendly owner is a fount of knowledge about the local area.

Clunie Lodge Guesthouse (☎ 741330; www.clunie lodge.com; Cluniebank Rd; d from £46; P ☒) A spacious Victorian villa set in beautiful gardens, the Clunie is a great place to relax after a hard day's hiking, with its comfortable residents lounge, bedrooms with views of the hills, and red squirrels scampering through the neighbouring woods. There's a drying room for wet weather gear, and secure storage for cycles.

Craiglea (☎ 741641; www.craigleabraemar.com; Hillside Dr; s/d £25/44; P ☒) Craiglea is a homely B&B set in a pretty stone-built cottage with three en-suite bedrooms. Vegetarian breakfasts are available, and the owners can give advice on local walks.

Braemar Lodge Hotel (☎ 741627; www.braemar lodge.co.uk; Glenshee Rd; dm/s/d £11/60/100; P ☒) The nicest place to stay in Braemar is this classy Victorian shooting lodge on the southern outskirts of the village. It has a good restaurant and a cosy lounge bar well stocked with a range of malt whiskies, plus a 12-berth hikers' bunkhouse in the hotel grounds.

Campers will find good facilities at **Invercauld Caravan Club Site** (☎ 741373; www.caravanclub .co.uk; tent sites £9-14; ☼ late Dec-Oct), or you can camp wild (no facilities) along the minor road on the east bank of the Clunie Water, 3 miles south of Braemar.

EATING

Fife Arms Hotel (☎ 741644; Mar Rd; bar meals £6-10; ☼ food served noon-2pm & 6-8pm) The Fife Arms is a climbers' favourite, a grand old pub with a roaring log fire in winter. Bar meals are served in the spacious lounge bar.

Gathering Place Bistro (☎ 741234; Mar Rd; mains £10-14; ☼ 6-10pm Tue-Sun) This bright and breezy bistro is an unexpected corner of culinary excellence, with a welcoming dining room and

NORTHEAST SCOTLAND

BRAEMAR GATHERING

There are Highland games in many towns and villages throughout the summer, but the best known is the **Braemar Gathering** (☎ 01339-755377; www.braemargathering.org), which takes place on a 12-acre site on the first Saturday in September. It's a major occasion, organised annually by the Braemar Royal Highland Society since 1817. Events include highland dancing, pipers, tug-of-war, a hill race up Morrone, tossing the caber, hammer- and stone-throwing and the long jump. International athletes are among those who take part.

These types of events took place informally in the Highlands for many centuries as tests of skill and strength, but they were formalised around 1820 due to the rise of Highland romanticism initiated by Sir Walter Scott and King George IV. Queen Victoria attended the Braemar Gathering in 1848, starting a tradition of royal patronage that continues to this day.

---

sunny conservatory, tucked below the main road junction at the entrance to the village.

Hungry Highlander (14 Invercauld Rd; ☺ 10am-9pm Tue-Thu & Sun, to 10pm Fri & Sat) If you're too late for a sit-down meal, this serves a range of take-away meals and hot drinks.

GETTING THERE & AWAY
Stagecoach Bluebird bus 201 runs from Aberdeen to Braemar (£7, 2¼ hours, hourly Monday to Saturday, six on Sunday). The drive from Perth to Braemar is beautiful, but there's no public transport on this route.

Inverey
Five miles west of Braemar is the tiny settlement of Inverey. Numerous mountain walks start from here, including the adventurous hike through the **Lairig Ghru** pass to Aviemore (see the boxed text, p330).

The **Glen Luibeg** circuit (15 miles, six hours) is a good day hike. Start from the woodland car park 250m beyond the Linn of Dee, a narrow gorge about 1.5 miles west of Inverey, and follow the footpath and track to Derry Lodge and Glen Luibeg – there are beautiful remnants of the ancient Caledonian pine forest here. Continue westwards on a pleasant path over a pass into Glen Dee,

then follow the River Dee back down to the linn. Take OS 1:50,000 map sheet No 43.

A good short walk (3 miles, 1½ hours) begins at the **Linn of Quoich** – a waterfall that thunders through a narrow slot in the rocks. Head uphill on a footpath on the east bank of the stream, past the impressive rock scenery of the **Punch Bowl** (a giant pothole), to a modern bridge that spans the narrow gorge and return via an unsurfaced road on the far bank.

The **Inverey Youth Hostel** (SYHA; ☎ 0870 004 1126; dm £10-12; ☺ May-Sep) provides basic digs in a cosy little cottage (only 14 beds, so book ahead).

A Royal Mail postbus runs from Braemar to Inverey Youth Hostel (15 minutes), Linn of Dee (20 minutes) and Luibeg (30 minutes), departing from Braemar post office at 1.20pm Monday to Saturday.

STRATHDON
The valley of River Don, home to many of Aberdeenshire's finest castles, stretches westward from Kintore, 13 miles northwest of Aberdeen, taking in the villages of Kemnay, Monymusk, Alford (pronounced *ah*-ford) and tiny Strathdon. The A944 parallels the lower valley; west of Alford, the A944, A97 and A939 follow the river's upper reaches.

Stagecoach Bluebird bus 220 runs from Aberdeen to Alford (£5, 1½ hours, seven a day Monday to Saturday, four on Sunday); bus 219 continues from Alford to Strathdon village (50 minutes, three daily Monday to Saturday) via Kildrummy. You'll need your own transport to reach Craigievar or Corgarff castles and the Lecht.

Alford
☎ 01975 / pop 1925
Alford has a **TIC** (☎ 562052; Old Station Yard, Main St; ☺ 10am-5pm Mon-Sat, 12.45-5pm Sun Jun-Aug, 10am-1pm & 2-5pm Mon-Fri, 10am-noon & 1.45-5pm Sat, 12.45-5pm Sun Apr, May & Sep), banks with ATMs and a supermarket.

The **Grampian Transport Museum** (☎ 562292; www.gtm.org.uk; adult/child £5/2.40; ☺ 10am-5pm Apr-Oct) houses a fascinating collection of vintage motorbikes, cars, buses and trams, including a Triumph Bonneville in excellent nick, a couple of Model T Fords (including one used by Drambuie), a Ferrari F40 and an Aston Martin V8 Mk II. Unusual exhibits include a 19th-century horse-drawn sleigh from Russia, a 1942 Mack snowplough and the Craigievar Express, a steam-powered tricycle built in 1895 by a local postman.

Next to the museum is the terminus of the narrow-gauge **Alford Valley Steam Railway** (☎ 562811; adult/child £2/1; ☸ trains run 1-4.30pm Jun-Aug, 1-4.30pm Sat & Sun Apr, May & Sep), a heritage line that runs from here to Haughton Country Park.

For B&B, you can't do better than **Frog Marsh** (☎ 571355; www.frogmarsh.com; Mossat; d/ste £60/100; ✗), a restored and extended cottage 6 miles west of Alford, which has two gorgeous doubles plus a luxury suite in the attic space.

Craigievar Castle

The most spectacular of the Strathdon castles, **Craigievar Castle** (NTS; ☎ 01339-883280; adult/child £10/7; ☸ noon-5.30pm Jul & Aug, noon-5.30pm Fri-Tue Easter-Jun & Sep), 9 miles south of Alford, has managed to survive pretty much unchanged since its completion in the 17th century, a superb example of the original Scottish Baronial style. The lower half is a plain tower house, the upper half sprouts corbelled turrets, cupolas and battlements – an extravagant statement of its builder's wealth and status. At time of research the castle was due to be closed for renovation until Easter 2007.

Kildrummy Castle

Nine miles west of Alford lie the extensive remains of the 13th-century **Kildrummy Castle** (HS; ☎ 01975-571331; adult/child £2.50/1; ☸ 9.30am-6.30pm Apr-Sep), former seat of the Earl of Mar and once one of Scotland's most impressive fortresses. After the 1715 Jacobite rebellion, the earl was exiled to France and his castle fell into ruin.

If you're in the mood for a night of luxury, head for **Kildrummy Castle Hotel** (☎ 01975-571288; www.kildrummycastlehotel.co.uk; s/d £90/156; ℗ ✗) just along the road, a splendid Baronial hunting lodge complete with original oak panelling, log fires and four-poster beds.

Corgarff Castle

In the wild upper reaches of Strathdon, near the A939 from Corgarff to Tomintoul, is the impressive tower house of **Corgarff Castle** (HS; ☎ 01975-651460; adult/child £3.30/1.30; ☸ 9.30am-6.30pm Apr-Sep, to 4.30pm Sat & Sun Oct-Mar). The tower house dates from the 16th century, but the star-shaped defensive cur-

tain wall was added in 1748 when the castle was converted to a military barracks in the wake of the Jacobite rebellion.

Jenny's Bothy (☎ 01975-651449; jenny@jenboth.go -plus.net; dm £8.50) is an excellent year-round bunkhouse set in a remote croft; look out for the sign by the main road, then follow the old military road (drivable) for 0.75 miles.

Lecht Ski Resort

At the head of Strathdon the A939 crosses the Lecht pass (637m), where there's a small skiing area with lots of short easy and intermediate runs. **Lecht 2090** (☎ 01975-651440; www .lecht.co.uk) hires out skis, boots and poles for £15, or a snowboard and boots for £18; a lift pass is £21 for a day. A two-day package, including ski hire, lift pass and instruction, costs £80.

The ski centre opens in summer, too, when you can ski or board on the dry ski slope (£11 for two hours, including equipment hire), or rent go-karts and quad bikes (£8.75 a session), or just take a trip up on the chairlift (£4.75 return).

NORTHERN ABERDEENSHIRE

North of Aberdeen, the Grampian Mountains fall away to rolling agricultural plains pocked with small, craggy volcanic hills. This fertile lowland corner of northeastern Scotland is known as Buchan, a region of traditional farming culture immortalised by Lewis Grassic Gibbon in his trilogy, *A Scots Quair*, based on the life of a farming community in the 1920s. The old Scots dialect called the Doric lives on in everyday use here – if you think the Glaswegian accent is difficult to understand, just try listening in to a conversation in Peterhead or Fraserburgh.

The Buchan coast alternates between rugged cliffs and long, long stretches of sand, dotted with picturesque little fishing villages such as Pennan, where parts of the film *Local Hero* were shot.

Peterhead

☎ 01779 / pop 17,950

Peterhead's sprawling harbour stands as testimony to a once-great fishing industry. Not much more than a decade ago the high-tech trawlers operating from here were so productive that they supported a Ferrari-driving fishing community with a large disposable income. Overfishing and EU quotas and restrictions have now led to a point where the entire industry is in danger of disappearing, and the town is turning to tourism and North Sea oil for salvation.

Peterhead Maritime Heritage (☎ 473000; The Lido, South Rd; admission free; ☉ 10.30am-5pm Mon-Sat, 11.30am-5pm Sun Jun-Sep) documents the town's involvement in the whaling and fishing industries and their replacement by North Sea oil; it overlooks a good sandy beach beside the marina. The central **Arbuthnot Museum** (☎ 477778; St Peter St; admission free; ☉ 11am-1pm & 2-4.30pm Mon-Sat, closes 1pm Wed) has wide-ranging displays on local history and Arctic whaling.

Stagecoach Bluebird buses run from Aberdeen to Peterhead every 30 minutes Monday to Saturday and hourly on Sunday (£4.80, 1¼ hours).

Fraserburgh
☎ 01346 / pop 12,450

Fraserburgh, affectionately known to locals as the Broch, is Europe's largest shellfish port. Like Peterhead, it has suffered from the general decline of the fishing industry. The harbour can be interesting when it's crowded with boats, and there are good sandy beaches east of the town. There's a **TIC** (☎ 518315; Saltoun Sq; ☉ 10am-1pm & 2-5pm Mon-Sat Apr-Oct), a supermarket and banks with ATMs.

The excellent **Scottish Lighthouse Museum** (☎ 511022; Kinnaird Head; adult/child £5/2.20; ☉ 10am-6pm Mon-Sat, 11am-6pm Sun Jul & Aug, 11am-5pm Mon-Sat, noon-5pm Sun Apr-Jun, Sep & Oct, 11am-4pm Mon-Sat, noon-4pm Sun Nov-Mar) provides a fascinating insight into the network of lights that have safeguarded the Scottish coast for over 100 years, and the men and women who built and maintained them (plus a sobering fact – that all the world's lighthouses are to be decommissioned by 1 January 2080). A guided tour takes you to the top of the old Kinnaird Head lighthouse, built on top of a converted 16th-century castle; the engineering is so precise that the 4.5-ton light assembly can be rotated by pushing with a single finger.

Maggie's Hoosie (☎ 514761; 26 Shore St, Inverallochy; admission free; ☉ 2-4.30pm May-Sep), 4 miles east of Fraserburgh, is a traditional fishwife's cottage with earthen floors and original furnishings, a timeless reminder of a bygone age.

Stagecoach Bluebird buses run hourly to Fraserburgh from Aberdeen (£5.20, 1½ hours) and Peterhead (£1.20, 40 minutes).

Pennan

Pennan is a picturesque harbour village tucked beneath red-sandstone cliffs, 12 miles west of Fraserburgh. The whitewashed houses are built gable-end to the sea, and the waves break just a few metres away on the other side of the village's only street. It's no longer a working fishing harbour; most of the cottages are now holiday homes.

The **Pennan Inn** (☎ 01346-561201; mains £7-12, d £50) featured in the film *Local Hero*, as did the red telephone box outside, though one of the houses further along the seafront to the east doubled for the exterior of the fictional hotel (the beach scenes were filmed on the other side of the country, in Arisaig, see p343). The rooms are comfy if a bit on the small side, but the restaurant is good and the bar is a lively little place on Friday nights and summer weekends. (Note, the hotel was up for sale at the time of research.)

Stagecoach Bluebird bus 273 from Fraserburgh to Banff stops at the Pennan road end (25 minutes, two a day, Saturday only), 350m south of (and a steep climb uphill from) the village.

Gardenstown & Crovie

The fishing village of Gardenstown (or Gamrie, pronounced *game*-rey), founded by Alexander Garden in 1720, is unusual in being built on a series of cramped terraces tumbling down the steep cliffs above the tiny harbour. Drivers should beware of severe gradients and hairpin bends in the village, parts of which can only be reached on foot. Crovie, 800m to the east, is even more claustrophobically picturesque.

Huntly
☎ 01466 / pop 4400

An impressive ruined castle and an attractive main square make this small town worth a stopover between Aberdeen and Elgin. The **TIC** (☎ 792255; The Sq; ☉ 10am-5.30pm Mon-Sat, to 3pm Sun Jul & Aug, 10am-1pm & 2-5pm Mon-Sat Easter-Jun, Sep & Oct) is on the main square, next to a bank with an ATM.

Castle St (beside the Huntly Hotel) runs north from the town square to an arched gateway and tree-lined avenue that leads to 16th-century **Huntly Castle** (HS; ☎ 793191; adult/child £3.30/1.30; ☉ 9.30am-6.30pm Apr-Sep, 9.30am-4.30pm Mon-Wed & Sat, 9.30am-1pm Thu, 2-4.30pm Sun Oct-Mar), the former stronghold of the Gordons on the banks of the River Deveron. Over the main door is a superb carving that includes the royal arms and the figures of Christ and St Michael.

There are a couple of hotels on the main square, and a handful of B&Bs in the surrounding streets; travellers have recommended the hospitable **Hillview** (☎ 794870; www .hillviewbb.com; Provost St; r per person £18; **P** ✕) and its tasty breakfast pancakes.

If you want to spoil yourself, continue along the drive beyond the castle to the **Castle Hotel** (☎ 792696; www.castlehotel.uk.com; s/d £67/100; **P** ✕), a splendid 18th-century mansion set amid acres of parkland. It's comfortably old-fashioned, with a grand wooden staircase, convoluted corridors, the odd creaky floorboard and rattling sash window, but must be among the most affordable country house hotels in Scotland.

Stagecoach Bluebird bus 10 from Aberdeen (£6, 1½ hours, hourly) to Inverness passes through Huntly. There are also regular trains from Aberdeen to Huntly (£9, one hour, every two hours), continuing to Inverness.

MORAY

The old county of Moray (pronounced murray), centred on the county town of Elgin, lies at the heart of an ancient Celtic earldom and is famed for its mild climate and rich farmland – the barley fields of the 19th century provided the raw material for the Speyside whisky distilleries, one of the region's main attractions for present-day visitors.

Elgin

☎ 01343 / pop 20,800

Elgin has been the provincial capital of Moray for the past eight centuries, and was an important town in medieval times. Dominated by a monument to the 5th duke of Gordon, erected in 1839, which crowns Lady Hill west of the town centre, Elgin's main attraction is its impressive ruined cathedral.

The **TIC** (☎ 542666; 17 High St; ✆ 9am-6pm Mon-Sat, 11am-4pm Sun Apr-Oct, 9am-5pm Mon-Sat Nov-Mar) is a short distance east of the pedestrianised High St, which splits to pass either side of St Giles' Kirk. The bus station is a block north of the High St, but the train station is 900m south of the town centre.

ELGIN

INFORMATION	
Post Office.................................	1 B2
Tourist Information Centre (TIC)........	2 C2

SIGHTS & ACTIVITIES	
Duke of Gordon Monument..............	3 B2
Elgin Cathedral............................	4 D1
Elgin Museum..............................	5 C2
Gordon & MacPhail........................	6 B2
St Giles' Kirk...............................	7 C2

SLEEPING	
Croft Guesthouse..........................	8 D2
Mansfield Hotel............................	9 B2
Southbank Guest House..................	10 C2

EATING	
Ashvale.....................................	11 C2
Mezzo.......................................	(see 9)
Tapas.......................................	12 C2

TRANSPORT	
Bus Station................................	13 B2

The **post office** (Batchen St; ⊗ 8.30am-6pm Mon-Fri, to 4pm Sat) is just south of High St.

SIGHTS

Many people think that the ruins of **Elgin Cathedral** (HS; ☎ 547171; adult/child £3.30/1.30, joint ticket with Spynie Palace £3.80/1.50; ⊗ 9.30am-6.30pm Apr-Sep, 9.30am-4.30pm Sat-Wed Oct-Mar), known as the 'lantern of the north', are the most beautiful and evocative in Scotland. Consecrated in 1224, the cathedral was burned down in 1390 by the infamous Wolf of Badenoch, the illegitimate son of Robert II, following his excommunication by the Bishop of Moray. The octagonal chapter house is the finest in the country.

Palaeontologists and Pict lovers will enjoy **Elgin Museum** (☎ 543675; 1 High St; adult/child £2/50p; ⊗ 10am-5pm Mon-Fri, 11am-4pm Sat Apr-Oct), where the highlights are its collections of fossil fish and Pictish carved stones.

Spynie Palace (HS; ☎ 546358; adult/child £2.50/1; ⊗ 9.30am-6.30pm Apr-Sep, 9.30am-4.30pm Sat & Sun Oct-Mar), 2 miles north of Elgin, was the residence of the medieval bishops of Moray until 1686. The massive tower house commands lovely views over Spynie Loch.

Not a sight as such, but a sight for sore eyes perhaps, **Gordon & MacPhail** (☎ 545110; www.gordonandmacphail.com; 58-60 South St; ⊗ 9am-5pm Mon-Sat) is the world's largest specialist malt whisky dealer. Over a century old and offering around 450 different varieties, its Elgin shop is a place of pilgrimage for whisky connoisseurs, as well as housing a mouthwatering delicatessen.

SLEEPING & EATING

Mansfield Hotel (☎ 540883; www.themansfield.com; Mayne Rd; s/d £80/120; P ⊠) Centred on a 19th-century manse (minister's house), but with extensive modern additions, the Mansfield offers elegant accommodation both in stylish modern rooms aimed at business travellers, and in more traditional rooms with four-poster beds.

Croft Guesthouse (☎ 546004; www.thecroftelgin.co.uk; 10 Institution Rd; s/d £45/60; P ⊠) The Croft offers a taste of Victorian high society, set in a spacious mansion built for a local lawyer back in 1848. The house is filled with period features – check out the cast-iron and tile fireplaces – and the three large bedrooms are equipped with easy chairs and crisp bed linen.

Southbank Guest House (☎ 547132; southbank@handbag.com; 36 Academy St; s/d from £26/44; P ⊠) The family-run, 12-room Southbank is set in a large Georgian town house in a quiet street south of Elgin's centre, just five minutes' walk from the cathedral and other sights.

Mezzo (☎ 540883; cnr Hay & South Sts; mains £6-10; ⊗ noon-2.30pm & 6-9.30pm Mon-Thu, noon-9.30pm Fri & Sat, 5-9.30pm Sun) This stylish bar and restaurant is part of the Mansfield Hotel complex, and serves tasty bistro fare, including pasta, pizza, burgers and various vegetarian dishes.

Tapas (☎ 549737; High St; mains £4-6; ⊗ 5-10pm) Part of Flanagan's Bar, tucked up a narrow wynd (lane) on the southern side of High St near the TIC, this place serves good Spanish food – it does an all-you-can-eat buffet for £10 on Wednesday and Sunday.

Ashvale (11 Moss St) For fish and chips, head for the excellent Ashvale.

GETTING THERE & AWAY

Stagecoach Bluebird buses run to Banff and Macduff (£8, one hour), Dufftown (£3.80, 30 minutes), Inverness (£7.50, one hour) and Aberdeen (£9, two hours).

Elgin is on the Aberdeen to Inverness railway line.

Lossiemouth

☎ 01343 / pop 9000

Lossie, as it's known locally, is the former port of Elgin, now better known as a fishing port, seaside resort, yachting harbour and air force base; it's also the birthplace of James Ramsay MacDonald (1866–1937), who was the UK's first Labour prime minister (served 1923–24 and 1929–31; there's a plaque at 1 Gregory Pl, where he was born).

Lossiemouth's main attraction is the **East Beach**, a beautiful golden-sand beach that stretches for several miles to the southeast of the town, reached via a footbridge over the River Lossie. The old harbour, now a yachting marina, is a pleasant place to stroll. It's also the home port of **Dolphinicity** (☎ 829244; www.sailingwild.com; East Pier; ⊗ office 11am-4pm Wed-Mon Jun-Sep), a 36ft sailing yacht that records data on marine mammals, and offers 1½- and 2½-hour wildlife-watching cruises (May to October is the best time for spotting bottlenose dolphins and porpoises, August to October for minke whales). Try to book a day or

---

TOP 10 SINGLE MALT WHISKIES – OUR CHOICE

After a great deal of diligent research (and not a few sore heads), Lonely Planet's *Scotland* authors and editors have selected their 10 favourite single malts from across the country (with the proviso that each offers a good distillery tour).

Bowmore (Islay) Smoke, peat and salty sea air – a classic Islay malt. One of the few distilleries that still malts its own barley (p289).

Bruichladdich (Islay) Peat, peat and more peat – not for the faint-hearted! A visitor-friendly distillery with a quirky, innovative approach (p289).

Clynelish (Highland) A smoky, fruity, sea-tinged malt, the heart of Johnnie Walker Gold Label. Modern distillery with sea views (p354).

Edradour (Highland) Smooth and sweet, with toffee, vanilla and honey notes. The country's smallest and prettiest distillery (p227).

Glenfiddich (Speyside) Fragrant, fruity and interesting, especially the special finishes. Distillery still in family ownership after 120 years (below).

Glenmorangie (Highland) Fruit, flowers, citrus and honey – a breath of springtime. Distillery has the tallest stills in Scotland (p352).

Glenturret (Highland) The backbone of the Famous Grouse blend. Pretty little distillery, with cute resident cat called Amber (p220).

Highland Park (Island) Full and rounded, with heather, honey, malt and peat. Award-winning distillery tour (p402).

Macallan (Speyside) The king of Speyside malts, with sherry and bourbon finishes. Distillery set amid waving fields of Golden Promise barley (p270).

Springbank (Campbeltown) Complex flavours – sherry, citrus, pear-drops, peat – with a salty tang. Entire production process from malting to bottling takes place on site (p286).

A visit to a whisky distillery should be part of any trip to Scotland – many distilleries around the country open their doors to visitors. For some, showing tourists around has become a slick marketing operation complete with promotional videos, gift shops that rival Harrods in size and glitziness, and an admission charge of around £3 to £5 (in most places this is refundable if you buy something in the shop).

See also How To Be A Malt Whisky Buff, p65.

---

two in advance. Cruises cost £17.50 to £25 per person, and sail daily from March to December.

Pleasant places for coffee and cake or a light lunch include the **Harbour Tearooms** (☎ 814622; 5 Pitgaveny Quay), overlooking the marina, and **La Caverna** (☎ 813027; 20 Clifton Rd; mains £7-10; ☻ noon-2pm & 5-9.30pm), a stone-vaulted Italian café and restaurant – the outdoor tables have a view of the beach.

Dufftown
☎ 01340 / pop 1450

Rome may be built on seven hills, but Dufftown's built on seven stills, say the locals. Founded in 1817 by James Duff, 4th earl of Fife, Dufftown is 17 miles south of Elgin and lies at the heart of the Speyside whisky-distilling region.

The **TIC** (☎ 820501; ☻ 10am-6pm Mon-Sat, 11am-3pm Sun Easter-Oct) is in the clock tower in the main square; the adjoining museum contains some interesting local items.

SIGHTS & ACTIVITIES

With seven working distilleries nearby, Dufftown has been dubbed Scotland's malt whisky capital. The **Whisky Shop** (☎ 821097; 1 Fife St) stocks hundreds of single malts and a huge range of bottled Scottish beers, and runs tasting sessions at 7pm on Wednesday evenings in July and August. Ask at the TIC for a **Malt Whisky Trail** (www.maltwhiskytrail .com) booklet, a self-guided tour around the seven stills plus the Speyside Cooperage.

At the northern edge of town is the **Glenfiddich Distillery Visitor Centre** (☎ 820373; www.glen fiddich.co.uk; admission free; ☻ 9.30am-4.30pm Mon-Fri mid-Oct–Easter, 9.30am-4.30pm Mon-Sat, noon-4.30pm Sun Easter–mid-Oct), where the guided tour includes a visit to the bottling plant – the only Highland distillery where bottling takes place on the premises. Your free dram is genuinely free, but enthusiasts can opt for the in-depth, 2½-hour Connoisseur's Tour (£12), which includes a 'nosing' of half a dozen whiskies under the supervision of an experienced taster.

The nearby **Speyside Cooperage** (☎ 871108; Craigellachie; adult/child £3.10/1.80; 🕑 9.30am-4pm Mon-Fri) turns out around 100,000 oak barrels a year for the maturing of Scottish malt whiskies; the visitor centre allows you to watch skilled coopers and apprentices at work. Across the River Spey from the cooperage lies the **Macallan Distillery** (☎ 872280; www.themacallan.com; Easter Elchies, Craigellachie; admission free; 🕑 9.30am-5pm Mon-Sat Apr-Oct, 11am-3pm Mon-Fri Nov-Mar), approached through waving fields of Golden Promise barley. The free tours last 30 minutes; again, there's a more detailed one-hour tour for enthusiasts (£15; must be booked in advance).

The **Keith and Dufftown Railway** (☎ 821181; www.keith-dufftown.org.uk; Dufftown Station) is a heritage railway line running for 11 miles from Dufftown to Keith. Trains hauled by 1950s diesel motor units run on Saturdays and Sundays from June to September, plus Fridays in July and August; a return ticket costs £8/4 for an adult/child. There are also two 1930s 'Brighton Belle' Pullman coaches on display, and a café housed in a 1957 British Rail cafeteria car.

FESTIVALS & EVENTS

The four-day **Spirit of Speyside Whisky Festival** (www.spiritofspeyside.com), held over the last weekend in April, takes in whisky tastings, tours, locally produced food and traditional music.

SLEEPING & EATING

Davaar B&B (☎ 820464; www.davaardufftown.co.uk; 17 Church St; s/d £35/50; ✗) Just along the street opposite the TIC, Davaar is a sturdy Victorian villa with three smallish but comfily kitted out rooms; the breakfast menu is superb, offering the option of Portsoy kippers instead of the traditional fry-up (which uses eggs from the owners' own chickens).

Fife Arms Hotel (☎ 820220; www.fifearmsdufftown .co.uk; 2 The Sq; mains £8-16, s/d £30/50; P ✗) This welcoming hotel offers slightly cramped but comfortable accommodation in a modern block around the back; its bar is stocked with a wide range of single malts, and the restaur-

ant dishes up sizzling steaks, homemade steak pies and locally farmed ostrich steaks.

A Taste of Speyside (☎ 820860; 10 Balvenie St; mains £14-16; 🕑 noon-2pm & 6-9pm Tue-Sun) This upmarket restaurant prepares traditional Scottish dishes using fresh local produce, including lamb, smoked salmon, venison, game and cheeses; typical dishes include sautéed loin of lamb, rabbit casserole and roast wood pigeon. A two-course Sunday lunch costs £12.50.

GETTING THERE & AWAY

Stagecoach Bluebird buses link Dufftown to Elgin (£4, 50 minutes, hourly), Huntly, Aberdeen and Inverness.

On summer weekends, you can take a train from Aberdeen or Inverness to Keith, and then ride the Keith and Dufftown Railway (left) to Dufftown.

Tomintoul

☎ 01807 / pop 320

This high-altitude (345m) village was built by the Duke of Gordon in 1775 on the old military road that leads over the Lecht pass from Corgarff, a route now followed by the A939, usually the first road in Scotland to be blocked by snow when winter closes in. The duke hoped that settling the dispersed population of his estates in a proper village would help to stamp out cattle stealing and illegal distilling.

Tomintoul (pronounced tom-in-towel) is a pretty, stone-built village with a grassy, tree-lined main square, where you'll find the **TIC** (☎ 580285; The Sq; 🕑 10am-4pm Mon-Sat Easter-Oct) and, next door, the **Tomintoul Museum** (☎ 673701; The Sq; admission free; 🕑 10am-4pm Mon-Sat Jun-Sep, 10am-4pm Mon-Fri May & Oct), which has displays on a range of local topics. The surrounding Glenlivet Estate (now the property of the Crown) has lots of walking and cycling trails – the estate's **information centre** (☎ 580283; www.crownestate.co.uk/glenlivet; Main St) distributes free maps of the area – and a spur of the **Speyside Way** long-distance footpath (see the boxed text, p58) runs between Tomintoul and Ballindalloch, 15 miles to the north.

Accommodation for walkers includes the **Tomintoul Youth Hostel** (SYHA; ☎ 0870 004 1152; Main St; dm £12.50; 🕑 Apr-Sep), housed in the old village school. The small, family-run **Glenavon Hotel** (☎ 580218; www.glenavon-hotel.co.uk; The Sq; s/d £27/50; P ✗) is a more comfortable alternative.

GETTING THERE & AWAY

There's an infrequent bus service from Tomintoul to Dufftown (£4.20, 40 minutes, one daily on Tuesday, two on Saturday) and to Elgin (£4.80, 1¼ hours, one daily Thursday only). The Speyside Stroller bus service (p232) also stops at Tomintoul.

Banff & Macduff

☎ 01261 / combined pop 7750

Banff is a handsome Georgian town and Macduff is a busy fishing port, the two lying either side of Banff Bay and separated only by the mouth of the River Deveron. The big attraction here is Banff Links – 800m of clean golden sand.

The **TIC** (☎ 812419; Collie Lodge, High St; ☉ 10am-1pm & 2-6pm Mon-Sat, 1-6pm Sun Jul & Aug, 10am-1pm & 2-5pm Mon-Sat Apr-Jun & Sep) is beside St Mary's car park in Banff.

SIGHTS

Duff House (☎ 818181; adult/child £5.50/4.50; ☉ 11am-5pm Apr-Oct, 11am-4pm Thu-Sun Nov-Mar) is an impressive baroque mansion on the southern edge of Banff (upstream from the bridge, and across from the TIC). Built between 1735 and 1740 as the seat of the earls of Fife, it was designed by William Adam and bears similarities to that Adam masterpiece, Hopetoun House (p112). Since being gifted to the town in 1906 it has served as a hotel, a hospital and a POW camp, but after extensive refurbishment it opened as an art gallery. One of Scotland's hidden gems, it houses a superb permanent collection of Scottish art. Nearby **Banff Museum** (☎ 622906; High St; admission free; ☉ 2-4.30pm Mon-Sat Jun-Sep) has award-winning displays on local wildlife, geology and history, and Banff silver.

The centrepiece of **Macduff Marine Aquarium** (☎ 833369; 11 High Shore; adult/child £4.50/2; ☉ 10am-5pm) is a 400,000L open-air tank, complete with kelp-coated reef and wave machine. Marine oddities on view include the brightly coloured cuckoo wrasse, the warty-skinned lumpsucker and the vicious-looking wolf fish.

SLEEPING & EATING

Bryvard Guest House (☎ 818090; www.bryvardguest house.co.uk; Seafield St, Banff; s/d £30/55; ✗) The Bryvard is an imposing Edwardian town house close to the town centre, with four bedrooms (two with en suite). Go for the 'suite', which has a four-poster bed and a sea view.

County Hotel (☎ 815353; www.thecountyhotel.com; 32 High St, Banff; s/d £38/70; P ✗) The County occupies an elegant Georgian mansion in the town centre, and is owned by a French chef – the hotel's bistro serves light meals, while the restaurant (L'Auberge) offers the finest French cuisine (the five-course *menu gourmand* is £25).

Banff Links Caravan Park (☎ 812228; Banff; tent/ campervan £7/13; ☉ Apr-Oct) This camp site is beside the beach, 800m west of town.

GETTING THERE & AWAY

Stagecoach Bluebird buses run from Banff to Elgin (£8, one hour, hourly) and Aberdeen, and less frequently to Fraserburgh.

Portsoy

☎ 01261 / pop 1730

The pretty fishing village of Portsoy has an atmospheric 17th-century harbour and a maze of narrow streets lined with picturesque cottages. An ornamental stone known as **Portsoy marble** – actually a beautifully patterned green and pale pink serpentine – was quarried near Portsoy in the 17th and 18th centuries, and was reputedly used in the decoration of some rooms in the Palace of Versailles.

Each year on the last weekend in June or first weekend in July, Portsoy harbour is home to the **Scottish Traditional Boat Festival** (☎ 842951; www.scottishtraditionalboatfestival.co.uk), a lively gathering of historic wooden sailing boats accompanied by sailing races, live folk music, crafts demonstrations, street theatre and a food festival.

The 12-room **Boyne Hotel** (☎ 842242; www .boynehotel.co.uk; 2 North High St; r per person from £25) is a cosy and atmospheric place to stay, while the **Shore Inn** (☎ 842831; Church St) is a cosy real-ale pub overlooking the harbour.

Portsoy is 8 miles west of Banff; the hourly bus between Elgin and Banff stops here.

Fordyce

pop 150

This well-preserved historic village lies about 3 miles southwest of Portsoy. The main attractions are the 13th-century **St Tarquin's Church**, with its extraordinary canopied Gothic tombs, and the impressive 16th-century tower house of **Fordyce Castle**. The castle is not open to the public, but

NORTHEAST SCOTLAND

its whitewashed west wing provides atmospheric **self-catering accommodation** (☎ 01261-843722; www.fordycecastle.co.uk; per week £375-450, 3 nights in low season £275) for up to four people.

The nearby **Joiner's Workshop & Visitor Centre** (☎ 01771-622906; admission free; ⏰ 10am-6pm Thu-Mon) has a collection of woodworking tools and machinery, and stages woodwork demonstrations by a master joiner.

Fochabers & Around
☎ 01343 / pop 1500

Fochabers sits beside the last bridge over the River Spey before it enters the sea. The town has a pleasant square, with a church and clock tower dated 1798, and a handful of interesting antique shops.

West of the bridge over the Spey is **Baxters Highland Village** (☎ 820666; admission free; ⏰ 9am-5.30pm Apr-Dec, 10am-4pm Jan-Mar), which charts the history of the Baxter family and their well-known brand of quality Scottish foodstuffs, which was founded in 1868 when they opened their first shop in Fochabers. There's a factory tour with cookery demonstrations on weekdays.

Four miles north of Fochabers, at the mouth of the River Spey, is the tiny village of **Spey Bay**, the starting point for the Speyside Way long-distance footpath (see p58). It's also home to the **Moray Firth Wildlife Centre** (☎ 820339; www.wdcs.org; admission free; ⏰ 10.30am-5pm Apr-Jun, Sep & Oct, to 7pm Jul & Aug), with an interesting display on the Moray Firth dolphins, which can occasionally be seen off the mouth of the river.

Bluebird Stagecoach buses run from Fochabers to Aberdeen (£8, two hours) and Inverness (£8, 1¾ hours).

Findhorn
☎ 01309 / pop 885

The attractive village of Findhorn lies at the mouth of the River Findhorn, just east of the Findhorn Bay nature reserve. It's a great place for bird-watching, seal-spotting and coastal walks.

Findhorn Heritage Centre (☎ 630349; admission free; ⏰ 2-5pm Wed-Mon Jun-Aug, 2-5pm Sat & Sun May & Sep), housed in a former salmon-fisher's bothy at the northern end of the village, records the history of the settlement. The beach is just over the dunes north of the

heritage centre – at low tide, you can see seals hauled out on the sandbanks off the mouth of the River Findhorn.

Hippies old and new should check out the **Findhorn Foundation** (☎ 690311; www.findhorn.org; ⏰ 9am-12.30pm & 2-5pm Mon-Fri, 2-5pm Sat & Sun May-Aug, 9am-12.30pm & 2-5pm Mon-Fri Mar, Apr, Sep & Oct, 9am-12.30pm Mon-Fri Nov-Feb), an international spiritual community, founded in 1962. There's a small permanent population of around 150, but the community receives thousands of visitors each year. With no formal creed, the community is dedicated to cooperation with nature, 'dealing with work, relationships and our environment in new and more fulfilling ways', and fostering 'a deeper sense of the sacred in everyday life'. Projects include ecofriendly houses, a biological sewage-treatment plant and a wind-powered generator. Guided tours (£1) are available at 2pm Monday, Wednesday and Friday from March to October, and on Saturday and Sunday as well from June to August.

The **Crown & Anchor** (☎ 690243; 44 Findhorn; r per person from £29, mains £7-12; **P**) is a friendly 18th-century hotel and pub that serves excellent bar meals, including fresh seafood. Kids will love the toy train that carries meal orders from the bar to the kitchen.

Findhorn's other pub, the **Kimberley Inn** (☎ 690492; mains £6-12; ⏰ food served noon-10pm), also does good bar meals.

Culbin Forest

On the western side of Findhorn Bay is Culbin Forest, a vast swathe of Scots and Corsican pine that was planted in the 1940s to stabilise the shifting sand dunes that buried the Culbin Estate in the 17th century. The forest is a unique wildlife habitat, and is crisscrossed by a maze of walking trails.

Forres

The tidy town of Forres, 4 miles south of Findhorn, is famous for **Sueno's Stone**, a remarkable, 6.5m-high Pictish stone. It is the tallest and most elaborately carved Pictish stone in Scotland, dating from the 9th or 10th century, and is thought to depict a battle between the Picts and invading Scots or Vikings. It's protected from the elements by a huge plate-glass box.

Southern Highlands & Islands

Nowhere else in Scotland are land and sea so intimately entwined as in the Highlands and islands of the southwest. Long sea lochs such as Loch Fyne and Loch Long penetrate up to 40 miles inland, and to the west, a flotilla of islands lies moored off the coast, as varied and fascinating as they are beautiful.

The region covered in this chapter corresponds with the old county of Argyll, whose name comes from the Gaelic *earra-ghaidheal* – the seaboard of the Gael. Though measuring only 155 miles north to south, Argyll's convoluted coastline is a staggering 2300 miles in length. This is a corner of Scotland where sea travel is as important as road and rail – a network of ferry crossings allows you to island-hop your way from the Firth of Clyde to Oban and beyond, via the whisky distilleries of Islay, the wild mountains of Jura and the scenic delights of little Colonsay.

Oban itself is the gateway to the isles – from the peaceful backwaters of Kerrera and Lismore to the dramatic coastal scenery of Mull and the wild, windswept beaches of Coll and Tiree. The very air feels balmy – warmed by the Gulf Stream, Argyll is famous for its mild climate. Palm trees grow on the promenades, and exotic subtropical species are cultivated in botanic gardens.

The region is rich in prehistoric sites and is home to important religious and political centres of the past, including Dunadd, the ancient crowning place of Scottish kings; Finlaggan, the lake-island headquarters of the medieval Lords of the Isles; and the sacred island of Iona, where St Columba based his mission to spread Christianity throughout Scotland.

HIGHLIGHTS

- Trying not to gawp open-mouthed as you walk through the opulent marble-clad halls of **Mount Stuart** (p281)
- Strolling along the **Crinan Canal** (p283) on a sunny day, stopping to help the yachties open and close the lock gates
- Riding a high-speed motorboat through the white water and tidal whirlpools of the **Gulf of Corryvreckan** (see the boxed text, p292)
- Sitting by a log fire, sampling some of the finest single malt whiskies of **Islay** (p286)
- Spotting your first minke whale off the west coast of **Mull** (p300)

- **POPULATION: 4.7 MILLION**
- **AREA: 227,420 SQ KM**

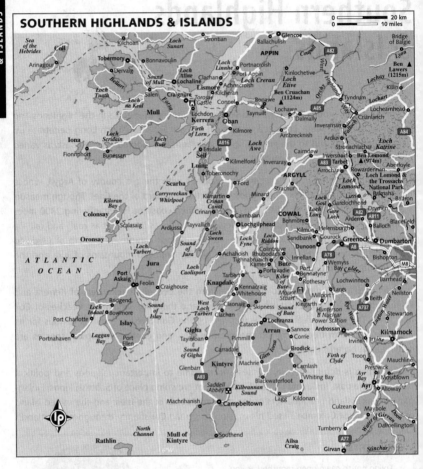

SOUTHERN HIGHLANDS & ISLANDS

SOUTHERN HIGHLANDS & ISLANDS

LOCH LOMOND & AROUND

The 'bonnie banks' and 'bonnie braes' of Loch Lomond have long been Glasgow's rural retreat – a scenic region of hills, lochs and healthy fresh air within easy reach of Scotland's largest city. Since the 1930s Glaswegians have made a regular weekend exodus to the hills, by car, by bike and on foot, and today the loch's popularity shows no sign of decreasing (Loch Lomond is within an hour's drive of 70% of Scotland's population).

The region's importance was recognised when it became the heart of the **Loch Lomond & the Trossachs National Park** (☎ 01389-722600; www.lochlomond-trossachs.org) – Scotland's first national park, created in 2002.

LOCH LOMOND

Loch Lomond is the largest lake in mainland Britain and, after Loch Ness, perhaps the most famous of Scotland's lochs. Its proximity to Glasgow (only 20 miles away) means that the tourist honeypots of Balloch, Loch Lomond Shores (a development near Balloch) and Luss get pretty crowded in summer. The main tourist focus is on the western shore of the loch, along the A82, and at the southern end, around Balloch, which can be a nightmare of Jet Skis and motorboats. The eastern shore is a little quieter.

GAELIC & NORSE PLACE NAMES

Throughout the Highlands and islands of Scotland the indigenous Gaelic language has left a rich legacy of place names. They're often intermixed with Old Norse names left behind by the Viking invaders who occupied the western and northern islands between the 8th and 13th centuries. The spelling is now anglicised but the meaning is still clear once you know what to look for. Here are a few of the more common Gaelic and Norse names and their meanings.

Gaelic Place Names

ach, auch – from *achadh* (field)
ard – from *ard* or *aird* (height, hill)
avon – from *abhainn* (river or stream)
bal – from *baile* (village or homestead)
ban – from *ban* (white, fair)
beg – from *beag* (small)
ben – from *beinn* (mountain)
buie – from *buidhe* (yellow)
dal – from *dail* (field or dale)
dow, dhu – from *dubh* (black)
drum – from *druim* (ridge or back)
dun – from *dun* or *duin* (fort or castle)
glen – from *gleann* (narrow valley)
gorm – from *gorm* (blue)
gower, gour – from *gabhar* (goat), eg Ardgour (height of the goats)
inch, insh – from *inis* (island, water-meadow or resting place for cattle)
inver – from *inbhir* (river mouth or meeting of two rivers)

kil – from *cille* (church), as in Kilmartin (Church of St Martin)
kin, ken – from *ceann* (head), eg Kinlochleven (head of Loch Leven)
kyle, kyles – from *caol* or *caolas* (narrow sea channel)
more, vore – from *mor* or *mhor* (big), eg Ardmore (big height), Skerryvore (big reef)
strath – from *srath* (broad valley)
tarbert, tarbet – from *tairbeart* (portage), meaning a narrow neck of land between two bodies of water, across which a boat can be dragged
tay, ty – from *tigh* (house), eg Tyndrum (house on the ridge)
tober – from *tobar* (well), eg Tobermory (Mary's well)

Norse Place Names

a, ay, ey – from *ey* (island)
bister, buster, bster – from *bolstaor* (dwelling place, homestead)
geo – from *gja* (chasm)
holm – from *holmr* (small island)
kirk – from *kirkja* (church)
pol, poll, bol – from *bol* (farm)
quoy – from *kvi* (sheep fold, cattle enclosure)
sker, skier, skerry – from *sker* (rocky reef)
ster, sett – from *setr* (house)
vig, vaig, wick – from *vik* (bay, creek)
voe, way – from *vagr* (bay, creek)

Loch Lomond straddles the Highland border and its character changes as you move north across it. The southern part is broad and island-studded and fringed by woods and Lowland meadows. However, north of Luss the loch narrows, occupying a deep trench gouged out by glaciers during the Ice Age, with 900m mountains crowding in on either side.

Orientation

Loch Lomond is 22 miles long and varies in width from 1 to 5 miles. The A82 along the western shore is the main road north from Glasgow to Fort William. The minor road along the eastern shore, reached from Balloch via Drymen, ends at Rowardennan. The West Highland Way walking trail also follows the eastern shore.

Information

Balloch Tourist Information Centre (TIC; ☎ 0870 720 0607; Balloch Rd; �
9.30am-6pm Jul & Aug, 10am-5pm May, Jun & Sep)
Balmaha National Park Centre (☎ 01360-870470; Balmaha; ☉ 10am-5pm Easter-Oct)
National Park Gateway Centre (☎ 0870 720 0631; www.lomondshores.com; Loch Lomond Shores, Balloch; ☉ 10am-7pm Apr-Jun & Sep, 10am-8pm Jul & Aug, 10.30am-4.30pm Oct-Mar)
Tarbet TIC (☎ 0870 720 0623; ☉ 9.30am-6pm Jul & Aug, 10am-5pm May, Jun & Sep) At the junction of the A82 and the A83.

Activities

WALKING

The big walk around here is the **West Highland Way** (see the boxed text, p278), which runs along the eastern shore of the loch.

There are shorter lochside walks at Firkin Point on the western shore and at several other places around the loch.

Rowardennan is the starting point for an ascent of **Ben Lomond** (974m), a popular five- to six-hour round trip. The route starts at the car park just past the Rowardennan Hotel.

OTHER ACTIVITIES
The mostly traffic-free **Clyde and Loch Lomond Cycle Way** links Glasgow to Balloch (20 miles), where it links with the **West Loch Lomond Cycle Path**, which continues along the loch shore to Tarbet (10 miles).

You can rent **rowing boats** at Balmaha Boatyard (see Tours, below) for £10/30 for a half-/full day, or £20/50 for a boat with outboard motor.

At Loch Lomond Shores (see Western Shore, right) you can hire canoes (£10/15 per half-/full hour) and bicycles (£7/10/15 per two hours/four hours/full day), take a **guided canoe trip** on the loch or go **pony trekking** (£1 a ride).

Tours
BOAT TRIPS
The main centre for boat trips is Balloch, where **Sweeney's Cruises** (☎ 01389-752376; Balloch Rd) offers a range of trips including a one-hour cruise around the islands (adult/child £5.50/3, departs hourly), and a daily 2½-hour cruise (£8/4, departs 2.30pm) to Luss village, allowing 30 minutes ashore. The terminal is directly opposite Balloch train station, beside the TIC. Sweeney's also runs hourly cruises from Loch Lomond Shores.

Cruise Loch Lomond (☎ 01301-702356) is based in Tarbet and offers trips to Inversnaid and Rob Roy MacGregor's cave (for more on Rob Roy, see the boxed text, p200).

The mail boat, run by **Balmaha Boatyard** (☎ 01360-870214; The Boatyard, Balmaha), cruises from Balmaha to the loch's four inhabited islands, departing at 11.30am and returning at 2pm with a one-hour stop on Inchmurrin (adult/child £8/4). Trips depart daily in July and August, and Monday, Thursday and Saturday in May, June and September.

Western Shore
The town of **Balloch**, which straddles the River Leven where it exits the southern end of Loch Lomond, is the loch's main popula-

tion centre and transport hub. A Victorian resort once thronged by day-trippers transferring between the train station and the steamer quay, it was sidelined somewhat by the A82 bypass in 1975. The bypass allows drivers to shoot through without stopping, but the town may be revived by the Loch Lomond Shores development.

Loch Lomond Shores (☎ 01389-722406; www.loch lomondshores.com), a half-mile north of Balloch, is a 'gateway centre' for Loch Lomond, offering a large national park information centre, various visitor attractions, outdoor activities and boat trips. However, in keeping with the times, the heart of the development is a large shopping mall. The vintage paddle steamer **Maid of the Loch** (☎ 01389-711865; admission free; ⏰ 11am-4pm May-Oct), built in 1953, is moored here while awaiting full restoration – you can nip aboard for a look around.

Unless it's raining, give Loch Lomond Shores a miss and head for the little picture-postcard village of **Luss**. Take a stroll among the pretty cottages with roses around their doors (cottages built by the local laird in the 19th century for the workers on his estate), and pop into the **Clan Colquhoun Visitor Centre** (☎ 01389-850564; adult/child £1/free; ⏰ 10.30am-6pm Easter-Oct) for some background history before enjoying a cuppa at the Coach House Coffee Shop.

SLEEPING & EATING
Loch Lomond Youth Hostel (SYHA; ☎ 0870 004 1136; Arden; dm £13-14.50; ⏰ Mar-Oct) Forget about roughing it, this is one of the most impressive hostels in the country – an imposing 19th-century country house set in beautiful grounds overlooking the loch. It's 2 miles north of Balloch and very popular, so book in advance in summer. And yes, it *is* haunted.

Drover's Inn (☎ 01301-704234; droversinn@visit-loch lomond.com; Inverarnan; s/d from £30/58, bar meals £6-9; ⏰ lunch & dinner; ⓟ) This is one howff (pub) you shouldn't miss – a low-ceilinged place with smoke-blackened stone, bare wooden floors spotted with candle wax, barmen in kilts and an ancient hallway festooned with moth-eaten stag's heads. Accommodation varies from basic rooms with shared bathroom in the old building to modern rooms (with bathrooms) in the annexe. The bar serves traditional Scottish dishes, including mince and tatties (potatoes), and haggis.

Ardlui Hotel (☎ 01301-704243; www.ardlui.co.uk; Ardlui; s/d £55/90; P) If the Drover's is a little rough for your taste, nip down the road to the plush Ardlui Hotel, a comfy country house hotel at the northern end of the loch.

Coach House Coffee Shop (☎ 01436-860341; Luss; snacks £2-4, mains £9; ☼ 10am-5pm) Fitted out with chunky pine furniture and a deep, deep sofa in front of a rustic fireplace, the Coach House is easily the best place to eat on Loch Lomond. The menu includes coffee and tea, home-baked cakes, scones and ciabattas, and more-substantial offerings such as haggis.

Viewing Gallery Café (☎ 01389-722416; Drumkinnon Tower, Loch Lomond Shores; snacks £3-5, mains £7-9) With tables arranged in front of floor-to-ceiling windows, this elegant café at the top of the Drumkinnon Tower makes the most of the superb views along the loch to Ben Lomond. The eating options range from tea and a scone to salads and smoked salmon.

Eastern Shore

The road along the loch's eastern shore passes through the attractive village of **Balmaha**, where you can hire boats or take a cruise on the mail boat (see Tours, opposite). There are several picnic areas along the lochside; the most attractive is at **Millarochy Bay** (1.5 miles north of Balmaha), which has a nice gravel beach and superb views across the loch to the Luss hills.

The road ends at **Rowardennan**, but the West Highland Way footpath continues along the shore of the loch. It's 7 miles to Inversnaid, which can be reached by road from the Trossachs (p197), and 15 miles to Inverarnan on the main A82 road at the northern end of the loch.

SLEEPING & EATING

Oak Tree Inn (☎ 01360-870357; www.oak-tree-inn.co .uk; Balmaha; s/d £48/68, 4-bed bunkroom £25, mains £7-14; ☼ food served noon-9pm; P ☒ ☖) An attractive traditional hotel built in slate and timber, the child-friendly Oak Tree has eight luxurious rooms with bathroom, and two four-bed bunkrooms. The rustic restaurant dishes up hearty meals such as sausage and mash, haggis, and vegetable lasagne; the house speciality is baked arctic char with lime-and-chive butter.

Passfoot Cottage (☎ 01360-870324; www.passfoot .com; Balmaha; r per person £23; ☼ Apr-Sep) Passfoot

is a pretty little whitewashed cottage decked out with colourful flower baskets, with a lovely location overlooking Balmaha Bay. The bright bedrooms have a homely feel, and there's a large lounge with wood-burning stove and loch view.

Rowardennan Youth Hostel (☎ 0870 004 1148; Rowardennan; dm £12-13.50; ☼ Mar-Oct) Housed in an attractive Victorian lodge, this hostel has a superb setting right on the loch shore.

Rowardennan Hotel (☎ 01360-870273; www.rowardennanhotel.com; Rowardennan; r £95-110, bar meals £7-12; ☼ lunch & dinner; P) Originally an 18th-century drovers' inn, the sprawling Rowardennan Hotel has comfy, refurbished rooms, two big bars (often crowded with rain-sodden hikers) and a beer garden (often crowded with midges).

Forestry Commission Cashel Campsite (☎ 01360-870234; Rowardennan; camp sites per 2 people £8-14; ☼ Apr-Oct) This is the most attractive camping ground in the area and is 3 miles north of Balmaha, by the loch.

Getting There & Away

First Glasgow buses 204 and 205 run from Argyle St in central Glasgow to Balloch and Loch Lomond Shores (1½ hours, at least two per hour). Scottish Citylink buses from Glasgow to Oban and Fort William stop at Luss (£5.60, 55 minutes, six daily), Tarbet (65 minutes) and Ardlui (1¼ hours).

There are frequent trains from Glasgow to Balloch (£3.55, 45 minutes, two per hour) and a less-frequent service on the West Highland line from Glasgow to Oban and Fort William, with stops at Arrochar & Tarbet, and Ardlui (£10, 1½ hours, three or four daily).

Getting Around

BUS

McColl's Coaches' (☎ 01389-754321) bus 309 runs from Balloch to Balmaha (20 minutes, every two hours). A Lomond Rural Rover ticket (£4) gives unlimited travel for a day on most buses in the Loch Lomond and Helensburgh area. Buy the ticket from the driver on the first bus you board.

FERRY

There are several passenger ferries on Loch Lomond, with fares ranging from £1 to £5 per person. These are mostly small motor-boats that operate on demand, rather than

WEST HIGHLAND WAY

This classic hike – the country's most popular long-distance path – stretches for 95 miles through some of Scotland's most spectacular scenery, from Milngavie (pronounced mull-guy), on the northwestern fringes of Glasgow, to Fort William.

The route begins in the Lowlands but the greater part of the trail is among the mountains, lochs and fast-flowing rivers of the western Highlands. After following the eastern shore of Loch Lomond and passing Crianlarich and Tyndrum, the route crosses the vast wilderness of Rannoch Moor and reaches Fort William via Glen Nevis, in the shadow of Britain's highest peak, Ben Nevis.

The path is easy to follow, making use of old drovers' roads (along which Highland cattle were once driven to Lowland markets), an old military road (built by troops to help subdue the Highlands in the 18th century) and disued railway lines.

Best done from south to north, you'll need about six or seven days to complete it. Many people round it off with an ascent of Ben Nevis (see the boxed text, p340).

You need to be properly equipped with good boots, maps, a compass and food and drink for the northern part of the walk. Midge repellent is also essential.

West Highland Way by Robert Aitken comes with a 1:50,000 Ordnance Survey (OS) route map and is the most comprehensive guidebook. The Harveys map West Highland Way is also handy and contains useful additional tourist information.

Accommodation shouldn't be too difficult to find, though between Bridge of Orchy and Kinlochleven it's limited. In summer, book B&Bs in advance. There are some youth hostels and bunkhouses on or near the path, and it's possible to camp in some parts. A list of accommodation is available for free from TICs.

For more information check out the website www.west-highland-way.co.uk.

to a set timetable – telephone, or call at the establishment listed for more information.

Ardlui to Ardleish (☎ 01307-704243; Ardlui Hotel) From 9am to 8pm on demand.

Balmaha to Inchcailloch (☎ 01360-870214; Balmaha Boatyard, Balmaha) From 9am to 8pm on demand.

Inverbeg to Rowardennan (☎ 01360-870273; Rowardennan Hotel) Three daily from April to September.

Inveruglas to Inversnaid (☎ 01877-386223; Inversnaid Hotel) On demand.

Tarbet to Inversnaid (☎ 01301-702356; Cruise Loch Lomond, Tarbet) If space is available on cruise boats; inquire at the Cruise Loch Lomond office, Tarbet.

HELENSBURGH

☎ 01436 / pop 16,500

With the coming of the railway in the mid-19th century, Helensburgh – named in the 18th century after the wife of Sir James Colquhoun of Luss – became a popular seaside retreat for wealthy Glaswegian families. Their spacious Victorian villas now populate the neat grid of streets that covers the hill-side above the Firth of Clyde, but none can compare with the splendour of **Hill House** (☎ 673900; Upper Colquhoun St; adult/child £8/5; ⏱ 1.30-5.30pm Easter-Oct). Built in 1902 for the Glasgow publisher Walter Blackie, it is perhaps architect Charles Rennie Mackin-

tosh's finest creation – its timeless elegance feels as chic today as it no doubt did when the Blackies moved in a century ago.

Helensburgh has a ferry connection with Gourock (p145) via Kilcreggan, and a frequent train service to Glasgow (£4.25, 40 minutes, two per hour).

ARROCHAR

☎ 01301 / pop 650

The village of Arrochar has a wonderful location, looking across the head of Loch Long to the jagged peaks of the **Cobbler** (881m). The mountain takes its name from the shape of its north peak (the one on the right), which looks like a cobbler hunched over his bench. The village has several hotels and shops, and a bank and a post office.

If you want to climb the Cobbler, start from the roadside car park at Succoth near the head of Loch Long. A steep uphill hike beside the woods is followed by an easier section as you traverse southwest into the valley below the triple peaks. Then it's steeply uphill again to the saddle between the north and central peaks. The central peak (to the south) is the highest point, but it's awkward to get to – scramble through the hole and along the ledge to reach the airy summit. The north peak (to the right/ north) is an easy walk. Allow five to six hours for the 5-mile return trip.

There's good camping at **Ardgartan Caravan & Campsite** (☎ 702293; Ardgartan; camp sites per 2 people £7.40-13; ☿ Apr-Oct) at the foot of Glen Croe.

The black-and-white, 19th-century **Village Inn** (☎ 702279; Arrochar; ☿ lunch & dinner) is a lovely spot for lunch, or just a pint of ale – the beer garden has a great view of the Cobbler.

Scottish Citylink buses from Glasgow to Inveraray and Campbeltown call at Arrochar and Ardgartan (£6.70, 1¼ hours, three daily). See p277 for trains to Arrochar & Tarbet station.

SOUTH ARGYLL

COWAL

The remote Cowal peninsula is cut off from the rest of the country by the lengthy fjords of Loch Long and Loch Fyne – it's an area more accessible by boat than by car. It's comprised of rugged hills and narrow lochs, with only a few small villages; the scenery around Loch Riddon is particularly enchanting. The only town on the mainland is the old-fashioned holiday resort of Dunoon.

From Arrochar, the A83 to Inveraray loops around the head of Loch Long and climbs up Glen Croe. The pass at the head of the glen is called the **Rest and be Thankful** – when the original military road through the glen was repaired in the 18th century, a stone was erected at the top inscribed 'Rest, and be thankful. This road was made, in 1748, by the 24th Regt…Repaired by the 93rd Regt. 1786'. A copy of the stone can be seen at the far end of the parking area at the top of the pass.

There's a Forest Enterprise **visitors centre** (☎ 702432; Ardgartan; admission free; ☿ 10am-5pm Apr-Oct) at the foot of the glen, with information on various walks in the Cowal peninsula.

As you descend Glen Kinglas on the far side of the Rest and be Thankful, the A815 forks to the left; this is the main overland route into Cowal. From Glasgow, the most direct route is by ferry from Gourock to Dunoon.

Dunoon & Around
☎ 01369
Like Rothesay on the Isle of Bute, Dunoon (population 9100) is a Victorian seaside re-

sort that owes its existence to the steamers that once carried thousands of Glaswegians on pleasure trips 'doon the watter' (down the water) in the 19th and 20th centuries. As with Rothesay, Dunoon's fortunes declined in recent decades when cheap foreign holidays stole its market – however, while the Bute resort appears to be recovering, Dunoon is still a bit down in the dumps.

The **TIC** (☎ 0870 720 0629; 7 Alexandra Pde; ☿ 9am-6pm Mon-Fri, 10am-5pm Sat & Sun) is on the waterfront 100m north of the pier.

SIGHTS & ACTIVITIES
The town's main attraction is still, as it was in the 1950s, strolling along the **promenade**, licking an ice-cream cone and watching the yachts at play in the Firth of Clyde. On a small hill above the seafront is a statue of **Highland Mary** (1763–86), one of the great loves of Robert Burns' life. She was born near Dunoon, but died tragically young; her statue gazes longingly across the firth to Burns' home territory in Ayrshire.

The **Benmore Botanic Garden** (☎ 706261; Benmore; adult/child £3.50/1; ☿ 10am-6pm Apr-Sep, to 5pm Mar & Oct), 7 miles north of Dunoon, was originally planted in the 19th and early 20th centuries. It contains the country's finest collection of flowering trees and shrubs, including Bhutanese and Chilean rainforest specimens, and is entered along a spectacular avenue of giant Californian redwoods (planted in 1863).

FESTIVALS & EVENTS
Dunoon hosts the annual **Cowal Highland Gathering** (☎ 703206; www.cowalgathering.com) in mid-August; the spectacular finale traditionally features 1000 bagpipers playing en masse.

SLEEPING & EATING
Belmont House (☎ 701287; www.belmont-house.co.uk; 2 Edward St, West Bay; s/d £35/50; P X) You can experience some of Dunoon's former elegance at this large Victorian villa that overlooks the bay south of the ferry pier. One of the rooms has a huge four-poster bed, and you can help yourself to the sherry decanter in the lounge.

Chatters (☎ 706402; 58 John St; mains £7-10; ☿ 10am-3pm & 6-10pm Wed-Sat) Chatters is a pretty little cottage restaurant serving traditional Scottish dishes, and is famous for its tempting desserts. The two-/three-course lunch (£10/12) is excellent value.

Black of Dunoon (☎ 702311; 113 George St) This bakery, halfway along the main street, is famous for its traditional Scottish shortbread.

GETTING THERE & AWAY

Dunoon is served by two competing ferry services from Gourock (p145) – the CalMac ferry is better if you are travelling on foot and want to arrive in the town centre.

Tighnabruaich

☎ 01700 / pop 200

Sleepy little Tighnabruaich (pronounced tinna-*broo*-ach), a small colony of seaside villas built by wealthy Glasgow families, was once a regular stop for Clyde steamers. It's also one of the most attractive villages on the Firth of Clyde.

The old wooden pier is still occasionally visited by the paddle steamer *Waverley*, and the link with the sea continues in the **Tighnabruaich Sailing School** (☎ 811717; www.tssargyll.co .uk; ☺ May-Sep). It offers dinghy-sailing and windsurfing courses – a half-day's instruction for an adult/child costs £33/28. Customers can pitch a tent at the school's own camping ground for £4 a night.

ISLE OF BUTE

☎ 01700 / pop 7350

The peaceful island of Bute lies pinched between the thumb and forefinger of the Cowal peninsula, separated from the mainland by a narrow, scenic strait known as the Kyles of Bute. The Highland Boundary Fault cuts through the middle of the island so that, geologically speaking, the northern half is in the Highlands and the southern half in the central Lowlands – a metal arch on Rothesay's Esplanade marks the fault line.

The **Isle of Bute Discovery Centre** (☎ 505156; www.visitbute.com; Esplanade, Rothesay; ☺ 9am-5.30pm) in Rothesay's restored Winter Garden provides tourist information.

The five-day **Isle of Bute Jazz Festival** (www .butejazz.com) is held over the first weekend of May, and in late July there's the **ButeLive** (www.butelive.co.uk) music and arts festival.

ACTIVITIES

The best **walk** on Bute is from the ferry pier at Rhubodach to the northern tip of the island (1.5 miles), where you can watch yachts negotiate the rocky narrows of the Burnt Islands.

Just around the point are the **Maids of Bute**, two rocks painted to look like old women. The story goes that the distinctively shaped (but then unpainted) rocks were first noticed by the skipper of a pleasure steamer in the early 20th century, who always pointed them out to the passengers on his boat. Frustrated that the tourists could never see the resemblance, he sent a deckhand ashore with a couple of tins of paint to give them some clothes and recognisable faces. No one is quite sure who now maintains the maids, but every time the paint begins to peel, it's not long before a fresh coat brightens them up.

You can retrace your steps to Rhubodach (allow two hours round trip), or continue south along the west coast of the island – there's some rough walking here – to Ettrick Bay (total 10 miles, allow four to five hours).

GETTING THERE & AROUND

CalMac ferries travel between Wemyss Bay (p145) and Rothesay (passenger/car £3.65/15, 35 minutes, hourly). Another ferry crosses the short stretch of water between Rhubodach in the north of the island and Colintraive (passenger/car £1.10/7.35, five minutes, frequent) in Cowal.

Stagecoach Western buses run several times a week from Rothesay to Tighnabruaich and Dunoon via the ferry at Colintraive. On Monday and Thursday a bus goes from Rothesay to Portavadie, where there's a ferry to Tarbert in Kintyre (passenger/car £3.05/15, 25 minutes, hourly April to September).

Cycling on Bute is excellent – the roads are well surfaced and fairly quiet. You can hire a bike from the **Mountain Bike Centre** (☎ 502333; 24 East Princes St, Rothesay) for £8/15 per half-/full day.

Rothesay

From the mid-19th century until the 1960s, Rothesay – once dubbed the Margate of the Clyde – was one of the most popular holiday resorts in Scotland. Its Esplanade thronged with day-trippers disembarking from the numerous steamers crowded round the pier, and its hotels were filled with elderly holidaymakers and convalescents taking advantage of the town's famously mild climate.

The fashion for foreign holidays that took off in the 1970s saw Rothesay's fortunes decline, and by the late 1990s it had become dilapidated and despondent. But in the last few years a nostalgia-fuelled resurgence of interest in Rothesay's holiday heyday has seen many of its Victorian buildings restored and a new feeling of optimism in the air.

Just two blocks inland from the pier are the splendid, moated ruins of 13th-century **Rothesay Castle** (☎ 502691; King St; adult/child £3/1.20; ☼ 9.30am-6.30pm Easter-Sep, 9.30am-4.30pm Sat-Wed Oct-Easter). Once a favourite residence of the Stuart kings, it is unique in Scotland in having a circular plan, with four massive round towers. The landscaped moat, with its manicured turf, flower gardens and lazily cruising ducks, makes a picturesque setting.

There aren't too many places where a public toilet would count as a tourist attraction, but Rothesay pier's **Victorian toilets** (adult/child 10p/free), dating from 1899, are a monument to lavatorial luxury, a disinfectant-scented temple of marbled black porcelain, glistening green and cream tiles and gleaming copper pipes. The attendant will escort ladies into the hallowed confines of the gents for a look around if those facilities are unoccupied. HRH Prince Charles, the prince of Wales, visited the loos in 1998 in his official capacity as the duke of Rothesay.

The most interesting displays in **Bute Museum** (☎ 505067; Stuart St; adult/child £1.20/40p; ☼ 10.30am-4.30pm Mon-Sat, 2.30-4.30pm Sun Apr-Sep, 2.30-4.30pm Tue-Sat Oct-Mar) are those recounting the history of the famous Clyde steamers. Other displays cover the natural history, archaeology and geology of the island.

Gardeners will enjoy the beautifully restored **Victorian Fernery** (☎ 504555; Ascog; adult/child £3/free; ☼ 10am-5pm Wed-Sun mid-Apr–mid-Oct) at Ascog Hall, on the southern edge of town.

SLEEPING & EATING

Commodore Guest House (☎ 502178; www.commodore bute.com; 12 Battery Pl; s/d from £25/40; ☒) This beautifully renovated harbour-side guesthouse has fine views at the front, a pleasant garden at the back and – Aussies take note – Vegemite on the breakfast table.

Moorings (☎ 502277; fjhbute@aol.com; 7 Mountstuart Rd; s/d £35/50; ℗) A little further east along the bay, this is a delightful Victorian lodge with good harbour views.

Ascog Farm (☎ 503372; Ascog; r per person £20; ℗) All four rooms at this peaceful farmhouse B&B have been laid out in accordance with the rules of feng shui. It's 3 miles from Rothesay, heading south on the A844 coastal road.

Waterfront Café (☎ 505166; 16 East Princes St; mains £6-10; ☼ 11am-5pm Mon-Sat, plus 6.30-10pm Fri & Sat, noon-4pm Sun) This smart, recently renovated eatery overlooks the harbour and offers everything from a good cappuccino to excellent haddock and chips. There are also good homemade veggie dishes.

Around Rothesay
MOUNT STUART

The Stuart earls of Bute are direct descendants of Robert the Bruce and have lived on the island for 700 years. When a large part of the family seat was destroyed by fire in 1877, the third marquess of Bute, John Patrick Crichton-Stuart (1847–1900) – one of the greatest architecture patrons of his day – commissioned Sir Robert Rowand Anderson to build **Mount Stuart** (☎ 503877; adult/child £7/3; ☼ 11am-5pm Sun-Fri, 10am-2.30pm Sat Easter & May-Sep). It's the finest neo-Gothic stately home in Scotland.

The heart of the house is the stunning **Marble Hall**, a three-storey extravaganza of Italian marble that soars 25m to a dark blue vault spangled with constellations of golden stars that represent the signs of the zodiac. The design and decoration reflect the third marquess' fascination with astrology, mythology and religion, a theme carried over into the grand **Marble Staircase** beyond (where wall panels depict the six days of the Creation), and the lavishly decorated **Horoscope Bedroom**. Here the central ceiling panel records the positions of the stars and planets at the time of the marquess' birth on 12 September 1847.

The present marquess (the seventh) is known, rather dashingly, as Johnny Dumfries (b 1958) and was once, even more dashingly, a Formula One and Le Mans racing driver. Mount Stuart hit the headlines in 2003 when Johnny's pal Stella McCartney – daughter of ex-Beatle Sir Paul – held her wedding there.

Yet another highlight is the **Marble Chapel**, built entirely out of dazzling white Carrara marble. It has a dome lit to spectacular effect by a ring of ruby-red stained-glass windows.

You could easily spend half a day here, wandering from one eye-poppingly magnificent room to the next; just keep one hand free to stop your jaw from repeatedly hitting the floor.

SOUTHERN HIGHLANDS
& ISLANDS

Mount Stuart is 5 miles south of Rothesay. **Western Buses** (☎ 502076) runs bus 90 hourly from Rothesay to Mount Stuart. You can buy a joint ticket (adult/child £17/8.50) that covers return train, ferry and bus travel from Glasgow to Mount Stuart, as well as admission. Ask at the Glasgow TIC.

Southern Bute

In the southern part of Bute you'll find the 12th-century ruin of **St Blane's Chapel**, with a 10th-century tombstone in the graveyard. There are good sandy **beaches** at Kilchattan Bay in the south, and at Scalpsie and Ettrick Bays on the west coast. You can often spot seals basking at low tide off **Ardscalpsie Point**.

INVERARAY

☎ 01499 / pop 700

You can spot Inveraray long before you get here – its neat, whitewashed buildings stand out from a distance on the shores of Loch Fyne. It's a planned town, built by the duke of Argyll when he revamped his nearby castle in the 18th century. The **TIC** (☎ 0870 720 0616; Front St; 🖳) is on the seafront, and has Internet access for £1 per 10 minutes.

Sights

Inveraray Castle (☎ 302203; adult/child £5.90/3.90; 🕑 10am-5.45pm Mon-Sat, 1-5.45pm Sun Jun-Sep, 10am-1pm & 2-5.45pm Mon-Thu & Sat, 1-5.45pm Sun Apr, May & Oct) has been the seat of the dukes of Argyll – chiefs of Clan Campbell – since the 15th century. The 18th-century building, with its fairytale turrets and fake battlements, houses an impressive armoury hall, its walls patterned with a collection of more than 1000 pole arms, dirks, muskets and Lochaber axes. The castle is 500m north of town, entered from the A819 Dalmally road.

The Georgian **Inveraray Jail** (☎ 302381; Church Sq; adult/child £5.95/3; 🕑 9.30am-6pm Apr-Oct, 10am-5pm Nov-Mar), in the centre of town, is an award-winning, interactive tourist attraction. You can sit in on a trial, try out a cell, and discover the harsh torture meted out to unfortunate prisoners. The attention to detail – including a life-sized model of an inmate squatting on a 19th-century toilet – more than makes up for the sometimes tedious commentary.

The ship *Arctic Penguin*, a three-masted schooner built in 1911 and one of the world's last surviving iron sailing ships, is permanently moored in Inveraray harbour

and houses the **Inveraray Maritime Museum** (☎ 302213; The Pier; adult/child £3/1.50; 🕑 10am-6pm Apr-Sep, 10am-5pm Oct-Mar). It has interesting photos and models of the old Clyde steamers and a display about Para Handy (see the boxed text, p44). Kids will love exploring below the decks – there's a special play area in the bowels of the ship.

Sleeping & Eating

Claonairigh House (☎ 302160; www.claonairighhouse .co.uk; Bridge of Douglas; r per person £18-25; 🅿 ⊠) This grand 18th-century house, built for the duke of Argyll in 1745, is set in 3 hectares of grounds on the bank of a river (salmon-fishing available). There are three homely en-suite rooms, one with a four-poster bed, and a resident menagerie of dogs, ducks, chickens and goats. It's 4 miles south of town on the A83.

George Hotel (☎ 302111; www.thegeorgehotel.co .uk; Main St East; s/d from £35/60; 🅿 ⊠) The recently renovated George Hotel boasts a magnificent choice of opulent rooms, complete with four-poster beds, period furniture, Victorian roll-top baths and private Jacuzzis. The cosy wood-panelled bar, with its rough stone walls, flagstone floor and peat fires, is a delightful place for a bar lunch.

Inveraray Youth Hostel (☎ 0870 004 1125; Dalmally Rd; dm £12.50; 🕑 Apr-Sep) To get to this hostel, which is housed in a comfortable, modern bungalow, go through the arched entrance on the seafront – it's set back on the left of the road about 100m further on.

Argyll Hotel (☎ 302466; www.the-argyll-hotel.co.uk; Front St; r per person £32-59; 🅿 ⊠) Dating from 1750, the large and comfortably modernised Argyll dominates Inveraray's seafront and offers elegant rooms with excellent views over the loch.

Loch Fyne Oyster Bar (☎ 600236; Clachan, Cairndow; mains £9-15; 🕑 9am-9pm) Six miles north of Inveraray in Cairndow, this rustic-themed restaurant serves excellent seafood, though the service can be hit-and-miss. It's housed in a converted byre, and the menu includes local seafood and salmon. The neighbouring shop sells packaged seafood to take away.

Getting There & Away

Scottish Citylink buses run from Glasgow to Inveraray (£8, 1¾ hours, six daily Monday to Saturday, two Sunday). Three of these buses continue to Lochgilphead and

Campbeltown (£8.60, 2½ hours); the others continue to Oban (£6.40, 1¼ hours).

LOCHGILPHEAD
☎ 01546 / pop 2600

Lochgilphead sits at the head of a long tidal flat, facing down Loch Fyne towards the peaks of Arran. There's not much to see in the town itself, but there's plenty of interest in the surrounding area. The Crinan Canal brushes the western edge of the village on its way to the west coast (you can easily walk from here to Crinan in a day), and Kilmartin Glen is just 8 miles to the north.

There's a **TIC** (☎ 602344; Lochnell St; ☼ Apr-Oct) on the seafront, a post office and a supermarket, and two banks with ATMs.

West Coast Motors (☎ 570500) bus 423 runs from Oban to Lochgilphead (£4, 1¾ hours, four daily Monday to Friday, two on Saturday) via Kilmartin Glen.

CRINAN CANAL
☎ 01546

The scenic Crinan Canal runs from Ardrishaig (2 miles south of Lochgilphead) to Crinan. Completed in 1801, the 9-mile canal allows seagoing vessels – mostly yachts – to take a short cut from the Firth of Clyde and Loch Fyne to the west coast of Scotland, avoiding the long and sometimes dangerous passage around the Mull of Kintyre. You can easily walk the full length of the canal towpath in a day.

Gemini Cruises (☎ 830238; www.gemini-crinan.co.uk; Kilmahuaig), a half-mile west of the Crinan Hotel, runs two-hour boat trips (adult/child £14/9) to the spectacular Gulf of Corryvreckan (see the boxed text, p292) where strong tidal currents create Britain's biggest whirlpool. It will also ferry groups across to Ardlussa on Jura (£60 for up to 12 passengers and bicycles, 30 minutes) by prior arrangement.

The plush **Cairnbaan Hotel** (☎ 603668; www .cairnbaan.com; Cairnbaan; s/d £73/125, mains £10-17; **P** ☼ ☐), halfway along the canal, serves delicious meals – including haddock and chips and chargrilled venison burgers – in a comfortable conservatory.

The even more luxurious **Crinan Hotel** (☎ 830261; www.crinanhotel.com; Crinan; s/d from £180/280, mains £16-25; **P** ☒), overlooking Loch Crinan at the northwestern end of the canal, has one of Scotland's finest seafood restaurants, although many consider it a tad overpriced.

The **coffee shop** (☼ 10am-5.30pm) on the western side of the canal basin at Crinan has great home-baked cakes and scones.

KILMARTIN GLEN
☎ 01546

This magical glen is the focus of one of the most concentrated areas of prehistoric sites in Scotland. Burial cairns, standing stones, stone circles, hill forts and cup-and-ring-marked rocks litter the countryside – within a 6-mile radius of Kilmartin village there are 25 sites with standing stones and over 100 rock carvings. In the 6th century Irish settlers founded the kingdom of Dalriada, which eventually united with the Picts in 843 to create the first Scottish kingdom; their capital was the hill fort of Dunadd.

There's a shop and post office in Kilmartin village.

Sights

The oldest monuments at Kilmartin date from 5000 years ago and comprise a linear cemetery of **burial cairns** that run south of Kilmartin village for 1.5 miles. There are also ritual monuments (two stone circles) at **Temple Wood**, three-quarters of a mile southwest of Kilmartin.

Kilmartin Churchyard contains some 10th-century Celtic crosses and lots of medieval grave slabs carved with the effigies of knights. Next door, the **Museum of Ancient Culture** (☎ 510278; www.kilmartin.org; Kilmartin House; adult/child £4.60/1.70; ☼ 10am-5.30pm) is a fascinating centre for archaeology and landscape interpretation with artefacts from the local sites; reconstructions; interactive displays; and guided tours. The project was partly funded by midges – the curator exposed himself in Temple Wood on a warm summer's evening and was sponsored per midge bite!

The hill fort of **Dunadd**, 3.5 miles south of Kilmartin village, was the royal residence of the first kings of Dalriada, and may have been where the Stone of Destiny (see the boxed text, p79) was originally located. The faint rock carvings of a wild boar and two footprints with an ogham inscription could have been used in some kind of inauguration ceremony. The prominent little hill rises straight out of the boggy plain of the Moine Mhor Nature Reserve. A slippery path leads to the summit where you can gaze out on much the same view that the kings of Dalriada enjoyed 1300 years ago.

At **Kilmichael Glassary** (a mile east of Dunadd) and **Achnabreck** (half a mile south) there are rock faces carved with elaborate designs – like ripples from a pebble dropped into a pond – known to archaeologists as cup-and-ring marks. Their purpose and meaning are unknown.

Just over a mile north of Kilmartin are the extensive remains of the 16th-century tower house **Carnassarie Castle**, former seat of the bishops of the Western Isles, with some excellent carved stonework.

Sleeping & Eating

Burndale B&B (☎ 510235; alan-hawkins@burndale-kilmartin.freeserve.co.uk; r per person £25) Set in an old manse (minister's house), this B&B is just three minutes' walk north from the Museum of Ancient Culture.

Kilmartin Hotel (☎ 510250; www.kilmartin-hotel.com; s/d £38/60; **P**) Though the rooms are bit on the small side, this attractively old-fashioned hotel is full of atmosphere and has a restaurant, and a real-ale bar where you can enjoy live folk music at weekends.

Cairn Bar & Restaurant (☎ 510254; mains £11-16; ☼ 6.30-10pm Wed-Mon Apr-Sep, 6.30-10pm Thu-Sun Oct-Mar) Just along the road from the Museum of Ancient Culture, this rustic-themed bar and restaurant serves traditional Scottish dishes such as smoked haddock, venison sausages, salmon and steak.

Getting There & Away

The Lochgilphead to Oban bus stops at Kilmartin (15 minutes, four daily Monday to Friday, two on Saturday), as does the return bus from Oban (£4, 1¼ hours).

KINTYRE

The Kintyre peninsula – 40 miles long and 8 miles wide – is almost an island, with only a narrow isthmus at Tarbert connecting it to the wooded hills of Knapdale. During the Norse occupation of the Western Isles, the Scottish king decreed that the Vikings could claim as their own any island they could circumnavigate in a longship. So in 1098 the wily Magnus Barefoot stood at the helm while his men dragged their boat across this neck of land, thus validating his claim to Kintyre.

Tarbert

☎ 01880 / pop 1500

The attractive fishing village and yachting centre of Tarbert is the gateway to Kintyre, and well worth a stopover for lunch or dinner. There's a **TIC** (☎ 820429; Harbour St; ☼ Apr-Oct), a Co-op supermarket and two banks with ATMs near the head of the harbour.

SIGHTS

The pretty harbour is overlooked by the crumbling, ivy-covered ruins of **Tarbert Castle**, built by Robert the Bruce in the 14th century. You can hike up to it via a signposted footpath beside the **Ann R Thomas Gallery** (Harbour St).

An Tairbeart Arts Centre (☎ 821116; Campbeltown Rd; admission free; ☼ 10am-5pm) is at the southern edge of the village and has galleries of crafts and contemporary arts. There are also displays about local natural history and human interaction with the environment.

FESTIVALS & EVENTS

Tarbert is a lively little place, and never more so than during the annual **Scottish Series Yacht Race** (www.clyde.org), held over five days around the last weekend in May, when the harbour is crammed with hundreds of visiting yachts. The **Tarbert Seafood Festival** (www.seafood-festival.com) is held on the first weekend in July, and the **Tarbert Music Festival** (www.auqn74.dsl.pipex.com) is on the third weekend in September.

SLEEPING & EATING

There are plenty of B&Bs and hotels, but be sure to book ahead during festivals and major events.

Springside B&B (☎ 820413; www.scotland-info.co.uk/springside; Pier Rd; s/d £25/44; **P** ✗) You can sit out the front of this pretty, whitewashed fisherman's cottage, which overlooks the entrance to the harbour, and watch the yachts and fishing boats come and go. There are four comfy rooms, three with en suite, and the house is just five minutes' walk from the village centre in one direction, and a short stroll from the Portavadie ferry in the other.

Columba Hotel (☎ 820808; www.columbahotel.com; East Pier Rd; s/d from £40/78, bar meals £7-12, 3-course dinner £25; ☼ lunch & dinner; **P**) A pleasant 10-minute walk from the village centre along the southern side of the harbour, this peaceful Victorian hotel has 10 en-suite rooms in period style, and a restaurant that serves top Scottish cuisine.

Corner House Bistro (☎ 820263; Harbour St; mains £12-20; ⏲ lunch & dinner) It's worth making the trip to Tarbert just to eat at this relaxed and romantic restaurant, with its log fires, candlelight and an award-winning French chef who knows exactly what to do with top quality local seafood – scallops seared to melt-in-the-mouth perfection, succulent sea bass flaking lightly from the bone. The entrance is on the side street around the corner from the Corner House pub – look for the green awning.

Victoria Hotel (☎ 820236; Barmore Rd; bar meals £6-12; ⏲ food served noon-2pm & 6-9.30pm) The bright yellow Victoria overlooks the head of the harbour and is popular with visiting yachties who flock here to enjoy the beer and decent bar meals.

GETTING THERE & AWAY

Tarbert is served by the Scottish Citylink buses that run from Campbeltown to Glasgow and Oban (Glasgow to Tarbert £11.20, 3½ hours; Tarbert to Campbeltown £5.10, 1¼ hours).

CalMac operates a small car ferry from Tarbert to Portavadie on the Cowal peninsula (passenger/car £3.05/15, 25 minutes, hourly April to September).

The Kennacraig ferry terminal on West Loch Tarbert, 5 miles south of Tarbert, has ferries to the islands of Islay (p288) and Colonsay (p294).

Skipness

☎ 01880 / pop 100
The tiny village of Skipness is on the east coast of Kintyre, about 13 miles south of Tarbert, in a pleasant and quiet setting with great views of Arran. There's a post office and general store in the village.

Beyond the village rise the substantial remains of 13th-century **Skipness Castle**, a former possession of the Lords of the Isles. It's a striking building, composed of dark green local stone and trimmed with red-brown Arran sandstone. The tower house was added in the 16th century and was occupied until the 19th. From the top you can see the roofless, 13th-century **St Brendan's Chapel** down by the shore; the kirkyard contains some excellent carved grave slabs.

There's a waymarked **forest walk** through the remote hills from Tarbert to Skipness (9 miles, four to five hours); pick up a free map from the TIC at Tarbert.

Skipness Seafood Cabin (☎ 760207; sandwiches £1-2, mains £5-8; ⏲ 11am-6pm Sun-Fri late May–Sep), in the grounds of nearby Skipness House, serves tea, coffee and home baking, as well as local fish and shellfish dishes. In fine weather you can eat at outdoor picnic tables with grand views of Arran.

Local bus 448 runs between Tarbert and Skipness (35 minutes, two to four daily Monday to Saturday).

At Claonaig, 2 miles west of Skipness, there's a daily car ferry to Lochranza (p171) on the Isle of Arran (passenger/car £4.45/20, 30 minutes, seven to nine daily).

Isle of Gigha

☎ 01583 / pop 120
Gigha (pronounced *ghee*-a) is a low-lying island that's 6 miles long by about a mile wide. It's famous for its sandy beaches and the subtropical plants that thrive in the mild climate at **Achamore Gardens** (☎ 505254; Achamore House; admission free, donation requested; ⏲ 9am-dusk). Locally made Gigha cheese is sold in many parts of Argyll. There are several varieties made on the island, including pasteurised goat's-milk cheese and oak-smoked cheddar.

The island's limited accommodation includes **Post Office House** (☎ 505251; www.gighastores .co.uk; r per person £22-25; P ✗), a Victorian house at the top of the hill above the ferry slip (it houses the island post office and shop as well as being a B&B), and the **Gigha Hotel** (☎ 505254; www.gigha.org.uk; r per person £35-45, 4-course dinner £28; ✗), 100m south of the post office.

There's also a range of self-catering cottages available (see www.gigha.org.uk for details). Camping is not allowed on the island.

CalMac runs a daily ferry from Tayinloan in Kintyre to Gigha (passenger/car £5.30/20 return, 20 minutes, hourly Monday to Saturday, six on Sunday) – only return fares are available. A bicycle costs an extra £2.

You can rent bikes from Post Office House or Gigha Hotel for £3 per hour or £10 per day.

Mid-Kintyre

At Glenbarr, 6 miles south of Tayinloan, is **Glenbarr Abbey Visitor Centre** (☎ 01583-421247; adult/child £3/2; ⏲ 10am-5pm Wed-Mon Easter-Oct), a centre for the Clan Macalister. This 18th-century house has a large collection of clothes, thimbles and china, and a pair of gloves worn by Mary, Queen of Scots. Angus Macalister, the laird of Glenbarr, will himself take you on an entertaining guided tour.

On the east coast of Kintyre is the pretty village of **Carradale**, with its mile-long sweep of golden beach on Carradale Bay. The **Network Heritage Centre** (☎ 01586-431296; admission free; ☽ 10am-5pm Mon-Sat, 12.30-5pm Sun Jul & Aug, 10am-5pm Tue, Wed, Fri & Sat, 12.30-4pm Sun Easter-Jun & Sep–mid-Oct) is housed in the old school house, and has fishing, farming and forestry displays.

There are several interesting ruins in the area, including a vitrified Iron Age fort on the eastern point of Carradale Bay, and the 12th-century **Saddell Abbey** (5 miles south), founded by Somerled, Lord of the Isles.

Campbeltown

☎ 01586 / pop 6000

Campbeltown, with its ranks of gloomy grey council houses, feels a bit like an Ayrshire mining town that's been placed incongruously on the shores of a beautiful Argyllshire harbour. Once a thriving fishing port and whisky-making centre, industrial decline and the closure of the former air force base at nearby Machrihanish has seen Campbeltown slip into decline.

The town feels a very long way from anywhere else, but the planned re-opening of the ferry link from Campbeltown to Ballycastle in Northern Ireland (due to begin service in summer 2006) should see an increase in visitor numbers. The spruced-up seafront, with its flower beds, smart Victorian buildings and restored Art-Deco cinema, lends the place a distinctly optimistic air.

The **TIC** (☎ 552056; ☽ 9am-5.30pm Mon-Sat) is beside the harbour. There are plenty of shops and banks in the nearby town centre.

SIGHTS & ACTIVITIES

There were once no fewer than 32 distilleries in the Campbeltown area, but most closed down in the 1920s. Today, **Springbank Distillery** (☎ 552085; tours £3; ☽ by arrangement 2pm Mon-Fri) is one of only two that survive (the other is Glen Scotia), and the only one open to the public. It is also one of the very few distilleries in Scotland that distils, matures and bottles all its whisky on the one site.

One of the most unusual sights in Argyll is in a cave on the southern side of the island of **Davaar**, at the mouth of Campbeltown Loch. On the wall of the cave is an eerie painting of the Crucifixion by local artist Archibald MacKinnon, dating from 1887. You can walk to the island at low tide across a shingle bar called the Dhorlinn (allow at least 1½ hours for the round trip), but make sure you're not caught by a rising tide – check tide times with the TIC before you set off.

Mull of Kintyre Seatours (☎ 0870 720 0609; www .mull-of-kintyre.co.uk) operates two-hour high-speed boat trips (adult/child from £25/12) out of Campbeltown harbour to look for wildlife – such as seals, porpoises, minke whales, golden eagles and peregrine falcons – in the turbulent tidal waters beneath the spectacular sea cliffs of the Mull of Kintyre.

The **Mull of Kintyre Music Festival** (☎ 551053; www.mokfest.com), held in Campbeltown in late August, is a popular event featuring traditional Scottish and Irish music.

GETTING THERE & AWAY

Scottish Citylink buses run from Campbeltown to Glasgow (£14, 4½ hours) via Tarbert, Inveraray, Arrochar and Loch Lomond. They also run to Oban (£15, four hours, three daily), changing buses at Inveraray.

Ask at the TIC for details of the new Campbeltown to Ballycastle ferry.

Mull of Kintyre

A narrow winding road, about 18 miles long, leads south from Campbeltown to the Mull of Kintyre, passing some good sandy beaches near Southend. The name of this remote headland has been immortalised in Paul McCartney's famous song – the former Beatle owns a farmhouse in the area. A lighthouse marks the spot closest to Northern Ireland, whose coastline, only 12 miles away, is often visible across the North Channel.

ISLE OF ISLAY

☎ 01496 / pop 3400

The most southerly island of the Inner Hebrides, Islay (pronounced *isle*-a) is best known for its single malt whiskies, which have a distinctive smoky flavour. There are eight working distilleries, all of which welcome visitors and offer guided tours.

With a list of over 250 recorded bird species, Islay also attracts bird-watchers. It's an

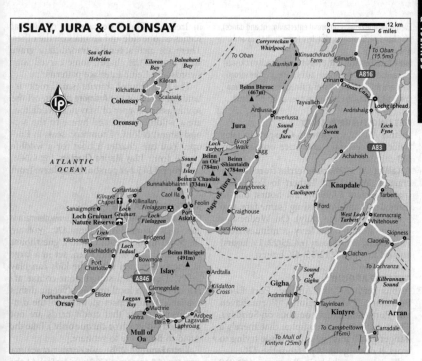

ISLAY, JURA & COLONSAY

important wintering ground for thousands of white-fronted and barnacle geese. As well as the whisky and wildfowl, there are miles of sandy beaches, great scenery and pleasant walking.

Islay's whisky industry contributes approximately £100 million a year to the government in excise duty and value-added tax (VAT); that's about £30,000 for every man, woman and child on the island. Little wonder that the islanders complain about the lack of government investment in the area.

ORIENTATION

There are two ferry terminals on the island, both served by ferries from Kennacraig in West Loch Tarbert – Port Askaig on the east coast, across from Jura, and Port Ellen in the south. Islay airport lies midway between Port Ellen and Bowmore.

There's a camping ground and bunkhouse at Kintra, near Port Ellen, and a youth hostel in Port Charlotte. If you want to camp elsewhere, ask permission first. Camping is prohibited on the Ardtalla and Dunlossit estates on the eastern side of Islay.

INFORMATION

Celtic House (☎ 810304; The Square, Bowmore) Bookshop.

MacTaggart Community CyberCafé (☎ 302693; 30 Mansfield Pl, Port Ellen; per 30min £1; ⏲ 11am-10pm Mon-Fri, 10am-10pm Sat, noon-9pm Sun; 🖳) Internet access is available here.

MacTaggart Leisure Centre (☎ 810767; School St, Bowmore) Coin-operated laundrette (wash £3, dry £1.50)

TIC (☎ 810254; The Square, Bowmore; ⏲ Mar-Oct)

TOURS

Islay Birding (☎ 850010; www.islaybirding.co.uk) Provides full-day bird-watching tours (adult/child £28/10) of the island, and will pick you up from your accommodation. There are also two-hour dawn and dusk tours (£15/6).

Islay Sea Safaris (☎ 07768 450000; www.islayseasafari .co.uk) Can arrange customised tours by sea to visit some or all of Islay and Jura's distilleries in a single day, as well as bird-watching trips, coastal exploration, and trips to Jura's remote west coast and the Corryvreckan whirlpool.

FESTIVALS & EVENTS

Islay Festival (Feis Ile; www.islayfestival.org) Held at the end of May, this is a week-long celebration of traditional Scottish music and includes the **Islay Whisky Festival**.

Events include *ceilidhs* (informal entertainment and dance), pipe band performances, distillery tours, barbecues and whisky tastings.

Islay Jazz Festival (☎ 810044; www.ileach.co.uk/jazz) This annual three-day festival takes place over the second weekend in September. It sees a varied line-up of international talent playing at various venues across the island.

GETTING THERE & AWAY
British Airways flies from Glasgow to Islay twice on weekdays and once on Saturday (40 minutes).

CalMac (☎ 302209) runs ferries from Kennacraig in West Loch Tarbert to Port Ellen (passenger/car £7.95/57, 2¼ hours, one to three daily) and Port Askaig (same fare, two hours, one to three daily). On Wednesday only in summer the ferry continues from Port Askaig to Colonsay (£4.25/22, 1¼ hours) and on to Oban (£12/55, 4¾ hours).

GETTING AROUND
A bus service links Ardbeg, Port Ellen, Bowmore, Port Charlotte, Portnahaven and Port Askaig (only one bus on Sunday). The timetable is so complex that there's a danger you'll miss your bus while trying to work it out – get a copy from the TIC.

Taxis are available in Bowmore (☎ 810 449) and Port Ellen (☎ 302155).

You can hire bikes in Bowmore (opposite) and Port Charlotte (opposite).

Port Ellen & Around
Port Ellen is the main point of entry for Islay. It has a **grocery store** (⊙ 8am-8pm Mon-Sat, noon-7.30pm Sun), a pub and a bank (no ATM, and it's closed most afternoons and all day Wednesday). While there's nothing to see in the town itself, the coast stretching northeast from Port Ellen is one of the loveliest parts of the island.

There are three **whisky distilleries** in close succession: **Laphroaig** (☎ 302418; ⊙ tours 10.15am & 2.15pm Mon-Fri by arrangement); **Lagavulin** (☎ 302400; ⊙ tours 9.30am, 11.15am & 2.30pm Mon-Fri); and **Ardbeg** (☎ 302244; ⊙ tours 10.30am, 11.30am, 2.30pm & 3.30pm Jun-Aug, 10.30am & 2.30pm Mon-Fri Sep-May). All guided tours are £3.

A pleasant bike ride leads past the distilleries to the atmospheric, age-haunted **Kildalton Chapel**, 8 miles northeast of Port Ellen. In the kirkyard is the exceptional late-8th-century **Kildalton Cross**, the only remaining Celtic high cross in Scotland (most surviving crosses are

in Ireland). There are carvings of biblical scenes on one side and animals on the other. There are also several extraordinary grave slabs around the chapel, some carved with swords and Celtic interlace patterns.

The kelp-fringed *skerries* (small rocky islands or reefs) of the **Ardmore Islands**, off the southeastern corner of Islay near Kildalton, are a wildlife haven and home to the second largest colony of common seals in Europe. You can charter a boat for a wildlife cruise from **Islay Marine Charters** (☎ 850436) for around £15 per person; boats leave from Port Askaig.

SLEEPING & EATING
Glenmachrie Farmhouse (☎ 305260; www.glenmachrie .com; d £80, dinner, B&B per person £70; ⊙ dinner; Ⓟ Ⓧ) This delightful country guesthouse is 4 miles north of Port Ellen, set in a large landscaped garden where the kids can play safely. Dinner is a superb four-course affair using fresh local produce (veggie dishes available) with sunset views from the dining room. (Note that credit cards are not accepted – it's cash or cheque only.) Take the A846 to Bowmore to get here.

Kintra Farm (☎ 302051; www.kintrafarm.co.uk; Kintra; camp sites £4-8, r per person £20-24; ⊙ Apr-Sep) At the southern end of Laggan Bay, Kintra offers three bedrooms in a homely farmhouse B&B, and a small but beautiful camping ground on buttercup-sprinkled turf amid the dunes (no electrical hook-up).

Old Kiln Cafe (☎ 302244; mains £5-8; ⊙ 10am-4pm Jul & Aug, 10am-4pm Mon-Fri Sep-Jun) Housed in the former malting kiln at Ardbeg Distillery, this is the area's best place to eat. It serves hearty homemade soups such as lentil and smoked ham, tasty light meals (try smoked salmon and asparagus quiche), and a range of home-baked desserts including traditional *clootie dumpling* (a rich steamed pudding filled with currants and raisins) with ice cream.

MacTaggart Community CyberCafe (☎ 302693; 30 Mansfield Pl, Port Ellen; mains £2-5; ⊙ food served 11am-6.30pm Mon-Fri, 10am-6.30pm Sat, noon-6.30pm Sun) Port Ellen's youth club and cybercafé offers snacks, salads, baked potatoes, tea, coffee and cakes to eat in or take away.

Other recommendations:

Trout Fly Guest House (☎ 302204; Charlotte St, Port Ellen; r per person £22-25; Ⓧ) Pleasant, four-room B&B just two minutes' walk from the ferry terminal.

Tigh na Suil (☎ 302483; Lagavulin; r per person £23-35; P ✗) Farmhouse B&B with coastal views, 3 miles east of Port Ellen.

Bowmore

The attractive Georgian village of Bowmore was laid out in 1768 to replace the village of Kilarrow, which was ruining the view from the laird's house. Its centrepiece is the distinctive **Round Church** at the top of Main St, built in circular form to ensure that the devil had no corners to hide in.

Bowmore is in the centre of the island, 10 miles from both Port Askaig and Port Ellen, and is the island's capital. It has a **TIC** (☎ 810254; The Square; ☾ Mar-Oct), two banks with ATMs, and a **Co-op supermarket** (☾ 8am-8pm Mon-Sat, noon-7.30pm Sun).

Bowmore Distillery (☎ 810441; School St; adult/child £2/1; ☾ tours 10.30am & 2pm Mon-Sat May-Sep, 10.30am & 2pm Mon-Fri Oct-Apr) is the only distillery on the island that still malts its own barley – the tour, which begins with an overblown 10-minute marketing video, is redeemed by a look at (and taste of) the germinating grain laid out in golden billows on the floor of the malting shed.

If the weather's bad, there's always the **MacTaggart Leisure Centre** (☎ 810767; School St; pool adult/child £2.20/1.40; ☾ 12.30-9.30pm Tue, 2-9pm Wed, 12.30-9pm Thu & Fri, 10am-6pm Sat, 10.30am-5.30pm Sun), with a 25m pool, a sauna and a fitness centre.

You can hire **bikes** at the post office, near the church at the top of Main St, for £10 per day.

SLEEPING & EATING

Lambeth House (☎ 810597; lambethguesthouse@tiscali .co.uk; Jamieson St; r per person £22; ✗) The Lambeth is a simple, good-value guesthouse with four bedrooms, and is a short stroll from the harbour. It also offers a two-course evening meal for £8.

Harbour Inn (☎ 810330; www.harbour-inn.com; The Square; s/d £75/110, mains £12-18; ☾ food served noon-2pm & 6-9pm; ✗) The plush seven-room Harbour Inn, smartly decorated with a nautical theme, is the poshest place in town. The restaurant has harbour views and serves fresh local oysters, lobster and scallops, Islay lamb and Jura venison.

Lochside Hotel (☎ 810244; www.lochsidehotel .co.uk; 19 Shore St; r per person from £40; ✗) The eight en-suite bedrooms at the Lochside have been recently refurbished with country pine furniture, and a new conservatory dining room provides sweeping views over Loch Indaal. The bar boasts a wide range of single malts, including a 29-year-old Black Bowmore (50% ABV) for £150 a nip!

Cottage Restaurant (☎ 810422; 45 Main St; mains £4-8; ☾ 10am-4pm Mon-Sat, plus 6-8pm Fri & Sat) This old-fashioned tearoom with tartan wallpaper does a line in healthy home-cooked food, as well as traditional artery-clogging café favourites such as sausage and chips.

Port Charlotte

Eleven miles from Bowmore, on the opposite shore of Loch Indaal, is the attractive village of Port Charlotte. It has a **shop** (☾ 9am-12.30pm & 1.30-5.30pm Mon-Sat, 11.30am-1.30pm Sun) and post office, and you can hire **bikes** from the house opposite the Port Charlotte Hotel.

Islay's long history is charted in detail in the **Museum of Islay Life** (☎ 850358; adult/child £2/1; ☾ 10am-5pm Mon-Sat, 2-5pm Sun Easter-Sep, 10am-4pm Mon-Sat Oct-Easter), housed in the former Free Church. Prize exhibits include an illicit still, 19th-century crofters' furniture, and a set of leather boots once worn by the horse that pulled the lawnmower at Islay House (so it wouldn't leave hoof-prints on the lawn!). There are also touch-screen computers displaying archive photos of Islay in 19th and early 20th centuries.

The **Islay Wildlife Information Centre** (☎ 850288; adult/child £2.50/1; ☾ 10am-3pm Mon, Tue, Thu & Fri Apr-Oct), next to the youth hostel, has exhibits explaining the island's natural history, and a useful reference library.

The **Bruichladdich Distillery** (☎ 850221; www .bruichladdich.com; tours £3; ☾ tours 10.30am & 2.30pm Mon-Sat) at the northern edge of the village re-opened in 2001 with all its original Victorian equipment restored to working condition. Independently owned and independently minded, Bruichladdich (pronounced brook-lah-day) produces an intriguing range of distinctive, very peaty whiskies. It also runs a whisky 'academy', a five-day course during which you learn to malt, mash, brew, distil, cask and bottle your own whisky (£795 per person, including food and accommodation for four nights).

SLEEPING & EATING

Islay Youth Hostel (SYHA; ☎ 0870 004 1128; dm £12.50; ☾ Apr-Sep) This modern and comfortable hostel is housed in a former distillery building with views over the loch.

Port Charlotte Hotel (☎ 850360; www.portcharlotte hotel.co.uk; s/d £65/110, bar meals £7-9, 3-course dinner £29; ☻ restaurant 6.30-9pm, bar meals noon-2pm & 5-8pm; P ☒) This lovely old Victorian hotel overlooking the sea has a stylish, candle-lit restaurant serving local seafood (seared scallops with Pernod and ginger sauce), Islay beef, venison and duck. The bar is well stocked with Islay malts and real ales, and has a nook at the back with a view over the loch.

Croft Kitchen (☎ 850230; mains lunch £5-9, dinner £11-14; ☻ snacks 10am-6pm, lunch noon-3pm, dinner 6.30-8.30pm) This laid-back little bistro acts as a café during the day and transforms into a restaurant serving quality meals in the evening.

Portnahaven

Six miles southwest of Port Charlotte the road ends at **Portnahaven**, another pretty village that was purpose-built as a fishing harbour in the 19th century. A mile north of the village is the pretty little shell-sand beach of **Currie Sands**, with a lovely view of Orsay island.

The next inlet to the north of the beach is occupied by the world's first commercially viable, wave-powered electricity generating station, built on cliffs that are open to the Atlantic swell. The 500kW plant – known as the **Limpet** (land-installed, marine-powered energy transformer) – provides enough electricity to power 200 island homes.

Loch Gruinart

Seven miles north of Port Charlotte is **Loch Gruinart Nature Reserve**, where you can hear corncrakes in summer and see huge flocks of migrating ducks, geese and waders in spring and autumn; there's a hide with wheelchair access. The nearby **RSPB Information Centre** (☎ 850505; admission free; ☻ 10am-5pm Apr-Oct, 10am-4pm Nov-Mar) offers two- to three-hour guided walks around the reserve (£2 per person, 10am Thursday and 6pm Tuesday in August).

Three miles north of the reserve, at **Kilnave Chapel**, is a Celtic stone cross made from an improbably thin slab; though less elaborate than the cross at Kildalton (p288), it is more delicate. The beach at **Killinallan**, northeast of the reserve, is one of Islay's best. You can walk for miles along the raised beaches on the coast to its north.

Kilchoman Distillery (☎ 850011; Kilchoman; ☻ 10am-5.30pm Mon-Sat May-Sep, plus 10am-5.30pm Sun Jul & Aug), 5 miles southwest of Loch Gruinart, is Islay's newest distillery, going into production in 2005. The distillery is growing its own barley on Islay, and the visitors centre explores the history of farmhouse distilling on the island. But it'll be at least 2010 before we get to taste the fruits of its labours...

Finlaggan

Lush meadows swathed in buttercups and daisies slope down to reed-fringed Loch Finlaggan, the medieval capital of the Lords of the Isles. This bucolic setting, 3 miles southwest of Port Askaig, was once the most important settlement in the Hebrides, the central seat of power of the Lords of the Isles from the 12th to the 16th centuries. From the little island at the northern end of the loch the descendants of Somerled administered their island territories and entertained visiting chieftains in their great hall. Little remains now except the tumbled ruins of houses and a chapel, but the setting is beautiful and the history fascinating. A wooden walkway leads over the reeds and water lilies to the island, where information boards describe the remains.

Finlaggan Visitor Centre (☎ 810629; admission free; ☻ 1-4.30pm May-Sep, 1-4.30pm Tue, Thu & Sun Apr, 1-4pm Tue & Thu Oct), in a nearby cottage, explains the site's history and archaeology. The island itself is open at all times.

Buses from Port Askaig stop at the road-end, from where it's a 15-minute walk to the loch.

Port Askaig & Around

Port Askaig is little more than a hotel, a shop and a ferry pier, set in a picturesque nook halfway along the Sound of Islay, the strait that separates the islands of Islay and Jura.

There are two distilleries within easy reach: **Caol Ila Distillery** (☎ 840207; ☻ tours by appointment Mon-Fri), pronounced cull ee-la, just a half-mile walk north of the ferry pier; and **Bunnahabhain Distillery** (☎ 840646; ☻ 9am-4.30pm Mon-Fri Mar-Oct, by appointment Nov-Feb), pronounced boo-na-ha-ven, 3 miles north of Port Askaig. Both enjoy a wonderful location with great views across to Jura.

Port Askaig Hotel (☎ 840245; www.portaskaig.co .uk; s/d £54/84; P) is beside the ferry pier. The hotel's beer garden is a popular spot to sit and watch the comings and goings at the quay.

ISLE OF JURA

☎ 01496 / pop 170

Jura lies off the coast of Argyll – it's long, dark and low like a vast Viking longship, its billowing sail the distinctive triple peaks of the Paps of Jura. A magnificently wild and lonely island, it's the perfect place to get away from it all – as George Orwell did in 1948. Orwell wrote his masterpiece *1984* while living at the remote farmhouse of Barnhill in the north of the island, describing it in a letter as 'a very un-get-at-able place'.

Jura takes its name from the Old Norse *dyr-a* (deer island) – an apt appellation, as the island supports a population of around 6000 red deer. The deer outnumber their human cohabitants by 30 to one. Most of the island is occupied by deer-stalking estates, and access to the hills may be restricted during the stalking season (July to February); Jura Hotel can provide details of areas to be avoided.

The community-run **Jura Service Point** (☎ 820161; Craighouse; ◷ 10am-1pm Mon-Fri; 🖳), 400m north of the Jura Hotel, provides tourist information and free Internet access. **Jura Stores** (☎ 820231; Craighouse; ◷ 9am-1pm & 2-5pm Mon-Fri, 9am-1pm & 2-4.30pm Sat) is the island's only shop.

Sights & Activities

Apart from the superb wilderness walking, there's not a whole lot to do on the island apart from visit the **Isle of Jura Distillery** (☎ 820240; admission free; ◷ by appointment) or wander around the attractive walled gardens of **Jura House** (adult/child £2/free; ◷ dawn-dusk) at the southern end of the island; a **tea tent** (◷ 11am-5pm Mon-Fri Jun-Aug) here sells hot drinks, home baking, crafts and plants.

There's also the **Feolin Study Centre** (www.the isleofjura.co.uk; admission free; ◷ 9am-5pm), just south of the ferry slip at Feolin, which has a small exhibition on Jura's history and provides information on all aspects of the island's history, culture and wildlife.

The bar at Jura Hotel is a very sociable place to spend the evening, and there are regular *ceilidhs* held throughout the year where visitors are made very welcome; check the notice board outside Jura Stores for announcements.

WALKING

There are few proper footpaths on Jura, and any off-the-beaten-path exploration will involve rough going through giant bracken, knee-deep bogs and thigh-high tussocks. The only real trail is **Evans' Walk**, a stalkers' path that leads for 6 miles from the main road through a pass in the hills to a hunting lodge above the beautiful sandy beach at Glenbatrick Bay. The path leaves the road 4 miles north of Craighouse (just under a mile north of the bridge over the Corran River); allow five hours for the 12-mile round trip.

Another good walk is to a viewpoint for the **Corryvreckan whirlpool** (see the boxed text, p292), the great tidal race at the northern end of the island between Jura and Scarba. From the northern end of the public road at Lealt you hike along a 4WD track past Barnhill to Kinuachdrachd Farm (6 miles). About 30m before the farm buildings a footpath forks left (there's an inconspicuous wooden signpost low down) and climbs up the hill-side before traversing rough and boggy ground to a point 50m above the northern tip of the island. A rocky slab makes a natural grandstand for viewing the turbulent waters of the Gulf of Corryvreckan; if you have timed it right (see the tide times at Jura Hotel), you will see the whirlpool as a writhing mass of white water diagonally to your left and over by the Scarba shore. Allow five to six hours for the round trip (16 miles) from the road end.

Climbing the **Paps of Jura** is a truly tough hill walk, over ankle-breaking scree, that requires good fitness and navigational skills (allow eight hours for the 11 long, hard, weary miles). A good place to start is by the bridge over the Corran River, 3 miles north of Craighouse. The first peak you reach is Beinn a'Chaolais (734m), the second is Beinn an Oir (784m) and the third is Beinn Shiantaidh (755m). Most people also climb Corra Bheinn (569m), before joining Evans' Walk to return to the road. If you succeed in bagging all four, you can reflect on the fact that the record for the annual Paps of Jura fell race is just three hours!

There are easier **short walks** (one or two hours) east along the coast from Jura House, and north along a 4WD track from Feolin *Jura – A Guide for Walkers* by Gordon Wright (£2) is available from the TIC in Bowmore, Islay.

Sleeping & Eating

Places to stay on the island are very limited, so book ahead – don't rely on just turning up and hoping to find a bed. Most of Jura's accommodation is in self-catering cottages that are let by the week.

Jura Hotel (☎ 820243; www.jurahotel.co.uk; Craighouse; s/d from £45/75, bar meals £6-10, 3-course dinner £20; ☯ food served noon-2pm & 6.30-9pm; ℗)) The 18-room Jura is the most comfortable place to stay on the island; ask for a room situated at the front with a view of the bay. The hotel also serves decent bar and restaurant meals.

Kinuachdrachd Farm (☎ 07899912116; joanmikekd@ hotmail.com; dm £7, d £35) There is a basic bunkhouse and more-luxurious farmhouse B&B accommodation at this remote farm in the far north of the island; you can hike or bike here, or arrange for the owner to come and pick you up from the end of the public road at Lealt.

You can camp for free in the field below Jura Hotel (ask at the bar first, and pop a donation in the bottle); there are toilets, hot showers (£1 coin needed) and a laundry in the block behind the hotel.

Getting There & Away

A small car ferry operated by **ASP Seascot** (☎ 840681) shuttles between Port Askaig (on Islay) and Jura (passenger return £2.40,

car and driver return £14, five minutes, hourly Monday to Saturday, every two hours Sunday).

Gemini Cruises (☎ 01546-830238; www.gemini-crinan .co.uk; Kilmahumaig, Crinan) operates a water-taxi service on demand and will take passengers from Crinan on the mainland to Ardlussa in Jura's northeast (£60 one way for up to 12 passengers).

From Easter to September, **Lorn Ferry Service** (☎ 01951-200320) runs a pedestrian- and bicycle-only ferry from Loch Tarbert on Jura to Colonsay (£15, two hours, one daily Tuesday and Friday). Prior booking is essential.

Getting Around

Charles MacLean (☎ 820314) runs a minibus service between Feolin and Craighouse, timed to coincide with ferry arrivals and departures at Feolin. One or two of the runs continue north as far as Inverlussa.

Mike Richardson (☎ 07899 912116) operates a Landrover taxi service from the road end at Lealt to Kinuachdrachd Farm for those wanting to shorten the hike to the Corryvreckan whirlpool (minimum £20 for two people, plus £5 a head).

You can hire bikes from the Jura Hotel.

THE SCOTTISH MAELSTROM

It may look innocuous on the map, but the Gulf of Corryvreckan – the 1km-wide channel between the northern end of Jura and the island of Scarba – is home to one of the three most notorious tidal whirlpools in the world (the others are the Maelstrom in Norway's Lofoten Islands, and the Old Sow in Canada's New Brunswick).

The tide doesn't just rise and fall twice a day, it flows – dragged around the earth by the gravitational attraction of the moon. On the west coast of Scotland, the rising tide – known as the flood tide – flows northwards. As the flood moves up the Sound of Jura, to the east of the island, it is forced into a narrowing bottleneck jammed with islands and builds up to a greater height than the open sea to the west of Jura. As a result, millions of gallons of sea water pour westwards through the Gulf of Corryvreckan at speeds of up to 8 knots – an average sailing yacht is going fast at 6 knots.

The Corryvreckan whirlpool forms where this mass of moving water hits an underwater pinnacle, which rises from the 200m-deep sea bed to within just 28m of the surface, and swirls over and around it. The turbulent waters create a magnificent spectacle, with white-capped breakers bulging boils and overfalls, and countless miniature maelstroms whirling around the main vortex.

Corryvreckan is at its most violent when a flooding spring tide, flowing west through the gulf, meets a westerly gale blowing in from the Atlantic. In these conditions, standing waves up to 5m high can form and dangerously rough seas extend more than 3 miles west of Corryvreckan, a phenomenon known as the Great Race.

You can see the whirlpool by making the long hike to the northern end of Jura (check tide times at Jura Hotel, and see Walking, p291, for walk details), or by taking a boat trip from Islay (see Tours, p287), Easdale (p299) or Crinan (p283).

ISLE OF COLONSAY

☎ 01951 / pop 100

Legend has it that when St Columba set out from Ireland in 563, his first landfall was Colonsay. But on climbing a hill he found he could still see the distant coast of his homeland, and pushed on further north to found his monastery in Iona, leaving behind only his name (Colonsay means 'Columba's Isle').

Colonsay is a connoisseur's island, a little jewel box of varied delights, none exceptional but each exquisite – an ancient priory, a woodland garden, a golden beach – set amid a Highland landscape in miniature: rugged, rocky hills, cliffs and sandy strands, machair and birch woods, even a trout loch. Here, hill walkers bag 'McPhies' – defined as 'eminences in excess of 300ft' (90m) – instead of Munros (see the boxed text, p60). There are 22 in all; the super-competitive will bag them all in one day.

Orientation & Information

The ferry pier is at **Scalasaig**, the main village, where you'll find a **shop** (⊙ 9am-5.30pm Mon-Fri, 9am-4pm Sat), post office and public telephone. There's no TIC and no bank or ATM on the island. General information is available at the CalMac waiting room beside the ferry pier.

The tiny **Colonsay Bookshop** (☎ 200232) at Kilchattan, on the west side of the island, has an excellent range of books on Hebridean history and culture.

Sights & Activities

If the tides are right, don't miss the chance to walk across the half-mile of cockleshell-strewn sand that links Colonsay to the smaller island of Oronsay. Here you can explore the 14th-century ruins of **Oronsay Priory**, one of the best-preserved medieval priories in Scotland. There are two beautiful late-15th-century stone crosses in the kirkyard, but the highlight is the collection of superb 15th- and 16th-century carved grave slabs in the Prior's House; look for the ugly little devil trapped beneath the sword-tip of the knight on the right-hand one of the two horizontal slabs. The island is accessible on foot for about 1½ hours either side of low tide, and it's a 45-minute walk from the road-end on Colonsay to the priory. There are tide tables posted at the ferry terminal in Scalasaig.

The **Woodland Garden** (☎ 200211; Kiloran; admission free; ⊙ garden dawn-dusk, terrace café 9am-5pm Wed & Fri Easter-Sep) at Colonsay House, 1.5 miles north of Scalasaig, is tucked in an unexpected fold of the landscape and is famous for its outstanding collection of hybrid rhododendrons and unusual trees. The formal walled garden around the mansion has a terrace café.

There are good sandy beaches at several points around the coast but **Kiloran Bay** in the northwest, a scimitar-shaped strand of dark golden sand, is outstanding. If there are too many people here for you, walk the 3 miles north to beautiful **Balnahard Bay**, accessible only on foot or by boat.

Kevin and Christa Byrne (☎ 200320; byrne@ colonsay.org.uk) offer guided tours on foot (£15 per hour per tour for up to eight people) or by minibus (£20 per hour per tour), and boat trips for fishing (£15 per person) or whale-watching (£20 per person).

Sleeping & Eating

Short-stay accommodation on Colonsay is limited and should be booked before coming to the island. Camping is not allowed.

Isle of Colonsay Hotel (☎ 200316; www.colonsay .org.uk/hotel.html; s/d from £59/83, mains £8-12; ⊙ food served noon-2pm & 6-9pm; P ✗) The island's most luxurious option is this wonderfully laid-back hotel – no TVs or phones in the rooms here – set in an atmospheric old inn dating from 1750. The bar is a convivial melting pot of locals, guests, hikers, cyclists and visiting yachties, and the restaurant offers down-to-earth cooking using good Scottish produce, from beefburgers to Colonsay oysters.

Seaview Guesthouse (☎ 200315; s/d £38/64; P) This peaceful farmhouse is in Kilchattan, at the southwestern end of Loch Fad, 3 miles from the pier. Packed lunches are available for an extra £4.

Isle of Colonsay Lodges (☎ 200320; byrne@colonsay .org.uk; peak season per week £380-540) These comfortable and modern self-catering holiday chalets are just 10 minutes' walk from the ferry pier at Scalasaig. You can check last-minute availability at www.colonsay.org .uk/newother/chalets.html.

Keepers Backpackers Lodge (☎ 200312; dm £10-12, tw £28) Set in a former gamekeeper's house near Colonsay House, this lodge is about 30 minutes' walk from the ferry terminal (you can arrange to be picked up at the pier). Bikes can be hired for £5 per day.

Pantry (☎ 200325; ☻ 9am-8pm Mon-Fri, 9am-6pm Sat, 2.30-8pm Sun Apr-Sep) Serves light meals, snacks and ice creams and is beside the ferry pier. It also opens from October to March, on the days that the ferry calls.

Getting There & Around

CalMac operates car ferries to Colonsay from Oban (passenger/car £12/54, 2¼ hours) once daily except on Tuesday and Saturday.

On Wednesday only, from April to September, there's a service from Colonsay to Islay's Port Askaig (passenger/car £4.25/22, 1¼ hours, one daily) and on to Kennacraig on the Kintyre peninsula. A day trip from Port Askaig or Kennacraig to Colonsay allows you about five hours on the island.

The island's only **bus** (☎ 200341) meets the ferry and makes a circular tour around the island.

OBAN & MULL

OBAN

☎ 01631 / pop 8120

Oban is a peaceful waterfront town on a delightful bay, with sweeping views to Kerrera and Mull. OK, that first bit about peaceful is true only in winter; in summer the town centre is a heaving mass of humanity, its streets jammed with holidaymakers, day-trippers and travellers headed for the islands.

There's not a huge amount to see in the town itself, but it's an appealingly busy place with some excellent restaurants and lively pubs, and it's the main gateway to the islands of Mull, Iona, Coll and Tiree.

Orientation

The bus, train and ferry terminals are all grouped conveniently together next to the harbour on the southern edge of the bay. Argyll Sq is one block east of the train station, and George St, the main drag, runs north along the promenade to North Pier. From the pier, Corran Esplanade runs round the northern edge of the bay.

Information

Esplanade post office (☎ 562340; Corran Esplanade)
Fancy That (☎ 562996; 13 George St; per 15min £1.25; ☻ 9am-5pm; ▣) Internet access.

Lorn & Islands District General Hospital (☎ 567500; Glengallan Rd) Southern end of town.
Main post office (☎ 510450; Lochside St; ☻ 8am-6pm Mon-Sat, 10am-1pm Sun) Inside the Tesco supermarket.
Ottakars (☎ 571455; 12 George St; ☻ 9am-5.30pm Mon-Sat, 11am-5pm Sun) Bookshop.
Police Station (☎ 510500; Albany St)
TIC (☎ 563122; www.oban.org.uk; Argyll Sq; per 10min £1; ☻ 9am-9pm Mon-Sat, 9am-7pm Sun Jul & Aug, 9am-5.30pm Mon-Sat, 9am-5pm Sun May, Jun & Sep, 9am-5.30pm Mon-Sat Oct-Apr; ▣) Just southeast of the train station, with Internet access.

Sights

Crowning the hill above the town centre is **McCaig's Tower** (admission free; ☻ 24hr). Its construction was commissioned in 1890 by local worthy John Stuart McCaig, an art critic, philosophical essayist and banker, with the philanthropic intention of providing work for unemployed stonemasons. To reach it on foot, make the steep climb up Jacob's Ladder (a flight of stairs) from Argyll St and then follow the signs. The views over the bay are worth the effort. **Pulpit Hill**, to the south of the bay, is another excellent viewpoint; the footpath starts to the right of Maridon House B&B on Dunuaran Rd.

Oban Distillery (☎ 572004; Stafford St; admission £4; ☻ 9.30am-8.30pm Mon-Fri, 9.30am-5pm Sat, noon-5pm Sun Jul-Sep, 9.30am-5pm Mon-Sat Easter-Jun & Oct, 9.30am-5pm Mon-Fri Nov-Easter) has been producing Oban single malt whisky since 1794. There are guided tours (£3 per person) available year-round (last tour begins one hour before closing time), but even without a tour it's still worth visiting the small exhibition in the foyer.

Military buffs should visit the little **War & Peace Museum** (☎ 564211; www.obanmuseum.org.uk; North Pier; admission free; ☻ 10am-4pm & 7-9pm Mon-Sat Jul & Aug, 10am-4pm Mon-Sat Sep-Jun), which chronicles Oban's role in WWII as a base for Catalina seaplanes and as a marshalling area for Atlantic convoys.

The **Oban Rare Breeds Farm Park** (☎ 770608; New Barran Farm, Glencruitten; adult/child £6/4; ☻ 10am-5.30pm late Mar-Oct, 10am-7.30pm mid-Jun-Aug) is a favourite with children, who get to meet all kinds of animals at close quarters, including rabbits, goats, cows, deer and even llamas. The farm maintains rare breeds of domesticated animals, including Tamworth pigs, Shetland and Soay sheep and longhorn cattle; it's 2 miles east of the town centre.

Activities

It's a pleasant 20-minute **walk** north from Oban Youth Hostel along the coast road to Dunollie Castle. The castle was built by the MacDougalls of Lorn in the 13th century and was unsuccessfully besieged for a year during the 1715 Jacobite rebellion. It's always open and very much a ruin. You can continue along this road to the beach at Ganavan Sands, 2.5 miles from Oban.

A TIC leaflet lists local **bike rides**. They include a 7-mile Gallanach circular tour, a 16-mile route to the Isle of Seil and routes to Connel, Glenlonan and Kilmore. You can hire mountain bikes from **Oban Cycles** (☎ 566996; 29 Lochside St; ☼ 9am-5.30pm

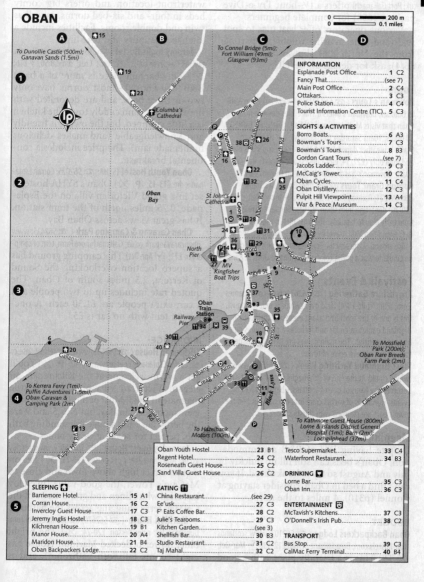

OBAN

0 ——————— 200 m
0 ——————— 0.1 miles

To Dunollie Castle (500m);
Ganavan Sands (1.5mi)

To Connel Bridge (5mi);
Fort William (49mi);
Glasgow (93mi)

Columba's Cathedral

Oban Bay

St John's Cathedral

North Pier

MV Kingfisher Boat Trips

Oban Train Station

Railway Pier

To Kerrera Ferry (1mi);
Puffin Adventures (1.5mi);
Oban Caravan & Camping Park (2mi)

To Hazelbank Motors (100m)

To Mossfield Park (200m);
Oban Rare Breeds Farm Park (2mi)

To Kathmore Guest House (800m);
Lorne & Islands District General Hospital (1mi); Barn (2mi);
Lochgilphead (37mi)

INFORMATION
Esplanade Post Office	1 C2
Fancy That	(see 7)
Main Post Office	2 C4
Ottakars	3 C3
Police Station	4 C4
Tourist Information Centre (TIC)	5 C3

SIGHTS & ACTIVITIES
Borro Boats	6 A3
Bowman's Tours	7 C3
Bowman's Tours	8 B3
Gordon Grant Tours	(see 7)
Jacobs Ladder	9 C3
McCaig's Tower	10 C2
Oban Cycles	11 C4
Oban Distillery	12 C3
Pulpit Hill Viewpoint	13 A4
War & Peace Museum	14 C3

SLEEPING
Barriemore Hotel	15 A1
Corran House	16 C2
Inverloy Guest House	17 C3
Jeremy Inglis Hostel	18 C3
Kilchrenan House	19 B1
Manor House	20 A4
Maridon House	21 B4
Oban Backpackers Lodge	22 C2
Oban Youth Hostel	23 B1
Regent Hotel	24 C2
Roseneath Guest House	25 C2
Sand Villa Guest House	26 C2

EATING
China Restaurant	(see 29)
Ee'usk	27 C3
F' Eats Coffee Bar	28 C3
Julie's Tearooms	29 C3
Kitchen Garden	(see 3)
Shellfish Bar	30 B3
Studio Restaurant	31 C2
Taj Mahal	32 C2
Tesco Supermarket	33 C4
Waterfront Restaurant	34 B3

DRINKING
Lorne Bar	35 C3
Oban Inn	36 C3

ENTERTAINMENT
McTavish's Kitchens	37 C3
O'Donnell's Irish Pub	38 C2

TRANSPORT
Bus Stop	39 C3
CalMac Ferry Terminal	40 B4

Mon-Sat), opposite Tesco supermarket, for £15 per day.

You can hire sailing dinghies, rowboats and motorboats at **Borro Boats** (☎ 563292; Gallanach Rd; ☯ 10am-6pm May-Sep). A Wayfarer sailing dinghy costs £25/50 per two hours/full day.

If you fancy exploring the underwater world, **Puffin Adventures** (☎ 566088; www.puffin.org .uk; Port Gallanach) offers a 1½-hour Try-a-Dive package (£58) for complete beginners.

Various operators offer **boat trips** to spot seals and other marine wildlife, departing from the North Pier slipway (adult/child £6/4); ask for details at the TIC.

Tours

Bowman's Tours (☎ 563221; Railway Pier) From April to October, Bowman's offers a Three Isles day trip from Oban that visits Mull, Iona and Staffa (adult/child £40/20, 10 hours, 10am Saturday to Thursday); the crossing to Staffa is weather dependent. A shorter day trip visits Mull and Iona only (£27/14, eight hours) and departs daily at 10am. Bowman's has a second office on Queens Park Pl.

Gordon Grant Tours (tickets from Bowman's Tours – ☎ 563221; Railway Pier) Runs a wildlife tour (adult/child £40/20) departing from Oban at 10am Sunday to Friday from early May to late July. The trip takes in a ferry crossing to Craignure on Mull, travel by coach to Fionnphort, and a cruise around Staffa and the Treshnish Isles, plus a landing on Lunga to visit a puffin colony, returning to Oban at 8pm.

Festivals & Events

Argyllshire Gathering (☎ 562671; www.obangames .com; adult/child £8/4) Held over two days in late August, this is one of the most important events on the Scottish Highland games calendar and includes a prestigious pipe band competition. The main games are held at Mossfield Park on the eastern edge of town.

West Highland Yachting Week (☎ 563309; www .whyw.co.uk) At the end of July/beginning of August, Oban becomes the focus of one of Scotland's biggest yachting events. Hundreds of yachts cram into the harbour and the town's bars are jammed with thirsty sailors.

Sleeping

Despite having lots of B&B accommodation, Oban's beds can still fill up quickly in July and August so try to book ahead. If you can't find a bed in Oban, consider staying at Connel (p310), 4 miles to the north.

BUDGET

Oban Backpackers Lodge (☎ 562107; www.scotlands -top-hostels.com; Breadalbane St; dm £12-13; ☯ Mar-Oct; ✗ ▣) This is a friendly place with a good vibe and an attractive communal area with lots of sofas and armchairs. From the train station, walk 800m north along George St, past the cinema, and veer right into Breadalbane St.

Corran House (☎ 566040; www.corranhouse.co.uk; 1 Victoria Cres; dm £12-14, tw £30-35; ℗ ▣ ⚹) The family-friendly Corran House has a nice waterfront location and offers big comfy beds in four- and six-bed dorms, as well as twin and double rooms. Facilities include a kitchen, a laundry and bike hire.

Jeremy Inglis Hostel (☎ 565065; jeremyinglis@mc tavishs.freeserve.co.uk; 21 Airds Cres; dm £8.50, s £16; ✗) This bargain place is more of a basic B&B than a hostel – most 'dorms' have only two or three beds, and are decorated with books, flowers and cuddly toys. The kitchen is a little cramped, but the owner is friendly and knowledgeable (and makes delicious homemade jam). The price includes a continental breakfast.

Oban Youth Hostel (SYHA; ☎ 562025; Corran Esplanade; dm £13-15; ℗ ✗) Oban's SYHA hostel is set in a grand Victorian villa on the Esplanade, 0.75 miles north of the train station. It has great views across Oban Bay.

Oban Caravan & Camping Park (☎ 562425; www .obancaravanpark.co.uk; Gallanachmore Farm; tent or campervan £11; ☯ Apr-Oct) This camping ground has a superb location overlooking the Sound of Kerrera, 2.5 miles south of Oban. The quoted rate includes up to two people and a car; extra people are £1.50 each. A one-person tent with no car is £5.

MIDRANGE

Kilchrenan House (☎ 562663; www.kilchrenanhouse.co .uk; Corran Esplanade; r per person £30-40; ℗ ✗) You'll get a warm welcome at the Kilchrenan, an elegant Victorian villa built for a textile magnate in 1883. Most of the 10 rooms have views across Oban Bay, but Nos 5 and 9 are the best – No 5 has a huge freestanding bath tub, perfect for soaking weary bones.

Invercloy Guest House (☎ 562058; www.invercloy .co.uk; Ardconnel Tce; r per person £20-25; ✗) Set on a quiet street high above town and close to McCaig's Tower, the good-value Invercloy has crisp white linen and grand views of the CalMac ferry chugging across the harbour.

Maridon House (☎ 562670; maridonhse@aol.com; Dunuaran Rd; r per person £20-24; ✗) The bright blue, flower-bedecked Maridon House has eight rooms (all with bathroom), and is only a few minutes' walk from the ferry terminal. The owners are very helpful and will provide a vegetarian breakfast if you ask.

Barriemore Hotel (☎ 566356; www.barriemore-hotel .co.uk; Corran Esplanade; s £32-50, d £64-84; P ☒) The Barriemore enjoys a grand location, overlooking the entrance to Oban Bay. There are 13 spacious rooms – ask for one with a sea view – a guest lounge with magazines and newspapers, and plump Loch Fyne kippers on the breakfast menu.

Other recommendations:

Kathmore Guest House (☎ 562104; www.kathmore .co.uk; Soroba Rd; s £25-35, d £40-50; P ☒)

Roseneath Guest House (☎ 562929; www.roseneath oban.com; Dalriach Rd; s £27-30, d £50-60; P ☒)

Sand Villa Guest House (☎ 562803; www.holiday oban.co.uk; Breadalbane St; r per person £23-28; ☒)

TOP END

Regent Hotel (☎ 562341; www.british-trust-hotels.com; Corran Esplanade; s/d £55/130) One part traditional Victorian and three parts 1930s Art Deco on the outside, and fully refurbished with all mod cons on the inside, the Regent has a great waterfront location right in the centre of town.

Manor House (☎ 562087; www.manorhouseoban .com; Gallanach Rd; s £60-95, d £70-130; P ☒) Built in 1780 for the duke of Argyll as part of his Oban estates, the Manor House is now one of Oban's finest hotels. It has small but elegant rooms in Georgian style, a posh bar frequented by local and visiting yachties, and a fine restaurant serving Scottish and French cuisine.

Eating

There's no shortage of places to eat in Oban. Most are strung out along the bay between the train station and North Pier, and along George St.

BUDGET

Shellfish Bar (Railway Pier; sandwiches £2.50-3; ☒ 9am-6pm) If you want to savour superb Scottish seafood without the expense of an upmarket restaurant, head for Oban's famous seafood stall – it's the green shack on the quayside. Here you can buy fresh and cooked seafood to take away – prawn sandwiches, dressed crab, and fresh oysters for only 55p each.

Julie's Tearooms (☎ 565952; 37 Stafford St; sandwiches £3-7; ☒ 10am-5pm Mon-Sat) Nip into Julie's (opposite the distillery) for coffee and cake,

tea and a scone, or some delicious Luca's ice cream.

Kitchen Garden (☎ 566332; 14 George St; snacks £2.50-5; ☒ 10am-5pm Mon, 10am-10pm Tue-Sat, noon-4pm Sun) This deli is packed with delicious picnic food, and also has a great little café on a mezzanine floor above the shop – good coffee, scones and cakes, homemade soups and sandwiches.

F'Eats Coffee Bar (☎ 571000; The Warehouse, John St; light meals £2-4; ☒ 9am-5pm Mon-Sat, 10am-4pm Sun) This stylish café and bar with comfy purple sofas serves tasty *paninis*, baguettes and focaccias, as well as homemade soup and great cappuccinos.

Self-caterers and campers can stock up at **Tesco** (Lochside St; ☒ 8am-10pm Mon-Sat, 9am-6pm Sun).

MIDRANGE

Ee'usk (☎ 565666; North Pier; mains £11-17; ☒ noon-3pm & 6-10pm) A new development on North Pier houses bright and modern Ee'usk (it's how you pronounce *iasg*, the Gaelic word for fish). Tall picture windows allow diners on two levels to enjoy views over the harbour to Kerrera and Mull, all while sampling a seafood menu ranging from crisp-battered haddock to Thai fish cakes. A little overpriced, perhaps, but both food and location are first class.

Waterfront Restaurant (☎ 563110; Waterfront Centre, Railway Pier; mains £8-20; ☒ 11.30am-2.15pm & 5.30-9.30pm) Housed in a converted seamen's mission, the Waterfront's stylish, minimalist décor – pale grey and lavender, with smart blue and white table linen – does little to distract from the superb seafood freshly landed at the quay just a few metres away. There's everything from humble haddock and chips to a splendid platter of scallops, sea bream and fat, pink langoustines.

Studio Restaurant (☎ 562030; Craigard Rd; mains £10-15; ☒ 6-10pm) This snug little place, up the hill off George St, deserves its good reputation, offering a menu of Scottish-French cuisine that includes pâté and oatcakes, scampi and scallops Provençale, roast Angus beef, and Scottish cheeses. A set three-course dinner costs £13/15 before/after 6.30pm.

For takeaway food, try the **Taj Mahal** (☎ 566400; 146 George St; mains £6-12; ☒ noon-2pm & 5pm-midnight) for Indian food, or **China Restaurant** (☎ 563575; 39 Stafford St; mains £7-10; ☒ noon-2pm & 5-10.30pm) for Chinese.

Drinking & Entertainment

Oban Inn (☎ 562484; Stafford St; bar meals £7; ☷ food served noon-8.30pm) The lively Oban Inn, overlooking the harbour by North Pier, is the best pub in town. It's a traditional bar with wood panelling, brass rails and stained glass, and has real ales, a wide range of single malt whiskies and good bar food – the *moules frites* (mussels and chips) are a local favourite.

Barn (☎ 564618; Lerags; ☷ 11am-11pm Mon-Sat, noon-11pm Sun Apr-Oct, 11am-11pm Mon-Sat Nov-Mar; ☷) This family-friendly pub, with an outdoor beer garden and children's play area, is in a lovely country setting 2 miles south of Oban. It does bar meals with a special children's menu and some good veggie options.

McTavish's Kitchens (☎ 563064; George St; adult/child £4.50/2 for show only, £2.50/1 for show if dining; ☷ show 8pm May-Sep) The nightly 'Scottish show' here caters to the kilts-and-tartan tourist market, with Scottish country dancing, live bands, piping, fiddle music and Gaelic songs.

O'Donnells Irish Pub (☎ 656421; Breadalbane St; ☷ 2pm-1am Sun-Thu, 2pm-2am Fri & Sat) This Irish bar, opposite Oban Backpackers, has live entertainment – usually Celtic music – most nights.

Lorne Bar (☎ 570020; Stevenson St) This lively bar is popular with Oban's late teens and twenty-somethings, and stays open till 2am Thursday to Saturday.

Getting There & Away

BOAT

CalMac (☎ 566688) ferries link Oban with the islands of Kerrera (opposite), Mull (p301), Coll (p308), Tiree (see Coll), Lismore (p311), Colonsay (p294), Barra (p384) and Lochboisdale (p384). See island entries for details.

BUS

Scottish Citylink buses run to Oban from Glasgow (£14, three hours, four daily) via Inveraray; from Fort William (£8.20, 1½ hours, four daily), with connections to Inverness; and from Perth (£9, three hours, twice daily Friday to Monday) via Tyndrum and Killin.

West Coast Motors (☎ 570500) bus 423 runs from Oban to Lochgilphead (£4, 1¾ hours, four daily Monday to Friday, two on Saturday) via Kilmartin Glen.

The **West Highland Flyer** (☎ 07780 724248) is a minibus service that links Oban with Fort William (£7, 1¼ hours) and Mallaig (£15, 2½ hours, one daily Monday to Saturday); it operates from Easter to late October. Bicycles can be carried for an extra £2 to Fort William and £3.50 to Mallaig.

TRAIN

Oban is at the end of a scenic route that branches off the West Highland line at Crianlarich. There are up to three trains daily from Glasgow to Oban (£17, three hours).

The train's not much use for travelling north from Oban. To reach Fort William requires a detour via Crianlarich – take the bus instead.

Getting Around

BUS

The main bus stop is outside the train station. **Oban & District Buses** (☎ 570500) is the local company; buses 1 and 401 run from the train station to Ganavan Sands via Oban Youth

---

THAR SHE BLOWS!

The North Atlantic Drift – a swirling tendril of the Gulf Stream – carries warm water into the cold, nutrient-rich seas off the Scottish coast, resulting in huge blooms of plankton. Small fish feed on the plankton, and bigger fish feed on the smaller fish. And this huge seafood smorgasbord attracts large numbers of marine mammals, from harbour porpoises and dolphins to minke whales and even – though sightings are rare – humpback and sperm whales.

In contrast to Iceland and Norway, Scotland has cashed in on the abundance of minke whales off its coast by embracing whale-watching rather than whaling. There are now dozens of operators around the coast offering whale-watching boat trips lasting from a couple of hours to all day; some have whale-sighting success rates of more than 95%.

While seals, porpoises and dolphins can be seen year-round, minke whales are migratory. The best time to see them is from June to August, with August being the peak month for sightings. A booklet titled *Is It a Whale?* is available from Tourist Information Centres (TICs) and bookshops, and provides tips on identifying the various species of marine mammal that you're likely to see.

Hostel (five minutes, every 20 minutes). Bus 431 connects the train station with the Kerrera ferry and Oban Caravan & Camping Park (15 minutes, two daily Monday to Saturday from late May to September).

CAR
Hazelbank Motors (☎ 566476; www.obancarhire.co.uk; Lynn Rd; ☼ 8.30am-5.30pm Mon-Sat) rents small cars from £40/225 per day/week including VAT, insurance and CDW (collision damage waiver).

TAXI
There's a taxi rank outside the train station. Otherwise, call **Oban Taxis** (☎ 564666) or **Kennedy's Taxis** (☎ 564172).

AROUND OBAN
Isle of Kerrera
☎ 01631 / pop 40
Some of the best **walking** in the area is on Kerrera, which faces Oban across the bay. There's a 6-mile circuit of the island (allow three hours), which follows tracks or paths (use OS map 49) and offers the chance to spot wildlife such as Soay sheep, wild goats, otters, golden eagles, peregrine falcons, seals and porpoises. At **Lower Gylen**, at the southern end of the island, there's a ruined castle.

Kerrera Bunkhouse & Tea Garden (☎ 570223; www.kerrerabunkhouse.co.uk; Lower Gylen; dm £10; ☼ tea garden 10.30am-4.30pm Wed-Sun Easter-Sep) is a charming seven-bed bothy (hut) in a converted 18th-century stable near Gylen Castle, a 2-mile walk south from the ferry (keep left at the fork just past the telephone box). Booking is recommended. You can get snacks and light meals at the nearby Tea Garden.

There's a daily passenger **ferry** (☎ 563665) to Kerrera from Gallanach, about 2 miles southwest of Oban town centre, along Gallanach Rd (adult/child £3.50/1.50 return, bicycle 50p, 10 minutes). From April to September it runs half-hourly from 10.30am to 12.30pm and 2pm to 6pm daily, plus 8.45am Monday to Saturday. Call to check winter ferry times.

Isle of Seil
☎ 01852 / pop 500
The small island of Seil, 10 miles south of Oban, is best known for its connection to the mainland – the so-called **Bridge over the Atlantic**, designed by Thomas Telford and

opened in 1793. The bridge has a single stone arch and spans the narrowest part of the tidal Clachan Sound.

On the west coast of the island is the pretty conservation village of **Ellanbeich**, with its whitewashed cottages, 4 miles from the bridge. The village was built to house workers at the local slate quarries, but the industry collapsed in 1881 when the sea flooded the main quarry pit – the pit can still be seen. The **Scottish Slate Islands Heritage Trust** (☎ 300449; Ellanbeich; adult/child £1.50/25p; ☼ 10.30am-5pm Apr-Jun & Sep, 10.30am-6pm Jul & Aug) displays fascinating old photographs illustrating life in the village in the 19th and early 20th centuries.

Coach tours flock to the **Highland Arts Studio** (☎ 300273; Easdale; ☼ 9am-9pm Apr-Sep, 10am-6pm Oct-Mar), a crafts and gift shop and a shrine to the eccentric output of the late 'poet, artist and composer' C John Taylor. Please, try to keep a straight face.

Just offshore from Ellanbeich is the small island of Easdale, which has more old slateworkers' cottages and the interesting **Easdale Island Folk Museum** (☎ 300370; adult/child £2.25/50p; ☼ 10.30am-5.30pm Apr-Oct). The museum has displays about the slate industry and life on the islands in the 18th and 19th centuries. Climb to the top of the island (a 38m peak!) for a great view of the surrounding area, then retire to the **Puffer Bar** (☼ 10.30am-5.30pm) for a cream tea or a prawn sandwich.

Sea.fari Adventures (☎ 300003; Easdale Harbour) runs a series of exciting two-hour boat trips in high-speed RIBs (rigid inflatable boats) to the Corryvreckan whirlpool (see the boxed text, p292), the slate island of Belnahua (see Isle of Luing, p300) and the remote Garvellach Islands (adult/child from £26/20).

Anyone who fancies their hand at ducks and drakes should try to attend the **World Stone-Skimming Championships** (www.stoneskimming.com), held each year in Easdale on the last Sunday in September.

GETTING THERE & AROUND
Oban & District Buses (☎ 01631-570500) runs buses at least twice daily, except Sunday, from Oban to Ellanbeich and on to North Cuan for the ferry to Luing (p300).

Argyll & Bute Council (☎ 01631-562125) operates the daily passenger-only ferry service from Ellanbeich to Easdale island (£1.40 return, bicycles free, five minutes). Most runs are on request, at the times displayed on the pier. To call the boat to Ellanbeich pier, sound the hooter during daylight, or switch on the light at night.

Isle of Luing

☎ 01852 / pop 180

Luing (pronounced ling), about 6 miles long and 1.5 miles wide, is separated from the southern end of Seil by the narrow Cuan Sound. There are two attractive villages – **Cullipool** at the northern end and **Toberonochy** in the east – but Luing's main pleasures are scenic.

The **slate quarries** of Cullipool were abandoned in 1965. About 1.5 miles out to sea you can see the remains of the extensively quarried slate island of **Belnahua** – workers used to live on this remote and desolate rock. You can get a closer look on a boat trip from Easdale (see Sea.fari Adventures, p299).

There are two Iron Age forts, the better being **Dun Leccamore**, about a mile north of Toberonochy. In Toberonochy itself are the ruins of the late medieval **Kilchatton Church** and a graveyard with unusual slate gravestones.

You can visit both villages, the fort, the ruined chapel and the scenic west coast on a pleasant 8-mile circular walk.

GETTING THERE & AROUND

A small **car ferry** (☎ 01631-562125) runs from Cuan (on Seil) to Luing (passenger/car £1.40/5.70 return, bicycles free, five minutes, two per hour Monday to Saturday); a passenger-only ferry runs on Sunday, too.

There's a Monday to Saturday **postbus** (☎ 01463-256200) service around Luing that connects to Ellanbeich on Seil.

Isle of Luing Bike Hire (☎ 314256) in Cullipool rents bikes for £6/10 per half/full day.

ISLE OF MULL

pop 2600

It's easy to see why Mull is so popular with tourists. As well as having superb mountain scenery, two castles, a narrow-gauge railway and being on the way to the sacred Isle of Iona, it's also a charming and endearing place.

Despite the number of visitors who flock to the island, it seems to be large enough to absorb them all; many stick to the well-worn route from Craignure to Iona, returning to Oban in the evening. If you're looking for budget accommodation, there's

not too much of it on Mull, so you'd be advised to take a tent.

The waters to the west of Mull provide some of the best whale-spotting opportunities in Scotland, with several operators offering whale-watching cruises (see Inter-Island Cruises, below and Sea Life Surveys, p302). See also the boxed text Thar She Blows (p298).

ORIENTATION

About two-thirds of Mull's population lives in and around Tobermory, the island's capital, in the north. Craignure, at the southeastern corner, has the main ferry terminal and is where most people arrive. Fionnphort is at the far western end of the long Ross of Mull peninsula, and is where the ferry to Iona departs.

INFORMATION

Clydesdale Bank (☎ 0345-826818; Main St, Tobermory; 9.15am-4.45pm Mon-Fri) Has a 24-hour ATM.

Craignure TIC (☎ 01680-812377; Craignure; 8.30am-5pm Mon-Sat, 10.30am-5pm Sun)

Dunaros Hospital (☎ 01680-300392; Salen) Has a minor injuries unit; the nearest casualty department is in Oban.

Post office (☎ 01688-302058; Main St, Tobermory; 9am-1pm & 2-5.30pm Mon, Tue, Thu & Fri, 9am-1pm Wed & Sat)

Tobermory TIC (☎ 01688-302182; The Pier, Tobermory; 9am-5pm Mon-Fri, noon-5pm Sat & Sun Apr-Oct)

TOURS

See Bowman's Tours, p296, for details of day tours from Oban to Mull, Staffa and Iona by ferry and bus. There are also several companies running wildlife and whale-watching tours – see Sea Life Surveys on p302 for details of whale-watching trips, and for a full listing see www.wildisles.co.uk. Booking for these is strongly advised.

Gordon Grant Marine (☎ 01681-700388; www.staffa tours.com) From Easter to mid-October, this outfit runs boat trips from Fionnphort to Staffa (adult/child £18/8.75, 2½ hours, daily March to October), and to Staffa and the Treshnish Isles (£35/18, five hours, Sunday to Friday May to August).

Inter-Island Cruises (☎ 01688-400264; www.whale watchingtrips.co.uk; Garadh Mor, Dervaig) Offers full-day whale-watching boat trips off the west coast of Mull for £45 per person; cruises depart from Croig pier, 3 miles west of Dervaig, in North Mull.

Mull Wildlife Expeditions (☎ 01688-500121; www .torrbuan.com; Ulva Ferry) Travellers have written to us to

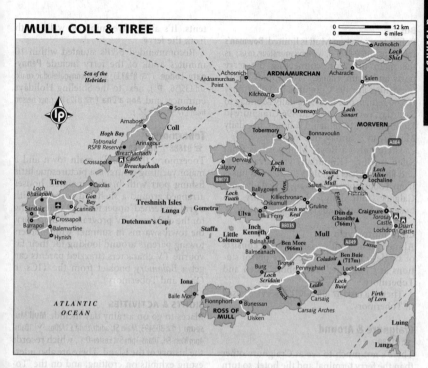

MULL, COLL & TIREE

recommend the 7½-hour Land Rover tours offered by this company. The cost (adult/child £33/27) includes a picnic lunch. You'll have a chance to spot golden eagles, peregrine falcons, hen harriers, red deer, seals and otters, and perhaps dolphins and porpoises. So that you can make this a day trip from Oban, tours leave from Tobermory at 10am and from Craignure an hour later, returning to Craignure for the 5pm Oban ferry.

Turus Mara (☎ 0800 085 8786; www.turusmara.com) Runs boat trips to Staffa and Iona from Ulva Ferry in central Mull (£18/9, four hours), giving you an hour ashore on the island. There are also longer trips that take in both Staffa and the Treshnish Isles (£35/18, 6½ hours), with an hour on Staffa and two hours on Lunga.

FESTIVALS & EVENTS
Mishnish Music Festival (☎ 01688-302383; www .mishnish.co.uk/musicfestival.htm) Last weekend of April. Three days of foot-stomping traditional Scottish and Irish folk music.
Mendelssohn on Mull (☎ 01688-301108; www.mull fest.org) Early July. A week-long festival of classical music.
Mull Highland Games (☎ 01688-302001; www .mishnish.co.uk/mhg.htm) Third Thursday in July.
Tour of Mull Rally (☎ 01688-302133; www.2300club .org) Early October. Part of the Scottish Championship;

around 150 cars are involved and public roads are closed for parts of the weekend.

GETTING THERE & AWAY
There are frequent CalMac ferries from Oban to Craignure (passenger/car £3.95/36, 40 minutes, every two hours). There's another car ferry link between Fishnish, on the east coast of Mull, and Lochaline (£2.45/11, 15 minutes, at least hourly).

A third **CalMac** (☎ 01688-302017) car ferry links Tobermory to Kilchoan on the Ardnamurchan peninsula (£3.80/20, 35 minutes, seven daily Monday to Saturday); from June to August there are also five sailings on Sunday.

GETTING AROUND
Bicycle
You can hire bikes for about £10 to £15 a day. In Salen, try **On Yer Bike** (☎ 01680-300501); it also has an outlet in the craft shop near the ferry terminal in Craignure. In Tobermory, try **Brown's Hardware Shop** (☎ 01688-302020; Main St) or Mrs MacLean at **Tom-A-Mhuillin** (☎ 01688-302164; Salen Rd).

Bus

Public transport on Mull is limited. **Bowman's Tours** (☎ 01680-812313; www.bowmanstours.co.uk) is the main operator, connecting the ferry ports and main villages. The routes useful for visitors are 495 Craignure to Tobermory (£6.60 return, one hour, six daily Monday to Saturday, two Sunday) and 496 Craignure to Fionnphort (£10 return, 1¼ hours, five daily Monday to Saturday, one Sunday).

There's also a Royal Mail postbus from Salen to Burg (Kilninian) via Ulva Ferry, and **RN Carmichael** (☎ 01688-302220) runs buses from Tobermory to Dervaig (five daily) and Calgary (four daily); there are only two buses on Saturday and none on Sunday.

Car & Motorcycle

Almost all of Mull's road network consists of single-track roads. There are petrol stations at Craignure, Fionnphort, Salen and Tobermory.

There's a **taxi** (☎ 01688-302204) service based in Tobermory.

Craignure & Around
☎ 01680

There's not much to see at Craignure other than the ferry terminal and the hotel, so turn left, walk 200m and hop onto the **Mull Railway** (☎ 812494; Old Pier Station; adult/child £4/3 return; ☼ May-Sep), a miniature steam train that will take you 1.5 miles south to Torosay Castle.

Torosay Castle & Gardens (☎ 812421; adult/child £5.50/2.25; ☼ house 10.30am-5pm Easter-Oct, gardens 9am-7pm Easter-Oct) is a rambling Victorian mansion in the Scottish Baronial style. 'Take your time but not our spoons' advises the sign, and you're left to wander at will.

Two miles beyond Torosay is **Duart Castle** (☎ 812309; adult/child £4.50/2.25; ☼ 10.30am-5.30pm May–mid-Oct, 11am-4pm Sun-Thu Apr), a formidable fortress dominating the Sound of Mull. The seat of the Clan Maclean, this is one of the oldest inhabited castles in Scotland – the central keep was built in 1360. It was bought and restored in 1911 by war hero Sir Fitzroy Maclean and has damp dungeons, vast halls and bathrooms equipped with ancient fittings.

SLEEPING

Shieling Holidays (☎ 812496; www.shielingholidays.co.uk; camp sites £10.50, with car £12.50, dm £10; ☼ late Mar-Oct) is a well-equipped camping ground with hostel beds available in large 'cottage'

tents. It's about five minutes' walk south from the ferry.

Recommended B&Bs situated within 10 minutes' walk of the ferry include **Pennygate Lodge** (☎ 812333; info@pennygatelodge.co.uk; s/d £35/56; P), next to the Shieling Holidays entrance, and **Aon a'Dha** (☎ 812318; r per person from £17.50; P ✗).

Tobermory
☎ 01688 / pop 750

Tobermory, the island's main town and a major yachting centre, is a picturesque little fishing port with brightly painted houses arranged around a sheltered harbour, with a grid-patterned 'upper town'. As the setting for the children's TV programme *Balamory*, the town swarms in summer with toddlers towing parents around looking for their favourite TV characters (frazzled parents can get a *Balamory* booklet from the TICs in Oban and Tobermory).

SIGHTS & ACTIVITIES

Places to go on a rainy day include **Mull Museum** (☎ 302493; Main St; adult/child £1/20p; ☼ 10am-4pm Mon-Fri, 10am-1pm Sat Easter-Oct), which records the history of the island. There are also interesting exhibits on crofting, and on the 'Tobermory galleon', a ship from the Spanish armada that sank in Tobermory Bay in 1588 and has been the object of treasure seekers ever since.

There's also **An Tobar Arts Centre** (☎ 302211; Argyll Tce; ☼ 10am-5pm Mon-Sat, 1-4pm Sun May-Sep, 10am-4pm Tue-Sat Oct-Apr), an art gallery and exhibition space, and the **Tobermory Distillery** (☎ 302645; adult/concession £2.50/1; ☼ 10.30am-4pm Mon-Fri Easter-Oct), which offers guided tours.

The Hebridean Whale & Dolphin Trust's **Marine Discovery Centre** (☎ 302620; 28 Main St; admission free; ☼ 10am-5pm Mon-Fri, 11am-4pm Sun Apr-Oct, 11am-5pm Mon-Fri Nov-Mar) has displays, videos and interactive exhibits on whale and dolphin biology and ecology.

Sea Life Surveys (☎ 400223; www.sealifesurveys.com; Ledaig) runs whale-watching trips from Tobermory harbour to the waters north and west of Mull. An all-day whale watch (£55) gives up to six hours at sea (not recommended for kids under 12), and has a 96% success rate for sightings. The four-hour family whale-watch is geared more towards children and costs £40/35 per adult/child. The booking office is next to MacGochan's pub, in the big car park at the southern end of the waterfront.

You can hire mountain bikes from **Archibald Brown** (☎ 302020; 21 Main St) for £10/15 per five/24 hours.

SLEEPING

Tobermory has dozens of B&Bs, but the place can still be booked solid in July and August, especially at weekends.

Baliscate Guest House (☎ 302048; www.baliscate.co .uk; Salen Rd; s/d £40/54; **P** **X**) A handsome 18th-century house set in beautiful gardens, Baliscate has four large en-suite bedrooms, a breakfast conservatory, a comfortable lounge with library, and an endearing resident cat. The welcoming owners are an interesting couple who not only breed horses but are also building their own aircraft in the nearby barn. The house is a mile south of the village centre, off the main road towards Craignure.

Ptarmigan (☎ 302863; www.bed-&-breakfast-tobermory.co.uk; The Fairways; r per person £35-45; **X** Mar-Nov; **P** **X** **R**) Here's a first – a B&B with a private, 10m swimming pool! Ptarmigan is a large modern house built by the former owners of the Western Isles Hotel, and offers luxury B&B in a beautiful setting with superb views over Tobermory Bay – ask for the upper turret bedroom, with its own balcony.

Brockville (☎ 302741; www.brockville-tobermory.co .uk; Raeric Rd; s/d £45/60; **P** **X**) This modern B&B enjoys a peaceful setting on the northern edge of the village There are two spacious en-suite bedrooms, complete with sofas and coffee tables, and great views across the Sound of Mull to the hills of Morvern.

Western Isles Hotel (☎ 302012; www.mullhotel .com; Western Rd; s/d from £53/106; **P** **X**) One of the top hotels on Mull, this grand Victorian pile commands the heights above the harbour. It has 28 luxurious rooms – the more-expensive doubles (£188) have great views over the harbour – and a conservatory bar-restaurant and terrace also with panoramic views.

Tobermory Youth Hostel (SYHA; ☎ 0870 004 1151; Main St; dm £13; **X** Mar-Oct) This smallish hostel (39 beds) has a great location, set in a Victorian house right on the waterfront. Bookings are recommended.

Tobermory Campsite (☎ 302624; www.tobermory campsite.co.uk; Newdale, Dervaig Rd; camp sites per person £4; **X** Mar-Oct) The nearest place to camp is this quiet, country camping ground a mile west of town on the road to Dervaig.

EATING & DRINKING

The regular summer influx of affluent yachties supports several top-notch seafood restaurants, including those in the Western Isles Hotel, the Tobermory Hotel, and Ulva House.

Anchorage (☎ 302313; 28 Main St; mains £14-20; **X** 10am-4pm & 6-9pm) Our current favourite among Tobermory's seafood restaurants is this nautical bistro decked out in smart navy blue and white, with bare stone walls and rope-wound pillars. The engine room is powered by a French chef who turns out adventurous dishes such as tuna sushi, smoked haddock, scallops *en papillotte*, and carpaccio of roe deer venison, as well as crowd-pleasers like kilo pots of mussels with a choice of *marinière* or Thai sauces.

Mishnish Hotel (☎ 302009; Main St; bar meals £8-10; **X** food served noon-2pm & 6-9pm) You can't miss the bright yellow façade of this hotel; it's a favourite hang-out for visiting yachties and a good place for a bar meal. The 'Mish', as it's known, is a fine traditional pub that has escaped the deluge of gambling machines afflicting so many of Scotland's watering holes. Toast your toes by the open fire, burrow into a booth with a book, or challenge the locals to a game of pool.

MacGochan's (☎ 302350; Ledaig; bar meals £6-10; **X** food served noon-10pm) A lively pub beside the car park at the southern end of the waterfront, MacGochan's does good bar meals, and often has outdoor barbecues on summer evenings; there's a more formal restaurant upstairs, and live music in the bar at weekends.

An Tobar Arts Centre (☎ 302211; Argyll Tce; **X** 10am-5pm Mon-Sat, 1-4pm Sun May-Sep, 10am-4pm Tue-Sat Oct-Apr) The village arts centre, set in a Victorian school building, has an attractive café that serves good coffee and home baking.

Campers can stock up on provisions at the **Co-op supermarket** (Main St; **X** 8am-8pm Mon-Sat, 12.30-7pm Sun), and the **Island Bakery** (☎ 302223; Main St; **X** 9am-5pm Mon-Sat), which sells delicious, locally baked wholegrain bread, cakes, biscuits and pastries as well as having a great deli counter.

North Mull
☎ 01688

With only 43 seats, **Mull Little Theatre** (☎ 302 828; www.mulltheatre.com; Dervaig; adult/child £10/6; ☺ shows 3pm & 8pm Apr-Sep) is Scotland's smallest theatre, but it enjoys a reputation for staging excellent productions. The theatre is 8 miles west of Tobermory at Dervaig, but the box office is on Main St in Tobermory.

The **Old Byre Heritage Centre** (☎ 400229; Dervaig; adult/child £4/2; ☺ 10.30am-6.30pm Wed-Sun Easter-Oct) brings Mull's heritage and natural history to life through a series of tableaux and a half-hour film show; prize for most bizarre exhibit goes to the 40cm-long model of a midge. The centre's tearoom serves good, inexpensive snacks, including soup, and *clootie dumplings*.

Mull's best silver-sand beach, flanked by cliffs and with views out to Coll and Tiree, is at **Calgary**, about 4 miles west of Dervaig. And yes – this is the place from which the more famous Calgary in Alberta, Canada, takes its name.

SLEEPING & EATING
Calgary Hotel (☎ 400256; www.calgary.co.uk; Calgary; r per person £33-48; P ☒) The Calgary provides delightfully rustic accommodation a few minutes' walk from the sandy beach at Calgary Bay. There are also two lovely self-catering loft apartments available for £390 per week (sleeping two to four people).

Bellachroy Hotel & Pub (☎ 400314; www.bella chroyhotel.co.uk; Dervaig; r per person £38, mains £7-12; ☺ lunch & dinner; P) The six-room Bellachroy is an atmospheric 17th-century droving inn; the bar, known as the Bear Pit, is a focus for good local social life and serves good-value bar meals.

Druimard Country House & Restaurant (☎ 400345; www.druimard.co.uk; Dervaig; r per person £45-63; ☺ dinner; P ☒) Along the road from Mull Theatre, this Victorian country house offers luxurious but homely accommodation, with a genteel lounge and conservatory with grand views. Its four-course dinners are available to non-guests for £31.50 a head (£30 for guests).

You can camp for free at the southern end of the beach at Calgary Bay – keep to the area south of the stream. There are no facilities other than the public toilets across the road; water comes from the stream.

Central Mull
☎ 01680

The central part of the island, between the Craignure–Fionnphort road and the narrow isthmus between Salen and Gruline, contains the island's highest peak, Ben More (966m) and some of its wildest scenery (see the Walking on Mull boxed text, opposite).

At Gruline, near the head of Loch na Keal, is the **MacQuarrie Mausoleum**, a monument to Sir Lachlan MacQuarrie (1762–1824) who was born on Mull and served as governor of New South Wales in Australia from 1809 to 1821.

The narrow B8035 road along the southern shore of Loch na Keal squeezes past some impressive cliffs before cutting south towards Loch Scridain. About a mile along the shore from Balmeanach, where the road climbs away from the coast, is **Mackinnon's Cave**, a deep and spooky fissure in the basalt cliffs that was once used as a refuge by Celtic monks; a big, flat rock inside, known as Fingal's Table, may have been their altar.

Balmeanach Park Caravan & Camping Site (☎ 300342; camp sites per adult/child £5/3, campervan £12-15; ☺ Mar-Oct) is a peaceful camping ground 10 minutes' walk from the Fishnish–Lochaline ferry, on the main road between Craignure and Tobermory.

There's also a very basic **camping ground** (camp sites per person £4) at Killiechronan, half a mile north of Gruline. Toilets and water are a five-minute walk away.

South Mull
☎ 01681

The road from Craignure to Fionnphort climbs through some wild and desolate scenery before reaching the southwestern part of the island, which consists of a long peninsula called the Ross of Mull. The Ross has a spectacular south coast lined with black basalt cliffs that give way further west to white-sand beaches and pink granite crags. The cliffs reach their highest at Malcolm's Point, near the superb **Carsaig Arches** (see the boxed text, opposite).

The little village of **Bunessan** has a hotel, tearoom, pub and some shops, and is home to the **Ross of Mull Historical Centre** (☎ 700659; admission £1; ☺ 10am-4.30pm Mon-Fri Apr-Oct), a Portakabin that houses displays on local history, geology, archaeology, genealogy and wildlife.

WALKING ON MULL

More information on the following walks can be obtained from the TICs in Oban (p294), Craignure (p300) and Tobermory (p300).

Ben More

The highest peak on the island, Ben More (966m) has spectacular views across to the surrounding islands when the weather is clear. A trail leads up the mountain from Loch na Keal, by the bridge on the B8035 over the Abhainn na h-Uamha (the river 8 miles southwest of Salen, Ordnance Survey (OS) 1:50,000 map sheet 49, grid reference 507368). Return the same way or continue down the narrow ridge to the eastern top, A'Chioch, then descend to the road via Gleann na Beinn Fhada. The glen can be rather wet and there's not much of a path. The round trip is 6.5 miles; allow five to six hours.

Carsaig Arches

One of the best walks on Mull is along the coast west of Carsaig Bay to the Carsaig Arches at Malcolm's Point. There's a good path below the cliffs all the way from Carsaig, but it becomes a bit rough and exposed near the arches – the route climbs and then traverses a very steep slope above a vertical drop into the sea (not for the unfit or faint-hearted). You'll see spectacular rock formations on the way, including one that looks like a giant slice of Christmas cake. The arches are two sea-cut rock formations. One, nicknamed the 'keyhole', is a freestanding rock stack; the other, the 'tunnel', is a huge natural arch. The western entrance is hung with curtains of columnar basalt – an impressive place. The round trip is 8 miles – allow three to four hours' walking time from Carsaig plus at least an hour at the arches.

Burg

At the tip of the remote Ardmeanach peninsula there is a remarkable 50-million-year-old **fossil tree** preserved in the basalt lava flows of the cliffs. A 4WD track leads from the car park at Tiroran to a house at Burg; the last 2.5 miles to the tree is on a very rough coastal path. About 500m before the tree, a metal ladder allows you to climb down to the foreshore, which is only accessible at low tide – check tide times at Tobermory TIC before setting off. Allow six to seven hours for the strenuous 14-mile round trip.

At the western end of the Ross, 38 miles from Craignure, is **Fionnphort** (pronounced *finn*-a-fort). The coast here is a beautiful blend of pink granite rocks, white sandy beaches and vivid turquoise sea. The **Columba Centre** (☎ 700660; admission free; ✆ 10am-5.30pm Apr-Oct) has displays about the life of St Columba, the Celts and the history of Iona.

SLEEPING & EATING

Pennyghael Hotel (☎ 704288; www.pennyghaelhotel .com; Pennyghael; r per person £55; 4-course dinner £23; ✆ dinner; Ⓟ ✗) This delightful, six-room country hotel is set in a 17th-century farmhouse, near the head of Loch Scridain and about halfway between Craignure and Fionnphort. Great views across the loch.

Seaview (☎ 700235; www.iona-bed-breakfast-mull .com; Fionnphort; r per person £19-29; Ⓟ ✗) Barely a minute's walk from the Iona ferry, the five-

bedroom Seaview has a breakfast conservatory with grand views across to Iona. The owner – a semiretired fisherman – is happy to take guests for a trip along the coast in his lobster boat.

Staffa House (☎ 700677; Fionnphort; r per person £25-40; Ⓟ ✗) Readers have recommended this family B&B for its charm and hospitality. The house is packed with antiques and period features, and like the Seaview offers breakfast in a conservatory with a view of Iona.

Keel Row (☎ 700458; Fionnphort; bar meals £7-9; ✆ food served noon-2.30pm & 6-8.30pm) It may look like an ordinary cottage, but Keel Row, next door to Seaview, is a cosy pub with wooden floors, stone walls, good bar meals and homemade snacks.

Fidden Farm (☎ 700427; camp sites per person £2; ✆ Apr-Sep) There's a basic but beautifully situated camping ground here, 1.25 miles south of Fionnphort (continue on the road past the Columba Centre).

Isle of Ulva

☎ 01688 / pop 30

Ulva, just off the west coast of Mull, has good walking and mountain-biking, a 9th-century Viking fort, and an old chapel with a graveyard. A short walk north of the ferry landing is **Sheila's Cottage Heritage Centre** (☎ 500241; admission included in ferry ticket; �

☺ 9am-5pm Mon-Fri Easter-Oct, plus 9am-5pm Sun Jun-Aug), a reconstruction of a traditional thatched crofter's cottage with displays about the history of the island.

At the Boathouse tearoom, beside the ferry landing, you can savour locally harvested oysters washed down with Guinness. An interpretative centre upstairs has information on walks and natural history.

The two-minute ferry crossing (adult/child £4.50/2 return) runs on demand during Heritage Centre opening hours.

Isle of Staffa

Felix Mendelssohn, who visited Staffa in 1829, was inspired to compose his Hebrides Overture after hearing waves echoing in the impressive and cathedral-like **Fingal's Cave**; the cave walls and surrounding cliffs are composed of vertical, hexagonal basalt columns that look like pillars (Staffa is Norse for 'Pillar Island'). You can land on the island and walk into the cave via a causeway. Nearby **Boat Cave** can be seen from the causeway, but you can't reach it on foot. Staffa also has a sizable puffin colony, north of the landing place.

Northwest of Staffa lies a chain of uninhabited islands called the **Treshnish Isles**. The two main islands are the curiously shaped **Dutchman's Cap** and **Lunga**. You can land on Lunga, walk to the top of the hill, and visit the shag, puffin and guillemot colonies on the west coast at **Harp Rock**.

GETTING THERE & AWAY

Unless you have your own boat, the only way to reach Staffa is on an organised boat trip – see Tours, p296, for details.

ISLE OF IONA

☎ 01681 / pop 130

There are few more uplifting sights on Scotland's west coast than the view of Iona from Mull on a sunny day – an emerald island set in a sparkling turquoise sea. From the

moment you step off the ferry you begin to appreciate the hushed, spiritual atmosphere that pervades this sacred island. Not surprisingly, the island attracts a lot of daytrippers, so if you want to experience the island's peace and quiet then the solution is to spend a night here. Once the crowds have gone for the day, you can wander in peace around the ancient graveyard where the kings of Scotland are buried, attend an evening service at the abbey, or walk to the top of the hill and gaze south towards Ireland, as St Columba must have done so many centuries ago.

There's a tiny post office on the right as you head uphill from the ferry, and a **Spar** (☺ 9am-5.30pm Mon-Sat, noon-5pm Sun) grocery store a little further along on the left. Turn left on leaving the ferry to find **Finlay Ross Ltd** (☺ 10am-5.15pm Mon-Sat, 11am-5pm Sun), which sells gifts, books and maps, rents out bikes, and provides a laundry service.

History

St Columba sailed from Ireland and landed on Iona in 563 before setting out to spread Christianity throughout Scotland. He established a monastery on the island and it was here that the *Book of Kells* – the prize attraction of Dublin's Trinity College – is believed to have been transcribed. It was taken to Kells in Ireland when Viking raids drove the monks from Iona.

The monks returned and the monastery prospered until its destruction during the Reformation. The ruins were given to the Church of Scotland in 1899, and by 1910 a group of enthusiasts called the **Iona Community** (www.iona.org.uk) had reconstructed the abbey. It's still a flourishing spiritual community that holds regular courses and retreats.

Sights & Activities

Head uphill from the ferry pier and turn right through the grounds of a ruined 13th-century **nunnery** with fine cloistered gardens, and exit at the far end. Across the road is the **Iona Heritage Centre** (☎ 700576; admission £1.50; ☺ 10.30am-4.30pm Mon-Sat Apr-Oct), which covers the history of Iona, crofting and lighthouses; the centre's coffee shop serves delicious home baking.

Turn right here and continue along the road to **Reilig Oran**, an ancient cemetery that holds the graves of 48 of Scotland's early kings, including Macbeth, and a tiny Romanesque chapel. Beyond rises the spiritual heart of the island – **Iona Abbey** (HS; ☎ 700512; adult/child £3.30/1.30; ��9.30am-6.30pm Apr-Oct, 9.30am-4.30pm Nov-Mar; ☐). The spectacular nave, dominated by Romanesque and early Gothic vaults and columns, contains the elaborate, white marble tombs of the 8th duke of Argyll and his wife. A door on the left leads to the beautiful Gothic cloister, where medieval grave slabs are displayed alongside modern religious sculptures. A replica of the intricately carved **St John's Cross** stands just outside the abbey – the massive 8th-century original is in the **Infirmary Museum** (around the far side of the abbey) along with many other fine examples of early Christian and medieval carved stones.

Back at the ferry slip, **Alternative Boat Hire** (☎ 700537; www.boattripsiona.com) offers cruises in a traditional wooden sailing boat to see, well, whatever you like – go fishing, birdwatching, picnicking, or just drift along admiring the scenery. Three-hour trips cost £13/7 per adult/child.

The **MV Volante** (☎ 700362) provides four-hour sea-angling trips (£30 per person including tackle and bait), as well as 1½-hour sightseeing cruises around Iona. (£10/5).

The **MV Iolaire** (☎ 700358) runs three-hour boat trips to Staffa (£18/7.50), departing Iona pier at 9.45am and 1.45pm.

Sleeping & Eating

Argyll Hotel (☎ 700334; www.argyllhoteliona.co.uk; Baile Mor; s/d from £65/90, mains £9-13; �� Feb-Nov, food served 12.30-2pm & 7-8.30pm; ☒) The terrace of cottages above the ferry slip houses this cute little hotel – it has 16 snug rooms (a sea view costs rather more – £129/146 for singles/doubles) and a country house restaurant with wooden fireplace and antique tables and chairs. The kitchen is supplied by a huge organic garden around the back, and the gourmet menu includes a delicately flavoured scallop chowder, a hearty cassoulet, and 'real beans on toast' (blackeye, lima and haricot beans in tomato and rosemary sauce on home-baked wholemeal toast).

Iona Hostel (☎ 700781; www.ionahostel.co.uk; Lagandorain; dm £15; �� check-in 4-7pm) This hostel is set in an attractive, modern timber building on a working croft, with stunning views out to Staffa and the Treshnish Isles. Rooms are

clean and functional, and the well-equipped lounge/kitchen area has an open fire. It's at the northern end of the island – to get here, continue along the road past the abbey for 1.5 miles (a 20- to 30- minute walk).

Shore Cottage (☎ 700744; www.shorecottage.co.uk; Baile Mor; r per person £23-30; ☒) Travellers have recommended this attractive modern house, just a few minutes' walk south from the ferry. There are three bedrooms (all with en suite), and breakfast is served in a sunroom with great views across the sea to Mull.

Iona Cottage (☎ 700358; Baile Mor; r per person £22; ☒) This pretty little whitewashed cottage sits directly in front of the ferry landing, with a neat garden looking across to the Ross of Mull.

Getting There & Around

The passenger ferry from Fionnphort to Iona (£3.70 return, five minutes, hourly) runs daily. There are also various interesting day trips available from Oban (p296) and Mull (p301) to Iona.

You can hire bikes from Finlay Ross Ltd (see opposite).

ISLE OF COLL
☎ 01879 / pop 170

Rugged and low-lying, Coll is Tiree's (p308) less fertile and less populous neighbour. The northern part of the island is a mix of bare rock, bog and lochans (small lochs) – the south is swathed in white shell-sand beaches and machairs up to 30m high.

Arinagour, at the ferry pier, is the only village, and has a post office, a grocery shop, some craft shops and a petrol pump.

Sights & Activities

The island's main attraction is the peace and quiet – empty beaches, bird-haunted coastlines, and taking long walks along the shore. The biggest and most beautiful sandy beaches are at **Crossapol** in the south, and **Hogh Bay** and **Cliad** on the west coast.

In summer, you may be lucky enough to hear the 'krek-krek-krek' of the corncrake at the **RSPB Nature Reserve** at Totronald in the southwest of the island; there's a free **information centre** (☎ 230301; �� year-round) here.

There are two ruined castles nearby, both known as **Breachachadh Castle**, built by the Macleans in medieval times.

Sleeping & Eating

Coll Hotel (☎ 230334; www.collhotel.com; Arinagour; r per person £30-50, mains £8-13; **P** ✗) The island's only hotel is an atmospheric old place. It has quirkily shaped rooms with white-painted, wood-panelled walls, some of which have lovely views over the manicured hotel gardens and the harbour. The hotel also has a really good restaurant that serves dishes ranging from venison casserole to lobster Thermidor.

First Port of Coll (☎ 230262; Arinagour; mains £5-6; ✓ lunch & dinner) This snug little café serves hearty, homemade meals such as sausage and mash with onion gravy; haddock and chips; and vegetarian cottage pie, all accompanied by organic beer, wine and cider.

Most accommodation on Coll is self-catering, but a few places offer B&B. These include **Taigh Solas** (☎ 230333; taigh.solas@virgin .net; r per person £22-25; ✗) in Arinagour, and **Caolas** (☎ 230438; caolasfarm@fsmail.net; r per person from £25; ✗), at the southern tip of the island (the owner can arrange to pick you up from the ferry).

Garden House Camping & Caravan Site (☎ 230374; Uig; camp sites per person £5; ✓ May-Sep) is a basic camping ground with toilets and cold water only, 4.5 miles south of Arinagour. Dogs are not allowed.

Getting There & Around

A CalMac car ferry runs from Oban to Coll (passenger/car £13/74, 2¾ hours, one daily) and continues to Tiree. You can also sail between Coll and Tiree (£3.25/20, one hour) on the same ferry.

Mountain bikes can be hired from **Tammie Hedderwick** (☎ 230382) for £10 per day in Arinagour.

ISLE OF TIREE

☎ 01879 / pop 765

Low-lying Tiree (pronounced tye-*ree*; from the Gaelic *tiriodh*, meaning 'land of corn') is a fertile sward of lush, green machair liberally sprinkled with yellow buttercups, much of it so flat that, from a distance, the houses seem to rise straight out of the sea. It is one of the sunniest places in Scotland, but also one of the windiest – cyclists soon find that although the island is flat, heading west usually feels like going uphill. One major benefit – the constant breeze keeps Tiree almost midge-free.

The surf-lashed coastline is scalloped with broad, sweeping beaches of white sand, hugely popular with windsurfers and kite-surfers. Most visitors, however, come for the bird-watching, beachcombing and lonely coastal walks.

Orientation & Information

The ferry arrives at Gott Bay, on the eastern side of the island. The airport is right in the centre. There's a bank (without ATM), post office and Co-op supermarket in Scarinish, the main village, a half-mile south of the ferry pier.

Tourist information is available from the new **visitors centre** (☎ 220074; An Talla, Crossapol; ✓ 10.30am-4.30pm Mon-Fri), and An Iodhlann (see Sights, following) has free Internet access.

Sights

In the 19th century Tiree's population was 4500, most of whom emigrated to Canada, the USA, Australia and New Zealand. **An Iodhlann** (☎ 220793; www.tireearchive.com; Scarinish; admission free; ✓ 10.30am-3.30pm Mon-Fri; 🖳) is a historical and genealogical library and archive, where many of the estimated 38,000 descendants of Tiree emigrants come to trace their ancestry. The centre stages a **summer exhibition** (adult/child £3/free; ✓ 2-5pm Jul-Sep) on island life and history.

At **Sandaig**, in the far west of the island, is the **Island Life Museum** (admission free; ✓ 2-4pm Mon-Fri Jun-Sep), a row of quaint thatched cottages each restored as a 19th-century crofter's home.

The picturesque harbour and hamlet of **Hynish**, near the southern tip of the island, was built in the 19th century to house workers and supplies for the construction of the Skerryvore Lighthouse, which stands 10 miles offshore. **Skerryvore Lighthouse Museum** (admission free; ✓ dawn-dusk) occupies the signal tower above the harbour, which was once used to communicate by semaphore with the lighthouse site.

For the best view on the island, walk up nearby **Ben Hynish** (141m), which is capped by a conspicuous radar station known locally as the Golf Ball.

Activities

Reliable wind and big waves have made Tiree one of Scotland's top windsurfing venues – the annual Tiree Wave Classic competition is held here in October. **Wild Diamond Windsurfing** (☎ 220399; www.tireewind surfing.com), based at Loch Bhasapoll in the northwest of the island, runs courses and rents equipment. A day's equipment hire costs from £20, and a beginners' course (five hours over two days) costs £60 including gear.

You can also try **sand-yachting** (☎ 220317; per hr £15) on Gott Bay beach at low tide.

Sleeping & Eating

Glebe House (☎ 220758; www.glebehousetiree.co.uk; Gott Bay; r per person £31-45; P ✕) This former manse, which stands foursquare above the foreshore of Gott Bay, has been beautifully renovated with a successful blend of period and modern styles.

Kirkapol (☎ 220729; www.kirkapoltiree.co.uk; Gott Bay; s/d £29/54; P ✕) The Kirkapol has six homely rooms and a big lounge room with leather-studded sofa, set in a converted 19th-century church overlooking the island's biggest beach.

Scarinish Hotel (☎ 220308; www.tireescarinish hotel.com; Scarinish; r per person £30-50; mains £9-15; ☾ lunch & dinner; P ✕) Enthusiastic new owners have given the bedrooms at the Scarinish Hotel a crisp and modern makeover, while retaining the cosy atmosphere of the old Lean-To Bar and reviving the restaurant menu with fresh local lamb and seafood.

Millhouse Hostel (☎ 220435; www.tireemillhouse.co .uk; Cornaigmore; dm £12, tw £30) Housed in a converted barn next to an old water mill, this small but comfortable hostel is 5 miles from the ferry pier.

There are no official camping grounds on Tiree but it's possible to camp for free almost anywhere on the island, provided that you ask permission from the farmer or crofter who owns the land.

Getting There & Around

British Airways flies from Glasgow to **Tiree airport** (☎ 220309) daily from Monday to Saturday. Ferry connections and fares are the same as for Coll (see Getting There & Around, opposite).

You can rent bicycles from **Neil MacLean** (☎ 220428; Kenovay) and also from Millhouse Hostel; **Tiree Motor Company** (☎ 220469; Crossapol) will rent you a car, and for a taxi, call **Island Cabs** (☎ 220344).

NORTH ARGYLL

LOCH AWE

Loch Awe is one of Scotland's most beautiful lochs, with rolling forested hills around its southern end and spectacular mountains in the north. It lies between Oban and Inveraray and is the longest loch in Scotland – about 24 miles long – but is less than a mile wide for most of its length.

At its northern end, the loch widens out and there are several islands you can visit: **Inishail** has a ruined church and **Fraoch Eilean** has a broken-down castle. You can hire boats from **Loch Awe Boats** (☎ 01866-833256; The Boat House, Ardbrecknish); a rowing boat costs £5/17 per hour/day, a motor boat with cabin £15/45. Ardbrecknish is on the south shore of the loch, 8 miles southwest of Dalmally.

Also at the northern end of Loch Awe are the scenic ruins of **Kilchurn Castle** (admission free; ☾ closed winter), built in 1440, which enjoys one of Scotland's finest settings. It's only accessible by boat from Lochawe village – **Loch Awe Steam Packet Company** (☎ 01838-200440; adult/child £6/2.50; ☾ 10am-5pm Apr-Nov) operates hourly trips by steam launch to the castle, allowing 40 minutes at the castle.

At its northern end, Loch Awe escapes to the sea through the narrow **Pass of Brander**, where Robert the Bruce defeated the Mac-Dougalls in battle in 1309. In the pass, by the A85, you can visit **Cruachan power station** (☎ 01866-822618; Lochawe; adult/child £3.50/1.50; ☾ 9.30am-5pm Easter-Jul & Sep-early Nov, 9.30am-6pm Aug). Electric buses take you more than half a mile inside Ben Cruachan, allowing you to see the pump-storage hydroelectric scheme in action.

Getting There & Away

Scottish Citylink buses from Glasgow to Oban go via Dalmally, Lochawe village and Cruachan power station. Trains from Glasgow to Oban stop at Dalmally and Lochawe village.

LOCH ETIVE

Loch Etive is one of Scotland's most beautiful sea lochs, extending for 17 miles from Connel to Kinlochetive and flanked by some impressive mountains. The area is easily explored on the way north from Oban to Glencoe.

Connel

☎ 01631 / pop 500

At Connel Bridge, 5 miles north of Oban, Loch Etive is joined to the sea by a narrow channel partly blocked by an underwater rock ledge. When the tide falls – as it does twice a day – millions of tons of water pour out of the loch and over the ledge, creating spectacular white-water rapids known as the **Falls of Lora**.

Dunstaffnage Castle (☎ 562465; Dunstaffnage; adult/child £2.50/1; �%9.30am-6.30pm Apr-Sep, 9.30am-4.30pm Sat-Wed Oct-Mar) is 2 miles west of Connel and easily reached by bus from Oban. It was built around 1260 on a rock plinth, and captured by Robert the Bruce during the Wars of Independence in 1309. The nearby ruins of the 13th-century **chapel** are slightly creepy – perhaps the skulls carved in the stonework are watching you?

Buses between Oban and Fort William or Glasgow, and trains between Oban and Glasgow, all stop in Connel.

Taynuilt

☎ 01866 / pop 700

One of the region's most unusual historical sights is **Bonawe Iron Furnace** (☎ 822432; adult/child £3/1.20; �%9.30am-6.30pm Easter-Sep), near Taynuilt. Dating from 1753, it was built by a Cumbrian iron-smelting company from the English Lake District because of the abundance of birchwood in the area. The wood was made into charcoal, which was needed for smelting the iron. To produce Bonawe's annual output of 700 tons of pig iron took 10,000 acres of woodland. A fascinating self-guided tour leads you around the various parts of the site.

Loch Etive Cruises (☎ 822430), at the end of the road that passes the entrance to Bonawe, runs cruises to the head of Loch Etive and back between one and three times daily from April to October. There are 1½-hour cruises (adult/child £6/4, departs noon) and three-hour cruises (£11/6, departs 2pm); you may spot eagles, otters, seals and deer, and at the head of the loch you can see the famous Etive slabs – usually dotted with rock climbers.

Aficionados of smoked salmon should pay a visit to **Inverawe Smokehouse & Fishery** (☎ 822274; www.smokedsalmon.co.uk; Inverawe; admission free; �%8am-5.30pm Mar-Oct), 2 miles east of Taynuilt, where local salmon (and trout, herring and venison) is smoked over split oak logs. There's also an angling school and trout fishery where you can learn to fly-fish, and a tearoom where you can sample the smokery's mouthwatering produce.

Taynuilt is 6 miles east of Connel. Scottish Citylink buses and trains to and from Oban stop here.

APPIN & AROUND

☎ 01631

The **Scottish Sea Life Sanctuary** (☎ 720386; Barcaldine; adult/child £9.50/6.95; �%9am-5pm Mar-Oct), 8 miles north of Oban on the shores of Loch Creran, provides a haven for orphaned seal pups. As well as the seal pools there are tanks with herring, rays and flatfish; touch pools for children; an otter sanctuary and displays on Scotland's marine environment.

Glen Creran, at the head of Loch Creran, is a scenic glen with several good walks. North of Loch Creran, at Portnacroish, there's a wonderful view of **Castle Stalker** perched on a tiny offshore island – Monty Python buffs will recognise it as the castle that appears in the final scenes of the film *Monty Python and the Holy Grail*. **Port Appin**, a couple of miles off the main road, is a pleasant spot with a passenger ferry to the island of Lismore.

The delightfully quaint **Pierhouse Hotel** (☎ 730302; pierhouse@btInternet.com; Port Appin; s £53-70, d £75-110, mains £15-20; �%lunch & dinner; P ☒) sits on the waterfront above the ferry pier for Lismore. Two of the 10 rooms have four-poster beds, and there's an atmospheric restaurant serving excellent seafood and game.

You can hire bikes from **Port Appin Bike** (☎ 730391) at the entrance to the village for £7/10 per half-/full day.

Scottish Citylink buses between Oban and Fort William stop at the marine sanctuary and Appin village.

LISMORE

☎ 01631 / pop 170

The first thing you notice about the island of Lismore is how green it is – there's no heather here. Much of the island consists of limestone, which makes for very fertile soil; the Gaelic name Lios Mor means 'Great Garden'.

Lismore is long and narrow – 10 miles long and just over a mile wide – with a road running almost its full length. There are a few scattered communities and two ferry terminals, one halfway up the east coast at

Achnacroish, the other at **Point**, the island's northernmost tip. **Clachan**, a scattering of houses midway between Achnacroish and Point, is the nearest the island has to a village. **Lismore Stores** (☎ 760272; ⌚ 9am-5.30pm Mon, Tue, Thu & Fri, 9am-1pm Wed & Sat; 🖳), between Achnacroish and Clachan, is a grocery store and post office, and has Internet access.

Lismore is a place to relax and enjoy the scenery. However, if you're feeling energetic, the best walk on the island runs from Kilcheran, at the southern end of the road, up to the top of **Barr Mor** (127m), then southwest along the ridge to the southern tip of the island, returning to Kilcheran by a 4WD track. It's about 6 miles for the round trip. Allow three to four hours to fully appreciate the fantastic views of the surrounding mountains.

The ruins of 13th-century **Castle Coeffin** have a lovely setting on the west coast, half a mile from Clachan. **Tirefour Broch**, a defensive tower with double walls reaching 3m in height, is directly opposite on the east coast.

There is very little short-stay accommodation on Lismore. However, there are several self-catering options advertised on www.isleoflismore.com.

Getting There & Around

A CalMac car ferry runs from Oban to Achnacroish, with two to five sailings Monday to Saturday (passenger/car £2.75/£24, 50 minutes).

Argyll & Bute Council (☎ 01546-604695) operates the passenger-only ferry from Port Appin to Point (£1.20, 10 minutes, hourly). Bicycles are carried free.

A Royal Mail postbus runs the length of the island daily Monday to Saturday, calling at Point at 12.40pm.

Central & Western Highlands

Seen from the summit of Cairngorm at sunset, the serried ridges of the central and western Highlands recede towards the horizon. Except for a small area of coastal plain around Inverness, this region is entirely mountainous, stretching from the high, subarctic plateau of the Cairngorms and the great, humpbacked hills of the Monadhliath to the more rugged, rocky peaks of Glen Coe, the Mamores and Ardgour. And, hunching its great, cliff-bound shoulders above the mass of lesser hills, is Ben Nevis (1344m), the highest summit in the British Isles.

Not surprisingly, this part of the country is an adventure playground for outdoor sports enthusiasts. Aviemore, Glen Coe and Fort William draw hordes of hill walkers and rock climbers in summer, and skiers, snowboarders and ice climbers in winter. There are purpose-built mountain-biking trails at Nevis Range and Laggan (near Newtonmore), the world's biggest indoor ice-climbing wall at Kinlochleven, and three of Scotland's five ski resorts at Nevis Range, Cairngorm and Glen Coe.

Inverness, the Highland capital, provides a spot of urban rest and relaxation before you strike south through the forests and lochs of the Great Glen, stopping perhaps to check Loch Ness for monsterish disturbances. The glens to the north of Loch Ness – Strathfarrar, Strathglass and Glen Affric – are among the most beautiful in the country, and offer a wealth of scenic low-level hiking.

From Fort William, the base camp for climbing Ben Nevis, the aptly named Road to the Isles skirts one of Europe's last great wilderness areas before reaching the gorgeous beaches of Arisaig and Morar, and the busy fishing and ferry port of Mallaig.

HIGHLIGHTS

- Wandering through the ancient Caledonian forest at **Rothiemurchus** (p326)
- Thundering across Glenfinnan Viaduct on the **Jacobite steam train** (p337)
- Watching the sun set behind the Small Isles from one of the silver-sand beaches of **Arisaig** (p343)
- Taking in the stunning views from the summit of the **Sgurr of Eigg** (p347)
- Hiking among the hills, lochs and forests of beautiful **Glen Affric** (p320)

★ Glen Affric

Rothiemurchus ★

Arisaig

★ Glenfinnan Viaduct

Sgurr of Eigg
(393m)

- POPULATION: 140,000
- AREA: 9660 SQ KM

CENTRAL & WESTERN HIGHLANDS

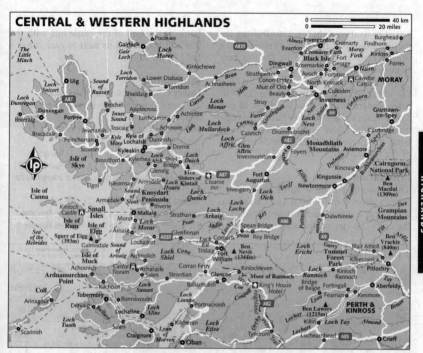

Getting Around

Scottish Citylink (☎ 0870 550 5050) runs buses from Perth to Inverness and from Glasgow to Fort William, and links Inverness to Fort William along the Great Glen. **Rapsons/Highland Country** (☎ 01463-710555; www.rapsons.com) is the main regional bus company, with offices in Aviemore, Inverness and Fort William. It has various Roverbus tickets (adult/child £6/4) for one day's unlimited travel on Rapsons/Highland Country buses in various regions, including Inverness–Nairn, the Black Isle, Aviemore and Fort William–Glencoe. Two rail lines serve the region: Perth–Aviemore–Inverness line in the east, and Glasgow–Fort William–Mallaig line in the west.

INVERNESS & THE GREAT GLEN

Inverness is the Highlands capital and one of the fastest growing towns in Britain. It's a transport hub and jump-off point for the central, western and northern Highlands, the Moray Firth coast and the Great Glen.

The Great Glen is a geological fault running in an arrow-straight line across Scotland from Fort William to Inverness. The glaciers of the last Ice Age eroded a deep trough along the fault line that is now largely filled by a series of lochs – Linnhe, Lochy, Oich and Ness. The glen has always been an important communication route – General George Wade built a military road along the southern side of Loch Ness in the early 18th century, and in 1822 the various lochs were joined together by the Caledonian Canal to create a cross-country waterway. The modern A82 road along the glen was completed in 1933 – a date that coincides neatly with the first modern sightings of the Loch Ness Monster (see the boxed text, p323).

INVERNESS

☎ 01463 / pop 44,500

Inverness, the primary city and shopping centre of the Highlands, has a great location astride the River Ness at the northern end of the Great Glen. In summer it overflows with visitors intent on monster-hunting at nearby Loch Ness, but it's worth a visit in its own right for a stroll along the picturesque River Ness and a cruise on the Moray Firth in search of its famous bottlenose dolphins.

The city was probably founded by King David in the 12th century, but thanks to its often violent history few buildings of real age or historical significance have survived – much of the older part of the city dates from the period following the completion of the Caledonian Canal in 1822.

Orientation

The broad and shallow River Ness, which flows a short 6 miles from Loch Ness into the Moray Firth, runs through the heart of the city. The city centre lies on the eastern

bank, at the foot of the castle hill, with the bus and train stations next to each other a little to the north.

Information

Leakey's (☎ 239947; Greyfriars Hall, Church St; 10am-5.30pm Mon-Sat) An excellent secondhand bookshop with a good café.

Main post office (9am-5.30pm Mon-Fri, to 6pm Sat) On Queensgate.

New City Laundrette (☎ 242507; 17 Young St; 8am-8pm Mon-Fri, to 6pm Sat, 10am-4pm Sun;) Charges £3 per load, £1.40 to dry, and has Internet access for £1 per 20 minutes.

Tourist Information Centre (TIC; ☎ 234353; inverness@host.co.uk; Castle Wynd; 9am-8pm Mon-Sat, 9.30am-5pm Sun;) Beside Inverness Museum,

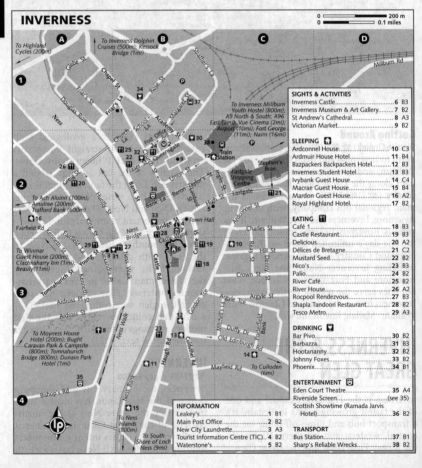

INVERNESS

0 —— 200 m
0 —— 0.1 miles

To Highland Cycles (200m)
To Inverness Dolphin Cruises (500m); Kessock Bridge (1mi)
Millburn Rd
To Inverness Millburn Youth Hostel (800m); A9 North & South; A96 East (2mi); Vue Cinema (2mi); Airport (10mi); Fort George (11mi); Nairn (16mi)
Train Station
Eastgate Shopping Centre
Stephen's Brae
Eastgate
To Ach Aluinn (100m); Amulree (200m); Trafford Bank (600m)
Fairfield Rd
Town Hall
To Winmar Guest House (200m); Clachnaharry Inn (1mi); Beauly (11mi)
Ness Bridge
Charles St
Hill St
Crown St
To Moyness House Hotel (200m); Bught Caravan Park & Campsite (800m); Tomnahurich Bridge (800m); Dunain Park Hotel (1mi)
Argyle Tce
Argyle St
Duffy Dr
Old Edinburgh Rd
Mayfield Rd
To Culloden (6mi)
To Ness Islands (800m)
Bishop's Rd
To South Shore of Loch Ness (9mi)

just off Bridge St. Contains a bureau de change, CalMac ferry office and accommodation booking service; it also sells tickets for tours and cruises. It has Internet access for £2 per 20 minutes.

Waterstone's (☎ 717474; 50-52 High St; ⊗ 9am-5.30pm Mon & Wed-Sat, 9.30am-5.30pm Tue, 10.30am-5pm Sun) The city's biggest bookshop.

Sights

The hill above the city centre is topped by the picturesque Baronial turrets of **Inverness Castle**, a pink-sandstone confection dating from 1847 that replaced a medieval castle blown up by the Jacobites in 1746; it serves today as the Sheriff's Court. Between the castle and the TIC is **Inverness Museum & Art Gallery** (☎ 237114; Castle Wynd; admission free; ⊗ 9am-5pm Mon-Sat), with wildlife dioramas, geological displays, period rooms with historic weapons, Pictish stones and a missable art gallery.

But save the museum for a rainy day – the main attraction in Inverness is a leisurely stroll along the river to the **Ness Islands**. Planted with mature Scots pine, fir, beech and sycamore, and linked to the river banks and each other by elegant Victorian footbridges, the islands make an appealing picnic spot. They're a 20-minute walk south of the castle – head upstream on either side of the river (the start of the Great Glen Way, see p322), and return on the opposite bank. On the way you'll pass the red-sandstone towers of **St Andrew's Cathedral**, dating from 1869, and the modern Eden Court Theatre (p318), which hosts regular art exhibits, both on the west bank.

If the rain does come down, you could opt for a spot of retail therapy in the **Victorian Market**, a shopping mall that dates from the 1890s and has rather more charm than its modern equivalents.

Tours

WALKING TOURS

Guided walking tours of the city (adult/child £4/2) leave from outside the TIC and last 1¼ hours; check with the TIC for details.

Davy the Ghost Tours (☎ 07730 831069; adult/child £7/5) offers 1¼-hour tours led by an '18th-century ghost' in period costume. Expect tales of the city's horrific past, including ghosts, witches, murders and hangings. Tours depart at 7pm from the blackboard outside the TIC.

BUS & TAXI TOURS

City Sightseeing (☎ 224000; adult/child £6/3; ⊗ 10am-4.30pm) From late May to September, 45-minute, hop-on, hop-off bus tours around Inverness, departing from Bridge St near the TIC every 30 minutes.

Discover Loch Ness (☎ 0800 731 5565; www .discoverlochness.com; ⊗ Easter-Oct) Four- to five-hour Loch Ness and Glen Affric tours (adult/child £25/19) go much deeper into history and background than the normal run of tourist excursions; recommended by readers.

John O'Groats Ferries (☎ 01955-611353; www .jogferry.co.uk; ⊗ departs 7.30am) From June to early September, daily tours (lasting 13½ hours; adult/child £46/23) by bus and passenger ferry from Inverness to Orkney.

Tartan Taxis (☎ 233033; www.tartantaxis.org) A wide range of day tours to places as far afield as Skye and the Cairngorms. Fares per car (with up to four people) include £42 for a three-hour trip to Fort George and Culloden, and £60 for a four-hour circular tour around Loch Ness.

CRUISES

Jacobite Cruises (☎ 233999; www.jacobite.co.uk; Glenurquhart Rd) Cruise boats depart at 10am and 2pm from Tomnahurich Bridge for a 3½-hour cruise (adult/child £12/10) on Loch Ness; you can buy tickets at the TIC and catch a free minibus to the boat (departs from TIC 9.30am, 10.30am and 1.15pm). A two-hour cruise to Urquhart Castle (p322), including admission fee and time ashore, costs £12/8 per adult/child (four daily).

Inverness Dolphin Cruises (☎ 717900; Shore St Quay, Shore St; ⊗ 10.30am-6pm Mar-Oct) Offers 1½-hour wildlife cruises (adult/child £12.50/9) to look for dolphins, seals and bird life. Sightings aren't guaranteed, but the commentaries are excellent, and on a fine day it's good just being out on the water. Follow the signs to Shore St Quay from the far end of Chapel St or catch the free shuttle bus that leaves from the TIC 15 minutes before sailings (every 1½ hours).

Sleeping

Inverness has a good range of backpacker accommodation, and there are lots of guesthouses and B&Bs along Old Edinburgh Rd and Ardconnel St on the east side of the river, and on Kenneth St and Fairfield Rd on the west bank; all are within 10 minutes' walk of the city centre.

The city fills up quickly in July and August, so either prebook your accommodation or get an early start looking for somewhere to stay.

BUDGET

Bazpackers Backpackers Hotel (☎ 717663; 4 Culduthel Rd; dm £10-12, tw £26-30; ✗ ⌨) This may be Inverness's smallest hostel (30 beds), but it's the most popular with Lonely Planet readers – a friendly, quiet place with a convivial lounge centred on a wood-burning stove, a small garden and great views, though the dorms can be a bit cramped. No email or online bookings.

Inverness Student Hotel (☎ 236556; www.scot lands-top-hostels.com; 8 Culduthel Rd; dm £12-13; 🖥) More of a lively party place than nearby Bazpackers, set in a rambling old house with comfy beds and views across the River Ness. It's a 10-minute walk from the train station, just past the castle.

Inverness Millburn Youth Hostel (SYHA; ☎ 0870 004 1127; Victoria Dr; dm £12-15; 🅿 ✕) Inverness' modern 166-bed hostel is 10 minutes' walk northeast of the city centre. With its comfy beds and flashy stainless-steel kitchen, some reckon it's the best hostel in the country. Booking is essential, especially at Easter and in July and August.

Bught Caravan Park & Campsite (☎ 236920; www.invernesscaravanpark.com; Bught Lane; tent £6-10, campervan £12; 🕑 Easter–mid-Nov) A mile southwest of the city centre near Tomnahurich Bridge, this is the nearest camping ground, and hugely popular with backpackers.

MIDRANGE

Ivybank Guest House (☎ 232796; www.ivybankguest house.com; 28 Old Edinburgh Rd; s £25-40, d £56-60; 🅿 ✕) Ivybank is a splendid detached villa – a mansion, really – with bags of character. Set in a large, wooded garden, it's been lovingly restored by its owner – a magnificent mahogany staircase leads from the wood-panelled lobby to luxurious bedrooms, one with a four-poster bed, another with a bathroom in a turret.

Trafford Bank (☎ 241414; www.traffordbankguest house.co.uk; 96 Fairfield Rd; s £45-60, d £70-80; 🅿 ✕) Lots of word-of-mouth rave reviews for Trafford Bank, an elegant Victorian villa that was once home to a bishop, just a mitre-toss from the Caledonian Canal and only 10 minutes' walk from the city centre. The luxurious rooms include fresh flowers and fruit, bathrobes and fluffy towels – ask for the Tartan Room, with its wrought-iron king-size bed and Victorian roll-top bath.

Ardconnel House (☎ 240455; www.ardconnel -inverness.co.uk; 21 Ardconnel St; s £30-45, d £50-60; ✕) The six-room Ardconnel is a readers' favourite, a terraced Victorian house with six comfortable en-suite rooms, a dining room

with crisp white table linen, and a breakfast menu that includes Vegemite for homesick Antipodeans.

Ach Aluinn (☎ 230127; www.achaluinn.com; 27 Fairfield Rd; s £25-35, d £45-60; 🅿 ✕) This large, detached Victorian house is bright and homely, and offers all you might want from a guesthouse – private bathroom, TV, reading lights, comfy beds with two pillows each, and an excellent breakfast. Five minutes' walk from city centre.

MacRae Guest House (☎ 243658; joycemacrae@ hotmail.com; 24 Ness Bank; s/d £35/50; 🅿 ✕) Travellers have recommended this pretty, flower-bedecked, Victorian house on the eastern bank of the river. One room is wheelchair accessible, and vegetarian breakfasts are available. Minimum two-night bookings in July and August.

Other recommendations:

Amulree (☎ 224822; amulree@supanet.com; 40 Fairfield Rd; s/d £30/54; ✕) Comfortable, four-bedroom Victorian B&B less than 10 minutes' walk west of the city centre.

Ardmuir House Hotel (☎ 231151; www.ardmuir.com; 16 Ness Bank; s/d from £36/60; ✕) Small, family-run Georgian hotel with a pleasant, riverside setting.

Mardon Guest House (☎ 231005; www.mardon -guest-house; 37 Kenneth St; r per person £20-25) Friendly B&B, with six cosy rooms (all with bathroom), just five minutes west of the city centre.

Moyness House Hotel (☎ 233836; www.moyness .co.uk; 6 Bruce Gardens; r per person £35-38; 🅿 ✕) Elegant Victorian villa with a beautiful garden and peaceful setting, 10 minutes' walk southwest of the city centre.

Winmar Guest House (☎ 239328; www.thewinmar .co.uk; 78 Kenneth St; s/d £20/40; 🅿 ✕) Another readers' recommendation; spacious sandstone villa with comfortable lounge, and kippers, croissants and fry-up on the breakfast menu.

TOP END

Royal Highland Hotel (☎ 231926; www.royalhigh landhotel.co.uk; Academy St; s/d from £90/130; 🅿 ✕) The refurbished Royal Highland has been restored to its former glory as the grandest hotel in Inverness. Located right next to the train station, it boasts an elegant lobby with serpentine columns and sweeping staircase, plush country house–style bedrooms, and friendly and efficient service.

Dunain Park Hotel (☎ 230512; www.dunain parkhotel.co.uk; Dunain Park; d £138-198; 🅿 ✕ 🖭) Staying at this sumptuous country house hotel is like living in an antiques showroom, what with its Victorian four-poster beds, Georgian-style furniture and Italian marble bathrooms, all set in beautiful wooded grounds just five minutes' stroll from the Caledonian Canal and River Ness. The hotel is on the A82 to Fort William a mile southwest of Inverness.

Eating

BUDGET

Délices de Bretagne (☎ 712422; 6 Stephen's Brae; mains £5-7; ☷ 9am-5pm Mon-Sat, 10am-5pm Sun) This café brings a little corner of France to the Highlands, with its Art-Nouveau décor and a menu of tasty *galettes* (savoury pancakes), crepes, Breton cider and excellent coffee.

River Café (☎ 714884; 10 Bank St; lunch mains £6-8 in café, in restaurant £9-17; ☷ 10am-9.30pm Tue-Sat, to 8.30pm Sun & Mon) This is good place to drop in for a pot of tea and a scone after a stroll along the river; there's a restaurant upstairs with more filling fare.

Shapla Tandoori Restaurant (☎ 241919; 2 Castle Rd; mains £8-12; ☷ noon-2.30pm & 6-11pm) Head upstairs and choose a table by the window, where you can enjoy a curry with a splendid view over the river. You can get a three-course lunch for £6 from noon to 2.30pm Monday to Saturday.

Tesco Metro (King St; ☷ 7.30am-10pm Mon-Sat, 9am-6pm Sun) Self-caterers should visit this supermarket.

Other good places for breakfast, coffee or a snack include the café in **Leakey's Bookshop** (☎ 239947; Greyfriars Hall, Church St; ☷ 10am-5.30pm Mon-Sat), the **Castle Restaurant** (☎ 230925; 41-43 Castle St; ☷ 9am-8.30pm) and **Delicious** (☎ 717172; 2 Greig St; ☷ 8am-6pm).

MIDRANGE & TOP END

Mustard Seed (☎ 220220; 16 Fraser St; mains £10-14; ☷ lunch & dinner) This bright and bustling bistro brings a dash of big-city style to Inverness and is one of the most popular restaurants in the city. The menu changes weekly, but focuses on Scottish and French cuisine with a modern twist. Grab a table on the upstairs balcony if you can – it's the best outdoor lunch spot in Inverness, with a great view across the river. It's best to book on weekends and any day in July and August.

Café 1 (☎ 226200; 75 Castle St; mains £9-14; ☷ noon-2pm & 6-9pm Mon-Sat) Café 1 is the Mustard Seed's main rival in the style stakes, with candle-lit tables amid elegant blonde-wood and wrought-iron décor, and an international menu based on quality Scottish produce, from succulent Aberdeen Angus steaks to seared halibut with *wasabi* and pickled ginger.

Nico's (☎ 234308; Glen Mhor Hotel, 9-12 Ness Bank; mains £10-18; ☷ noon-2pm & 5-9.30pm Sun-Thu, noon-2pm & 5-10.30pm Fri & Sat) A snug, wood-panelled bistro where the menu concentrates on Scottish shellfish and steaks, Nico's is a long-standing local favourite. On Sunday from 12.30pm to 3.30pm you can enjoy brunch or a roast for £7.

River House (☎ 222033; 1 Greig St; 2-/3-course dinner £25/29; ☷ noon-2pm & 5.30-9.30pm Tue-Sat, 6-9.30pm Sun) The River House is an elegant restaurant of the polished-wood and crisp white-linen variety, serving the best of British venison, beef, lamb, duck and seafood. An early evening menu is available from 5.30pm to 7pm (mains £8 to £10).

Rocpool Rendezvous (☎ 717274; 1 Ness Walk; mains £10-16; ☷ noon-2.30pm & 6-10pm) Navy-blue leather, white walls and linen, and walnut wood panelling lend a nautical air to this relaxing bistro beside the river, offering a Mediterranean-influenced menu that makes the most of quality Scottish produce, especially seafood (there's a special seafood menu on Friday). The bar, with a tapas menu, is open all day, from noon until late.

Palio (☎ 711950; 26 Queensgate; pizza £5-10, mains £10-17; ☷ noon-late Mon-Sat, noon-5.30pm Sun) If you're looking for the best pizza in the city (10in, stone baked), look no further than this stylish Italian restaurant, which also offers chargrilled steaks and baked langoustines.

Drinking

Phoenix (☎ 233685; 108 Academy St) This is the best of the traditional pubs in the city centre, with a mahogany horseshoe bar, a comfortable, family-friendly lounge, and good food at both lunchtime and in the evening. Real ales on tap include the rich and fruity Orkney Dark Island.

Hootananny (☎ 233651; 67 Church St) Hootananny is the city's best live-music venue, with traditional Celtic and/or rock music sessions nightly, including big-name bands from all over Scotland (and, indeed, the world). The bar is well stocked with a range of beers from the local Black Isle Brewery.

Barbazza (☎ 243342; 5-9 Young St) Barbazza continues to pull in a young crowd – it probably has the highest pierced belly-button

CENTRAL & WESTERN HIGHLANDS

count in Inverness – with regular DJs, drinks promos from 8pm to 11pm Wednesday and Sunday, and rock karaoke on Thursday from 9pm. It also offers a menu of booze-absorbing grub, such as baked potatoes, burgers and nachos.

Bar Pivo (☎ 713307; 38-40 Academy St) This Czech-themed pub – half of the industrial-chic bar area is made up to look like a Prague metro station – offers no fewer than three Czech beers on draught, plus another six in bottles, as well as Scottish-made Belhaven real ales. DJs play from 9pm Thursday to Sunday, and there's a Sunday brunch with live jazz (11am to 2pm).

Johnny Foxes (☎ 236577; 26 Bank St) Stuck beneath the ugliest building on the riverfront, Johnny Foxes is a big and boisterous Irish bar, with a wide range of food served all day and live music nightly.

Clachnaharry Inn (☎ 239806; 17-19 High St; Clachnaharry) Just over a mile northwest of the city centre, on the bank of the Caledonian Canal just off the A862, this is a delightful old coaching inn serving good food and excellent real ales.

Entertainment

Eden Court Theatre (☎ 234234; www.eden-court .co.uk; Bishop's Rd; ☯ box office 10am-8.30pm Mon-Sat) Inverness' main cultural venue has a busy programme of drama, dance and music, an excellent cinema (see Riverside Screen, below), and a good bar and restaurant. Pick up a programme from the foyer or check its website. (The theatre will be closed until early 2007 for a major refurbishment.)

Scottish Showtime (☎ 830930; www.nessie.org .uk; Ramada Jarvis Hotel, Church St; tickets £16; ☯ 8.30pm Mon-Thu Jun & Jul, 8.30pm Mon-Fri Aug-early Sep) From June to early September the Inverness Suite at the Ramada Jarvis Hotel stages 'Scottish Showtime', an evening of traditional Scottish music, song and dance aimed squarely at tourists. Tickets available from the TIC.

Riverside Screen (☎ 221718; Bishop's Rd; adult/child £4.80/3) Part of the Eden Court Theatre complex, Inverness' art-house cinema screens both recent films and old classics. (Closed until early 2007.)

Vue Cinema (☎ 08712-240240; Inverness Retail & Business Park, Eastfield Way; adult/child £6.10/4.40) This is a seven-screen multiplex cinema way out on the eastern edge of the city, just south of the A96 to Nairn.

Getting There & Away

AIR

Ten miles east of the city on the A96 to Aberdeen, **Inverness airport** (☎ 01667-464000; www.hial.co.uk) is at Dalcross. There are scheduled flights to London, Belfast, Glasgow, Edinburgh, Stornoway, Benbecula, Orkney, Shetland and several other British airports. For more information, see p446.

BOAT

A new high-speed ferry service, the **Loch Ness Express** (☎ 0800 328 6426; www.lochnessexpress .com), runs from Dochgarroch (2 miles south of Inverness, free shuttle bus from city centre) along the length of Loch Ness to Fort Augustus, twice daily from May to October, once daily in November and December (adult/child £13/8 one way, one hour 20 minutes).

BUS

National Express (☎ 0870 580 8080; www.national express.com) operates a direct overnight bus from London to Inverness (£39, 13 hours, one daily), with more frequent services requiring a change at Glasgow.

Scottish Citylink (☎ 0870 550 5050; www.citylink .co.uk) has direct connections to Glasgow (£17, four hours, four daily), Edinburgh (£17, four hours, five daily), Fort William (£10, two hours, five daily), Ullapool (£7.70, 1½ hours, two daily except Sunday), Portree on the Isle of Skye (£12, 3½ hours, two daily) and Thurso (£13, 3½ hours, four daily).

Megabus (☎ 0900 160 0900; www.megabus.com) offers fares from as little as £3 for buses from Inverness to Glasgow and Edinburgh, £1 to Perth and £16 to London.

Buses to Aberdeen (£12, 3¾ hours, hourly) are operated by Stagecoach Bluebird, while Rapsons/Highland Country bus 15 serves Aviemore (£5, 1¾ hours, three daily Monday to Friday) via Grantown-on-Spey.

TRAIN

There is one direct train daily from London to Inverness (£110, eight hours); others (nine hours, five daily) require a change at Edinburgh. There are several direct trains a day from Glasgow (£34, 3½ hours), Edinburgh (£34, 3¼ hours) and Aberdeen (£21, 2¼ hours), and three daily Monday to Saturday (one or two on Sunday) to Thurso and Wick (£14, four hours).

The line from Inverness to Kyle of Lochalsh (£16, 2½ hours, four daily Monday to Saturday, two Sunday) offers one of Britain's great scenic train journeys.

Getting Around
TO/FROM THE AIRPORT
Rapsons/Highland Country (☎ 710555; www.rapsons.com) bus 11 runs from the airport to Queensgate in the city centre (£2.80, 20 minutes, at least hourly). A taxi costs around £12.

BICYCLE
There are some great cycling opportunities out of Inverness. Rental outlets include **Highland Cycles** (☎ 234789; 16a Telford St; ⊗ 8.30am-5.30pm Mon-Sat), which charges £12 a day.

BUS
Local services and buses to places around Inverness, including Nairn, Forres, the Culloden battlefield, Beauly, Dingwall and Lairg, are available with **Rapsons/Highland Country** (☎ 710555; www.rapsons.com). A Tourist Trail Roverbus ticket costs £6 and gives unlimited travel for a day on buses serving Culloden, Cawdor Castle, Fort George and Nairn.

CAR
The TIC has a handy Car Hire leaflet. The big boys charge from around £35 per day, or you could try **Sharp's Reliable Wrecks** (☎ 236694; www.sharpsreliablewrecks.co.uk; Inverness train station) for cheaper cars from £20 per day.

TAXI
Call **Central Taxis** (☎ 222222).

AROUND INVERNESS
Culloden
The Battle of Culloden in 1746, the last pitched battle ever fought on British soil, saw the defeat of Bonnie Prince Charlie and the end of the Jacobite dream; 1200 Highlanders were slaughtered by government forces in a 68-minute rout. The duke of Cumberland, son of the reigning king George II and leader of the Hanoverian army, won the label Butcher Cumberland for his brutal treatment of the defeated Scottish forces. The battle sounded the death knell of the old clan system, and the

horrors of the Clearances soon followed. The sombre moor where the conflict took place has scarcely changed in the ensuing 260 years.

The **Culloden visitor centre** (☎ 01463-790607; adult/child £5/4; ⊗ 9am-6pm Jun-Aug, 9am-5.30pm Easter-May, Sep & Oct, 11am-4pm Nov, Dec, Feb & Mar) screens a 15-minute audiovisual presentation on the battle, but it's hardly worth the money – the guided tours of the battlefield (adult/child £3/2) are much better value.

Culloden is 6 miles east of Inverness. See left for details of bus services.

Fort George
The headland guarding the Moray Firth narrows opposite Fortrose is occupied by the magnificent and virtually unaltered 18th-century artillery fortification of **Fort George** (☎ 01667-462777; adult/child £6/2.40; ⊗ 9.30am- 6.30pm Easter-Sep, to 4.30pm Oct-Mar). One of the finest examples of its kind in Europe, it was completed in 1769 as a base for George II's army of occupation in the Highlands – the cost, in today's money, was around £1 billion. The mile-plus walk around the ramparts offers fine views out to sea and back to the Great Glen. Given its size, you'll need at least two hours to do the place justice. The fort is off the A96 about 11 miles northeast of Inverness.

Nairn
☎ 01667 / pop 11,000
Nairn is a popular golfing and seaside resort with a good sandy beach. The town has a **TIC** (☎ 452763; 62 King St; ⊗ Apr-Oct), banks with ATMs and a post office.

The most attractive part of Nairn is the old fishing village of **Fishertown**, down by the harbour. **Nairn Museum** (☎ 458531; Viewfield House; adult/child £2/50p; ⊗ 10am-4.30pm Mon-Sat Easter-Oct), a few minutes' walk from the TIC, has displays on the history of Fishertown, as well as on local archaeology, geology and natural history.

You can spend many pleasant hours wandering along the **East Beach**, which is one of the finest in Scotland.

The big event in the town's calendar is the **Nairn Highland Games** (www.nairnhighlandgames.co.uk), held in mid-August. Also in August is the week-long **Nairn International Jazz Festival**. Contact the TIC for details of both events.

SLEEPING & EATING

Ceol Mara B&B (☎ 452495; www.ceolmara.co.uk; The Links; r per person £20-26; **P**) This B&B has a great location looking over the Links and the town beach to the Moray Firth. The three bedrooms are decorated in flouncy, flowery style – the rose-patterned double has a great view over the beach.

Sunny Brae Hotel (☎ 452309; www.sunnybrae hotel.com; Marine Rd; s £79-99, d £94-124; **P** **X**) Beautifully decked out with fresh flowers and pot plants, the nine-room Sunny Brae enjoys an enviable location with great views across the Moray Firth. The hotel restaurant specialises in Scottish produce cooked with Continental flair, such as warm salad of scallops with lemon and tarragon dressing and breast of pheasant with red cabbage and a mustard, honey and whisky sauce.

Havelock House Hotel (☎ 455500; www.havelock househotel.co.uk; Crescent Rd; r per person from £30; **P** **X**) Originally built as a summer residence for the emir of Jaipur after he was exiled from India in 1857, this hotel is right in the centre of town and has five recently refurbished rooms, all with en suite. There's also a neat little restaurant specialising in Scottish seafood and game.

GETTING THERE & AWAY

Stagecoach Bluebird buses run hourly (less frequently on Sunday) from Inverness to Aberdeen via Nairn. The town also lies on the Inverness to Aberdeen railway line; there are five to seven trains a day from Inverness (£4, 20 minutes).

Cawdor

The 14th-century home of the Thanes of Cawdor, **Cawdor Castle** (☎ 01667-404615; adult/child £6.80/4; ☷ 10am-5.30pm May–mid-Oct) is reputedly the castle of Shakespeare's *Macbeth* and was the scene of Duncan's murder in the play – a bit of poetic licence from the bard, since the central tower dates from the 14th century (the wings were 17th-century additions) and Macbeth died in 1057. The castle is 5 miles southwest of Nairn.

Cawdor Tavern (☎ 01667-404777; bar meals £5-9) in the nearby village is worth a visit, though it can be difficult deciding what to drink as it stocks over 100 varieties of whisky. There's also good pub food, with tempting daily specials.

Brodie Castle

Set in 70 hectares of parkland, **Brodie Castle** (☎ 01309-641371; adult/child £8/5; ☷ noon-4pm Easter-Apr, Jul & Aug, noon-4pm Sun-Thu May, Jun & Sep) has several highlights, including a library with more than 6000 peeling, dusty volumes. There are wonderful clocks, a huge Victorian kitchen and a 17th-century dining room with wildly extravagant moulded plaster ceilings depicting mythological scenes. The Brodies have been living here since 1160, but the present structure dates mostly from 1567, with many additions over the years.

The castle is 8 miles east of Nairn. Stagecoach Bluebird buses run from Inverness to Brodie (£4.90, 45 minutes, hourly) via Culloden.

WEST OF INVERNESS
Beauly
☎ 01463 / pop 1160

In 1584 Mary, Queen of Scots is said to have given this village its name when she exclaimed, in French: *'Quel beau lieu!'* (What a beautiful place!). Founded in 1230 the red-sandstone **Beauly Priory** (☎ 01667-460232; admission free; ☷ 9.30am-6.30pm mid-Jun–Sep) is now an impressive, mostly roofless ruin. A small information kiosk next door has information on the history of the priory.

The attractive and centrally located **Priory Hotel** (☎ 782309; www.priory-hotel.com; The Sq; s/d £48/90; **P** **X**) has bright, modern rooms and an excellent restaurant. For B&B, try **Ellangowan** (☎ 782273; Croyard Rd; r per person £16-25; **P**), a few minutes' walk from the priory.

Stagecoach Inverness runs buses from Inverness to Beauly (£3.50, hourly Monday to Saturday, four on Sunday), and the town lies on the Inverness–Thurso railway line.

Strathglass & Glen Affric
☎ 01456

The broad valley of **Strathglass** extends about 18 miles inland from Beauly, followed by the A831 road to **Cannich**, the only village in the area, where there's a grocery store and a post office.

About 5 miles west of Beauly, at the Aigas Dam on the River Beauly, there's a **fish lift** (☷ 10am-3pm Mon-Fri mid-Jun–early Oct) where you can watch migrating salmon take advantage of a dam bypass.

Several long and narrow valleys lead west from Strathglass into an almost roadless wilderness. **Glen Affric**, one of the most beautiful glens in Scotland, extends deep into the hills beyond Cannich. The upper reaches of the glen, now designated as Glen Affric National Nature Reserve, is a scenic wonderland of shimmering lochs, rugged mountains and native Scots pine, home to pine marten, wildcat, otter, red squirrel and golden eagle.

From the parking area and picnic site at the eastern end of **Loch Affric** there are several short walks along the river and the loch shore. The circuit of Loch Affric (10 miles, allow five hours) follows good paths right around the loch and takes you deep into the heart of some very wild scenery. Contact Inverness TIC (p314) for more information.

It's possible to walk all the way from Cannich to Glen Shiel (p372) on the west coast (35 miles) in two days, spending the night at the remote Glen Affric Youth Hostel (below).

SLEEPING & EATING
Cougie Lodge (☎ 415459; www.cougie.com; Cougie; dm £10, tent sites per person £5) This tiny, six-bed timber lodge is hidden away in the forest to the south of Loch Beinn a'Mheadhoin, 9 miles southwest of Cannich (go through Tomich and continue on a forest road beyond Plodda Falls car park). It makes a good overnight stop if you're walking from Cannich to Glen Affric Youth Hostel. You can also camp here.

Glen Affric Youth Hostel (SYHA; ☎ 0870 155 3255; Allt Beithe, Glen Affric; dm £13; ☯ Apr-Oct) This remote and rustic hostel is set amid magnificent scenery at the halfway point of the cross-country walk from Cannich to Ratagan Youth Hostel on the west coast. Facilities are basic and you'll need to take all supplies with you. Book in advance.

Kerrow House (☎ 415243; www.kerrow-house.co.uk; Cannich; s £27-32, d £44-60; **P** ✗) This wonderful Georgian hunting lodge has bags of old-fashioned character – it was once the home of Highland author Neil M Gunn (see the boxed text, p44), and has spacious grounds with 3.5 miles of private trout fishing. It's a mile south of Cannich on the minor road along the east side of the River Glass.

Tomich Hotel (☎ 415399; www.tomichhotel.co.uk; Tomich; s £58-64, d £85-97; **P** ✗ ☺) About 3 miles southwest of Cannich on the southern side of the river, this Victorian hunting lodge has a blazing log fire, a Victorian restaurant,

eight comfortable en-suite rooms and – a bit of a surprise out here in the wilds – a small, heated indoor swimming pool.

Other recommendations:
Cannich Youth Hostel (SYHA) Closed for renovation at time of research.
Glen Affric Backpackers (☎ 415263; Charrein Lodge, Cannich; dm £10)
Cannich Caravan Park (☎ 415364; www.highlandcamping.co.uk; Cannich; tent sites per person £4 plus per car £1)

GETTING THERE & AWAY
Rapsons/Highland Country buses run from Inverness to Cannich (45 minutes, five a day Monday to Friday, two Saturday) via Drumnadrochit.

From July to mid-September, **Ross's Minibuses** (☎ 01463-761250) runs from Beauly train station to Cannich (30 minutes, one or two a day), and from Cannich to Loch Affric car park (30 minutes, two a day). The rest of the year there are only two buses a week from Beauly to Cannich, on Tuesday and Thursday.

Black Isle
The Black Isle – a peninsula rather than an island – is linked to Inverness by the Kessock Bridge.

Rapsons/Highland Country runs buses from Inverness to Fortrose and Rosemarkie (30 minutes, hourly Monday to Saturday); most continue to Cromarty (£5.40, 55 minutes).

FORTROSE & ROSEMARKIE
At **Fortrose Cathedral** you'll find the vaulted crypt of a 13th-century chapter house and sacristy, and a ruinous 14th-century southern aisle and chapel. **Chanonry Point**, 1.5 miles to the east, is a favourite dolphin-spotting vantage point – there are one-hour dolphin-watching cruises (adult/child £10/7) departing from the harbour at Avoch (pronounced 'auch'), 3 miles southwest.

In Rosemarkie, the **Groam House Museum** (☎ 01381-620961; admission free; ☯ 10am-5pm Mon-Sat, 2-4.30pm Sun Easter & May-Sep, 2-4pm Sat & Sun Oct-Apr) has a superb collection of Pictish stones engraved with designs similar to those on Celtic Irish stones.

From the northern end of Rosemarkie's High St a short but pleasant signposted walk leads you through the gorges and waterfalls of the **Fairy Glen**.

CROMARTY

The Cromarty Firth, north of the Black Isle, is often dotted with huge offshore oil rigs lying at anchor; some are mothballed, others waiting for maintenance work at the Nigg Bay shipyards before being towed out to the North Sea.

The pretty village of Cromarty at the northeastern tip of the Black Isle has lots of 18th-century stone houses, two stores, a post office and a bank with ATM.

The 18th-century **Cromarty Courthouse** (☎ 01381-600418; Church St; adult/child £3/2; ☽ 10am-5pm Easter-Oct) details the town's history using contemporary references. It's very engaging – kids will love the talking mannequins.

Next to the Courthouse is **Hugh Miller's Cottage** (NTS; ☎ 01381-600245; Church St; adult/child £5/4; ☽ noon-5pm Easter-Sep, noon-5pm Sun-Wed Oct), the thatched birthplace of Hugh Miller (1802–56), a local stonemason and amateur geologist who later moved to Edinburgh and became a famous journalist and newspaper editor. A brand-new **museum** (☽ noon-5pm Easter-Sep, noon-5pm Sun-Wed Oct) celebrating his life and achievements has opened in the nearby Georgian villa that was built by his father.

From Cromarty harbour, **Ecoventures** (☎ 01381-600323; www.ecoventures.co.uk) runs 2½-hour boat trips (adult/child £20/15) into the Moray Firth to see bottlenose dolphins and other wildlife.

LOCH NESS

Deep, dark and narrow, Loch Ness stretches for 23 miles between Inverness and Fort Augustus. Its bitterly cold waters have been extensively explored in search of Nessie, the elusive Loch Ness monster, and although some visitors get lucky, most see only her cardboard cutout form at the monster exhibitions. The busy A82 road runs along the northwestern shore, while the more tranquil and picturesque B862 follows the southeastern shore. A complete circuit of the loch is about 70 miles – travel anticlockwise for the best views.

Activities

The 73-mile **Great Glen Way** (www.greatglenway.com) long-distance footpath stretches from Inverness to Fort William, where walkers can connect with the West Highland Way (see the boxed text, p278). It is described in

detail in *The Great Glen Way* by Jacquetta Megarry and Sandra Bardwell.

The footpath shares some sections with the 80-mile **Great Glen Mountain Bike Trail**, a waymarked mountain-bike route that follows canal towpaths and gravel tracks through forests, avoiding roads where possible.

The climb to the summit of **Meallfuarvonie** (699m), on the northwestern shore of Loch Ness, makes an excellent short hill walk: the views along the Great Glen from the top are superb. It's a 6-mile round trip, so allow about three hours. Start from the car park at the end of the minor road leading south from Drumnadrochit to Bunloit.

Drumnadrochit

☎ 01456 / pop 800

Seized by monster madness, its gift shops bulging with Nessie cuddly toys, Drumnadrochit is a hotbed of beastie fever, with two monster exhibitions battling it out for the tourist dollar.

The **Loch Ness 2000 Exhibition Centre** (☎ 450573; www.loch-ness-scotland.com; adult/child £6/3.50; ☽ 9am-8pm Jul & Aug, 9am-6pm Jun & Sep, 9am-5.30pm Oct, 9.30am-5pm Easter-May, 10am-3.30pm Nov-Easter; ☒) is the better of the two Nessie-themed attractions, featuring a 40-minute audiovisual presentation, plus exhibits of equipment used in the various underwater monster hunts.

The more homely **Original Loch Ness Monster Centre** (☎ 450342; www.lochness-centre.com; adult/child £4/3.50; ☽ 9am-8pm Jul & Aug, 10am-5.30pm Apr-Jun, Sep & Oct, 10am-4pm Nov-Mar) shows a superficial 30-minute Loch Ness video (with multilingual headsets), but its main function is to sell you tacky Loch Ness Monster souvenirs.

One-hour monster-hunting cruises, complete with sonar and underwater cameras, aboard the **Nessie Hunter** (☎ 450395; www.loch ness-cruises.com), operate from Drumnadrochit. Cruises depart hourly from 9am to 6pm daily from Easter to October, and cost £10/6 for an adult/child.

Urquhart Castle

Commanding a brilliant location with outstanding views (on a clear day), **Urquhart Castle** (HS; ☎ 450551; adult/child £6/2.80; ☽ 9.30am-6.30pm Apr-Sep, 9.30am-4.30pm Mon-Sat, 2-4.30pm Sun Oct-Mar; ☒) is a popular Nessie-sighting hot spot. A controversial new visitor centre (most of which is beneath ground level) includes a video theatre (with a dramatic 'unveiling' of the castle at the end of the film), displays of medieval items discovered in the castle, a huge gift shop and a restaurant.

The castle was repeatedly sacked and rebuilt over the centuries, but was finally blown up in 1692 to prevent the Jacobites from using it. The five-storey tower house at the northern point is the most impressive remaining fragment and offers wonderful views across the water.

Sleeping & Eating

Loch Ness Backpackers Lodge (☎ 450807; www .lochness-backpackers.com; Coiltie Farmhouse, East Lewiston; dm/d £11.50/29) This neat, friendly hostel has six-bed dorms, one double and a large barbecue area. It's about 0.75 miles from Drumnadrochit, along the A82 towards

Fort William; turn left where you see the sign for Loch Ness Inn, just before the bridge.

Loch Ness Youth Hostel (SYHA; ☎ 0870 004 1138; dm £12-13; ☺ Apr-Oct) This hostel is housed in a big lodge overlooking Loch Ness, and many dorms have loch views. It's on the A82 road, 13 miles southwest of Drumnadrochit, and 4 miles northeast of Invermoriston. Buses from Inverness to Fort William stop nearby.

Gillyflowers (☎ 450641; gillyflowers@cali.co.uk; s/d from £35/44; P ✗) This B&B is a renovated 18th-century farmhouse on the southern edge of Drumnadrochit village, with three luxury en-suite rooms, one with a tartan-draped four-poster bed. Walkers and cyclists are welcome.

STRANGE SPECTACLE ON LOCH NESS

Highland folklore is filled with tales of strange creatures living in lochs and rivers, notably the kelpie (water horse) that lures unwary travellers to their doom. The use of the term 'monster', however, is a relatively recent phenomenon whose origins lie in an article published in the *Inverness Courier* of 2 May 1933, entitled 'Strange Spectacle on Loch Ness'.

The article recounted the sighting of a disturbance in the loch by Mrs Aldie Mackay and her husband: 'There the creature disported itself, rolling and plunging for fully a minute, its body resembling that of a whale, and the water cascading and churning like a simmering cauldron.'

The story was taken up by the London press and sparked off a rash of sightings that year, including a notorious on-land encounter with London tourists Mr and Mrs Spicer on 22 July 1933, again reported in the *Inverness Courier*:

It was horrible, an abomination. About fifty yards ahead, we saw an undulating sort of neck, and quickly followed by a large, ponderous body. I estimated the length to be 25 to 30 feet, its colour was dark elephant grey. It crossed the road in a series of jerks, but because of the slope we could not see its limbs. Although I accelerated quickly towards it, it had disappeared into the loch by the time I reached the spot. There was no sign of it in the water. I am a temperate man, but I am willing to take any oath that we saw this Loch Ness beast. I am certain that this creature was of a prehistoric species.

The London newspapers couldn't resist. In December 1933 the *Daily Mail* sent Marmaduke Wetherall, a film director and big-game hunter, to Loch Ness to track down the beast. Within days he found 'reptilian' footprints in the shoreline mud (soon revealed to have been made with a stuffed hippopotamus foot, possibly an umbrella stand). Then in April 1934 came the famous 'long-necked monster' photograph taken by the seemingly reputable Harley St surgeon Colonel Kenneth Wilson. The press went mad and the rest, as they say, is history.

In 1994, however, Christian Spurling – Wetherall's 90-year-old stepson – revealed that the most famous photo of Nessie ever taken was in fact a hoax, perpetrated by his stepfather with Wilson's help. Today, of course, there are those who claim that Spurling's confession is itself a hoax. And, ironically, the researcher who exposed the surgeon's photo as a fake still believes wholeheartedly in the monster's existence.

Hoax or not, there's no denying that the bizarre mini-industry that has grown up around Loch Ness and its mysterious monster since that eventful summer 70 years ago is the strangest spectacle of all.

Borlum Farm Caravan & Camping Park (☎ 450 220; tent/campervan sites per person £4.40; ☺ Mar-Oct) This campsite is 800m southeast of Drumnadrochit.

Near Drumnadrochit's village green are the pleasant **Glen Café Bar** (☎ 450282) and the more expensive, nonsmoking **Fiddler's Café Bar** (☎ 450678; mains £9-16), which serves traditional Highland fare, such as venison casserole, and a wide range of bottled Scottish beers.

Getting There & Away

Scottish Citylink buses from Inverness to Fort William run along the Great Glen; those headed for Skye turn off at Invermoriston. There are bus stops at Drumnadrochit (£5, 30 minutes), Urquhart Castle car park (£5, 35 minutes) and Loch Ness Youth Hostel (£7, 45 minutes, seven or eight daily).

FORT AUGUSTUS

☎ 01320 / pop 510

Fort Augustus, at the junction of four old military roads, was originally a government garrison and the headquarters of General George Wade's road-building operations in the early 18th century. Today it's a neat and picturesque little place, often overrun by tourists in summer.

There's a **TIC** (☎ 366367; ☺ 9am-6pm Mon-Sat, 10am-4pm Sun Easter-Oct) in the central car park, and an ATM and bureau de change (in the post office) beside the canal. **Neuk Café** (☎ 366208; ☐), a few doors along from the post office, has Internet access for £1.50 per 15 minutes.

Sights & Activities

At Fort Augustus, boats using the **Caledonian Canal** are raised and lowered 13m by a 'ladder' of five consecutive locks. It's fun to watch, and the neatly landscaped canal banks are a great place to soak up the sun or compare accents with fellow tourists. The **Caledonian Canal Heritage Centre** (☎ 366493; admission free; ☺ 10am-5pm Apr-Oct), beside the lowest lock, showcases the history of the canal.

The **Clansman Centre** (☎ 366444; admission free; ☺ 10am-6pm Apr-Oct) has an exhibition on 17th-century Highland life, with live demonstrations of how to put on a plaid (the forerunner of the kilt) and how the claymore (Highland sword) was made and

used. There's also a workshop where you can buy handcrafted reproduction swords, dirks and shields.

The **Royal Scot** (☎ 366277; ☺ 10am-5pm Mar-Nov) offers 50-minute cruises (adult/child £8/4) on Loch Ness accompanied by the latest high-tech sonar equipment so you can keep an underwater eye open for Nessie. Departures are hourly.

Sleeping & Eating

Morag's Lodge (☎ 366289; www.moragslodge.com; Bunnoich Brae; dm/d £12.50/32; ☒) This large and well-run hostel is set in a big Victorian house with great views of Fort Augustus' hilly surrounds; at the time of research an extension was being built. It's hidden away up the steep side road just north of the TIC car park.

Stravaigers Lodge (☎ 366257; stravaigerslodge@aol.com; Glendoe Rd; tw per person £15; ⓟ ☒) This modern, purpose-built hostel offers comfortable accommodation in twin rooms only – no dorms. There's a well-equipped kitchen and laundry, and the owners can arrange horse-riding trips. It's south of the village, just off the B862 road.

Lorien House (☎ 366736; www.lorien-house.co.uk; Station Rd; s/d £30/50) Lorien is a cut above your usual B&B – the bathrooms come with bidets and the breakfasts with smoked salmon, and there's a library of walking, cycling and climbing guides in the lounge.

Lovat Arms Hotel (☎ 0845 450 1100; www.lovat arms-hotel.com; Main Rd; s £40-65, d £80-100; ⓟ ☒) The bedrooms in this grand old hotel are spacious and elegantly furnished, while the lounge is equipped with a log fire, comfy armchairs and grand piano. It's up the hill to the south of the canal bridge.

Fort Augustus Caravan & Camping Park (☎ 366 618; tent/campervan sites per person £4.50) This campsite is just south of the village on the western side of the road to Fort William.

Lock Inn (☎ 366302; bar meals £5-6; ☺ food served noon-5pm) A superb little pub on the canal bank, the Lock Inn has a vast range of malt whiskies, and a tempting menu of bar lunches that includes Orkney salmon and Highland venison.

Getting There & Away

Scottish Citylink buses from Inverness to Fort William stop at Fort Augustus (£8, 1¼ hours, five or six daily).

THE CAIRNGORMS

The Cairngorms National Park encompasses the highest landmass in Britain – a broad mountain plateau, riven only by the deep valleys of the Lairig Ghru and Loch Avon, with an average altitude of over 1000m and including five of the six highest summits in the UK. This wild mountain landscape of granite and heather has a sub-Arctic climate and supports rare alpine tundra vegetation and high-altitude bird species, such as snow bunting, ptarmigan and dotterel.

The harsh mountain environment gives way lower down to scenic glens softened by beautiful open forests of native Caledonian pine, home to rare animals and birds, such as pine marten, wildcat, red squirrel, osprey, capercaillie and crossbill.

This is prime hill-walking territory, but even couch potatoes can enjoy a taste of the high life by taking the Cairngorm Mountain Railway (p329) up to the edge of the Cairngorm plateau.

AVIEMORE

☎ 01479 / pop 2400

Aviemore is the gateway to the Cairngorms, the region's main centre for transport, accommodation, restaurants and shopping. It's not the prettiest town in Scotland by a long stretch – the main attractions are in the surrounding area – but when bad weather puts the hills off limits, Aviemore fills up with hikers, cyclists and climbers (plus skiers and snowboarders in winter) cruising the outdoor equipment shops or recounting their latest adventures in the cafés and bars. Add in tourists and locals and the eclectic mix makes for a lively little place.

Orientation

Aviemore is on a loop off the A9 Perth-Inverness road; almost everything of note is to be found along the main drag, Grampian Rd. The train station and bus stop are towards the southern end.

The Cairngorm skiing area and mountain railway lie 9 miles east of Aviemore along the B970 and its continuation through Coylumbridge and Glenmore.

CENTRAL & WESTERN HIGHLANDS

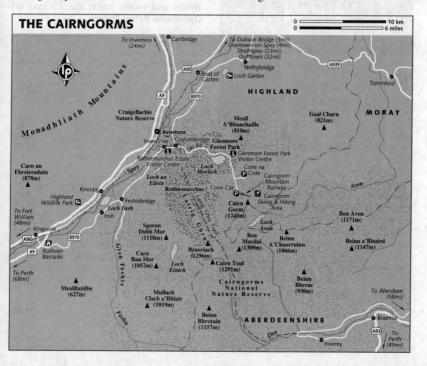

THE CAIRNGORMS

Information

There's a cluster of ATMs outside the Tesco supermarket on Grampian Rd, and there's currency exchange at the post office and the TIC.

Aviemore Photographic (☎ 810371; The Mall, Grampian Rd; per 10min £1; ☼ 8.30am-8pm; 💻) You can check email here.

Old Bridge Inn (☎ 811137; 23 Dalfaber Rd; per 30min £1; ☼ 11am-11pm Sun-Thu, to midnight Fri & Sat; 💻) Internet access is available here.

Ottakar's (☎ 810797; 87 Grampian Rd; ☼ 9am-5.30pm Mon-Sat, 11am-5pm Sun) For books and maps.

TIC (☎ 810363; aviemoretic@host.co.uk; The Mall, Grampian Rd; ☼ 9am-5pm Mon-Sat, 10am-4pm Sun) Next door to Aviemore Photographic.

Sights

Aviemore's train station is home to the **Strathspey Steam Railway** (☎ 810725; www.strathspeyrailway.co.uk; Station Sq), which runs steam trains on a section of restored line between Aviemore and Broomhill, 10 miles to the northeast, via Boat of Garten (p330). There are four or five trains daily from June to September, and a more limited service in April, May, October and December; a return ticket from Aviemore to Broomhill is £9/4.50 per adult/child. An extension to Grantown is planned.

The former Aviemore Centre to the west of Grampian Rd has been completely overhauled and is now home to the **Aviemore Highland Resort** (☎ 0845 223 6217; www.aviemorehighlandresort.com), a complex including hotels, chalets, restaurants, a swimming pool, gym, spa, computer games arcade and a huge, shiny shopping mall. The **swimming pool** (adult/child £6/3; ☼ 8am-10pm) and other leisure facilities are open to nonresidents.

Activities

WALKING

A trail leads west from Aviemore Youth Hostel and passes under the A9 into the **Craigellachie Nature Reserve**, a great place for short hikes across steep hill-sides covered in natural birch forest. Look out for birds and other wildlife, including the peregrine falcons that nest on the crags from April to July. If you're very lucky, you may even spot a capercaillie.

The **Rothiemurchus Estate Visitor Centre** (☎ 812345; www.rothiemurchus.net; Inverdruie; admission free; ☉ 9am-5.30pm), a mile southeast of Aviemore along the B970, has a free *Visitor Guide & Footpath Map* detailing access to 50 miles of footpaths through the estate's beautiful Caledonian pine forests, including the wheelchair-accessible 4-mile trail around **Loch an Eilein**, with its ruined castle and peaceful pine woods. See also the Mountain Walks in the Cairngorms boxed text, p330.

FISHING
Fishing permits for salmon, sea trout and brown trout on the Aviemore stretch of the River Spey are available from **Speyside Sports** (☎ 810656; 2 Station Sq); they're only available to people who are staying in local accommodation. A day permit costs around £20; numbers are limited, so it's best to book in advance.

Rothiemurchus Fishery (☎ 810703; Rothiemurchus Estate, Inverdruie) at the southern end of the village has a loch where you can cast for rainbow trout; buy permits (from £12 to £25 a day, plus £3.50 for tackle hire) at the Fish Farm Shop in Inverdruie. If you're a fly-fishing virgin, it offers a one-hour beginner's package, including tackle hire and basic instruction, for £12.50.

You can also fish for brown trout and pike on **Loch Morlich** (p329) – permits are available from the warden's office at Glenmore Caravan & Camping Site (p329).

SKIING
Aspen or Val d'Isere it ain't, but with 19 runs and 23 miles of piste **Cairngorm Mountain** (☎ 861261; www.cairngormmountain.com) is Scotland's biggest ski area. When the snow is at its best and the sun is shining you can close your eyes and imagine you're in the Alps; sadly, low cloud and horizontal sleet are more common. The season usually runs from December until the snow melts, which may be as late as the end of April, but snowfall here is unpredictable – in some years the slopes can be open in November, but closed for lack of snow in February.

The mountain railway (p329) and most ski tows start from the main Coire Cas car park. A ski pass for one/five days is £26/106 for adults and £16/66 for those under 16. Ski or snowboard rental is around £16/12 per adult/child a day; there are lots of rental outlets at Coire Cas, Glenmore and Aviemore.

During the season the TIC displays snow conditions and avalanche warnings. You can check the latest snow conditions on the **Ski Hotline** (☎ 861261) and at http://ski.visitscotland.com, or tune into Cairngorm Radio Ski FM on 96.6MHz.

OTHER ACTIVITIES
If bad weather keeps you off the hills, there are other ways to get wet and dirty. You can burn some rubber go-karting at the **Aviemore Kart Raceway** (☎ 810722; Aviemore Centre; per session £5; ☉ 9am-10pm Jun-Sep, 10am-5pm Oct-May), or join a cross-country quad bike trek at **Alvie & Dalraddy Estate** (☎ 810330; Dalraddy Holiday Park; per person £30), 3 miles south of Aviemore on the B9152 (call first).

If you prefer the smell of wet dog to the whiff of petrol, **Cairngorm Sled-Dog Centre** (☎ 07767 270526; www.sled-dogs.co.uk; Ski Rd) can take you on a two- to three-hour sled tour of local forest trails in the wake of a team of huskies (adult/child £45/30). The sleds have wheels, so snow is not necessary. There are also one-hour guided tours of the kennels (adult/child £7.50/3.50).

Sleeping
BUDGET
Aviemore Bunkhouse (☎ 811181; www.aviemore-bunkhouse.com; Dalfaber Rd; dm/tw/f £12/29/38; P ☒ ⬛) This independent hostel, next door to the Old Bridge Inn, provides accommodation in bright, modern six- or eight-bed dorms, each with private bathroom, and one twin/family room. There's a drying room, secure bike storage and wheelchair-accessible dorms. From the train station, cross the pedestrian bridge and walk south on Dalfaber Rd.

Aviemore Youth Hostel (SYHA; ☎ 0870 004 1104; 25 Grampian Rd; dm £12-14; P ☒ ⬛) Offers upmarket hostelling in a well-equipped building, five minutes' walk from the village centre. There are four- and six-bed rooms, and the doors stay open until 2am.

Kinapol Guest House (☎ 810513; kinapol@ecosse.net; Dalfaber Rd; s/d £30/40; P ☒) The Kinapol is a modern bungalow offering basic but comfortable B&B accommodation, across the tracks from the train station. All three rooms have shared bathrooms.

Rothiemurchus Caravan Park (☎ 812800; Coylumbridge; tent/campervan sites per person £5/15) The nearest camping ground to Aviemore is this year-round park at Coylumbridge, 1.5 miles along the B970.

MIDRANGE

Old Minister's House (☎ 812181; www.theoldministershouse.co.uk; Rothiemurchus; r per person £30-40; P 🗶) This former manse dates from 1906 and has four rooms with a homely, country farmhouse feel. It's in a lovely setting amid Scots pines on the banks of the River Druie, just 0.75 miles southeast of Aviemore.

Ardlogie Guest House (☎ 810747; www.ardlogie.co.uk; Dalfaber Rd; s/d £35/60; P 🗶) Handy for the train station, the five-room Ardlogie has great views over the Spey towards the Cairngorms, and guests get free use of the local Country Club's pool, spa and sauna.

Dunroamin (☎ 810698; lorraine.sheffield@virgin.net; Craig na Gower Ave; s/d £40/55; P 🗶) Dunroamin is a family-run B&B in a pleasant modern bungalow, with three bedrooms with TV and private bathroom, set on a quiet street a short walk north of the village centre.

Ravenscraig Guest House (☎ 810278; ravenscrg@aol.com; Grampian Rd; r per person £25-35; P 🗶) Ravenscraig is a large, flower-bedecked Victorian villa with six spacious en-suite rooms, plus another six in a modern annexe at the back (one wheelchair accessible). It serves traditional and veggie breakfasts in an attractive conservatory dining room.

Cairngorm Hotel (☎ 810233; www.cairngorm.com; Grampian Rd; s/d £40/70; P 🖵) Better known as the Cairn, this long-established hotel is set in the fine old granite building with the pointy turret opposite the train station. It's a welcoming place with comfortable rooms and a determinedly Scottish atmosphere, all tartan carpets and stags' antlers.

TOP END

Hilton Coylumbridge (☎ 810661; www.coylumbridge.hilton.com; Coylumbridge; s/d from £78/94; P 🗶 🐾) This modern, low-rise Hilton, set amid the pine woods just outside Aviemore, is a wonderfully child-friendly family hotel, with bedrooms for up to two adults and two

children, indoor and outdoor play areas, a crèche and a baby-sitting service.

Eating & Drinking

Old Bridge Inn (☎ 811137; 23 Dalfaber Rd; bar meals £7, mains £10-14; 🕑 food served noon-2pm & 6-9pm, to 9.30pm Fri & Sat) The Old Bridge has a snug bar, complete with roaring log fire in winter, and a cheerful, chalet-style restaurant at the back serving quality Scottish cuisine.

Ski-ing Doo (☎ 810392; 9 Grampian Rd; mains £6-10, steaks £13-15; 🕑 1pm-late Mon, Tue & Thu-Sat, 5.30pm-late Sun) A long-standing Aviemore institution, the child-friendly Ski-ing Doo (it's a pun… oh, ask the waiter!) is a favourite with family skiers. An informal place offering a range of hearty, homemade burgers, chillis and juicy steaks.

Cairngorm Hotel (☎ 810233; Grampian Rd; mains £6-13; 🕑 food served 9am-9.30pm) The Cairn has a coffee shop that serves full fry-up breakfasts (9am to noon), and a lounge and restaurant (with snazzy new outdoor terrace) that does decent bar meals and dinners. The bar is a popular meeting place for locals, and often has folk-music sessions in the evenings.

Café Mambo (☎ 811670; The Mall, Grampian Rd; mains £6-8; 🕑 food served noon-8.30pm Mon-Thu, to 7.30pm Fri & Sat, 12.30-8.30pm Sun) The Mambo is the snowboarders' alternative to the crustily traditional Cairn – a chill-out café in the afternoon, serving burgers, steaks and Tex-Mex grub, it turns into a clubbing and live-band venue in the evenings.

Coffee Corner (☎ 810564; 85 Grampian Rd; snacks £2-4; 🕑 9am-5pm) This cosy café is a good place to relax with newspapers and a steaming mug of coffee on a rainy day. It does good breakfasts, scones and ice-cream sundaes.

Tesco (Grampian Rd; 🕑 8am-10pm Mon-Sat, 9am-6pm Sun) This supermarket is massive.

Rothiemurchus Larder (☎ 810858; Rothiemurchus Estate Visitor Centre, Inverdruie) A mile along Ski Rd, head here for smoked trout, venison, pâté and other picnic delicacies.

Getting There & Away

BUS

Buses stop on Grampian Rd; buy tickets at the TIC. Scottish Citylink connects Aviemore with Inverness (£5, 45 minutes), Newtonmore (£5, 25 minutes), Pitlochry (£7, 1¼ hours), Perth (£11, two hours), Glasgow (£15, 3¼ hours) and Edinburgh (£15, 3¼ hours).

Rapsons/Highland Country buses link Aviemore with Carrbridge (15 minutes), Grantown-on-Spey (£3.90, 35 minutes, hourly) and Inverness (£5, 1¾ hours, three daily Monday to Friday) via the town of Grantown-on-Spey.

TRAIN
There are direct train services to Glasgow/Edinburgh (£34, 2½ hours, three daily) and Inverness (£8, 40 minutes, nine daily).

Getting Around
BIKE
Several places in Aviemore, Rothiemurchus Estate and Glenmore have mountain bikes for hire, including **Bothy Bikes** (☎ 810111; www.bothybikes.co.uk; Ski Rd); most charge around £15/10 per day/half day.

BUS
There is service available with **Rapsons/Highland Country** (☎ 811211) from Aviemore to Cairngorm (£3, seven daily June to September and mid-December to April, three daily Monday to Friday May and October to mid-December) and to Coylumbridge (every 40 minutes Monday to Saturday).

AROUND AVIEMORE
Loch Morlich
☎ 01479
Six miles east of Aviemore, Loch Morlich is surrounded by some 2000 hectares of pine and spruce forest that make up the Glenmore Forest Park. Its attractions include a sandy beach (at the east end) where you'll find the popular **Loch Morlich Watersports Centre** (☎ 861221; Glenmore; ☼ 9am-5pm May-Oct), which rents out Canadian canoes (£15 an hour), kayaks (£8), windsurfers (£15), sailing dinghies (£18) and rowing boats (£14).

The park's **visitor centre** (☎ 861220) has a small exhibition on the Caledonian forest and sells the *Glen More Forest Guide Map*, detailing local walks. The circuit of Loch Morlich (one hour) makes a pleasant outing; the trail is pram- and wheelchair-friendly.

The warden at the neighbouring **Cairngorm Reindeer Centre** (☎ 861228; Glenmore; adult/child £8/4) will take you on a tour to see and feed Britain's only herd of reindeer, who are very tame and will even eat out of your hand. Walks take place at 11am, plus another at 2.30pm from May to September.

Glenmore Lodge (☎ 861256; www.glenmorelodge .org.uk; Glenmore; s/d £30/40; **P**) is one of Britain's leading adventure sports training centres, offering courses in hill walking, rock climbing, ice climbing, canoeing, mountain biking and mountaineering. The centre's comfortable B&B accommodation is available to all, even if you're not taking a course, as is the indoor-climbing wall, gym and sauna.

Cairngorm Lodge Youth Hostel (SYHA; ☎ 0870 004 1137; Glenmore; dm £12-14; ☼ closed Nov–mid-Dec) is set in a former shooting lodge and enjoys a great location at the east end of Loch Morlich; prebooking is essential.

Glenmore Caravan & Camping Site (☎ 861271; Glenmore; tents & campervans £8.20-16.90; ☼ closed Nov–mid-Dec) Campers can set up a base at this attractive lochside site with pitches amid the Scots pines; rates include up to four people per tent/campervan.

Cairngorm Mountain Railway
Aviemore's newest attraction is the **Cairngorm Mountain Railway** (☎ 01479-861261; ☼ 10am-4.30pm May-Oct), a funicular train that will whisk you to the edge of Cairngorm plateau (1085m) in just eight minutes (adult/child return £8.50/5). The bottom station is at the Coire Cas car park at the end of Ski Rd; at the top is an exhibition, a shop (of course) and a restaurant. Unfortunately, for environmental and safety reasons, you're not allowed out of the top station in summer, not even to walk down – you must return to the car park on the funicular.

The **Ptarmigan Restaurant** (☎ 01479-861336; 3-course dinner incl train fare £32; ☼ 6.30-10.30pm Fri & Sat late Jun-Sep) in the top station is Britain's highest restaurant, and offers – weather permitting – a spectacular sunset dining experience. The menu combines traditional Scottish ingredients with contemporary styles. On Thursdays in July and August there is also a buffet dinner and *ceilidh* (evening of traditional Scottish entertainment including music, song and dance; adult/child £20/10). Bookings recommended.

Kincraig & Glen Feshie
The **Highland Wildlife Park** (☎ 01540-651270; Kincraig; adult/child £8.50/6; ☼ 10am-7pm Jun-Aug, to 6pm Apr-May & Sep-Oct, to 4pm Nov-Mar, last entry 2hr before closing) near Kincraig, 6 miles southwest of Aviemore, features a drive-through safari

park and animal enclosures that offer the chance to get close to rarely seen native wildlife, such as wildcat, capercaillie, pine marten, white-tailed sea eagle and red squirrel, as well as species that once roamed the Scottish hills but have long since disappeared, including wolf, lynx, wild boar, beaver and European bison. Visitors without cars get driven around by staff (at no extra cost).

At Kincraig the Spey widens into Loch Insh, home of the **Loch Insh Watersports Centre** (☎ 01540-651272; www.lochinsh.com; Kincraig), which offers canoeing, windsurfing, sailing, bike hire and fishing, as well as B&B accommodation from £21 per person. The food here is good, especially after 6.30pm when the lochside café metamorphoses into a cosy restaurant.

Beautiful, tranquil **Glen Feshie** extends south from Kincraig, deep into the Cairngorms, with Scots pine woods in its upper reaches surrounded by big, heathery hills. The 4WD track to the head of the glen makes a great mountain-bike excursion (25 miles round trip).

Glen Feshie Hostel (☎ 01540-651323; glenfeshie hostel@totalise.co.uk; Glen Feshie; dm £9.50), about 5 miles south of Kincraig, is a cosy, independent 14-bed hostel popular with hikers. Rates include bed linen and a steaming bowl of porridge to start the day.

Carrbridge
☎ 01479 / pop 540
Carrbridge, 7 miles northeast of Aviemore, is a good alternative base for exploring the region. It takes its name from the graceful old bridge (spotlit at night), built in 1717, over the thundering rapids of the Dulnain.

The **Landmark Forest Heritage Park** (☎ 01479-841613; adult/child £8.95/6.90; ☼ 10am-5pm, to 6pm Apr–mid-Jul, to 7pm mid-Jul–Aug; ⓓ), set in a forest of Scots pines, is a theme park with a difference; the theme is timber. The main attractions are the Treetop Trail, a raised walkway through the forest canopy that allows you to view red squirrels, crossbills and crested tits, the wooden viewing tower and the steam-powered sawmill.

Good places to stay include the **Struan House Hotel** (☎ 841242; www.struanhousehotel.co.uk; s/d £30/53; ℗), with its snug bar and roaring log fire, and the similarly styled **Cairn Hotel** (☎ 841212; www.cairnhotel.co.uk; Main Rd; s/d £28/48; ℗).

Carrbridge Bunkhouse Hostel (☎ 841250; jones bunk@aol.com; dm £7.50) is a cosy, wood-panelled forest cabin, complete with hot showers, drying room and sauna. It's just off the A938 at Bogroy, on the western edge of the village.

Rapsons/Highland Country runs four or five buses daily (Monday to Saturday) from Inverness to Carrbridge (£3.70, 45 minutes) and onwards to Grantown-on-Spey (£2.50, 20 minutes).

Boat of Garten
☎ 01479 / pop 570
Boat of Garten is known as the Osprey Village because these rare and beautiful birds of prey nest nearby at the **RSPB Loch Garten Osprey Centre** (☎ 831694; Tulloch, Nethybridge; adult/child £2.50/50p; ☼ 10am-6pm Apr-Aug; ⓓ). The ospreys migrate here each spring from Africa and nest in a tall pine tree – watch from a hide as the birds feed their young. The centre is signposted about 2 miles east of the village.

MOUNTAIN WALKS IN THE CAIRNGORMS

The climb from the car park at the Coire Cas ski area to the summit of **Cairn Gorm** (1245m) takes about two hours (one way). From there, you can continue south across the high-level plateau to Ben Macdui (1309m), Britain's second-highest peak. This takes eight to 10 hours return from the car park and is a serious undertaking, for experienced and well-equipped walkers only.

The **Lairig Ghru trail**, which can take eight to 10 hours, is a demanding 24-mile walk from Aviemore across the Lairig Ghru pass (840m) to Braemar. An alternative to doing the full route is to make the six-hour return hike up to the summit of the pass and back to Aviemore. The path starts from Ski Rd, a mile east of Coylumbridge, and involves some very rough going.

Warning – the Cairngorm plateau is a sub-Arctic environment where navigation is difficult and weather conditions can be severe, even in midsummer. Hikers must have proper hill-walking equipment, and know how to use a map and compass. In winter it is a place for experienced mountaineers only.

Fraoch Lodge (☎ 831331; Deshar Rd; r per person £14-16; P ✗) provides luxury hostel-style accommodation in a Victorian town house, in twin or family rooms. There's a lounge with an open fire and a self-catering kitchen.

The **Old Ferryman's House** (☎ 831370; s/d £25/50; P ✗) is a charming cottage B&B on the riverbank on the far side of the bridge to the east of the village (follow the signs to Nethybridge), while the **Boat Hotel** (☎ 831258; www .boathotel.co.uk; s/d £55/80; P ✗) is a luxurious country hotel with a superb restaurant.

Boat of Garten is 8 miles northeast of Aviemore. The most interesting way to get here is on the Strathspey Steam Railway (p326).

GRANTOWN-ON-SPEY
☎ 01479 / pop 2170

Grantown (pronounced granton) is an elegant Georgian town on the banks of the Spey geared towards the needs of anglers and retirees. Thronged with tourists in summer, it reverts to a quiet backwater in winter. Most hotels can kit you out for a day of fly-fishing or put you in touch with someone who can. There's a **TIC** (☎ 872773; 54 High St; ☯ Mar-Oct), a bank, ATMs and a post office.

Sleeping & Eating
Brooklynn (☎ 873097; www.woodier.com; Grant Rd; r per person £22-30; P ✗) This beautiful Victorian villa features original stained glass and wood panelling, and seven spacious, luxurious rooms (all doubles have en suites). The food – dinner is available as well as breakfast – is superb, too.

Culdearn House Hotel (☎ 872106; www.culdearn .com; Woodlands Tce; r per person £45-60; P ✗) Yet another plush Victorian villa (Grantown is full of them) with corniced ceilings, marble fireplaces and original wood panelling, this hotel has an excellent restaurant, with a log fire and candle-lit tables. Note that children under 10 are not welcome.

Good B&Bs include the welcoming, nine-room **Willowbank Guest House** (☎ 872089; www .willowbankguesthouse.co.uk; High St; r per person £19-28; ✗) and **Bank House** (☎ 873256; farleys@breathemail .net; 1 The Sq; r per person £25-30) in a former Bank of Scotland building (entrance at the back).

The **Coffee House & Ice Cream Parlour** (High St) is a traditional family café that sells delicious homemade ice cream; the Garth Hotel, on the north end of the town square, is a pleasant place for a drink or a bar meal.

Getting There & Away
Rapsons/Highland Country buses run between Grantown-on-Spey and Aviemore (£4.20, 35 minutes, hourly) and Inverness (£4.60, 1¼ hours, two or three daily except Sunday).

KINGUSSIE
☎ 01540 / pop 1410

The gracious old Speyside town of Kingussie (pronounced kin-yewsie) sits at the foot of the great heather-clad humps of the Monadhliath Mountains. The town is best known as the home of the excellent Highland Folk Museum.

Sights
The open-air **Highland Folk Museum** (☎ 661307; Duke St; adult/child £2.50/1.50; ☯ 9.30am-5pm Mon-Sat Apr-Aug, to 4pm Mon-Sat Sep & Oct) comprises a collection of historical buildings and relics revealing many aspects of Highland culture and lifestyle. The museum is laid out like a village and has a traditional thatch-roofed Isle of Lewis *blackhouse* (low-walled stone cottage), a water mill and a 19th-century corrugated-iron shed for smoking salmon. Actors in period costume give demonstrations of traditional crafts. There's another section of the museum at nearby Newtonmore.

Perched dramatically on a river terrace and clearly visible from the main A9 road, the roofless **Ruthven Barracks** (admission free; ☯ 24hr) was one of four garrisons built by the British government after the first Jacobite rebellion of 1715 as part of a Hanoverian scheme to take control of the Highlands. Ironically, the barracks were last occupied by Jacobite troops awaiting the return of Bonnie Prince Charlie after the Battle of Culloden. Learning of his defeat and subsequent flight, they destroyed the barracks before taking to the glens. The ruins are spectacularly floodlit at night.

Activities
The Monadhliath Mountains, northwest of Kingussie, attract fewer hikers than the nearby Cairngorms and make an ideal destination for walkers seeking peace and solitude. However, during the deer-stalking season (August to October), you'll need to check with the TIC before setting out.

The recommended six-hour circular walk to the 878m summit of **Carn an Fhreiceadain**, above Kingussie, begins north of the village. It continues to Pitmain Lodge and along the Allt Mor river before climbing to the cairn on the summit. You can then follow the ridge east to the twin summits of Beinn Bhreac before returning to Kingussie via a more easterly track.

Sleeping & Eating

Lairds Bothy Hostel (☎ 661334; 68 High St; dm £10) Tucked behind the Tipsy Laird pub in the main street, this hostel has four family rooms and several plain eight-bed dorms.

Homewood Lodge (☎ 661507; www.homewood -lodge-kingussie.co.uk; Newtonmore Rd; s/d £25/40; P ✗) This elegant Victorian lodge on the western outskirts of town offers double rooms with exquisite views of the Cairngorms – a nice way to wake up in the mornings!

Hermitage (☎ 662137; Spey St; r per person from £24; P ✗) The five-bedroom Hermitage is a lovely old house with plenty of character, filled with Victorian period features. The lounge has a log fire, and there are good views of the Cairngorms from the garden.

Osprey Hotel (☎ 661510; www.ospreyhotel.co.uk; Ruthven Rd; r per person £25-39; P ✗) Overlooking the town's flower-filled memorial gardens, this cosily old-fashioned Victorian town house has eight brightly refurbished rooms, and serves tasty home cooking at breakfast and dinner.

Cross (☎ 661166; www.thecross.co.uk; Tweed Mill Brae, Ardbroilach Rd; d £130-190, 3-course dinner £35; ✆ dinner Tue-Sat; P ✗) Housed in a converted water mill beside the Allt Mor burn, the Cross is one of the finest restaurants in the Highlands. The intimate, low-raftered dining room has an open fire and a patio overlooking the stream, and serves the likes of Scottish seafood and local lamb accompanied by a superb wine list. If you want to stay the night, there are eight stylish bedrooms to choose from.

Getting There & Away

Kingussie is on the Edinburgh/Glasgow to Inverness rail and bus routes, and all trains and many Scottish Citylink buses stop here.

There are Scottish Citylink buses to Aviemore (£4, 25 minutes, five to seven daily) and Inverness (£7, one hour, six to eight Monday to Saturday, three Sunday). Rapsons/ Highland Country runs a once-daily service (Monday to Friday only) between Newton-

more and Inverness, calling at Kingussie, Kincraig, Aviemore and Carrbridge, with more frequent buses (school days only) between Kingussie and Aviemore.

From the train station at the southern end of town there are trains to Edinburgh (£33, 2½ hours, seven a day Monday to Saturday, two Sunday) and Inverness (£8, one hour, eight a day Monday to Saturday, four Sunday).

NEWTONMORE
☎ 01540 / pop 980

Three miles southwest of Kingussie lies the peaceful backwater of Newtonmore, home to the excellent **Highland Folk Museum** (☎ 661307; adult/child £5/3; ✆ 10.30am-5.30pm Apr-Aug, 11am-4.30pm Sep & Oct), a sister establishment to the museum of the same name in Kingussie. The Newtonmore site includes a reconstructed village with wattle and daub cottages, a school and a farm, and on-site demonstrations of woodcarving, spinning and peat-fire baking. You'll need two to three hours to make the most of a visit here.

Ten miles southwest of Newtonmore, on the A86 road towards Spean Bridge, is **Laggan Wolftrax** (☎ 01528-544786; Strathmashie Forest, Laggan; ✆ 10am-6pm Mon-Wed & Fri, to 9pm Thu, 9am-8pm Sat, 9am-6pm Sun), a new mountain-biking centre with purpose-built trails ranging from open-country riding to black-diamond downhills. Cycle hire is available on-site, from £18 a day for an ordinary mountain bike to £35 for a full-suspension downhill rig.

Sleeping

Eagleview Guest House (☎ 673675; www.eagle view-guesthouse.co.uk; Perth Rd; r per person £23-30; P ✗) The family-friendly Eagleview is one of the nicest places to stay in the area, with beautifully decorated bedrooms, spacious bathrooms with power showers, and nice little touches like wall-mounted flat-screen TVs, cafetieres with real coffee on your hospitality tray, and real milk rather than yucky UHT stuff.

As a popular hill-walking base camp, Newtonmore is well endowed with budget accommodation, including **Newtonmore Hostel** (☎ 673360; www.highlandhostel.co.uk; Main St; dm £10-12, s/d £20/24; P ▯), a bright, modern, bungalow-style place, and **Strathspey Mountain Hostel** (☎ 673694; strathspey@newtonmore.com; Main St; dm £11; P ✗ ▯), a snug 19th-century cottage with two six-bunk dorms and two triple rooms.

Getting There & Around

Rapsons/Highland Country runs a twice-daily service Monday to Friday (once on Saturday) between Newtonmore and Aviemore (£2.80, 25 minutes).

You can rent bikes (from £5 a day) from Strathspey Mountain Hostel.

DALWHINNIE

The remote village of Dalwhinnie, bypassed by the main A9 road, straggles along its single street in glorious isolation amid wild and windswept scenery. From a distance you can spot the distinctive twin pagoda-shaped roofs of the malt kiln at **Dalwhinnie Distillery** (☎ 01540-672219; ⏰ 9.30am-5pm Mon-Sat Jun & Sep, 9.30am-5pm Mon-Sat, 12.30-4pm Sun Jul & Aug, 11am-4pm Mon-Sat Oct, 9.30am-5pm Mon-Fri Easter-May, 1-4pm Mon-Fri Nov-Easter), which offers tours for £3.50. It is the highest in Scotland (326m above sea level) and one of the most remote.

Three or four trains a day on the Glasgow/Edinburgh to Inverness line stop at Dalwhinnie's tiny station, 600m from the distillery.

WEST HIGHLANDS

This area extends from the bleak blanket-bog of Rannoch Moor to the west coast beyond Glen Coe and Fort William, and includes the southern reaches of the Great Glen. The scenery is grand throughout, with high and wild mountains dominating the glens. Great expanses of moor alternate with lochs and patches of commercial forest. Fort William, at the inner end of Loch Linnhe, is the only sizable town in the area.

GLEN COE

Scotland's most famous glen is also one of the grandest and, in bad weather, the grimmest. The approach to the glen from the east, watched over by the rocky pyramid of Buachaille Etive Mor – the Great Shepherd of Etive – leads over the Pass of Glencoe and into the narrow upper valley. The southern side is dominated by three massive, brooding spurs, known as the Three Sisters, while the northern side is enclosed by the continuous steep wall of the knife-edged Aonach Eagach ridge. The main road threads its lonely way through the middle of all this mountain grandeur, past deep gorges and crashing waterfalls, to the more pastoral lower reaches of the glen around Loch Achtriochtan and Glencoe village.

Glencoe was written into the history books in 1692 when the resident MacDonalds were murdered by Campbell soldiers in what became known as the Glencoe Massacre (see the boxed text, p335).

Activities

There are several short, pleasant walks around **Glencoe Lochan**, near the village. To get there, turn left off the minor road to the youth hostel, just beyond the bridge over the River Coe. There are three walks (40 minutes to an hour), all detailed on a signboard at the car park. The artificial lochan was created by Lord Strathcona in 1895 for his homesick Canadian wife Isabella and is surrounded by a North American–style forest.

A more strenuous hike, but well worth the effort on a fine day, is the climb to the **Lost Valley**, a magical mountain sanctuary still haunted by the ghosts of murdered MacDonalds (only 2.5 miles round trip, but allow three hours). A rough path from the car park at Allt na Reigh (on the A82, 6 miles east of Glencoe village) bears left down to a footbridge over the river, then climbs up the wooded valley between Beinn Fhada and Gearr Aonach (the first and second of the Three Sisters). The route leads steeply up through a maze of giant, jumbled, moss-coated boulders before emerging – quite unexpectedly – into a broad, open valley with an 800m-long meadow as flat as a football pitch. Back in the days of clan warfare, the valley – invisible from below – was used for hiding stolen cattle; its Gaelic name, Coire Gabhail, means 'corrie of capture'.

The summits of Glen Coe's mountains are for experienced mountaineers only. Details of hill-walking routes can be found in the Scottish Mountaineering Club's guidebook *Central Highlands* by Peter Hodgkiss.

East of the Glen

A few miles east of Glencoe proper, on the south side of the A82, is the car park and base station for the **Glencoe Mountain Resort** (☎ 01855-851226; www.glencoemountain.com), where commercial skiing in Scotland first began back in 1956. The Lodge Café-Bar has comfy sofas where you can soak up the view through the floor-to-ceiling windows.

The **chairlift** (adult/child £5/3; ⊙ 9.30am-4.30pm Thu-Mon May-Sep) continues to operate in summer – there's a grand view over Rannoch Moor from the top station. In winter a lift pass costs £24 a day and equipment hire is £18 a day.

Two miles west of the ski centre, a minor road leads along peaceful and beautiful **Glen Etive**, which runs southwest for 12 miles to the head of Loch Etive (p309). On a hot summer's day the River Etive contains many tempting pools for swimming in, and there are lots of good picnic sites. Wild camping is allowed here, too.

The remote **King's House Hotel** (☎ 01855-851259; www.kingy.com; Glencoe; s/d from £25/50, bar meals £6-10; P) claims to be one of Scotland's oldest licensed inns, dating from the 17th century. It lies on the old military road from Stirling to Fort William (now followed by the West Highland Way; see the boxed text, p278), and after the Battle of Culloden – it was used as a Hanoverian garrison – hence the name. The hotel serves good pub food – it's famous for its haggis, neeps and tatties (haggis, mashed turnip and mashed potato), and the lounge has a picture window with a stupendous view of Buachaille Etive Mor, a great place to sit and admire the scenery with a glass of malt whisky.

Glencoe Village

☎ 01855 / pop 360

The little village of Glencoe stands on the south shore of Loch Leven at the western end of the glen, 16 miles south of Fort William. The small, thatched **Glencoe Folk Museum** (☎ 811664; Glencoe; adult/child £2/free; ⊙ 10am-5.30pm Mon-Sat mid-May–Sep) houses a varied collection of military memorabilia, farm equipment, and tools of the woodworking, blacksmithing and slate-quarrying trades.

About 1.5 miles east of the village, towards the glen, is the **Glencoe Visitor Centre** (NTS; ☎ 811307; Inverigan; adult/child £5/4; ⊙ 9.30am-5.30pm Apr-Aug, 10am-5pm Sep & Oct, 10am-4pm Thu-Sun Nov-Feb; ♿). A modern facility with an ecotourism angle, the centre provides comprehensive information on the geological, environmental and cultural history of Glencoe via high-tech interactive and audiovisual displays, and tells the story of

the Glencoe Massacre (see the boxed text, opposite) in all its gory detail.

SLEEPING & EATING

Glencoe Youth Hostel (SYHA; ☎ 811219; Glencoe; dm £12.50-14; ▯) The 62-bed Glencoe hostel is very popular with hikers, though the atmosphere is a little institutional. It's a 1.5-mile walk from the village along the minor road on the northern side of the river.

Glencoe Hostel & Bunkhouse (☎ 811906; www .glencoehostel.co.uk; Glencoe; dm £8-12, tent sites per person £4.50) New owners have refurbished this handily located hostel, just 10 minutes' walk from the Clachaig. It's set in an old farmhouse with three six-bed dorms, and another 10 beds in the neighbouring cottage. There's also a separate bunkhouse, with 24 spaces in communal, Alpine-style bunks, and a camping area.

Clachaig Inn (☎ 811252; www.clachaig.com; Clachaig, Glencoe; r per person £38-42, bar meals £6-9; P ✕) The Clachaig has long been a favourite haunt of hill walkers and climbers. As well as comfortable en-suite accommodation, there's a smart, wood-panelled lounge bar, with lots of studded leather sofas and armchairs, mountaineering photos and climbing magazines to leaf through. Climbers usually head for the lively Boots Bar on the other side of the hotel – it has log fires, serves real ale and good pub grub, and has live Scottish, Irish and blues music every Wednesday and Saturday nights.

GETTING THERE & AWAY

Rapsons/Highland Country and Scottish Citylink buses run between Fort William and Glencoe (£4.30, 30 minutes, up to seven a day Monday to Saturday). Scottish Citylink buses also run to Glasgow (£13, 2½ hours, four a day).

KINLOCHLEVEN

☎ 01855 / pop 900

Kinlochleven is hemmed in by high mountains at the head of the beautiful fjord-like Loch Leven, about 7 miles east of Glencoe village. The aluminium smelter that led to the town's development in the early 20th century has now closed, and the opening of the Ballachulish Bridge in the 1970s allowed the main road to bypass the place completely. A ray of hope was provided by the opening of the West Highland Way,

---

THE GLENCOE MASSACRE

The brutal murders that took place here in 1692 were particularly shameful, perpetrated as they were by one Highland clan upon another, with whom they were lodging as guests.

In an attempt to quash remaining Jacobite loyalties among the Highland clans, King William III had ordered that all chiefs take an oath of loyalty to him by the end of the year (1691). Maclain, the elderly chief of the MacDonalds of Glencoe, was late in setting out to fulfil the king's demand and going first to Fort William rather than Inveraray made him later still.

The secretary of state for Scotland, Sir John Dalrymple, declared that the MacDonalds should be punished as an example to other Highland clans, some of whom had not bothered to take the oath. A company of 120 soldiers, mainly of the Campbell clan, were sent to the glen. It was a long-standing tradition for clans to provide hospitality to passing travellers and, since their leader was related to Maclain by marriage, the troops were billeted in MacDonald homes.

After they'd been guests for 12 days, the order came for the soldiers to put to death all MacDonalds aged under 70. Some Campbells alerted the MacDonalds to their intended fate, while others turned on their hosts at 5am on 13 February, shooting Maclain and 37 other men, women and children. Some died before they knew what was happening, while others fled into the snow, only to die of exposure.

The ruthless brutality of the incident caused a public uproar, and after an inquiry several years later Dalrymple lost his job. There's a monument to Maclain in Glencoe village and members of the MacDonald clan still gather here on 13 February each year.

---

which now brings a steady stream of hikers through the village.

Sights & Activities

The final section of the **West Highland Way** stretches for 14 miles from Kinlochleven to Fort William. The village is also the starting point for easier walks up the glen of the River Leven, through pleasant woods to the Grey Mare's Tail waterfall, and harder mountain hikes into the Mamores.

If you fancy trying your hand at ice-climbing, even in the middle of summer, head for the **Ice Factor** (☎ 831100; www.ice-factor.co.uk; Leven Rd; ⏰ 9am-late), the world's biggest indoor ice-climbing wall; a three-hour beginner's course costs £35. There's also a rock-climbing wall, sauna and steam room, and kids' adventure play area.

The **Aluminium Story Visitor Centre** (☎ 831663; Linnhe Rd; admission free; ⏰ 10am-1pm & 2-5pm Mon-Fri Apr-Sep, 10am-1pm Mon, Wed & Fri, 10am-2pm & 6-8pm Tue & Thu Oct-Mar) tells the interesting story of the British Aluminium Company smelter (which opened in 1908) and the Blackwater Reservoir hydroelectric scheme that powered it.

Sleeping

Blackwater Hostel (☎ 831253; www.blackwaterhostel .co.uk; Lab Rd; dm £12, tent sites per person £5) This 40-bed hostel has spotless, pine-panelled dorms with en-suite bathrooms and TV, and an adjacent camping ground.

Mamore Lodge Hotel (☎ 831213; www.mamore lodgehotel.co.uk; Kinlochleven; s £25-38, d £52-78; P ⊠) This hotel occupies a spectacular situation, perched high on a hill-side 200m above Kinlochleven. Built in 1905 as a shooting lodge for shipping magnate Frank Bibby, its guest list included Viscount Churchill and King Edward VII. The rooms retain their original and ageing pine panelling, and the whole place is very much the worse for wear – if it rains, expect to lend a hand placing buckets under the drips – but the place has a certain eccentric charm and the gorgeous views make up for the spartan décor.

Getting There & Away

Rapsons/Highland Country buses run to Kinlochleven from Fort William (£3.20, 15 minutes, seven a day Monday to Saturday) and Glencoe village.

FORT WILLIAM
☎ 01397 / pop 9910

Basking on the shores of Loch Linnhe amid magnificent mountain scenery, Fort William has one of the most enviable settings in the country. If it wasn't for the busy dual carriageway crammed between the town centre and the loch, and one of the highest rainfall records in the country, it would

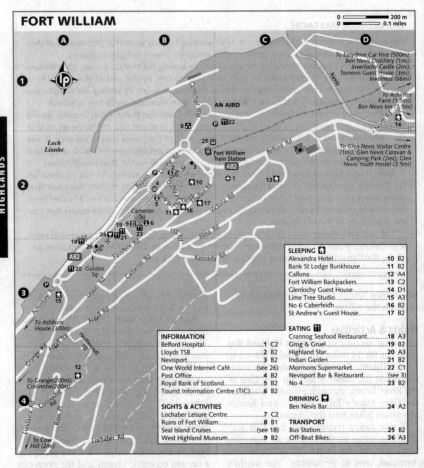

FORT WILLIAM

0 _____ 200 m
0 _____ 0.1 miles

To Easydrive Car Hire (500m);
Ben Nevis Distillery (1mi);
Inverlochy Castle (2mi);
Torlevis Guest House (3mi);
Inverness (66mi)

To Achintee
Farm (1.5mi);
Ben Nevis Inn (1.5mi)

To Glen Nevis Visitor Centre
(1mi); Glen Nevis Caravan &
Camping Park (2mi); Glen
Nevis Youth Hostel (2.5mi)

To Ashburn
House (300m)

To Grange (200m);
Crolinnhe (200m)

To Cow
Hill (2mi)

INFORMATION
Belford Hospital	1	C2
Lloyds TSB	2	B2
Nevisport	3	B2
One World Internet Café	..........(see 26)	
Post Office	4	B2
Royal Bank of Scotland	5	B2
Tourist Information Centre (TIC)	6	B2

SIGHTS & ACTIVITIES
Lochaber Leisure Centre	7	C2
Ruins of Fort William	8	B1
Seal Island Cruises	..............(see 18)	
West Highland Museum	9	B2

SLEEPING 🏠
Alexandra Hotel	10	B2
Bank St Lodge Bunkhouse	11	B2
Calluna	12	A4
Fort William Backpackers	13	C2
Glenlochy Guest House	14	D1
Lime Tree Studio	15	A3
No 6 Caberfeidh	16	B2
St Andrew's Guest House	17	B2

EATING 🍴
Crannog Seafood Restaurant	18	A3
Grog & Gruel	19	A3
Highland Star	20	A3
Indian Garden	21	B2
Morrisons Supermarket	22	C1
Nevisport Bar & Restaurant	........(see 3)	
No 4	23	B2

DRINKING 🍷
| Ben Nevis Bar | ....24 | A2 |

TRANSPORT
| Bus Station | ....25 | B2 |
| Off-Beat Bikes | ....26 | A3 |

be almost idyllic. Even so, it's not a bad little town, and its easy access by rail and bus makes it a good place to base yourself for exploring the surrounding mountains and glens.

Magical Glen Nevis begins near the northern end of the town and wraps itself around the southern flanks of Ben Nevis (1344m) – Britain's highest mountain and a magnet for hikers and climbers. The glen is also popular with movie makers – parts of the films *Braveheart*, *Rob Roy* and *Harry Potter & the Sorcerer's Stone* were filmed here.

History
There's little left of the original fort from which the town takes its name – it was

pulled down in the 19th century to make way for the railway. The first castle here was built by General Monk in 1654 and called Inverlochy, but the meagre ruins by the loch are those of the fort built in the 1690s by General Mackay and named after King William III. In the 18th century it became part of a chain of garrisons (along with Fort Augustus and Fort George) that controlled the Great Glen in response to the Jacobite rebellions.

Originally a tiny fishing village called Gordonsburgh, the town took its present name with the opening of the railway in 1901, which, along with the building of the Caledonian Canal, soon saw it grow into a tourist centre. This has been consolidated in the last three decades by the huge increase in popularity of climbing, skiing and other outdoor sports.

Orientation

The town straggles along the shore of Loch Linnhe for around 3 miles. The compact town centre is clustered around High St and Cameron Sq, 200m southwest of the train and bus stations, and is easy to get around on foot. Glen Nevis (p340) and Ben Nevis (see the boxed text, p340) are 3 miles north of the town centre.

Information

Belford Hospital (☎ 702481; Belford Rd) Opposite the train station.

Lloyds TSB (☎ 0845 303 0109; 6 Tweedale, High St; ⏰ 9.30am-4pm Mon & Tue, 10am-4pm Wed, 9.30am-5.30pm Thu, 9.30am-5pm Fri)

Nevisport (☎ 704921; Airds Crossing, High St; ⏰ 9am-5.30pm Mon-Sat, 9.30am-5pm Sun; 🖳) Has a huge range of outdoor equipment, and books and maps for mountaineers. There is Internet access in the downstairs bar (per 10 minutes £1).

One World Internet Café (☎ 07976 961695; 123 High St; per 15min £1; ⏰ 10am-9pm; 🖳) Net access, printing.

Post office (☎ 0845 722 3344; 5 High St)

Royal Bank of Scotland (☎ 705191; 6 High St; ⏰ 9.15am-4.45pm Mon, Tue, Thu & Fri, 10am-4.45pm Wed)

TIC (☎ 703781; fortwilliam@host.co.uk; Cameron Sq; ⏰ 9am-8pm Mon-Sat, 10am-6pm Sun; 🖳) Has a good range of books and maps. There's Internet access here (per 20 minutes £1).

Sights

The small but fascinating **West Highland Museum** (☎ 702169; Cameron Sq; adult/child £3/50p; ⏰ 10am-5pm Mon-Sat Jun & Sep, 10am-5pm Mon-Sat, 2-5pm Sun Jul & Aug, 10am-4pm Mon-Sat Oct-May) is packed with all manner of Highland memorabilia. Look out for the secret portrait of Bonnie Prince Charlie – after the Jacobite rebellions all things Highland were banned, including pictures of the exiled leader, and this tiny painting looks like nothing more than a smear of paint until placed next to a cylindrical mirror, which then reflects a credible likeness of the prince.

A tour of the **Ben Nevis Distillery** (☎ 702476; Lochy Bridge; ⏰ 9am-7.30pm Mon-Fri, 10am-4pm Sat Jul & Aug, 9am-5pm Mon-Fri Sep-Jun) makes for a warming rainy-day alternative to exploring the hills; the tour costs £4/2 per adult/child.

From late May to early October, the **Jacobite Steam Train** (☎ 01463-239026; www.steamtrain .info) makes the scenic two-hour run from Fort William to Mallaig, departing from Fort William train station at 10.20am Monday to Friday (plus Sunday in August), returning from Mallaig at 2.10pm (adult/child £26/15 day return). There's a brief stop at Glenfinnan station (p343), and you get 1½ hours in Mallaig (p344). Classed as one of the great railway journeys of the world, the route crosses the historic Glenfinnan Viaduct, made famous in the *Harry Potter* films – the Jacobite's owners supplied the steam locomotive and rolling stock used in the film.

Activities

The **Lochaber Leisure Centre** (☎ 704359; Belford Rd; pool £2.30, wall £2.70; ⏰ 10am-9pm Mon-Fri, to 6pm Sat & Sun) has a swimming pool, indoor climbing wall, gym and other leisure facilities.

You can hike from the town centre to the summit of **Cow Hill** (287m) for a superb view of Ben Nevis, the Great Glen and Loch Linnhe. From the roundabout at the end of High St, head south along Lundavra Rd for 0.75 miles and turn left after Lochview Dr onto an unsurfaced road that leads to the TV mast at the top of the hill. Halfway to the summit another path descends on the far side of the hill into Glen Nevis, from where you can return to town along the road (6 miles total, allow 2½ hours).

For details of walking and cycling routes through the Great Glen, see p322.

Tours

Glengarry Mini Tours (☎ 01809-501297; tours@ glengarry.net) Half- or full-day tours around Lochaber and Glencoe, starting at £10 for a four-hour afternoon tour.

Seal Island Cruises (☎ 703919) Operates 1½-hour boat trips (adult/child £7.50/4) on the loch from the Town Pier, visiting a seal colony and a salmon farm. There are four trips a day mid-May to mid-September, and two a day from March to mid-May.

Sleeping

It's best to book well ahead in summer, especially for hostels. See also the Glen Nevis Sleeping & Eating section (p340).

BUDGET

Fort William Backpackers (☎ 700711; www.scot lands-top-hostels.com; Alma Rd; dm £11-15; ✂ 🖳)

A 10-minute walk from the bus and train stations, this lively and welcoming hostel is set in a grand Victorian villa, perched on a hill-side with great views over Loch Linnhe.

Calluna (☎ 700451; www.fortwilliamholiday.co.uk; Heathercroft, Connochie Rd; dm/tw £10.50/24; P ✗) Run by well-known mountain guide Alan Kimber and wife, Sue, the Calluna is geared to hikers and climbers, with three four-bed bunkrooms, five twin rooms, a fully equipped kitchen and an excellent drying room for your soggy hiking gear.

Bank Street Lodge Bunkhouse (☎ 700070; bank streetlodge@btconnect.com; Bank St; dm/tw £12/40) Part of a modern hotel and restaurant complex, the Bank Street Lodge offers the most central budget beds in town, only 250m from the train station. It has kitchen facilities and a drying room.

MIDRANGE

Lime Tree Studio (☎ 701806; www.limetreestudio.co.uk; Achintore Rd; s/d £40/70; P ✗) Much more interesting than your average B&B is this 19th-century former manse overlooking Loch Linnhe, now an 'art gallery with rooms', decorated throughout with the artist-owner's atmospheric Highland landscapes.

St Andrew's Guest House (☎ 703038; www .standrewsguesthouse.co.uk; Fassifern Rd; r per person £20-25; P) Set in a lovely 19th-century building that was once a rectory and choir school, St Andrew's retains period features, such as carved masonry, wood panelling and stained-glass windows, and has six spacious bedrooms, some with stunning views.

Tornevis Guest House (☎ 772868; www.tornevis .co.uk; Banavie; r per person £30-45; P ✗) This luxury B&B is set in a spacious modern house with a great location, enjoying an uninterrupted view of Ben Nevis. The friendly and knowledgeable owners have been in the business for many years, and can recommend local walks (the Caledonian Canal is a few minutes' walk) and attractions. Closed from December to February.

Glenlochy Guest House (☎ 702909; www.glenlochy .co.uk; Nevisbridge; s/d £35/60; P ✗) Set in a huge garden beside the River Nevis, and convenient to Glen Nevis and the end of the West Highland Way, the Glenlochy is a sprawling modern place, with 12 en-suite rooms.

Alexandra Hotel (☎ 702241; www.strathmore hotels.com; The Parade; r per person £30-45; P ✗) A large, traditional, family-oriented hotel

bang in the middle of town, the recently refurbished Alexandra is a comfortable and convenient choice, despite the tourist-oriented tartan-toned décor.

Other recommendations:

No 6 Caberfeidh (☎ 703756; www.6caberfeidh.com; 6 Caberfeidh, Fassifern Rd; r per person £18-30; ✗) Friendly B&B; vegetarian breakfast on request.

Ashburn House (☎ 706000; www.highland5star.co.uk; Achintore Rd; r per person £35-50; P ✗) Grand Victorian villa opposite the sailing club.

TOP END

Grange (☎ 705516; www.grangefortwilliam.com; Grange Rd; r per person £43-48; P ✗) An exceptional 19th-century villa set in its own landscaped grounds, the Grange is crammed with antiques and fitted with log fires, chaise longues and Victorian roll-top baths. The Turret Room, with its window seat in the turret overlooking Loch Linnhe, is our favourite.

Crolinnhe (☎ 702709; www.crolinnhe.co.uk; Grange Rd; r per person £45-60; P ✗) If you can't get into the Grange try the neighbouring Crolinnhe, another grand 19th-century villa, with lochside location, beautiful gardens and sumptuous accommodation. A vegetarian breakfast is provided on request.

Eating & Drinking

No 4 (☎ 704222; 4 Cameron Sq; lunch mains £6-9, dinner mains £9-16; ⏱ 11am-5pm & 6.30-9.30pm) No 4 has a relaxing, farmhouse atmosphere, with an attractive, sunny conservatory and a couple of outdoor tables squeezed out the back. The food is wholesome and fresh, ranging from hearty homemade soups to steaks and seafood, with lots of inventive vegetarian dishes (such as veggie stroganoff, with brandy and cream sauce served with basmati rice).

Crannog Seafood Restaurant (☎ 705589; Town Pier; mains £13-16; ⏱ noon-2.30pm & 6-9.30pm) The Crannog vies with No 4 for the accolade of Fort William's best restaurant, but easily wins the prize for best location. It's perched on the Town Pier, giving diners an uninterrupted view down Loch Linnhe as they feast on fresh seafood. (The restaurant was badly damaged by storms in 2005, and was operating from a site on An Aird at the time of research, but should have returned to the Town Pier by this book's publication.)

Grog & Gruel (☎ 705078; 66 High St; mains £8-14; ⏱ bar meals noon-9pm, restaurant 5pm-late) The Grog & Gruel is a traditional-style, wood-

---

SOMETHING SPECIAL

Inverlochy Castle Hotel (☎ 702177; www
.inverlochycastlehotel.co.uk; Torlundy; s/d £290/435;
Ⓟ ✕) If your pockets are deep enough
you can hobnob with celebrities in the wonderfully grand Inverlochy Castle, an opulent
Victorian creation completed in 1865. One
of Scotland's finest country house hotels,
it has everything you'd expect to find in
a Victorian gentleman's country retreat –
hunting trophies, log fires, a billiard room
and a walled garden. It's set in 200 hectares of private grounds, 3 miles north of
Fort William.

---

panelled pub with an excellent range of
cask ales from regional Scottish and English microbreweries. Upstairs is a lively Tex-
Mex restaurant, with a crowd-pleasing (and
belly-bursting) menu of tasty enchiladas,
burritos, fajitas, burgers, steaks and pizza.

Nevisport Bar & Restaurant (☎ 704921; Airds
Crossing; mains £6-9; ✆ bar 11am-late, restaurant 9am-
5pm Mon-Sat, to 4.30pm Sun) The downstairs bar-
restaurant at this outdoor equipment shop
is a mountaineering extravaganza, festooned
with climbing memorabilia and portraits of
celebrity climbers. Chicken, fish and steak
dominate the menu, but there are several
veggie dishes, too. The bar tempts walkers
and climbers in with locally brewed real ales
and, on the second Saturday of each month,
free blues, folk and jazz performances.

For takeaway grub, try the **Indian Garden**
(☎ 705011; 88 High St; mains £5-8) for curries, or
the **Highland Star** (☎ 703905; 155 High St; mains
£5-8) for Chinese food.

Morrisons Supermarket (An Aird; ✆ 8.30am-8pm
Mon-Wed, to 9pm Thu & Fri, 8am-8pm Sat, 9am-6pm Sun)
Self-caterers can stock up at this supermar-
ket, next to the train station.

Ben Nevis Bar (☎ 702295; 105 High St) The Ben
Nevis, whose lounge bar enjoys a good
view over the loch, exudes a relaxed, jovial
atmosphere where climbers and tourists
can work off leftover energy jigging to live
music (several nights a week) or belting out
their karaoke favourites (Tuesday).

Getting There & Away

Fort William lies 146 miles from Edinburgh,
104 miles from Glasgow and 66 miles from
Inverness.

BUS

Direct buses are available with **Scottish Citylink** (☎ 0870 550 5050) to Glasgow (£14, three
hours, four daily), Edinburgh (£20, four
hours, one daily) – both via Glencoe and
Crianlarich – Oban (£8.20, 1½ hours, four
daily), Inverness (£8.90, two hours, five
daily) and Portree on the Isle of Skye (£17,
three hours, three daily).

Shiel Buses (☎ 01967-431272) runs one bus
daily, except Sunday, to/from Mallaig (£4.50,
1¼ hours) via Glenfinnan (35 minutes).

Rapsons/Highland Country (☎ 702373) runs
buses to Kinlochleven (£3.30, 50 minutes,
six daily) via Inchree, Onich, Ballachulish
and Glencoe.

See also p298 for details of the minibus
service between Oban and Fort William.

CAR

The TIC has a leaflet listing car-hire companies. **Easydrive Car Hire** (☎ 701616; www.easy
drivescotland.co.uk; Unit 36a, Ben Nevis Industrial Estate,
Ben Nevis Dr) has small cars from £32/180 a
day/week, including tax and unlimited
mileage.

TRAIN

The spectacular West Highland line runs
from Glasgow to Mallaig via Fort William.
There are two or three trains daily from
Glasgow to Fort William (£23, 3¾ hours),
and four or five daily between Fort William
and Mallaig (£8.10, 1½ hours). Travelling
from Edinburgh (£34, five hours), you have
to change at Glasgow's Queen St station.

There's no direct rail connection between Oban and Fort William – you have
to change at Crianlarich, so it's faster to
use the bus.

The overnight Caledonian Sleeper service connects Fort William and London
Euston (£73 seated, £119 sharing a twin-
berth cabin, 13 hours).

Getting Around

From late May to late September **Rapsons/
Highland Country** (☎ 702373) bus 42 runs from
the bus station up Glen Nevis to the Glen
Nevis Youth Hostel (£1.40, 10 minutes,
every 80 minutes Monday to Saturday, four
daily Sunday) and on to the Lower Falls
(20 minutes).

There's a **taxi rank** (☎ 702545, 773030) on the
corner of High St and The Parade.

Off-Beat Bikes (☎ 704008; 117 High St; ⏰ 9am-5.30pm) rents out mountain bikes for £15/10 for a day/half-day.

AROUND FORT WILLIAM
Glen Nevis
☎ 01397

You can walk the 3 miles from Fort William to scenic Glen Nevis in about an hour or so. The **Glen Nevis Visitor Centre** (☎ 705922; ⏰ 9am-5pm Easter–mid-Oct) is situated a mile up the glen, and provides information on walking as well as specific advice on climbing Ben Nevis.

From the car park at the far end of the road along Glen Nevis, there is an excellent walk (1.5 miles) through the spectacular Nevis Gorge to **Steall Meadows**, a verdant valley dominated by a 100m-high bridal-veil waterfall. You can reach the foot of the falls by crossing the river on a wobbly, three-cable wire bridge – one cable for your feet and one for each hand – a real test of balance!

SLEEPING & EATING

Glen Nevis Youth Hostel (SYHA; ☎ 0870 004 1120; Glen Nevis; dm £14; ▣) Large, impersonal and reminiscent of a school camp, this hostel is 3 miles from Fort William, beside one of the starting points for the tourist track up Ben Nevis.

Ben Nevis Inn (☎ 702240; www.ben-nevis-inn.co.uk; Achintee; dm £11-12; P ▣) A good alternative to the youth hostel is this great barn of a pub (bar meals available), with a comfy 20-bed hostel downstairs. It's at the Achintee start of the path up Ben Nevis, and only a mile from the end of the West Highland Way.

Achintee Farm (☎ 702240; www.achinteefarm.com; Achintee; dm £11-13, r per person £30; ✗) This attractive farmhouse not only offers B&B but also has a small bunkhouse attached. It's just 100m from the Ben Nevis Inn, and ideally positioned for climbing Ben Nevis.

Glen Nevis Caravan & Camping Park (☎ 702191; www.glen-nevis.co.uk; tent £5.70, tent & car £8.60, campervan £9, plus per person £2.50; ⏰ Mar-Oct) This

---

CLIMBING BEN NEVIS

As the highest peak in the British Isles, Ben Nevis (1344m) attracts many would-be ascensionists who would not normally think of climbing a Scottish mountain – a staggering (often literally) 100,000 people reach the summit each year.

Although anyone who is reasonably fit should have no problem climbing Ben Nevis on a fine summer's day, an ascent should not be undertaken lightly. Every year people have to be rescued from the mountain. You will need proper walking boots (the path is rough and stony, and there may be soft, wet snowfields on the summit), warm clothing, waterproofs, a map and compass, and plenty of food and water.

Here are a few facts to mull over before you go racing up the tourist track: the summit plateau is bounded by 700m-high cliffs and has a sub-Arctic climate; at the summit it can snow on any day of the year; the summit is wrapped in cloud nine days out of 10; in thick cloud, visibility at the summit can be 10m or less; and in such conditions the only safe way off the mountain requires careful use of a map and compass to avoid walking over those 700m cliffs.

The tourist track (the easiest route to the top) was originally called the Pony Track. It was built in the 19th century for the pack ponies that carried supplies to a meteorological observatory on the summit (now in ruins) that was manned continuously from 1883 to 1904.

There are three possible starting points for the tourist track ascent – Achintee Farm; the footbridge at Glen Nevis Youth Hostel; and, if you have a car, the car park at Glen Nevis Visitor Centre. The path climbs gradually to the shoulder at Lochan Meall an t-Suidhe (known as the Halfway Lochan), then zigzags steeply up beside the Red Burn to the summit plateau. The highest point is marked by a trig point on top of a huge cairn beside the ruins of the old observatory; the plateau is scattered with countless smaller cairns, stones arranged in the shape of people's names and, sadly, a fair bit of litter.

The total distance to the summit and back is 8 miles; allow four or five hours to reach the top, and another 2½ to three hours for the descent. Afterwards, as you celebrate in the pub with a pint, consider the fact that the record time for the annual Ben Nevis Hill Race is just under 1½ hours – up and down. Then have another pint.

big, well-equipped site is a popular base camp for Ben Nevis and the surrounding mountains.

GETTING THERE & AWAY
From June to September Rapsons/Highland Country bus 42 runs from Fort William bus station to Glen Nevis Youth Hostel (10 minutes, 11 a day Monday to Saturday, four Sunday) and continues to the Lower Falls (3 miles beyond the hostel).

Nevis Range
The **Nevis Range ski area** (☎ 01397-705825; www .nevisrange.com), 6 miles north of Fort William, spreads across the northern slopes of Aonach Mor (1221m). The gondola that gives access to the bottom of the ski area at 655m operates year-round from 10am to 5pm; a return trip costs £8/4.90 for an adult/child (15 minutes each way). At the top there's a restaurant and a couple of walking routes through nearby **Leanachan Forest**. During the ski season a one-day lift pass costs £23/13.50 per adult/child; a one-day package, including equipment hire, lift pass and four hours' instruction, costs £39.

A competition-class **downhill mountain bike trail** (☼ 11am-3pm mid-May–mid-Sep) – for experienced riders only – runs from the Snowgoose restaurant to the base station; bikes are carried on a rack on the gondola cabin. A single trip with your own bike costs £10; including bike hire it's £26. There are also 25 miles of waymarked mountain-bike trails in the nearby forest.

Rapsons/Highland Country buses run from Fort William's bus station to Nevis Range (15 minutes, three or four a day).

Corpach to Loch Lochy
Corpach lies at the southern entrance to the Caledonian Canal, 3 miles north of Fort William. There's a classic picture-postcard view of Ben Nevis from the mouth of the canal. Nearby is the award-winning **Treasures of the Earth** (☎ 01397-772283; Corpach; adult/child £3.50/3; ☼ 9.30am-7pm Jul-Sep, 10am-5pm Oct-Dec & Feb-Jun) exhibition, a rainy-day diversion, with a great collection of gemstones, minerals, fossils and other geological curiosities.

A mile east of Corpach, at Banavie, is **Neptune's Staircase**, an impressive flight of eight locks that allows boats to climb 20m to the main reach of the Caledonian Canal.

The B8004 road runs along the west side of the canal to Gairlochy at the south end of Loch Lochy, offering superb views of Ben Nevis; the canal towpath on the east side makes a great walk or bike ride (6.5 miles).

From Gairlochy the B8005 continues along the west side of Loch Lochy to Achnacarry and the **Clan Cameron Museum** (☎ 01397-712480; adult/child £3/free; ☼ 11am-5pm Jul & Aug, 1.30-5pm Easter-Jun & Sep–mid-Oct), which records the history of the clan and its involvement with the Jacobite rebellions, including items of clothing that once belonged to Bonnie Prince Charlie.

From Achnacarry the Great Glen Way and Great Glen Mountain Bike Trail (p322) continue along the roadless western shore of Loch Lochy, and a dead-end minor road leads west along lovely **Loch Arkaig**.

Glen Spean & Glen Roy
Near Spean Bridge, at the junction of the B8004 and A82, 2.5 miles east of Gairlochy stands the **Commando Memorial**, which commemorates the WWII special forces soldiers who trained in this area.

Four miles further east, at Roy Bridge, a minor road leads north up Glen Roy, which is noted for its intriguing, so-called **parallel roads**. These prominent horizontal terraces contouring around the hill-side are actually ancient shorelines formed during the last Ice Age by the waters of an ice-dammed glacial lake. The best viewpoint is 3 miles up Glen Roy.

ARDGOUR & ARDNAMURCHAN
The drive from **Corran Ferry**, 8 miles south of Fort William, to Ardnamurchan Point, the most westerly place on the British mainland, is one of the most beautiful in the western Highlands, especially in late spring and early summer when much of the narrow, twisting road is lined with the bright pink and purple blooms of rhododendrons. A car ferry (car £5.20, passenger free, 10 minutes, two an hour) crosses to Ardgour at Corran Ferry.

The road clings to the northern shore of Loch Sunart, going through the pretty villages of **Strontian** – which gave its name to the element strontium, first discovered in ore from nearby lead mines in 1790 – and **Salen**.

The mostly single-track road from Salen to Ardnamurchan Point is only 25 miles long, but it'll take you 1½ hours each way.

CENTRAL & WESTERN HIGHLANDS

It's a dipping, twisting, low-speed roller coaster of a ride through sun-dappled native woodlands draped with lichen and fern. Just when you're getting used to the views of Morvern and Mull to the south, it makes a quick detour to the north for a panorama over the islands of Rum and Eigg.

Sights

Midway between Salen and Kilchoan is the fascinating **Ardnamurchan Natural History Centre** (☎ 01972-500209; Glenmore; adult/child £3/2; ☺ 10.30am-5.30pm Mon-Sat, noon-5.30pm Sun Easter-Oct). Devised by local photographer Michael MacGregor, it brings you face to face with the flora and fauna of the Ardnamurchan peninsula – the Living Building is designed to attract local wildlife, and you'll have the opportunity to see pine marten, red deer and local bird life.

The scattered crofting village of **Kilchoan**, the only village of any size west of Salen, is best known for the scenic ruins of 13th-century **Mingary Castle**. The village has a **TIC** (☎ 01972-510222; Pier Rd; ☺ Easter-Oct), a shop and a hotel.

The final 6 miles of road ends at the 36m-high, grey granite tower of **Ardnamurchan Lighthouse**, built in 1849 by the Stevensons to guard the westernmost point of the British mainland. The **Kingdom of Light Visitor Centre** (☎ 01972-510210; adult/child £2.50/1.50; ☺ 10am-5pm Apr-Oct), by Kilchoan, will tell you more than you'll ever need to know about lighthouses, with lots of hands-on stuff for kids; the guided tour (£5) includes a trip to the top of the lighthouse. But the main attraction here is the expansive view over the ocean – this is a superb sunset viewpoint, provided you don't mind driving back in the dark.

Sleeping & Eating

Salen Hotel (☎ 01967-431661; www.salenhotel.co.uk; Salen; r per person from £25; ℙ) A traditional Highland pub with views over Loch Sunart, the newly renovated Salen Hotel has three rooms upstairs in the pub and another three rooms (each with en suite) in a modern chalet out the back. The cosy lounge has a roaring fire and comfy sofa, and the bar meals, including seafood, venison and other game dishes, are very good.

Inn at Ardgour (☎ 01855-841225; www.ardgour.biz; Ardgour; s £45-65, d £70-110, mains £7-12; ℙ ✕) This pretty, whitewashed coaching inn, draped in colourful flower baskets, makes a great place for a lunch or dinner stop. The restaurant is set in the row of cottages once occupied by the Corran ferrymen, and serves traditional, homemade Scottish dishes.

You can camp at **Resipole Caravan Park** (☎ 01967-431235; www.resipole.co.uk; Resipole; tent sites £7.50, with car £12). Alternatively, the **Kilchoan House Hotel** (☎ 01972-510200; www.kilchoanhouse hotel.co.uk; Kilchoan; d £60, tent sites per person £2.50; ☺ Mar-Oct; ℙ) will let you pitch a tent in its garden; ask at the bar first.

Getting There & Away

The bus company **Shiel Buses** (☎ 01967-431272) runs between Fort William and Kilchoan (one daily Monday to Saturday). For details of ferries between Kilchoan and Tobermory, see p302.

SALEN TO LOCHAILORT

The A861 road from Salen to Lochailort passes through the low, wooded hills of Moidart. A minor road (signposted Dorlin) leads west from the A861 at Shiel Bridge to a picnic area looking across to the picturesque roofless ruin of 13th-century **Castle Tioram** (admission free; ☺ 24hr). The castle sits on a tiny island in Loch Moidart, connected to the mainland by a narrow strand that is submerged at high tide (the castle's name, pronounced *chee*-ram, means 'dry'). It was the ancient seat of the Clanranald Macdonalds, but the Clanranald chief ordered it to be burned (to prevent it falling into the hands of Hanoverian troops) when he set off to fight for the Jacobite side in the 1715 rebellion. At the time of research it was closed to the public while the owner and Historic Scotland wrangled over plans for its future.

As the A861 curls around the north shore of Loch Moidart you will see a line of five huge beech trees between the road and the shore. Known as the **Seven Men of Moidart** (two have been blown down by gales and replaced with saplings), they were planted in the late 18th century to commemorate the seven local men who accompanied Bonnie Prince Charlie from France and acted as his bodyguards at the start of the 1745 rebellion.

Shiel Buses (☎ 01967-431272) has a service from Fort William to Acharacle via Lochailort.

ROAD TO THE ISLES

The 46-mile A830 from Fort William to Mallaig is traditionally known as the Road to the Isles, as it leads to the jumping-off point for ferries to the Small Isles and Skye. This is a region steeped in Jacobite history, having witnessed both the beginning and the end of Bonnie Prince Charlie's doomed attempt to regain the British throne.

The final section of this scenic route, between Arisaig and Mallaig, has recently been upgraded to a fast straight road. Unless you're in a hurry, opt for the old coastal road (signposted Alternative Coastal Route).

Between the A830 and the A87 far to the north lies Scotland's 'Empty Quarter', a rugged landscape of wild mountains and lonely sea lochs roughly 20 miles by 30 miles in size, mostly uninhabited and penetrated only by two minor roads (along Lochs Arkaig and Quoich). If you want to get away from it all, this is the place to go.

Glenfinnan

☎ 01397 / pop 100

Glenfinnan is hallowed ground for fans of Bonnie Prince Charlie, and its central shrine is the **Glenfinnan Monument**. This tall column, topped by a statue of a kilted Highlander, was erected in 1815 on the spot where the Young Pretender first raised his standard and rallied the clans on 19 August 1745, marking the start of the ill-fated campaign that would end in disaster 14 months later. The setting, at the north end of Loch Shiel, is hauntingly beautiful.

The nearby **Glenfinnan Visitor Centre** (☎ 722 250; adult/child £3/2; ☿ 9.30am-5.30pm Jul & Aug, 10am-5pm Easter-Jun, Sep & Oct, 10am-4pm Sat & Sun Nov; ☁) recounts the story of the '45, as the Jacobite rebellion of 1745 is known, when the prince's loyal clansmen marched and fought from Glenfinnan south to Derby, then back north to final defeat at Culloden.

A half-mile west of the visitor centre is **Glenfinnan Station Museum** (☎ 722295; adult/child £1/50p; ☿ 9.30am-4.30pm Jun-Sep), a shrine of a different kind whose object of veneration is the great days of steam on the West Highland line. The famous 21-arch **Glenfinnan Viaduct**, just east of the station, was built in 1901, and featured in the movie *Harry Potter & the Chamber of Secrets*. A pleasant walk of around 0.75 miles leads to a viewpoint for the viaduct and the loch.

The **Glenfinnan Highland Games** (☎ 722324) are held on the Saturday nearest to 19 August.

Two converted railway carriages at Glenfinnan Station house the 10-berth **Sleeping Car Bunkhouse** (☎ 722295; dm £8-10) and the atmospheric **Dining Car** (☎ 722295; snacks £1-4; ☿ 9.30am-5pm), which serves home-baked cakes and pots of tea with superb views along Loch Shiel.

Prince's House Hotel (☎ 722246; www.glenfinnan .co.uk; s £40-50, d £70-90; ℗ ☒) is a delightful old coaching inn from 1658; it's a good place to pamper yourself – ask for the tartan-clad, spacious Stuart Room if you want to stay in the oldest part of the hotel. There's no documentary evidence that Bonnie Prince Charlie stayed here in 1745, but it was the only sizable house in Glenfinnan at that time, so…

Arisaig & Morar

☎ 01687

The 5 miles of coast between Arisaig and Morar is a fretwork of rocky islets, inlets and gorgeous silver-sand beaches backed by dunes and machair, with stunning sunset views across the sea to the silhouetted peaks of Eigg and Rum. The **Silver Sands of Morar**, as they are known, draw crowds of bucket-and-spade holidaymakers in July and August, when the many camping grounds scattered along the coast are filled to over-flowing.

Fans of the movie *Local Hero* still make pilgrimages to **Camusdarach Beach**, just south of Morar, which starred in the film as Ben's beach. To find it, look for the car park 800m north of Camusdarach camp site; from here, a wooden footbridge and a 400m walk through the dunes lead to the beach.

Loch nan Uamh (pronounced loch nan oo-ah, meaning the loch of the caves) washes the southern shores of Arisaig; this was where Bonnie Prince Charlie first set foot on the Scottish mainland on 11 August 1745, on the shingle beach at the mouth of the Borrodale burn. Just 2 miles to the east of this bay, on a rocky point near a parking area, the **Prince's Cairn** marks the spot where he finally departed Scottish soil, never to return, on 19 September 1746.

SLEEPING & EATING

There are at least half a dozen camping grounds between Arisaig and Morar; all are open in summer only, and are often full in July and August, so book ahead.

Old Library Lodge & Restaurant (☎ 450651; www.oldlibrary.co.uk; Arisaig; r per person £35-45, 3-course dinner £24; ☒ 11.30am-2.30pm Wed-Mon, 6.30-9.30pm daily) The Old Library is a charming restaurant with rooms set in converted 200-year-old stables overlooking the waterfront in Arisaig village. The lunch menu concentrates on soups and freshly made sandwiches, while dinner is a more sophisticated affair offering local seafood and lamb.

Garramore House (☎ 450268; garramorehouse@aol.com; South Morar; r per person £20-28, mains £9-12; ℗) Built as a hunting lodge in 1840, it served as a Special Operations Executive HQ during WWII. Today it's a wonderfully atmospheric, child- and pet-friendly guesthouse and restaurant set in lovely woodland gardens with great views to the Small Isles and Skye.

Camusdarach Campsite (☎ 450221; www.camusdarach.com; South Morar; camp sites £8-13; ☒ Mar-Oct) A small and beautiful site with good facilities, only three minutes' walk from the *Local Hero* beach.

Mallaig
☎ 01687 / pop 800

If you're travelling between Fort William and Skye you may find yourself overnighting in the bustling fishing and ferry port of Mallaig. Indeed, it makes a good base for a series of day trips by ferry to the Small Isles and Knoydart. There's a **TIC** (☎ 462170; ☒ 10am-4pm Mon-Fri, 10.15am-3.45pm Sat, 1.45-3.45pm Sun; ☐) with Internet access, a post office, a bank with ATM and a **Co-op supermarket** (☒ 8am-10pm).

The village's rainy-day attractions consist of **Mallaig Marine World** (☎ 462292; The Harbour; adult/child £3/1.50; ☒ 9am-7pm Mon-Sat, 11am-6pm Sun Jul & Aug, 9am-6pm Mon-Sat, 11am-6pm Sun Mar-Jun, Sep & Oct, 9am-6pm Mon-Sat Nov-Feb), a child-friendly aquarium with touch-pools and hands-on exhibits, and **Mallaig Heritage Centre** (☎ 462085; Station Rd; adult/child £1.80/free; ☒ 11am-4pm Mon-Sat, 12.30-4.30pm Sun), which covers the archaeology and history of the region, including the heart-rending tale of the Highland Clearances in Knoydart.

The **MV Grimsay Isle** (☎ 462652) provides entertaining, customised sea-fishing trips and seal-watching tours, while the **Brightwater** (☎ 07747 034767; www.seaotter.co.uk) offers high-speed boat trips to Skye, the Small Isles and Mull.

SLEEPING & EATING
Sheena's Backpacker's Lodge (☎ 462764; Harbour View; dm £13, mains £2-6; ☒) Sheena's is a friendly, 12-bed hostel in a lovely old house overlooking the harbour. On a sunny day the hostel's garden terrace café, with its flowers, greenery and cosmopolitan backpacker staff, feels more like the Med than Mallaig. The speciality of the house is a pint-glass full of Mallaig prawns with dipping sauce (£8.50).

Moorings Guest House (☎ 462225; mooringsguesthouse@talk21.com; East Bay; s/d £25/44; ☒) Just beyond the tourist office, this four-bedroom B&B has grand views over the harbour, not only from the upstairs bedrooms but also from the conservatory-style breakfast room, which doubles as a tearoom open to the public from Easter to September.

Springbank Guest House (☎ 462459; www.springbank-mallaig.co.uk; East Bay; r per person £19; ℗) A little further around the bay, the Springbank is a traditional West Highland house with seven homely guest bedrooms, again with superb views across the harbour to the Cuillin of Skye.

Fish Market (☎ 462299; Station Rd; mains £9-16; ☒ 11.45am-2.45pm & 6-9pm) There are at least half a dozen signs in Mallaig advertising 'seafood restaurant', but this bright, modern bistro-style place right next to the harbour is our favourite, serving simply prepared scallops, langoustines, lobster, sole and salmon, as well as the most delicious *Cullen skink* (soup made with smoked haddock, potato, onion and milk) on the west coast.

GETTING THERE & AWAY
There are services with **Shiel Buses** (☎ 01967-431272) and Scottish Citylink coaches from Fort William to Mallaig (£4.20, 1¼ hours, one a day Monday to Friday) via Glenfinnan (35 minutes), Arisaig and Morar. See also Getting There & Away (p298) for details of the summer minibus service linking Mallaig, Fort William and Oban.

The beautiful West Highland railway links Mallaig to Fort William (£8.10, 1½ hours) and Glasgow (£23, 5¼ hours, four a day Monday to Saturday, two Sunday). In summer vintage steam trains (p337) operate between Fort William and Mallaig.

Ferries run from Mallaig to the Small Isles (right), the Isle of Skye (p373) and Knoydart (below).

KNOYDART PENINSULA

☎ 01687 / pop 70

The Knoydart Peninsula is the only sizable area in Britain that remains inaccessible to the motor car, cut off by miles of rough country and the embracing arms of Lochs Nevis and Hourn – Gaelic for the lochs of Heaven and Hell. No road penetrates this wilderness of rugged hills – **Inverie**, its sole village, can only be reached by ferry from Mallaig, or on foot from the remote road-end at Kinloch Hourn (a tough 16-mile hike).

The main reasons for visiting are to climb the remote 1020m peak of **Ladhar Bheinn** (pronounced *laar*-ven), which affords some of the west coast's finest views, or just to enjoy the feeling of being cut off from the rest of the world. There are no shops, no TV and no mobile phone reception.

There are a couple of walkers' bunkhouses near Inverie, including the recently renovated **Knoydart Foundation Bunkhouse** (☎ 462242; info@knoydart.org; Inverie; dm £10), 15 minutes' walk east of the ferry pier, and the atmospheric **Torrie Shieling** (☎ 462669; torrie@knoydart.org; Inverie; dm £15), a 20-minute walk to the west.

The very basic **Barrisdale Bothy** (☎ 01764-684946; www.barisdale.com; Barrisdale; dm £3, tent sites per person £1), 6 miles west of Kinloch Hourn on the footpath to Inverie, has sleeping platforms without mattresses – you'll need your own sleeping bag and foam mat.

The **Pier House** (☎ 462347; www.thepierhouse knoydart.co.uk; Inverie; r per person £30; ✉) is the first place you'll see when you walk off the ferry. A guesthouse and restaurant, it offers B&B in its four homely bedrooms, and is famous for its superb seafood, venison and vegetarian dishes.

The neighbouring **Old Forge** (☎ 462267; Inverie) is listed in the *Guinness Book of Records* as Britain's most remote pub. It's very sophisticated – as well as having real ale on tap, there's an Italian coffee machine for those wilderness lattes and cappuccinos, and the house special is a platter of langoustines with aïoli dipping sauce. In the evening you can sit by the fire, pint of beer in hand and join the impromptu *ceilidh* that seems to take place just about nightly.

Getting There & Away

A Royal Mail postbus runs from Invergarry post office (on the A82, halfway along the Great Glen) to Kinloch Hourn (two hours, one a day Monday, Wednesday and Friday), departing at 11.55am.

A passenger ferry operated by **Bruce Watt Cruises** (☎ 462320; www.knoydart-ferry.co.uk) links Mallaig to Inverie (£8/10 single/return, 45 minutes, two a day) daily from mid-May to mid-September, on Monday, Wednesday and Friday only the rest of the year. Taking the morning boat gives you four hours ashore in Knoydart.

SMALL ISLES

The scattered jewels of the Small Isles – Rum, Eigg, Muck and Canna – lie strewn across the silvery-blue cloth of the Cuillin Sound to the south of the Isle of Skye. Their distinctive outlines enliven the glorious views from the beaches of Arisaig and Morar.

Rum is the biggest and boldest of the four, a miniature Skye of pointed peaks and dramatic sunset silhouettes. Eigg is the most pastoral and populous, dominated by the miniature sugarloaf mountain of the Sgurr. Muck is a botanist's delight with its wildflowers and unusual alpine plants, and Canna is a craggy bird sanctuary made of magnetic rocks.

If your time is limited and you can only visit one island, choose Eigg; it has the most to offer on a day trip.

Getting There & Away

The main ferry operator is **CalMac** (☎ 01687-462403; www.calmac.co.uk), which operates the passenger-only ferry from Mallaig to Eigg (£9.45 return, 1¼ hours, five a week), Muck (£14.50 return, 1½ hours, four a week), Rum (£14 return, 1¼ hours, five a week) and Canna (£17.60 return, two hours, four a week). You can also hop between the islands without returning to Mallaig, but the timetable is complicated and it requires a bit of planning – you would need at least five days to visit all four. A bicycle costs £2 extra on all routes.

From May to September **Arisaig Marine** (☎ 01687-450224; www.arisaig.co.uk) operates day cruises from Arisaig harbour to Eigg (£15 return, one hour, six a week), Rum (£20 return, 2½ hours, two or three a week) and Muck (£16 return, two hours, three a week). The trips include whale-watching, with up to an hour for close viewing. Sailing times allow four or five hours ashore on Eigg, two hours on Muck or Rum.

ISLE OF RUM
☎ 01687 / pop 30

The Isle of Rum – the biggest and most spectacular of the Small Isles – was once known as the Forbidden Island. Cleared of its crofters in the early 19th century to make way for sheep, from 1888 to 1957 it was the private sporting estate of the Bulloughs, a nouveau riche Lancashire family whose fortune was made in the textile industry. Curious outsiders who ventured too close to the island were liable to find themselves staring down the wrong end of a gamekeeper's shotgun.

The island was sold to the Nature Conservancy in 1957. Since then it has been a reserve noted for its deer, wild goats, ponies, golden and white-tailed sea eagles, and a 120,000-strong nesting colony of Manx shearwaters. Its dramatic, rocky mountains – known as the Rum Cuillin for their similarity to the peaks on neighbouring Skye – draw hill walkers and climbers.

Kinloch, where the ferry lands, is the island's only settlement; it has a small grocery shop, post office and public telephone. There's a tearoom in the village hall, which is open for day-trippers. The hall itself is open at all times for people to shelter from the rain (or the midges!).

Sights & Activities
When George Bullough – a dashing, Harrow-educated cavalry officer – inherited Rum along with half his father's fortune in 1891, he became one of the wealthiest bachelors in Britain. He blew half his inheritance on building his dream bachelor pad – the ostentatious **Kinloch Castle** (☎ 462037; adult/child £3/1.50; ☒ guided tours only, to coincide with ferry times). He shipped in pink sandstone from Dumfriesshire and 250,000 tonnes of Ayrshire topsoil for the gardens, and paid his workers a shilling extra a day to wear tweed kilts – just so they'd look more picturesque. He kept hummingbirds in the greenhouses and alligators in the garden, and entertained

guests with an orchestrion, the Edwardian equivalent of a Bose hi-fi system. Since the Bulloughs left, the castle has survived as a perfect time capsule of upper-class Edwardian eccentricity. The guided tour should not be missed.

The only part of the island that still belongs to the Bullough family is the **Bullough Mausoleum** in Glen Harris, a miniature Greek temple that wouldn't look out of place on the Acropolis; Lady Bullough was laid to rest here alongside her husband and father-in-law in 1967, having died at the age of 98.

There's some great coastal and mountain walking on the island, including a couple of easy, waymarked **nature trails** in the woods around Kinloch. Glen Harris is a 10-mile round trip from Kinloch, on a rough 4WD track – allow four to five hours' walking. The climb to the island's highest point, **Askival** (812m), is a strenuous hike and involves a bit of rock scrambling (allow six hours for the round trip from Kinloch).

Sleeping & Eating
Accommodation on Rum is strictly limited, and if you want to stay overnight on the island, you have to contact the **reserve office** (☎ 462026) in advance.

Kinloch Campsite (tent sites per person £3) Near the castle, this is the only place on the island where camping is allowed. The only facilities are toilets and a water supply, and there's not much in the way of level ground! Book in advance with the reserve office.

Kinloch Castle (☎ 462037; dm/d £13/60) The castle has 45 hostel beds and four double bedrooms in its rear wing. There's also a small restaurant offering breakfast (£3 to £6) and dinner (£12) to guests and nonguests alike.

ISLE OF EIGG
☎ 01687 / pop 70

The Isle of Eigg made history in 1997 when it became the first Highland estate to be bought out by its inhabitants. The island is now owned and managed by the **Isle of Eigg Heritage Trust** (www.isleofeigg.org), a partnership among the islanders, Highland Council and the Scottish Wildlife Trust.

The ferry landing is at Galmisdale in the south. **An Laimhrig** (☎ 482416), the building above the pier, houses a post office, grocery store, craft shop and tearoom. You can hire bikes here, too.

Activities

The island takes its name from the Old Norse *egg* (edge), a reference to the **Sgurr of Eigg** (393m), an impressive mini-mountain that towers over Galmisdale. Ringed by vertical cliffs on three sides, it's composed of pitchstone lava with columnar jointing similar to that seen on the Isle of Staffa and at the Giant's Causeway in Northern Ireland.

The climb to the summit (4.5 miles round trip; allow three to four hours) begins on the stony road leading up from the pier, which continues uphill through the woods to a red-roofed cottage. Go through the gate to the right of the cottage and turn left; just 20m along the road a cairn on the right marks the start of a boggy footpath that leads over the eastern shoulder of the Sgurr, then traverses beneath the northern cliffs until it makes its way up onto the summit ridge.

On a fine day the views from the top are magnificent – Rum and Skye to the north, Muck and Coll to the south, Ardnamurchan Lighthouse to the southeast and Ben Nevis shouldering above the eastern horizon. Take binoculars – on a calm summer's day there's a good chance of seeing minke whales feeding down below in the Sound of Muck.

A shorter walk (2 miles; allow 1½ hours round trip, and bring a torch) leads west from the pier to the spooky and claustrophobic **Uamh Fraing** (Massacre Cave). Start as for the Sgurr of Eigg, but 800m from the pier turn left through a gate and into a field. Follow the 4WD track and fork left before a white cottage to pass below it. A footpath continues across the fields to reach a small gate in a fence; go through it and descend a ridge towards the shore.

The cave entrance is tucked inconspicuously down to the left of the ridge. The entrance is tiny – almost a hands-and-knees job – but the cave opens out inside and runs a long way back. Go right to the back, turn off your torch, and imagine the cave packed shoulder to shoulder with terrified men, women and children. Then imagine the panic as your enemies start piling firewood into the entrance. Almost the entire population of Eigg – around 400 people – sought refuge in this cave when the MacLeods of Skye raided the island in 1577. In an act of inhuman cruelty, the raiders lit a fire in the narrow entrance and everyone inside died of asphyxiation. There are more than a few ghosts floating around in here.

Other good walks are to the deserted crofts of **Grulin** on the southwest coast (5 miles, two hours round trip), and north to Laig Beach with its famous **singing sands** – the sand makes a squeaking noise when you walk on it (8 miles, three hours return). You can get more information on island walks from the craft shop in An Laimhrig.

Sleeping & Eating

All accommodation should be booked in advance. For a full listing of self-catering accommodation, see www.iselofeigg.org.

Glebe Barn (☎ 482417; www.glebebarn.co.uk; Galmisdale; dm/tw £12/26) The Glebe has excellent bunkhouse accommodation – a smart, maple-floored lounge with central fireplace, modern kitchen, laundry, drying room, and bright, clean dorms and bedrooms.

Sandavore Bothy (☎ 482480; Sandavore; per night/ week £25/150) This tiny, one-room bothy, a 15-minute walk from the pier, has space for four people in one double bed and two bunk beds. It's a real Hebridean experience – accessible only on foot, no electricity (just gaslight and candles), cold running water only and outside toilet.

An Laimhrig (☎ 482416; www.isleofeigg.org; Galmisdale) There's a good café here. The neighbouring craft shop takes fees for camping near the head of the bay at Galmisdale (£3 a tent); you use the showers and toilets at the pier.

You can also camp at **Sue Holland's Croft** (☎ 482480; sueholonds@talk21.com; per tent £4) at Cleadale in the north of the island.

ISLE OF MUCK

☎ 01687 / pop 30

The tiny island of Muck, measuring just 2 miles by 1 mile, has exceptionally fertile soil, and the island is carpeted with wildflowers in spring and early summer. It takes its name from the Gaelic *muc* (pig), and pigs are still raised there.

Ferries call at the southern settlement of **Port Mor**. There's a tearoom and craft shop above the pier, which also acts as an information centre.

CENTRAL & WESTERN
HIGHLANDS

It's an easy 15-minute walk along the island's only road from the pier to the sandy beach at **Gallanach** on the northern side of the island. A longer and rougher hike (1½ hours round trip) goes to the top of **Beinn Airein** (137m) for the best views. Puffins nest on the cliffs at the western end of Camas Mor, the bay to the south of the hill. On Wednesday in summer you can take a **guided tour** (£1) around the island by tractor and trailer; it departs at 1.30pm.

The cosy six-bed **Isle of Muck Bunkhouse** (☎ 462042; dm £11.50), with its oil-fired Rayburn stove, is just above the pier, as is the welcoming eight-room **Port Mhor Guesthouse** (☎ 462365; r per person £35); the evening meals are available to nonguests (£15, book in advance).

You can camp on the island for free – ask at the craft shop first.

ISLE OF CANNA
☎ 01687 / pop 16

The roadless island of Canna is a moorland plateau of black basalt rock, just 5 miles long and 1.25 miles wide. **Compass Hill** (143m), at the northeastern corner, contains enough magnetite (an iron oxide mineral) to deflect the magnetic compasses in passing yachts.

The ferry arrives at the hamlet of **A'Chill** at the eastern end of the island, where tourists have left extensive graffiti on the rock face south of the harbour. There's a tearoom and craft shop by the harbour, and a tiny post office in a hut.

You can walk to **An Coroghon**, just east of the ferry pier, a medieval stone tower perched atop a sea cliff, and continue to Compass Hill, or take a longer hike along the southern shore past a **Celtic cross** and the remains of the 7th-century **St Columba's Chapel**.

The island is owned by the National Trust for Scotland (NTS) and there are no hotels or B&Bs. Contact the **warden** (☎ 462466) for permission to camp, or write to the Holidays Secretary, NTS, Wemyss House, 28 Charlotte Sq, Edinburgh EH2 4ET for self-catering accommodation details.

Northern Highlands & Islands

The northern Highlands epitomises most visitors' romantic notion of Scotland. Vast, wild expanses punctuated by sparkling, steely blue lochs, and towering mountain ranges veined with snow, their summits often lost in swirling cloud and mist. This is powerful country, and you can almost feel the desolation and tragedy of the Clearances – the silence can be deafening. But the romanticism of the region is inescapable too, and if you've ever heard the call of the wild, you're likely to be mesmerised here. There's something unique and Scottish in all of this – it's the ethereal light that squeezes through the clouds and tangos over Europe's northern fringe, illuminating its rugged splendour and changing its appearance by the hour, or even by the minute.

The stunning scenery extends offshore to the Isle of Skye, where the jagged peaks of the Cuillin Hills tear at the mist, and the ghosts of Bonnie Prince Charlie and Flora MacDonald haunt the hallways of Dunvegan Castle. Skye is a paradise for walkers, climbers and wildlife enthusiasts, with its dramatic mountains, lonely lochs and scenic coastlines, home to golden eagles, peregrine falcons, otters, deer and seals.

And that magical light intensifies as you head west to the Outer Hebrides with their harsh landscapes of peat bog, lochans (small lochs) and bare, glaciated gneiss, the terrain softened by glittering shell-sand beaches, wildflower-strewn dunes, and buttercup meadows where the outlines of ruined crofts settle into the turf like fossilised shells in a slab of rock. This necklace of remote islands is a last bastion of Gaelic culture, where the hardships of life in the old *blackhouses* remain within living memory.

NORTHERN HIGHLANDS & ISLANDS

HIGHLIGHTS

- Driving over the moonscape of the Bealach na Ba pass to the gorgeous wooded village of **Applecross** (p371)

- Grappling with the Highlands' mighty peaks in the stunning mountainous playgrounds of **Inverpolly Nature Reserve** (p366), **Assynt** (p365) and **Glen Torridon** (p370)

- Walking among the jagged peaks of Skye's spectacular **Cuillin Hills** (p378)

- Taking a boat trip to experience the brooding grandeur of **Loch Coruisk** (p378)

- Pondering the past amid the mysterious prehistoric standing stones of **Callanish** (p390)

Callanish Standing Stones ★

Assynt ★
★ Inverpolly Nature Reserve

★ Glen Torridon
★ Applecross

Cuillin Hills & ★
Loch Coruisk

- **POPULATION: 175,000**
- **AREA: 20,000 SQ KM**

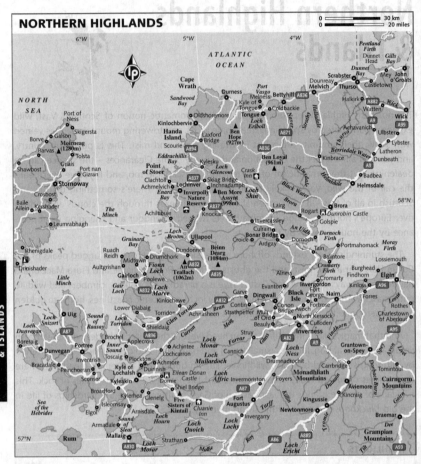

NORTHERN HIGHLANDS

EAST COAST

In both landscape and character, the east coast is where the real barrenness of the Highlands begins to unfold. A gentle splendour and a sense of escapism mark the route along the twisting A9, as it heads north for the last of Scotland's far-flung, mainland population outposts. With only a few exceptions the tourism frenzy is left behind once the road traverses Cromarty Firth and snakes its way along wild and pristine coastline.

While the interior is dominated by the vast and mournful Sutherland mountain range, along the coast great heather-covered

hills heave themselves out of the wild North Sea. Rolling farmland, dominated by miles of stone fencing, crawls its way over hills and pastureland and drops suddenly into the icy waters, and the only interruptions en route are the small, historic towns moored precariously on the coast's edge.

Getting Around

Call **Traveline** (☎ 0870 608 2608) for public transport information. The region is well served by buses, and trains follow the coast up to Wick then across to Thurso. **Scottish Citylink** (☎ 0870 550 5050) runs regular services from Inverness through to Wick, stopping at most towns on the A9 and A99 along the way, before taking the short cut inland to Thurso.

TOP 10 PLACES TO GET OFF THE EATEN TRACK

Here's a selection of some of the best eating you'll find as you journey through the northern Highlands; often in remote, less touristed communities.

Oyster Catcher Restaurant (p352) – Portmahomack, east coast, northern Highlands
Le Bistro (p362) – Thurso, north coast, northern Highlands
Ben Loyal Hotel (p363) – Tongue, north coast, northern Highlands
Summer Isles Hotel (p366) – Achiltibuie, west coast, northern Highlands
Coul House Hotel (p369) – Contin, northern Highlands
Strath Stores (p370) – Gairloch, west coast, northern Highlands
Tigh an Eilean Hotel (p371) – Shieldaig, west coast, northern Highlands
Applecross Inn (p371) – Applecross, west coast, northern Highlands
Kishorn Seafood & Snack Bar (p371) – Kishorn, west coast, northern Highlands
Waverley (p372) – Kyle of Lochalsh, west coast, northern Highlands

---

Rapsons/Highland Country (☎ 01463-222244) operates buses from Wick to Thurso, via the coast and John o'Groats. **Stagecoach Inverness** (☎ 01463-239292) runs services to towns close to (including north of) Inverness.

STRATHPEFFER
☎ 01997 / pop 918

Charming Strathpeffer has a certain faded grandeur in its creaking old pavilions and grandiose hotels – there's a whisper of days gone by in the streets, which are interspersed with some lush greenery.

The village was a fashionable spa in Victorian and Edwardian times, when chic society folk congregated here to splash about in the sulphurous waters.

The self-service **Tourist Information Centre** (TIC; ☎ 421000; The Square; ☿ 10am-6pm Mon & Wed-Sat, to 4pm Sun Easter-Nov) is in Square Wheels Bike Shop, which also hires mountain bikes for £12 per day. You'll find a supermarket and a post office nearby.

Sights

The renovated **Pump Room** (☎ 421415; adult/child £2/1.50; ☿ 10am-6pm Mon-Sat, 2-5pm Sun May-Oct) has some splendid displays showing the bizarre lengths Victorians went to in the quest for a healthy glow.

At the old Victorian train station is the **Highland Museum of Childhood** (☎ 421031; adult/child £2/1.50; ☿ 10am-5pm Mon-Sat, 2-5pm Sun Apr-Jun, Sep & Oct, 10am-7pm Mon-Fri, to 5pm Sat, 2-5pm Sun Jul & Aug). It has a wide range of social history displays about childhood in the Highlands, and also has activities for children, including a dressing-up box and a toy train.

Sleeping & Eating

Craigvar (☎ 421622; www.craigvar.com; The Square; s/d £35/64) Luxury living with a refined touch is what you'll find in this delightful Georgian town house. All the little extras that mark out a classy place are here, such as a welcome drink, bathrobes and fresh fruit. Couples should go for the 'Blue Room' with its sensational four-poster bed – you'll need to collapse back into it after the gourmet breakfast.

Highland Hotel (☎ 421457; www.shearingsholidays .com; r per person £30-50) Many of the old spa hotels have fallen into neglect, but this one has been renovated. It's a magnificent, European chateau–style building overlooking the TIC, with a wood-panelled lobby and lounge, plus lovely wooded grounds. Book in advance for the best deals.

Maya (☎ 420008; Main St; box of chocs £1.50-20) Ohhhh, this place is dangerous. Bringing Belgian chocolates to the Highlands, Maya is the ultimate in sweet indulgence. It also serves up hot drinks, including hot chocolate…

Also recommended:

Strathpeffer Hotel (☎ 421200; strathpeffer.hotel @virgin.net; s/d from £25/45) Solid pub rooms.
Museum Coffeeshop (light meals £2-4; ☿ 10am-5pm) In the old Victorian train station, a good pit stop for a toastie or *panini*.

Getting There & Away

Stagecoach Inverness operates buses from Inverness to Strathpeffer (45 minutes, hourly Monday to Saturday, four on Sunday). The Inverness to Gairloch and Durness buses, plus some Inverness to Ullapool buses, also run via Strathpeffer.

TAIN

☎ 01862 / pop 3511

Tain is Scotland's oldest royal burgh (town) and was an important pilgrimage centre. It has a couple of excellent attractions, making it a desirable spot to break a journey along the east coast. The high street has a post office and banks.

Tain Through Time (☎ 894089; adult/child £3.50/2.50; ☉ 10am-5pm Apr-Jun, Sep & Oct, to 6pm Jul & Aug) is a fascinating heritage centre that describes the history of Tain as a place of pilgrimage, tracing events from the time of St Duthac through to the Reformation. St Duthac was born in Tain, died in Armagh (Ireland) in 1065, and is commemorated by the 12th-century ruins of **St Duthac's Chapel**, as well as by St Duthus Church.

On the northern edge of town is the excellent **Glenmorangie Distillery & Visitor Centre** (☎ 892477; ☉ 9am-5pm Mon-Fri Sep-May, 9am-5pm Mon-Fri, 10am-4pm Sat, noon-4pm Sun Jun-Aug), which produces some of the finest single malts in the Highlands. For proof, knock back a dram of the sherry- or Madeira-wood finish. There are also excellent tours (£2.50).

Rooms are of a high standard at the bustling **St Duthus Hotel** (☎ 894007; Tower St; r per person £20-30, mains £7-9; ⚓). The bathrooms are spotless and the snazzy dining area has a cheery vibe; there's also a beer garden that doubles as a playground for the kids.

Scottish Citylink buses from Inverness to Thurso pass through Tain (five daily). Stagecoach Inverness runs frequent express buses from Inverness (£6, one hour).

There are up to three trains daily to Inverness (£9.30, one hour) and Thurso (£11.40, 2½ hours).

PORTMAHOMACK

☎ 01862 / pop 608

Portmahomack is a former fishing village in a picture-perfect spot – right off the beaten track and gazing across the water at snow-capped peaks. The best place to enjoy the town is the grassy foreshore at the far end of Main St, near the little harbour.

The intriguing **Tarbat Discovery Centre** (☎ 871351; Tarbatness Rd; adult/child £3.50/1; ☉ 10am-5pm May-Sep, 2-5pm Mar, Apr & Oct, 2-4pm Fri & Sat Nov; ⚓) has some excellent carved Pictish stones. When 'crop circles' appeared a few years ago, the foundations of an Iron Age settlement were discovered around the village church.

The church then became the centre of excavations – it's now the discovery centre.

There are good coastal walks at **Tarbat Ness**, 3 miles northeast of the village; the headland is marked by a tall, red-and-white-striped lighthouse.

If you're staying, try the friendly and comfortable **Caledonian Hotel** (☎ 871345; www.caley hotel.co.uk; Main St; s/d £38/65) overlooking the village's sandy beach. Only two rooms overlook Dornoch Firth, so book early. Seafood aficionados shouldn't miss the bright and cheerful **Oyster Catcher Restaurant** (☎ 871560; Main St; starters £6-9, mains £9-17; ☉ lunch & dinner Wed-Sun) – the seafood buffet for £22 is wonderful and there are many delectable lobster dishes.

Stagecoach Inverness runs from Tain to Portmahomack (30 minutes, one daily).

BONAR BRIDGE & AROUND

The A9 crosses the Dornoch Firth, on a bridge and causeway, near Tain. An alternative route goes around the firth via the tiny settlements of **Ardgay**, where you'll find a train station, shop and hotel, and **Bonar Bridge**, where the A836 to Lairg branches west.

From Ardgay, a single-track road leads 10 miles up Strathcarron to **Croick**, the scene of notorious evictions during the 1845 Clearances (see the boxed text, p355). You can still see the sad messages scratched by refugee crofters from Glencalvie on the eastern windows of Croick Church.

If a youth hostel could attract a five-star rating, opulent **Carbisdale Castle Youth Hostel** (SYHA; ☎ 0870 004 1109; Culrain; dm adult/child £15.50/12; ☉ Mar-Oct) would score six. Carbisdale Castle was built in 1914 for the dowager duchess of Sutherland – it is now Scotland's biggest and most luxurious hostel, its halls studded with statues. It's 10 minutes' walk north of Culrain train station. Advance bookings are recommended.

Trains from Inverness to Thurso stop at Ardgay and Culrain (£11.20, two or three times daily), half a mile from Carbisdale Castle.

LAIRG

☎ 01549 / pop 904

Lairg is an attractive village strung out quite a way – it makes for an idyllic afternoon wander, although the tranquillity can be rudely interrupted by the sound of military jets heard whining and cracking overhead.

THE HIGHLANDS' JURASSIC PARK

In a pristine spot in the northern Highlands a revolutionary project is set to change the concept of wildlife conservation in Scotland. **Alladale Wilderness Lodge & Reserve** (☎ 01863-755338; www .alladale.com; Ardgay), home to the country's most northerly tuft of ancient Scots pine forest, is set to release formerly extinct species to roam on its vast estate. The plan is to replace deer-stalking with former predators, once abundant in Scotland, including grey wolves, European brown bears and Eurasian lynx. There are also plans to reintroduce moose and wild boar.

Visitors can stay in the lodge, where accommodation is very exclusive; there are eight luxury rooms accommodating 16 guests with a minimum of six required for a booking. Call the lodge or see the website for tariff details, which includes all meals. Activities at the time of writing included guided nature walks, 4WD safaris, fishing and mountain biking. The main draw card however – the reintroduction of this wildlife – looks set to kick off in spring 2006.

Alladale is approximately 40 miles north of Inverness. From the A836 (heading to Bonar Bridge from Tain) take the side road at Ardgay, heading along Strathcarron to Croick; Alladale is about 8 miles down this road.

At the southern end of Loch Shin, it's the gateway to the remote mountains and loch-speckled bogs of central Sutherland. The A836 from Lairg to Tongue passes Ben Klibreck (961m) and Ben Loyal (764m).

Lairg has a seasonal **TIC** (☎ 402160; Ferrycroft Countryside Centre; ☉ 10am-4pm Mar-May, to 5pm Jun-Aug, to 4pm Sep & Oct; ☐) on the far side of the river from the village, with Internet access available. There are also shops, a bank (with ATM) and a post office.

From June to September, just south of Lairg, you can watch salmon leaping the **Falls of Shin** on their way upstream to spawn. There are easy forest walks leaving from the Lairg TIC (ask inside for details), and the bench seating outside the centre makes a good spot for lunch.

Sleeping & Eating

Sleeperzzz (☎ 01408-641343; www.sleeperzzz.com; Rogart Station; r per person £10; ☉ Mar-Nov) Nine miles east of Lairg (and a short stumble to the village pub) is this charming and unique hostel. Ten compartments in two 1st-class railway carriages have been fitted with two comfortable bunks each; there's also a compartment with a little kitchen and another with a dining room. Bike hire is free to guests and there's a 10% discount for cyclists and train travellers.

Crask Inn (☎ 411241; Crask; r per person £22, 3-course dinner £12) The small and remote Crask Inn, 13 miles north of Lairg on the A836, is notorious for being the coldest place in Scotland. In December 1995 a record low of -30°C was recorded here, but peat-burning stoves

and central heating keep the inn cosy. Roast venison is often on the menu.

Nip Inn (☎ 402243; www.nipinn.co.uk; Main St; r per person £25-30, bar meals £7, restaurant mains £9-13; ☉ lunch & dinner) Rooms are surprisingly modern and very good value at this solid old inn. The décor is bright, en suites are sparkling and the inn caters for solo travellers. Downstairs, sip a beer at a window table while watching the hustle and bustle of Highland life.

Getting There & Away

From Lairg, single-track roads run north to Tongue, Laxford Bridge (between Durness and Kylesku) and Ledmore (between Kylesku and Ullapool).

Stagecoach Inverness buses run from Inverness to Tain (£6, one hour, frequent); MacLeods then picks up the link from Tain to Lairg (30 minutes, four daily Monday to Saturday). Buses also run to Helmsdale (three daily Monday to Friday).

Trains from Inverness to Thurso stop at Lairg (£11.20, 1¾ hours) and Rogart (£11.20, two hours) two or three times daily in each direction.

DORNOCH

☎ 01862 / pop 1206

It's difficult to believe that Scotland's last executed witch perished in a vat of boiling tar in Dornoch in 1722, because today this graceful village is all happy families. On the coast, 2 miles off the A9, this symphony in sandstone bewitches visitors with flowers, greenery and affable locals at every turn.

The **TIC** (☎ 810916; ☼ 9.30am-5.30pm Mon-Sat, 10am-4pm Sun Apr-Oct, call for winter hrs; 🖳) in the main square doubles as a coffee shop, and offers Internet access.

Sights

The town is clustered around the 13th-century **Dornoch Cathedral**, which is shaped like a crucifix. The crisscross of light streaming through adjacent stained-glass windows creates a powerful effect. The original building was destroyed in 1570 during a clan feud. Despite some patching up, it wasn't completely rebuilt until 1837.

South of Dornoch, seals are often visible on the sand bars of **Dornoch Firth**.

Sleeping & Eating

Trevose Guest House (☎ 810269; trevose@amserve .net; Cathedral Sq; s/d £25/45) A gorgeous stone cottage claiming primo location, spilling out onto the village green across from the cathedral. Firm mattresses and a selection of shared and en-suite bathrooms make this place a good choice, and there's a smokers' guest lounge. Someone here takes their garden ornaments very seriously.

Dornoch Castle Hotel (☎ 810216; www.dornochcastle hotel.com; Castle St; garden s/d from £65/80, castle s/d from £140/150, bar meals £5-7, dinner mains £12-16; ☼ lunch & dinner) Fancy a night in a castle? Then try this grand, 16th-century former bishop's palace. The stately rooms vary considerably, but you're unlikely to be disappointed no matter what you choose – ask for a room number at random! In the evening toast your toes in the cosy bar before dining in style at the first-rate restaurant.

Eagle Hotel (☎ 810008; Castle St; bar meals £6-10; ☼ lunch & dinner) Chow down at this top little boozer complete with eccentric ornamentation and man-sized meals. Wash it all down with a Dornoch Ale.

Also recommended:

Rosslyn Villa (☎ 810237; Castle St; r per person £19) The best B&Bs come with simplicity and a smile.

Auchlea (☎ 811524; www.auchlea.co.uk; B9168; s/d £25/45) A purpose-built lodging with three en-suite rooms; it's near the A9 turn-off to Dornoch, about 1.5 miles from town.

Getting There & Away

Scottish Citylink has services to/from Inverness (£6.80, 1¼ hours, four to five daily)

WORTH THE TRIP

On the northern edge of Brora is **Clynelish Distillery** (☎ 01408-623000; Brora; ☼ 10am-5pm Mon-Fri Easter-Sep, 11am-4pm Mon-Fri Oct, by arrangement Nov-Feb), which produces an earthy, peaty, slightly smoky single malt reminiscent of the famous Islay whiskies. Fruits, spices and malted barley are all distinguishable. Tours (£4) leave at least hourly and take about 40 minutes; you'll also get a £3 voucher to spend on a bottle of whisky.

The distillery is at the northern end of Brora off the A9, on the road to Balnacoil.

and Thurso (£10.30 2¼ hours, four to five daily), stopping in the square at Dornoch.

GOLSPIE

☎ 01408 / pop 1404

Golspie is an attractive town off the main drag, and would be a congenial option for a day or two (particularly if you feel like pulling on the walking boots or exploring a castle).

One mile north of town is mighty **Dunrobin Castle** (☎ 633177; adult/child £6.60/4.70; ☼ 10.30am-5.30pm Jul & Aug, 10.30am-4.30pm Mon-Sat, noon-5.30pm Sun Jun & Sep, 10.30am-4.30pm Mon-Sat, noon-4.30pm Sun Apr, May & Oct), the largest house in the Highlands (187 rooms). Although it dates back to around 1275, most of what you see today was built in French style between 1845 and 1850. One of the homes of the earls and dukes of Sutherland, it's richly furnished and offers an intriguing insight into their opulent lifestyle. The house also displays innumerable gifts from farm tenants (probably grateful they weren't victims of the Clearances – see the boxed text, opposite).

Golspie is the starting point for some good walks. One trail leads north along the coast for 5 miles to Brora, passing the remains of the Iron Age broch (defensive tower) of **Carn Liath** about halfway along. The other trail climbs steeply above the village to the summit of **Ben Bhraggie** (394m), which is crowned by a massive monument to the duke of Sutherland that was erected in 1834 and is visible for miles around.

Sutherland Arms Hotel (☎ 633234; Main St; s/b £35/70, mains £6-9; ☼ lunch & dinner) claims to be Sutherland's oldest coaching inn (the wallpaper in the rooms backs its claim) and is well situated at the northern end of the village, close to Dunrobin Castle. Flowery, en-suite rooms are in good shape and there's a range of decent meals available.

Buses between Inverness and Thurso stop in Golspie. There are also trains from Inverness (£12.40, two hours, two or three daily).

HELMSDALE

☎ 01431 / pop 861

Backed by gorse-bedecked hills and set on a wide river mouth, Helmsdale has an enviable location. It's surrounded by stunning, undulating coastline and the River Helmsdale – one of the best salmon rivers in the Highlands.

For tourist information and Internet access, go to the **Strath Ullie Crafts & Information Centre** (☎ 821402; The Harbour, Shore St; 🕙 9am-5.30pm Mon-Sat Apr-Oct, 10am-4.30pm Mon-Sat Nov-Mar; 🖳).

Sights & Activities

The excellent **Timespan Heritage Centre** (☎ 821327; Dunrobin St; adult/child £4/2; 🕙 10am-5pm Mon-Sat, noon-5pm Sun Easter-Oct; 🖧) has a gallery relating the Gartymore Story – hundreds of families were forcibly removed from their native homes by the House of Sutherland in the early 19th century. The gallery is intriguing because it's a collection of stories based on people in the area, their possessions and, importantly, their memories. There's also a free gallery upstairs overlooking the river, featuring fine exhibitions from local artists.

Helmsdale is known for its salmon fishing and if you feel like throwing in a line, drop into **Bridge Hotel Tackle Shop** (☎ 821102; Dunrobin St). It rents out fly rods for £20 per day, and sells trout or salmon river-fishing permits for £18 per day (loch fishing is cheaper).

CROFTING & THE CLEARANCES

In many parts of the Highlands and islands you will see clusters of ruined cottages crumbling amid the bracken – all that remains of deserted farming communities. Up until the 19th century the most common form of farming settlement here was the *baile,* a group of a dozen or so families who farmed the land granted to them by the local chieftain in return for military service and a portion of the harvest. The arable land was divided into strips called *rigs,* which were allocated to different families by annual ballot so that each took turns at getting the poorer soils; this system was known as *runrig.* The families worked the land communally, and their cattle shared the grazing land.

But this lifestyle was swept away in the wake of the Highland Clearances, which took place between around 1750 and the 1880s. Following the ban on private armies, clan chiefs no longer needed military service from their tenants, and saw sheep farming as far more profitable than collecting rent from poverty-stricken farmers. Tens of thousands of tenant farmers were evicted from their homes and their land.

Those who chose not to emigrate or move to the cities to find work were forced to eke a living from narrow plots of marginal agricultural land, often close to the coast. This was a form of smallholding that became known as crofting. The small patch of land barely provided a living, and had to be supplemented by other work such as fishing and kelp-gathering. The close-knit community of the *baile* was replaced by the widely scattered cottages of the crofting settlements that you can still see today.

When economic depression hit in the late 19th century, many crofters couldn't pay their rent. This time, however, they resisted expulsion, instead forming the Highland Land Reform Association and their own political party. Their resistance led to several of their demands being acceded to by the government; the Crofters' Holdings Act of 1886 provided for security of tenure, fair rents and eventually the supply of land for new crofts.

Today the Scottish Highlands are, in many parts, a graveyard of broken communities, communities that ceased living and breathing more than 200 years ago. Evidence of the cruel evictions is everywhere and the human tragedy has scarred this majestic landscape. While economic recovery is in full swing, the human cost is irrecoverable and the desolation of the countryside is in harmony with the poor souls lost to starvation, poverty and estrangement from their ancestral lands.

Crofting tenancies still exist and complex regulations now protect the crofters. The Land Reform Act, passed in 2003, gave crofters the absolute right to buy their tenancy, and a law abolishing feudal tenure come into effect in late 2004, ending 900 years of feudalism.

Sleeping & Eating

Belgrave Arms Hotel (☎ 821242; www.belgravearms hotel.com; cnr Dunrobin St & A9; s/d £20/48) The Belgrave has a genuine feel to it, with a slightly musty odour and creaky floorboards. Importantly, though, the rooms are fresh and well maintained.

Bridge Hotel (☎ 821100; www.bridgehotel.net; Dunrobin St; s/d £80/105) Ideally located, this early-19th-century lodging is a top place to stay. The suite (£145) is more like a mini flat and the luxurious doubles with polished wood furniture have great hill and river views. For some, the only drawback may be the hunting theme, with numerous 'trophies' on the wall.

Helmsdale Youth Hostel (SYHA; ☎ 0870 004 1124; cnr A9 & Old Caithness Rd; dm adult/child £11.75/8.25; ✷ May-Sep) This hostel is particularly good for groups and has large, 12-bed dorms and a cavernous dining hall. It gets busy; book well ahead for July and August.

La Mirage (☎ 821615; 7 Dunrobin St; light meals £3-5, mains £7-13) Former proprietor Nancy Sinclair (La Mirage changed ownership in 2005) has gone to great lengths to become Barbara Cartland's double (Cartland holidayed here for over 60 years). Accordingly, her restaurant's décor oozes pink kitsch, and is a draw card in itself. The menu boasts standard grills and vegetarian options, as well as fish done both cheap and classy. Nancy still drops in to admire her handiwork.

Getting There & Away

Buses from Inverness and Thurso stop in Helmsdale, as do trains (from Thurso £11.20, 1¼ hours, four daily).

HELMSDALE TO LATHERON

About 7 miles north of Helmsdale, a 15-minute walk east from the A9 (signposted) takes you to **Badbea**. It's here that the ruins of crofts are perched on the cliff top. The **Berriedale Braes**, 2.5 miles beyond the Badbea parking area, is a difficult section of the A9, with steep gradients and hairpin bends.

Dunbeath has a spectacular setting in a deep glen – it makes a good stop on the way to the northern towns. There are a couple of shops and a **heritage centre** (☎ 01593-731233; www.dunbeath-heritage.org.uk; The Old School; adult/child £2/1; ✷ 10am-5pm Easter-Oct), with displays about the history of Caithness, including crofting and fisheries. There are also exhibitions, including one on the crash of the Sunderland flying boat near Dunbeath in 1942.

The friendly and laid-back **Kingspark Llama Farm** (☎ 01593-751202; Berriedale; s/d from £20/40), a working llama farm, 4 miles south of Dunbeath, has cosy rooms with low-slung ceilings and shared bathrooms. Guests are greeted with a cheery smile and sent on their way with a happy stomach.

At the **Clan Gunn Heritage Centre & Museum** (☎ 01593-741700; adult/child £2.50/50p; ✷ 11am-1pm & 2-4pm Mon-Sat Jun & Sep, 11am-1pm & 2-4pm Mon-Sat, 2-4pm Sun Jul & Aug) in Latheron, 3 miles northeast of Dunbeath on the A9, you'll learn that a Scot, not Christopher Columbus, discovered America – but you might take this claim with a pinch of salt! Even if you don't want to go in, it's worth pulling into the car park on a fine day to admire the stunning views.

LYBSTER
☎ 01593

Lybster is a purpose-built fishing village dating from 1810, with a stunning harbour area surrounded by grassy cliffs.

The major crowd-pleaser here is the **Waterlines Visitor Centre** (☎ 721520; adult/child £2.50/50p; ✷ 11am-5pm May-Sep; ♿ ♨). It has a heritage exhibition, a smokehouse (giving visitors a whiff of the kippering process) and CCTV beaming live pictures of nesting sea birds from nearby cliffs. After a visit you can sit on outdoor benches and munch on some home baking while admiring the views across the stunning harbour setting.

The warm and welcoming **Portland Arms Hotel** (☎ 721721; www.portlandarms.co.uk; s/d £55/80), on the A9 main road in town, is an atmospheric old pub with log fires and a farmhouse feel. There's a mix of older and refurbished rooms – all are pretty good.

Scottish Citylink buses between Thurso and Inverness run via Lybster (one hour, up to five daily), Latheron and Dunbeath. Rapsons/Highland Country runs four times daily from Wick to Ulbster, Lybster, Dunbeath and Berriedale.

AROUND LYBSTER

At Ulbster, 5 miles north of Lybster on the A99, is **Whaligoe Steps**, a spectacular staircase cut into the cliff face. It provides access to a tiny natural harbour ringed by vertical cliffs and echoing with the cackle of nesting fulmars. The path begins at the end of the minor road beside the telephone box, opposite the road signposted 'Cairn of Get'. The **Cairn o'Get**, a prehistoric burial cairn, is a mile northwest of Ulbster. From the car park cross the stile and follow the black-and-white marker poles for approximately 1 mile. Wear decent shoes as the ground is boggy.

There are several interesting prehistoric sites near Lybster. Five miles to the northwest of Lybster, on the minor road to Achavanich, just south of Loch Stemster, are the unsigned 30 **Achavanich Standing Stones**. In a desolate setting, these crumbling monuments of the distant past still capture the imagination with their evocative location. It's all about colours: blue skies, a steely grey loch, and the soft browns and greens of the land. The setting and bypass of modern tourism makes this place special.

A mile east of Lybster on the A99, a turn-off leads north to the **Grey Cairns of Camster**. Dating from between 4000 BC and 2500 BC, these burial chambers are hidden in long, low mounds rising from an evocatively desolate stretch of moor. The Long Cairn measures 60m by 21m. You can enter the main chamber, but must first crawl into the well-preserved Round Cairn, which has a corbelled ceiling. You can then continue 7 miles north on this remote road to approach Wick on the A882.

Back on the A99, the **Hill o'Many Stanes**, 2 miles beyond the Camster turn-off, is a curious, fan-shaped arrangement of 22 rows of small stones that probably date from around 2000 BC. Staggeringly, there were 600 in the original pattern. On a sunny day, the views from this hill are stunning.

WICK

☎ 01955 / pop 7333

While we wouldn't quite say that Wick has turned a corner, the town appears to be a little less dismal than it once was. In any case, you should spend at least a night, as it takes a wee while to dig under the town's economically depressed façade to enjoy its fascinating history, grittiness and admirable attractions.

Information

Bank of Scotland (Bridge St) Has ATM.

Cafe Net (☎ 604600; 102 High St; per 15min/1hr £1/3.25; ⏰ 9am-6pm Mon-Sat; ⛁) Internet access.

Royal Bank of Scotland (Bridge St) Has ATM.

TIC (☎ 603344; St Fergus Rd) Provides an unattended station in the Norseman Hotel.

Sights

WICK HERITAGE CENTRE

The town's award-winning local **museum** (☎ 605393; 18-27 Bank Row; adult/child £2/50p; ⏰ 10am-5pm Mon-Sat May-Sep, outside these months call for hrs) deserves all the praise heaped upon it. Tracking the rise and fall of the herring industry, it displays everything from fishing equipment to complete herring fishing boats. It's a fantastic museum – without doubt one of the best in the country – and is absolutely huge inside, crammed with memorabilia and extensive displays describing the days when Wick was the largest herring port in Europe (in the mid-19th century).

The dedicated volunteers who run the place are desperate to save Wick's heritage from development and are constantly bringing in new exhibits and expanding the museum. Try to get one of them to show you around – their in-depth knowledge of the exhibits is riveting. The Johnston photographic collection is the museum's star exhibit. From 1863 to 1977, three generations of Johnstons photographed everything that happened around Wick, and the 70,000 photographs are an amazing portrait of the town's life. Prints of the early photos are for sale.

CASTLES

A path leads a mile south of town to the ruins of 12th-century **Old Wick Castle**, with the spectacular cliffs of the **Brough** and the **Brig**, as well as **Gote o'Trams**, a little further south. In good weather, it's a fine coastal walk to the castle, but take care on the final approach. Three miles northeast of Wick is the magnificently located cliff-top ruin of **Castle Sinclair**.

DISTILLERY

Old Pulteney (☎ 602371; www.oldpulteney.com; Huddart St) is the most northerly distillery on mainland Scotland and runs excellent tours (£3.50) at 11am and 2pm from Monday to Friday (closed in July). Old Pulteney whisky has a light, earthy character with a hint of sea air and sherry. The visitors centre is free and gives an interesting, abbreviated account of the distilling process.

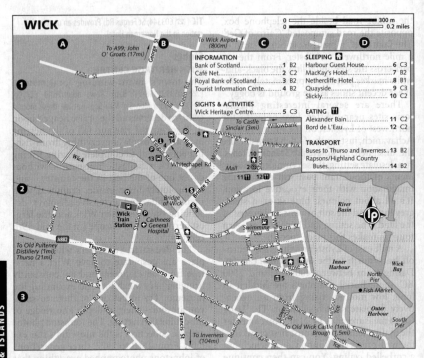

WICK

INFORMATION	
Bank of Scotland.....................1 B2	
Café Net..................................2 C2	
Royal Bank of Scotland..........3 B2	
Tourist Information Centre......4 B2	

SIGHTS & ACTIVITIES	
Wick Heritage Centre..............5 C3	

SLEEPING	
Harbour Guest House..............6 C3	
MacKay's Hotel.......................7 B2	
Nethercliffe Hotel....................8 B1	
Quayside.................................9 C3	
Slickly...................................10 C2	

EATING	
Alexander Bain......................11 C2	
Bord de L'Eau........................12 C2	

TRANSPORT	
Buses to Thurso and Inverness..13 B2	
Rapsons/Highland Country Buses.................................14 B2	

Sleeping & Eating

Slickly (☎ 602356; 2 Shore Lane; r per person £17) Just off High St, Slickly is a traditional, welcoming house with good-value rooms that share a bathroom. There's a communal breakfast in the morning in a light-filled glass conservatory.

Quayside (☎ 603229; www.quaysidewick.co.uk; 25 Harbour Quay; r per person £20-25) This homely, efficient place overlooking the harbour has neat rooms and is handy for the heritage centre and the chippy a couple of doors down. Note that the single is *very* small.

MacKay's Hotel (☎ 602323; www.mackayshotel.co.uk; Union St; s/d £65/90) The renovated MacKay's is Wick's best hotel. Rooms vary in layout and size so ask to see a few; prices drop if you're staying more than one night. The 2.75m-long Ebenezer Pl, the shortest street in Britain, runs past one end of the hotel.

Bord de L'Eau (☎ 604400; 2 Market St; starters £5, mains £10-12; ☽ lunch Tue-Sat, dinner Tue-Sun) This serene, upmarket French restaurant is the best place to eat in Wick, by a mile. It overlooks the river and serves dishes such as *escargot*, and roasted rabbit legs served with French mustard. The menu is very meat-driven.

Alexander Bain (☎ 609920; Market Pl; dishes £5.50-7; ☽ lunch & dinner) This is the only pub in town that serves food on weeknights. It's a cavernous place in the middle of the pedestrianised High St, attracting a mix of tourists, families and ragtag locals. The food dabbles in pastas, salads, burgers, steaks and wraps, and it's very reasonably priced.

Also recommended:

Harbour Guest House (☎ 603276; harbour.guest house@supanet.com; 6 Rose St; s/d £22/40) Decent digs for a decent price.

Nethercliffe Hotel (☎ 602044; fax 605691; Louisburgh St; s/d £40/55;) A very friendly, small hotel with good-value rooms exhibiting warmth and a flowery old-fashioned décor.

Getting There & Away

Wick is a transport gateway to the surrounding area. **Logan Air** (☎ 602294; www.loganair.co.uk) flies between Edinburgh and Wick airport (from £70 return, one hour, one daily Monday to Saturday) and on to the Shetland Islands. **Eastern Airways** (☎ 01652-680600; www

.easternairways.com) flies to Aberdeen (£135 return, 35 minutes, four daily).

Scottish Citylink operates buses to/from Inverness (£11, three hours, four daily) and Thurso (£2.50, 40 minutes, four daily).

Rapsons/Highland Country runs the connecting service to John o'Groats (40 minutes, up to five daily Monday to Saturday) for the passenger ferry to Burwick, Orkney.

Trains service Wick from Inverness (£14, four hours, one or two daily).

JOHN O'GROATS

☎ 01955 / pop 512

Why would you pay 20p to go to a public toilet? That's the dilemma you'll be faced with at John o'Groats, Scotland's worst and most embarrassing tourist attraction. Falsely believed to be the most northerly point on the British mainland (it's actually Dunnet Head; right), John o'Groats has been milking this geographical extremity for years. It's not worth the trip here and it's hardly worth including this text about the place – but we did want to warn you! The main attraction is basically a car park surrounded by shoddy craft and souvenir shops. For accommodation, try Wick (opposite), Mey (right) or Thurso (p361), all nearby.

Two miles east of John o'Groats is the much better **Duncansby Head**, which is home to many sea birds at the start of summer. A path leads to **Duncansby Stacks**, spectacular natural rock formations soaring 60m above the sea. There is a series of narrow inlets and deep coves on this wonderful stretch of coast.

Getting There & Away

Rapsons/Highland Country runs buses between John o'Groats and Wick (40 minutes, up to five daily Monday to Saturday). There are also up to five services Monday to Saturday to/from Thurso.

From May to September, the passenger ferry MV *Pentland Venture*, operated by **John o'Groats Ferries** (☎ 611353; www.jogferry.co .uk), shuttles across to Burwick in Orkney (adult/child return £26/13); a coach tour of Orkney mainland, including the ferry fare, is £36/18. Ninety-minute wildlife cruises to the island of Stroma or Duncansby Head cost £15.

MEY

☎ 01847 / pop 200

Castle of Mey (☎ 851473; www.castleofmey.org.uk; adult/child £7/free; ⏲ 10.30am-4pm Sat-Thu May-Jul & mid-Aug–Sep), a big crowd-puller, is about 6 miles from John o'Groats, off the A836 to Thurso. It's the former home of the late Queen Mother, and hardened royal buffs will get a kick out of items of memorabilia and pictures of the Queen Mum, but for everyone else there's not that much to see inside. Outside in the castle grounds, though, there's an unusual walled garden that's worth a stroll around, and there are lovely views over the Pentland Firth.

The nearby **Castle Arms Hotel** (☎ 851244; www .castlearms.co.uk; s/d £48/76), a former 19th-century coaching inn, has a friendly bar downstairs and decent rooms upstairs. Or try **Hawthorns** (☎ 851710; www.thehawthornsbnb.co.uk; s/d £24/48), where rooms are huge and the owner's cheery smile is just as big.

DUNNET HEAD

Let's put a common misconception to rest. Contrary to popular belief, naff John o'Groats is not the British mainland's most northerly point; that honour goes to Dunnet Head, 10 miles to the west. The head is marked by a lighthouse dating from 1832.

Not only is Dunnet Head the real 'most northerly point', it's also well worth coming out here for the views of the startling sea cliffs and the vista over to Orkney and beyond, all near the lighthouse. The lonely car park (with plaques about local flora and fauna and a self-guided tour of the area) is a welcome relief from the con of John o'Groats.

Just southwest of Dunnet Head there is a magnificent stretch of sandy beach, at the southern end of which lies the tiny harbour of **Castlehill**. It's here that a heritage trail explains the evolution of the local flagstone industry.

NORTH & WEST COAST

Quintessential Highland country such as this, marked by single-track roads, breathtaking emptiness and a wild, fragile beauty, is a rarity on the modern, crowded, highly urbanised island of Britain. You could get lost up here for weeks – and that still wouldn't be enough time.

Carving its way from Thurso to Glencoul, the north and northwest coastline is a feast of deep inlets, forgotten beaches and surging peninsulas. Within the rugged confines, the deep interior is home to vast, empty spaces, enormous lochs and some of Scotland's highest peaks.

The remarkable thing about the landscape is that it makes you feel special. Whether it's blazing sunshine or a murky greyness, the character of the land is totally unique and constantly changing – for that window of time in which you glimpse it, you capture an exclusive snapshot of this ancient area in your mind (or on your camera!). Park the car and gaze. This northernmost slab of the Highlands is the stuff of coastal-drive dreams.

Getting Around

Public transport in the northwest is, well, pretty awful. There's no doubt that this region is best explored by car – you'll be able to reach the sites and towns far more easily and, doing it all in your own time, you'll get a lot more from the experience. Getting to Thurso or Kyle of Lochalsh by bus or train is easy, but following the coast between these places, especially from October to May, is when the fun really starts. **Royal Mail postbuses** (☎ 0845 774 0740; www.postbus.royalmail.com) run year-round; fares vary, but long journeys are usually good value at around £4 or £5. See its website for details of routes, which cover most towns in this section. **Rapsons/Highland Country** (☎ 01847-893123) runs services to major towns.

To travel across the north coast, from Thurso to Durness, the Monday to Saturday postbus services are your only option.

From late April to late September, **Tim Dearman Coaches** (☎ 01349-883585; www.timdearmancoaches.co.uk) runs buses from Inverness to Durness (£17, five hours, one daily Monday to Saturday, plus Sunday in July and August) via Ullapool and Lochinver.

An alternative is to come up from Inverness via Lairg. Apart from trains (Monday to Saturday in winter), **Stagecoach Inverness** (☎ 01463-239292) operates to/from Tain (£6, 1¼ hours, half-hourly) and **MacLeods Coaches** (☎ 01408-641354) operates a connecting service to Lairg (£3, 45 minutes, four daily Monday to Saturday). A postbus will then get you from Lairg through to Durness via Kinlochbervie (one daily Monday to Saturday).

There are regular Scottish Citylink buses between Inverness and Ullapool.

Westerbus (☎ 01571-84473) runs every Thursday year-round between Ullapool and Gairloch.

The once-daily (except Sunday) Westerbus service from Inverness to Gairloch, runs via Achnasheen and Kinlochewe, or via Dundonnell on Monday, Wednesday and Saturday. The route via Dundonnell provides a link between Ullapool and Gairloch (via Braemore Junction). The Achnasheen–Kinlochewe–Torridon postbus can be used in conjunction with the Westerbus, taking you from Gairloch to Kinlochewe and Torridon (at least one day after the Ullapool to Gairloch leg).

From Torridon, the **MacLennan** (☎ 01520-755239) bus service goes to Strathcarron (£3, once daily Monday to Saturday) from June to September, or Monday, Wednesday and Friday the rest of the year.

THURSO & SCRABSTER
☎ 01847 / pop 7737

The mainland's most northerly town, Thurso is a bleak, rather depressing place where prams seem to rule the streets – you get the impression that young people here either leave or have bairns (children) as soon as they're able. Note the young 'uns doing bog laps of the centre in their little cars. It's useful as a service centre, though, and as an overnight stop en route to Orkney – the view across Pentland Firth to Hoy beckons visitors to a more appealing location.

Ferries cross from Scrabster, 2.5 miles west of Thurso, to Orkney. Tiny Scrabster, little more than a collection of BP oil storage containers, revolves around its port.

Information

ATM (cnr Olrig & Rotterdam Sts)
Dunbar Hospital (☎ 893263; Ormlie Rd)
Laundrette (Riverside Pl; wash £4)
Library (☎ 893237; Davidson's Lane; ♥ 10am-6pm Mon & Wed, to 8pm Tue & Fri, to 1pm Thu & Sat; ▣) Free Internet access.
Riverbank medical centre (☎ 892027; Janet St)
TIC (☎ 892371; thurso@visitscotland.com; Riverside Rd; ♥ Mon-Sat Apr & Oct, daily late May-Sep)

Sights & Activities

Thurso Heritage Museum (☎ 892459; High St; adult/child £1.50/50p; ♥ 10am-1pm & 2-5pm Mon-Sat Jun-

THURSO

Sep) displays Pictish and Christian fossils and carved stones, and a reconstruction of a croft interior. There's also an excellent photographic display.

Thurso is an unlikely **surfing** centre, but the nearby coast has arguably the best and most regular surf on mainland Britain. There's an excellent right-hand reef break on the eastern side of town, directly in front of Lord Thurso's castle (closed to the public), and another shallow reef break 5 miles west at Brimms Ness.

Thurso's idyllic country **riverside walk** will make you feel miles away from town. Access is near Waterside House and you can walk upstream, cross a bridge and come back on the other side. It's a beautiful walk, taking about 45 minutes at a stroll, and is a very popular local pursuit in decent weather. You can also walk all the way to Scrabster along cliffs for brilliant views (40 minutes). Take care in windy weather.

Sleeping

Waterside House (☎ 894751; www.watersidehouse.info; 3 Janet St; r per person £17-22) Opposite the river

and just around the corner from the centre, Waterside House is classy, cool and comfortable with well-kept rooms (more-expensive ones with en suite). The breakfast system here is excellent – you get a list the night before and you just tick what you want (the list includes filled rolls).

Murray House (☎ 895759; 1 Campbell St; s/d £25/50) Everything smells new in this recently refurbished place. Rooms are spick-and-span, modern if floral (it's an obsession in this country!), and the ones on the top floor have more space and draw in the best light.

Pentland Hotel (☎ 893202; fax 892761; Princes St; s/d £41/80) The business-style rooms in this place are great value. They're big enough to have a couch and a separate nook with a desk. It's a stylish place, and surprisingly tranquil inside, given its central location. There are plenty of open areas for lounging around while you wait for the ferry to Orkney.

Thurso Hostel (Ormlie Lodge; ☎ /fax 896888; Ormlie Rd; s/d £9/15) This scruffy hostel is a students' hall of residence a few minutes' walk from the train station. It has an excellent, if slightly ragged, range of budget accommodation, is great value, and seems to be undergoing constant renovations.

Eating

Cafe Cardosi (☎ 896212; cnr Olrig & Traill Sts; dishes £2.50-3.50; ☺ 9am-6pm Mon-Sat) Stylishly decked out in warm colours and a trendy, minimalist décor, Cardosi pumps out decent coffee, salads, light hot meals (such as hot smoked salmon and Brie) and sandwiches. The decadent home-baked cakes are a standout, but the best thing about this joint is people-watching, both inside and on the busy street outside.

Le Bistro (☎ 893737; 2 Traill St; lunch £4-6, dinner mains £9-12; ☺ lunch & dinner Tue-Sat) One of our faves in northern Scotland, this bright, Mediterranean-style bistro with top-notch food wins our 'best place to eat in town' award, hands down. The kitchen whips up both traditional (local haggis parcels) and exotic (Mexican chilli bean crepe) fare, and service comes with a smile. Seafood dishes feature on the blackboard, meals are made to order and vegetarians are catered for.

Captain's Galley (☎ 894999; The Harbour, Scrabster; 3-course dinner £30; ☺ dinner Tue-Sat) This classy diner, metres from the pier, dishes out posh seafood and has a changing menu, depending on the day's catch. If you're a serious seafood connoisseur, try the medley of Scrabster market fish.

Also recommended:

Central Hotel (☎ 893129; Traill St; mains £2-6; ☺ lunch & dinner; 🐾) Paninis, sandwiches, grills, pizzas and curries on offer.

St Clair Hotel (☎ 896481; Sinclair St; mains £7-12; ☺ lunch & dinner) Tasty seafood, Mexican and classy pub faves.

Getting There & Around

Thurso is 130 miles from Inverness and 21 miles from Wick.

From Inverness, Scottish Citylink buses operate via Wick to Thurso (£13, 3½ hours, three to five daily).

Rapsons/Highland Country runs a service to Wick (45 minutes, hourly) and also to John o'Groats (one hour, hourly Monday to Friday, three Saturday).

There are two or three daily train services from Inverness in summer (£13.50, 3½ hours), but space for bicycles is limited so book ahead.

It's a 2-mile walk from Thurso train station to the ferry port at Scrabster, or there are buses from Olrig St (80p). **William Dunnet & Co** (☎ 893101; Manson's Lane; ☺ 8am-5.30pm Mon-Fri, 9am-1pm Sat) rents cars; a small car starts at £25 per day, plus 10p per mile – you can drop it off in Wick if you're heading that way.

THURSO TO DURNESS

It's 80 winding and often spectacular coastal miles from Thurso to Durness.

Dounreay & Melvich

On the coast 10 miles west of Thurso, the **Dounreay Nuclear Power Station Visitor Centre** (☎ 01847-802572; Dounreay; admission free; ☺ 10am-4pm Easter-Nov) spews company propaganda that only Homer Simpson would swallow. It's actually rather humorous, and worth dropping into if you're in the area. The plant is being decommissioned and cleaning up the site and storing the waste safely will take until 2036 and cost 2.7 billion pounds (see p54). Just beyond Dounreay, **Reay** has a shop and an interesting little harbour dating from 1830. **Melvich** overlooks a fine beach and there are great views from **Strathy Point** (a 2-mile drive from the coast road, then a 15-minute walk).

Bettyhill (Am Blaran Odhar)

☎ 01641 / pop 553

The panorama of a sweeping, sandy beach and surrounding velvety green hills with bulbous, rocky outcrops makes a sharp contrast to the sad history of this area. Bettyhill is a crofting community of resettled tenant farmers kicked off their land during the Clearances (see the boxed text, p355).

Bettyhill **TIC** (☎ 521244; ☺ 10.30am-5pm Mon-Sat Apr-Oct) has limited information on the area but Elizabeth's Cafe (mains £6) here serves good home-cooked food. There's also a shop and post office.

Strathnaver Museum (☎ 521418; Clachan; adult/child £1.90/50p; ☺ 10am-1pm & 2-5pm Mon-Sat Apr-Oct, by arrangement at other times), in an old church, tells the sad story of the Strathnaver Clearances. The museum contains memorabilia of Clan Mackay, various items of crofting equipment and a 4000-year-old beaker.

Dunveaden (☎ 521273; r per person £18-20, camp sites £8) is a friendly B&B and camping ground on the main road, opposite the grocery store. Traditional **Bettyhill Hotel** (☎ /fax 521352;

enquiries@bettyhill.info; r per person £20-30, mains £8; ⓨ lunch & dinner) has a range of renovated rooms with en suites – they're stylishly decorated with a cool summer feel. There are rip-roaring views from some (such as No 2) over the sandy beach fringing Torrisdale Bay. The restaurant here churns out some interesting cuisine, including lobster bites.

From Bettyhill, the B871 turns south for Helmsdale, through **Strathnaver**, where the Clearances took place.

Coldbackie & Tongue

☎ 01847 / pop 445

Coldbackie has outstanding views over the sandy beach, turquoise waters and offshore islands. If you haven't seen that magical Scottish light at work yet, there's a good chance you'll see it here – park the car for a few minutes and watch. Only 2 miles further on is Tongue, with the evocative 14th-century ruins of **Castle Varrich**, once a Mackay stronghold. To get to the castle, take the trail next to the Royal Bank of Scotland, near Ben Loyal Hotel – it's an easy stroll. Tongue has a shop, post office, bank and petrol station.

Ben Loyal Hotel (☎ 611216; www.benloyal.co.uk; s/d from £35/60, mains £7-12; ⓨ lunch & dinner) has great rooms – they have magic views where you'll probably catch sight of the water and Ben Loyal in one big sweeping panorama (room No 1 is a fave) – and the restaurant seems to drag patrons from miles around with its delicious, filling meals prepared with local produce. Try the local Kyle of Tongue oysters. Marvellous Murphys stout is on tap.

Vying for the position of best-located B&B in Scotland, **Cloisters** (☎ 601286; www.cloistertal.demon.co.uk; Talmine; r per person £25-30; ��) has three en-suite twin rooms with brilliant views over the Kyle of Tongue and offshore islands. Tastefully furnished, this place would suit older visitors or families. To get here from Tongue, cross the causeway and take the turn-off to Melness, almost immediately on your right.

Tongue to Durness

From Tongue it's 37 miles to Durness – you can take the causeway across the **Kyle of Tongue** or the beautiful old road that goes around the head of the kyle. A detour to **Melness** and **Port Vasgo** may be rewarded with the sight of seals on the beach.

SOMETHING SPECIAL

Strathtongue Old Manse (☎ 01847-611252; www.strathtongue.co.uk; Tongue; r per person £23) Have we got something special for you! Just a half-mile east of Coldbackie, set back from the A836, is this old manse – and it's a ripper of a B&B. The host knows her business and there's a choice of an en-suite double or a double and twin sharing a private bathroom (good for families). The private bathroom is the *pièce de résistance* – it's huge. Breakfast here is one of the best you'll get at a B&B and offers alternatives (such as fruit and kippers) away from bacon and eggs. It's a real nook-and-cranny house and there's a friendly mutt on hand to greet new arrivals. You'll find this place behind the old parish church.

Continuing west, the road crosses a desolate moor past **Moine House** (a ruin built as a shelter for travellers in 1830) to the northern end of **Loch Hope**. A 10-mile detour south along the loch leads to **Dun Dornaigil**, a well-preserved broch in the shadow of **Ben Hope** (927m). If you'd like to bag this Munro (ie reach the top of this summit – for more about this term, see the boxed text, p60), it's a 4.5-mile, four-hour round trip along the route from the car park, which is 2 miles before the broch, near a large barn. It's a relatively easy walk but often cold at the exposed top.

Beyond Loch Hope, on the main road, **Heilam** has stunning views out over **Loch Eriboll**, Britain's deepest sea inlet and a shelter for ships during WWII.

DURNESS (DIURANAIS)

☎ 01971 / pop 353

The scattered village of Durness (www.durness.org) is strung out along cliffs, which rise from a series of pristine beaches. It has one of the finest locations in Scotland. When the sun shines, the effects of blinding white sand, the cry of sea birds and the lime-coloured seas combine in a magical way. The only blight is the sometimes constant thumping from the Ministry of Defence (MOD) range on Cape Wrath, which can shatter the tranquillity of this northern outpost.

Orientation & Information

What's known as Durness is really two villages strung along the main road: Durness, in the west, and Smoo, a mile to the east.

Durness has two stores (Mace has an ATM), and a petrol station.

Durness Community Building (1 Bard Tce; per 30min £1; 🖵) Self-serve Internet access, opposite MacKays Hotel.

Health centre (☎ 511273)

TIC & visitor centre (☎ 511368; durnesstic@visit scotland.com; ☼ 10am-5pm Mon-Sat Apr, May, Sep & Oct, 10am-5pm Mon-Sat, to 4pm Sun Jun-Aug, 10am-1.30pm Nov-Mar) Organises guided walks in summer.

Sights & Activities

A mile east of the village centre is a path, near the SYHA hostel, down to **Smoo Cave**. The vast cave entrance stands at the end of an inlet, or geo, and a river cascades through its roof into a flooded cavern, then flows out to sea. There's evidence the cave was inhabited about 6000 years ago. You can take a **boat trip** (adult/child £3/1.50) into the floodlit cave, although after heavy rain the waterfall can make it impossible to get into the cave.

If you're a Beatles fan, drop by the **John Lennon memorial** in the garden by the village hall. His 'In my Life' song, from the *Rubber Soul* album, is about Durness.

The village has several beautiful **beaches**. One of the best is Sangobeg, but there's also a 'secret beach' just to the east, which can't be seen from the road. Around the coast, there are wrecks, caves, seals and whales. Inquire at the TIC for **trout-fishing** permits.

The old radar station at **Balnakeil**, less than a mile up a minor road from Durness, has been turned into a hippy craft village, with a bookshop, restaurants, art and craft workshops and the innovative **Lotte Globe Pottery Studio** (☎ 511354).

Sleeping & Eating

Smoo Falls (☎ 511228; www.smoofalls.com; Smoo; s £25, d £18-22; ☼ Mar-Oct) Friendly Smoo Falls is a working croft that has tastefully furnished rooms with a touch of class; the breakfast uses local produce and is a fine way to start the day.

MacKays Hotel (☎ 511202; www.visitmackays .com; Durness; d £70) This refurbished hotel has tastefully decorated rooms and an air of sophistication. The deluxe rooms have super king-size beds and big showers – they're worth the extra 10 quid.

Lazy Crofter Bunkhouse (☎ 511202; fiona@visit mackays.com; Durness; dm £10) This hostel has neat snug-as-a-bug bunks and great facilities. There are hot showers, no curfews and small dorms. Check in at MacKays Hotel next door.

Sango Sands Oasis (☎ 511222; fax 511205; Durness; camp sites per person £4.50) Pitch your tent on the northern edge of the country and dangle your feet over the precipice, admiring the sweeping views over the Atlantic's twinkling waters.

Loch Croispol Bookshop & Restaurant (☎ 511777; 17c Balnakeil Craft Village; lunch & snacks £2.50-5; ☼ 10am-5pm Mon-Sat, to 4pm Sun; ♿) At this place you can feed your body and your mind. Set among books featuring all things Scottish are a few tables where you can enjoy an all-day breakfast, and sandwiches and other standard fare at lunch. The Sunday traditional lunch with Yorkshire pudding (£8) is a highlight.

Also recommended:

Caberfiedh Guest House (☎ 511215; Durness; r per person £17) Basic digs, good value.

Puffin Cottage (☎ /fax 511208; www.puffincottage .com; Durness; d per person £18-22; ☼ Apr-Sep) A fine B&B.

Balnakeil Bistro (☎ 511232; Balnakeil Craft Village; mains £7-10; ☼ lunch & dinner; 🖵) Dine on rainbow trout, Lochinver pies and British lamb. Come for the food, not the décor.

DURNESS TO ULLAPOOL

It's 69 miles from Durness to Ullapool, with plenty of diversions along the way. The road to Ullapool has jaw-dropping scenery – dangerous on single-track roads as drivers struggle to tear their eyes away from vast, desolate plains spliced with rivulets of burns (streams), towering peaks and giant rocky outcrops.

Rugged **Cape Wrath** is crowned by a lighthouse (dating from 1827) and stands close to the sea-bird colonies on Clo Mor Cliffs, the highest coastal cliffs on the mainland. Getting to Cape Wrath involves a **ferry** (☎ 01971-511376) ride across the Kyle of Durness (£4.30 return, two hours) and a connecting **minibus** (☎ 01971-511287) for the 11 miles to the cape (£7 return, 40 minutes one way). Contact the TIC before setting out to make sure the ferry is running.

Kinlochbervie was one of Scotland's premier fish-landing ports and there's a lovely beach at **Oldshoremore**, a crofting settlement about 2 miles northwest of Kinlochbervie.

South of Cape Wrath, **Sandwood Bay** boasts one of Scotland's best and most isolated beaches, guarded at one end by the spectacular rock pinnacle Am Buachaille. Sandwood Bay is about 2 miles north of the end of a track from Blairmore (approach from Kinlochbervie), or you could walk south from the cape (allow eight hours) and on to Blairmore. Sandwood House is a creepy ruin reputedly haunted by the ghost of a 17th-century shipwrecked sailor.

The outlook from the **Kinlochbervie Hotel** (☎ 01971-521275; www.thekinlochberviehotel.com; r per person £35-45) must be the envy of almost every hotel in Scotland! Traditionally furnished, room Nos 1 and 2 are the best with simply magnificent water views. **Braeside** (☎ 01971-521325; r per person £21) is a friendly well-established B&B in a modern bungalow. There's no surcharge for solo travellers.

Scourie is a pretty crofting community. If you're looking to spoil yourself, **Scourie Lodge** (☎ 01971-502248; s/d £45/70, dinner £20), in a gorgeous building overlooking the bay, has three luxurious rooms and a garden with possibly the most northerly palm trees in the world.

Ferries (adult/child £8/4, half-hourly, 9.30am to 2pm Monday to Saturday April to mid-September) go to the important **Handa Island** sea-bird sanctuary from Tarbet, 6 miles north of Scourie; call ☎ 01971-502347.

Kylesku & Loch Glencoul
☎ 01971

Cruises on Loch Glencoul pass treacherous-looking mountains, seal colonies and the 213m-drop of **Eas a'Chual Aulin**, Britain's highest waterfall. In summer, the **MV Statesman** (☎ 502345) runs two-hour trips twice daily (except Saturday) from Kylesku Old Ferry Pier for £12.50/5 per adult/child. There are also trips to the lovely **Kerrachar Gardens** (ferry £10, admission £2.50), which are only accessible by boat from Kylesku.

While you wait for the ferry you can enjoy a pint (decent ales on tap) and tuck into a superb bar meal at the **Kylesku Hotel** (☎ 502231; www.kyleskuhotel.co.uk; Kylesku; s/d £45/75, bar mains £4.50; ❍ lunch & dinner), overlooking the pier. Seafood is the speciality including local mussels and salmon fish cakes.

Old Man of Stoer

It's roughly a 30-mile detour off the A894 to the Point of Stoer and the Rhu Stoer Lighthouse (1870) and back to the main road again. Along the coast road you need to be prepared for single-track roads, blind bends, summits and sheep. The rewards are spectacular views, pretty villages and excellent beaches. From the lighthouse, it's a good one-hour cliff walk to the Old Man of Stoer, a spectacular sea stack.

There are more good beaches between Stoer and Lochinver, including one at Achmelvich. **Achmelvich Youth Hostel** (SYHA; ☎ 0870 004 1102; dm adult/child £12/9; ❍ Apr-Sep) is about 1.5 miles from the Lochinver–Drumbeg postbus route, and 4 miles from Lochinver. Sheltered by rocky hills and found close to the beach, it's a small place with basic dorms.

Lochinver & Assynt
☎ 01571

The distinctive region of Assynt comprises a landscape of spectacular peaks rising from the moorland. Lochinver (population 639) is the main settlement. The busy little fishing port is a popular port of call for tourists, with its laid-back attitude, good facilities, striking scenery and award-winning visitor centre.

The **TIC & visitor centre** (☎ 0845 225 5121; Main St; ❍ 10am-5pm Jun-Oct, 10am-5pm Mon-Sat late Mar-May) has an interpretive display on the story of Assynt, from flora and fauna to clans, conflict and controversy. There's a supermarket in town, as well as a post office, bank (with an ATM), petrol station and **doctor** (☎ 844755).

The Lochinver–Lairg road (A837) meets the Durness road (A894) at **Skiag Bridge**, by Loch Assynt, about 10 miles east of Lochinver. Half a mile south of here, by the loch, there's the ruin of the late 15th-century Mac-Leod stronghold, **Ardvreck Castle**. There are wonderful summer sunsets over the castle and the loch.

The stunningly shaped hills of Assynt are popular with walkers and include peaks such as Suilven (731m), Quinag (808m), Ben More Assynt (998m) and Canisp (846m). The TIC has a free leaflet with brief details of walks in the area. For a more in-depth guide, pick up a copy of *Walks: West Sutherland* (£2.50) or *Making More of Assynt* (£2).

SLEEPING & EATING

Mrs Ross (☎ 844401; 1 Bayview Tce, Lochinver; r per person £17) This B&B has home-spun vibes and tidy rooms – a double and twin share a bathroom and overlook the water from the main drag.

Ardglas (☎ 844257; www.ardglas.co.uk; Inver, Lochinver; r per person £20) The comfortable Ardglas is a bastion in the hospitality trade with modern rooms, a decent-sized single and top views from the guests' lounge. It's expected to undergo significant renovations. All rooms share a bathroom.

Inchnadamph Lodge (☎ 822218; www.inch-lodge.co.uk; Inchnadamph; dm/d £12.50/18.50; ⬛ ♻) By the Lochinver–Lairg road, this place is a friendly 50-bed lodge with lots of rustic accommodation. Most rooms are spacious and clean and there's a separate music/TV lounge for late partying. The facilities are excellent and it's very popular with groups.

Albannach (☎ 844407; www.thealbannach.co.uk; Baddidarroch, Lochinver; d per person £105-125) The Albannach is sheer indulgence, on a grand scale. You'll discover roaring fireplaces, furniture found only in antique shops and a demure, sophisticated atmosphere. The restaurant here uses organic, wild produce and is highly recommended.

Lochinver Larder & Riverside Bistro (☎ 844356; 3 Main St; pies £5.75, mains £8-12; ⏲ lunch & dinner) With an outstanding ensemble of inventive food made with local produce, Lochinver pies are a particular standout here and are famous in this part of the world: try the apple and rhubarb, or wild boar and apricot – very tasty. The bistro here also churns out delicious seafood dishes in the evening, including hot spicy prawns. If you get addicted to the pies, don't worry – they deliver throughout Britain.

Inverpolly Nature Reserve

The Inverpolly Nature Reserve has numerous glacial lochs and the three peaks of Cul Mor (849m), Stac Pollaidh (613m) and Cul Beag (769m). **Stac Pollaidh** provides one of the most exciting walks in the area, with some good scrambling on its narrow sandstone crest. It takes just three hours on a round trip from the car park at Loch Lurgainn.

Achiltibuie

☎ 01854 / pop 290

With sheep nibbling the grassy roadside verges, the gorgeous Summer Isles moored just off the coast and the silhouettes of mountains skirting the bay, this town personifies idyllic Scottish beauty and is the perfect place for some serious relaxation.

About 5 miles northwest of town, the **Achiltibuie Smokehouse** (☎ 622353; Altandhu; admission free; ⏲ 9.30am-5pm Mon-Sat Easter-Oct) smokes all sorts of things, from cheese to eel to salmon. You can watch the processing and then buy the delectable results in the shop.

Summer Isles Cruises (☎ 622200) operates boat trips to the Summer Isles from Achiltibuie – you'll see some magnificent island scenery. The 3½-hour trips cost £20/10 per adult/child, and you get one hour ashore on **Tanera Mor**, where the post office issues its own stamps.

Summer Isles Hotel (☎ 622282; www.summerisleshotel.co.uk; Achiltibuie; s £75-150, d £120-185, bar meals £4-10, 5-course dinner £47; ⏲ Easter-Oct) is the Russian caviar of country hotels, exuding class, comfort and rustic sophistication. It makes a great spot to take a break from urban dwelling. The bar has quality bar meals ranging from sandwiches to the local speciality – seafood (try the platter for a taste of everything).

The rudimentary 20-bed **Achininver Youth Hostel** (SYHA; ☎ 0870 004 1101; Achininver, Achiltibuie; dm adult/child £12/9; ⏲ May-Sep) is designed for walkers and outdoor enthusiasts – you have to walk half a mile off the main road to reach it. Its remote, serene location has to be one of the best in the country.

Spa Coaches (☎ 01997-421311) operates buses Monday to Saturday from Reiff, Badenscallie (half a mile from the hostel) and Achiltibuie to Ullapool (one hour, two daily Monday to Friday, one Saturday).

ULLAPOOL

☎ 01854 / pop 1308

Ullapool's harbour-side façade is postcard-perfect and, on a sunny day, its surrounding rocky slopes are mirrored in the glassy veneer of the bay. A ferry service links Ullapool to Stornoway on the Isle of Lewis, churning a consistent trade of overnighters in its wake. There are few attractions, but heaps of great walking, piles of accommodation, mountains of delectable seafood and a couple of good watering holes.

Information

Bank of Scotland (West Argyle St) Has an ATM.
Laundrette (Broomfield Holiday Park; wash £3)
Library (☎ 612543; Mill St; ⏲ 9am-5pm Mon, Wed & Fri, 9am-5pm & 6-8pm Tue & Thu, closed Mon & Wed during holidays; ⬛) Free Internet access.

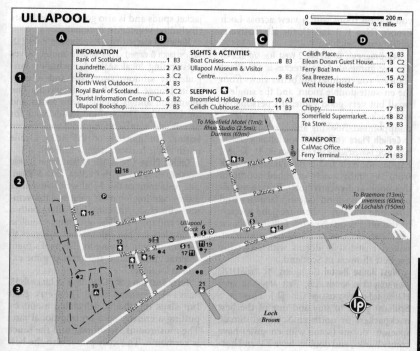

ULLAPOOL

INFORMATION	
Bank of Scotland	1 B3
Laundrette	2 A3
Library	3 C2
North West Outdoors	4 B3
Royal Bank of Scotland	5 C2
Tourist Information Centre (TIC)	6 B2
Ullapool Bookshop	7 B3

SIGHTS & ACTIVITIES	
Boat Cruises	8 B3
Ullapool Museum & Visitor Centre	9 B3

SLEEPING	
Broomfield Holiday Park	10 A3
Ceilidh Clubhouse	11 B3

Ceilidh Place	12 B3
Eilean Donan Guest House	13 C2
Ferry Boat Inn	14 C2
Sea Breezes	15 A2
West House Hostel	16 B3

EATING	
Chippy	17 B3
Somerfield Supermarket	18 B2
Tea Store	19 B3

TRANSPORT	
CalMac Office	20 B3
Ferry Terminal	21 B3

To Morefield Motel (1mi); Rhue Studio (2.5mi); Durness (69mi)

To Braemore (13mi); Inverness (60mi); Kyle of Lochalsh (150mi)

Loch Broom

NORTHERN HIGHLANDS & ISLANDS

Royal Bank of Scotland (cnr Ladysmith & Argyle Sts) Has an ATM.

TIC (☎ 612486, 0845 225 5121; ullapool@host.co.uk; 6 Argyle St; ⏰ 9.30am-5pm Mon-Sat May, 9.30am-5pm Jun-Sep, 9am-3pm Mon-Fri Oct-Apr) Efficient and helpful.

Ullapool Bookshop (☎ 612918; Quay St; ⏰ 9am-6pm Mon-Sat, 10am-4pm Sun; 🖥) Lots of books on Scottish topics, and maps of the area.

Sights

Ullapool Museum & Visitor Centre (☎ 612987; 7-8 West Argyle St; adult/child £3/50p; ⏰ 10am-5pm Mon-Sat Apr-Oct) is in a converted Telford Parliamentary church. An audiovisual presentation, interactive exhibits and various other displays chart the history of Loch Broom and its people.

Rhue Studio (☎ 612460; www.rhueart.co.uk; Rhue; admission free; ⏰ 10am-6pm Mon-Sat Apr-Sep, call for details Oct-Mar), 2.5 miles northwest of Ullapool, displays and sells the excellent art of contemporary landscape painter James Hawkins. The vivid and reflective works take a moment to adjust to, but they are wonderful interpretations. His work on the Outer Hebrides is breathtaking.

Activities

Ullapool is a great centre for hill walking. A good path up **Gleann na Sguaib** heads for the top of Beinn Dearg from Inverlael, at the inner end of Loch Broom. Ridge-walking on the **Fannichs** is relatively straightforward and many different routes are possible. The TIC can supply you with all the information and maps you need.

Good walking books sold at the TIC include *Walks in Wester Ross* (£2.50), or you can pick up a copy of the freebie guide to local woodland walks.

Tours

There are regular trips to the Summer Isles departing from the ferry terminal (adult/child £22/10, four hours).

Sleeping

Ferry Boat Inn (☎ 612366; www.ferryboat-inn.com; Shore St; r per person £36) The vivacious Ferry Boat is the liveliest place in town. The stylish, tastefully furnished rooms – a contrast to the grubby corridors – get snapped up quickly in summer. Book in advance if you want a room with a view across Loch Broom (Nos 1, 3 and 4); the alternative is looking at a brick wall.

Sea Breezes (☎ 612148; 2 West Tce; s/d £15/45) The recommended Sea Breezes is a brilliant choice – you couldn't buy better views from the en-suite double room, and the single is small but very good value. It's personable, laid-back and virtually impossible to leave disappointed. Booking ahead is advisable.

Ceilidh Place (☎ 612103; reservations@ceilidh.de mon.co.uk; 14 West Argyle St; r per person £45-65; ⬚ ♿) Exudes warmth and class. Take your pick from the individually designed rooms in this nook-and-cranny hotel. Price depends upon size, position (view), facilities and how long you stay – there are good specials in the off season. Nearby, **Ceilidh Clubhouse** (☎ 612103; West Lane; dm £15-20) has upmarket, pokey, rustic-style dorms with reputedly the best showers in Scotland.

West House Hostel (Scotpackers; ☎ /fax 613126; www.scotpackers-hostels.co.uk; West Argyle St; dm/d £12/30, self-catering cottage £75; ⬚) This is a brilliant place to stay and one of the best backpackers in northern Scotland. Small, spacious dorms (some with en suite) have comfy bunks, and doubles have TV and hot-drink facilities. It's clean, well run and very friendly – the owner has the right attitude.

Eilean Donan Guest House (☎ 612524; edonan@ ullapoolholidays.com; 14 Market St; s/d £25/50, 2-/3-course dinners £16.50/20) This top-class guesthouse has an open fire in the sitting room for those blustery evenings, a full-blown restaurant and excellent rooms with bathroom. It's in a lovely, tree-lined street a few minutes' walk from the seafront.

Broomfield Holiday Park (☎ 612664; West Lane; camp sites £8-12; ♥ May-Oct) On an inviting verge of Loch Broom, this camping ground has pesky midges, good facilities (including a laundrette) and lawns manicured with nail scissors.

Eating & Drinking

Chippy (Quay St; fish & chips £4; ♥ lunch & dinner) A previous winner of a best UK takeaway award. The grub here really is a cut above your average greasy chippy – the chips are freshly sliced and the fish is freshly cooked.

Tea Store (☎ 612995; Argyle St; snacks & light meals £2-5; ♥ 8am-8pm Mon-Sat, 10am-4pm Sun) A decent coffee nook for a light meal and a read of the newspaper. It serves filled rolls, toasties,

jacket spuds and is also good for breakfasts (including vegetarian options).

Morefield Motel (☎ 612161; North Rd; mains £12-18; ♥ lunch & dinner) This sedate motel serves outstanding local seafood, including langoustine, salmon, swordfish and lobster, in its lounge bar. It has a deservedly fine reputation and is popular with locals and tourists alike. The Seafood Rendezvous for two should only be attempted if you've been fasting. The motel is off the A835, a mile north of the harbour (follow Mill St).

Ceilidh Place (☎ 612103; 14 West Argyle St; light meals £6, mains £13-18; ♥ breakfast, lunch & dinner) The restaurant of this hotel serves inventive dishes catering for most palates – the venison with chilli and chocolate offers both a sweet and spicy fix. The restaurant's soulless setting lets the place down, but it comes to life in summer, serving as Ullapool's main entertainment centre and serving some excellent local ales.

Ferry Boat Inn (☎ 612366; Shore St; bar meals £8, mains £7-12; ♥ lunch & dinner) The Ferry Boat Inn slaps together a delectable menu by putting a creative spin on traditional fare. The mushrooms are shiitake and the sauce is vermouth. This cosy pub is also the best watering hole in town. New management has recently taken over and hopefully the excellent kitchen does not skip a beat.

For self-catering, you'll find a large Somerfield supermarket next to the car park north of Seaforth Rd.

Shopping

North West Outdoors (☎ 613323; West Argyle St) Good for outdoor equipment.

Getting There & Around

Ullapool is 215 miles from Edinburgh and 60 miles from Inverness. Scottish Citylink has two daily buses, Monday to Saturday, from Inverness to Ullapool (£7.70, 1½ hours), connecting with the ferry. See p384 for details of the ferry to Stornoway on the Isle of Lewis.

Bikes can be hired from West House Hostel (left).

ULLAPOOL TO THE EAST COAST

The A835 goes south from Ullapool to Braemore Junction, then continues over the wild Dirrie More to the Glascarnoch dam, with great views of Beinn Dearg on the way. This section is sometimes closed by snow in winter.

Five miles south of Inchbae, there's a junction where the A832 goes west to Gairloch through pleasant **Strath Braan**. The A835 continues southeast, past Garve village and Loch Garve to **Contin**.

Coul House Hotel (☎ 01997-421487; www.coulhouse hotel.com; Contin; s £55-75, d £90-130, mains £15-17; ☺ dinner) is a very fine country mansion dating from 1821. Set in its own private wilderness, this charming country hotel with blazing log fire will entice you to linger. Luxury rooms include mountain views and four-poster beds. Its restaurant serves eclectic modern fusion. Interpreted: everything's delicious.

Ullapool to Inverness buses follow this route and stop off at Contin, Garve and Aultguish. Trains from Inverness to Kyle of Lochalsh stop at Garve.

ULLAPOOL TO KYLE OF LOCHALSH

Although it's less than 50 miles as the crow flies from Ullapool to Kyle of Lochalsh, it's more like 150 miles along the circuitous coastal road – but don't let that put you off. It's a deliciously remote region and there are fine views of beaches and bays backed by mountains all the way along.

Falls of Measach

The A832 doubles back to the coast from the A835, 12 miles from Ullapool. Just before the junction, the Falls of Measach ('ugly' in Gaelic) spill 45m into the spectacularly deep and narrow Corrieshalloch Gorge. You can cross from side to side on a wobbly suspension bridge, built by Sir John Fowler of Braemore. The thundering falls and misty vapours rising from the gorge are very impressive – a shame about the logging in the plantation forest on the far side.

Dundonnell & Around
☎ 01854 / pop 169

Dundonnell appears half-drowned after a good soaking, with a combination of imposing ridges overlooking the lowlands of this tiny settlement. **An Teallach** (1062m) is a magnificent mountain – the highest summit can be reached by a path starting less than 500m southeast of the Dundonnell Hotel (six hours return). Traversing the ridge to Sail Liath is a more serious proposition, with lots of scrambling in precarious

places and difficult route-finding. Carry Ordnance Survey (OS) map No 19, food, water and waterproofs – it's amazing how quickly the weather can turn foul here.

Badrallach Bothy (☎ 633281; www.badrallach.com; Croft 9, Badrallach; bothy per person £4, camp sites per 2 people £9, r per person £25), 7 miles from the A832, has a good range of accommodation, as well as boats, bikes and fishing gear for hire. It's the perfect place to get away from it all and acquaint yourself with the rural beauty of this country.

Dundonnell Hotel (☎ 633204; www.dundonnellhotel .com; Dundonnell; r per person £50-80, bar meals £5-8) provides good refuge from the elements and has elegant, traditionally furnished rooms; the loch-and mountain-facing premier rooms have great views. Adventurous menus and attentive service ensure an enjoyable culinary experience too. Try the clam chowder or the local mussels.

Gairloch & Around
☎ 01445 / pop 1061

Gairloch is a group of villages (comprising Auchtercairn, Strath and Charlestown) around the inner end of a loch of the same name. The surrounding area has beautiful sandy beaches, good trout-fishing and bird-watching. Hill walkers also use Gairloch as a base for the Torridon hills and An Teallach.

The **TIC** (☎ 0845 225 5121; gairlochticadmin@tiscali .co.uk; ☺ daily Easter-Sep, Mon-Sat Oct-Easter) is at the car park in Auchtercairn, next to the museum, where a road branches off to the main centre at Strath.

There is a bank (with ATM) between Auchtercairn and Charlestown. For a doctor, call the **Auchtercairn health centre** (☎ 712229).

SIGHTS & ACTIVITIES
The excellent **Heritage Museum** (☎ 712287; www .gairlochheritagemuseum.org.uk; Auchtercairn; adult/child £3/50p; ☺ 10am-5pm Mon-Sat Mar-Sep, 10am-1pm Mon-Sat Oct), near the TIC, creates a vivid impression of life in the west Highlands from the time of the Picts to the present. You can see a typical crofting cottage, school room and shop.

The **Gairloch Marine Life Centre** (☎ 712636; Pier Rd, Charlestown; admission free; ☺ 10am-4pm Easter-Sep) has audiovisual and interactive displays, lots of charts and photos, and knowledgeable staff.

TOURS

From the Gairloch Marine Life Centre, **Gairloch Marine Cruises** (☎ 712636; www.porpoise-gairloch.co.uk; cruises per adult/child £15/13) sails up to three times daily (weather permitting) from Easter to September; during the two-hour trips you may see basking sharks, porpoises and Minke whales.

SLEEPING & EATING

Rua Reidh Lighthouse Hostel (☎ 771263; ruareidh@netcomuk.co.uk; dm/d £10/26) By Melvaig, and 13 miles from Gairloch (at the end of the road), this excellent hostel will give you a taste of a lighthouse-keeper's life. It also does good meals for £12.50 (by reservation). Buses from Gairloch run as far as Melvaig, then it's a 3-mile walk along the road to the lighthouse. En-suite doubles, twins and family rooms are also available.

Wayside Guest House (☎ 712008; Strath; s/d £25/40) If you're looking for a place to hole up for the night, this central B&B has water views from its two cosy rooms, which share a bathroom. It's right next to Strath Stores.

Musn't Grumble Cafe-Bar (☎ 771212; www.mustnt-grumble.com; B8021, Melvaig; mains £6-10; ☽ 11am-11pm Wed & Fri-Mon; ♿) Recommended for families, this eatery is café by day and classier restaurant by evening, specialising in chargrills and spit roasts. It's also home to rare breeds of animal such as Soay sheep, white wallabies and emus – wonderful entertainment for the kids.

Strath Stores (☎ 712499; Strath; lunch £2.40; 🖳) Drop into this first-rate grocery store for a

---

SOMETHING SPECIAL

Old Inn (☎ 01445-712006; www.theoldinn.net; Charlestown; s/d £40/90, mains £6-13) The sounds of honking geese, water rushing past in the burn (stream) and the twittering of birds greet patrons as they cross an old stone bridge and walk into the rustic Old Inn. It has a great feel, and a range of excellent snug rooms, some (such as No 4) beautifully furnished with polished dark-wood furniture. There are also rooms with four-poster beds. Downstairs, the bar is an atmospheric nook-and-cranny affair, with a great beer garden and serving recommended bar meals of the delectable seafood variety. The inn is just opposite Gairloch Pier.

---

freshly prepared sandwich or baguette. It also stocks some homemade mouthwatering pies and sausage rolls, including some stuffed with haggis.

Loch Maree & Victoria Falls

Loch Maree is sprinkled with islands, and a series of peaks line its northern shore, culminating in 980m-high Slioch. The A832 runs alongside the loch.

The Victoria Falls (commemorating the visit of Queen Victoria in 1877) tumble down to the loch between Slattadale and Talladale. Look for the 'Hydro Power' signs to find it.

Kinlochewe to Torridon

KINLOCHEWE & AROUND

☎ 01445

Tiny Kinlochewe is a good base for outdoor activities. You'll find an outdoor-equipment shop, a petrol station with a tearoom and a shop/post office that runs a café in summer. Check out the **Beinn Eighe Visitor Centre** (☎ 760254; admission free; ☽ 10am-5pm Easter-Oct), a mile north of Kinlochewe, with interactive displays (good for kids, too) on local geography, ecology, flora and fauna, and walking routes.

There's a basic, free **camping ground** (☎ 760 254) 1.5 miles north of the village. **Hillhaven** (☎ 760204; www.kinlochewe.info; Kinlochewe; s/d £32/54) is an excellent, friendly B&B that organises hawk-flying displays.

Kinlochewe Hotel (☎ 760253; kinlochewehotel@tinyworld.co.uk; Kinlochewe; dm £10, r per person £27.50, with bathroom £30, bar meals £5-£12; ☽ lunch & dinner) has a bunkhouse with one no-frills, 12-bed dorm, a decent kitchen and clean bathrooms. Make sure you check in at the hotel before venturing into the bunkhouse. Rooms inside the hotel aren't flash but are perfectly adequate – downstairs, the hotel dishes out traditional bar meals.

East of Kinlochewe, the single-track A832 continues to Achnasheen, where there's a train station.

TORRIDON & AROUND

Southwest from Kinlochewe, the A896 follows **Glen Torridon**, overlooked by multiple peaks, including Beinn Eighe (1010m) and Liathach (1055m). The drive along Glen Torridon is one of the most breathtaking in Scotland. Mighty, brooding mountains, often partly obscured by clumps of passing clouds, seemingly drawn to their peaks like magnets, loom over the tiny, winding, single-track road.

The road reaches the sea at Torridon, where there is a **Countryside Centre** (☎ 01445-791221; Torridon Mains; donation adult/child £3/2; ☯ 10am-6pm May-Sep) offering information on walks in the rugged area. There's an unstaffed **Deer Museum** (☯ daylight hrs year-round) nearby, which contains a collection of photos and odds and ends put together by a previous ranger.

The **camping ground** (☎ 01381-621252; Torridon; camp sites free) here has good showers and you get a grassy patch to pitch your tent, along with stunning views and wide-open, exhilarating space.

The modern, squat **Torridon Youth Hostel** (SYHA; ☎ 0870 004 1154; Torridon; dm adult/child £13/10; ☯ Mar-Oct) is in a magnificent location near the countryside centre and is used mainly by outdoor enthusiasts.

Ferroch (☎ 01445-791451; www.ferroch.co.uk; Annat, Loch Torridon; s/d £40/60), just southwest of Torridon village, is a guesthouse that, once you've woken up to the views, you'll never want to leave.

Magnificent **Loch Torridon Country House Hotel** (☎ 01445-791242; www.lochtorridonhotel.com; Torridon; s £64-110, d £101-331, 4-course dinner £45; ☒), complete with clock tower, is a class act and one of the best places to stay in Scotland. Everything about this property screams luxury…in a very quiet, refined way.

The A896 continues westwards to lovely **Shieldaig**, which boasts an attractive main street of whitewashed houses. **Tigh an Eilean Hotel** (☎ 01520-755251; Shieldaig; bar meals £7-12, 3-course dinner £38; ☯ lunch & dinner) dishes out locally caught seafood so fresh that it may still be squirming on your plate.

Applecross
☎ 01520 / pop 183

A long side trip abandons the A896 to follow the coast road to the delightfully remote seaside village of Applecross. Or you can continue a bit further down the A896 to one of the best drives in the country (best in terms of the remote and incredibly rugged and spectacular scenery, not the actual road, which winds and twists and balances on sheer precipices). The road climbs steeply to the Bealach na Ba pass (626m), then drops dramatically to the village. This drive is pure magic and a must if you're in the area. Note,

this road can be closed in winter. Applecross itself is a delightful wooded village gazing across to the peaks of Skye.

You can pitch your tent at the **Applecross Camp Site & Flower Tunnel** (☎ 744268; camp sites from £6, pizzas from £4; ☯ Easter-Oct), which also has a licensed pizza restaurant in a flower-filled conservatory.

The family-run **Applecross Inn** (☎ 744262; applecrossinn@globalnet.co.uk; Shore St; r per person £25-35, bar meals £7-10; ☒) is the kind of pub you could easily spend all day in. You'll find excellent food, real ales (Red Cuillen on tap) and usually a mix of locals and tourists. You couldn't ask for a better place to hole up.

Back on the main road, the A896 runs south from Shieldaig to **Kishorn**, where there's a general store and post office, and spectacular views westwards to the steep sandstone Applecross hills.

Kishorn Seafood & Snack Bar (☎ 733240; Kishorn; seafood dishes £5-15; ☯ 10am-5pm Mon-Sat, noon-5pm Sun Apr-Jun, Sep & Oct, 10am-9pm Mon-Sat, noon-9pm Sun Jul & Aug) has outstanding seafood in a simple eatery. The squat lobster (£5) is particularly good and the shellfish platter (£17) allows a taste of some of its best dishes.

Lochcarron
☎ 01520 / pop 920

The appealing, whitewashed village of Lochcarron is a veritable metropolis with two supermarkets, a bank (with an ATM), post office and petrol station. A long shoreline footpath at the loch's edge provides the perfect opportunity for a stroll to walk off breakfast.

Milmar (☎ 722406; stubbs-lc@tiscali.co.uk; Croft Rd; s/d £25/50) is one of the best-value B&Bs in the northern Highlands. There are views to die for in absolutely huge, pristine rooms – rooms that are truly immaculate. There's also no surcharge for solo travellers. The only slight blemish is breakfast, but they need something to work on…

If you stay at the small, quiet **Rockvilla Hotel** (☎ 722379; rockvillahotel@btInternet.com; Main St; r £60-65, mains £8-12; ☯ lunch & dinner) choose room Nos 1 or 2 – they are slightly cheaper, and have private facilities and dreamy views. The hotel kitchen does wonderful fresh seafood and is renowned for its scallops.

If only small Scottish towns had more places like **Waterside Cafe** (☎ 722303; Main St; mains £4-7; ☯ breakfast, lunch & dinner Mon-Sat, 10am-6pm Sun).

Serving a range of delicious meals at reasonable prices, including fresh seafood (try the local prawns), you can eat in the bright café or take food away at this friendly, humming little place.

Plockton

☎ 01599 / pop 428

Plockton is so idyllic that it could be designed by Hollywood, but there's nothing fake about the grandeur and beauty of this set. The place is overrun with tourists. However, its design around the harbour – a small, protected bay dotted with mini islands – means it gets cramped. It's especially popular with over 55s and we'd recommend a visit out of season (ie not in summer).

Cycling is a great way to explore the area and **Plockton Cycle Hire** (☎ 544255; Plockton Cottages, Frithard Rd) rents bikes for £8/12 per half/full day.

Calum's Seal Trips (☎ 544306; cruises adult/child £6/4) runs seal-watching cruises; there are swarms of seals just outside the harbour and the trip comes with an excellent commentary. Trips leave daily at 10am, noon, 2pm and 4pm. You may even spot an otter.

Plockton Station Bunkhouse (☎ 544235; mickcoe@btInternet.com; Nessun Dorma; dm £8.50-10) is in the former station building with excellent, clean facilities and comfy four-bed dorms. It's modern, and very convenient for the train.

The black-painted **Plockton Hotel** (☎ 544274; www.plocktonhotel.co.uk; Harbour St; r per person £30-45, starters £4.50, mains £7-14; ✆ lunch & dinner) has comfy rooms and serves popular pub food – rustic dining in an elegant pub setting.

KYLE OF LOCHALSH

☎ 01599 / pop 739

Before the Skye Bridge opened, Kyle of Lochalsh (normally just called Kyle) was the main jumping-off point for trips to the Isle of Skye. Now, however, its many B&B owners watch most of their trade whiz past without stopping.

The **TIC** (☎ 534198, 534390; ✆ 9.30am-5pm Mon-Fri, 10am-4pm Sat & Sun Easter-Oct), beside the main seafront car park, stocks information on Skye.

There's a string of B&Bs just outside of town on the road to Plockton. **Clais an Torrain** (☎ 530205; Church Rd; s/d £30/50) has two excellent, en-suite rooms in a rustic, down-to-earth place. It's all very homely,

unlike some of the soulless B&Bs in this town.

For a bit more luxury, **Kyle Hotel** (☎ 534204; www.thekylehotel.co.uk; Main St; r per person from £40) has deluxe doubles with spa bath that are deliciously decadent.

The best place at which to eat is the **Waverley** (☎ 534337; Main St; starters £5, mains £9-15; ✆ dinner Fri-Wed). This superb restaurant is an intimate place with excellent service; try the Indonesian chicken satay (skewers).

Kyle can be reached by bus from Inverness (£12, 2½ hours), and by three daily direct Scottish Citylink buses from Glasgow (£22, 5½ hours).

The 82-mile train ride between Inverness and Kyle of Lochalsh (£16, 2½ hours, up to four daily) is one of Scotland's most scenic rail routes.

KYLE TO THE GREAT GLEN

It's 55 miles southwest via the A87 from Kyle to Invergarry, which lies between Fort William and Fort Augustus, on Loch Oich.

Eilean Donan Castle

Photogenically sited at the entrance to Loch Duich, near Dornie village, **Eilean Donan Castle** (☎ 01599-555202; Dornie; adult/child £4.75/1.50; ✆ 10am-5.30pm mid-Mar–Nov, call for winter hrs) is one of Scotland's most evocative castles, and must be represented in millions of photo albums. It's on an offshore islet, magically linked to the mainland by an elegant, stone-arched bridge. It's very much a re-creation inside with an excellent introductory exhibition. Keep an eye out for the photos of castle scenes from the movie *Highlander*. There's also a sword used at the battle of Culloden in 1745. The castle was ruined in 1719 after Spanish Jacobite forces were defeated at the Battle of Glenshiel, and it was rebuilt between 1912 and 1932.

Scottish Citylink buses from Fort William and Inverness to Portree stop opposite the castle and by the bridge at Dornie.

Glen Shiel & Glenelg

From Eilean Donan Castle, the A87 follows Loch Duich into spectacular Glen Shiel, with 1000m-high peaks soaring up on both sides of the road. At Shiel Bridge, a narrow side road goes over the **Bealach Ratagain** (pass) to Glenelg, where there's still a ferry to Skye.

There are several good walks in the area, including the low-level route from Morvich to Glen Affric Youth Hostel (p321), via spectacular **Gleann Lichd** (17 miles). A traverse of the **Five Sisters of Kintail** is a classic and none-too-easy expedition; start a mile east of the Glen Shiel battle site and finish at Shiel Bridge (eight to 10 hours). For more information on these walks, contact the TIC at Kyle of Lochalsh.

From the Bealach Ratagain, there are great views of the Five Sisters. Continue past Glenelg to the two fine ruined Iron Age **brochs** – Dun Telve and Dun Troddan. Dun Telve still stands to a height of 10m, making it the second-best-preserved broch in Scotland, after Mousa (p423) in the Shetlands.

From Glenelg round to the road-end at **Arnisdale**, the scenery becomes even more spectacular, with great views across Loch Hourn to Knoydart.

Ratagan Youth Hostel (SYHA; ☎ 0870 004 1147; Shiel Bridge; dm adult/child £12.50/9.50; ☺ Mar-Oct; ▣) is a particularly good hostel. It has excellent facilities and a to-die-for spot by Loch Duich. If you want a break from Munro bagging, this is the place.

Kintail Lodge Hotel (☎ 01599-511275; www.kintaillodgehotel.co.uk; Shiel Bridge; bunkhouse bed £12.50, r per person £35-45, bar meals £8; ☺ lunch & dinner) has two bunkhouses, with self-catering facilities, sleeping six people each. With 10 of the 12 fine rooms facing the loch, you'd be unlucky not to get a decent outlook from a room inside the hotel. The tasty bar meals include local venison and salmon.

Scottish Citylink buses between Fort William, Inverness and Skye operate along the A87. There's a postbus operating once daily, except Sunday, from Kyle to Arnisdale via Shiel Bridge and Glenelg.

Cluanie Inn

Beyond the top of Glen Shiel, the A87 passes the remote, but welcoming, **Cluanie Inn** (☎ 01320-340238; www.cluanieinn.com; Glenmoriston; r per person £30-58, bar meals £6-15; ☺ lunch & dinner), which has a great lived-in feel to it, providing shelter and good cheer from the elements. It's a classy lodge and very popular with outdoor enthusiasts. There's even a four-poster bed, spa and sauna in here. Bar meals for hungry walkers include freshly shot haggis. From the inn, you can walk along several mountain ridges, bagging

Munros to your heart's content. There's a low-level route through to Glen Affric Youth Hostel (p321), which takes three hours, but it gets very wet at certain times of year.

ISLE OF SKYE

pop 8850

The Isle of Skye (an t-Eilean Sgiathanach in Gaelic) takes its name from the old Norse *sky-a*, meaning 'cloud island' – no doubt a reference to the often mist-enshrouded Cuillin Hills. It's the biggest of Scotland's islands, a 50-mile-long smorgasbord of velvet moors, jagged mountains, sparkling lochs and towering cliffs. The stunning scenery is the main attraction, but when the mist closes in there are plenty of castles, crofting museums and cosy pubs and restaurants to retire to.

Along with Edinburgh and Loch Ness, Skye is one of Scotland's top three tourist destinations. However, the hordes tend to stick to Portree, Dunvegan and Trotternish, and it's almost always possible to find peace and quiet in the island's farther-flung corners. Come prepared for changeable weather: when it's fine it's very fine indeed, but all too often it isn't.

Information

Portree and Broadford are the main population centres on Skye.

INTERNET ACCESS

Columba 1400 Community Centre (☎ 01478-611400; Staffin, Trotternish; per 20min £1.50; ☺ 10.30am-4.30pm Mon-Sat)

Portree TIC (☎ 01478-612137; portree@host.co.uk; Bayfield Rd, Portree; per 20min £1)

Skye Cobbler (☎ 01471-822880; Sutherland's Garage, Broadford; per 15min £1; ☺ 9am-5pm Tue-Fri)

Sligachan Hotel (☎ 01478-650204; www.sligachan .co.uk; Sligachan; per 15min £1)

MEDICAL SERVICES

Hospital (☎ 01478-613200; Portree) There's a casualty department and dental surgery here.

MONEY

Only Portree and Broadford have banks with ATMs. Portree's TIC has a currency exchange desk.

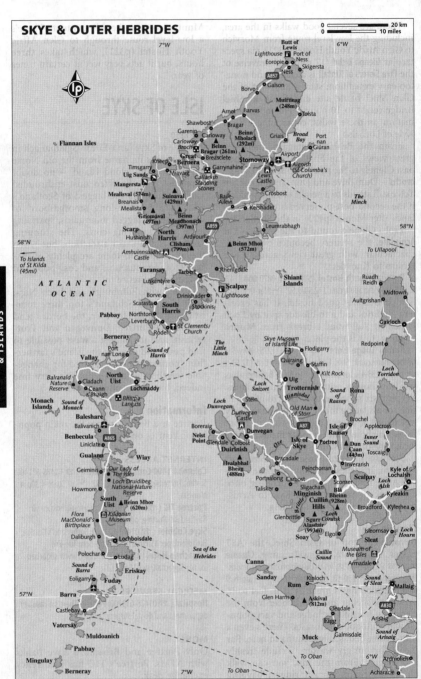

SKYE & OUTER HEBRIDES

| 0 | 20 km |
| 0 | 10 miles |

NORTHERN HIGHLANDS & ISLANDS

TOURIST INFORMATION

Broadford TIC (☎ 01471-822361; The Car Park, Broadford; ☒ 9.30am-5pm Mon-Fri, 10am-4pm Sat & Sun Apr-Oct, 9.30am-4.30pm Mon-Sat Nov-Mar)

Dunvegan TIC (☎ 01470-521581; 2 Lochside, Dunvegan; ☒ 9.30am-5pm Mon-Fri, 10am-4pm Sat & Sun Apr-Oct, 9.30am-4.30pm Mon-Sat Nov-Mar)

Portree TIC (☎ 01478-612137; portree@host.co.uk; Bayfield Rd, Portree; ☒ 9.30am-5pm Mon-Fri, 10am-4pm Sat & Sun Apr-Oct, 9.30am-4.30pm Mon-Sat Nov-Mar)

Activities
WALKING

Skye offers some of the finest – and in places the roughest and most difficult – walking in Scotland. There are many detailed guidebooks available, including a series of four walking guides by Charles Rhodes, available from the Aros Centre and the TIC at Portree. You'll need OS 1:50,000 maps Nos 23 and 32. Don't attempt the longer walks in bad weather or in winter.

Easy low-level routes include: through Strath Mor from Luib (on the Broadford–Sligachan road) to Torrin (on the Broadford–Elgol road, allow 1½ hours, 4 miles); from Sligachan to Kilmarie via Camasunary (four hours, 11 miles); and from Elgol to Kilmarie via Camasunary (2½ hours, 6.5 miles). The walk from Kilmarie to Coruisk via Camasunary and the 'Bad Step' (allow five hours, 11 miles round trip) is superb but slightly harder (the Bad Step is a rocky slab poised above the sea that you have to scramble across; it's easy in fine, dry weather, but some walkers find it intimidating nevertheless).

Skye Walking Holidays (☎ 01470-552396; www .skyewalks.co.uk; Duntulm Castle Hotel, Trotternish) organises week-long walking holidays, but individual walkers are welcome to join their guided walks for £25 a day.

CLIMBING

The Cuillin Hills is a playground for rock climbers, and the traverse of the Cuillin Ridge – a two-day expedition – is the finest mountaineering expedition in the British Isles. There are several mountain guides who can provide instruction and safely introduce inexperienced climbers to the harder routes. Agencies include **Cuillin Guides** (☎ 01478-640289; www.cuillin-guides.co.uk) and **Skye Guides** (☎ 01471-822116; www.skyeguides .co.uk). A five-day basic rock-climbing course costs around £275, and a private mountain

guide for one or two clients can be hired for around £80 a day.

WATER SPORTS

The sheltered coves and sea lochs around the coast of Skye provide magnificent sea-kayaking opportunities. **Whitewave Outdoor Centre** (☎ 01470-542414; www.white-wave.co.uk; Linicro, Kilmuir; ☒ Mar-Oct) and **Skyak Adventures** (☎ 01471-833428; www.skyakadventures.com; 13 Camus cross, Isleornsay) provide kayaking instruction, guiding and equipment hire for beginners and experts. It costs around £22 for a half-day kayak hire with instruction.

Tours

There are several operators who offer guided tours of Skye, covering history, culture and wildlife, including **Red Deer Travel** (☎ 01478-612142) and **Isle of Skye Tour Guide Co** (01471-844440; www.isle-of-skye-tour-guide.co.uk). Rates are around £10 an hour for up to six people.

Getting There & Away
BOAT

Despite there being a bridge, there are still a couple of ferry links between Skye and the mainland.

CalMac (☎ 01471-844248; www.calmac.co.uk) operates the Mallaig to Armadale ferry (driver or passenger £3.25, car £17.65, 30 minutes, eight or nine a day). It's very popular in July and August, so book ahead if you're travelling by car.

For details of ferries from Uig on Skye to the Outer Hebrides, see p384.

Skye Ferry (☎ 01599-511302; www.skyeferry.co.uk) runs a tiny vessel (six cars only) on the short Glenelg to Kylerhea crossing, from Easter to October only (car and up to four passengers £7, motorcycle £4, pedestrian £1, bicycle £1.50, five minutes, on demand). The ferry operates from 9am to 7.45pm Monday to Saturday and 10am to 5.45pm Sunday from mid-May to August (until 5.45pm Monday to Saturday in September and October). From Easter to mid-May it operates from 9am to 5.45pm Monday to Saturday only.

By summer 2006 a passenger-only ferry service between Portree and Gairloch should be open, operated by **West Highland Seaways** (☎ 0800 328 6426; www.overtheseatoskye.com); check the website for the latest details.

BUS

Scottish Citylink runs direct buses from Glasgow to Portree and Uig (£25, seven hours, three daily) via Crianlarich, Fort William, Kyle of Lochalsh and Thurso. Buses also run from Inverness to Portree (£15, 3½ hours, twice daily).

CAR & MOTORCYCLE

The Isle of Skye became permanently tethered to the Scottish mainland when the Skye Bridge opened in 1995. The controversial bridge tolls were abolished in 2004 and the crossing is now free.

There are petrol stations at Broadford (open 24 hours), Armadale, Portree, Dunvegan and Uig.

Getting Around

Getting around the island by public transport can be a pain, especially if you want to explore away from the main Kyleakin–Portree road. Here, as in much of the Highlands, public transport dwindles to nothing at weekends, particularly in winter and even more dramatically (or so it seems) when it rains.

Rapsons/Highland Country (☎ 01478-612622; www.rapsons.co.uk) operates the main bus routes on the island, linking all the main villages and towns. It offers a good-value Skye Roverbus ticket, giving unlimited travel for one/three days for £6/16.

You can order a taxi from **Kyle Taxi Company** (☎ 01599-534323), or rent a car from **Portree Coachworks** (☎ 01478-612688; www.portree coachworks.co.uk) from around £36 a day.

KYLEAKIN (CAOL ACAIN)
☎ 01599 / pop 100

Poor wee Kyleakin had the carpet pulled from under it when the Skye Bridge opened – it went from being the gateway to the island to a backwater bypassed by the main road. It's now a pleasant, peaceful little place, with a harbour used by yachts and fishing boats.

The village is something of a backpacker ghetto, with three hostels in close proximity. The homely **Dun Caan Independent Hostel** (☎ 534087; www.skyerover.co.uk; Castle View; dm £11-12; ✗), in a fine old pine-panelled house overlooking the harbour, has the most attractive location.

Friendly **Skye Backpackers** (☎ 534510; www .scotlands-top-hostels.com; Benmhor; dm £12-13) pulls in the party crowd, but the boxy **Kyleakin International Hostel** (SYHA; ☎ 0870 004 1134; dm £12-14), which looks more like a 1930s seaside hotel, lacks atmosphere despite its sea views.

Harry's Café (☎ 534641; mains £5; ☻ 9am-5.30pm Mon, Tue & Thu-Sat, 10am-5.30pm Sun), down by the harbour, is the place to go for tea and scones.

A shuttle bus runs half-hourly between Kyle of Lochalsh and Kyleakin (£1.90, five minutes), and there are eight to 10 buses daily (except Sunday) to Broadford and Portree.

BROADFORD (AN T-ATH LEATHANN)
☎ 01471 / pop 1050

Broadford is a service centre for the scattered communities of southern Skye. The long, straggling village has a **TIC** (☎ 822361; The Car Park; ☻ 9.30am-5pm Mon-Fri, 10am-4pm Sat & Sun Apr-Oct, 9.30am-4.30pm Mon-Sat Nov-Mar), a 24-hour petrol station, a large **Co-op supermarket** (☻ 8am-10pm Mon-Fri, 10am-4pm Sat & Sun), a laundrette, a bank with ATM, and a **hospital** (☎ 822137). **Broadford Books** (☎ 822748; Old Post Office; ☻ 9.15am-5pm Mon-Sat) sells a wide range of fiction as well as books of local interest.

Activities

The little harbour at Broadford is a base for **SkyeJet** (☎ 0800 783 2175; www.skyejet.co.uk), which offers high-speed boat trips in search of marine wildlife. You can also take cruises on the glass-bottomed boat **Family's Pride II** (☎ 0800 783 2175; www.skyejet.co.uk). One- or two-hour trips for both run most days from March to October; book in advance the previous evening, or between 7.30am and 9.30am on the day of the tour.

Sleeping & Eating

There are lots of B&Bs in and around Broadford, and the village is well placed for exploring southern Skye by car. Recommended B&Bs include **Berabhaigh** (☎ 822372; berabhaigh@freeuk.com; 3 Limepark; s £25-35, d £40-52; ℗ ✗), a lovely old croft house with views over the bay, and neighbouring **Limestone Cottage** (☎ 822142; 4 Lime Park; r per person £28-35; ✗), a delightful ivy-clad cottage. Both lie between the main road and the sea.

Broadford has several places at which to eat, but one really stands out. **Creelers** (☎ 822281; Lower Harrapool; mains £8-13; ☻ 4-10pm Thu-Tue) is a small, bustling, no-frills restaurant that serves some of the best seafood on Skye. Book ahead, and if you can't get a table then nip around to the back door, where you'll find Ma Doyle's Takeaway, for fish and chips (£4.50) to go.

Getting There & Around

Daily Scottish Citylink buses to Portree stop at Broadford. You can hire bikes from **Fairwinds Bicycle Hire** (☎ 822270) near the Broadford Hotel for £7 a day.

SLEAT

If you cross over the sea to Skye on the ferry from Mallaig you arrive in Armadale, at the southern end of the long, low-lying peninsula known as Sleat (pronounced slate). The landscape of Sleat itself is not exceptional, but it provides a grandstand for ogling the magnificent scenery on either side – take the steep and twisting minor road that loops through **Tarskavaig** and **Tokavaig** for stunning views of the Isle of Rum, the Cuillin Hills and Bla Bheinn.

Armadale

☎ 01471 / pop 150

Armadale has a grocery store and post office. Just along the road is the part-ruined Armadale Castle, former seat of Lord Macdonald of Sleat and home to the **Museum of the Isles** (☎ 844305; adult/child £4.80/3.50; ☼ 9.30am-5.30pm Easter-Oct). The museum will tell you all you ever wanted to know about Clan Donald, as well as providing an easily digested history of the Lordship of the Isles. Prize exhibits include rare portraits of clan chiefs, and a wine glass that was once used by Bonnie Prince Charlie. The ticket also gives admission to the lovely castle gardens.

Sea.fari (☎ 822361; www.seafari.co.uk) runs two- and three-hour boat trips in a high-speed RIB (rigid inflatable boat) for £22/32 per person. These trips have a high success rate for spotting Minke whales in summer, with rarer sightings of bottlenose dolphins and basking sharks – even a humpback whale was spotted in August 2004.

The no-frills **Armadale Youth Hostel** (SYHA; ☎ 0870 004 1103; dm £12; ☼ Apr-Sep) has a great location on the north side of the ferry harbour, while the rustic **Flora MacDonald Hostel** (☎ 844440; The Glebe, Kilmore; dm/tw £11/25) is 3 miles north of the ferry, on a farm full of Highland cattle and Eriskay ponies.

The **Pasta Shed** (☎ 844264; The Pier, Armadale; mains £5-9), beside the ferry pier, is a cute little

---

SOMETHING SPECIAL

Toravaig House Hotel (☎ 01471-820200; www.skyehotel.co.uk; Sleat; r per person £55-69, mains £13-18; ☼ lunch & dinner; P ✗) The owners of this gorgeous country house hotel know a thing or two about hospitality – as soon as you arrive you'll feel right at home, whether relaxing on the plump sofas by the log fire in the lounge, or admiring the view across the Sound of Sleat from the lawn chairs in the garden. The spacious bedrooms – ask for room No 1, with its enormous sleigh bed – are luxuriously equipped, from the rich and heavy bed linen to the huge, high-pressure shower-heads, and the elegant restaurant serves the best of local fish, game and lamb. After dinner, you can retire to the lounge with a single malt and flick through the yachting magazines, or try your hand at tickling the ivories on the baby grand in the corner. The hotel is on the A851 road, 7 miles north of Armadale and 10 miles south of Broadford.

---

conservatory with some outdoor tables. It serves good seafood dishes, pizza, chips and sandwiches – you can sit in or take away.

There are six or seven buses a day (Monday to Saturday) from Armadale to Broadford and Portree.

Isleornsay

This pretty harbour, 8 miles north of Armadale, is opposite Sandaig Bay on the mainland, where Gavin Maxwell lived and wrote his much-loved memoir *Ring of Bright Water*. **Gallery An Talla Dearg** (☎ 01767-650444; admission free; ☼ 10am-6pm Mon-Fri, to 4pm Sat & Sun) exhibits the works of local artists.

Hotel Eilean Iarmain (☎ 01471-833266; s/d £90/110, bar meals £7-10; P) is a charming old Victorian hotel with log fires, an excellent restaurant and 12 luxurious rooms, many with sea views. The hotel's cosy, wood-panelled bar serves delicious, gourmet-style bar meals – try the grilled langoustines or pork-neck steaks.

ELGOL (EALAGHOL)

On a clear day, the journey along the road from Broadford to Elgol is one of the most scenic on Skye. It takes in two classic postcard panoramas – the view of Bla Bheinn

FLORA MACDONALD

The Isle of Skye was home to Flora MacDonald, who became famous for helping Bonnie Prince Charlie escape his defeat at the Battle of Culloden.

Flora was born in 1722 at Milton in South Uist, where a memorial cairn marks the site of one of her early childhood homes. After her mother's abduction by Hugh MacDonald of Skye, Flora was reared by her brother and educated in the home of the Clanranald chiefs.

In 1746, she helped Bonnie Prince Charlie escape from Benbecula to Skye, disguised as her Irish maidservant. With a price on the prince's head, their little boat was fired on, but they managed to land safely and Flora escorted the prince to Portree where he gave her a gold locket containing his portrait before setting sail for Raasay.

Waylaid on the way home, the boatmen admitted everything. Flora was arrested and imprisoned in the Tower of London. She never saw or heard from the prince again.

In 1747, she returned home, marrying Allan MacDonald of Skye and having nine children. Dr Samuel Johnson stayed with her in 1773 during his trip the Western Isles, but later poverty forced her family to emigrate to North Carolina. There her husband was captured by rebels. Flora returned to Kingsburgh on Skye where she died in 1790. She was buried in Kilmuir churchyard, wrapped in the sheet in which both Bonnie Prince Charlie and Dr Johnson had slept.

across Loch Slapin (near Torrin), and the superb view of the entire Cuillin range from Elgol pier.

Bella Jane (☎ 0800 731 3089; www.bellajane.co.uk; adult/child £20/6; ☼ Easter–mid-Oct) offers a three-hour cruise from Elgol harbour to the remote **Loch na Cuilce**, an impressive inlet surrounded by soaring peaks and acres of bare rock slabs. On a calm day, you can clamber ashore here to make the short walk to **Loch Coruisk** in the heart of the Cuillin Hills. You get 1½ hours ashore, and visit a seal colony en route.

Aquaxplore (☎ 0800 731 3089; www.aquaxplore.co .uk) runs 2½-hour high-speed boat trips from Elgol to Loch na Cuilce and an abandoned shark-hunting station on the island of Soay (adult/child £23/17). There are longer trips (£28/20) to Rum, Canna and Sanday to visit breeding colonies of puffins, with the chance of seeing Minke whales on the way.

There's a Royal Mail postbus from Broadford to Elgol (£4, 40 minutes, two daily Monday to Friday, one Saturday), departing Broadford at 10.45am and 3.40pm, and departing Elgol at 2.40pm and 8.07am.

CUILLIN HILLS
☎ 01478

The Cuillin Hills are Britain's most spectacular mountain range. Though small in stature (**Sgurr Alasdair**, the highest summit, is only 993m), the peaks are near-alpine in character, with knife-edge ridges, jagged pinnacles, scree-filled gullies and acres of naked rock. While they are a paradise for experienced mountaineers, the higher reaches of the Cuillin are off limits to the majority of walkers.

There are plenty of good low-level walks within the ability of most walkers. One of the best (on a fine day) is the steep climb from Glenbrittle camping ground to **Coire Lagan** (6 miles round trip; allow at least three hours). The impressive upper corrie contains a lochan for bathing (for the hardy!), and the surrounding cliffs are a playground for rock climbers – bring along your binoculars.

There are two main bases for exploring the Cuillin – Sligachan to the north, and Glenbrittle to the south.

Sleeping & Eating
Sligachan Hotel (☎ 650204; www.sligachan.co.uk; Sligachan; dm/s/d £10/50/70; ⓟ ☒ 🖥) The Slig, as it has been known to generations of climbers, is a near village in itself, encompassing a posh hotel, a bunkhouse, self-catering cottages, a big barn of a bar (complete with kids' playroom) and an adventure playground. **Seamus's Bar** (mains £5-11; ☼ food served 8am-11pm) dishes up decent bar meals, but if you fancy something a little more up-market, the hotel's **Cairidh Seafood Restaurant** (mains £10-17; ☼ noon-2pm & 7-9pm) can oblige.

Across the road from the hotel there's a basic **camping ground** (☎ 650333; camp sites per person £4.50).

At the southern end of the Cuillin you have the choice of the Scandinavian-style, timber **Glenbrittle Youth Hostel** (SYHA; ☎ 0870 004 1121; Glenbrittle; dm £12; ☼ Apr-Sep), or the **camping** ground (☎ 640404; camp sites per person £3.50, plus per car £1.75) down by the sea. Beware – the midges can be diabolical.

Getting There & Away

Sligachan, on the main Kyle–Portree road, is easily accessible by bus. Glenbrittle is a bit harder to reach. From Monday to Saturday, local buses run twice a day from Portree to Glenbrittle via Sligachan and Carbost. Hitching to Glenbrittle can be slow, especially late in the day.

MINGINISH

☎ 01478

Loch Harport, to the north of the Cuillin, divides the Minginish peninsula from the rest of Skye. On its southern shore lies the village of Carbost, home to the smooth, sweet and smoky Talisker malt whisky, produced at **Talisker Distillery** (☎ 614308; Carbost; admission £4; ☢ 9.30am-5pm Mon-Sat Easter-Oct, 2-5pm Mon-Fri Nov-Easter). This is the only distillery on Skye; the guided tour includes a free dram. Magnificent **Talisker Bay**, 5 miles west of Carbost, has a sandy beach, sea stack and waterfall.

The **Old Inn** (☎ 640205; Carbost; dm/s/d £12/30/58; ☢ food served 6.30-10pm; **P**) has a lovely location overlooking Loch Harport. Its bright, refurbished rooms are complemented by a comfortable chalet-style bunkhouse. The bar is a favourite with walkers and climbers from Glenbrittle.

Three miles northwest of Carbost is the **Skyewalker Independent Hostel** (☎ 640250; Fiskavaig Rd, Portnalong; dm £8.50), housed in the old village school. There's a tiny **camping ground** (camp sites per person £2.50) out the back.

There are two or three buses a day from Portree to Carbost via Sligachan.

PORTREE (PORT RIGH)

☎ 01478 / pop 1920

Portree is Skye's largest and liveliest town. It has a pretty harbour lined with gaily painted houses, and there are great views of the surrounding hills. Its name (from the Gaelic for King's Harbour) commemorates James V, who came here in 1540 to pacify the local clans.

Information

Bank of Scotland (☎ 0845 720 3040; Somerled Sq; ☢ 9am-12.30pm & 1.30-5pm Mon-Fri) Has an ATM.

Post office (☎ 612533; Wentworth St; ☢ 9am-5.30pm Mon-Sat) Offers currency exchange.
Royal Bank of Scotland (☎ 612822; Bank St; ☢ 9.15am-4.45pm Mon, Tue, Thu & Fri, 10am-4.45pm Wed) Has ATMs.
TIC (☎ 612137; Bayfield Rd; ☢ 9.30am-5pm Mon-Fri, 10am-4pm Sat & Sun Apr-Oct, 9.30am-4.30pm Mon-Sat Nov-Mar; ☐) Provides Internet access (£1 per 20 minutes) and currency exchange.

Sights & Activities

On the southern edge of Portree, the **Aros Experience** (☎ 613649; Viewfield Rd; adult/child £3/2; ☢ 9am-6pm) is a combined visitor centre, book and gift shop, restaurant, theatre and cinema. The price of a ticket gets you a look at some fascinating, live CCTV images from local sea eagle and heron nests, and a viewing of a strangely commentary-free wide-screen video of Skye's impressive scenery (it's worth waiting for the aerial shots of the Cuillin). The centre is a useful rainy-day retreat, with an indoor soft play area for children.

An Tuireann Art Centre (☎ 613306; www.antuire ann.org.uk; Struan Rd; admission free; ☢ 10am-5pm Mon-Sat), half a mile west of town on the B885, is an appealing gallery that hosts changing exhibitions of contemporary art. It also has an excellent café.

Festivals & Events

The annual **Isle of Skye Highland Games** (☎ 612608; www.skye-highland-games.co.uk) are held in Portree in early August.

Sleeping

Portree is well supplied with B&Bs, but most of them are in bland modern bungalows that, though comfortable, are often lacking in character. Accommodation fills up fast in July and August, so be sure to book ahead.

BUDGET

Portree Independent Hostel (☎ 613737; skyehostel@ yahoo.co.uk; The Green; dm £12-13; ☒) Housed in the former post office near the town square, this is a rambling two-storey hostel with cosy dorms and a huge open kitchen and dining area. Phone bookings are preferred to those made by email.

Bay View House (☎ 613340; Bayfield; r per person £17; **P** ☒) This is a modern house with spartan but sparklingly clean rooms, some with sea and mountain views, and bathrooms with power showers. At this price and location, it's a bargain.

Torvaig Camping (☎ 612209; Torvaig; camp sites per adult/child £4/1; ☼ Apr–mid-Oct) This is the closest camping ground to Portree. It's a mile north of town on the A87 to Uig.

MIDRANGE & TOP END

Rosedale Hotel (☎ 613131; www.rosedalehotelskye .co.uk; Beaumont Cres; s £35-50, d £70-100; ☼ Mar–Nov; ✗) The Rosedale is an atmospheric old hotel delightfully situated down by the harbour. Its three converted fishermen's cottages are linked by a maze of narrow stairs and corridors. Readers have commented approvingly on its friendly and helpful staff, and on its fine restaurant with harbour views.

Pink Guest House (☎ 612263; www.pink-guest -house.co.uk; 1 Quay St; r per person £35; ✗) You can't miss the bright pink façade of this waterfront B&B. The pink theme continues in the bedrooms (all have en suites), many of which have spectacular views across the harbour.

Grenitote B&B (☎ 612808; e.a.matheson@amserve .net; 9 Martin Cres; s/d £30/50) Readers have appreciated the warm welcome at this attractive, modern, two-room bungalow. It's in a quiet residential area, just uphill from the town centre.

Royal Hotel (MacNab's Inn; ☎ 612525; www.royal -hotel-skye.com; Bank St; s/d £65/100; ✗) The historic Royal Hotel was visited by James V in 1540, and Bonnie Prince Charlie and Flora MacDonald parted company in a room here

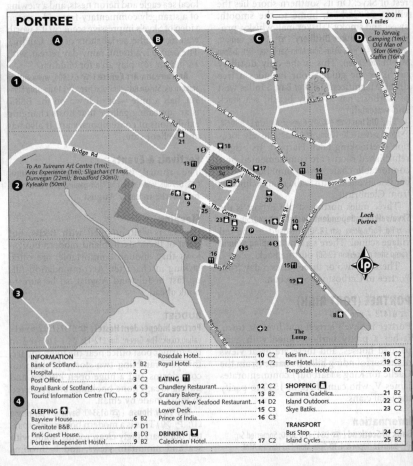

shortly before the prince left for Raasay. Recently refurbished, it's now a luxurious, modern place with a sauna and gym; most of the 21 rooms have a view across the harbour.

Eating

Harbour View Seafood Restaurant (☎ 612069; 7 Bosville Tce; mains £13-18; ☻ noon-2.30pm & 5.30-10pm) The Harbour View is Portree's most congenial place at which to eat. It has a homely dining room with a log fire in winter, books on the mantelpiece and bric-a-brac on the shelves. And on the table, superb Scottish seafood dishes such as fresh Skye oysters, seafood chowder, king scallops, langoustines and lobster.

Chandlery Restaurant (☎ 612846; 1 Bosville Tce; mains £9-15, 3-course dinner £37; ☻ noon-2.30pm & 6-10pm) The restaurant at the Bosville Hotel offers a relaxed atmosphere, and an award-winning chef, and a menu that uses Skye-sourced produce including lamb, game, seafood, cheese, organic vegetables and berries. Signature dishes include seared loin of lamb on a cassoulet of barley and root vegetables with a thyme jus; and pan-fried venison and poached oysters on julienne vegetables and salad leaves, with a balsamic and dill dressing. You can also dine on good lunches in the hotel's Merchant Bar.

An Tuireann Art Centre Café (☎ 613306; Struan Rd; sandwiches £3-5, mains £4-7; ☻ snacks 10am-4.30pm Mon-Sat, lunch Mon-Sat) It's well worth making the short journey out of town (a mile west on the B885) to eat at the art centre's organic café. You can enjoy homemade soups (such as sweet potato, cauliflower, or *Cullen skink*) and imaginative vegetarian and vegan dishes, as well as a few seafood and chicken specials.

Granary Bakery (☎ 612873; Somerled Sq; light meals £3-5; ☻ 8.30am-5pm Mon-Sat) Most of Portree seems to congregate at the Granary's cosy coffee shop at breakfast and lunch, to snack on tasty sandwiches, filled rolls, pies, cakes and pastries.

Portree's favourite fish and chip shop is **Lower Deck** (Quay St; ☻ noon-2.30pm & 6-9pm) down by the harbour; for a curry (takeaway or sit-in), try **Prince of India** (☎ 612681; Bayfield Rd; mains £5-8).

Drinking

Isles Inn (☎ 612129; Somerled Sq) A mix of young locals and backpackers head to the inn's Jacobean-themed bar with its flagstone floor and open fires.

Tongadale Hotel (☎ 612115; Wentworth St) The lively bar at the Tongadale pulls in a similar crowd to that of the Isles Inn.

Caledonian Hotel (☎ 612641; Wentworth St) Popular with locals, the bar here has live music from Thursday to Saturday.

Pier Hotel (☎ 612094; Quay St) You can almost guarantee a weekend sing-song at this waterfront hotel.

Shopping

Skye Batiks (☎ 613331; The Green; ☻ 9am-6pm May, Jun & Sep, to 9pm Jul & Aug, to 5pm Mon-Sat Oct-Apr) A cut above the average gift shop, selling a range of interesting crafts such as carved wood, jewellery and batik fabrics with Celtic designs.

Island Outdoors (☎ 611073; The Green; ☻ 9am-6pm Mon-Sat) Next door to Skye Batiks, this store stocks equipment and clothing for climbing, walking, camping and kayaking.

Carmina Gadelica (☎ 612585; 4 Wentworth St; ☻ 9am-5.30pm Mon-Sat, to 8pm Jul & Aug) Browse the shelves here for CDs of Gaelic music and books on local subjects.

Getting There & Around

The main bus stop is in Somerled Sq. There are three to five buses a day from Portree to Sligachan (15 minutes), Broadford (35 minutes) and Dunvegan Castle (40 minutes), and six a day on a circular route around Trotternish (in both directions) taking in Flodigarry (20 minutes), Kilmuir (1¼ hours) and Uig (30 minutes). See p376 for details of buses from the mainland.

You can hire bikes at **Island Cycles** (☎ 613121; The Green; ☻ 9am-5pm Mon-Sat) for £7.50/12 per half-/full day.

DUNVEGAN (DUN BHEAGAIN)
☎ 01470

Skye's most famous historic building, and one of its most popular tourist attractions, is **Dunvegan Castle** (☎ 521206; Dunvegan; adult/child £6.50/4; ☻ 10am-5pm Easter-Oct, 11am-4pm Oct-Easter), seat of the chief of Clan MacLeod. It has played host to Samuel Johnson, Sir Walter Scott and, most famously, Flora MacDonald (see the boxed text, p378). The oldest parts are the 14th-century keep and dungeon, but most of it dates from the 17th to 19th centuries.

In addition to the usual castle stuff – swords, silver and family portraits – there are some interesting artefacts, most famous being the **Fairy Flag**, a diaphanous silk banner that dates from some time between the 4th and 7th centuries. Bonnie Prince Charlie's waistcoat and a lock of his hair, donated by Flora MacDonald's granddaughter, share a room with **Rory Mor's Drinking Horn**, a beautiful 16th-century vessel of Celtic design that could hold half a gallon of claret. Upholding the family tradition in 1956, the present chief downed the contents in one minute and 57 seconds 'without setting down or falling down' – note that in his portrait in the dining room he is most definitely sitting down.

DUIRINISH
☎ 01470

The Duirinish peninsula, to the west of Dunvegan, has some of Skye's most atmospheric hotels and restaurants. It's worth making the long drive beyond Dunvegan on single-track roads to Waterstein to see the spectacular sea cliffs of **Waterstein Head**, and to walk down to **Neist lighthouse** with its views to the Outer Hebrides. This part of the island also has some of Skye's most atmospheric hotels and restaurants.

Sleeping & Eating

Stein Inn (☎ 592362; www.steininn.co.uk; Stein, Waternish; s/d £32/50; **P**) This old country tavern dates from 1790, with a handful of rooms (all with sea views), a lively little bar, and a delightful beer garden – a real suntrap on summer afternoons – beside the loch. It's on the B886 road along the Waternish peninsula, about 8 miles north of Dunvegan.

Lochbay Seafood Restaurant (☎ 592235; Stein, Waternish; mains £9-20; ☻ noon-2.30pm & 6.30-9pm Mon-Fri Easter-Oct, plus 6.30-9pm Sat Aug-Oct) Next door to the Stein Inn is one of Skye's most romantic restaurants, a cosy farmhouse kitchen with terracotta tiles and a wood-burning stove, and a menu that includes most things that either swim in the sea or live in a shell – from fillet of hake to sautéed scallops to lobster.

Three Chimneys (☎ 511258; www.threechimneys .co.uk; Colbost, Dunvegan; d £240, 3-course lunch/dinner £24/45; ☻ 12.30-2pm & 6.30-9pm Mon-Sat; **P** ✗) In Colbost, halfway between Dunvegan and Waterstein, is another superb romantic retreat combining a gourmet restaurant in a candle-lit crofter's cottage with sumptuous five-star rooms in the modern house next door. Book well in advance.

TROTTERNISH
☎ 01470

The Trotternish peninsula to the north of Portree has some of Skye's most beautiful – and bizarre – scenery.

East Coast

First up is the 50m-high, potbellied pinnacle of crumbling basalt known as the **Old Man of Storr**, prominent above the road 6 miles north of Portree. Walk up to its foot from the car park in the woods at the northern end of Loch Leathan (one hour round trip, 2 miles). This seemingly unclimbable pinnacle was scaled in 1955 by English mountaineer Don Whillans. North again, near Staffin (Stamhain), is spectacular **Kilt Rock**, a stupendous cliff of columnar basalt whose vertical ribbing is fancifully compared to pleats of a kilt.

Staffin Bay is dominated by the dramatic basalt escarpment of the **Quiraing**, whose impressive land-slipped cliffs and pinnacles constitute one of Skye's most remarkable landscapes. From a parking area at the highest point of the minor road between Staffin and Uig you can walk north to the Quiraing in half an hour. The adventurous (and energetic) can scramble up to the left of the slim pinnacle called the **Needle** to find a hidden, grass-topped plateau known as the **Table**.

SLEEPING & EATING

Flodigarry Country House Hotel (☎ 552203; www .flodigarry.co.uk; Flodigarry; d £130-190; ☻ lunch & dinner; **P** ✗) Flora MacDonald (see the boxed text, p378) lived in a farmhouse cottage at Flodigarry in northeast Trotternish from 1751 to 1759. The cottage and its pretty garden are now part of this delightful hotel – you can stay in the cottage itself (there are two bedrooms), or in the more spacious rooms in the hotel itself. The hotel bar – whose décor is strangely reminiscent of a Turkish bathhouse – has great views over the Inner Sound, and serves excellent haddock and chips for lunch.

Dun Flodigarry Hostel (☎ 552212; hostel.flodi garry@btopenworld.com; Flodigarry; dm/d £11/25; ✗ ▣) If the hotel is too expensive for you, this nearby hostel shares the same superb views, and you can still visit the hotel bar for a pint – it's only a 100m walk away.

West Coast

The peat-reek of crofting life in the 18th and 19th centuries is preserved in thatched cottages at **Skye Museum of Island Life** (☎ 552206; Kilmuir; adult/child £1.75/1; ☺ 9am-5.30pm Mon-Sat Apr-Oct). Behind the museum is Kilmuir Cemetery, where a tall Celtic cross marks the **grave of Flora MacDonald**; the cross was erected in 1955 to replace the original, of which 'every fragment was removed by tourists'.

Whichever way you arrive at **Uig** (pronounced oo-ig), the picture-perfect bay, ringed by steep hills, rarely fails to impress. If you've time to kill while waiting for a ferry to the Outer Hebrides, visit the **Isle of Skye Brewery** (☎ 542477; The Pier, Uig; ☺ 9am-5pm Mon-Fri), which sells local cask ales and bottled beers.

Just south of Uig, a minor road (signposted 'Sheader and Balnaknock') leads in a mile or so to the **Fairy Glen**, a strange and enchanting natural landscape of miniature conical hills, rocky towers, ruined cottages and a tiny roadside lochan.

There's a cluster of B&Bs in Uig, as well as the **Uig Youth Hostel** (SYHA; ☎ 0870 004 1155; Uig; dm £12; ☺ late Apr-Sep) and a lovely old coaching inn, the **Uig Hotel** (☎ 542205; Uig; s/d £38/73; Ⓟ).

ISLE OF RAASAY

☎ 01478 / pop 160

Raasay is the rugged, 10-mile-long island that lies off Skye's east coast. There are several good walks here, including one to the flat-topped conical hill of **Dun Caan** (443m). Forest Enterprise publishes a free leaflet (available from the TICs in Portree or Kyle of Lochalsh) with suggested walks and forest trails.

The extraordinary ruin of **Brochel Castle**, perched on a pinnacle at the northern end of Raasay, was home to Calum Garbh Mac-Leod, an early-16th-century pirate. At the battle of Culloden in 1746, Raasay supplied Bonnie Prince Charlie with around 100 fighting men and 26 pipers, but the people paid dearly for their Jacobite sympathies when victorious government forces arrived and proceeded to murder, rape and pillage their way across the island.

Sleeping

Raasay Outdoor Centre (☎ 660266, 660200; Raasay House; B&B per person £23, camp sites per person £6) Set in the former laird's residence, the centre welcomes campers and overnight guests as well as those attending outdoor activity courses.

Raasay Youth Hostel (SYHA; ☎ 660240; Creachan Cottage; dm £11; ☺ Apr-Sep) Set in a rustic cottage high on the hill overlooking Skye, this hostel is a fair walk from the ferry pier (2.5 miles) but is a good base for exploring the island.

Other island accommodation includes the picturesquely situated **Isle of Raasay Hotel** (☎ 660222; www.isleofraasayhotel.co.uk; Borodale House, Inverarish; s/d £35/65; Ⓟ), just above the ferry pier, and **Churchton Guest House** (☎ 660260; Suisnish; r per person £30), half a mile to the north.

Getting There & Away

A CalMac **ferry** (bicycle/passenger/car £1/2.60/10.25) runs from Sconser, on the road from Portree to Broadford, to the southern end of Raasay (15 minutes, hourly Monday to Saturday, twice daily Sunday). There are no petrol stations on the island.

OUTER HEBRIDES

pop 26,500

A professor of Spanish and a professor of Gaelic met at a conference and began discussing the relative merits of their respective languages. 'But tell me,' said the Spanish professor, 'do you have a Gaelic equivalent for the Spanish phrase *mañana, mañana*?' The Hebridean professor thought for a while, then replied, 'No, I do not think that we have in the Gaelic a word that conveys such a pressing sense of urgency'.

An old joke perhaps, but one that hints at the slower pace of life you can expect to find in the Gaelic-speaking communities of the Outer Hebrides, a place where the morning papers arrive in the afternoon and almost everything – in Lewis and Harris at least – closes down on Sundays.

Isolated, windswept and irresistibly romantic, the Outer Hebrides – also known as the Western Isles, or Na h-Eileanan an Iar in Gaelic – are a 130-mile-long string of islands lying off the northwest coast of Scotland. It's Europe's most isolated frontier.

The ferry crossing from Ullapool or Uig marks an important cultural divide – more than a third of Scotland's registered crofts are in the Outer Hebrides, no less than 60% of the population are Gaelic speakers, and the rigours of life in the old island *blackhouses* (low-walled stone cottages with thatch or turf roofs and earth floors) are less than distant memories. Religion still plays a prominent part in public and private life, especially in the Protestant north where shops and pubs close their doors on Sundays and some accommodation providers prefer guests not to arrive or depart on the Sabbath. The Roman Catholic south is a little more relaxed about these things.

The name Hebrides is not Gaelic, and is probably a corruption of Ebudae, the Roman name for the islands. But the alternative derivation from the Norse *havbredey* (isles at the edge of the sea) has a much more poetic ring, alluding to the broad vistas of sky and sea that characterise the islands' often bleak and treeless landscapes. But there is beauty here too, in the machair (wildflower-coated dunes) and dazzling white-sand beaches, majesty in the rugged hills and sprawling lochs, and mystery in the islands' fascinating past. It's a past signalled by Neolithic standing stones, Viking place names, deserted crofts and folk memories of the Clearances (see the boxed text, p355).

If you only have a short time, head straight for the west coast of Lewis with its prehistoric sites, preserved *blackhouses* and beautiful beaches. There are five main inhabited islands in the Outer Hebrides. From north to south they are: Lewis and Harris (two parts of a single island, although often described as if they are separate islands), North Uist, Benbecula, South Uist and Barra. The middle three (often referred to simply as 'the Uists') are joined by road-bearing causeways.

Information

INTERNET ACCESS

Community Library (☎ 01871-810471; Community School, Castlebay, Barra; per 30min £2; ☒ 9am-4.30pm Mon & Wed, 9am-4.30pm & 6-8pm Tue & Thu, 9am-3.30pm Fri, 10am-12.30pm Sat)

Stornoway Public Library (☎ 01851-708631; 19 Cromwell St, Stornoway, Lewis; per 30min £2; ☒ 10am-5pm Mon-Wed & Sat, to 6pm Thu & Fri)

Taigh Chearsabhagh (☎ 01876-500293; Lochmaddy, North Uist; per 20min 50p; ☒ 10am-5pm Mon-Sat Feb-Jun & Sep-Dec, 10am-5pm Mon-Thu & Sat, to 8pm Fri Jul & Aug)

MEDICAL SERVICES

Both hospital have casualty departments.

Uist & Barra Hospital (☎ 01870-603603; Balivanich, Benbecula)

Western Isles Hospital (☎ 01851-704704; MacAulay Rd, Stornoway, Lewis)

MONEY

There are banks with ATMs situated in Stornoway (Lewis), Tarbert (Harris), Lochmaddy (North Uist), Balivanich (Benbecula), Lochboisdale (South Uist) and Castlebay (Barra).

TOURIST INFORMATION

Castlebay TIC (☎ 01871-810336; Main St, Castlebay, Barra; ☒ 9am-1pm & 2-5pm Mon-Sat, noon-4pm Sun Apr-Oct)

Lochboisdale TIC (☎ 01878-700286; Pier Rd, Lochboisdale, South Uist; ☒ 9am-1pm & 2-5pm Mon-Fri, 9.30am-1pm & 2-5pm Sat Apr-Oct)

Lochmaddy TIC (☎ 01876-500321; Pier Rd, Lochmaddy, North Uist; ☒ 9am-1pm, 2-5pm & 7.30-8.30pm Mon, Wed & Fri, 9am-1pm & 2-5pm Tue & Thu, 9.30am-1pm & 2-5.30pm Sat)

Stornoway TIC (☎ 01851-703088; 26 Cromwell St, Stornoway, Lewis; ☒ 9am-6pm & 8.30-9.30pm Mon, Tue & Thu, 9am-8pm Wed & Fri, 9am-5pm & 8.30-9.30pm Sat)

Tarbert TIC (☎ 01859-502011; Pier Rd, Tarbert, Harris; ☒ 9am-5pm Mon, Wed & Fri, to 5pm & 8-9pm Tue, Thu & Sat)

Getting There & Away

AIR

There are airports at Stornoway (Lewis), and on Benbecula and Barra.

There are flights to Stornoway from Edinburgh (daily), Inverness (daily) and Glasgow (Monday to Saturday). There are two flights a day (weekdays only) between Stornoway and Benbecula. Standard one-way fares are about £150, but can be as low as £30.

There are daily flights from Glasgow to Barra and Benbecula. At Barra, the planes land on the hard-sand beach at low tide, so the timetable depends on the tides.

Airlines serving the Western Isles:

bmi (☎ 0870 607 0555; www.flybmi.com)

British Airways/Loganair (☎ 0845 779 9977; www.britishairways.com)

Highland Airways (☎ 01851-701282; www.highlandairways.co.uk)

BOAT

Ferry

CalMac (☎ 0870 565 0000; www.calmac.co.uk) runs car ferries from Ullapool to Stornoway (Lewis); from Uig (Isle of Skye) to Lochmaddy (North Uist) and Tarbert (Harris); and from Oban to Castlebay (Barra), continuing to Lochboisdale (South Uist).

Crossing	Duration	Car	Driver/Passenger
Ullapool-Stornoway	2¾hr	£70	£15
Uig-Lochmaddy	1¾hr	£45	£9.40
Uig-Tarbert	1½hr	£45	£9.40
Oban-Castlebay	4¾hr	£76	£21
Oban-Lochboisdale	6¾hr	£76	£21

From Monday to Saturday there are two or three CalMac ferries a day to Stornoway, two a day to Tarbert and Lochmaddy, and one a day to Castlebay and Lochboisdale; on Sundays there are ferries (same frequency) to Castlebay, Lochboisdale and Lochmaddy, but none to Tarbert and Stornoway. Advance booking for cars is essential in July and August; foot and bicycle passengers should have no problems. The fare for a bicycle is only £1 or £2, as well as the passenger fare.

CalMac has 12 different Island Hopscotch tickets for set routes in the Outer Hebrides, offering a saving of around 10% (tickets are valid for one month).

Getting Around

Despite their separate names, Lewis and Harris are actually one island. Berneray, North Uist, Benbecula, South Uist and Eriskay are all linked by road bridges and causeways. There are car ferries between Harris and Berneray, and between Eriskay and Barra.

The local council publishes two booklets of timetables (one covering Lewis and Harris, the other the Uists and Barra) that list all bus, ferry and air services in the Outer Hebrides. Timetables can also be found online at www.cne-siar.giv.uk/travel.

BICYCLE

Many visiting cyclists plan to cycle the length of the archipelago, but if you're one of them, remember that the wind is often strong (you may hear stories of people pedalling downhill and freewheeling uphill), and the prevailing direction is from the southwest – so south to north is usually the easier direction. There are few serious hills, except for a stiff climb on the main road just north of Tarbert.

Bikes can be hired for around £8.50 a day or £30 a week in Stornoway, Howmore (South Uist) and Castlebay (Barra).

BUS

The bus network in the Outer Hebrides has been much improved in recent years, with around four to six buses a day on all the main routes; however, there are still no buses at all on Sundays. You can pick up timetables from the TICs, or call **Stornoway bus station** (☎ 01851-704327) for information about Lewis and Harris services. Visitors without their own transport should anticipate a fair amount of hitching and walking.

KEEPING THE SABBATH

Religion still plays a complex and central role in island life, especially on predominantly Protestant Lewis and Harris, where the Sabbath is still strictly observed.

The Protestant church is divided into three main sects with convoluted, emotionally charged histories. The Church of Scotland, the main Scottish church, is state recognised or 'established'. The Free Church of Scotland (known as the 'Wee Frees'), and the Free Presbyterian Church of Scotland, which both split from the Church of Scotland in 1843 and 1893 respectively, are far more conservative, permitting no ornaments, organ music or choirs. Their ministers deliver uncompromising sermons (usually in Gaelic) from central pulpits, and precentors lead the congregation in unaccompanied but fervent psalm singing. Visitors are welcome to attend services, but due respect is essential.

The Protestants of the Outer Hebrides have succeeded in maintaining a distinctive fundamentalist approach to their religion, with Sunday being devoted largely to religious services, prayer and Bible reading. On Lewis and Harris, the last bastion of Sabbath observance in the UK, almost everything closes down on a Sunday. But a few cracks have begun to appear in recent years.

There was outrage when British Airways/Loganair introduced Sunday flights from Edinburgh and Inverness to Stornoway in 2002, with members of the Lord's Day Observance Society spluttering that this was the thin end of the wedge. They were probably right – in 2003 a Stornoway petrol station began to open on a Sunday (see Information, p386), and now does a roaring trade in Sunday papers and takeaway booze.

CAR & MOTORCYCLE

Most roads are single track, but the main hazard is posed by sheep wandering about or sleeping on the road. Petrol stations are far apart (almost all of those on Lewis and Harris are closed on Sunday), and fuel is about 10% more expensive than on the mainland.

There are petrol stations at Stornoway, Barvas, Borve, Uig, Tarbert and Ness on Lewis and Harris; at Lochmaddy and Cladach on North Uist; at Balivanich on Benbecula; at Howmore, Lochboisdale and Daliburgh on South Uist; and at Castlebay on Barra.

Cars can be hired from around £23 per day from **Lewis Car Rentals** (☎ 01851-703760; www .lewis-car-rental.co.uk; 52 Bayhead St, Stornoway) and **Ask Car Hire** (☎ 01870-602818; enquiries@askcarhire .com; Liniclate, Benbecula).

LEWIS (LEODHAIS)

☎ 01851 / pop 19,600

The northern part of Lewis is dominated by the desolate expanse of the Black Moor, a vast, undulating peat bog dimpled with glittering lochans, seen clearly from the Stornoway–Barvas road. The coastal fringes have some arable land and are surprisingly densely populated, though not that attractive.

The old *blackhouses* may have gone, but most smallholdings still follow a traditional pattern dating back to medieval times. Most are narrow strips of land, designed to give all an equal share of good and bad soil, running from the foreshore (with its valuable seaweed, used as fertiliser), across the machair (the grassy sand dunes that provide the best arable land) to the poorer sheep-grazing land on hill or moor. Today, few crofts are economically viable, so most islanders supplement their income with fishing, tweed-weaving, and work on oil rigs and fish farms.

Lewis' finest scenery is on the west coast, from Barvas southwest to Mealista, where the rugged landscape of hill, loch and sandy strand is reminiscent of the northwestern Highlands. The Outer Hebrides' most evocative historic sites – Callanish Standing Stones, Dun Carloway, and Arnol Blackhouse Museum – are also to be found here.

Stornoway (Steornabhagh)

pop 6000

Stornoway is the bustling 'capital' of the Outer Hebrides and the only real town in the whole archipelago. It's a surprisingly busy lit-

tle place, with cars and people swamping the centre on weekdays. Though set on a beautiful natural harbour, the town isn't going to win any prizes for beauty or atmosphere, but it's a pleasant enough introduction to this remote corner of the country.

Stornoway is the Outer Hebrides' administrative and commercial centre, home to the Western Isles Council (Comhairle nan Eilean Siar) and the islands' Gaelic TV and radio stations. It turns into a bit of a ghost town on Sundays, especially between 11am and 12.30pm when almost everyone is at church.

There's an airport and a car ferry link with Ullapool (see p384).

INFORMATION

There are banks with ATMs near the tourist office.

Baltic Bookshop (☎ 702802; 8-10 Cromwell St; ⏰ 9am-5.30pm Mon-Sat) Good for books and maps.

Post office (☎ 0845 722 3344; 16 Francis St)

Sandwick Rd Petrol Station (☎ 702304; Sandwick Rd) The only shop in town that's open on a Sunday (⏰ 10am-4pm); the Sunday papers arrive around 2pm.

Stornoway Public Library (☎ 708631; 19 Cromwell St; per 30min £2; ⏰ 10am-5pm Mon-Wed & Sat, to 6pm Thu & Fri; 🖳) Has Internet access.

TIC (☎ 703088; www.witb.co.uk; 26 Cromwell St; ⏰ 9am-6pm & 8.30-9.30pm Mon, Tue & Thu, 9am-8pm Wed & Fri, 9am-5pm & 8.30-9.30pm Sat) A short walk from the ferry pier; opens late for ferry arrivals.

SIGHTS

The **Museum nan Eilean** (☎ 703773; Francis St; admission free; ⏰ 10am-5.30pm Mon-Sat, shorter winter hrs) should be your first stop on a visit to Lewis. The main exhibition strings together a loose history of the Outer Hebrides from the earliest human settlements some 9000 years ago to the 20th century, exploring traditional island life and the changes inflicted by progress and technology.

An Lanntair Art Centre (☎ 703307; www.lanntair .com; Kenneth St) is housed in a brand-new, purpose-built arts centre, complete with theatre, cinema and restaurant, opposite the ferry terminal; it hosts changing exhibitions of contemporary art.

The **Lewis Loom Centre** (☎ 704500; 3 Bayhead; adult/child £1/50p; ⏰ 9am-6pm Mon-Sat) houses an exhibition on the history of Harris tweed; the 40-minute guided tour (£2.50 extra) includes spinning and weaving demonstrations.

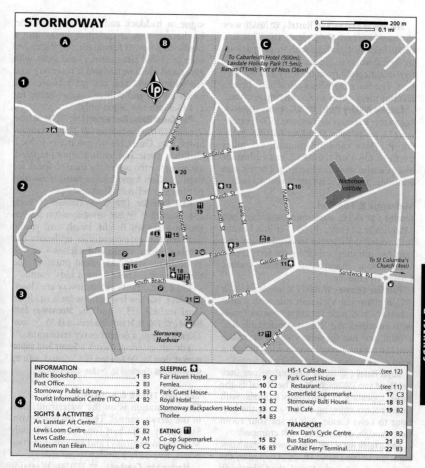

STORNOWAY

To Cabarfeidh Hotel (500m);
Laxdale Holiday Park (1.5mi);
Barvas (11mi); Port of Ness (26mi)

Nicholson Institute

To St Columba's Church (4mi)

Stornoway Harbour

INFORMATION			SLEEPING			HS-1 Café-Bar........................(see 12)
Baltic Bookshop..........................	1	B3	Fair Haven Hostel........................	9	C3	Park Guest House
Post Office...................................	2	B3	Fernlea......................................	10	C2	Restaurant.........................(see 11)
Stornoway Public Library...........	3	B3	Park Guest House.....................	11	C3	Somerfield Supermarket............ 17 C3
Tourist Information Centre (TIC).......	4	B2	Royal Hotel..............................	12	B2	Stornoway Balti House............... 18 B3
			Stornoway Backpackers Hostel.......	13	C2	Thai Café.................................. 19 B2
SIGHTS & ACTIVITIES			Thorlee.......................................	14	B3	
An Lanntair Art Centre................	5	B3				TRANSPORT
Lewis Loom Centre.....................	6	B2	EATING			Alex Dan's Cycle Centre............ 20 B2
Lews Castle.................................	7	A1	Co-op Supermarket..................	15	B2	Bus Station................................ 21 B3
Museum nan Eilean.....................	8	C2	Digby Chick..............................	16	B3	CalMac Ferry Terminal.............. 22 B3

Lews Castle, the baronial mansion across the harbour, was built in the 1840s. It was home to the local college for 40 years but has lain empty since 1997. The beautiful grounds are open to the public, and host the Hebridean Celtic Festival. The roofless ruin of the 14th-century **St Columba's Church** (Aignish; admission free; ⏲ 24hr), 4 miles east of town on the Eye peninsula, features the grave slabs of Roderick McLeod, 7th clan chief (around 1498), and his daughter (1503). Hourly buses (not Sunday) from Stornoway to Point pass nearby.

FESTIVALS & EVENTS
The **Hebridean Celtic Festival** (www.hebceltfest .com) is a four-day extravaganza of folk/rock/ Celtic music held in the second half of July.

SLEEPING
Budget
Fair Haven Hostel (☎ 705862; www.hebrideansurf .co.uk; 17 Keith St; dm/s/d £10/15/30) The Fair Haven is a friendly, easy-going hostel run by Hebridean Surf Holidays. It is often used by groups who don't mind squeezing in together – for the rest of us it can be a bit cramped. You can hire bikes and surfing equipment, and arrange transport and historical bus tours.

Thorlee (☎ 705466, 706300; www.thorlee.com; 1-3 Cromwell St; d £30) The family-orientated Thorlee has bright and cheerful rooms and a great central location with views over the harbour – an absolute bargain. If there's no answer at the guesthouse, ask at the Stag Bakery next door.

Stornoway Backpackers Hostel (☎ 703628; www .stornoway-hostel.co.uk; 47 Keith St; dm £10) This is a small, laid-back cottage with three spacious six-bed dorms (single-sex and mixed). It's a five-minute walk from the ferry and bus station. The price includes a fairly basic breakfast but there's also a self-catering kitchen.

Laxdale Holiday Park (☎ 703234; www.laxdaleholi daypark.com; 6 Laxdale Lane; camp sites £5.50-7, campervans £7-8, plus per person £1.50-2, dm/d £11/40; ◯ Apr-Oct; **P**) This camping ground, 1.5 miles north of town off the A857, has a pleasant and peaceful woodland setting. There's also a bunkhouse that stays open year-round.

Midrange & Top End

Fernlea (☎ 702125; maureenmacmillan@amserve.com; 9 Matheson Rd; s/d £30/50; **P** ✕) Set in a beautifully restored Victorian terraced house, and only five minutes' walk from the ferry, Fernlea has four characterful en-suite rooms. Closed in January.

Park Guest House (☎ 702485; 30 James St; s/d £48/76; ✕) A charming Victorian villa with a conservatory and nine luxurious rooms (most with en suite), the Park is comfortable and central and has the advantage of an excellent restaurant. Rooms overlooking the main road can be noisy on weekday mornings.

Royal Hotel (☎ 702109; www.calahotels.com; Cromwell St; s/d from £50/80; **P** ✕) The Royal is the most appealing of Stornoway's hotels, with many rooms enjoying a view across the harbour to Lews Castle. Ask to see your room first, though, as some are a bit cramped.

Cabarfeidh Hotel (☎ 702604; www.calahotels.com; Manor Park; s/d from £70/100; **P** ✕) Owned by the same company as the Royal, the Cabarfeidh is bigger and more luxurious and is handy for the golf course, but lacks the Royal's old-fashioned character. It has one room that is wheelchair accessible.

EATING

Thai Café (☎ 701811; 27 Church St; mains £5-6; ◯ noon-2.30pm & 5-11pm Mon-Sat) Here's a surprise – authentic, inexpensive Thai food in the heart of Stornoway. This spick-and-span little restaurant has a genuine Thai chef, and serves some of the most delicious, best-value Asian food in the Hebrides. There's no liquor licence, so BYOB (bring your own bottle).

Digby Chick (☎ 700026; 28 Point St; mains £14-17; ◯ noon-10pm Mon-Sat) A modern restaurant that dishes up family favourites such as la-

sagne or haddock and chips at lunchtime. In the evenings, it metamorphoses into a candle-lit gourmet restaurant, serving dishes such as grilled langoustines, and steak with garlic and chilli butter and a rosemary and red wine gravy. You can get a two-course lunch for £8, and a three-course dinner for £14 (5.30pm to 6.30pm only).

Park Guest House Restaurant (☎ 702485; 30 James St; mains £12-17; ◯ 6-9pm Tue-Sat) The restaurant at the Park Guest House specialises in local shellfish, game and lamb, simply prepared, allowing the flavour of the food to speak for itself. It offers a good-value two-course dinner for £13 between 6pm and 7pm.

HS-1 Café-Bar (☎ 702109; Cromwell St; snacks £3-6, mains £6-8; ◯ food served noon-4pm & 5-9pm Mon-Sat, 4-9pm Sun) Bright, brash and young at heart, this café-bar dishes up hearty bar meals – fajitas, steaks and nachos – as well as healthier stuff like baked potatoes and tortilla wraps. There's also a kids' menu.

Most restaurants in Stornoway are closed Sundays, but the few options for a sit-down meal include HS-1 and the **Stornoway Balti House** (☎ 706116; 24 South Beach; mains £6-10; ◯ noon-2.30pm & 6-11pm), a decent curry restaurant.

For self-catering, there's a **Somerfield supermarket** (Ferry Rd; ◯ 8am-8pm Mon-Sat) and a **Co-op supermarket** (Cromwell St; ◯ 8am-8pm Mon-Sat).

GETTING THERE & AROUND

The bus station is on the waterfront, next to the ferry terminal. There are buses from Stornoway to Tarbert (one hour, five daily Monday to Saturday) and Leverburgh (two hours, five daily Monday to Saturday).

Maclennan Coaches (☎ 702114) Westside Circular bus W2 runs a circular route from Stornoway through Callanish, Carloway, Garenin and Arnol; the timetable means you can visit one or two of the sites in a day. A one-day Rover ticket costs £5.

For details on CalMac ferries, see p384.

You can hire bikes from **Alex Dan's Cycle Centre** (☎ 704025; www.hebrideancycles.co.uk; 67 Kenneth St).

Butt of Lewis (Rubha Robhanais)

The Butt of Lewis (no snickering, please) – the extreme northern tip of the Hebrides – is windswept and rugged, with a very imposing lighthouse, pounding surf and large colonies of nesting fulmars on the high cliffs. There's a bleak sense of isola-

FOR PEAT'S SAKE

As you travel through the Outer Hebrides you will notice peat stacks next to many houses. These carefully constructed stacks are designed to allow the wind to blow through the stack, helping the peat to dry out so that it can be used as fuel.

Peat in its raw state is extremely wet and it can take a couple of months to dry out. It is cut from roadside bogs, where the cuttings are at least a metre deep. Rectangular blocks of peat are cut using a long-handled tool called a *tairsgeir* (Gaelic for peat-iron); this is extremely hard work and can cause blisters even on hands that are used to manual labour.

Different types of *tairsgeir* are used on different islands. In Lewis, they cut relatively short brick-shaped blocks, while in Uist the blocks are somewhat longer. The peat blocks are transported to the cutter's house, then carefully assembled into a *cruach-mhonach* (peat stack), each balanced on top of the other in a grid pattern and thus creating maximum air space. Once the peat has dried out it is stored in a shed.

Peat burns much more slowly than wood or coal and produces a not unpleasant smell, but in the old *blackhouses* (which had no chimney) it permeated every corner of the dwelling, not to mention the inhabitants' clothes and hair (hence the expression 'peat-reek' – the ever-present smell of peat smoke that was long associated with island life). Peat also produces quite a lot of heat, but peat fires are becoming increasingly rare in Hebridean homes due to the popularity and convenience of oil-fuelled central heating.

tion here, with nothing but the grey Atlantic between you and Canada.

Just before the turn-off to the Butt at Eoropie (Eoropaidh), you'll find **St Moluag's Church** (Teampull Mholuidh), an austere, barn-like structure believed to date from the 12th century but still used by the Episcopal Church. The main settlement here is **Port of Ness** (Port Nis) with its attractive harbour. To the west of the village is the sandy beach of **Traigh**, which is popular with surfers and has a kids' adventure playground nearby.

Arnol
ARNOL BLACKHOUSE MUSEUM

One of Scotland's most evocative historic buildings, the **Arnol Blackhouse Museum** (☎ 710395; adult/child £4/1.60; ☉ 9.30am-6.30pm Mon-Sat Apr-Sep, to 4.30pm Mon-Sat Oct-Mar, last admission 30min before closing; ﴾₰﴿) is not so much a museum as a perfectly preserved fragment of a lost world. Built in 1885, this traditional *blackhouse* – a combined byre, barn and home – was inhabited until 1964 and has not been changed since the last inhabitant moved out. The staff faithfully rekindle the central peat fire every morning so you can experience the distinctive peat-reek; there's no chimney, and the smoke finds its own way out through the turf roof, windows and door – spend too long inside and you might feel like you've been kippered! The museum is just off the A858, about 3 miles west of Barvas.

At nearby **Bragar**, a pair of whalebones form an arch by the road, with the rusting harpoon that killed the whale dangling from the centre.

Garenin (Na Gearrannan)

The picturesque and fascinating **Gearrannan Blackhouse Village** is a cluster of nine restored thatch-roofed *blackhouses* perched above the exposed Atlantic coast. One of the cottages is home to the **Blackhouse Museum** (☎ 643416; adult/child £2.50/1; ☉ 10am-5.30pm Mon-Sat Apr-Oct), a traditional 1955 *blackhouse* with displays on the village's history, while another houses the **Taigh an Chocair Restaurant** (☎ 643416, 710506; ☉ 11am-5pm Mon-Sat, dinner Thu-Sat). Dinner is by booking only.

Garenin Crofters' Hostel (www.gatliff.org.uk; dm adult/child £8/5.50) occupies one of the village *blackhouses*, and is one of the most atmospheric hostels in Scotland (or anywhere else for that matter).

The other houses in the village are let out as self-catering **holiday cottages** (☎ 643416; www .gearrannan.co.uk; per week for 5 people £276-456), offering the chance to stay in a unique and luxurious modernised *blackhouse* with attached kitchen and lounge. There's a minimum five-night let from June to August.

Carloway (Carlabhagh)

Dun Carloway (Dun Charlabhaigh) is a 2000-year-old dry-stone broch, perched defiantly above a beautiful loch with views to the mountains of North Harris. The site is clearly signposted along a minor road off the A858, a mile southwest of Carloway village. One of the best-preserved brochs in Scotland, its double walls (with internal staircase) still stand to a height of 9m and testify to the engineering skills of its Iron Age architects.

The tiny, turf-roofed **Doune Broch Centre** (☎ 643338; admission free; ⏰ 10am-5pm Mon-Sat late May–mid-Sep) nearby has interpretative displays and exhibitions about the history of the broch and the life of the people who lived there.

Callanish (Calanais)

The **Callanish Standing Stones** (☎ 621422; admission free), 15 miles west of Stornoway on the A858 road, form one of the most complete stone circles in Britain, and one of the most atmospheric prehistoric sites anywhere. Its ageless mystery, impressive scale and undeniable beauty leave a lasting impression. Sited on a wild and secluded promontory overlooking Loch Roag, 13 large stones of beautifully banded gneiss are ranged, as if in worship, around a central monolith that's 4.5m high. Some 40 smaller stones radiate from the circle in the shape of a cross, with the remains of a chambered tomb at the centre. Dating from

3800 to 5000 years ago, the stones are roughly contemporary with the pyramids of Egypt.

The nearby **Calanais Visitor Centre** (☎ 621422; admission free; ⏰ 10am-6pm Mon-Sat Apr-Sep, to 4pm Mon-Sat Oct-Mar) is a *tour de force* of discreet design. Inside is a small **exhibition** (adult/child £2/1) that speculates on the origins and purpose of the stones, and an excellent **café** (snacks £1-4).

If you plan to stay the night, you have a choice of **Eshcol Guest House** (☎ 621357; www .eshcol.com; 21 Breascleit; r per person £31-33; P ✗) and neighbouring **Loch Roag Guest House** (☎ 621357; www.lochroag.com; 22a Breascleit; r per person £28-32; P ✗), half a mile north of Callanish. Both are modern bungalows with the same friendly owner who is very knowledgeable about the local area.

Tigh Mealros (☎ 621333; Garrynahine; mains £8-15; ⏰ 7-9pm Mon-Sat), a private family home set in a sculpture garden, offers a tasty à la carte seafood menu including not-to-be-missed local scallops. Bookings are essential.

Great Bernera

This rocky island is connected to Lewis by a bridge built by the local council in 1953 – the islanders had originally planned to destroy a small hill with explosives and use the mater-

---

INVASION OF THE KILLER HEDGEHOGS

In 1974, a couple of hedgehogs were introduced to South Uist by a local gardener in an attempt to control the slugs in his garden. Hedgehogs had never been native to the islands, and the incomers waddled innocently into a vacant ecological niche. They spread like wildfire, and by 2002, it was estimated that there were around 5000 of the spiny slug-munchers in the Uists. But what's more, they were posing a mortal threat to important colonies of rare ground-nesting birds – eggs are a favourite hedgehog food.

In 2002, Scottish Natural Heritage (SNH) announced that a cull was the only way to preserve the bird population, and since then each summer has seen a battle between the SNH culling teams and animal rights organisations. While SNH combed the fields at night with flashlights, hog-spotters and lethal injections, the British Hedgehog Preservation Society and other campaign groups were offering £20 a head for live hedgehogs, which they transported to the mainland for release into the wild. One enterprising islander set up as a 'bounty hunter' and turned in more than 100 live hedgehogs, collecting a tidy sum for his efforts.

If the Uist invaders had been rats rather than cute Mrs Tiggywinkles, the public reaction might have been different, as the inhabitants of Canna, in the Small Isles, will confirm. Rats were accidentally introduced to the tiny island (population 14) by a ship a century ago – by 2005 the rodent raiders numbered more than 10,000. As in the Uists, the incomers began to force out native species including wood mice and birds – the island's population of burrow-nesting Manx shearwaters has declined by 90% in the last 30 years.

Canna's owner, the National Trust for Scotland, called in a crack team of rat-trappers from New Zealand, who hoped to have destroyed 90% of the rat population by summer 2006, with a mopping-up exercise planned for the following year. Any public outcry? Not a squeak.

ial to build their own causeway. On a sunny day, it's worth making the long detour to the island's northern tip for a picnic at the perfect little sandy beach of **Bosta** (Bostadh).

To the west of the beach, an entire Iron Age village has been excavated. A guide will show you around a restored **Iron Age house** (☎ 612331; Bosta; adult/child £2/50p; ☑ noon-4pm Tue-Sat May-Sep).

There are four or five buses a day (Monday to Saturday) between Stornoway and the hamlet of Breacleit on Great Bernera; the bus will continue to Bosta if you ask the driver.

Miavaig (Miabhaig) & Mealista (Mealasta)

The B8011 road (signposted Uig, on the A858 Stornoway–Callanish road) from Garrynahine to Timsgarry (Timsgearraidh) meanders through scenic wilderness to some of Scotland's most stunning beaches. At **Miavaig**, a loop road detours north through the Bhaltos Estate to the pretty, mile-long white strand of **Traigh na Cnip**; there's a basic **camping ground** in the machair behind the beach.

From May to September, **Sea Trek** (☎ 672464; www.seatrek.co.uk; Miavaig Pier) runs two-hour boat trips (adult/child £25/15) to spot seals and nesting sea birds, and more-adventurous all-day trips (£80 per person) in a high-speed RIB to the **Flannan Isles**, a remote group of tiny, uninhabited islands 25 miles northwest of Lewis. Puffins, seals and a ruined 7th-century chapel are the main attractions, but the isles are most famous for the mystery of the three lighthouse keepers who disappeared without trace in December 1900.

From Miavaig the road continues west through a rocky defile to Timsgarry and the vast, sandy expanse of **Traigh Uige** (Uig Beach) – famous 12th-century Lewis chesspieces made of walrus-ivory were discovered in the sand dunes here in 1831; of the 78 pieces, 67 are in the British Museum in London, with 11 in Edinburgh's Museum of Scotland and Royal Museum (p84). You can buy replicas at various outlets on the island. There's a very basic **camping ground** (☎ 672248; camp & campervan sites per person £1) on the south side of the bay (signposted 'Ardroil Beach').

The minor road that continues south from Timsgarry to **Mealista** passes a few smaller, but still spectacular, white-sand beaches; beware, though – the surf can make swimming treacherous.

SLEEPING & EATING

Bonaventure (☎ 672474; www.bonaventurelewis.co.uk; Aird Uig; 3-course dinner £27, r per person £23; ☑ noon-2pm Wed-Sat, 7-9pm Tue-Sat, closed Nov & Feb) This has to be the most remote French restaurant in Europe. It's housed in a converted, pine-clad military prefab that's perched above a wild, cliff-bound Atlantic cove 3 miles north of Timsgarry. The food is superb – local seafood, lamb and venison prepared by the resident French chef/owner – and the setting unique. Booking is essential for both lunch and dinner. If you want to stay the night, there are three comfy double rooms.

HARRIS (NA HEARADH)

☎ 01859 / pop 1870

Harris, the southern part of the Outer Hebrides' largest island, is the scenic jewel in the necklace of islands that comprises the Outer Hebrides, and combines mountains, pristine beaches, expanses of machair and weird rocky hills and coastline. The mountains of North Harris rise forbiddingly above the peat moors south of Stornoway – Clisham (799m) is the highest point. South Harris, across the isthmus at Tarbert, has a fascinating variety of landscapes and lovely snow-white beaches.

Harris is famous for Harris Tweed, high-quality woollen cloth still hand-woven in islanders' homes. The industry employs around 400 weavers; staff at Tarbert TIC can tell you about weavers and workshops that you can visit.

Tarbert (An Tairbeart)

pop 480

Tarbert is a harbour village with ferry connections to Uig on Skye. It's a serene and pretty place with a spectacular location, overshadowed by mountains on the narrow neck of land that links North and South Harris.

The **TIC** (☎ 502011; Pier Rd; ☑ 9am-5pm Mon, Wed & Fri, 9am-5pm & 8-9pm Tue, Thu & Sat) is signposted up the hill and stays open for late ferry arrivals. Village facilities include a petrol station, bank, ATM and two general stores. The **Harris Tweed Shop** (☎ 502493; Main St) stocks a wide range of books on the Hebrides and sells the famous cloth.

SLEEPING & EATING

Rockview Bunkhouse (☎ 502626; imacaskill@aol.com; Main St; dm £10) This hostel on the street above the harbour is a bit cell-like with its cramped dorms, but it's close to the ferry and has good facilities.

Harris Hotel (☎ 502154; www.harrishotel.com; s/d £60/110; ℗) Run since 1903 by four generations of the Cameron family, Harris Hotel is a 19th-century sporting hotel, originally built for deer-stalkers visiting the North Harris Estates. It has spacious, comfy rooms and a good restaurant; look out for JM Barrie's initials scratched on the dining room window (the author of *Peter Pan* visited in the 1920s). The hotel is on the way out of the village, on the road north towards Stornoway.

Firstfruits (☎ 502439; Pier Rd; ☼ 10.30am-8pm Mon-Sat Jul & Aug, 10.30am-6.30pm Mon-Sat Jun, 10am-4.30pm Mon-Sat Apr, May & Sep) This is a cosy little cottage tearoom near the TIC – handy while you wait for a ferry.

North Harris

Magnificent North Harris is the most mountainous region of the Outer Hebrides. There are few roads, but many opportunities for climbing, walking and bird-watching.

The B887 leads west to **Hushinish**, where there's a lovely silver-sand beach. Just northwest of Hushinish is the uninhabited island of **Scarp**, the scene of bizarre attempts to send mail by rocket in 1934, a story recounted in the movie *The Rocket Post* (2001), which was shot in Harris.

Rhenigidale Crofters' Hostel (www.gatliff.org.uk; dm adult/child £8/5.50) can be reached on foot from Tarbert (6 miles, allow three hours). It's an excellent walk, but take all the necessary supplies for a mountain walk (map, compass, protective clothing etc). Take the road towards Kyles Scalpay for 2 miles and, at a bend in the road just beyond Laxdale Lochs, veer off to the left on a signposted track across the hills (marked on OS maps). The hostel is a white building standing above the road on the eastern side of the glen; the warden lives in the house closest to the shore.

The remote hamlet of Rhenigidale can also be reached by road; the **Rhenigidale Taxi Bus** (☎ 502221) will take you there, but you'll have to book in advance.

South Harris

If you think Scotland has no decent beaches, wait till you see the west coast of South Harris. The blinding white sands and turquoise waters of **Luskentyre** and **Scarasta** beaches would be major holiday resorts if they were

transported to somewhere with a warm climate; as it is, they're usually deserted.

The culture and landscape of the Hebrides are celebrated in the exhibition at **Seallam! Visitor Centre** (☎ 520258; Northton; adult/child £2.50/2; ☼ 9am-5pm Mon-Sat). Seallam is Gaelic for 'Let me show you'. The centre, which is in Northton, just south of Scarasta, also has a genealogical research centre for people who want to trace their Hebridean ancestry.

The east coast is a complete contrast to the west – a strange, rocky moonscape of hillocky gneiss pocked with tiny lochans, the bleakness lightened by the occasional splash of green around the few crofting communities. Film buffs will know that the psychedelic sequences depicting the surface of Jupiter in *2001: A Space Odyssey* were shot from an aircraft flying low over the east coast of Harris.

The narrow, twisting road that winds its way along this coast is known locally as the Golden Rd, because of the vast amount of money it cost per mile. It was built in the 1930s to link all the tiny communities known as 'The Bays'. The **MV Lady Catherine** (☎ 530310), based at Flodabay harbour halfway down the east coast, offers three-hour wildlife cruises (adult/child £12/6) from May to September.

At the southernmost tip of this coastline stands the impressive 16th-century **St Clement's Church** (Rodel/Roghadal; admission free), which was abandoned in 1560 after the Reformation. Inside the echoing nave is the fascinating tomb of Alexander MacLeod, the man responsible for the church's construction. Crude carvings show hunting scenes, a castle, a galleon, and various saints, including St Clement clutching a skull.

The town of **Leverburgh** (An t-Ob) is named after Lord Leverhulme (the creator of Sunlight soap, and the founder of Unilever), who bought Lewis and Harris in 1918. He had grand plans for the islands, and for Obbe, as Leverburgh was then known. It was to be a major fishing port with a population of 10,000, but the plans died with Lord Leverhulme in 1925 and the village reverted to a sleepy backwater.

SLEEPING & EATING

Am Bothan (☎ 520251; www.ambothan.com; Leverburgh; dm £13-14; ℗ ✗ 🕭) This attractive, chalet-style hostel has small, neat dorms and a great porch where you can enjoy morning coffee with views over the creek.

Sorrel Cottage (☎ 520319; www.sorrelcottage.co.uk; 2 Glen, Leverburgh; r per person £20-30) Sorrel Cottage is a pretty crofter's house, about 1.5 miles west of the ferry at Leverburgh. Evening meals can be provided (£15 a head), and vegetarians and vegans are happily catered for.

Carminish Guest House (☎ 520400; www.carmin ish.com; 1a Strond, Leverburgh; s/d £44/54; P ⊠) One of the few B&Bs in Harris that is open all year, the welcoming Carminish is a modern house with three comfy guest bedrooms. There's a view of the ferry from the dining room, and lots of nice little touches such as handmade soaps, a tin of choccy bickies in the bedroom, and the latest weather forecast posted on the breakfast table.

Rodel Hotel (☎ 520210; www.rodelhotel.co.uk; Rodel; s £65-90, d £90-120, mains £12-17; P ⊠) Don't be put off by the rather grey and grim exterior of this remote hotel – the interior has been recently refurbished and offers four large, luxurious bedrooms; the one called Iona has the best view, across the little harbour. The hotel restaurant serves delicious local seafood and game, with dishes such as seared scallops with creamed leeks and crushed buttered potatoes.

GETTING THERE & AROUND
A CalMac car ferry zigzags through the reefs of the Sound of Harris from Leverburgh to Berneray (pedestrian/car £5.30/24.30, 1¼ hours, three or four daily Monday to Saturday). You can hire bicycles from Sorrel Cottage for £10 a day.

BERNERAY (BEARNARAIGH)
☎ 01876 / pop 140
The superb beaches of western Berneray are unparalleled in Scotland. The causeway to North Uist opened in October 1998, but hasn't altered the peace and beauty of this place.

The atmospheric, thatch-roofed **Gatliff Hostel** (www.gatliff.org.uk; Baile; dm adult/child £8/5.50) is just under 2 miles from the causeway.

In summer, snacks are available at the Lobster Pot, the tearoom attached to Ardmarree Stores (a grocery shop near the causeway).

There are **Royal Mail postbus** (☎ 01246-546329) services and **Grenitote Travel** (☎ 560244) buses from Berneray (Gatliff Hostel and Harris ferry) to Lochmaddy (six or seven daily Monday to Saturday). For details of ferries to Leverburgh (Harris), see above.

NORTH UIST (UIBHIST A TUATH)
☎ 01876 / pop 1400
North Uist, an island half-drowned by lochs, is famed for its fishing but also has some magnificent beaches on its north and west coasts. For bird-watchers this is an earthly paradise, with huge populations of wading birds – oystercatchers, lapwings, curlews and redshanks – at every turn. The landscape is less wild and mountainous than Harris, but it has a sleepy, subtle appeal.

Lochmaddy (Loch nam Madadh)
There's not much to keep you in tiny Lochmaddy, but it's the first village you hit after arriving on the ferry from Skye. There's a **TIC** (☎ 500321; Pier Rd; ⏲ 9am-1pm, 2-5pm & 7.30-8.30pm Mon, Wed & Fri, 9am-1pm & 2-5pm Tue & Thu, 9.30am-1pm & 2-5.30pm Sat), a couple of stores, a Bank of Scotland with ATM, a petrol station, a post office and a pub.

Taigh Chearsabhagh (☎ 500293; admission free, donation requested for museum, mains £2-4; ⏲ 10am-5pm Mon-Sat Feb-Jun & Sep-Dec, 10am-5pm Mon-Thu & Sat, to 8pm Fri Jul & Aug; ▣) is a museum and arts centre that preserves and displays the history and culture of the Uists, and is also a thriving community centre and meeting place. The centre's lively café dishes up lovely homemade soups, sandwiches and cakes, and provides Internet access at 50p for 20 minutes.

Buses from Lochmaddy to Langass, Clachan na Luib, Benbecula and Lochboisdale run five or six times a day Monday to Saturday.

SLEEPING & EATING
Old Courthouse (☎ 500358; r per person £25; P ⊠) This charming Georgian-style villa has four guest rooms; it's within walking distance of the ferry, north of the main road, on the road that leads to Uist Outdoor Centre.

Uist Outdoor Centre (☎ 500480; www.uistoutdoor centre.co.uk; Cearn Dusgaidh; dm £11) This shore-side activity centre has clean, four-bed dorms and offers a range of activities including canoeing, walking, rock climbing and diving.

Lochmaddy Hotel (☎ 500331; www.lochmaddyhotel .co.uk; r per person £35-45, mains £7-11; P) This is a traditional anglers' hotel (you can buy fishing permits here) with comfy, old-fashioned rooms, many with harbour views. The lively hotel bar pulls in anglers, locals and tourists, and serves excellent pub grub including seafood, venison and king-size steaks.

Bharpa Langass & Pobull Fhinn

A waymarked circular path beside the Langass Lodge Hotel (just off the A867, 6 miles southwest of Lochmaddy) leads to the chambered Neolithic burial tomb of **Bharpa Langass** and the stone circle of **Pobull Fhinn** (Finn's People); both are reckoned to be around 5000 years old. There are lovely views over the loch, where you may be able to spot seals and otters.

The delightful six-bedroom **Langass Lodge Hotel** (☎ 580285; langasslodge@btconnect.com; Locheport; s/d £60/90, 2-/3-course dinner £20/25; P) is a former shooting lodge set in splendid isolation overlooking a sea loch. The restaurant is noted for its fine seafood and game, including grouse, snipe and woodcock.

Balranald Nature Reserve

Bird-watchers flock to this Royal Society for the Protection of Birds (RSPB) nature reserve, 18 miles west of Lochmaddy, in the

hope of spotting the rare red-necked phalarope or hearing the distinctive call of the corncrake. There's a **visitors centre** (☎ 510372; admission free; ✆ Apr-Sep; &) with a resident warden who offers 2½-hour guided walks (£3, 10am Tuesday and Wednesday from May to August).

BENBECULA (BEINN NA FAOGHLA)
☎ 01870 / pop 1880

Squeezed between North Uist and South Uist and connected to both by causeways, Benbecula is a low-lying island that's almost as much water as land. The flat, lochan-studded landscape is best appreciated from the summit of **Rueval** (124m), the island's highest point – there's a path around the south side of the hill (signposted from the main road; park beside the landfill site) that is said to be the route taken to the coast by Bonnie Prince Charlie and Flora MacDonald during the prince's escape in 1746.

THE EVEN FURTHER OUTER HEBRIDES

St Kilda (www.kilda.org.uk) is a collection of spectacular sea stacks and cliff-bound islands about 45 miles west of North Uist. The largest island, Hirta, measures only 2 miles by 1 mile, with huge cliffs along most of its coastline. Owned by National Trust for Scotland (NTS), the islands are a Unesco World Heritage site and are the biggest sea-bird nesting site in the North Atlantic, home to more than a million birds.

History

Hirta was inhabited by a Gaelic-speaking population of around 200 until the 19th century, when the arrival of church missionaries and tourists began the gradual breakdown of St Kilda's traditional way of life. By the 1920s, disease and emigration had seen the islands' economy collapse, and the 35 remaining islanders were evacuated, at their own request, in 1930. The people had survived here by keeping sheep, fishing, growing a few basic crops such as barley, and climbing the cliffs barefoot to catch sea birds and collect their eggs. Over the centuries, this resulted in a genetic peculiarity – St Kilda men had unusually long big toes.

Visiting St Kilda

Boat tours to St Kilda are a major undertaking. For a full listing of tour operators, check out the website at www.kilda.org.uk. **Western Edge Charters** (☎ 01506-204053; www.westernedge.co.uk) operates leisurely six-day expeditions on a 12m sailing yacht departing from Berneray (North Uist) for around £550 per person.

The only way to spend any time in the islands is to join one of the two-week NTS work parties that visit St Kilda from mid-May to August. The NTS charges volunteers for doing archaeological and conservation work in and around the village ruins – you have to be physically fit and prepared to work for up to 36 hours per week. And you have to pay for the privilege – from £555 to £645 (including transport from Oban in a converted lifeboat and full board in dorm accommodation). To get an application form, send a stamped, self-addressed envelope to St Kilda Work Parties, NTS, Balnain House, 40 Huntly St, Inverness IV3 5HR. The closing date for applications is 31 January.

The control centre for the British army's Hebrides Missile Range (located on the northwestern tip of South Uist) is the island's main source of employment, and **Balivanich** (Baile a'Mhanaich) – looking like a corner of a Glasgow housing estate planted incongruously on the machair – is the commercial centre serving the troops and their families. The village has a bank with an ATM, a post office and a large **Co-op supermarket** (8am-8pm Mon-Sat, 12.30-6pm Sun).

SOUTH UIST (UIBHIST A DEAS)
pop 2060
South Uist is the second-largest island in the Outer Hebrides, and saves its choicest corners for those who explore away from the main north–south A865 road. The low-lying west coast is an almost unbroken stretch of white-sand beach and flower-flecked machair, while the multitude of inland lochs provide excellent trout fishing. The east coast, riven by four large sea lochs, is hilly and remote, with spectacular **Beinn Mhor** (620m) the highest point.

As you drive south from Benbecula you cross from the predominantly Protestant northern half of the Outer Hebrides into the mostly Roman Catholic south, a religious transition marked by the granite statue of **Our Lady of the Isles** on the slopes of Rueval (the hill with the military radomes on its summit), and the presence of many roadside shrines.

The North
The northern part of the island is mostly occupied by the watery expanses of Loch Bee and Loch Druidibeg. **Loch Druidibeg National Nature Reserve** is an important breeding ground for birds like dunlin, redshank, ringed plover, greylag goose and corncrake; you can take a 5-mile self-guided walk through the reserve (pick up a leaflet from Lochmaddy or Lochboisdale TICs).

Situated two miles south of Loch Druidibeg is the attractive hamlet of **Howmore** (Tobha Mor), with several restored, thatched *blackhouses,* one of which houses the **Tobha Mor Crofters' Hostel** (www.gatliff.org.uk; dm adult/child £8/5.50).

You can rent bikes from **Rothan Cycles** (01870-620283; www.rothan.com; 9 Howmore; per day/week £8/35) where the road to the hostel leaves the main road.

The South
Kildonan Museum (01878-710343; Kildonan; adult/child £1.50/free; 10am-5pm Mon-Fri, 2-5pm Sun Easter-Oct), 6 miles south of Howmore, explores the lives of local crofters through its collection of artefacts – an absorbing exhibition of black-and-white photography and first-hand accounts of harsh Hebridean conditions.

Amid the ruined *blackhouses* of Milton, half a mile south of the museum, a cairn marks the site of **Flora MacDonald's birthplace**.

LOCHBOISDALE (LOCH BAGHASDAIL)
01878
The ferry port of Lochboisdale in the southeast is the island's largest settlement, with a **TIC** (700286; 9am-1pm & 2-5pm Mon-Fri, 9.30am-1pm & 2-5pm Sat Apr-Oct), a bank with ATM, a grocery store and a petrol station. There's a **Co-op supermarket** (8am-8pm Mon-Sat, 12.30-6pm Sun) at Daliburgh, 3 miles west of the village.

For details of ferries from Oban to Castlebay (Barra) and Lochboisdale see p384.

Sleeping & Eating
Lochside Cottage (700472; r per person £22;) This friendly B&B, 1.5 miles west of the ferry, has appealing rooms and a sun lounge barely a fishing-rod's length from its own trout loch.

Lochboisdale Hotel (700332; www.lochboisdale .com; s/d £55/80, bar meals £8-12;) This old-fashioned huntin'-and-fishin' hotel is right above the ferry terminal, with recently modernised rooms, many of which have stunning views across the Minch to the island of Rum. The lounge bar has a roaring fire in winter, and hosts regular traditional music sessions – it also serves decent bar meals.

ERISKAY (EIRIOSGAIGH)
01878 / pop 170
In 1745, Bonnie Prince Charlie first set foot in Scotland on the west coast of Eriskay, on the sandy beach (immediately north of the ferry terminal) still known as **Prince's Strand** (Coilleag a'Phrionnsa).

More recently, the SS *Politician* sank just off the island in 1941. The islanders salvaged much of its cargo of around 250,000 bottles of whisky and, after a binge of dramatic proportions, the police intervened and a number of the islanders landed in jail. The story was immortalised by Sir Compton Mackenzie in his comic novel *Whisky Galore*, later made

NORTHERN HIGHLANDS & ISLANDS

into a famous film (at the time of writing there were plans underway for a remake).

A CalMac car ferry links Eriskay with Ardmhor at the northern end of Barra (pedestrian/car £5.80/18, 40 minutes, four or five daily).

BARRA (BARRAIGH)

☎ 01871 / pop 1200

With its beautiful beaches, wildflower-clad dunes, rugged little hills and strong sense of community, little Barra – just 14 miles in circumference – is the Outer Hebrides in miniature. For a great view of the island, walk up to the top of **Heaval** (383m), a mile northeast of Castlebay.

Castlebay (Bagh a'Chaisteil), in the south, is the largest village. There's a TIC (☎ 810336; Main St; 9am-1pm & 2-5pm Mon-Sat, noon-4pm Sun), a bank with ATM, a post office and two grocery stores. There's Internet access at the **Community Library** (☎ 810471; Community School, Castlebay; per 30min £2; 9am-4.30pm Mon & Wed, 9am-4.30pm & 6-8pm Tue & Thu; 9am-3.30pm Fri, 10am-12.30pm Sat;).

Sights & Activities

Castlebay takes its name from **Kisimul Castle** (HS; ☎ 810313; Castlebay; adult/child incl ferry £3.70/2.50; 9.30am-6.30pm Apr-Oct), first built by the MacNeil clan in the 11th century. It was sold in the 19th century and restored in the 20th by American architect Robert MacNeil, who became the 45th clan chief; he gifted the castle to Historic Scotland in 2000 for an annual rent of £1 and a bottle of whisky (Talisker single malt, if you're interested).

The **Barra Heritage Centre** (☎ 810413; Castlebay; adult/child £2/1; 11am-4pm Mon-Sat May-Aug, 11am-4pm Mon, Wed & Fri Apr & Sep) has Gaelic-themed displays about the island, local art exhibitions and a tearoom. The centre also manages a restored 19th-century thatched cottage, the **Black Shieling** (adult/child £2/75p; 1-4pm Mon-Fri May-Sep), 3 miles north of Castlebay on the west side of the island.

Traigh Mor (the Big Strand), in the north of the island, is a vast expanse of firm golden sand that serves as Barra's airport (a mile across at low tide, and big enough for three 'runways'), the world's only beach airport to handle scheduled flights. Watching the little Twin Otter aircraft come and go is a favourite spectator sport.

Sleeping & Eating

Accommodation on Barra is limited, so make a reservation before committing to a night on the island.

Faire Mhaoldonaich (☎ 810441; www.fairemhaoldonaich.com; Nasg; r per person £23-25; Mar-Oct;) This B&B is a modern house with spacious, comfortable rooms with great views over Bagh Beag to the isle of Mhaoldonaich; it's a mile west of Castlebay on the road to Vatersay.

Dunard Hostel (☎ 810443; www.dunardhostel.co.uk; Castlebay; dm/d £11/30;) Dunard is a friendly, family-run hostel with 16 beds, just five minutes' walk from the ferry terminal. The hostel can organise sea-kayaking tours for £20/30 a half-/full day.

Craigard Hotel (☎ 810200; www.isleofbarra.com/craigard.html; Castlebay; s/d £65/90, mains £7-10;) The Craigard has snug rooms and a conservatory restaurant with grand views across the harbour to the islands south of Barra; the house speciality is cockles gathered from the airport beach.

Getting There & Around

See p384 for details of CalMac ferries from Castlebay to Oban and Lochboisdale (South Uist) and flights to the Scottish mainland, and p395 for the ferry from Ardmhor, at the northern end of Barra, to Eriskay.

A **Royal Mail postbus** (☎ 01246-546329) makes a regular circuit of the island, and connects with flights at the airport.

You can hire bikes from **Barra Cycle Hire** (☎ 810284; 29 St Brendan's Rd, Castlebay).

PABBAY (PABAIDH), MINGULAY (MIUGHALAIGH) & BERNERAY (BEARNARAIGH)

These three uninhabited islands, gifted to the National Trust for Scotland (NTS) in 2000, are important breeding sites for seabird species such as fulmar, black guillemot, common and Arctic tern, great skua, puffin and storm petrel. **Allan MacNeil** (☎ 01871-810449) in Castlebay, Barra, operates bird-watching cruises to Mingulay in settled weather for £15 per person, including a landing on the beautiful beach of Mingulay Bay; ask at Barra TIC (☎ 01871-810336; Main St, Barra; 9am-1pm & 2-5pm Mon-Sat, noon-4pm Sun) for details. The puffin season lasts from June to early August.

Orkney & Shetland Islands

Moored off the country's remote northeast coast, the Orkney and Shetland Islands are a plaything for the raging northern Atlantic Ocean, which cuts them from the Scottish mainland, mercilessly buffets their coastline and, in times of relative calm, reflects their raw beauty. Together, these diverse and captivating archipelagos form an antithesis to modern urban grit, and for visitors offer a unique insight into ancient and modern Scotland.

Devolution came to these islands long before the rest of Scotland. Their geographical isolation, unique cultural flavour, Norse roots and distinctive island geography gives each group its own identity. This character is accentuated by echoes of the past; the islands are a living, breathing museum, with distant ancestors leaving behind an extraordinary diary of human development. It's this sort of fusion that makes a trip to Scotland's far-flung northern outposts not only compelling but also a highlight of any visit to the country.

In many ways the landscape is untamed, as mother nature lashes it with snarling gales. Breathtaking scenery means walking and cycling are both popular and (with sometimes ferocious headwinds) challenging island pursuits. The wildlife spectacle here is unparalleled in the British Isles, and visitors may spot porpoises, elusive otters and seal colonies – but it is the thriving bird population that is a real draw card, with millions of sea birds breathing life into forbidding coastal areas. And who can resist sitting among colonies of comical puffins as they totter about their daily business?

HIGHLIGHTS

- Gasping at the skill used to construct incredibly well-preserved prehistoric sites such as **Skara Brae** (p410) and **Maes Howe** (p409), which predate the pyramids

- Gazing out towards the Arctic Circle amid the colourful puffins at **Hermaness** (p428)

- Feeling the power of an ancient faith in the deafening silence of Kirkwall's majestic **St Magnus Cathedral** (p401)

- Walking or cycling the raw, desolate and intensely beautiful landscapes of the **Shetlands** (p416)

- Scuba diving in Europe's premier underwater museum of sunken warships in **Scapa Flow** (p406)

★ Hermaness

Shetlands ★

Skara Brae ★ · ★ St Magnus
Maes Howe ★ Cathedral
★ Scapa Flow

■ POPULATION: Orkney 19,250; Shetland 22,000   ■ AREA: Orkney 990 sq km; Shetland 1466 sq km

ORKNEY & SHETLAND ISLANDS

ORKNEY ISLANDS

Orcadians are known to be fiercely independent of mainland Scotland, even though their magical archipelago is situated a mere 6 miles off the north coast. Indeed, stepping off the boat leaves visitors in no doubt that they have entered a different realm – it is all part of the allure of these enchanting islands. They are a glittering centrepiece in Scotland's treasure chest of attractions, and only 17 of Orkney's 70 islands are inhabited. The dramatic coastal scenery sees 300m cliffs plunge into white, sandy beaches.

Orkney contains a sliver of mankind's ancient existence that's found nowhere else. Prehistoric sites are sprinkled throughout the islands – Europe's greatest concentration – their stone walls immune to 5000 years of climatic onslaught. The Flinstonesque furniture of Skara Brae, the tomb of Maes Howe and numerous standing stones provide a mystical milieu while providing a snapshot of the way people have worshipped, lived and perished since ancient times. The real magnetism of Orkney, though, is today's civilisation, which can be found in its animated contemporary culture – expressed through fine cuisine, inviting drinking holes, chatty locals and rollicking festivals.

Tours

Orkney Island Holidays (☎ 01856-711373; www .orkneyislandholidays.com; Furrowend, Shapinsay) offers holidays based on Shapinsay, with guided tours of archaeological sites, bird-watching trips, wildlife trips and excursions to other islands. One-week, all-inclusive packages cost £850.

Wildabout Orkney (☎ /fax 01856-851011, 07776 378966; wildabout@orkney.com) operates tours covering Orkney's history, ecology, folklore and wildlife. Day trips operate year round and cost £25. The minibus tours pick you up at Stromness ferry terminal, and at Palace Rd and Kirkwall Youth Hostel in Kirkwall.

Discover Orkney (☎ /fax 01856-872865; 44 Clay Loan, Kirkwall, Mainland) caters to individuals and small groups, offering guided tours and walks throughout the islands in the company of a qualified guide.

Getting There & Away

AIR
British Airways/Loganair (☎ 0845 773 3377; www .loganair.co.uk) flies at least twice daily (except Sunday) from Kirkwall airport to Aberdeen (one hour), Edinburgh (1¾ hours), Glasgow and Inverness (45 minutes), with connections to London Heathrow, Birmingham, Manchester and Belfast. There is one daily flight from Kirkwall to Sumburgh airport on Shetland (35 minutes). You can book on the website; fares fluctuate depending on date and time of departure.

BOAT
Car ferries to and from Orkney can be very busy in July and August – it's best to book ahead at these times.

From Scrabster, Shetlands & Aberdeen
Northlink Ferries (☎ 0845 600 0449; www.north linkferries.co.uk) operates ferries from Scrabster to Stromness (passenger return £25 to £29, car return £80 to £90, 1½ hours, three daily Monday to Friday, two on weekends). Northlink also sails from Aberdeen to Kirkwall (passenger return £31 to £48, car return £120 to £165, up to 7¼ hours, one daily) and on to Lerwick (passenger return £26 to £38, car return £94 to £150, up to 7½ hours, two to four weekly) on the Shetland Islands. Note that there are only three services weekly from Lerwick to Kirkwall and on to Aberdeen.

Fares vary according to low, mid- and peak season (we've provided low and peak fares), and travel times vary due to winds.

From Gills Bay
Pentland Ferries (☎ 01856-831226; www.pentland ferries.com) offers a shorter and less expensive car-ferry crossing than the Northlink trip. Boats leave from Gills Bay, about 3 miles west of John o'Groats, and head to St Margaret's Hope in Orkney (passenger/car £11/28, one hour). There are three to four crossings daily in summer and usually three in winter.

From John o'Groats
During the summer period, **John o'Groats Ferries** (☎ 01955-611353; www.jogferry.co.uk) operates a passenger-only ferry (p359) from John o'Groats to Burwick, on the southern tip of South Ronaldsay.

BUS

Scottish Citylink (☎ 0870 550 5050; www.citylink .co.uk) has daily coaches from Inverness to Scrabster (£14, three hours), connecting with the ferries to Stromness. Early-morning departures from Glasgow or Edinburgh, and overnighters from London, connect with the Scrabster bus at Inverness.

John o'Groats Ferries (☎ 01955-611353; www .jogferry.co.uk) operates the summer-only Orkney bus service from Inverness to Kirkwall. Tickets (one way/return £30/42, five hours) include bus travel from Inverness to John o'Groats, passenger ferry to Burwick and another bus from Burwick to Kirkwall. There's one bus daily in May and two daily from June to early September.

Getting Around

Orkney Islands Council (☎ 01856-873535) publishes the *Orkney Public Transport Timetable*, a detailed schedule of all bus, ferry and air services around and to/from Orkney. The timetable is available free from Tourist Information Centres (TICs).

The largest island, Mainland, is joined by road-bearing causeways to Burray and South Ronaldsay. The other islands can be reached by air and ferry services.

TO/FROM THE AIRPORT

British Airways/Loganair (☎ 01856-872494; orkney res@loganair.co.uk) operates inter-island flights between Kirkwall airport and North Ronaldsay, Westray, Papa Westray, Stronsay, Sanday and Eday. For details, see each island's entry in this chapter.

BICYCLE

You can hire bikes from various locations on Mainland, including **Cycle Orkney** (☎ 01856-875777; Tankerness Lane, Kirkwall; per day/week £8/60) and **Orkney Cycle Hire** (☎ 01856-850255; 54 Dundas St, Stromness; per day £6-9).

BOAT

Orkney Ferries (☎ 01856-872044; www.orkneyferries .co.uk; Shore St, Kirkwall) operates car ferries from Mainland to Hoy, Flotta and the northern Orkney islands; for details see each island's section later in the chapter.

CAR

There are several car-hire companies on Mainland, including **Orkney Car Hire** (☎ 01856-

---

> **TOP FIVE PUBS FOR LUSCIOUS ORCADIAN SEAFOOD**
>
> **Kirkwall Hotel** (p403) – Kirkwall, Mainland
> **Stromness Hotel** (p407) – Stromness, Mainland
> **Creel Inn & Restaurant** (p406) – South Ronaldsay
> **Stronsay Hotel** (p414) – Stronsay
> **Pierowall Hotel** (p415) – Westray

872866; Junction Rd, Kirkwall) and **Norman Brass Car Hire** (☎ 01856-850850; Blue Star Filling Station, North End Rd, Stromness). Small-car rates begin at around £34/165 per day/week.

Star Rent-a-Car (in Orkney ☎ 01856-831832, in Lerwick 01595-692075; www.starrentacar.co.uk; 22 Commercial Rd, Lerwick) offers to collect/return vehicles from all northern island ports and airports, a great combined way to get around the Orkney and Shetland Islands.

To hire a camper van, contact **Orkney Motorhome Hire** (☎ 01856-874391; www.orkney -motorhome-hire.co.uk). The vans sleep two adults comfortably, but two adults and three kids at a pinch. Weekly rates are £390 from November to March, £490 in July and August, and £440 all other months.

PUBLIC TRANSPORT

Orkney Coaches (☎ 01856-870555) runs bus services on Mainland and South Ronaldsay. Most buses don't operate on Sunday. Day Rover (£6) and 3-Day Rover (£15) tickets will save you money, allowing unlimited travel on Orkney Coaches' bus routes. **Causeway Coaches** (☎ 01856-831444) runs to St Margaret's Hope on South Ronaldsay.

KIRKWALL

☎ 01856 / pop 6206

With its streets pounded by the footsteps of tourists on their summer Orcadian pilgrimage, Kirkwall has an energy that ebbs and flows along its busy streets. It's set back from a wide bay, and its vigour, combined with the atmospheric paved streets and twisting wynds (lanes), gives Orkney's capital a distinctive character. Magnificent St Magnus Cathedral takes pride of place in the centre of town, and the nearby Earl's and Bishop's Palaces are also worth a ramble through. Founded in the early 11th century, the original part of Kirkwall is one of the best examples of an ancient Norse town.

ORKNEY &
SHETLAND ISLANDS

KIRKWALL

0 — 300 m
0 — 0.2 miles

To Northlink Ferry
Office & Terminal (1mi)

To Shapinsay (4mi);
Eday (16mi); Westray (19mi);
Stronsay (21mi); Papa Westray (28mi);
North Ronaldsay (37mi)

Wide Firth

Ayre Rd

Peerie Sea

East Rd

Berstane Rd

To Sanderlay
(200m)

King St

Mill St

Palace Rd

Watergate

Dundas Cres

Junction Rd

Union St

Main

Clay Loan

Glaitness Rd

Wellington St

New Scapa Rd

Scapa Rd Old

To Foveran Hotel (2mi);
Orphir (8mi); Houton
Ferry Terminal (9mi)

To Highland Park Distillery (800m);
Royal Oak Guest House (800m);
Airport (3mi), Deerness (11mi);
Burray; South Ronaldsay (11mi)

SLEEPING 🏠	
Albert Hotel	10 B1
Ayre Hotel	11 B1
Kirkwall Youth Hostel	12 A4
Kirkwell Hotel	13 B1
Mrs Flett's	14 C1
Mrs Muir	15 C2
Peedie Kirkwall Hostel	16 B1
Pickaquoy Centre Caravan & Camping Site	17 A2

EATING 🍽	
Bothy Bar	(see 10)
Busters Diner	18 B2
International Takeaway	19 C1
Matchmakers Lounge	(see 10)
Somerfield Supermarket	20 B2
St Magnus Café	21 B2
Stables Restaurant	(see 10)
Trenabies Cafe	22 C2

ENTERTAINMENT 🎭	
Fusion Nightclub	23 B1

SHOPPING 🛍	
Longship	24 B2

TRANSPORT	
Bus Station	25 B2
Cycle Orkney	26 B2
Northern Isles Ferry Terminal	27 B1
Orkney Car Hire	28 B1
Orkney Ferries Office	29 B1
Shapinsay Ferry Terminal	30 B1

INFORMATION	
Balfour Hospital	1 B3
Launderama	2 B2
Orkney Library	3 B2
Support Training	4 B2
Tourist Information Centre (TIC)	5 B2

SIGHTS & ACTIVITIES	
Bishop's Palace	6 B2
Earl's Palace	7 B2
St Magnus Cathedral	8 B2
Tankerness House & Orkney Museum	9 B2

ORKNEY &
SHETLAND ISLANDS

Orientation

Kirkwall is fairly compact and it's easy enough to get around on foot. The cathedral and most of the shops are on Broad St, which changes name several times along its length.

Information

There are banks with ATMs on Broad St and Albert St.

Balfour Hospital (☎ 888000; New Scapa Rd)
Launderama (☎ 872982; 47 Albert St; ☽ 8.30am-5.30pm Mon-Fri, 9am-5pm Sat) Service wash and dry £7.
Orcadian Bookshop (☎ 878888; www.orcadian.co.uk; 50 Albert Street) Great selection of local books and newspapers.
Orkney Library (☎ 873166; 44 Junction Rd; ☽ 9am-

8pm Mon-Thu, 9am-6pm Fri, 9am-5pm Sat; 🖳) Fast and free Internet access (one hour maximum).
Post office (Junction Rd)
Support Training (☎ 873582; cnr Junction Rd & West Tankerness Lane; per hr £5; ☽ 8.30am-7pm Mon, Wed & Fri, 8.30am-9.30pm Tue, 10am-5pm Sat, 10am-4pm Sun; 🖳) Internet access.
TIC (☎ 872856; www.visitorkney.com; 6 Broad St; ☽ 9am-5pm Mon-Fri & 10am-4pm Sat Oct-Apr, 9am-6pm May & Sep, 8.30am-8pm Jun-Aug) Very helpful. Has a good range of publications on Orkney.

Sights

ST MAGNUS CATHEDRAL

Founded in 1137 and constructed from local red sandstone and yellow Eday stone, fabulous **St Magnus Cathedral** (☎ 874894; Broad

St; admission free; 9am-6pm Mon-Sat & 2-6pm Sun Apr-Sep, 9am-1pm & 2-5pm Mon-Sat Oct-Mar) should not be missed. The powerful atmosphere of an ancient faith pervades the impressive interior. Epitaphs of the dead, written in a lyrical and melodramatic way, line the walls inside and emphasise the serious business of 17th- and 18th-century bereavement.

Earl Rognvald Brusason commissioned the cathedral in the name of his martyred uncle, Magnus Erlendsson, who was killed by Earl Hakon Paulsson on Egilsay in 1117. Work began in 1137, but the building is actually the result of 300 years of construction and alteration, and includes Romanesque, transitional and Gothic styles.

During summer only, 40-minute tours of the cathedral's upper levels start at 11am and 2pm on Tuesday and Thursday and cost £5.50 per person.

EARL'S PALACE & BISHOP'S PALACE
Near the cathedral, and on opposite sides of the street, these two ruined Historic Scotland (HS) **palaces** (☎ 871918; Watergate; adult/child £2.50/1; 9.30am-6.30pm Apr-Sep) are worth poking around. The Earl's Palace was once known as the finest example of French Renaissance architecture in Scotland. It's the better of the two palaces, with many lower rooms still intact. One room features an interesting history of its builder, Earl Patrick Stewart, who was executed in Edinburgh for treason. He started construction in about 1600, but he ran out of money and it was never completed.

The Bishop's Palace was built in the mid-12th century to provide comfortable lodgings for Bishop William the Old. There's a good view of the cathedral from the tower, and a plaque showing the different phases of the cathedral's construction.

TANKERNESS HOUSE & ORKNEY MUSEUM
This fine restored **merchant's house** (☎ 873191; Broad St; admission free; 10.30am-5pm Mon-Sat & 2-5pm Sun May-Sep, 10.30am-5pm Mon-Sat Oct-Apr) gives an intriguing glimpse into Orkney's archaeological treasure chest, starting from the first settlers, who arrived over 5000 years ago. Exhibits include Pictish stones, 'bone' pins and Iron Age jewellery. The highlight is the photo archive downstairs, which offers snapshots of a technologically distant past. Keep an eye out for the temporary exhibitions.

HIGHLAND PARK DISTILLERY
Not only is Highland Park a very fine single malt, but the tour (£5) of the world's most northerly **whisky distillery** (☎ 874619; Holm Rd; 10am-5pm Mon-Fri Apr, Sep & Oct, 10am-5pm Mon-Sat & noon-5pm Sun May-Aug, 1-5pm Mon-Fri Nov-Mar) is also one of the best. You'll see the whole whisky-making process – this is one of the few distilleries that still does its own barley malting, known as floor malting. Tours are run half-hourly.

Festivals & Events
The **St Magnus Festival** (☎ 871445; www.stmagnus festival.com) takes place in June and is a colourful celebration of music and the arts.

Sleeping
BUDGET
Kirkwall Youth Hostel (SYHA; ☎ 0870 004 1133; Old Scapa Rd; dm adult/child £13/10; Apr-Sep) Kirkwall's well-equipped hostel is a 10-minute walk south of the bus station. Though no architectural gem, it's large (with plenty of four-bed dorms), has decent facilities and is very friendly. You'll probably get a room to yourself.

Peedie Kirkwall Hostel (☎ 875477; 1 Ayre Houses, Ayre Rd; dm from £12) This clean, compact, independent hostel has small dorms with comfy wooden bunks (four beds to a room), washbasin and TV in each room. It's on the waterfront next to Ayre Hotel, five minutes' walk west of the town centre.

Also recommended:
Pickaquoy Centre Caravan & Camping Site (☎ 879 900; Pickaquoy Rd; camp sites £4-7.20) Plenty of grass and decent facilities.
Mrs Flett's (☎ 873160; Cumliebank, Cromwell Rd; r per person from £18) Small, traditional and very friendly B&B.

MIDRANGE
Mrs Muir (☎ 874805; 2 Dundas Cres; s/d £25/40) This highly recommended mansion, the old manse for the church, has some of the best accommodation in town. Cavernous rooms have huge windows that flood the place with light. Bathrooms are shared, but these lodgings are something special.

Albert Hotel (☎ 876000; www.alberthotel.co.uk; Mounthoolie Lane; s/d £52/85, with dinner £67/115;) Central, child-friendly Albert Hotel has a pleasant, traditional feel to it. Functional, tidy rooms have king-size beds and you'll get a discount if you stay more than three nights.

Excellent meals are served downstairs, and one of the best pubs in town is also here.

Kirkwall Hotel (☎ 872232; www.kirkwallhotel.com; Harbour St; s/d from £35/50) A grand old bastion of Orcadian hospitality, this hotel sits in a prime location gazing proudly over the harbour. Executive rooms face the front, have magnificent views as well as refurbished en suites and have enough room to park your car next to your bed – they're huge! You're paying for the grandeur, but once you're snuggled into the downstairs bar, you won't care.

Also recommended:

Sanderlay (☎ 875587; www.sanderlay.co.uk; 2 Viewfield Drive; s/d £25/48; 🖳) Sombre Sanderlay is a classy guesthouse in a family home, with understated and first-rate rooms.

Royal Oak Guest House (☎ /fax 877177; www.royaloakhouse.co.uk; Holm Rd; s/d £30/50; 🖳) Has modern rooms that would suit business travellers or families.

TOP END

Ayre Hotel (☎ 873001; www.ayrehotel.co.uk; Ayre Rd; s £56-70, d £98-108) The Ayre Hotel is a very busy 200-year-old town-house hotel. The service can be surly, sure, but this four-star affair is the classiest joint in town. Modern bedrooms are tastefully decked out and the executive rooms are spacious, with views over the harbour.

Foveran Hotel (☎ 872389; www.foveranhotel.co.uk; St Ola; s/d from £57/94, mains £12-18; 🕓 lunch & dinner)

Two miles southwest of Kirkwall, modern Foveran Hotel enjoys a peaceful location overlooking Scapa Flow. The hotel would suit families or older visitors, and rooms are spotless and slightly sterile but very comfortable. The restaurant here is also excellent.

Eating

Trenabies Café (☎ 874336; 16 Albert St; mains £3.50-5; 🕓 8am-6pm Mon-Sat & noon-5pm Sun, plus dinner Fri) Infused with local produce such as homemade chutney and Orkney cheddar, this café menu is the best in town. The combo of booth seating and comfy couches gives it a cosy and relaxed ambience in a homely setting – perfect when the rain is lashing outside. It also has the best coffee in Kirkwall, and Friday night is Mexican madness (mains £10).

Busters Diner (☎ 876717; 1 Mounthoolie Lane; mains £5-11; 🕓 5-10pm Mon-Fri, noon-9pm Sat, 5-9pm Sun) A perpetually busy, American-style diner churning out generous portions of hot dogs, pizza and burgers, and Tex-Mex such as enchiladas and tacos. Busters is popular with the younger crowd.

Albert Hotel (☎ 876000; Mounthoolie Lane; bar suppers £7, Stables Restaurant starters £6, mains £12; 🕓 lunch & dinner) The Albert offers a fine range of places to eat. The lively, friendly Bothy Bar and the more sedate Matchmakers Lounge dish out high-quality, scrumptious bar suppers including chickpea wraps, fajitas and Orkney crab cakes. Or, if you're in the mood for something a bit more stylish, Stables Restaurant offers an intimate ambience and gourmet cuisine using local produce – try heavenly dishes such as baked Orkney salmon with Moroccan sauce.

Kirkwall Hotel (☎ 872232; Harbour St; mains £8-13; 🕓 lunch & dinner) Although catering for most diners, with a mix of beef, lamb, game and veggie dishes, the seafood is the highlight at this hotel restaurant, with sauces that bring out the flavour of the sea. Locals reckon it's the best tucker in town. Dining here is a sedate experience, not for those with food fights on their minds.

Somerfield supermarket (Pickaquoy Rd) is the best place to stock up on provisions.

Also recommended:

St Magnus Café (☎ 873354; Broad St; light meals under £2; 🕓 9.30am-6pm & 7-10pm Mon-Fri, 9.30am-4pm

---

KIRKWALL MADNESS

Kirkwall is transformed into a seething swell of islanders and tourists on New Year's Day and Christmas Day, when the boisterous and chaotic (read: frankly crazy) ball game known as the **Ba'** takes place. Two teams – the Uppies and the Doonies – chase a leather ball, and each other, through the streets, with the aim of getting the ba' into their opponents' goal. The streets become a heaving mass of people, striking this way and that as the ba' moves through the throng. The game can go on for hours, especially if the ba' finds its way into a small lane with the mobs jammed in and neither side willing to give up. It's not unknown for teams to take short cuts through shops and houses, or even across rooftops. It's an extraordinary spectacle, but prepare to be jostled!

Sat) Old-fashioned food hall serving cheap, honest food such as toasties and bacon rolls.

International Takeaway (☎ 874773; Bridge St; fish supper £3.75; ☼ lunch & dinner Mon-Sat) Fires out some kicking kebabs.

Drinking & Entertainment

Bothy Bar (☎ 876000; Mounthoolie Lane) Found in the Albert Hotel, this cosy nook is the best bar in town, with tourists and locals rubbing shoulders and agreeing that the weather is unpredictable. It's a very convivial place and a good chance to strike up a conversation. Matchmakers, in the same building, is more sedate and, with its comfy horseshoe seating, is good for groups.

Fusion Nightclub (☎ 879489; Ayre Rd; admission club nights £2-6; ☼ from 10pm Thu-Sat, last entry 11.45pm) A rocking club catering to most musical tastes – from retro and cheesy chart numbers to soul, funk and hip-hop. Local DJs also spin the latest dance tunes and the club sometimes hosts live gigs. The dress code is smart casual.

Shopping

Kirkwall has some gorgeous jewellery and crafts in shops along Albert St. Try **Longship** (☎ 888790; 7 Broad St; ☼ 9am-5.30pm Mon-Sat) for Orkney-made crafts and gifts, and especially for exquisite designer jewellery.

Getting There & Away

The **airport** (☎ 886210) is 2.5 miles east of the town centre. For information on flying into Orkney, see Getting There & Away, p398. For flights and ferries from Kirkwall to the northern islands, see the island sections.

Bus 91 runs direct from Kirkwall to Stromness (40 minutes, four to 12 daily); 92 runs to Orphir and Houton (20 minutes, four or five Monday to Saturday); and there are also buses from Kirkwall to Stromness via Birsay (one hour).

Bus 96 runs from Kirkwall to Tingwall (30 minutes, three to five daily Monday to Saturday) and the ferry to Rousay, and on to Evie (40 minutes, four daily Monday to Saturday).

From May to September, bus 90 runs between Kirkwall and the John o'Groats ferry at Burwick (45 minutes, two to five daily). From June to September, a special tourist service (bus 98A) runs twice daily Monday to Friday between Kirkwall and Stromness

via Stenness standing stones, the Ring of Brodgar and Skara Brae.

EAST MAINLAND TO SOUTH RONALDSAY

☎ 01856

The sinking of the battleship HMS *Royal Oak* in 1939 – torpedoed by a German U-boat that snuck through Kirk Sound into Scapa Flow – prompted Winston Churchill to commission better defences for this important naval harbour. Causeways made of concrete blocks were laid across the channels on the eastern side of Scapa Flow, linking Mainland to the islands of Lamb Holm, Glimps Holm, Burray and South Ronaldsay. The **Churchill Barriers**, flanked by the rusting wrecks of the old blockships that once guarded the channels, now carry the main road from Kirkwall to Burwick. There are good sandy beaches by barrier Nos 3 and 4.

GETTING THERE & AWAY

Orkney Coaches bus 94 from Kirkwall runs to Deerness in East Mainland (30 minutes, two to four daily Monday to Saturday), with one bus calling at Tankerness. From May to September, bus 90 runs from Kirkwall to Burwick (45 minutes, two to five daily).

Causeway Coaches travels from Kirkwall to South Ronaldsay's St Margaret's Hope (30 minutes, four daily Monday to Friday, two on Saturday, one on Sunday).

East Mainland

On a farm at Tankerness is the mysterious Iron Age site of **Mine Howe** (☎ 861234; adult/child £2.50/1.50; ☼ 10am-3pm Wed, Fri & Sun May, 10am-5pm daily Jun-Aug, 11am-4pm daily early Sep, 10am-2pm Wed, Fri & Sun late Sep), discovered in 1946 but reopened by farmer Douglas Paterson in September 1999. The Howe is an eerie underground chamber whose function is unknown – staff from the Channel 4 TV series *Time Team* carried out an archaeological dig here in 2000 and concluded that it may have had some ritual significance, perhaps as an oracle or shrine. Be careful as you climb down – the stairs are narrow and wet. There are other archaeological works situated in the area and, presumably, many historical mysteries yet to be uncovered.

On the far eastern shore of Mainland, a mile north of Skaill, is the **Gloup**, a spectacular natural arch and sea cave. There are large colonies of nesting sea birds at **Mull Head**, and the shores of **Deer Sound** attract wildfowl.

Lamb Holm

On the tiny island of Lamb Holm, the **Italian Chapel** (☎ 781268; admission free; 🕙 9am-10pm Apr-Sep, 9am-4.30pm Oct-Mar) is all that remains of a POW camp that housed the Italian soldiers who worked on the Churchill Barriers. They built the chapel in their spare time, using two Nissen huts, scrap metal and their considerable artistic and decorative skills. One of the artists returned in 1960 to restore the paintwork. It's quite extraordinary inside and definitely worth seeing.

Burray

Sleepy Burray village, on the southern side of this island, has a general store, a post office and a couple of places to stay.

Nearby, **Orkney Fossil & Vintage Centre** (☎ 731255; Viewforth; adult/child £3/2; 🕙 10am-6pm Apr-Sep) has a quirky collection of household and farming relics and 360-million-year-old fish fossils. The fossils are from the Devonian period, which predates the dinosaurs (Jurassic period) by about 200 million years. There are also galleries devoted to the world wars.

Ankersted (☎ 731217; ankersted@tinyworld.co.uk; r per person £20) is a great place to stay, with fine rooms, all with private bathroom. The upstairs lounge and balcony area overlook Watersound Bay and barrier No 4, and are exclusively for guests' use.

Sands Hotel (☎ /fax 731298; www.thesandshotel .co.uk; Burray; s/d £50/70, mains £11-15, bar meals £6.50; 🕙 lunch & dinner) is a spiffy, refurbished 19th-century herring station, right on the pier. Very modern rooms have stylish furnishings, some with superb views over the water. The restaurant with its genteel, nautical feel dishes out decent nosh, and tables in the sunlit conservatory migrate outside in sunny weather.

South Ronaldsay

The main village on South Ronaldsay is **St Margaret's Hope**, named after Margaret, the Maid of Norway, who died here in 1290 on the way from her homeland to marry Edward II of England. There are two grocery stores, a post office and several pubs.

SIGHTS

Tomb of the Eagles

This 5000-year-old chambered **tomb** (☎ 831 339; Liddle Farm; adult/child £5/3; 🕙 10am-noon Mar, 9.30am-6pm Apr-Oct, by arrangement Nov-Feb), at the southern tip of South Ronaldsay, is run as a visitor attraction by local farmers. Their entertaining and informative tour is a real draw card and an excellent way to experience this relic. It's possible that sky burials occurred here; there's evidence that the bodies of people had been stripped of their flesh before being put in the tomb, possibly by being placed on top of wooden platforms just outside the tomb entrance and providing the eagles with a feast. You'll also see a **burnt mound**, an impressive Bronze Age kitchen. The tomb is a 20-minute walk east of Burwick.

Orkney Marine Life Aquarium

The newest attraction in Orkney, this **aquarium** (☎ 831700; B9044, Grimness; adult/child £4/3; 🕙 10am-6pm) showcases the fascinating and diverse collection of marine animals found in Scapa Flow and Orcadian coastal waters. Giant shellfish such as lobsters are a feature, and there's a rock pool that allows up-close and personal inspections of local creatures – great for everyone, but especially kids. Injured seals that have been nursed back to health can be viewed in open-air pools, and there's also an old creel boat to clamber about on.

SLEEPING & EATING

Bankburn House (☎ 831310; St Margaret's Hope; r per person £25) On the A961, just outside town, this place has four smashing upstairs rooms in a large rustic house. Two rooms have en suite, all are a brilliant size, and a lot of thought has been put into guests' comfort. There's also a huge stretch of lawn out the front, which overlooks the town and bay – perfect for sunbathing on those shimmering, summery Orkney days.

Murray Arms Hotel & Backpacker's Hostel (☎ 831205; murrayarms@freeuk.com; St Margaret's Hope; dm £11, hotel s/d £33/66) Run by the neighbouring Murray Arms Hotel, the backpackers here is a lovely stone cottage and has one single, two twins and a six-bed dorm with comfy bunks. There's a great lounge, a kitchen and good hot showers. It's an excellent setup, particularly as the pub is right outside the front door! Book ahead for weekends. If you prefer a bit more comfort, the hotel has adequate upstairs rooms, and does bar food all day.

Creel Inn & Restaurant (☎ 831311; Front Rd, St Margaret's Hope; s/d £60/90, mains £18; ☼ dinner) Arguably the best restaurant in Orkney, the Creel serves fresh local produce – simply prepared, but delicious. Try the roasted torsk and pan-fried monkfish and round it off with a chocolate mascarpone torte. There are also first-class rooms, some with panoramic views of the small harbour.

SOUTH MAINLAND

☎ 01856

With its gently rolling landscape, South Mainland may not have the archaeological treasures of the north, but it does have its share of the island's history. There are a few things to see at **Orphir**, a scattered community with no shop, about 9 miles west of Kirkwall. The town's **Orkneyinga Saga Centre** (admission free; ☼ 9am-5pm) has displays relating to the Orkneyinga Saga (a story dating from 1136 about the Vikings in Orkney), and a wide-screen video show.

Just behind the centre is the **Earl's Bu** (admission free; ☼ 24hr), the foundations of a 12th-century manor house belonging to the Norse earls of Orkney. There are also the remains of **St Nicholas' Church**, a unique circular building that was originally 9m in diameter. Built before 1136 and modelled on the rotunda of the Church of the Holy Sepulchre in Jerusalem, it was popular with pilgrims after the capture of the Holy Land during the First Crusade.

If it's sunny and you're thinking about a picnic, head to **Waulkmill Bay**, between Kirkwall and Orphir. The huge sandy beach is perfect for strolling along and there is bench seating with impressive views.

Roving Eye Enterprises (☎ 811360; adult/child £25/12.50) offers terrific boat trips, with the opportunity to view some of the rusting hulks of the German High Seas Fleet at the bottom of Scapa Flow – and you don't even

---

DIVING SCAPA FLOW'S WRECKS

The many wrecks that litter the floor of Scapa Flow make it one of the most popular diving locations in Europe. Enclosed by Mainland, Hoy and South Ronaldsay, this is one of the world's largest natural harbours and has been used by vessels as diverse as King Hakon's Viking ships in the 13th century and members of today's NATO fleet.

It was from Scapa Flow that the British Home Fleet sailed to meet the German High Seas Fleet at the Battle of Jutland on 31 May 1916. After the war, 74 German ships were interned in Scapa. Conditions for the German sailors were poor, and there were several mutinies as the negotiations for the fate of the ships dragged on. When the terms of the armistice were agreed on 6 May 1919, with the announcement of a severely reduced German navy, Admiral von Reuter (who was in charge of the German fleet in Scapa Flow) decided to take matters into his own hands. On 21 June, a secret signal to scuttle the ships was passed from vessel to vessel, and the British watched incredulously as every German ship began to sink.

Most of the ships were salvaged but seven remain on the sea floor, attracting divers from all over the world. There are three battleships – the *König*, the *Kronprinz Wilhelm* and the *Markgraf* – which are all over 25,000 tonnes. The first two were subjected to blasting for scrap metal, but the *Markgraf* is undamaged and considered one of the best dives in the area. Four light cruisers (4400 to 5600 tonnes) – the *Karlsruhe*, *Dresden*, *Brummer* and *Köln* – are particularly interesting, as they lie on their sides and are very accessible to divers. The *Karlsruhe*, though severely damaged, is only 10m below the surface. Its twisted superstructure has now become a huge metal reef encrusted with diverse sea life.

As well as the German wrecks, numerous other ships rest on the sea bed in Scapa Flow. HMS *Royal Oak*, which was sunk by a German U-boat in October 1939, with the loss of 833 crew, is an official war grave.

Recommended contacts for diving in Scapa Flow:

Diving Cellar (☎ 01856-850055; www.divescapflow.co.uk; 4 Victoria St, Stromness)
European Technical Dive Centre (ETDI; ☎ 01856-731269; www.technicaldivers.com; Garisle, Burray)
Scapa Scuba (☎ /fax 01856-851218; www.scapascuba.co.uk; Lifeboat House, Dundas St, Stromness)

get your feet wet! The boat uses a video camera attached to a ROV (remotely operated vehicle). The trips, which must be booked in advance, depart from Houton Pier at 1.20pm from May to September, last around three hours and include a visit to the Scapa Flow Visitor Centre (p411) at Lyness.

Sleeping

Foinhaven (☎ 811249; foinhavenbandb@orphir1.free serve.co.uk; Germiston Rd, Orphir; r per person £25; ☒) For a farm stay, old-fashioned hospitality and one of the best breakfasts around, try the solitude at this place, 1.5 miles from Orphir, overlooking Waulkmill Bay. Rooms are traditional and bathrooms modern – a speck of dirt would feel lonely in here. The rate comes down if you stay more than one night.

Houton Bay Lodge (☎ 811320; www.houtonbay lodge.com; Houton; s/d/f from £35/50/75; ☐ ☒) Particularly good for families or business folk, this old seaplane base has been extensively refurbished, and the cool, stylish, contemporary rooms decked out with pine furniture are top notch (No 5 is a fave). Slick leather chairs, comfy beds and en suites complete the happy picture. The lodge is right behind the ferry terminal with departures for Flotta and Hoy.

Getting There & Away

Bus 92 runs from Kirkwall to Houton (25 minutes, three to five daily Monday to Saturday) via Orphir. For details of ferries from Houton to Hoy, see p411.

STROMNESS

☎ 01856 / pop 1609

An elongated little port with the atmosphere of a bygone era, Stromness lacks Kirkwall's size and punch but makes up for that with bucket-loads of character. The rambling, winding streets flanking the town have changed little since the 18th century and the flagstone-paved main street curves along the waterfront, amid attractive stone cottages. Guesthouses, pubs and eateries interrupt traditional trade along the main street, where cars and pedestrians move at the same pace as each other.

Information

Bank of Scotland (Dundas St) Has an ATM.
Royal Bank of Scotland (Victoria St) Near the pier; has an ATM.

Stromness Community Centre (Church Rd; per hr £3-5; ☒) Cheaper rates for Internet access in the evenings.
Sutherlands Pharmacy (Victoria St)
TIC (☎ 850716; stromness@visitorkney.com; ☒ 9am-5pm Jun-Aug, 9.30am-3.30pm Mon-Fri & 8.30am-2.30pm Sat Sep-May) Small and friendly office in the ferry terminal building.

Sights

The main recreation in Stromness is simply strolling back and forth along the narrow, atmospheric main street. The **Pier Arts Centre** (☎ 850209; 30 Victoria St) is an exquisite gallery that, at the time of writing, was undergoing a major extension and refurbishment – it's due to reopen in summer 2006.

The superb **Stromness Museum** (☎ 850025; 54 Alfred St; adult/child £2.50/50p; ☒ 10am-5pm Apr-Sep) is full of knick-knacks from maritime and natural-history exhibitions covering whaling, the Hudsons Bay Company and the sunk German fleet. You can happily nose around the place for a couple of hours. Across the street from the museum is the house where local poet and novelist **George Mackay Brown** lived from 1968 until his death in 1996.

Festivals & Events

The annual **Orkney Folk Festival** (☎ 851331; www.orkneyfolkfestival.co.uk) is a four-day event based in Stromness in the third week of May, with a programme of folk concerts, *ceilidhs* (evenings of traditional Scottish entertainment including music, song and dance) and casual pub sessions.

Sleeping

Stromness Hotel (☎ 850298; www.stromnesshotel .com; Victoria St; r per person £48) The grandest place in town, 19th-century Stromness Hotel lords it over the harbour. Everything seems on a very imposing scale and the rooms are a bit old-fashioned, but stupendous views from the almost floor-to-ceiling windows more than compensate for the building's faded splendour. Room No 2 is a beauty, with brilliant harbour vistas.

Ferry Inn (☎ 850280; www.ferryinn.com; John St; s/d £32/60) The Ferry Inn is a great pub to stay at. Rooms are cutesy, except No 9, which is spacious and has good views. The lively bar downstairs will alleviate all symptoms of boredom. The Ferry Inn also runs the annexe (15 John St) across the road, which

ORKNEY & SHETLAND ISLANDS

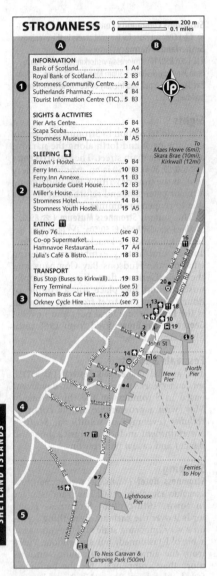

STROMNESS

0 ————— 200 m
0 ————— 0.1 miles

INFORMATION
Bank of Scotland........................... 1 A4
Royal Bank of Scotland................. 2 B3
Stromness Community Centre..... 3 A4
Sutherlands Pharmacy................. 4 B4
Tourist Information Centre (TIC).. 5 B3

SIGHTS & ACTIVITIES
Pier Arts Centre............................. 6 B4
Scapa Scuba................................... 7 A5
Stromness Museum....................... 8 A5

SLEEPING 🛏
Brown's Hostel.............................. 9 B4
Ferry Inn....................................... 10 B3
Ferry Inn Annexe.......................... 11 B3
Harbourside Guest House............ 12 B3
Miller's House............................... 13 B3
Stromness Hotel........................... 14 B4
Stromness Youth Hostel.............. 15 A5

EATING 🍴
Bistro 76....................................(see 4)
Co-op Supermarket..................... 16 B2
Hamnavoe Restaurant................. 17 A4
Julia's Café & Bistro.................... 18 B3

TRANSPORT
Bus Stop (Buses to Kirkwall)....... 19 B3
Ferry Terminal..........................(see 5)
Norman Brass Car Hire................ 20 B3
Orkney Cycle Hire....................(see 7)

To Maes Howe (6mi);
Skara Brae (10mi);
Kirkwall (12mi)

New Pier

North Pier

Ferries to Hoy

Lighthouse Pier

To Ness Caravan &
Camping Park (500m)

ORKNEY &
SHETLAND ISLANDS

---

desperately requires an interior decorator, but these rooms may be cheaper.

Miller's House (☎ 851969; millershouse@orkney.com; 7 John St; s/d £28/45) Miller's House also runs Harbourside Guest House, a couple of doors down at 13 John St (same prices). They're both lovely historical houses that have been extensively renovated inside to fully exploit their light and space. The rooms in Harbourside are better, but all are quite luxurious. Expect a cracking breakfast in the morning. Over summer you'll need to book in advance.

Stromness Youth Hostel (SYHA; ☎ 0870 004 1150; Hellihole Rd; dm adult/child £12/10; ☺ May-Sep) This sedate hostel is a 10-minute walk from the ferry terminal and is a comfortable spot, but it's not for party animals. Facilities are clean and well looked after; note that it was closed at the time of research, pending improvement works – call before coming here.

Brown's Hostel (☎ 850661; 45 Victoria St; dm £10) Brown's is a popular 14-bed independent hostel, just five minutes' walk from the ferry. It opens year-round and there's no curfew. There are single, double and family rooms, all clean but small. The location is excellent for getting around town.

Ness Caravan & Camping Park (☎ 873535; camp sites £4-7.20) This breezy, fenced-in camping ground overlooks the bay at the southern end of town and is as neat as a pin.

Eating

Julia's Café & Bistro (☎ 850904; 20 Ferry Rd; mains lunch £4-8, dinner £10-15; ☺ café breakfast & lunch daily, bistro dinner Wed-Sun May-Sep) This light and airy eatery can get frantic when the tour buses converge. Featuring local produce wherever possible, meals are not sophisticated affairs but they are tasty, filling and reasonably priced. For lunch, chow down on melts, open crab or salmon sandwiches, crisp salads and a homemade nut roast for vegetarians. Follow up with Orkney fudge cheesecake. Dinners have a more formal ambience in the evening.

Bistro 76 (☎ 851803; 76 Victoria St; starters £5, mains £9-13; ☺ dinner Mon-Sat) This is an intimate cellar restaurant with a standout menu that will entice most palates through the door (particularly those of vegetarians). It's located under the Orca Hotel.

Stromness Hotel (bar meals £7, restaurant mains £7-15; ☺ lunch & dinner) The Stromness Hotel does excellent seafood dishes fused with tastes of the Orient (try the seafood chow mein). It also serves a fiery-hot peri peri chicken, and there are vegetarian options. You can toast the toes in the Flattie Bar downstairs.

Hamnavoe Restaurant (☎ 850606; 35 Graham Pl; starters £6, mains £12-15; ☺ dinner Tue-Sat Apr-Sep) Taking itself pretty seriously, Stromness' gourmet restaurant uses local Orcadian produce and is especially good for seafood. Dining takes place among the crisp linen of its elegant dining room.

Self-caterers can stock up at the **Co-op supermarket** (North End Rd).

Getting There & Away

For information on ferries to Scrabster, Lerwick and Aberdeen, see p398. For bus services, see p404.

WEST & NORTH MAINLAND

☎ 01856

This part of Orkney is sprinkled with outstanding prehistoric monuments, many of them in the care of HS.

Stenness

The scattered village of Stenness, about 4 miles northeast of Stromness, consists of little more than some houses, a petrol station and a hotel. Around it, however, are some of the most absorbing prehistoric monuments on Orkney, easily accessible using the regular bus service between Stromness and Kirkwall (p404). For an idea of the wealth of Orkney's prehistoric past, keep an eye out for single standing stones in pastureland around Stenness and Brodgar – weird sentry-like figures whose past relevance has been long forgotten.

Just 500m north of the Stenness crossroads, on the B9055, are the **Standing Stones of Stenness**. Only four of the original 12 mighty slabs of this prehistoric stone circle remain erect. Fenced off from the world outside, just like the sheep in the next field, the stones are impressive for their sheer size (one is over 5m high) and of course, age – they were erected around 2500 BC.

A short walk to the east are the excavated remains of **Barnhouse Neolithic Village**, thought to have been inhabited by the builders of Maes Howe.

If you want a bit of solitude, **Upper Nisthouse** (☎ 761378; upper.nisthouse@btinternet.com; Upper Nisthouse; r per person £18-21;) could be just the thing. It's very friendly and you can muse over your day's explorations while gazing out to the hills and lochs that surround the property. From Stenness, take the A965 to Kirkwall for 1.5 miles and turn right at the road to Orphir. The B&B is 2 miles up this road.

Maes Howe

Egypt has the pyramids, Scotland has **Maes Howe** (HS; ☎ 761606; adult/child £4/1.60; 9.30am-6.30pm Apr-Sep, 9.30am-4.30pm Oct-Mar). Constructed about 5000 years ago, it's the finest chambered tomb in Western Europe. A long, low stone passage leads into a chamber in the centre of an earth-covered mound, which is over 6.7m high and 35m across. The size of the local sandstone slabs used, and the skill with which they were laid, is mind-boggling. During the winter solstice, Maes Howe takes on Indiana Jones–esque qualities as blood-red sunsets align themselves with the passage, striking a cairn entrance at the rear of the chamber with alarming precision. These sunsets are recorded live at www.maeshowe.co.uk in December and January.

In the 12th century, Vikings returning from the Crusades broke into the tomb, searching for treasure. They found none but left a wonderfully earthy collection of graffiti, carved in runes on the walls of the tomb, including 'Thorni bedded Helgi' – some things never change. There's also some Viking artwork here, including a crusader cross, a lion, a walrus and a knotted serpent.

Entry is through a timed ticketing system (due to the popularity of the site) and includes an excellent 45-minute guided tour, filling your mind with both awe and questions about this astonishing place. Buy your ticket across the road at Tormiston Mill. Maes Howe is about 10 minutes' walk east of the Stenness crossroads.

Ring of Brodgar

Situated about a mile north of Stenness, along the road towards Skara Brae, is this wide circle of **standing stones** (admission free; 24hr), some over 5m tall. Twenty-two of the original 60 stones still stand among the heather. These mysterious giants in their curious shapes, mutilated by years of climatic onslaught, fire the imagination – what were they for? On a grey day with dark clouds thudding low across the sky, the stones look secretive and seem to be almost sneering at the jostling summer crowds. Raised skyward 4500 years ago, the stones still attract the forces of nature – on 5 June 1980 one was struck by lightning.

Skara Brae & Skaill House

A visit to extraordinary **Skara Brae** (HS; ☎ 841 815; Bay of Skaill; adult/child £5/2, joint ticket with Skaill House £6/2.40; ⏰ 9.30am-6.30pm Apr-Sep, 9.30am-4.30pm Mon-Sat & 2-4.30pm Sun Oct-Mar) offers the best opportunity in Scotland for a glimpse of Stone Age life. Idyllically situated by a sandy bay 8 miles north of Stromness, and predating the pyramids of Giza and Stonehenge, Skara Brae is northern Europe's best-preserved prehistoric village.

Even the stone furniture – beds, boxes and dressers – has survived the 5000 years since a community lived and breathed here. It was hidden until 1850, when waves whipped up by a severe storm eroded the sand and grass above the beach, exposing the houses underneath. There's an excellent interactive exhibit and short video, arming visitors with facts and theory, which will enhance the impact of the site. The official guidebook, available from the visitors centre, includes a good self-guided tour.

The joint ticket will also get you into **Skaill House** (closed Oct-Mar), an early-17th-century mansion and the former home of the laird of Breckness, who discovered Skara Brae. The library here has secret shelves behind the book shelves – straight out of a spy movie! The porthole window exemplifies just how thick the outer walls are and the property is built on the site of a Pictish graveyard. Upstairs rooms afford lovely views.

Buses run on Monday and Thursday to Skara Brae from Kirkwall and Stromness (May to September only). It's possible to walk along the coast from Stromness to Skara Brae via Yesnaby and the Broch of Borwick (9 miles).

Yesnaby Sea Stacks

Six miles north of Stromness are some spectacular but easy coastal walks (the Stromness TIC has details). Less than half a mile south of the car park at Yesnaby is the Yesnaby Castle sea stack. Watch out during the nesting season in early summer when dive-bombing sea birds determinedly protect their nests.

Birsay

The small village of Birsay, with a shop and a post office, is 6 miles north of Skara Brae. The ruins of the **Earl's Palace** (admission free; ⏰ 24hr), built in the 16th century by the despotic Robert Stewart, earl of Orkney, dominate the village centre. Today it's a mass of half walls and crumbling columns, the latter climbing like dilapidated chimney stacks. Nevertheless, the size of the palace is impressive, matching the reputed ego and tyranny of its former inhabitant.

At low tide (check tide times at the shop in Earl's Palace) you can walk out to the **Brough of Birsay** (HS; ☎ 841815; adult/child £2/80p; ⏰ 9.30am-6.30pm mid-Jun–Sep), about three-quarters of a mile northwest of the Earl's Palace. On the island, you'll find the extensive ruins of a Norse settlement and the 12th-century St Peter's Church.

There's **self-catering accommodation** (☎ 721 321; per wk £80-100) in a couple of excellent properties scraping the water's edge. One is a small, sunlit studio-flat that sleeps two. Or try the family-run **Barony Hotel** (☎ 721327; fax 721302; Birsay; r per person £30; ⏰ May-Sep), overlooking the Loch of Boardhouse, about half a mile south of Birsay. This groaning old place has seen better days, but it's a lot better on the inside than it looks from the outside. It also has a beautiful, tranquil, loch-side location – recommended for anglers.

Evie

On an exposed headland at Aikerness, a 1.5-mile walk northeast from the straggling village of Evie, you'll find the **Broch of Gurness** (HS; ☎ 751414; adult/child £3.30/1.30; ⏰ 9.30am-6.30pm Apr-Sep). Built around 100 BC, it's the best-preserved example of a fortified stone tower in Orkney. Surrounding it are the shells of houses, discernable by the hearths in the centre of each. The small visitors centre helps unravel the mysteries of this ancient culture.

Eviedale Cottages & Campsite (☎ /fax 751270; colin.richardson@orkney.com; Dyke Farm, Evie; camp sites £4-7, bothy bunks £5, self-catering cottages per wk £190-310; ⏰ camping ground Apr-Sep), at the northern end of the village, has a small, basic bothy (hut) with four beds (with toilet and stove, but no showers or bed linen). There's also a good grassed area for camping, with picnic tables. Next door is self-catering accommodation in excellent, renovated farm cottages.

Woodwick House (☎ 751330; www.woodwick house.co.uk; Evie; s £32, d £56-84, dinner £25) has large, stark rooms in a relaxed country house. The building is set in gorgeous gardens, where guests can catch glimpses of the sea. When you're feeling peckish, there are three-course homemade dinners.

HOY
☎ 01856

Orkney's second-largest island, Hoy (the name means 'High Island'), got the lion's share of this archipelago's scenic beauty. Shallow turquoise bays lace the perimeter, while peat and moorland cover Orkney's highest hills. The highest point is Ward Hill (479m), in the north of Hoy. This dramatic landscape can be accessed on foot or by wheels, and will tempt hands to cameras.

Sights

The northern part of the island boasts spectacular coastal scenery, including some of Britain's highest vertical cliffs – St John's Head on the northwest coast rises 346m. Hoy is probably best known for the **Old Man of Hoy**, a 137m-high rock stack that can be seen from the Scrabster–Stromness ferry. The northern part of Hoy has been maintained as a nature reserve by the Royal Society for the Protection of Birds (RSPB) since 1983.

Lyness, on the eastern side of Hoy, was an important naval base during both world wars, when the British Grand Fleet was based in Scapa Flow. With the dilapidated remains of buildings and an uninspiring outlook towards the oil terminal on Flotta Island, this isn't a pretty place. However, the **Scapa Flow Visitor Centre** (Lyness Interpretation Centre; ☎ 791300; admission by donation; ☼ 9am-4.30pm Mon-Fri & 10am-4pm Sun May-Sep) is a fascinating naval museum and photographic display, located in an old pumphouse that once fed fuel to the ships.

Activities

First scaled in 1966, the **Old Man of Hoy** is a rock climber's delight. The easiest approach to the Old Man is from Rackwick Bay, a two- to three-hour walk by road from Moaness Pier (in Hoy village on the east coast, where the ferries dock) through the beautiful **Rackwick Glen**. You'll pass the 5000-year-old **Dwarfie Stone**, the only example of a rock-cut tomb in Scotland and, according to Sir Walter Scott, the favourite residence of Trolld, a dwarf from Norse legend. On your return you can take the path via the **Glens of Kinnaird** and **Berriedale Wood**, Scotland's most northerly tuft of native forest.

The most popular walk climbs steeply westwards from Rackwick Bay, then curves northwards, descending gradually to the edge of the cliffs opposite the Old Man of Hoy. Allow seven hours for the return trip from Moaness Pier, or three hours from Rackwick, a village on the west coast – there's a hostel here from where the walk begins.

Sleeping & Eating

Hoy Youth Hostel (☎ 873535 ext 2415 office hrs only; Moaness; dm adult/child £11/8; ☼ May–mid-Sep) This recently refurbished place has an enviable location, around 15 minutes' walk from Moaness Pier, at the base of the rugged Cuilags. You'll need your own sleeping bags and supplies for the en-suite six-bed dorms.

Rackwick Youth Hostel (☎ 873535 ext 2415 office hrs only; Rackwick; dm adult/child £8.50/7.10; ☼ Apr-Sep) The Rackwick, 6 miles from the ferry at Moaness, is a snug (two four-bed dorms), clean place, popular with walkers. As with the Hoy Youth Hostel, you'll need your own sleeping bag and supplies. The warden will collect your dosh in the evening.

There are several B&Bs on the island, including welcoming **Stoneyquoy Farm** (☎ 791 234; www.visithoy.com; Lyness; s/d £26/42), a charming farmhouse with Dutch-Orcadian hosts, comfy rooms and 'special' breakfasts – call ahead as they may be moving location soon. **St John's Manse** (☎ 791240; r per person £25; ▯), between Lyness and Longhope, is a recommended guesthouse for some serious relaxation – there's a superb double and a delightful twin.

Stromabank Hotel (☎ 701494; Longhope; bar meals £6-10; ☼ lunch Sat & Sun, dinner Fri-Wed) The small, atmospheric Stromabank offers tasty home-cooked meals from its small menu; try the chicken breast stuffed with haggis in a whisky ginger sauce.

Groceries can be bought at the shops in Lyness and Longhope.

Getting There & Away

Orkney Ferries (☎ 850624) runs passenger ferries between Stromness and Moaness Pier (£3, 30 minutes, two to five daily May to September). There's a reduced schedule from October to April. In the other direction, the service departs 30 minutes after its arrival on Hoy.

There's also a frequent **car ferry** (☎ 811397) to Lyness (Hoy) from Houton on Mainland (passenger/car £3/9, 40 minutes, up to six daily Monday to Friday, two or three Saturday and Sunday). The more limited Sunday service runs from May to September.

Getting Around

Transport on Hoy is very limited. **North Hoy Transport** (☎ 791315) runs a minibus service between Rackwick and Moaness, meeting the 10am weekday ferry from Stromness. Otherwise, call the same number for a taxi service.

You can hire mountain bikes at **Moaness pier** (☎ 791225; per day £8). Hitching is possible, but on this island there are more sheep than cars.

NORTHERN ISLANDS

The group of windswept islands north of Mainland provides a refuge for migrating birds and a nesting ground for sea birds; there are several RSPB reserves. Some of the islands are also rich in archaeological sites, but it's the beautiful scenery, with wonderful white-sand beaches and lime-green to azure seas, that is the main attraction.

The TICs in Kirkwall and Stromness have the useful *Islands of Orkney* brochure with maps and details of these islands. Note that the 'ay' at the end of each island name (from the Old Norse for 'island') is pronounced 'ee' (Shapinsay is pronounced *shap*-in-see).

Orkney Ferries (☎ 01856-872044) enables you to make day trips to many of the islands from Kirkwall on most days of the week (Friday only to North Ronaldsay), but it's really worth staying for at least a few nights.

Shapinsay

☎ 01856 / pop 300

Just 20 minutes by ferry from Kirkwall, Shapinsay is a low-lying, intensively cultivated island with a superb castle. There are two general stores and a post office.

Balfour Castle (☎ 711282; adult/child £18/9), completed in 1848 in the turreted Scottish Baronial style, is Shapinsay's most impressive draw card. Guided tours (2.15pm Sunday from May to September) must be booked in advance; the price includes the ferry, admission to the castle and afternoon tea. It's also possible to stay at **Balfour Castle** (☎ 711282; www.balfourcastle.com; Balfour Village; dinner, B&B per person from £85), in the grand, old-fashioned Victorian rooms, with the added

attraction that you are, of course, spending the night in a castle. A boat is available for guests for island trips, bird-watching and sea fishing.

About 4 miles from the pier, at the far northeastern corner of the island, is the Iron Age **Burroughston Broch** (admission free; ⏲ 24hr), one of the best-preserved brochs (defensive towers) in Orkney.

Girnigoe (☎ 711256; jean@girnigoe.f9.co.uk; Girnigoe; s/d £25/44) is a friendly, traditional farmhouse at the northern end of the island. The breakfasts (with Mrs Wallace's homemade bread and jam) and local kippers are excellent and dinner is also available.

Orkney Ferries operates a ferry from Kirkwall (passenger/car £3/9, 25 minutes, six daily Monday to Friday, four or five Saturday and Sunday May to September). Services are limited in winter.

Rousay

☎ 01856 / pop 200

History buffs will adore this hilly island. Lying close to Mainland's northeast, it's known as 'the Egypt of the North' for its numerous archaeological sites. Most of the island is classed as a Site of Special Scientific Interest (SSSI), but it also has the important **Trumland RSPB Reserve** and three trout-fishing lochs.

Marion's shop, and a post office that looks like a hen coop, are at Sourin, 2.5 miles north of the pier.

SIGHTS

West of the pier are the prehistoric burial cairns (piles of stones to mark a path or junction) of **Taversoe Tuick**, **Blackhammer**, **Knowe of Yarso** and Midhowe Cairn.

Midhowe Cairn is an extraordinary burial cairn, containing the remains of 25 people. Dating from the 3rd millennium BC, the 'Great Ship of Death', as it's called, is the longest chambered cairn in Orkney. Bird and animal bones accompany the human remains, perhaps meant as food for the deceased. It's housed inside a modern barn-like building, about 5.5 miles west of the pier, and a half-mile walk down from the road.

Nearby **Midhowe Broch** (admission free; ⏲ 24hr) is the best example of a broch in Orkney. The TICs on Mainland have a useful leaflet *(Westness Walk)* describing the mile-long walk from Midhowe Cairn to Westness

Farm. It outlines 5000 years of Orkney history and includes Viking and Pictish burial sites.

Trumland House (gardens £1.50; ⏲ 10am-5pm Mon-Fri May-Sep) is probably the largest private house in Orkney and is currently undergoing extensive restoration. When we passed through, just the lovely gardens were open to the public.

SLEEPING & EATING

Taversoe Hotel (☎ 821325; d £60) This hotel recently reopened and is about 2 miles southwest of the pier. There's a twin, a double and a family room (only the family has en suite); all are beautifully furnished. There are panoramic views from the dining room – the perfect place to munch on a home-cooked pizza. Takeaway food is also available.

Trumland Farm Hostel (☎ 821252; Trumland Farm; camp sites £3, dm £8, bedding extra £2) On an organic farm half a mile west of the ferry, this hostel offers great views and accommodation in two tidy but cramped six-bed dormitories (and one single room). Excellent self-catering facilities are also available.

Pier Restaurant (☎ 821359; meals £4-8; ⏲ 11am-9pm Mon-Sat), by the pier, is an ideal spot for a bar meal, snack or dram of whisky to warm the insides while you wait for the ferry.

GETTING THERE & AROUND

A small **car ferry** (☎ 751360) connects Tingwall on Mainland with Rousay (passenger/car £3/9, 30 minutes, up to six daily) and the nearby islands of Egilsay and Wyre.

Bikes can be rented for £7 per day from Trumland Farm. The island's one road makes a pleasant circuit of about 14 miles.

Egilsay & Wyre

These two small islands lie east of Rousay. On **Egilsay** (population 37), a cenotaph marks the spot where Earl Magnus was murdered in 1117. After his martyrdom, pilgrims flocked to the island, and **St Magnus Church**, now roofless, was built. Today it provides a rare example of a round-towered Viking church. Much of Egilsay is an RSPB reserve; listen for the corncrakes at the southern end of the island.

Wyre (population 18) is even smaller than Egilsay. It was the domain of the Viking baron Kolbein Hruga ('Cubbie Roo'); the ruins of his castle, built around 1145, and

the nearby 12th-century **St Mary's Chapel**, can be visited free. Seal sightings at the beach on Wyre's western sliver are virtually guaranteed. These two islands are reached on the Rousay–Tingwall ferry (see left).

Stronsay

☎ 01857 / pop 340

A peaceful and attractive island, Stronsay draws seals, migratory birds and tourists, the latter coming to walk or pedal over its beautiful landscapes and four curving bays. In the 19th century, Whitehall harbour became one of Scotland's major herring ports, but then the fisheries collapsed in the 1930s.

SIGHTS & ACTIVITIES

The old **Stronsay Fish Mart** (☎ 616386; Whitehall; admission free; ⏲ 11am-6pm Mon & Wed, 11am-7pm Thu-Sat & 10am-7pm Sun May-Sep) now houses a herring industry interpretation centre, designed to take visitors back (figuratively speaking) to the herring boom days. There's also a hostel and café here.

Just across the harbour from Whitehall is the small island of **Papa Stronsay**, where Earl Rognvald Brusason was murdered in 1046. The island is owned by a monastic order, the Transalpine Redemptorists; the monks will provide **boat trips** (☎ 616389) to the island by prior arrangement.

There are good coastal walks on the island and, in the east, the **Vat o'Kirbuster** is the best example of a *gloup* (natural arch) in Orkney.

At the southern end of the island, you can visit the **seal-watch hide** on the beach near the Torness Camping Barn. There's also a chance to see otters at nearby **Loch Lea-shun**.

SLEEPING & EATING

Torness Camping Barn (☎ 616314; bunkhouse per person £6; 🐾) Down at the southern end of the island, the environmentally friendly Holland Farm offers bunkhouse accommodation only a few metres from the beach. It's an excellent place – more like a bungalow – that sleeps about eight and has a toilet and kitchen, but you'll need a sleeping bag. Phone from the pier for a lift. Bubs are free and kids half-price.

Stronsay Fish Mart (☎ 616386; Whitehall; dm £10) Part of the island's former herring station has been converted into a 10-bed hostel with shower and kitchen. It's clean and well run, but pretty basic. Bedding is an extra £3 if you don't have a sleeping bag. The neighbouring café serves takeaways, snacks and meals all day.

Stronsay Hotel (☎ 616213; www.stronsayhotel.com; Whitehall; s/d from £35/70, pub meals from £7; ♥ lunch & dinner; 🕭) The island's watering hole has immaculate refurbished rooms. There's also recommended pub grub in the bar, with excellent seafood (including paella and lobster) in particular. There are good deals for multinight stays.

Stronsay Bird Reserve (☎ 616363; Castle, Mill Bay; full board/B&B per person £30/20) Birders in particular will enjoy staying at the friendly, comfortable Stronsay Bird Reserve, a 40-minute walk south from the ferry pier. Rates include all the tea and coffee you can drink and ensure hours of conversation with the chatty owners.

GETTING THERE & AWAY

British Airways/Loganair (☎ 01856-872494) flies from Kirkwall to Stronsay (one way/return £31/62, 20 minutes, two daily Monday to Saturday).

A **car ferry** (☎ 01856-872044) links Kirkwall with Stronsay (passenger/car £6/14, 1½ hours, two to three daily) and Eday.

Eday
☎ 01857 / pop 121

Eday has a hilly centre, with cultivated fields situated around the coast. There is the impressive standing **Stone of Setter** and close by, the chambered cairns of **Braeside**, **Huntersquoy** and **Vinquoy**. Huntersquoy is a two-storey cairn, like Taversoe Tuick (p412) on Rousay. The early-17th-century **Carrick House** (☎ 622260; adult/child £2.50/1; ♥ by appointment), with its floor bloodstained from a pirate skirmish, is worth a visit; tours of the house run in summer with advance notice.

It's worth getting hold of the *Eday Heritage Walk* leaflet from Kirkwall TIC, which details an interesting four-hour ramble from the Community Enterprises shop up to the cliffs of Red Head in the north of the island.

Eday Minibus Tour (☎ 622206) offers 2¼-hour guided tours (£8) from the ferry pier on Monday, Wednesday and Friday from May to August. Tickets don't include lunch, and Friday is the best day, as you get more time on the island.

SLEEPING & EATING

Eday Hostel (SYHA; ☎ 622283; Bay of London; dm adult/child £9/8) Four miles north of the ferry pier, this simple, renovated, 24-bed hostel is like a cross between an army barracks and a church hall. You'll need your own sleeping bag, although cotton bags are provided.

Mrs Popplewell's (☎ 622248; Blett, Carrick Bay; dinner, B&B per person £28, croft house per person £23) Mrs Popplewell has a charming cottage opposite the Calf of Eday. There's also a fully equipped self-catering croft house nearby for three people. Mrs Popplewell bakes fresh bread daily, and she serves snacks and meals at her craft shop.

GETTING THERE & AROUND

There are two flights from Kirkwall (one way/return £31/62, 30 minutes) to London airport – that's London, Eday – on Wednesday only. The ferry service from Kirkwall usually sails via Stronsay (passenger/car £6/13.50, 1¼ to two hours, two to three daily), but occasionally it's direct. There's also a link between Sanday and Eday (20 minutes).

Alan Stewart (☎ 622206) runs the local minibus and taxi service. He charges around £4 for a trip along the length of Eday.

Sanday
☎ 01857

Aptly named, blissfully quiet Sanday is ringed by Orkney's best beaches – with dazzling white sand of the sort you'd expect in the Caribbean. The island is almost entirely flat apart from a colossal sand dune and the cliffs at Spurness; the dunes are 12 miles long and growing, due to sand build-up.

There are several archaeological sites here, the most impressive being the **Quoyness chambered tomb** (admission free; ♥ 24hr), similar to Maes Howe and dating from the 3rd millennium BC. It has triple walls, a main chamber and six smaller cells. At the northeastern tip of Sanday, there's **Tafts Ness**, with around 500 prehistoric burial mounds.

There are shops and post offices at Kettletoft, Lady and Rusness. A bank service is available at Kettletoft on Tuesday only.

SLEEPING & EATING

With permission, you can camp anywhere on the island.

Kettletoft Hotel (☎ /fax 600217; www.kettletofthotel.co.uk; Kettletoft; r per person £20-25) The welcoming and family-friendly Kettletoft is a refurbished elderly statesman located near the centre of the island. The pub here serves tasty bar meals for around £7, with particularly good puddings.

Belsair (☎ 600206; emma@white1935.freeserve.co.uk; Kettletoft; r per person £25; ☽ dinner) The Belsair overlooks the harbour and has tidy en-suite rooms that are good value. Its bar meals and evening dinner feature Orcadian produce, and staff will even do you a packed lunch.

GETTING THERE & AROUND

There are flights from Kirkwall to Sanday (one way/return £31/62, 20 minutes, twice daily Monday to Saturday). There are ferries between Kirkwall and Sanday (passenger/car £6/13.50, 1½ hours, two daily May to September), and a link to Eday.

Bernie Flett (☎ 600284) hires out bicycles for £7 per day.

Westray

☎ 01857 / pop 700

The largest of the northern islands, Westray is a jewel in the archipelago's crown. With prehistoric sites, sandy beaches and lovely cliff scenery, this island is a favourite. The friendly locals, great places to stay and fresh seafood will entice visitors to linger. The ferry docks at Rapness in the south of the island, but Pierowall, 7 miles to the northwest, is the main village. It has grocery shops, a post office and a hotel. For information about island facilities, call the **Westray & Papa Westray Tourist Association** (☎ 677404; www.westraypapawestray.com).

SIGHTS

Pierowall has one of the best natural harbours in Orkney – it was once an important Viking base. The **Westray Heritage Centre** (☎ 677414; Pierowall; adult/child £2/50p; ☽ 10am-noon & 2-5pm Tue-Sat & 11.30am-5pm Sun & Mon May-Sep) has interesting displays on local history and nature.

A half-mile west of Pierowall lie the ruins of creepy **Noltland Castle** (HS; admission free; ☽ 9.30am-6.30pm mid-Jun–Sep), a 16th-century fortified Z-plan tower house. The RSPB reserve at **Noup Head** coastal cliffs, in the northwest of the island, attracts vast numbers of breeding sea birds from April to July. There are big puffin colonies here and at **Castle o'Burrian**, a mile north of Rapness.

SLEEPING & EATING

With permission, you can camp almost anywhere.

Barn (☎ 677214; www.thebarnwestray.com; Chalmersquoy, Pierowall; dm adult/child £11.75/8.80, camp sites from £3; ☒) This excellent, intimate, modern, 13-bed hostel is an Orcadian gem. It's heated throughout and has an inviting lounge. The price includes bed linen, shower and pristine kitchen facilities. Local advice comes free.

Bis Geos Hostel (☎ 677420; www.bis-geos.co.uk; Bis Geos; dm £11; ☐) This is a snug 16-bed hostel in spectacular surrounds. Guests can enjoy the latter from the conservatory. Another excellent budget option, it's about 2 miles west of Pierowall and 30 minutes' hike from Noup Head. Ask here about self-catering cottages.

Pierowall Hotel (☎ 677472; www.orknet.co.uk/pierowall; Pierowall; s/d £23/40, with bathroom £28/52) The comfortable, eight-room Pierowall Hotel is famous throughout Orkney for its popular fish and chips – the fish is caught fresh by the hotel's boats and is available to eat in or takeaway. Toast your toes by the coal fire in the lounge.

Mrs Groat (☎ 677374; Sand o'Gill; r per person £22) Friendly Mrs Groat, at the northern end of Pierowall, has two properties that she lets out as B&B or self-catering accommodation. Each property has a double plus a two-bunk bedroom – good for families.

GETTING THERE & AWAY

There are flights from Kirkwall to Westray (one way/return £31/62, 20 minutes, twice daily Monday to Saturday). A ferry service links Kirkwall with Rapness (passenger/car £6/13.50, 1½ hours, two to three daily May to September). There are one to two ferries daily in winter.

There's also a passenger-only ferry from Pierowall to Papa Westray (£3, 25 minutes, three to six daily in summer); the crossing is free if you travel direct from the Rapness ferry. From October to April the boat sails by arrangement; phone ☎ 677216.

Papa Westray

Known locally as Papay (*pa-pee*), this exquisitely peaceful, tiny island (4 miles long by a mile wide) attracts superlatives. It is home to Europe's oldest domestic building, the **Knap of Howar** (built about 5500 years ago), and to Europe's largest colony of arctic terns (about 6000 birds) at North Hill. Even the two-minute hop from Westray airfield is featured in *Guinness World Records* as the world's shortest scheduled air service. The island was also the cradle of Christianity in Orkney – **St Boniface's Church** was founded in the 8th century, though most of the recently restored structure is from the 12th century.

From May to September, **Jim Davidson** (☎ 644259) runs boat trips to the **Holm of Papay**, a small island about a half-mile east of Papa Westray, for £5 per person. The main reason for a visit is to see the huge **chambered cairn**, with 16 beehive cells, and wall carvings. You enter through the roof – there's a torch so you can light your way as you crawl around in the gloomy interior.

Beltane House Hotel (☎ 644267; papaybeltane2@ hotmail.com; dm £10, s/d £27/50, meals from £7; ☺ lunch & dinner), owned by the local community co-op, is the best place to stay on the island. It comprises a 16-bed Scottish Youth Hostel Association (SYHA)– approved hostel and a guesthouse with four simple and immaculate rooms with en suite. There is also a small shop and generous lunches and dinners on offer using Orkney beef, seafood, lamb and veggies. The hotel is just over a mile north of the ferry.

GETTING THERE & AWAY

There are two daily (three on Monday and Wednesday) flights to Papa Westray (£15, 15 minutes) from Kirkwall, Monday to Saturday; it's an amazing deal compared with other flights in Orkney – about twice the distance for a fraction of the price (taxes not included). For ferry details, see p415.

North Ronaldsay

☎ 01857 / pop 50

All of 3 miles long and almost completely flat, North Ronaldsay is a real outpost surrounded by rolling seas and big skies. The delicious peace and quiet and excellent birdwatching lures visitors here; the island is home to cormorant and seal colonies and is an important stopover for migratory birds.

There's also a piteous colony of sheep, kept off the rich farmland by a 13-mile-long wall all around the island and forced to feed only on seaweed, which is said to give their meat a unique flavour.

Powered by wind and solar energy, **Observatory Guest House** (☎ 633200; alison@nrbo.prestel .co.uk; dm £10, s/d £31/60) is a working croft next to the ferry pier, and offers first-rate accommodation and ornithological activities. Note that under-15s are half-price, and under-fours are free. Dinner is an extra £10, and there are also a shop, a café and a licensed lounge bar.

Garso Guest House (☎ /fax 633244; christine@garso .fsnet.co.uk; dinner, B&B per person £33, cottage per night £33) is a comfortable B&B and self-catering cottage sleeping five. It's at the northern end of the island, about 3 miles from the pier. Mrs Muir, one of the owners, also offers a taxi and minibus service.

There are two daily (three on Monday and Wednesday) flights to North Ronaldsay (£15, 20 minutes) from Kirkwall, Monday to Saturday. There's a weekly ferry from Kirkwall on Friday (passenger/car £6/14, 2½ hours).

SHETLAND ISLANDS

The rugged and remote Shetland Islands – a collection of mighty, wind-ravaged clumps of brown and green earth rising from the frigid waters of the North Sea – are Scotland's northerly outpost and feel miles away from anywhere. They were under Norse rule until 1469, when they were given to Scotland as part of a Danish princess's dowry.

Far more desolate and cut off than Orkney, the light here is even more changeable than on mainland Scotland. Different parts of the island are variously illuminated at any given hour – the window for that perfect photo can be short. The setting is still uniquely Scottish, though, with deep, naked glens flanked by steep hills, twinkling, sky-blue lochs and, of course, sheep with no comprehension of the 'right of way' on the roads.

The island's far-flung location is belied by the activity and charisma of the capital, Lerwick, causing you to forget the 60-plus oceanic miles between you and the mainland. But once you're outside the humming capital, the isolation sweeps you off your feet – frequent thundering gales thrash across the

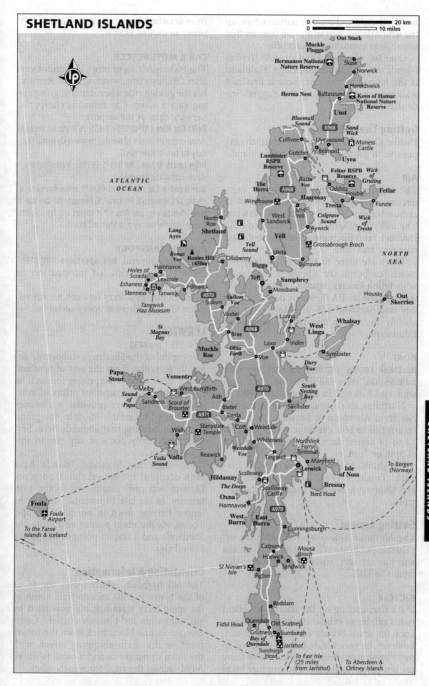

raw landscape and mother nature whips up the wild Atlantic into white-cap frenzies that smash into imposing coastal cliffs.

Over 100 windswept and virtually treeless islands make up this archipelago. Mainland is the biggest island and there is first-rate walking, especially along the rugged, indented coastline.

Getting There & Away

Unlike Orkney, Shetland is relatively expensive to get to from mainland Scotland.

AIR

The oil industry ensures that air connections are good. The main airport is at Sumburgh, 25 miles south of Lerwick. The following flights can be booked on the Internet; fares fluctuate according to departure date and time.

There are three to five flights daily between Sumburgh and Aberdeen (one hour) with **British Airways/Loganair** (☎ 0845 773 3377; www.loganair.co.uk). BA flies daily between Orkney and Shetland (35 minutes). You can also fly direct from Inverness, Glasgow and Edinburgh.

BOAT

Northlink Ferries (☎ 0845 600 0449; www.north linkferries.co.uk) runs car ferries between Lerwick and Kirkwall in Orkney (see p398).

Northlink also operates overnight car ferries from Aberdeen to Lerwick (passenger return £40 to £61, car return £165 to £220, 12 to 14 hours, daily) departing Aberdeen at 5pm or 7pm.

For details of the ferry link between Lerwick, Torshavn (Faroe Islands) and Bergen (Norway), see the Transport chapter, p446.

Getting Around

The *Shetland Transport Timetable,* an invaluable publication listing all local air, sea and bus services, costs £1 and is available from the TIC.

BICYCLE

If it's fine, cycling on the islands' excellent roads can be an exhilarating way to experience the stark beauty of Shetland. It can, however, be very windy (wind speeds of up to 194mph have been recorded!) and there are few places to shelter. You can hire bikes

from **Grantfield Garage** (☎ 01595-692709; North Rd, Lerwick; per day/week £7.50/45).

CAR & MOTORCYCLE

The wide roads seem more like motorways after Orkney's tiny, winding lanes. Remember the golden rule when driving, give passing cars a wave. Car rental is cheaper in Lerwick than at the airport.

Bolts Car Hire (☎ 01595-693636; 26 North Rd, Lerwick) Small cars start from £22 per day for a weekly rental (£25 daily for two or three days).

John Leask & Son (☎ 01595-693162; leasks@zetnet .co.uk; Esplanade, Lerwick)

Star Rent-a-Car (☎ 01595-692075; www.starrentacar .co.uk; 22 Commercial Rd, Lerwick) Opposite the bus station; offers pick-up and drop off at airport and ferry points throughout the Orkney and Shetland Islands.

PUBLIC TRANSPORT

There are several **bus operators** (☎ 01595-694100). Call for detailed information on services.

For inter-island ferry services, see the relevant Getting There & Away sections.

LERWICK

☎ 01595 / pop 6830

The capital of the Shetlands stubbornly defies its seclusion from the rest of Scotland with a vitality that's surprising for such an isolated town. The constant influx of tourists and oil workers provides a vibrancy and energy, breathing life into the grand Victorian housing that abounds here. Lerwick is the only place of any size in this island group.

Although the Shetland Islands have been occupied for several thousand years, Lerwick was only established in the 17th century. In the late 19th century it was the largest herring town in northern Europe. Today, it's the main port of entry into the Shetlands and a transit point to the North Sea oil rigs.

Orientation & Information

The old harbour, which forms the focus of the town, is a 20-minute walk south of the main ferry terminal; it's now used by visiting yachts and pleasure cruisers. Commercial St, one block back from the waterfront, is the main shopping street, with the town's post office and a bank (with an ATM) across the road from each other.

Bank of Scotland (Commercial St) Has an ATM.

Gilbert Bain Hospital (☎ 743000; South Rd)

Lerwick Health Centre (☎ 693201; South Rd)

Manson's Dry Cleaners (☎ 695335; Kantersted Rd)
Charges £8 for a wash and dry.

Shetland Library & Museum (☎ 693868; Lower
Hillhead; ✿ 10am-7pm Mon, Wed & Thu, 10am-5pm Tue,
Fri & Sat; ▣) Free Internet access.

Shetland Times Bookshop (☎ 695531; 71 Commercial
St) Has every book you could possibly want to read about
the Shetlands, with topics from the famous WWII Shetland
Bus to how to spot adorable puffins around the islands.

Support Training (☎ 695026; 6a Mounthooly St; per
30min £1; ✿ 9am-1pm & 2-5pm Mon-Fri; ▣) Internet
access.

TIC (☎ 693434; www.visitshetland.com; Market Cross;
✿ 8am-6pm Mon-Fri, 8am-4pm Sat & Sun Apr-Oct,

9am-5pm Mon-Fri Nov-Mar) This friendly office has a good
range of books and maps, and a comprehensive selection of brochures detailing Shetlands' activities. *Walks on
Shetland* (£6.99), by Mary Welsh, is a good walking guide.
For in-depth advice on walking, look for the *Walking the
Coastline of Shetland* series (£8.99 each). There's also a
bureau de change here.

Sights

Above the town, there are excellent views
from the battlements of **Fort Charlotte** (Charlotte
St; admission free; ✿ 9.30am-sunset), built in 1665 to
protect the harbour from the Dutch navy.

The bad news is that the excellent Shetland Museum was closed in 2005 – the good
news is that a new multimillion-pound museum is being built near the new harbour, a

LERWICK

INFORMATION	
Bank of Scotland	1 A3
Gilbert Bain Hospital	2 B4
Lerwick Health Centre	3 B4
Shetland Library	4 C3
Shetland Times Bookshop	5 A3
Support Training	(see 26)
Tourist Information Centre (TIC)	6 A3

SIGHTS & ACTIVITIES	
Clickimin Broch	7 A4
Fort Charlotte	8 C3
New Museum Complex	9 B2
Up-Helly-Aa Exhibition	10 B2

SLEEPING	
Alder Lodge	11 C3
Carradale Guest House	12 B3
Clickimin Caravan & Camp Site	13 A3
Fort Charlotte Guesthouse	14 C3
Grand Hotel	15 A2
Lerwick Youth Hostel	16 B3
Solheim Guest House	(see 12)

EATING	
Co-op Supermarket	17 A2
Fort Café	18 C3
Havly Centre	19 C3
Island Fine Foods	20 A3
La Piazza	(see 22)
Monty's Bistro	21 A3
Osla's Café	22 A2
Peerie Shop Café	23 A3
Raba Indian Restaurant	24 C2

DRINKING	
Captain Flint's	25 A3
Lounge	26 A3
Posers	(see 15)

SHOPPING	
Jamieson's Knitwear	27 A3
Spider Web	28 B3

TRANSPORT	
Bolts Car Hire	29 B2
Grantfield Garage	30 A2
Holmsgarth Ferry Terminal	31 A1
John Leask & Son	32 A2
Star Rent-a-Car	(see 24)
Viking Bus Station	33 C2

**ORKNEY &
SHETLAND ISLANDS**

short walk from the bus station, and should be open in 2006. It all looks very promising, especially given the wonderful exhibits that were in the old museum. Ask staff at the TIC whether it's open, or check www .shetland-museum.org.uk.

There's a lot of memorabilia and an authentic feel to the **Böd of Gremista** (☎ 695057; Gremista; admission free; ◷ 10am–1pm & 2-5pm Wed-Sun May–mid-Sep), a restored 18th-century fishing booth located 1 mile north of the centre; the highlight is the chatty guide who shows visitors around.

The fortified site of **Clickimin Broch** (admission free; ◷ 24hr), just under a mile southwest of the town centre, was occupied from the 7th century BC to the 6th century AD. It's impressively large and its setting on a small loch gives it a feeling of being removed from the present day – unusual given the surrounding urban encroachment.

The **Up-Helly-Aa Exhibition** (St Sunniva St; adult/ child £3/1; ◷ 2-4pm & 7-9pm Tue, 7-9pm Fri, 2-4pm Sat mid-May–mid-Sep) explains the truly bizarre, annual Viking fire festival (see the boxed text, opposite).

Festivals & Events

It's well worth being here for the **Folk Festival** (www.shetlandfolkfestival.com) in the last week of April, or the **Fiddle & Accordion Festival** in mid-October. See the boxed text, opposite, for a description of the wacky **Up-Helly-Aa** festival, which takes place on the last Tuesday in January.

Sleeping
BUDGET
Lerwick Youth Hostel (SYHA; ☎ 692114; King Harald St; dm adult/child £12/10; ◷ Apr-Sep) This hostel, in a grand building with modern facilities, has spacious dorms and is clean and well maintained, although the kitchen is small. It's very popular with groups, so book ahead.

Clickimin Caravan & Camp Site (☎ 741000; Lochside; camp sites per small/large tent £6.70/9) By the loch on the western edge of town, Clickimin is a small and tidy park with good grassy sites. Rates include the use of the ablutions facility in the adjacent Clickimin Leisure Centre.

MIDRANGE
Fort Charlotte Guesthouse (☎ 692140; www.fort charlotte.co.uk; 1 Charlotte St; s £25-35, d £55) This place is like *Dr Who*'s tardis – much bigger

inside than it looks from the outside. In a quiet, central part of Lerwick, it has bright and cheery rooms and the best single accommodation in town. Book ahead, as it's very popular. The family room is particularly good value for three people (£55).

Carradale Guest House (☎ 692251; 36 King Harald St; s £22-27, d £46-60) It's very friendly here, and perpetually busy. The rooms, although a mix of old and new, are large and well furnished and provide a concoction of comforts for visitors. Couples should ask for the huge family room, which is traditionally decked out and has a private bathroom. Carradale is located next door to Solheim, but try here first.

Solheim Guest House (☎ /fax 695275; 34 King Harald St; s £22-35, d £40-52) An excellent place. Solheim offers a filling breakfast, and the rooms, with shared bathrooms, are clean and bright. Although they aren't huge, the rooms make intelligent use of space and the whole place is very laid-back.

Alder Lodge (☎ 695705; 6 Clairmount Pl; s £25-35, d £50) This large stone building, a former bank, is a delightful place to stay. Imbued with a sense of space and light, common in these gracious old buildings, the rooms are large and, in this particular case, well-furnished.

TOP END
Grand Hotel (☎ 692826; www.kgqhotels.co.uk; 24 Commercial St; s £68, d £93-123) With its air of faded grandeur, this bastion of hospitality is 'grand' indeed. Rooms are mostly twins and singles, but there are four double rooms – couples should go straight for No 330, which is an enormous room (recently refurbished with four-poster bed) with dazzling harbour views. You'll feel like royalty.

Kveldsro House Hotel (☎ 692195; reception@ kveldsrohotel.co.uk; Greenfield Pl; s/d £85/105) Shetland's most luxurious hotel overlooks the harbour. It's a dignified small hotel that will appeal to older visitors or couples looking for a treat. Room Nos 415 and 417 are doubles with striking views over the harbour, or if after a twin, try No 413, which has two walls of windows and Shetland views.

Eating
Monty's Bistro (☎ 696555; 5 Mounthooly St; mains lunch £4-7, dinner £10-17; ◷ lunch & dinner Tue-Sat)

Highly recommended, Monty's Bistro, with its seasonally changing menu, is the best place to eat in Lerwick. The bright Mediterranean décor, cheery staff and delicious local produce combine to make it an excellent dining experience. Vegetarians are catered for with dishes such as goats-cheese, leek and pumpkin-seed tart.

La Piazza (☎ 696005; 88 Commercial St; mains £6-10; ☺ dinner Mon-Sat) Upstairs from Osla's is La Piazza, dishing out healthy portions of pasta, and authentic, thin-crust pizza just like Papa used to make…well, almost. It's quite stylish (note: stylish for Shetland means it scrubs up just fine) and it also does pizza home-deliveries and takeaways.

Osla's Café (☎ 696005; 88 Commercial St; pancakes £2.50-3.50; ☺ breakfast Mon-Sat, lunch & dinner daily) Osla's is a sparky little joint that does a roaring trade dishing out a range of decent nosh. It's good for a bite at any time of the day, and the scrumptious sweet and savoury pancakes are a highlight (beware: servings are huge). Try the funky chicken – chicken in cumin and homemade chutney sauce.

Peerie Shop Café (☎ 692817; Esplanade; light meals from £3.50; ☺ 9am-6pm Mon-Sat) The place to head for a cup of tea and a toasty when you get off the ferry. A trendy spot with a stark, industrial décor that interior designers would kill for, it's as close as Lerwick comes to stylish. Peerie also makes a good spot for a lunchtime beer and does a mean carrot cake.

Island Fine Foods (☎ 690606; Harrison Sq; light meals £2.60; ☺ 9am-4pm Mon-Sat) This clean, modern place is the best spot in town for a freshly roasted coffee. It also does *paninis*, bagels, tasty pita breads, and wraps with a variety of fillings (the Moroccan orange chicken is recommended).

Self-caterers should head for the **Co-op supermarket** (Holmsgarth Rd).

Also recommended:

Fort Café (☎ 693125; 2 Commercial Rd; fish supper £4; ☺ lunch Mon-Sat, dinner daily) Reliable place for a fish supper, and has won praise from vegetarians.

Havly Centre (☎ 692100; 9 Charlotte St; light meals £2-5; ☺ 10am-3pm Mon-Fri, 10am-4.45pm Sat) Comfy couches and toys for the kids – a good spot for a read of the newspaper.

Raba Indian Restaurant (☎ 695585; 26 Commercial Rd; mains £4.50-8; ☺ lunch & dinner) Highly recommended curry house; Sunday buffet is a bargain at £8.50.

Drinking & Entertainment

The Shetland Fiddlers play at a number of locations, and it's worth attending their sessions – inquire at the TIC.

Lounge (☎ 692231; 4 Mounthooly St) A friendly bar patrolled by Andy Capp characters during the day, Lounge features a variety of live music performances several nights a week, including informal jam sessions.

Captain Flint's (☎ 692249; 2 Commercial Rd) This lively bar throbs with happy conversation and has a distinctly nautical, creaky-wooden feel. There's a cross-section of young 'uns, tourists and older locals. The upstairs bar has a pool table and more seating, and attracts younger punters. There's live music some nights.

Posers (☎ 692826; 24 Commercial St; admission £5) At the Grand Hotel, Posers is Lerwick's only nightclub. Show the locals your latest moves to the booming, dated dance music. Random drug searches are carried out here.

Shopping

Best buys are the woollen jerseys, cardigans and sweaters for which Shetland is world-famous. **Spiders Web** (☎ 695246; 51 Commercial St) is worth dropping into as much for a chat as for the store's excellent array of hand-knitted garments, which are very high quality. The shop is opposite the Queen's Hotel. At **Jamieson's Knitwear** (☎ 693114; 93 Commercial St) you'll find real Fair Isle sweaters with the distinctive OXOXO pattern, from £45.

VIKING MAYHEM

Given the connections with their Scandinavian neighbours, it's not surprising that islanders wish to honour their Norse heritage. And what better way to do it than by burning a replica Viking longship? The **Up-Helly-Aa festival** is all about fancy dress and pageantry: costumed revellers with flaming torches lug a wooden galley through Lerwick to the designated torching site. Leading the charge is a horde of Vikings wearing sheepskins and winged helmets (think *Asterix*) and armed with axes and shields. This festival dates back to Norse times, when Vikings celebrated the rebirth of the sun at yule by torching a longship in the bay.

Getting There & Around

See Getting There & Away, p418, for details of services to Lerwick. Ferries dock at Holmsgarth terminal, a 20-minute walk from the town centre. From Sumburgh airport, Leask's runs regular buses that meet flights (£2.20 one way).

If you need a taxi, call **Sinclair's Taxis** (☎ 694617).

BRESSAY & NOSS

☎ 01595 / pop 353

Two islands lie across Bressay Sound east of Lerwick. The 34-sq-km island of Bressay (bress-ah) has some interesting walks, especially along the cliffs and up Ward Hill (226m), which has good views of the island.

Colonies of birds can be seen at the Ord and Bard Head cliffs in the south. For serious **bird-watching**, though, it's worth visiting Noss, a National Nature Reserve east of Bressay, to see the huge number of sea birds nesting on the island's 183m cliffs. Noss can only be visited from mid-May to August, when Scottish Natural Heritage (SNH) operates a small visitor centre at Gungstie.

From Lerwick, **Seabirds & Seals** (☎ 693434) runs three-hour cruises (9.30am and 2pm mid-April to mid-September) around Bressay and Noss for £30; book with the TIC. It also runs the Shetland Submarine, which is a remote-controlled minisub bringing live, colour feeds of underwater wildlife from the caves of Bressay (£25, two hours).

Maryfield Hotel (☎ 820207; mains £7-10), by the ferry quay, offers bar meals with seafood specialities.

Getting There & Away

From Lerwick there are daily ferries (passenger/car return £3/7, seven minutes, frequent) to Bressay. It's then 2.5 miles across the island (some people bring rented bikes from Lerwick) to take the inflatable dinghy to Noss (adult/child £3/1.50, 10am to 5pm Tuesday, Wednesday and Friday to Sunday mid-May to August) – but check with **SNH** (☎ 0800 107 7818) before leaving Lerwick, as the dinghy doesn't operate in bad weather.

CENTRAL & WEST MAINLAND

Scalloway

☎ 01595 / pop 812

The former capital of Shetland, Scalloway (scall-o-wah), on the west coast 6 miles from Lerwick, is now a busy fishing village set around bare, rolling hills. It's a little shabby but has an air of authenticity away from the tourist hordes. During WWII, the Norwegian resistance movement operated the Shetland Bus (see the boxed text, below) from here, carrying arms and transporting refugees in fishing boats.

The small, volunteer-run **Scalloway Museum** (☎ 880675; Main St; donation requested; ☒ 9.30-11.30am & 2-4.30pm Mon & 10am-noon & 2-4.30pm Tue-Sat May-Sep) is best visited for its Shetland Bus displays, and a peek at Scalloway's glory days.

Down in the village close to the waterfront, the **Scalloway Hotel** (☎ 880444; Main St; s/d £49/79) has modern, spotless rooms with small en suites. Some rooms have good views over the harbour and the Scalloway may be a decent option if everything in Lerwick is full.

Being in the North Atlantic Fisheries College, it's no surprise that the **Da Haaf Restaurant** (☎ 880747; Port Arthur; fish dishes £9;

ALL ABOARD THE SHETLAND BUS

In early April 1940, Nazi Germany mounted an unprovoked attack on Norway. Ill-prepared, Norway was quickly overrun and many small craft fleeing the German advance ended up in Shetland. The penny soon dropped that if small boats could sail to Shetlands they could also return – so began the Shetland Bus. At first fishing boats were used, but the Germans and the weather took their toll and eventually the boats were replaced by three more-formidable American sub-chasers. The trips were very successful, carrying agents, wireless operators and military supplies for the resistance movement and returning with refugees, recruits for the Free Norwegian Forces and, in December, Christmas trees for the treeless Shetlands!

The **Shetland Bus Memorial** in Scalloway is a moving tribute on the waterfront, built of stones from both countries. The Norwegian stones are sourced from the home areas of 44 Norwegian men who died running the gauntlet between Norway and the Shetland Islands.

For more information on the Shetland Bus, see www.shetland-heritage.co.uk/shetlandbus.

lunch & dinner) specialises in seafood – excellent local seafood at that. It's easily the best place to eat in town.

Buses run from Lerwick (25 minutes, roughly hourly Monday to Saturday) to Scalloway.

Weisdale

☎ 01595

It's worth dropping into the Bonhoga Gallery in the restored **Weisdale Mill** (☎ 830400; www.bonhoga.com; Weisdale; admission free; 10.30am-4.30pm Tue-Sat, noon-4.30pm Sun). The first purpose-built gallery in the Shetlands, it has monthly, changing exhibitions, and everything – jewellery, crafts and paintings – is on sale. It's an excellent place to visit, very friendly, and you're likely to meet some resident artists. There's also a café that's ideal for tucking into Orcadian produce, in a sunlit conservatory overlooking the burn (stream).

On the western shore of Weisdale Voe, south of the mill, are the ruins of the house where John Clunies Ross (1786–1853) was born. In 1827 he settled in the Indian Ocean's Cocos Islands, where he proclaimed himself king.

Western Side

☎ 01595

The western side of Mainland is notable for its varied scenery: bleak moors, sheer cliffs, rolling green hills, and numerous cobalt-blue lochs and inlets. It's ideal for walking, cycling and fishing.

Out in the Atlantic Ocean, about 15 miles southwest of Walls, is the 8-sq-km island of **Foula** (Bird Island), which competes with Fair Isle for the title of Scotland's most isolated inhabited island. Foula supports 42 people, 1500 sheep and 500,000 sea birds, including the rare Leach's petrel and Scotland's largest colony of great skuas. It's all amid dramatic cliff scenery, particularly the awesome, sheer Kame (372m). There isn't a shop on the island, but centrally located **Mrs Taylor's** (☎/fax 753226; Leraback; dinner, B&B per person £30-34) offers accommodation and good food.

Foula is reached by thrice-weekly **ferries** (☎ 753226, 743976) from Walls or Scalloway (passenger return £2.60, car and driver return £13, four hours) and **flights** (☎ 840246) from Tingwall and Sumburgh (return £50 to £56).

Northwest from Walls, the road crosses desolate moorland and then descends through green fields before arriving at the small crofting community of **Sandness**. Visible about a mile offshore is the island of **Papa Stour**, home to huge colonies of auks, terns and skuas. It's mostly made up of volcanic rock that has eroded to form sea caves, underground passages, arches and columns. Access to the island is by ferry from West Burrafirth (passenger return £2.60, car and driver return £3.50, 40 minutes, daily except Tuesday and Thursday), east of Sandness; book with **W Clark** (☎ 810460).

SOUTH MAINLAND

From Lerwick, the main road south winds 25 miles down the eastern side of this long, narrow, hilly tail of land that ends at Sumburgh Head. The waters lapping against the cliffs are an inviting turquoise in many places. If it weren't for the raging Arctic gales, you may almost be tempted to have a dip.

Sandwick & Around

☎ 01950 / pop 1352

Opposite the small, scattered village of Sandwick is the **Isle of Mousa**, an RSPB reserve. The impressive double-walled **Mousa Broch** (13m) stands on the island – this well-preserved broch was built from local sandstone between 100 BC and AD 100 and features in two Viking sagas as a hide-out for eloping couples! The island is also home to many sea birds and waders; around 6000 storm petrels nest on Mousa, but they're only on the island at night. Common and grey seals can be seen on the beach and among the rocks at West Voe.

From mid-April to mid-September, **Tom Jamieson** (☎ 431367; www.mousaboattrips.co.uk) runs daily boat trips (adult/child return £9/4, 15 minutes) from Leebitton harbour in Sandwick, allowing two hours on Mousa. He also conducts night trips to view the petrels.

Back on Mainland, **Hoswick Visitor Centre** (☎ 431406; Hoswick; admission free; 10am-5pm Mon-Sat & 11am-5pm Sun May-Sep) has a great collection of old wirelesses (including the daddy of them all – the Murphy-type wireless). There are displays on fishing, whaling, weaving and peat casting.

The old-style rooms with shared bathroom are pretty average at the friendly

Barclay Arms Hotel (☎ 431226; fax 431262; Hoswick; s/d £25/50), but you come here for the *craic* (conversation, gossip, fun), not the comforts – there's traditional live music at night in a great bar overlooking the water, and there are real ales on tap.

If you'd prefer a cosy B&B, try **Solbrekke** (☎ 431410; Park Rd, Sandwick; r per person £20-22), which overlooks Mousa Broch.

There are buses between Lerwick and Sandwick (25 minutes, three to seven daily).

Bigton & Around

Buses from Lerwick stop twice daily (Monday to Saturday) in Bigton on the west coast, but it's another couple of miles to the **tombolo** (a narrow isthmus) that connects Mainland with St Ninian's Isle. This geologically important site is the largest shell-and-sand tombolo in Britain and is an SSSI.

Across the tombolo is **St Ninian's Isle**, where you'll find the ruins of a 12th-century church, beneath which are traces of an earlier Pictish church. During excavations in 1958, Pictish treasure, probably dating from AD 800 and consisting of 27 silver objects, was found beneath a broken sandstone slab. They're now kept in the Museum of Scotland (p84) in Edinburgh.

Boddam

From this small village there's a side road that leads to the **Shetland Crofthouse Museum** (☎ 01595-695057; South Voe; admission free; ⏱ 10am-1pm & 2-5pm mid-Apr–Sep). When you enter, the years clunk by the wayside as you step back into a primitive existence. Built in 1870, it has been restored, thatched and furnished with 19th-century furniture and utensils. The Lerwick–Sumburgh bus stops right outside.

Quendale

☎ 01950

South of Boddam, a minor road runs southwest to Quendale. Here you'll find the small but excellent, restored and fully operational 19th-century **Quendale Watermill** (☎ 460969; adult/child £2/50p; ⏱ 10am-5pm May-Sep), the last of Shetland's water mills.

The village overlooks a long, sandy beach to the south in the Bay of Quendale. West of the bay there's dramatic cliff scenery and

diving in the waters between Garth's Ness and Fitful Head and to the wreck of the oil tanker *Braer* off Garth's Ness.

From Lerwick there are two buses daily to Quendale from Monday to Saturday.

Sumburgh

☎ 01950

With its clear waters, sea cliffs, and grassy headlands jutting out into sparkling blue waters, Sumburgh is one of the most scenic places to stay on the island. The sandy beach fringed with turquoise waters makes this place seem more like an idyllic Pacific holiday destination…when the sun shines.

SIGHTS

At the southern tip of Mainland, this village is home to the international airport and **Jarlshof** (HS; ☎ 460112; adult/child £3.30/1.30; ⏱ 9.30am-6.30pm Apr-Sep), Shetland's most impressive archaeological attraction. This large settlement, with buildings from prehistory through Norse times to the 16th century, was hidden under the sand until it was exposed by a gale at the end of the 19th century. It's a thought-provoking place, mainly in ruins, but with a fascinating, intact wheelhouse that defies time. You should buy the short guide, which interprets the ruins from a number of vantage points (otherwise a fair bit of imagination is required).

Near Jarlshof you can visit **Sumburgh Head**, an RSPB reserve. The lighthouse here isn't open to the public, but you can view the many birds that inhabit the cliffs below. At various times there are puffins (over 2000 pairs), kittiwakes (1000 pairs), fulmars, guillemots (over 13,000 breed here), razorbills and cormorants. The other important bird-watching area is the **Pool of Virkie**, the bay just east of the airport.

The best thing about a visit to the remarkable excavation at **Old Scatness** (☎ 01595-694688; Dunrossness; adult/child £2/1; ⏱ 10am-5.30pm Sat-Thu Apr-Aug, call for winter hr) is that it's very much a work in progress. A broch from around 300 BC is the centrepiece of the site, which is surrounded by wheelhouses and evidence of later Viking occupation. It's all compelling stuff and ideal for kids. Guides dressed in period costume take visitors into reconstructions of Iron Age houses and divulge all kinds of fascinating facts about life a couple of thousand years ago.

BIRD-WATCHING IN SHETLAND

For bird-watchers, Shetland is paradise. This island group is internationally famous for its bird life. As well as being a stopover for migrating Arctic species, there are huge sea-bird breeding colonies.

Out of the 24 sea-bird species that nest in the British Isles, 21 are found here; June is the height of the breeding season. The **Royal Society for the Protection of Birds** (RSPB; www.rspb.org.uk) maintains several reserves on south Mainland and on the island of Fetlar. There are National Nature Reserves at **Hermaness** (where you can't fail to be entertained by the clownish antics of the almost tame puffins) and on the **Isle of Noss**. **Fair Isle** also supports large sea-bird populations.

A useful bird-watching website is www .wildlife.shetland.co.uk/birds/where.html. Take care when bird-watching as the cliff-edge sites can be dangerous. Also watch out for skuas (bonxies) that will dive-bomb you if you go near their nests. Since they aim for the highest part of your body, it's wise to walk with a stick, pointing it above your head if they approach. And don't get too close to nesting fulmars or you'll be the target for their smelly, oily spittle!

SLEEPING & EATING

Sumburgh Hotel (☎ 460201; www.sumburgh-hotel .zetnet.co.uk; Sumburgh; s/d from £50/65; bar meals £7; ☼ lunch & dinner) Next to Jarlshof is an upmarket, country-style hotel with a high standard of accommodation. For a treat go for the St Ninian room with its four-poster bed and stunning views. The bar meals here are delicious and the servings ample. Pub faves such as steak-and-Guinness pie feature alongside seafood dishes (the platter gives a taste of everything), and vegetarians are catered for.

Betty Mouat's Cottage (☎ 460249; Old Scatness, Dunrossness; beds £8) This is a simple 10-bed camping *böd* (basic accommodation for walkers) affair with potbelly stove, fuel for sale and coin-operated showers. It's by Old Scatness – book at Lerwick TIC and pay the warden on site.

GETTING THERE & AWAY

To get to Sumburgh from Lerwick, take the airport bus (45 minutes, five daily Monday to Saturday, three on Sunday) and get off at the second-last stop.

FAIR ISLE

☎ 01595 / pop 68

About halfway to Orkney, Fair Isle is one of Scotland's most remote inhabited islands. It's only 3 miles by 1.5 miles in size and is probably best known for its patterned knitwear, still produced in the island's co-operative, Fair Isle Crafts.

It's also a paradise for bird-watchers, who form the bulk of the island's visitors. Fair Isle is in the flight path of migrating birds, and thousands breed here. They're monitored by the **Bird Observatory**, which collects and analyses information year-round; visitors are more than welcome to participate.

The small **George Waterston Memorial Centre** (☎ 760244; Taft; donations welcome; ☼ 2-4pm Mon, 10.30am-noon Wed & 2-4pm Fri May-Sep) has photos and exhibits on the island's natural history, crofting, fishing, archaeology and knitwear.

Fair Isle Lodge & Bird Observatory (☎ /fax 760258; www.fairislebirdobs.co.uk; full-board dm/s/d £30/44/78) offers home cooking and free guided walks; it's located about 400m from the ferry terminal.

Getting There & Away

There are **flights** (☎ 840246) to Fair Isle from Tingwall (£56 return, 25 minutes, twice daily Monday, Wednesday and Friday). There's also a return flight from Sumburgh on Saturday.

From May to September, the *Good Shepherd IV* ferry sails from Grutness (near Sumburgh) to Fair Isle (£2.60 return, three hours) on Tuesday, Saturday and alternate Thursdays, and from Lerwick (£2.60 return, 4½ hours) on alternate Thursdays. In winter, there's one return trip on Tuesday. Book with **JW Stout** (☎ 760222).

NORTH MAINLAND

The north of Mainland is very photogenic – jumbles of cracked, peaty, brown hills blend with grassy pastureland and extend like bony fingers of land into numerous lochs, and out into the wider, icy, grey waters of the North Sea. Different shades of light give it a variety of characters. Get the camera primed.

Voe
☎ 01806

Lower Voe is a pretty collection of buildings beside a tranquil bay on the southern shore of Olna Firth.

In previous incarnations, red-painted **Sail Loft** (☎ 588392, 588708; Lower Voe; beds £8), by the pier, was a fishing shed and knitwear factory, but it's now a camping *böd*, with coin-operated showers and fuel for sale. Book at Lerwick TIC and pay the warden on site.

Try the excellent seafood, including local salmon, in the appealing, wood-panelled **Pierhead Restaurant & Bar** (☎ 588332; Lower Voe; starters £5, mains £9-15; ⊗ lunch & dinner), opposite Sail Loft. Eat in the restaurant or go for the cheaper bar meals. How do mussels and a pint sound?

There are buses from Lerwick to Voe (35 minutes, up to six daily Monday to Saturday and two on Sunday during school terms).

Whalsay & Out Skerries
☎ 01806 / pop 1043

South of Voe, the B9071 branches east to Laxo, the ferry terminal for the island of **Whalsay**. This is one of the most prosperous of Shetland's islands, due to its large fishing industry whose fleet is based at the modern harbour of **Symbister**.

Whalsay is popular for sea angling, and for trout fishing in its lochs. There are also scenic walks in the south and east where colonies of sea birds breed and where you may catch sight of seals.

Grieve House (☎ 566341; Sodom; beds £6), the former home of famous poet Hugh Mac-Diarmid, is now a simple camping *böd*. There's no electricity or shower, but there is fuel for sale. Book through Lerwick TIC.

There are regular **ferries** (☎ 566259) between Laxo and Symbister (£3 return, 30 minutes, daily).

Northeast of Whalsay, another thriving fishing community occupies the 2 sq miles of **Out Skerries** (or just Skerries). It's made up of the three main islands of Housay, Bruray (these two connected by a road bridge) and Grunay, plus a number of islets. Their rugged cliffs teem with bird life.

There are **ferries** (☎ 515226) between Out Skerries and Lerwick on Tuesday and Thursday (passenger return £2.60, car and driver return £3.50, 2½ hours), and Friday to Monday to Vidlin (passenger return £2.60, car and driver return £3.50, 1½ hours), about 3 miles northeast of Laxo.

Brae & Around
☎ 01806

With its accommodation options, Brae makes a good base. However, you should book in advance – guesthouses are often full, as they mainly cater to oil workers (the upside for solo travellers is that there are plenty of single beds). Pack a bottle of your favourite poison (single malts recommended) to keep you company on those stormy nights.

There's fine **walking** on the peninsula west of Brae, and to the south on the red-granite island of **Muckle Roe**, which is connected to the peninsula by a bridge. Muckle Roe also offers good **diving** off its west and north coasts.

Valleyfield Guest House (☎ 522563; marinani colson@hotmail.com; r per person £35-40) has good-sized rooms with en suite and is run more like a small hotel. For families there's a double and a single with a separate entrance, giving good privacy. Valleyfield also has a couple of chalets on the property for self-catering and is located 1.5 miles south of Brae on the A970. **Drumquin Guest House** (☎ 522621;

SOMETHING SPECIAL

Busta House Hotel (☎ 522506; www.busta house.com; s/d from £75/100, 4-course dinner extra £25; ⊗ dinner) Just outside Brae and built in 1588, this luxurious, genteel, country house hotel with a fine restaurant is a gem and would make a great place to splash out. The building itself is a draw and sloping floors in the passageways add to the character: remember to take some pebbles for finding your way back to reception. Recently refurbished rooms are tastefully decked out, and retain a classy but homely charm. They're all individually designed and named after places in Shetland. Linga and Foula, the former with four-poster bed, are both delightful rooms. Bar meals are around £9 and the menu changes daily depending on availability of local produce. The upstairs lounge is the perfect nook for a quiet read, a hot drink and some contemplation on the stunning views out of the palatial windows.

Brae; r per person £25-35) is a large, laid-back place with good rooms (mix of en-suite and shared bathrooms) and chilled hosts. Breakfast is served in a light-flooded conservatory.

The town's only restaurant, **Brae Indian Takeaway** (☎ 522500; A970; dishes £5-8; ⏲ 4-11pm Tue-Sun), is an offshoot of the Raba Indian Restaurant (p421) in Lerwick. The chefs' considerable culinary skills give diners a choice of excellent curries. You will need somewhere to chow down as there's no dining on site.

Brae Stores, near the junction in the village centre, is a supermarket and post office.

Buses from Lerwick to Eshaness and North Roe stop in Brae (35 minutes, up to seven daily Monday to Saturday).

Eshaness & Hillswick
☎ 01806

About 11 miles northwest of Brae the road ends at the red basalt cliffs of Eshaness, which form some of the most impressive, wild, coastal scenery in Shetland. Howling Atlantic gales whip the ocean into a white-cap frenzy before it crashes into the base of the cliffs. When the wind subsides there is superb **walking** and panoramic views from the lighthouse (closed to the public) on the headland.

A mile east of Eshaness, a side road leads south to the **Tangwick Haa Museum** (☎ 503389; Tangwick Haa; admission free; ⏲ 1-5pm Mon-Fri & 11am-7pm Sat & Sun May-Sep), located in a restored 17th-century house. The wonderful collection of ancient black-and-white photos capture the sense of community here.

At **Hamnavoe**, which you reach from another side road heading north, about 3.5 miles east of Eshaness, is the basic (no showers or electricity), stone **Johnny Notions Camping Böd** (☎ 503362; beds £6); book through Lerwick TIC. This was the birthplace of Johnny 'Notions' Williamson, an 18th-century blacksmith who inoculated several thousand people against smallpox using a serum and method he had devised himself.

Almara B&B (☎ /fax 503261; almara@zetnet.co.uk; Urafirth; r per person £25), just before Hillswick, is a friendly family home with spiffy rooms decked out in wood furnishings. The elevation of the property provides the real draw and the views are just stunning. Everything is very clean and the single and one of the doubles share a bathroom that has a long, deep tub – perfect for soothing weary bones.

Down on the quay, **Booth** (☎ 503348; Hillswick; dishes £3-8; ⏲ 11am-late Sat & Sun May & Sep, 11am-late Tue-Sun Jun-Aug) serves vegetarian food in a hippy crofters' house – actually a 300-year-old former Hanseatic trading-post house and one of Shetland's oldest buildings. All proceeds go to the local wildlife sanctuary.

Buses from Lerwick run (evenings only) to Hillswick (1¼ hours) and Eshaness (1½ hours).

THE NORTH ISLES
Yell, Unst and Fetlar make up the three islands of the North Isles, all connected to each other by ferry.

Yell
☎ 01957 / pop 1083

Yell is all about colours: the browns and vivid, lush greens of the peaty moor, grey clouds thudding through the skies and the steely blue waters of the North Atlantic, which are never far away. The peat makes the ground look cracked and parched, although it's swimming most of the year, and you'll see peat cuttings – wedges of land with rows of peat clumps drying in the fleeting sun – everywhere. It's a desolate island with some good coastal and hill walks, especially around the **Herra peninsula**, about halfway up the west coast.

Across Whale Firth from the peninsula is **Lumbister RSPB Reserve**, where red-throated divers (called rain geese in Shetland), merlins, bonxies, Arctic skuas and other bird species breed. The area is home to a large otter population, too. The otters are best viewed near the shores of Whale Firth, where you may also spot common and grey seals.

South of Lumbister, on the hill-side above the main road, stand the reputedly haunted ruins of **Windhouse**, dating from 1707. About a mile east of here is **Mid Yell**, the island's largest village and a natural harbour. The road north to Gutcher passes **Basta Voe**, where many otters inhabit the shores. In the north, around the village of **Cullivoe**, there's more good walking along the attractive coastline.

From Ulsta ferry terminal, the road leads 5 miles east to Burravoe. The **Old Haa Museum**

(☎ 722339; Burravoe; admission free; ⏰ 10am-4pm Tue-Thu & Sat, 2-5pm Sun Apr-Sep) has a fascinating exhibition on local flora, fauna and military history, and there's a small gallery. It's given authenticity by the musty old stone building (Yell's oldest building, built in 1672) in which it's housed, and there's a genealogy centre for those whose ancestors came from these parts. Yell Crafts is here too, selling Fair Isle woollen garments and some vivid (and reasonably priced) paintings of Shetland scenery.

SLEEPING & EATING

Hillhead (☎ 722274; rita.leask@btopenworld.com; Burravoe; r per person £19, with dinner £29) The stupendous views and attractive garden give this place an air of tranquillity. With two appealing rooms and large beds, this is a fine, traditional place, just around the corner from the ferry. The peat fire inside will keep you toasty on those chilly evenings.

Gutcher Post Office (☎ 744201; fax 744366; Gutcher; r per person £20, dinner £10) This friendly place has cosy rooms and is a stone's throw from the ferry pier. The owner has a definite piggy fetish! It's very cheerful and has been recommended by travellers. Note that the singles are *very* small.

Windhouse Lodge (☎ 702231; Mid Yell; beds £8) Below the haunted ruins of Windhouse, and on the A968, you'll find this well-kept, clean, snug camping *böd* with a pot belly stove to warm your toes. You can book beds at Lerwick TIC.

Wind Dog Cafe (☎ 744321; Gutcher; snacks & light meals £3; ⏰ 8.30am-6.30pm Mon-Fri, 10am-6.30pm Sat & Sun, dinner May-Sep; 🖳) While you're waiting for the ferry to Unst, you can snack at this warm, eclectic little café. It serves up *paninis*, burgers and hot drinks. There's also a small library inside, ideal if the rain is pelting outside.

Hilltop Restaurant & Bar (☎ 702333, Mid Yell; bar meals £5; ⏰ lunch & dinner) An inviting spot to hunker down, here simple bar meals (of the fish and chip variety) are served, although the puller is the wonderful views. The bar is a good spot to meet chatty locals.

There are grocery stores in Mid Yell, Aywick and Ulsta.

GETTING THERE & AWAY

Yell is connected with Mainland by **ferry** (☎ 722259) between Toft and Ulsta (pas-

senger return £3, car and driver return £7, 20 minutes, frequent). Although you don't need to book, traffic is constant from May to September so it's wise to do so during those months.

Buses leave Lerwick for Toft ferry pier (one hour, two to five daily, Sunday during school terms only). There are connecting buses at Ulsta for other parts of the island.

Unst
☎ 01957 / pop 1067
Unst is a lot smaller but prettier than Yell with bare, velvety-smooth hills and clusters of settlements that cling to their waterside locations, fiercely resisting the buffeting winds. It also feels less isolated and has more of a community. With an area of 45 sq miles it's Scotland's northernmost inhabited island. There's a wide variety of vegetation – over 400 different plant species. Some of the most unusual examples can be seen at the 30-hectare **Keen of Hamar National Nature Reserve** northeast of Baltasound.

In the northwest is the wonderfully wild and windy National Nature Reserve of **Hermaness**. Here you can sit on the high cliffs, commune with the thousands of sea birds and Shetland's largest colony of puffins (best seen in May and June), and gaze across the sea towards the Arctic Circle. The more energetic should take on the superb **cliff-top walk** along the west coast.

The **Hermaness Visitor Centre** (☎ 711278; Shore Station, Burrafirth; admission free; ⏰ 9am-5pm early Apr–mid-Sep), near the reserve's entrance, has an interactive sea-bird exhibit and provides information on the island's wildlife.

Robert Louis Stevenson wrote *Treasure Island* while living on Unst and the map in the novel is reputedly based on the island. Stevenson's uncle built the lighthouse on **Muckle Flugga**, one of the group of rocks off Hermaness; another of the rocks is **Out Stack**, Scotland's most northerly point.

Unst Heritage Centre (☎ 711528; Haroldswick; adult/child £2/free, joint Unst Boat Haven ticket £3; ⏰ 1.30-5pm May-Sep) houses a modern museum with a history of the Shetland pony, and a nostalgic look at the past. There's a re-creation of a croft house complete with box bed and, for weather-obsessed Brits, a summary of the last 170 years of weather in the Shetlands.

Unst Boat Haven (☎ 711528; Haroldswick; adult/child £2/free, joint Unst Heritage Centre ticket £3; ☒ 1.30-5pm May-Sep) is housed in a large shed and is every boaty's delight, with rowing and sailing boats, photographs of more boats, and maritime artefacts.

Scotland's oddest **bus shelter**, complete with sofa, TV, books, flower box and decorative ornaments, is at Baltasound – it looks as though someone just got kicked out of home. It even has its own website (www.unstbusshelter.shetland.co.uk). If this was a few hundred miles further south it would be ripped off and graffitied within hours – it speaks volumes of the community spirit that still exists throughout these islands.

SLEEPING & EATING

Clingera Guest House (☎ 711579; clingera@btopenworld.com; Baltasound; r per person £18-25) This is one of the best places to stay on the island. It has affable hosts and huge, immaculate rooms with en suites. The twin has a separate sitting room and is terrific value. The owners also rent out a couple of self-catering croft houses.

Gardiesfauld Hostel (☎ 755279; www.gardiesfauld.shetland.co.uk; Uyeasound; dm adult/child £10/8, tent & 2 people £6; ☒ Apr-Sep) This 35-bed hostel is very clean, has excellent kitchen facilities and has sun-drenched common areas for relaxing. There are dorms with a maximum of 10 beds, a twin and a family room with en suite. Non-residents are welcome to use common areas. It's always open and is the place to go if you miss the ferry. The bus stops right outside.

Prestegaard (☎ 755234; www.prestegaard.shetland.co.uk; Uyeasound; r per person £20, with dinner £30) The rooms at the front of this large Victorian house are excellent with lovely views over the water. It's a well-kept place with a friendly host. To get here from the village, take East Rd and look for the sign straightaway.

Baltasound Hotel (☎ 711334; www.baltasound-hotel.shetland.co.uk; Baltasound; s/d £46/72) The cottage-style rooms inside this solid place are better than the rooms in the nearby chalets, which are a bit cramped. It's also a decent watering hole with a lovely country outlook, and it's popular with tourist buses. During the day it's soup and sandwiches, while dinner at night is decent nosh from £5.50. Try the local real ale White Wife, named after a ghostly figure seen by the A968, just south of Baltasound.

Self-caterers can stock up at Skibhoul Store & Bakery (Baltasound) or at Haroldswick Shop, where you can heat up and eat your purchase (eg pie or pizza) in its little kitchen.

GETTING THERE & AWAY

Unst is connected with Yell by a small car **ferry** (☎ 722395) between Gutcher and Belmont (passenger £3, car and driver £7, 10 minutes, frequent).

Haroldswick is 55 miles from Lerwick and, if you don't have a car, you must spend the night on Unst as buses only run once daily.

Fetlar

☎ 01957 / pop 87

Fetlar is the smallest (5 miles by 2 miles) but most fertile of the North Isles. Much of the island is designated an SSSI. There's great bird-watching here, and the 705 hectares of grassy moorland around Vord Hill (159m) in the north form the **Fetlar RSPB Reserve**. Large numbers of auks, gulls and shags breed in the cliffs. Common and grey seals can also be seen on the shores. The reserve is closed during the breeding season, from May to August; contact the **warden** (☎ 733246) at Baelans.

Scenic **walking** is possible on much of the island, especially around the bay near Tresta, at Urie and Gruting in the north, and Funzie in the east.

There's no petrol on Fetlar, but there's a shop and a post office in Houbie, the main village. The excellent **Fetlar Interpretive Centre** (☎ 733206; Houbie; adult/child £2/free; ☒ 1-5pm Mon-Fri & 2-5pm Sat & Sun May-Sep), near the post office, has photos, audio recordings and videos on the island and its history.

Garth's Campsite (☎ 733227; Gord; camp sites £4-7.40), 2.5 miles from the ferry, overlooks the beach at Tresta and has great facilities. Nearby is the friendly **Gord B&B** (☎ 733227; lynboxall@zetnet.co.uk; Gord; r per person £25, dinner, B&B £37) with terrific sea views and two twin rooms and one double, all with en suite.

The shop/café in Houbie serves homemade food, including lemon chicken pie and pasta dishes.

Regular ferries (passenger return £3, car and driver return £7, 25 minutes) from Oddsta in the island's northwest connect with Gutcher on Yell and Belmont on Unst.

DIRECTORY

Directory

CONTENTS

ACCOMMODATION

For a peaceful night's slumber, Scotland provides a comprehensive choice of accommodation to suit all visitors. For budget travel (£5 to £20 per person a night), the options are camping grounds, bothies or *böds* (see Something Different, p432), hostels and cheap B&Bs. Midrange travellers will find a plethora of comfortable B&Bs and guesthouses (£20 to £50 per person a night). For top-end lodgings (£50-plus per person a night) there are some superb hotels, the most interesting being converted castles and mansions. In Glasgow midrange and top-end travellers can experience unique, cutting-edge design accommodation – even in some pubs!

Almost all B&Bs, guesthouses and hotels (and even some hostels) provide breakfast; if this is not the case then it is mentioned in individual reviews throughout the guide.

Prices tend to increase over the peak tourist season (June to September) and are at their highest in July and August. Outside of these months, and particularly in winter, special deals are often available at guesthouses and hotels. Smaller establishments will often close from around November to March, particularly in more remote areas. If you're going to be in Edinburgh in the festival month of August or at Hogmanay (New Year), book as far in advance as you can – a year if possible – as the city will be packed.

Tourist Information Centres (TICs) have an accommodation booking service (£2 to £3, local and national), which can be handy over summer. We have listed hundreds of accommodation options throughout the book, but if you're stuck, try **VisitScotland** (www.visitscotland.com/accommodation) for help in booking accommodation across the country.

B&Bs & Guesthouses

B&Bs are a Scottish institution. At the bottom end you get a bedroom in a private house, a shared bathroom and a fry-up (juice, coffee or tea, cereal and cooked breakfast – bacon, eggs, sausage, baked beans and toast). Midrange B&Bs have en-suite bathrooms, TVs in each room and more variety (and healthier options) for breakfast. Almost all B&Bs provide hospitality trays (tea- and coffee-making facilities) in bedrooms. An excellent option are farm B&Bs, which offer traditional Scottish hospitality, huge breakfasts and a quiet rural setting – good for discharging urban grit. Pubs may also offer cheap (and sometimes noisy) B&B and can be good fun.

Guesthouses, often large converted private houses, are an extension of the B&B concept. They are normally more upmarket than B&Bs, offering quality food and more luxurious accommodation.

Camping & Caravan Parks

Free 'wild' camping became a legal right under the Land Reform Bill. However, campers are obligated to camp on unenclosed land, in small numbers and away from buildings and roads (see the boxed text, p55).

Commercial camping grounds are geared to caravans and vary widely in quality. A tent site is £4 to £12. If using a tent regularly, buy *Scotland: Caravan & Camping* (£4.99), available from most TICs. VisitScotland has a free map showing caravan and camping parks around Scotland, also at TICs.

Homestays

A convenient and increasingly popular holiday option is to join an international house-exchange organisation. You sign up for a year and place your home on a website giving details of what you're looking for, where and for how long. You organise the house-swap yourself with people in other countries and arrange to swap homes, rent free, for an agreed period. Shop around, as registration costs vary between organisations. Check out **Home Base Holidays** (www.homebase-hols.com) and **Home Link International** (www.homelink.org.uk).

Hostels

If you're on a budget, the numerous hostels offer cheap accommodation and are great centres for meeting fellow travellers – in Scotland the standard of facilities is generally very good. In recent years there's been a trend in the more upmarket hostels to have en-suite bathrooms in their dorms.

Hostels have facilities for self-catering, and many provide Internet access and can usually arrange activities and tours.

From May to September and on public holidays, hostels can be booked out, sometimes by large groups, so phone in advance.

INDEPENDENT & STUDENT HOSTELS

There are a large number of independent hostels, most with prices around £10 to £15. Facilities vary considerably, but some of the best are listed in this guide and because they are aimed at young backpackers, they can often be great places to party. The free *Independent Backpackers Hostels Scotland* guide (www.hostel-scotland.co.uk), available from TICs, lists over 100 hostels in Scotland.

SCOTTISH YOUTH HOSTEL ASSOCIATION

The **Scottish Youth Hostel Association** (SYHA; ☎ 0870 155 3255; www.syha.org.uk; 7 Glebe Cres, Stirling FK8 2JA) has a network of decent, reasonably priced hostels and produces a free booklet

---

PRACTICALITIES

■ Leaf through Edinburgh's *Scotsman* newspaper or Glasgow's *Herald*, the oldest daily in the English-speaking world.

■ Have a giggle at the popular Labour tabloid, the *Daily Record*, or try the *Sunday Post* for rose-tinted nostalgia.

■ Watch and listen to the advertising-free national BBC TV and radio networks.

■ BBC Radio Scotland (AM 810kHz, FM 92.4–94.7MHz) provides a Scottish point of view.

■ Zone out in front of the box to BBC1 and BBC2 and three commercial channels (ITV1, Channel Four and Channel Five). Regional ITV channels, Scottish Television and Grampian TV, give a Scottish perspective.

■ Buy or watch videos on the PAL system.

■ Plug into a square three-pin adaptor (different from the Australian three-pin) before plugging into the electricity supply (240V, 50Hz AC).

■ Use the metric system for weights and measures, with the exception of road distances (in miles) and beer (in pints).

---

listing details of more than 70. Some such as Loch Lomond and Carbisdale Castle are fabulous – more like hotels, with magnificent interiors. The booklet is available from SYHA hostels and TICs. Average prices are about £12 an adult, £9 a child, more in summer.

Hotels

Hotels normally service the top end of the scale and there are some wonderfully luxurious places, including country house hotels in fabulous settings, and castles complete with crenellated battlements, grand staircases and the obligatory rows of stags' heads. Expect all the perks at these places, often including a gym, sauna, pool and first-class service.

Interestingly, midrange hotels, independent or chain, have not really caught on in Scotland and apart from the bigger cities, midrange travellers will often have to splurge if they want a night away from a B&B or guesthouse. The exception is Glasgow, which has many chic, stylish city hotels that fall into the upper midrange and top-end class – these are listed in detail in the Glasgow chapter.

Rental Accommodation

Self-catering accommodation is very popular in Scotland and staying in a house in a city or cottage in the country gives you an opportunity to get a feel for a region and its community. The minimum stay is usually one week in the summer peak season, three days or less at other times. Details are in the regional accommodation guides available from TICs. Alternatively, buy a copy of VisitScotland's *Scotland: Self-Catering* (£5.99). Expect a week's rent for a two-bedroom cottage to cost from £150 in winter, £175 April to June, and £250 July to September. Places in the city range from £175 to over £700 per week.

The following are good places to start your search:

CKD Galbraith (☎ 0131-556 4422; www.ckdgalbraith .co.uk; 17 Dublin St, Edinburgh EH1 3PG) Offers a wide range of self-catering accommodation, from cottages to castles.

Ecosse Unique (☎ 01835-870779; www.unique scotland.com; Lilliesleaf, Melrose, Roxburghshire TD6 9JD) Offers furnished holiday homes all over the country.

Highland Hideaways (☎ 01631-562056; www.high landhideaways.co.uk; Alliance House, 1 George St, Oban, Argyll PA34 5RU) Has self-catering properties in Argyll, the west Highlands and the southern islands of the Hebrides.

Landmark Trust (☎ 01628-825925; www.landmark trust.org.uk; Shottesbrooke, Maidenhead, Berkshire SL6 3SW England) A building-preservation charity that restores historic buildings and lets them out as accommodation.

Something Different

Scotland offers a surprising diversity of accommodation and it's possible to bunk down on a cruise around the Hebrides (a good way to see remote St Kilda) or the Caledonian Canal; in converted churches (spooky!); in a *blackhouse* (primitive 19th-century living); and in an art gallery, wigwam or lighthouse. Information on specific establishments is littered throughout this guide and can also be found on the VisitScotland website www .visitscotland.com/accommodation.

Simple, alternative accommodation can be found at bothies – basic shelters, often in remote places. They're not locked, there's no charge, and you can't book. A camping barn (*böd* in Shetland) – usually a converted farm building – is where walkers can stay for around £6 to £8 per night. Take your own cooking equipment, sleeping bag and mat.

We have listed many bothies and *böds* in this guide; TICs also have lists.

University Accommodation

Many Scottish universities offer their student accommodation to visitors during the holidays. Most rooms are comfy, functional, single bedrooms, some with shared bathroom, but there are also twin and family units, self-contained flats and shared houses. Full-board, half-board, B&B and self-catering options are often available. Rooms are usually let out late June to late September. B&B costs around £25 to £30 per person. Details are provided throughout regional chapters.

BUSINESS HOURS

Shops open at least 9am to 5pm Monday to Friday, and most open Saturday too. A growing number also open Sunday, typically 11am to 5pm. Even in small towns, supermarkets stay open to 8pm daily and a few city supermarkets open 24 hours. In country towns, some shops have an early-closing day – usually Tuesday, Wednesday or Thursday.

In the Highlands and islands followers of the Free Church of Scotland and the Free Presbyterian Church often observe the Sabbath strictly, and in some areas, notably Harris and Lewis, all shops and petrol stations are closed Sundays, and there are no ferries.

Approximate standard opening hours:

Banks 9.30am to 4pm Monday to Friday, plus some are open 9.30am to 12.30pm Saturday.

Cafés 9am to 5pm; in large towns and cities some open for breakfast from about 7am. If licensed they may stay open for dinner too.

Post offices 9am to 5.30pm Monday to Friday, 9am-12.30pm Saturday.

Pubs & Bars 11am to 11pm (some places to midnight or 1am) Monday to Saturday, 12.30pm to 11pm Sunday; lunch is served noon to 2.30pm, dinner 6pm to 9pm daily.

Restaurants Lunch noon to 3pm, dinner 6pm to 9pm or 10pm; in small towns and villages the chippy (fish and chip shop) is often the only place to buy cooked food after 8pm.

CHILDREN

Throughout this book we have listed child-friendly accommodation and recommended places and activities suitable for families.

It's well worth asking in TICs for local family-based publications. The *List* magazine (available at newsagents and bookshops) has a section on children's activities and events in and around Glasgow and Edinburgh; also check local newspapers. If going to Orkney, pick up a copy of the excellent *Child Friendly Orkney* book (free) from Kirkwall TIC, which is jam-packed full of activities, sightseeing and accommodation suggestions.

Children are well-received around Scotland, particularly in more traditional areas such as the Highlands and islands. Another great destination for families is Dumfries & Galloway in southern Scotland (see the boxed text, p178), which has many child-friendly attractions and B&Bs.

A lot of pubs are family-friendly and some have great beer gardens where kids can run around and exhaust themselves while you have a quiet pint. However be aware that most Scottish pubs, even those that serve bar meals, are forbidden by law to admit children under 14; even in family-friendly pubs (ie those in possession of a Children's Certificate), under-14s are only admitted between 11am and 8pm, and only when accompanied by an adult aged 18 or over.

Children under a certain age can often stay free with their parents in hotels, but be prepared for hotels and B&Bs that won't accept children; call ahead to get the lowdown. More hotels and guesthouses these days provide child-friendly facilities including cots. Many restaurants (especially the larger ones) have highchairs available. Nappy-changing facilities can be found in shopping centres.

The larger car-hire companies can provide safety seats for children – ask when booking. Note that attitudes towards breast-feeding in public are generally a little conservative.

See Edinburgh for Children, p91, and Glasgow for Children, p130, for more on travel in those two cities. See also Lonely Planet's *Travelling with Children*, by Cathy Lanigan, and check out the website www.kids-scotland.co.uk, which is a great site packed with useful suggestions and lots of advice.

CLIMATE CHARTS

'Variable' is a vague but appropriate way to describe the many moods of Scotland's cool, temperate climate. Considering how far north the country lies you might expect a colder climate, but the winds from the Atlantic are warmed by the Gulf Stream.

See the climate charts, p433, for an indication of temperature and rainfall around the country. See also the When to Go section, p17, in the Getting Started chapter.

COURSES

With the remarkable revival of Scottish Gaelic since the 1980s, a number of courses on the language and culture are available:

Cothrom na Fèinne (☎ 01599-566240; Balmacara Mains, Kyle IV40 8DN) Residential language courses take place during the first week of the month, year-round. Individually tailored weekends are £90; courses start at £250.

Royal Scottish Country Dance Society (☎ 0131-225 3854; www.rscds.org) In July and August, this society holds a summer school in St Andrews; fees from £107 a week.

Sabhal Mór Ostaig (☎ 01471-888000; www.smo.uhi .ac.uk; Sleat, Isle of Skye IV44 8RQ) Offers courses in Gaelic language, song, piping and the fiddle. Courses cost from £125 per week plus accommodation.

CUSTOMS

Travellers arriving in the UK from other EU countries don't have to pay tax or duty on goods for personal use. The maximum amounts of tobacco and alcohol that each person can bring in duty-free are 3200 cigarettes, 400 cigarillos, 200 cigars, 3kg of smoking tobacco, 10L of spirits, 20L of fortified wine (eg port or sherry), 90L of wine and 110L of beer. Those under 17 cannot import any alcohol or tobacco. Some newer EU member countries (such as Estonia, Poland, Hungary, Latvia, Lithuania, Slovakia, the Czech Republic and Slovenia) have different allowances concerning tobacco products – check the website following for further details.

Travellers from outside the EU can bring in, duty-free, a maximum of 200 cigarettes *or* 100 cigarillos *or* 50 cigars *or* 250g of tobacco; 2L of still table wine; 1L of spirits *or* 2L of fortified wine, sparkling wine or liqueurs; 60mL of perfume; and £145 worth of all other goods, including gifts and souvenirs. Anything over this limit must be declared to customs officers on arrival.

For details of restrictions and quarantine regulations, see the website of **HM Customs and Excise** (www.hmrc.gov.uk).

DANGERS & ANNOYANCES
Crime

Scotland has the usual big-city crimes (often alcohol and/or drug related), mainly in Edinburgh and Glasgow, so normal caution is advised. Don't wander unlit city streets at night, and be aware of who is around you late at night anywhere on the streets. Pickpockets and bag snatchers operate in crowded places, but this isn't a common problem.

Never leave valuables in a car, and remove all luggage overnight. Report thefts to the police and ask for a statement, or your travel insurance won't pay out; bear in mind that thefts from cars may be excluded.

Midges & Clegs

The most painful problems facing visitors to the Highlands and islands are midges and clegs. The midge is a tiny, 2mm-long blood-sucking fly. Midges are at their worst during the twilight hours, and on still, overcast days. They proliferate from late May to mid-September, but especially mid-June to mid-August – which unfortunately coincides with the main tourist season. Cover up, particularly in the evening, wear light-coloured clothing (midges are attracted to dark colours) and, most importantly, use a reliable insect repellent containing DEET or DMP.

The cleg, or horse fly, is 13mm long and slate grey in colour. A master of stealth, it loves to land unnoticed on neck or ankle, and can give a painful bite. It can even bite through hair or light clothing. Unlike midges, they are most active on warm, sunny days, and are most common in July and August.

Military Jets

One of the most annoying and frightening aspects of touring the Highlands is the sudden appearance and sound of military jets. It's something you never get used to.

DISABLED TRAVELLERS

For many disabled travellers, Scotland is a strange mix of user-friendliness and unfriendliness. Most new buildings are accessible to wheelchair users, so large, new hotels and modern tourist attractions are usually fine. However, most B&Bs and guesthouses are in hard-to-adapt older buildings. This means that travellers with mobility problems may pay more for accommodation than their more able-bodied fellows.

It's a similar story with public transport. Newer buses sometimes have steps that lower for easier access, as do trains, but it's wise to check before setting out. Tourist attractions sometimes reserve parking spaces near the entrance for disabled drivers.

Many ticket offices, banks etc are fitted with hearing loops to assist the hearing-impaired; look for the symbol of a large ear.

A few tourist attractions, such as Glasgow Cathedral, have Braille guides or scented gardens for the visually impaired.

VisitScotland produces a guide, *Accessible Scotland*, for wheelchair-bound travellers, and many TICs have leaflets with accessibility details for their area. Perthshire TICs have the *Access For All* brochure that provides info on transport, parking, activities and accommodation in the Perthshire region.

Many regions have organisations that hire wheelchairs – contact the local TIC for details. There are many countryside rambles in Perthshire that have been adapted for wheelchair users – see www.perthshire.co.uk.

Historic Scotland (HS; ☎ 0131-668 8600; www.historic-scotland.gov.uk; Longmore House, Salisbury Pl, Edinburgh EH9 1SH) has a free leaflet outlining access and facilities for the disabled to HS properties, and also produces a large-print version of HS's promotional brochure.

The **Royal Association for Disability & Rehabilitation** (RADAR: ☎ 020-7250 3222; www.radar.org.uk; Information Dept, 12 City Forum, 250 City Rd, London EC1V 8AF) publishes a guide (£8 including postage) on travelling in the UK and has an accommodation website. **Holiday Care Service** (☎ 0845 124 9971; www.holidaycare.org.uk; Holiday Care Information Unit, 7th fl Sunley House, 4 Bedford Park, Croydon, Surrey CR0 2AP) publishes regional information guides (£5) to Scotland and can offer general advice.

Rail companies offer a Disabled Persons Railcard (see p449).

DISCOUNT CARDS
Hostel Cards
If travelling on a budget, membership of the **Scottish Youth Hostel Association/Hostelling International** (SYHA/HI; ☎ 01786 891400; www.syha.org.uk) is a must (annual membership over/under 18 is £6/2.50, life membership is £60).

Senior Cards
Discount cards for those over 60 are available for train travel (see p449).

Student & Youth Cards
The most useful card is the International Student Identity Card (ISIC), which displays your photo. This can perform wonders, including producing discounts on entry to attractions and on many forms of transport.

There's a global industry in fake student cards, and many places now stipulate a maximum age for student discounts or substitute a 'youth discount' for 'student discount'. If under 26 but not a student, you can apply for the Euro/26 card, which goes by various names in different countries, or an International Youth Travel Card (IYTC) issued by the International Student Travel Confederation (ISTC; www.istc.org). These cards are available through student unions, hostelling organisations or youth travel agencies.

EMBASSIES & CONSULATES
Scottish/UK Embassies Abroad
The following is a selection of British embassies and high commissions abroad.

Australia (☎ 02-6270 6666; www.britaus.net; Commonwealth Ave, Yarralumla, Canberra, ACT 2600)

Canada (☎ 613-237 1530; www.britainincanada.org; 80 Elgin St, Ottawa, Ontario K1P 5K7)

France (☎ 01 44 51 31 00; www.amb-grandebretagne.fr; 35 rue du Faubourg St Honoré, 75383 Paris)

Germany (☎ 030-20457-0; www.britischebotschaft.de; Wilhelmstrasse 70, 10117 Berlin)

Ireland (☎ 01-205 3700; www.britishembassy.ie; 29 Merrion Rd, Ballsbridge, Dublin 4)

Japan (☎ 03-5211 1100; www.uknow.or.jp; 1 Ichiban-cho, Chiyoda-ku, Tokyo 102-8381)

Netherlands (☎ 070-427 0427; www.britain.nl; Lange Voorhout 10, 2514 ED, The Hague)

New Zealand (☎ 04-924 2888; www.britain.org.nz; 44 Hill St, Wellington)

South Africa (☎ 012-421 7500; www.britain.org.za; 255 Hill St, Arcadia, 0002 Pretoria)

USA (☎ 202-588 7800; www.britainusa.com; 3100 Massachusetts Ave NW, Washington, DC 20008)

Consulates in Scotland
Most foreign diplomatic missions are in London, but many countries also have consulates in or near Edinburgh:

Australia (Map pp72-3; ☎ 0131-624 3333 69; George St, EH2 2JG) Passport applications and document witnessing only; for emergencies contact the Australian High Commission in London (☎ 020-7887 5335).

Canada (Map pp72-3; 0131-473 6320; Festival Sq, 50 Lothian Rd, EH3 9WJ)

Denmark (Map p69; ☎ 0131-220 0300; 48 Melville St, EH3 7HF)

France (Map pp70-1; ☎ 0131-225 7954; 11 Randolph Cres, EH3 7TT)

Germany (Map pp70-1; ☎ 0131-337 2323; 16 Eglinton Cres, EH12 5DG)

Ireland (Map pp70-1; ☎ 0131-226 7711; 16 Randolph Cres, EH3 7TT)

Japan (Map pp70-1; ☎ 0131-225 4777; 2 Melville Cres, EH3 7HW)

DIRECTORY

Netherlands (Map pp72-3; ☎ 0131-220 3226; Thistle Ct, 1-2 Thistle St, EH2 1DD)
USA (Map pp70-1; ☎ 0131-556 8315; 3 Regent Tce, EH7 5BW)

Eight countries have consulates in Lerwick, Shetland Islands. Denmark, Iceland, Netherlands and Sweden are based at **Hay & Co** (☎ 01595-692533; 66 Commercial Rd) and Finland, France, Germany and Norway at **Shearer Shipping Services** (☎ 01595-692556; off Commercial Rd).

FESTIVALS & EVENTS

Countless diverse events are held around the country all year. Even small villages have weekly markets, and many still enact traditional customs and ceremonies, some dating back hundreds of years.

VisitScotland publishes a comprehensive list, *Events in Scotland*, twice a year.

The **Traditional Music & Song Association** (☎ 0131-667 5587; www.tmsa.info) publishes an excellent annual listing of music, dance and cultural festivals around Scotland.

Highlights of Scotland's many festivals and events are listed here. There's more on these and other events in the Edinburgh chapter (p94) and the regional chapters throughout the book.

JANUARY
Burns Night Suppers all over the country (and the world for that matter) are held on 25 January to celebrate Robbie Burns.
Celtic Connections (www.grch.com) A celebration of Celtic music and culture, held mid- to late January in Glasgow.
The Ba' A seething swell of islanders and tourists take part in this boisterous and chaotic ball game, held on New Year's Day in Kirkwall, Orkney.
Up Helly Aa Re-enactment of a Viking fire festival (think Asterix); held last Tuesday in January in Lerwick, Shetland.

FEBRUARY
Six Nations Rugby Tournament (www.6nations .co.uk) Between Scotland, England, Wales, Ireland, France and Italy, held February to March; home games played at Murrayfield, Edinburgh.

MARCH
Shetland Folk Festival (www.shetlandfolkfestival.com) Folk music festival featuring local and international acts, held in late March.
Whuppity Scourie Chasing away the winter blues in Lanark; held 1 March.

APRIL
Rugby Sevens Seven-a-side rugby tournament, held April and May in various towns throughout the Borders region – the first is in Galashiels and Melrose in early April.

MAY
Beltane Fire Festival (www.beltane.org) An incredibly popular, wild and wacky pagan fire festival celebrating the end of winter; 10,000 people descend upon Calton Hill, Edinburgh on 30 April.
Burns An' A' That (www.burnsfestival.com) This Ayr festival has really taken off in the last two years.
Spirit of Speyside Whisky Festival (www.spiritof speyside.com) Four days of distillery tours, knocking back the 'water of life', food, art and outdoor activities; held late April to early May in Moray and Speyside.
Orkney Folk Festival (www.orkneyfolkfestival.com) A brilliant time to be in these islands with concerts, *ceilidhs* (evenings of traditional Scottish entertainment), impromptu music sessions and workshops; held in late May.
Scottish FA Cup Final (www.scottishfa.co.uk) Deciding match in Scotland's premier football tournament; held at Glasgow's Hampden Park.

JUNE
Caledonian Brewery Beer Festival (www.caledonian -brewery.co.uk) Taste tens of local Scottish brews and learn more about CAMRA – Campaign for Real Ale; held early June in Edinburgh.
Glasgow Jazz Festival (www.jazzfest.co.uk) A growing event with big-name jazz acts in venues all over the city – George Sq is particularly good for free jazz; held mid-June in Glasgow.
Riding of the Marches Horse riding, with parades, brass bands etc, commemorating conflict with England; held in various Border towns, Selkirk is one of the biggest and best.
Royal Highland Show (www.royalhighlandshow.org) Scotland's national agricultural show; held late June in Edinburgh.
St Magnus Festival (www.stmagnusfestival.com) A midsummer celebration of the arts; music, literature and visual arts; held mid-June in Orkney.
West End Festival (www.westendfestival.co.uk) Two-week festival of music and the arts; Glasgow's biggest festival.

JULY
T in the Park (www.tinthepark.com) Music festival in the footsteps of Glastonbury; held over a mid-July weekend at Balado, by Kinross.

AUGUST
Edinburgh Book Festival (www.edbookfest.co.uk) A celebration of literature held in Charlotte Sq featuring talks from various literary people and local authors; held mid- to late August.

Edinburgh International and Fringe Festivals
(www.eif.co.uk, www.edfringe.com) Premier international arts festivals, running for three weeks; the city's largest annual event attracting millions each year; held mid-August to early September.

Edinburgh International Film Festival
(www.edfilmfest.org.uk) A truly international selection of films sourced from all over the world; from West Africa, to Iran to Peru; held mid- to late August.

Edinburgh Military Tattoo
(www.edintatoo.co.uk) Pageantry and military displays running for three weeks – an impressive spectacle and an unforgettable night if you like the bagpipes.

World Pipe Band Championships
Gathering of over 100 pipe bands in Glasgow.

SEPTEMBER

Braemar Gathering
(www.braemargathering.org) Kilts, cabers and bagpipes, attended by the Queen; held early September in Deeside.

OCTOBER

Royal National Mod
(www.the-mod.co.uk) Gaelic music festival competition; held mid-October in various locations.

DECEMBER

Hogmanay
Celebrations to greet the New Year, including a huge street party – Edinburgh is the biggest (it's heaving), but there are festivities all over the country on 31 December.

Stonehaven Fireball Festival
(31 December; Stonehaven) Large procession of fireball-swinging locals who fling their flaming orbs into the sea on 31 December.

FOOD

In larger towns and cities we have ordered places to eat in this guide by neighbourhood, then price (by dinner main course: budget up to £6, midrange £6 to £15, top end above £15), and then by the author's favourite choices in each category. Note though that lunch mains are often cheaper. In other places, listings are by price and then by author choice. When there are no budget breakdowns, venues are in author preference. See p432 for restaurant opening hours, and the Food & Drink chapter (p62) for information about tucking into Scottish cuisine.

GAY & LESBIAN TRAVELLERS

Although many Scots are fairly tolerant of homosexuality, overt displays of affection aren't wise if conducted away from acknowledged 'gay' venues or districts –

hostility may be encountered. The age of homosexual consent is 16.

Edinburgh and Glasgow have small but flourishing gay scenes. The website www.gayscotland.com and the monthly magazine *Scotsgay* (www.scotsgay.com) keep gays, lesbians and bisexuals informed about gay-scene issues. Another good info source is the **GLGBT Centre** (☎ 0141-221 7203; www.glgbt.org.uk; 11 Dixon St, Glasgow); otherwise, contact the **Gay & Lesbian Switchboard** (☎ 0141-332 8372; info@lgls.org). See also the boxed texts in the Glasgow (p139) and Edinburgh (p108) chapters.

HOLIDAYS
Public Holidays

Although bank holidays are general public holidays in the rest of the UK, in Scotland they only apply to banks and some other commercial offices. Bank holidays occur at the start of January, the first weekend in March, the first and last weekend in May, the first weekend in August and Christmas Day and Boxing Day. Christmas Day, New Year's Day and 2 January, Good Friday and Easter Monday are also general public holidays. Scottish towns normally have their own spring and autumn holiday; dates vary from year to year and from town to town.

School Holidays

School holidays (two weeks at Easter, early July to late August, one week in October and two or three weeks at Christmas) are always a busy time, particularly in summer when families often go on their annual break to the countryside. As this coincides with peak tourist season, accommodation is harder to come by and it's often worth booking ahead.

INSURANCE

This not only covers you for medical expenses, theft or loss, but also for cancellation of, or delays in, any of your travel arrangements. There's a variety of policies and your travel agent can give recommendations. The international student travel policies handled by STA Travel and other reputable student travel organisations are usually good value.

Make sure the policy includes health care and medication in the countries you may visit on your way to/from Scotland. See also Health (p450).

Always read the small print carefully. Some policies specifically exclude 'dangerous activities' such as scuba diving, motorcycling, skiing, mountaineering and even trekking.

You may prefer a policy that pays doctors or hospitals directly rather than forcing you to pay on the spot and claim the money back later. If you have to claim later, make sure you keep all documentation. Some policies ask you to call back (reverse charges) to a centre in your home country where an immediate assessment of your problem is made.

Not all policies cover ambulances, helicopter rescue or emergency flights home. Most policies exclude cover for pre-existing illnesses.

INTERNET ACCESS

If you're travelling in Scotland with a laptop you should be able to connect to the Internet via a hotel room phone socket for the cost of a local call by registering with an Internet roaming service such as MaGlobe (www.maglobe.com). Many upmarket hotels offer in-room Internet connections via RJ-11 Ethernet sockets or wi-fi. For help and information on getting online from hotel rooms see www.kropla.com.

There is a growing number of wi-fi hot spots around Scotland where you can access the Internet with a wi fi–enabled laptop, including McDonald's restaurants, Starbucks coffee shops, and anywhere within 50m of blue-topped BT Internet payphones; search for wi-fi hot spots on www.jiwire.com.

If you don't have a laptop, the best places to check email and surf the Internet in Scotland are public libraries – almost every town and village in the country has at least a couple of computer terminals devoted to the Internet, and they are free to use. In bigger towns and cities the libraries may well have cyber centres, which mean fast connections and lots of terminals – details are given under destination headings throughout this guidebook. In some regions you will be given a user name and password so you can access the Internet easily at any library in the area (the Highlands for example).

Internet cafés also exist in the cities and larger towns and are generally good value, charging approximately £2 to £5 per hour. Always check the minimum charge though before you settle in – sometimes it's not worth the 10 minutes it takes to check your emails. Keep in mind that many of the larger TICs across the country have Internet access.

LEGAL MATTERS

The 1707 Act of Union preserved the Scottish legal system as separate from the law in England and Wales.

Police have the power to detain anyone suspected of having committed an offence punishable by imprisonment (including drugs offences) for up to six hours. They can search you, take photos and fingerprints, and question you. You are legally required to provide your correct name and address – not doing so, or giving false details, is an offence – but you are not obliged to answer any other questions. After six hours, the police must either formally charge you or let you go. If you are detained and/or arrested, you have the right to inform a solicitor and one other person, though you have no right to actually see the solicitor or to make a telephone call. If you don't know a solicitor, the police will inform the duty solicitor for you.

In the wake of September 11, the UK parliament passed the anti-terrorism crime and security act. It makes it possible for the government to detain foreigners suspected of terrorist activities, without trial. Since the London Underground and bus bombings in July 2005 further laws are being considered.

If you need legal assistance contact the **Scottish Legal Aid Board** (☎ 0131-226 7061; www .slab.org.uk; 44 Drumsheugh Gardens, Edinburgh).

Possession of a small amount of cannabis is an offence punishable by a fine, but possession of a larger amount of cannabis, or any amount of harder drugs, is much more serious, with a sentence of up to 14 years in prison. Police have the right to search anyone they suspect of possessing drugs.

You're allowed to have a maximum blood-alcohol level of 35mg/100mL when driving.

WHEN YOU'RE LEGAL

The following legal minimum ages apply in Scotland:

- Drinking alcohol – 18 years
- Driving – 17 years
- Heterosexual/homosexual sex – 16 years
- Smoking – 16 years
- Marriage – 16 years
- Voting – 18 years

Traffic offences (illegal parking, speeding etc) usually incur a fine for which you're usually allowed 30 to 60 days to pay. In Glasgow and Edinburgh the parking inspectors are numerous and without mercy – NEVER leave your car around the city centres without a valid parking ticket, or you risk a hefty fine – upwards of £30.

MAPS

Most bookshops stock a range of decent road atlases. If you plan to go off the beaten track, you'll need one that shows at least 3 miles to the inch (1.9km to 1cm).

Alternatively, TICs have free maps at a scale of at most 10 miles to one inch (6.4km to 1cm) which are adequate for most purposes. For general touring the clear *Collins Touring Map of Scotland* (£3.99) shows most tourist attractions.

If you're about to tackle Munros you'll require maps with far greater detail than the maps in this guide, or the ones supplied by TICs. Look out for the Collins map of the *Munros* (£4.99). The Ordnance Survey (OS) caters to walkers, with a wide variety of maps at different scales. Alternatively, look out for the excellent walkers' maps published by Harveys; they're at scales of 1:40,000 and 1:25,000.

MONEY

The British currency is the pound sterling (£), with 100 pence (p) to a pound. 'Quid' is the slang term for pound.

Several Scottish banks issue their own banknotes. You shouldn't have trouble changing them in shops etc immediately south of the Scotland–England border, but elsewhere it may be difficult. All UK banks will accept them, but foreign banks will not.

Sterling is a stable currency and was strong against the US dollar and steady against the euro in 2005; there were predictions that the currency would weaken in 2006. Euros are accepted in Scotland only at some major tourist attractions and a few upmarket hotels – it's always better to have sterling cash. For exchange rates see the inside front cover of this book. For information on costs see the Getting Started chapter, p18.

ATMs

Automatic teller machines (ATMs – called cashpoints in Scotland) are widespread and

you'll usually find at least one in small towns and villages. You can use Visa, MasterCard, Amex, Cirrus, Plus and Maestro to withdraw cash from ATMs belonging to most banks and building societies in Scotland.

Cash withdrawals from some ATMs may be subject to a small charge (about £1.50), but most are free.

Cash

Nothing beats cash for convenience – or risk. It's still a good idea, though, to travel with some local currency in cash, if only to tide you over until you get to an exchange facility. There's no problem if you arrive at Edinburgh, Glasgow, Glasgow Prestwick or Aberdeen airports; all have good-value exchange counters open for incoming flights.

Credit Cards

Visa, MasterCard, Amex and Diners Club cards are widely recognised, although some places will charge for accepting them (generally for small transactions). Charge cards such as Amex and Diners Club may not be accepted in small establishments or off the beaten track. Credit and credit/debit cards like Visa and MasterCard are more widely accepted. Combine plastic and travellers cheques so you have something to fall back on if an ATM swallows your card or the local banks don't accept it.

International Transfers

Money sent by telegraphic transfer (usually at a cost of about £15) should reach you within a week; by mail, allow at least two weeks. When it arrives, it'll most likely be converted into local currency. You can also transfer money by either Moneygram or Thomas Cook. US travellers can also use **Western Union** (☎ 0800 833833; www.westernunion.com).

Moneychangers

Be careful using bureaux de change; they may offer good exchange rates but frequently levy outrageous commissions and fees. The bureaus de change at international airports are exceptions to the rule. They charge less than most high-street banks, and cash sterling travellers cheques for free.

US dollars are probably the best currency to carry (especially if you intend further travel outside Europe), although the euro is an attractive alternative.

Travellers Cheques

Amex or Thomas Cook cheques are widely accepted and have efficient replacement policies. Bring pounds sterling to avoid changing currencies twice. In Scotland, travellers cheques are usually only accepted by banks.

Take most cheques in large denominations, say £100; commission is usually charged per cheque.

PHOTOGRAPHY & VIDEO

Both print and slide film are widely available; if there's no specialist photographic shop around, Boots, the chemist chain, is the most likely stockist. The cost for a roll of 36-exposure print film starts from £4, excluding processing; processing print films ranges from £4 to £8.50, depending on how quickly you want it back. A 36-exposure slide film costs from £7.79 (excluding processing) to £10.50 (including processing). A three-pack of 90-minute Digital 8/Hi8 video cassettes costs around £15; a three-pack of 30-minute DV-Mini cassettes costs £9.

Mathers (☎ 01204-522186) offers bulk-buy mail-order film at very good prices. A 10-pack of 24-exposure print film is £11.40, plus £2.95 postage. Most towns have several shops where you can get print films processed in as little as one hour.

With dull, overcast conditions common throughout the whole of Scotland, high-speed film (ISO 200 or ISO 400) is useful. In summer, the best times of day for photography are usually early in the morning and late in the afternoon when the glare of the sun has passed. For expert guidance pick up a copy of Lonely Planet's *Travel Photography*.

Many tourist attractions either charge for taking photos or ban photography altogether. Use of a flash is often forbidden to protect delicate pictures and fabrics. Video cameras are often not allowed because of the inconvenience they can cause to other visitors.

POST

Mail sent within the UK can go either 1st or 2nd class. First-class mail is faster (normally next-day delivery) and more expensive (30/46p for up to 60/100g) than 2nd-class mail (21/35p). An airmail postcard/letter (60g) to European countries costs 42/78p, to South Africa, the USA and Canada 47p/£1.42 and Australia and New Zealand 47p/£1.56. An air-mail letter generally takes five days

to get to the USA or Canada and around a week to Australia or New Zealand.

If you don't have a permanent address, mail can be sent to poste restante in the town or city where you're staying. Amex offices also hold card-holders' mail for free.

SOLO TRAVELLERS

Travelling solo in Scotland is quite easy and relatively common. Note that we do not recommend solo hitching anywhere in Scotland. The biggest nuisance for midrange solo travellers is finding single rooms in B&Bs and guesthouses. Many accommodation owners are reluctant to let a double room (even when it's quiet) to one person without charging a supplement, particularly in the peak season when a solo traveller may be asked to pay double rates. To avoid difficulties, book ahead when you can and seek out places with single rooms. We've made many such recommendations throughout this guide.

The easiest place to meet other people, be it locals or tourists, is in the many pubs around the country. In small towns and villages they're usually the centre of social interaction. Although most Scots are not extroverts, they are generally very friendly and welcoming to foreign visitors (especially after a few beers). For budget travellers, hostels are an excellent way to meet other travellers.

Women travelling by themselves should encounter no extra difficulties, as long as sensible precautions observed in most western countries are adhered to – see Women Travellers, p442, for more information.

TELEPHONE

The famous red telephone boxes are a dying breed now, surviving mainly in conservation areas.

To call Scotland from abroad dial your country's international access code then ☎ 44 (the UK country code), then the area code (dropping the first 0) followed by the telephone number.

You'll mainly see two types of phone booth in Scotland: one takes money (and doesn't give change), while the other uses prepaid phone cards and credit cards. Some phones accept both coins and cards. The minimum charge is 20p.

All phones come with reasonably clear instructions in several languages. British Telecom (BT) offers phonecards for £3, £5, £10 and £20; they're widely available from retailers, including post offices and newsagents.

Some codes worth knowing:
- ☎ 0345 – local call rate
- ☎ 0800 – toll-free call
- ☎ 0845 – local call rate
- ☎ 0870 – national call rate
- ☎ 0891 – premium rate
- ☎ 9064 – premium call rate

International Calls

Dial ☎ 155 for the international operator. To get an international line (for international direct dialling) dial ☎ 00, then the country code, area code (drop the first zero if there is one) and number. Direct dialling is cheaper, but some budget travellers prefer operator-connected reverse-charge (collect) calls.

You can also use the Home Country Direct service to make a reverse-charge or credit-card call via an operator in your home country.

Local & National Calls

Local calls are charged by time; national calls are charged by time and distance. Daytime rates are from 8am to 6pm, Monday to Friday; cheaper rates are from 6pm to 8am Monday to Friday, and the cheap weekend rate is from midnight Friday to midnight Sunday. The last two rates offer substantial savings.

For directory inquiries call ☎ 118500 (free from public telephones but 40p per call from a private phone). To get the operator call ☎ 100. The *Yellow Pages* business directory (with maps) is at www.yell.co.uk.

Mobile Phones

Codes for mobile phones usually begin with ☎ 07. The UK uses the GSM 900/1800 network, which covers the rest of Europe, Australia and New Zealand, but isn't compatible with the North American GSM 1900 (though some North Americans have GSM 1900/900 phones that work in Scotland). If you have a GSM phone, check with your service provider about using it in the UK, and beware of calls being routed internationally (very expensive for a 'local' call). You can rent a mobile phone – ask a TIC for details – or buy a 'pay-as-you-go' phone for as little as £40.

TIME

See the World Time Zones map, p457.

TOURIST INFORMATION

The Scottish Tourist Board, known as **Visit-Scotland** (☎ 0845 2255 121; www.visitscotland.com; Ocean Point One, 94 Ocean Dr, Leith, Edinburgh EH6 6JH), deals with inquiries made by post and telephone only.

Most larger towns have Tourist Information Centres (TICs) that open 9am or 10am to 5pm Monday to Friday, and at weekends in summer. In small places, particularly in the Highlands, TICs only open from Easter to September.

Recently, VisitScotland took control of all TICs throughout Scotland (previously they were independently managed through regional tourist boards). This won't affect visitors dropping in on TICs to pick up local information (the same cheery staff work in them), although note that many now have a central telephone number. This means that like banks and many other large organisations, TICs are now afflicted with that 21st-century disease: if you call a local office you'll be connected to a central call centre instead to deal with your query. An audit of all offices is due to be carried out in 2005/06, which may result in some closures.

USEFUL ORGANISATIONS

Membership of Historic Scotland (HS) and the National Trust for Scotland (NTS) is worth considering, especially if you're going to be in Scotland for a while. Both are non-profit organisations dedicated to the preservation of the environment, and both care for hundreds of spectacular sites. Throughout this guide the abbreviations HS and NTS are used to indicate places which are under the care of these organisations.

Historic Scotland (HS; ☎ 0131 668 8600; www.historic-scotland.gov.uk; Longmore House, Salisbury Pl, Edinburgh EH9 1SH) A year's membership costs from £34/39 for an adult/family, and gives free entry to HS sites (half-price entry to sites in England and Wales). Also offers short-term 'Explorer' membership – three/seven/10 days for £17/23.50/28. Standard HS property opening times are 9.30am to 6.30pm daily April to September, closing two hours earlier October to March. (Note, some properties have extended hours in October.)

National Trust for Scotland (NTS; Map pp72-3; ☎ 0131-243 9300; www.nts.org.uk; 28 Charlotte Sq, Edinburgh EH2 4ET) A year's membership of the NTS, costing £35 (£12 for those aged under 25, £26 for seniors), offers free access to all NTS and National Trust properties (in the rest of the UK).

DIRECTORY

VISAS

Visa regulations are always subject to change so it's essential to check with your local British embassy, high commission or consulate before leaving home. Currently, if you're a citizen of Australia, Canada, New Zealand, South Africa or the USA, you can stay for up to six months (no visa required), but are not allowed to work. The Working Holidaymaker scheme, for Commonwealth citizens aged 17 to 30 inclusive, allows visits of up to two years but arrangements must be made in advance through a British embassy.

Commonwealth citizens with a UK-born parent may be eligible for a Certificate of Entitlement to the Right of Abode, which entitles them to live and work in the UK. Commonwealth citizens with a UK-born grandparent could qualify for a UK Ancestry-Employment Certificate, allowing them to work full time for up to four years in the UK. EU citizens can live and work in Britain free of immigration control and don't need a visa to enter the country.

All other nationalities should contact their nearest British diplomatic mission to obtain a visa. Six month/one year multiple-entry visas cost from £50/85.

British immigration authorities have always been tough; dress neatly and carry proof that you have sufficient funds with which to support yourself. A credit card and/or an onward ticket will help.

No visas are required for Scotland if you arrive from England or Northern Ireland. For more info, see www.ukvisas.gov.uk or the **Lonely Planet** (www.lonelyplanet.com) website.

Visa Extensions

To inquire about extending your stay in the UK, contact the **Home Office, Immigration & Nationality Directorate** (☎ 0870 606 7766; Lunar House, 40 Wellesley Rd, Croydon, London CR9 2BY) *before* your existing permit expires.

WOMEN TRAVELLERS

Women are unlikely to have problems in Scotland, but common-sense caution should be observed, especially in towns and cities. Women can enter most pubs alone, but there are still a few places where this may attract unwanted attention. Cosmopolitan city pubs and most rural pubs are fine – you'll get a pretty good idea when you enter. Sticking to pubs frequented by tourists is a safe bet.

Many parts of central Edinburgh and Glasgow are best avoided late at night. Be aware of red-light districts in both cities – between Salamander St and Leith Links (Leith, Edinburgh) and Anderston/Blythswood Sq (Glasgow).

The National Office of **Rape Crisis** (☎ 0141 552 3200 in Glasgow, ☎ 0131 556 9437 in Edinburgh; www.rapecrisisscotland.org.uk; 1st fl, Central Chambers, 93 Hope Street, Glasgow) has a website with details of local offices around the country.

The contraceptive pill is available only on prescription, however, the 'morning-after' pill (effective against conception for up to 72 hours after unprotected sexual intercourse) is available over-the-counter at chemists.

For general advice on health issues, contraception and pregnancy, visit a Well Woman clinic – ask at local libraries or doctors' surgeries. In Edinburgh, contact **Well Woman Services** (☎ 0131 332 7941; 18 Dean Tce, Stockbridge).

WORK

Whatever your skills, it's worth registering with a number of temporary employment agencies – there are plenty in the cities.

Hostel notice boards sometimes advertise casual work. Without skills, it's difficult to find a job that pays enough to save money. Pick up the free *TNT* (www.tntmagazine.co.uk), found in larger cities – it lists jobs and employment agencies aimed at travellers.

Low-paid seasonal work is available in the tourist industry, usually in restaurants and pubs. This was once the domain of Australian, South African and New Zealand travellers but the recent membership enlargement of the EU has seen many Eastern Europeans also travel to Scotland for these jobs. In particular, you'll probably meet Poles and Slovenians working in pubs, hotels and restaurants in the Highlands.

EU citizens don't need a work permit – see also Visas earlier for details about the Working Holidaymaker scheme for Commonwealth citizens.

Students from the USA who are at least 18 years old and studying full time at a college or university can get a Blue Card permit allowing them to work for six months in the UK. It's available through the **British Universities North America Club** (BUNAC; www.bunac.org.uk). The club also runs programmes for Australians, Canadians and New Zealanders. For more details, check out the website.

Transport

CONTENTS

GETTING THERE & AWAY

AIR

There are direct flights to Scottish airports from England, Wales, Ireland, the USA, Canada, Scandinavia and several countries in western and central Europe. From the rest of the world you'll probably have to fly into a European hub and catch a connecting flight to a Scottish airport – London, Amsterdam, Frankfurt and Paris have the best connections. If flying from North America, it's worth looking at Icelandair, which often has good deals to Glasgow via Reykjavik.

Airports & Airlines

Scotland has four main international airports of its own. London is the main UK gateway for long-haul flights.

Aberdeen (ABZ; ☎ 0870 040 0006; www.aberdeen airport.com)

Edinburgh (EDI; ☎ 0870 040 0007; www.edinburgh airport.com)

Glasgow (GLA; ☎ 0870 040 0008; www.glasgowairport .com)

Glasgow Prestwick (PIK; ☎ 0871 223 0700; www .gpia.co.uk)

London Gatwick (LGW; ☎ 0870 000 2468; www .gatwickairport.com)

London Heathrow (LHR; ☎ 0870 000 0123; www .heathrowairport.com)

A few short international flights land at **Dundee** (DND; ☎ 01382-662200; www.dundeecity.gov.uk /airport), **Inverness** (INV; ☎ 01667-464000; www.hial .co.uk) and **Sumburgh** (LSI; ☎ 01950-461000; www .hial.co.uk).

There are many airlines serving Scottish airports. The main ones:

Aer Lingus (EI; ☎ 0845 973 7747; www.aerlingus.com)

Air France (AF; ☎ 0845 084 5111; www.airfrance.com)

Air Malta (KM; ☎ 0845 607 3710; www.airmalta.com)

Air Scotland (GRE; ☎ 0141-222 2363; www .air-scotland.com)

Air Transat (TS; ☎ 0870 556 1522; www.airtransat.com)

American Airlines (AA; ☎ 0845 778 9789; www.aa.com)

Atlantic Airways (RC; ☎ 0845 758 111; www.atlantic.fo)

bmibaby (WW; ☎ 0870 264 2229; www.bmibaby.com)

Braathens (BU; ☎ 0191-214 0991; www.braathens.no)

British Airways (BA; ☎ 0845 773 3377; www .britishairways.co.uk)

British European (BE; ☎ 0870 567 6676; www .flybe.com)

British Midland (BD; ☎ 0870 607 0555; www .flybmi.com)

Continental Airlines (CO; ☎ 0845 607 6760; www .continental.com)

Czech Airlines (OK; ☎ 0870 444 3747; www.czech airlines.com)

Eastern Airways (T3; ☎ 0870 366 9100; www .easternairways.com)

easyJet (U2; ☎ 0870 600 0000; www.easyjet.com)

Globespan (GSM; ☎ 0870 556 1522; www.flyglobe span.com)

Icelandair (FI; ☎ 0845 758 1111; www.icelandair.com)

KLM UK (UK; ☎ 0870 507 4074; www.klmuk.com)

Lufthansa (LH; ☎ 0845 773 7747; www.lufthansa.com)

Ryanair (FR; ☎ 0870 156 9569; www.ryanair.com)

Scandinavian Airlines (SK; ☎ 0870 60 727 727; www
.scandinavian.net)
ScotAirways (CB; ☎ 0870 606 0707; www.scot
airways.co.uk)
Wideroe (WF; ☎ 01224-795895; www.wideroe.no)
Zoom Airlines (OOM; ☎ 0870 240 0055; www.flyzoom
.com)

Australia & New Zealand

Many airlines compete on flights between
Australia and New Zealand and the UK and
there is a wide range of fares. Round-the-
world (RTW) tickets are often real bargains
and can sometimes work out cheaper than
a straightforward return ticket.

Expect to pay anything from A$2000 to
A$3000. Adding a connecting flight from
London to Edinburgh should only add
around A$100 to the cost of the ticket.

AUSTRALIA
Flight Centre (☎ 131 133; www.flightcentre.com.au)
STA Travel (☎ 1300 733 035; www.statravel.com.au)

NEW ZEALAND
Flight Centre (☎ 0800 243544; www.flightcentre.co.nz)
STA Travel (☎ 0508 782 872; www.statravel.co.nz)

Canada

Zoom Airlines flies direct to Glasgow from
Vancouver and Toronto (up to five a week,
year-round), and from Calgary and Halifax
(once or twice a week, May to October only).
Charter operator Air Transat has one direct
flight a week from Toronto to Edinburgh
(May to October) and Glasgow (April to October), and weekly flights to Glasgow from
Calgary and Vancouver (May to October).

Travel CUTS (☎ 1-866 246 9762; www.travelcuts
.com) is Canada's national student travel
agency and has offices in all major cities.

Continental Europe

Major airlines run several direct flights a day
into Edinburgh from Amsterdam, Brussels,
Frankfurt, Geneva, Hamburg, Madrid, Mos-
cow, Paris, Prague and Rome. Budget airlines
fly directly to Glasgow and/or Edinburgh
from Alicante, Barcelona, Cologne–Bonn,
Fuerteventura, Geneva, Malaga, Milan, Nice,
Oslo, Rome and Zurich.

England & Wales

There are over a hundred flights a day between London and Edinburgh and Glasgow,
and several daily from other UK airports. BA
has flights to Glasgow and Edinburgh from
London, Bristol, Birmingham, Cardiff, Manchester, Plymouth and Southampton, and to
Aberdeen and Inverness from London.

EasyJet flies from London to Edinburgh,
Glasgow, Inverness and Aberdeen. ScotAirways flies from London City to Edinburgh
and Dundee; bmibaby has flights from
East Midlands and Cardiff to Edinburgh
and Glasgow. Eastern Airways flies from
Norwich to Edinburgh, and from various
English airports to Aberdeen and Inverness.
Prices vary a lot. A standard economy return ticket from London to Edinburgh or
Glasgow is around £250, while budget airlines offer flights for as little as £20 one way,
travelling midweek and booking a month or
two in advance.

Dependable UK travel agencies include
STA Travel (☎ 0131-226 7747; www.statravel.co.uk) and
Trailfinders (☎ 0141-353 2224; www.trailfinders.com).

Ireland

BA flies from Belfast and Londonderry to
Glasgow, and from Belfast to Aberdeen and
Edinburgh. EasyJet has direct flights from
Belfast to Glasgow and Edinburgh. There
are daily flights from Dublin to Edinburgh
and Glasgow with Aer Lingus and BA. Ryan-
air flies from Dublin to Glasgow Prestwick,
Edinburgh and Aberdeen. British European
flies from Cork and Shannon airports to
Glasgow and Edinburgh via Birmingham.

The Irish youth and student travel agency
usitNOW (☎ 01-602 1904; www.usitnow.ie) has offices in most major cities in Ireland.

Scandinavia

British Midland and SAS fly from Copen-
hagen to Edinburgh and Glasgow, and Braathens has flights to Aberdeen from Bergen,
Stavanger and Malmo. Ryanair flies from
Oslo and Stockholm to Glasgow Prestwick,
and Wideroe flies Oslo to Sumburgh (summer only) and Bergen to Aberdeen.

Icelandair has daily flights between Reykjavik and Glasgow. Atlantic Airways links
the Faroe Islands to Aberdeen and Glasgow.

USA

Continental flies daily from New York (Newark) to Glasgow and Edinburgh. Flight time
from New York to Glasgow is 7½ hours, and
return fares range from US$440 to US$700.

STA Travel (☎ 800 781 4040; www.statravel.com) has offices in major cities.

LAND
Bus
Buses are usually the cheapest way to get to Scotland from other parts of the UK. The main operators are **National Express** (☎ 0870 580 8080; www.gobycoach.com) and its subsidiary **Scottish Citylink** (☎ 0870 550 5050; www.citylink.co.uk), with regular services from London and other cities in England, Wales and Northern Ireland.

Silver Choice Travel (☎ 0141-333 1400; www.silverchoicetravel.co.uk) operates a daily overnight service from London to Glasgow/Edinburgh, charging from £24 for an Apex (advanced purchase) return. **Megabus** (☎ 0900 160 0900; www.megabus.com) has one-way fares from London to Glasgow from as little as £10. For info on bus passes and discount cards, see p447.

Scottish Citylink runs a daily bus service to Edinburgh from Belfast (£35 return, 7½ hours) and Dublin (£45 return, 10½ hours).

BACKPACKER BUSES
Several companies run hop-on, hop-off bus services between London or Ireland and Scotland, visiting places of interest en route:
Celtic Connection (☎ 0131-225 3330; www.celticconnectiontours.com)
Haggis Backpackers (☎ 0131-557 9393; www.haggisadventures.com)
Wild in Scotland (☎ 0131-478 6500; www.wild-in-scotland.com)

Car & Motorcycle
Drivers of EU-registered vehicles will find bringing a car or motorcycle into Scotland fairly easy. The vehicle must have registration papers and a nationality plate, and you must have insurance. The International Insurance Certificate (Green Card) isn't compulsory, but is excellent proof that you're covered. If driving from mainland Europe via the Channel Tunnel or ferry ports, head for London and follow the M25 orbital road to the M1 motorway, then follow the M1 and M6 north.

Train
Travelling to Scotland by train is usually faster and more comfortable, but more expensive, than the bus. Taking into account check-ins and travel time between city centre and airport, the train is a competitive alternative to air travel on the London to Edinburgh

route. You can get timetable and fares info for all UK trains from the **National Rail Enquiry Service** (☎ 0845 748 4950; www.nationalrail.co.uk).

CONTINENTAL EUROPE
You can travel from Paris or Brussels to London Waterloo on the **Eurostar** (www.eurostar.com; UK ☎ 0870 518 6186; France ☎ 0892 35 35 39), but to reach Scotland you'll have to take the tube from Waterloo to Kings Cross or Euston stations to connect with the Edinburgh or Glasgow train. Total journey time from Paris is about eight hours.

UK
GNER (☎ 0845 722 5225; www.gner.co.uk) operates a fast and frequent rail service between London Kings Cross and Edinburgh (four hours). A standard open return costs around £200 but special offers sometimes have fares as low as £55. The **Virgin Trains** (☎ 0845 722 2333; www.virgintrains.co.uk) service between London Euston and Glasgow is slower at 5½ hours.

First ScotRail (☎ 0845 755 0033; www.firstscotrail.com) runs the Caledonian Sleeper service connecting Edinburgh, Glasgow, Stirling, Perth, Dundee, Aberdeen, Fort William and Inverness with London Euston. A standard sleeper (sharing a twin cabin) from London to Edinburgh is £98 a single and £140 return, and to Inverness, Aberdeen or Fort William is £119 a single, £160 return. Services to Edinburgh from other parts of England and Wales usually mean changing trains at some point. First ScotRail also has Rail & Sail deals between Edinburgh and Glasgow and Belfast via the ferry crossings at Stranraer and Troon.

SEA
Continental Europe
Superfast Ferries (☎ 0870 410 6040; www.superfast.com) runs a car ferry between Rosyth, 12 miles northwest of Edinburgh, and Zeebrugge in Belgium (17½ hours, one daily). Return passenger fares in high season (July and August) range from €170 in an aircraft-style seat to €566 in a luxury cabin. A car is €239 return.

Northern Ireland
Car ferry links between Northern Ireland and Scotland are run by **Stena Line** (☎ 0870 570 7070; www.stenaline.com) and **P&O Irish Sea** (☎ 0870 242 4777; www.poirishsea.com). Stena Line travels the Belfast–Stranraer route and P&O Irish Sea the Larne–Troon and Larne–Cairnryan routes.

There are standard and high-speed ferries on the Stranraer and Cairnryan routes.

The following prices are open return fares for a foot passenger/car with driver, in high season; fares vary with time and day of departure, and are often less than quoted here.

Crossing	Duration	Frequency	Fare (£)
Belfast-Stranraer	3¼hr	2-4 daily	46/230
Belfast-Stranraer	1¾hr	4 daily	46/260
Larne-Cairnryan	1¾hr	8 daily	48/270
Larne-Cairnryan	1hr	2 daily (Mar-Sep)	48/270
Larne-Troon	1¾hr	2 daily (Mar-Sep)	48/270

Scandinavia

From May to early September, **Smyril Line** (☎ 01595-690845; www.smyril-line.com) operates a weekly car ferry between Shetland (Lerwick), the Faroe Islands (Torshavn), Iceland (Seydisfjordur), Norway (Bergen) and Denmark (Hantsholm). It leaves from Lerwick on Monday for Bergen, and on Wednesday for Torshavn and Seydisfjordur. The Lerwick to Bergen crossing takes 13½ hours, Lerwick to Torshavn is 13 hours, and Torshavn to Seydisfjordur is 15 hours.

GETTING AROUND

Public transport is generally good, but it can be costly compared with other European countries. Buses are usually the cheapest way to get around, but also the slowest. With a discount pass, trains can be competitive; they're also quicker and often take you through beautiful scenery.

Traveline (☎ 0870 608 2608; www.travelinescotland .com) provides timetable info for all public transport services in Scotland, but can't provide fare information or book tickets.

AIR

Most domestic air services are geared to business needs, or are lifelines for remote island communities. Flying is a pricey way to cover relatively short distances, and only worth considering if you're short of time and want to visit the Hebrides, Orkney or Shetland.

Airlines in Scotland

British Airways/Loganair (☎ 0870 850 9850; www .loganair.co.uk)
British Midland (☎ 0870 607 0555; www.flybmi.com)

Eastern Airways (☎ 0870 366 9100; www.eastern airways.com)
Highland Airways (☎ 01851-701282; www .highlandairways.co.uk)

British Airways/Loganair is the main domestic airline in Scotland, with flights from Glasgow to Barra, Benbecula, Campbeltown, Inverness, Islay, Kirkwall, Sumburgh, Stornoway and Tiree; from Edinburgh to Inverness, Kirkwall, Sumburgh, Stornoway and Wick; from Aberdeen to Kirkwall and Sumburgh; and from Inverness to Kirkwall, Stornoway and Sumburgh. They also operate interisland flights in Orkney and Shetland, and from Barra to Benbecula.

British Midland flies from Edinburgh to Stornoway, and Eastern Airways from Aberdeen to Wick. Highland Airways has flights from Inverness to Sumburgh and Stornoway, and from Stornoway to Benbecula.

BOAT

The main ferry operators are **Caledonian MacBrayne** (CalMac; ☎ 0870 565 0000; www.calmac.co.uk) for the west coast and islands, and **Northlink Ferries** (☎ 0845 600 0449; www.northlinkferries.co.uk) for Orkney and Shetland. CalMac's Island Rover ticket gives unlimited travel on its ferry services, and is £49/71 for a foot passenger for eight/15 days, plus £234/350 for a car, and £117/175 for a motorbike. Bicycles travel free with a foot passenger's Island Rover ticket. There are also more than two dozen Island Hopscotch tickets, which give lower fares for various combinations of crossings; these are listed on the website and in the CalMac timetables booklet available from Tourist Information Centres (TICs) throughout Scotland. Northlink ferries sail from Aberdeen and Scrabster (near Thurso) to Orkney, from Orkney to Shetland and from Aberdeen to Shetland. See the relevant destinations for full details of ferry services and fares.

BUS

The national network is operated by **Scottish Citylink** (☎ 0870 550 5050; www.citylink.co.uk), with comfy, reliable buses serving all main towns. Off main roads, you'll have to switch to local services. If planning a journey off the main routes, phone **Traveline** (☎ 0870 608 2608; www .travelinescotland.com) for up-to-date timetables.

Many remote villages can only be reached by **Royal Mail postbuses** (☎ 0845 774 0740; www

TRANSPORT

.postbus.royalmail.com). These are minibuses, or sometimes four-seater cars, driven by postal workers delivering and collecting the mail. They follow circuitous routes through some of the loveliest areas of Scotland, and are useful for walkers – there are no official stops, and you can hail a postbus anywhere on its route. Fares are usually £2 to £5 one way.

Haggis Backpackers (☎ 0131-557 9393; www .haggisadventures.com) and **Macbackpackers** (☎ 0131-558 9900; www.macbackpackers.com) offer jump-on, jump-off minibuses, running from Edinburgh to Inverness, Ullapool, Skye, Fort William, Glencoe, Oban and Glasgow. A ticket, valid for up to three months, is about £65.

Bus Passes

The Scottish Citylink Explorer Pass can be bought in the UK by both UK and overseas citizens. It offers unlimited travel on all Scottish Citylink services within Scotland for three consecutive days (£39), for any five days out of 10 (£62), or any eight days out of 16 (£85). It also gives discounts on various regional bus services and on Northlink ferries. It is not valid on National Express coaches.

Scottish Citylink offers discounts to holders of the Euro/26 card, and the **Young Scot card** (☎ 0870 513 4936; www.youngscot.org), which gives discounts all over Scotland and Europe. There are no discount passes for seniors.

CAR & MOTORCYCLE

Travelling by car or motorcycle allows you to get to remote places, and to travel quickly,

independently and flexibly. Unfortunately, the independence you enjoy tends to isolate you, and cars are nearly always inconvenient in city centres. Scotland's roads are generally good and far less busy than in England, so driving is more enjoyable.

Motorways (designated 'M') are toll-free dual carriageways, limited mainly to central Scotland. Main roads ('A') are dual or single carriageways and are sometimes clogged with slow-moving trucks or caravans; the A9 from Perth to Inverness is notoriously busy.

Life on the road is more relaxed and interesting on the secondary roads (designated 'B') and minor roads (undesignated). These wind through the countryside from village to village. You can't travel fast, but you won't want to. In many country areas, and especially in the Highlands and islands, roads are only single track with passing places. Remember that passing places are not only for allowing oncoming traffic to pass, but also for overtaking – check your rear-view mirror often, and pull over to let faster vehicles to pass if necessary. It's illegal to park in passing places. In the Highlands and islands there's the added hazard of suicidal sheep wandering onto the road (be particularly wary of lambs in spring).

At around 90p per litre (equivalent to just over US$6 for a US gallon), petrol is expensive by American or Australian standards, and diesel costs even more. Distances, however, aren't as great. Prices tend to rise as you get further from the main population centres,

ROAD DISTANCES (MILES)

	Aberdeen	Dundee	Edinburgh	Fort William	Glasgow	Inverness	Kyle of Lochalsh	Mallaig	Oban	Scrabster	Stranraer
Dundee	70										
Edinburgh	129	62									
Fort William	165	121	146								
Glasgow	145	84	42	104							
Inverness	105	131	155	66	166						
Kyle of Lochalsh	188	177	206	76	181	82					
Mallaig	189	161	180	44	150	106	34				
Oban	180	118	123	45	94	110	120	85			
Scrabster	218	250	279	185	286	119	214	238	230		
Stranraer	233	171	120	184	80	250	265	232	178	374	
Ullapool	150	189	215	90	225	135	88	166	161	125	158

TRANSPORT

and are more than 10% higher in the Outer Hebrides. In remote areas petrol stations are rare and sometimes closed on Sunday.

Driving Licence

A foreign licence is valid in Britain for up to 12 months from time of entry into the country. If bringing a car from Europe make sure you're adequately insured.

Hire

Car rental is relatively costly and often you'll be better off making arrangements in your home country for a fly/drive deal. The international rental companies charge from around £135 a week for a small car (Ford Fiesta, Peugeot 106); local companies, such as **Arnold Clark** (☎ 0845 607 4500; www.arnoldclarkrental.co.uk), start from £23 a day or £110 a week.

The main international hire companies:

Avis (☎ 0870 606 0100; www.avis.co.uk)

Budget (☎ 0870 153 9170; www.budget.co.uk)

Europcar (☎ 0870 607 5000; www.europcar.co.uk)

Hertz (☎ 0870 844 8844; www.hertz.co.uk)

Thrifty Car Rental (☎ 01494-751600; www.thrifty.co.uk)

TICs have lists of local car-hire companies.

To rent a car, drivers must usually be aged 23 to 65 – outside these limits special conditions or insurance requirements may apply.

If planning to visit the Outer Hebrides, Orkney or Shetland, it'll often prove cheaper to hire a car on the islands, rather than pay to take a rental car across on the ferry.

Road Rules

Anyone using the roads a lot should get the *Highway Code*, which is widely available in bookshops. Vehicles drive on the left-hand side; front-seat belts are compulsory and if belts are fitted in the back seat then they must be worn; the speed limit is 30mph in built-up areas, 60mph on single carriageways and 70mph on dual carriageways; you give way to your right at roundabouts (traffic already on the roundabout has right of way). Motorcyclists must wear helmets.

It is a criminal offence to use a hand-held mobile phone or similar device while driving; this includes while you are stopped at traffic lights, or stuck in traffic, when you can expect to be moving again at any moment.

See also p438 for information on drinking and driving and other legal matters.

HITCHING

Hitching is never entirely safe in any country and we don't recommend it. Travellers who hitch take a small but potentially serious risk. However, many people choose to hitch, and the advice that follows should help to make their journeys as fast and safe as possible.

Hitching is fairly easy in Scotland, except around big cities and built-up areas, where you'll need to use public transport. Although the northwest is more difficult because there's less traffic, waits of over two hours are unusual (except on Sunday in 'Sabbath' areas). On some islands, where public transport is infrequent, hitching is so much a part of getting around that local drivers may stop and offer you lifts without you even asking.

It's against the law to hitch on motorways or their immediate slip roads; make a sign and use approach roads, nearby roundabouts or service stations.

TOURS

There are lots of companies in Scotland offering all kinds of tours, including historical, activity-based and backpacker tours. It's a question of picking the tour that suits your requirements and budget. More companies are listed in destination chapters under Tours.

Heart of Scotland Tours (☎ 558 8855; www.heartofscotlandtours.co.uk) Recommended day-tour operator specialising in central Scotland and the Highlands.

Mountain Innovations (☎ 0845 095 6174; www.scotmountain.co.uk; Fraoch Lodge, Deshar Rd, Boat of Garten PH24 3BN) Good-value activity holidays in the Highlands; walking, mountain biking, kayaking, skiing and horse riding.

Rabbie's Trail Burners (☎ 0131-226 3133; www.rabbies.com; 207 High St, Edinburgh) One- to five-day tours of the Highlands in 16-seat minibuses.

Saltire Tours (☎ 0131-558 7374; www.saltiretours.co.uk; Suite 130, 12 South Bridge, Edinburgh EH1 1DD) Small company providing a wide range of imaginative tours from art and architecture to Sir Walter Scott. The golfing tours take in the lesser-known courses around the country.

Scot-Trek (☎ 0141-334 9232; www.scot-trek.co.uk; 9 Lawrence St, Glasgow G11 5HH) Guided walks for all levels; ideal for solo travellers wanting to link up with others.

TRAIN

Scotland's rail network extends to all major cities and towns, but the railway map has a lot of large, blank areas in the Highlands and the Southern Uplands where you'll need to switch to bus or car. The West Highland line from Glasgow to Fort William and Mallaig, and the Inverness to Kyle of Lochalsh line are two of the world's most scenic journeys.

For info on train timetables call the **National Rail Enquiry Service** (☎ 0845 748 4950; www.national rail.co.uk) or look at www.firstscotrail.com.

Bikes are carried free on all First ScotRail trains, but space is sometimes limited. Reservations are compulsory on certain rail routes, including the Glasgow–Oban–Fort William–Mallaig line and the Inverness–Kyle of Lochalsh line; they are recommended on many others. You can make reservations for your bicycle from eight weeks to two hours in advance at main train stations, or when booking tickets by phone (☎ 0845 755 0033).

There are two classes of train travel: first and standard. First class is 30% to 50% more than standard but, except on very crowded trains, isn't really worth the extra money.

Costs & Reservations

Rail travel is more expensive than the bus: a standard return from Edinburgh to Inverness is about £68 compared with £29 on the bus.

First ScotRail (☎ 0845 755 0033; www.firstscotrail .com) operates most train services in Scotland. Reservations are recommended for intercity trips, especially on Fridays and public holidays; for shorter journeys, just buy a ticket at the station before you go. On certain routes, including the Glasgow–Edinburgh express, and in places where there's no ticket office at the station, you can buy tickets on the train.

Children under five travel free; those five to 15 usually pay half. On weekends on some intercity routes you can upgrade a standard-class ticket to first class for £1.50 per single journey – ask the conductor on the train.

There's a bewildering array of ticket types.

Single Valid for a single (ie one-way) journey at any time on the particular day specified; expensive.

Day Return Valid for a return journey at any time on the particular day specified; relatively expensive.

Cheap Day Return Valid for a return journey on the day specified on the ticket, but there are time restrictions (you're not usually allowed to travel on a train that leaves before 9.15am); relatively cheap.

Open Return For outward travel on a stated day and return on any day within a month.

Apex One of the cheapest return fares; standard class only; reservations compulsory and you must travel on the booked services; must book at least 48 hours in advance, but limited seats so book as soon as possible (up to eight weeks ahead).

SuperSaver The cheapest ticket where advance purchase isn't necessary; can't be used on Friday after 2.30pm, Saturday in July and August or on bank holidays, or on days after these before 2.30pm; the return must be within a calendar month.

Saver Higher priced than the SuperSaver, but can be used any day and there are fewer time restrictions.

SuperAdvance Similarly priced to SuperSaver but with fewer time/day restrictions; however, you must buy tickets before 6pm on the day before travel and specify both outward and return journey times; limited availability so book early.

Discount Cards

Discount **railcards** (www.railcard.co.uk) are available for people 60 and over, for people 16 to 25 (or mature full-time students), and for those with a disability (☎ 0191-218 8103, textphone ☎ 0191-269 0304). The Seniors Railcard (£20), Young Persons Railcard (£20) and Disabled Persons Railcard (£14) are each valid for one year and give one-third off most train fares in Scotland, England and Wales. Fill in an application at any major train station. You'll need proof of age (birth certificate, passport or driving licence) for the Young Persons and Seniors railcards (proof of enrolment for mature-age students), and proof of entitlement for the Disabled Persons Railcard.

Train Passes

First ScotRail has a range of good-value passes for train travel. You can buy them at BritRail outlets in the USA, Canada and Europe, at the British Travel Centre in Regent St, London, at train stations throughout Britain, at certain UK travel agents and from **First ScotRail Telesales** (☎ 0845 755 0033).

The Freedom of Scotland Travelpass gives unlimited travel on all ScotRail and Strathclyde Passenger Transport trains, all CalMac ferry services, and on certain Scottish Citylink coach services (on routes not covered by rail). It's available for four days' travel out of eight (£92) or eight days out of 15 (£124).

The Highland Rover pass gives travel from Glasgow to Oban, Fort William and Mallaig, and from Inverness to Kyle of Lochalsh, Aviemore, Aberdeen and Thurso; it also gives free travel on the Oban/Fort William to Inverness bus, and a discount on ferries to Mull and Skye. It allows four days' travel out of eight (£60). The Central Scotland Rover covers train travel between Glasgow, Edinburgh, North Berwick, Stirling and Fife. It's £30 for three days' travel out of seven.

Note that Travelpass and Rover tickets are not valid for travel on certain (mainly commuter) services before 9.15am weekdays.

TRANSPORT

Health

CONTENTS

BEFORE YOU GO

While Scotland has excellent health care, prevention is the key to staying healthy while travelling in the country. A little planning before departure, particularly for pre-existing illnesses, will save trouble later. Bring medications in their original, clearly labelled containers. A signed, dated letter from your physician describing your medical conditions and medications, including generic names, is also a good idea. If carrying syringes or needles, be sure to have a physician's letter documenting their medical necessity. Carry a spare pair of contact lenses and glasses, and take your optical prescription with you.

INSURANCE

If you're an EU citizen, a European Health Insurance Card (EHIC), available from health centres or, in the UK, post offices, covers you for most medical care. EHIC will not cover you for nonemergencies, or emergency repatriation. Citizens from non-EU countries should find out if there is a reciprocal arrangement for free medical care between their country and the UK. If you do need health insurance, make sure you get a policy that covers you for the worst possible case, such as an accident requiring an emergency flight home. Find out in advance if your insurance plan will make payments directly to providers or reimburse you later for overseas health expenditures.

RECOMMENDED VACCINATIONS

No jabs are required to travel to Scotland. The World Health Organization, however, recommends that all travellers should be covered for diphtheria, tetanus, measles, mumps, rubella, polio and Hepatitis B, regardless of their destination.

IN TRANSIT

DEEP VEIN THROMBOSIS (DVT)

Blood clots may form in the legs during plane flights, chiefly because of prolonged immobility. The longer the flight, the greater the risk. The chief symptom of deep vein thrombosis is swelling or pain in the foot, ankle or calf, usually but not always on just one side. When a blood clot travels to the lungs, it may cause chest pain and difficulty breathing. Travellers with any of these symptoms should immediately seek medical attention.

To prevent the development of DVT on long flights you should walk about the cabin, contract the leg muscles while sitting, drink plenty of fluids and avoid alcohol and tobacco.

JET LAG & MOTION SICKNESS

To avoid jet lag (common when crossing more than five time zones) try drinking plenty of nonalcoholic fluids and eating light meals. Upon arrival, get exposure to natural sunlight and readjust your schedule (for meals, sleep etc) as soon as possible.

Antihistamines such as dimenhydrinate (Dramamine) and meclizine (Antivert, Bonine) are usually the first choice for treating motion sickness. A herbal alternative is ginger.

IN SCOTLAND

AVAILABILITY & COST OF HEALTH CARE

Excellent health care is readily available and for minor self-limiting illnesses pharmacists can give valuable advice and sell over-the-counter medication. They can also advise when more specialised help is required and point you in the right direction.

TRAVELLER'S DIARRHOEA

If you develop diarrhoea, be sure to drink plenty of fluids, preferably in the form of an oral rehydration solution such as dioralyte. If diarrhoea is bloody, persists for more than 72 hours or is accompanied by fever, shaking, chills or severe abdominal pain you should seek medical attention.

ENVIRONMENTAL HAZARDS

Midges and clegs can be annoying problems in the Scottish Highlands and islands; see p434.

Heat Illness

Heat exhaustion (yes, it can happen in Scotland!) occurs following excessive fluid loss with inadequate replacement of fluids and salt. Symptoms to look out for include headache, dizziness and tiredness. Dehydration is already happening by the time you actually feel thirsty – aim to drink sufficient water to produce pale, diluted urine. To treat heat exhaustion drink water and/or fruit juice, and cool the body with cold water and fans.

Cold Illness

Hypothermia occurs when the body loses heat faster than it can produce it. As ever, proper preparation will reduce the risks of getting it. Even on a hot day in the mountains, the weather can change rapidly, so carry waterproof garments, warm layers and a hat and inform others of your route.

Hypothermia starts with shivering, loss of judgment and clumsiness. Unless rewarming occurs, the sufferer deteriorates into apathy, confusion and coma. Prevent further heat loss by seeking shelter, warm dry clothing, hot sweet drinks and shared bodily warmth.

TRAVELLING WITH CHILDREN

Make sure the children are up to date with routine vaccinations, and discuss possible travel vaccines well before departure as some vaccines are not suitable for children under a year. See also Lonely Planet's *Travelling with Children* by Cathy Lanigan.

HEALTH

Language

CONTENTS

Scottish Gaelic (*Gàidhlig* – pronounced *gallic* in Scotland) is spoken by about 80,000 people in Scotland, mainly in the Highlands and islands, and by many native speakers and learners overseas. It is a member of the Celtic branch of the Indo-European family of languages, which has given us Gaelic, Irish, Manx, Welsh, Cornish and Breton.

Although Scottish Gaelic is the Celtic language most closely associated with Scotland it was quite a latecomer to those shores. Other Celtic languages in the form of Pictish and Brittonic had existed prior to the arrival and settlement by Gaelic-speaking Celts (Gaels) from Ireland from the 4th to the 6th centuries AD. These Irish settlers, known to the Romans as Scotti, were eventually to give their name to the entire country. Initially they settled in the area on the west coast of Scotland in which their name is perpetuated, Earra Ghaidheal (Argyll). As their territorial influence extended so did their language, and from the 9th to the 11th centuries Gaelic was spoken throughout the country. For many centuries the language was the same as the language of Ireland; there is little evidence of much divergence before the 13th century. Even up to the 18th century the bards adhered to the strict literary standards of Old Irish.

The Viking invasions from AD 800 brought linguistic influences which are evident in many of the coastal place names of the Highlands.

Gaelic culture flourished in the Highlands until the 18th century and the Jacobite rebellions. After the Battle of Culloden in 1746 many Gaelic speakers were forced from their ancestral lands; this 'ethnic cleansing' by landlords and governments culminated in the Highland Clearances of the 19th century. Although still studied at academic level, the spoken language declined, being regarded as a mere 'peasant' language of no modern significance.

It was only in the 1970s that Gaelic began to make a comeback with a new generation of young enthusiasts who were determined that it should not be allowed to die. People from all over Scotland, and indeed worldwide, are beginning to appreciate their Gaelic heritage.

After two centuries of decline, the language is now being encouraged through financial help from government agencies and the EU. Gaelic education is flourishing from playgroups to tertiary levels. This renaissance flows out into the field of music, literature, cultural events and broadcasting.

The Gaelic language has a vital role to play in the life of modern Scotland.

MAKING CONVERSATION

Good morning.
   Madainn mhath.   madding va
Good afternoon/Good evening.
   Feasgar math.   fesskurr ma
Good night.
   Oidhche mhath.   uh eech uh va
How are you?
   Ciamar a tha thu?   kimmer uh ha oo?
Very well, thank you.
   Glè mhath, tapadh leat.   gley va, tappuh let
I'm well, thank you.
   Tha mi gu math,   ha mee goo ma,
   tapadh leat.   tappuh let
That's good.
   'S math sin.   sma shin
Please.
   Mas e do thoil e.   mahs eh doh hawl eh
Thank you.
   Tapadh leat.   tappuh let
Many thanks.
   Mòran taing.   moe ran ta eeng
You're welcome.
   'Se do bheatha.   sheh doh veh huh
I beg your pardon.
   B'àill leibh.   baaluv
Excuse me.
   Gabh mo leisgeul.   gav mo lishk yal
I'm sorry.
   Tha mi duilich.   ha mee dooleech
Do you speak (have) Gaelic?
   A bheil Gàidhlig agad?   uh vil ga lick ackut?

Yes, a little.
Tha, beagan.   ha, beg an
Not much.
Chan eil mòran.   chan yil moe ran
What's your name?
De an t ainm a tha ort?   jae an tannam uh ha orsht?
I'm ...
Is mise ...   is meeshuh ...
Good health/Cheers!
Slàinte mhath!   slahntchuh va!
Goodbye. (lit: Blessings go with you)
Beannachd leat.   b yan achd let
Goodbye. (The same with you)
Mar sin leat.   mar shin let

FOOD & DRINK
I'm hungry.
Tha an t-acras orm.   ha an tac russ orrom
I'm thirsty.
Tha am pathadh orm.   ha am pah ugh orrom
I'd like ...
Bu toigh leam ...   boo tawl lehum
I don't like ...
Cha toigh leam ...   chah tawl lehum
That was good.
Bha siud math.   va shood ma
Very good.
Glè mhath.   gley va

a biscuit	*brioscaid*	briskatch
bread	*aran*	aran
broth/soup	*brot*	broht
butter	*ìm*	eem
cheese	*càise*	kashuh
cream	*bàrr*	baahrr
dessert	*mìlsean*	meehlshuhn
fish	*iasg*	eeusk
meat	*feòil*	fehyawl
oatcakes	*aran coirce*	aran korkuh
peas	*peasair*	pessir
porridge	*lee lite*	chuh
potatoes	*buntàta*	boontahtuh
salmon	*bradan*	brahdan
vegetables	*glasraich*	glasreech

a cup of coffee	*cupa cofaidh*	coopa cawfee
a cup of tea	*cupa tì*	coopa tee
black coffee	*cofaidh dubh*	cawfee dooh
black tea	*tì dhubh*	tee dhooh
with milk	*le bainne*	leh bahnyuh
with sugar	*leh le siùcar*	shooh car
a glass of water	*glainne uisge*	glahnyuh ooshkuy
a glass of wine	*glainne fìon*	glahnyuh feeuhn
beer	*leann*	lyawn
red wine	*fìon dearg*	feeuhn jerrack
white wine	*fìon geal*	feeuhn gyahl
whisky	*uisge beatha*	ooshkuy beh huh

Glossary

bag – reach the top of (as in to 'bag a couple of peaks' or 'Munro bagging')

bailey – the space enclosed by castle walls

bairn – child

ben – mountain

birlinn – Hebridean galley

blackhouse – low-walled stone cottage with thatch or turf roof and earth floors; shared by both humans and cattle and typical of the Outer Hebrides until the early 20th century

böd – once a simple trading booth used by fishing communities, today it refers to basic accommodation for walkers etc

bothy – hut or mountain shelter

brae – hill

broch – defensive tower

burgh – town

burn – stream

buttie – sandwich

cairn – pile of stones to mark path or junction, also peak

camanachd – Gaelic for *shinty*

ceilidh – pronounced *kay*-lay; evening of traditional Scottish entertainment including music, song and dance

Celtic High Cross – a large, elaborately carved stone cross decorated with biblical scenes and Celtic interlace designs dating from the 8th to 10th centuries

chippy – fish and chip shop

close – entrance to an alley

corrie – circular hollow on a hill-side

craig – exposed rock

Cullen skink – soup made with smoked haddock, potato, onion and milk

dene – valley

dirk – dagger

doocot – dovecote

dun – fort

firth – estuary

glen – valley

gloup – natural arch

Hogmanay – New Year's Eve

howff – pub or shelter

HS – Historic Scotland

kirk – church

kyle – narrow strait of water

laird – estate owner

land – tenement

law – round hill

linn – waterfall

lochan – small loch

machair – grass-and wildflower-covered dunes

makar – maker of verses

Mercat Cross – a symbol of the trading rights of a market town or village, usually found in the centre of town and usually a focal point for the community

motte – early Norman fortification consisting of a raised, flattened mound with a keep on top; when attached to a *bailey* it is known as a motte-and-bailey

Munro – mountain of 3000ft (914m) or higher

Munro bagger – a hill walker who tries to climb all the Munros in Scotland

ness – headland

neuk – corner

NNR – National Nature Reserve, managed by the SNH

NTS – National Trust for Scotland

nyvaig – Hebridean galley

OS – Ordnance Survey

pap – breast-shaped hill

pend – arched gateway

Picts – early inhabitants of north and east Scotland (from Latin *pictus*, or 'painted', after their body paint decorations)

provost – mayor

rhinn or **rhin** – headland

RIB – rigid inflatable boat

rood – an old Scots word for a cross

RSPB – Royal Society for the Protection of Birds

Sassenach – from Gaelic *Sassannach*, meaning anyone who is not a Highlander (including Lowland Scots)

sett – tartan pattern, or cobblestone

shinty – fast and physical ball-and-stick sport similar to Ireland's hurling

SMC – Scottish Mountaineering Club

SNH – Scottish Natural Heritage, a government organisation directly responsible for safeguarding and improving Scotland's natural heritage

sporran – purse worn around waist with the kilt

SSSI – Site of Special Scientific Interest

strath – valley

SYHA – Scottish Youth Hostel Association

TIC – Tourist Information Centre

tor – bare, rocky hill, or outcrop of granite

wynd – lane

Behind the Scenes

THIS BOOK

This is the 4th edition of Lonely Planet's *Scotland*. The 1st edition was written by Tom Smallman and Graeme Cornwallis. Neil Wilson coordinated the 2nd edition, with contributions from Graeme, and the 3rd edition, with fellow author Alan Murphy. Neil and Alan updated this edition. This guidebook was commissioned in Lonely Planet's London office and produced by the following:

Commissioning Editors Sam Trafford, Amanda Canning
Coordinating Editor Sasha Baskett
Coordinating Cartographer Kusnandar
Coordinating Layout Designer Jessica Rose
Assisting Layout Designers Jacqui Saunders, Pablo Gastar, Wibowo Rusli, Laura Jane, Michael Ruff
Managing Cartographer Mark Griffiths
Assisting Editors Joanne Newell, Kristin Odijk, Monique Choy, Sarah Bailey, Helen Koehne
Project Managers Charles Rawlings-Way, Sarah Sloane, Nancy Ianni
Language Content Coordinator Quentin Frayne

Thanks to Simon Tillema, Bruce Evans, Sally Darmody, Adriana Mammarella

THANKS
Neil Wilson

Many thanks to all the helpful and enthusiastic staff at TICs throughout the country, and to the many travellers I met on the road who chipped in with advice and recommendations. Thanks also to Carol Downie for keeping me company in restaurants and for providing ad-

vice on shopping (never my strong point), and to Carolyn Macdonald for some useful tips about Campbeltown restaurants. Finally, thanks to coauthor Alan – lovely stuff, that Clynelish – and to the ever-helpful and patient editors and cartographers at Lonely Planet. *Slainte!*

Alan Murphy

Every trip to Scotland is a treat for me as I not only get to travel around one of the best countries in the world, but also get to catch up with some of my best friends in the world. The support of my family and friends was as usual rock solid, and the cornerstone of this project. I'd like to give special mention to Ben and Matthew, my two gorgeous nephews in Melbourne whose addition to my family has been a gift. In Edinburgh thanks to Bryan McRitchie foremost a friend, but also musician and writer of the *Scotland's Live-Music Capital* piece, which added significantly to the Glasgow chapter. Still in Edinburgh, thanks to journalist Nial Briggs for research tips on Scotland, pints in the Cumberland Bar and curries in Kebab Mahal – usually in that order. Those two people also helped with invaluable telephone research on the ground after my departure. Tourist Information Centres around the country were, as usual, a welcoming fountain of information, particularly the friendly gang in Dunkeld (consistently one of my favourite in the country), St Andrews, Glasgow, Aberfeldy, Lerwick and Jedburgh. The special thing about travelling around Scotland really is its people – and once again my appreciation for their friendly patter and hospitality. I'd also like to thank my publishing girls in the Lonely Planet UK office for putting up with me in 2004 and in particular Sam Trafford who commissioned me for this title. Lastly, thanks to my coauthor Neil who is himself a great resource on Scotland – I couldn't wish for a better coauthor and after this trip I'm far more knowledgeable about *Sandy Bells* and single malts. Hopefully, I'll see you for the next edition…

OUR READERS

Many thanks to the hundreds of travellers who used the last edition and wrote to us with helpful hints, useful advice and interesting anecdotes:

A Dorothee Ackermann, Lindsay Amey **B** Peter Barr, Leigh Baumann, Tobias Bege, Stuart Bell, Mary Bickmore, Danie Blais, Sharon Brotherhood, Andrew Brown, Jerome Brown, Julian Bryers, Nikki Buran **C** Alan Cameron, Francesco Cavalli, Christine Centmayer, Pam Chamberlain, S Connuck, Mike Crook, Rebecca Cutri-Kohart **D** Nicole Delong, Nick Domke, Gina Doubleday, Y Dudinski, Julie Dyer **E** Sally Edwards, Hanne Espolin Johnson **F** Gunda Feddersen, Dana Foster **G** Andy Gabe, Chiara Gallanti, Fiona Grant, George Gray, Kate Green **H** Ian Harrison, Allan Henderson, Marieke Hohnen, Mark Holmes, Leon Hoogsteen, Lana Horn, Margaret Horton, Maggie Huber, Carol Hutton **J** Sarah Jameson, Mark Jenkins, Linda Johnston, Muijel Juittio, Debbie Junk **K** Jordan Karol, Mary Koster, Ivana Kotalova **L** Elsa Lafferty, June Lashmar, Peter Lemtis, Simon Lock, Steve Loughlin, Mandy Loutrel, Colin Love, Daniela & Andrea Lussana, Ian Lynch **M** Rosie Macdonald, Kristina Macku, Eirini Maltezou, Kristin Maltman, Paul Mandigers, Ianthe Mantingh, Brent Marshall, Renee Mason, Marie Mattsson, Jamie McBride, Ian McCay, Harry Mcdonald, Murray Mcgibbon, Than McIntosh, Frazer Mclachlan, Catherine Mclean, Leslie McMichael, Andrew & Chris Mcpheason, Langdon Miller, Brenda Miskie, Elisabeth Mitter, Sheila Moore **N** Eran Nachlieli, Stasia Napierska, Voury Nelly, Haydee Notholt Borel, Jan Nunnink **P** Dan Perkins, Sharon Perry, Tomaz Pintar, William Ponissi, Johanna Puesche, Balazs Pula **R** Stewart Reddaway, Elizabeth Reid, Craig Richmond, Valentina Riva, Duncan Robertson, Rebecca Ross **S** Chris Schenk, Andreas Schwarz, Gerhard Schweng, Millicent Scott, Rachel Sides, Elizabeth Silva, Uta Simon, Kathie Simpson, Timothy So, Mary Stacey, Stefano Stefanucci, Paul Stephenson, Ann-Marie Sullivan, Douglas Suter, Thor & Mary Swope **T** Sandra Tegtmeier, Francoise Trine **V** Juha Valimaki **W** Natali Wall, Heather Walsh, Alan & Liz Walter, JanWatten, Joshua Welbaum, Jane Wenman, Jamie Westcott, John & Deborah Wheaton, Steve White, Kathy Wilhelm, Chris Wood, Laura Wood, David Woodhouse **Y** Andrew Young, Jennifer Young **Z** Susan Zimmerman

ACKNOWLEDGMENTS

Many thanks to the following for the use of their content: Globe on back cover © Mountain High Maps 1993 Digital Wisdom, Inc.

Index

INDEX

000 Map pages
000 Photograph pages

INDEX

000 Map pages
000 Photograph pages

INDEX

INDEX

MAP LEGEND
ROUTES

Tollway	One-Way Street
Motorway	Street Mall/Steps
Primary Road	Tunnel
Secondary Road	Walking Tour
Tertiary Road	Walking Tour Detour
Lane	Walking Trail
Under Construction	Walking Path
Track	Pedestrian Overpass
Unsealed Road	

TRANSPORT

Ferry	Rail
Metro	Rail (Underground)
Bus Route	Tram

HYDROGRAPHY

River, Creek	Canal
Intermittent River	Water

BOUNDARIES

International	Regional, Suburb
State, Provincial	Ancient Wall
Marine Park	Cliff

AREA FEATURES

Airport	Land
Area of Interest	Mall
Beach, Desert	Market
Building	Park
Campus	Reservation
Cemetery, Christian	Rocks
Cemetery, Other	Sports
Forest	Urban

POPULATION

◎ CAPITAL (NATIONAL)	⦿ CAPITAL (STATE)
● Large City	◎ Medium City
● Small City	○ Town, Village

SYMBOLS

Sights/Activities
- Beach
- Castle, Fortress
- Christian
- Diving, Snorkelling
- Monument
- Museum, Gallery
- Point of Interest
- Pool
- Ruin
- Skiing
- Zoo, Bird Sanctuary

Eating
- Eating

Drinking
- Drinking
- Café

Entertainment
- Entertainment

Shopping
- Shopping

Sleeping
- Sleeping
- Camping

Transport
- Airport, Airfield
- Border Crossing
- Bus Station
- Cycling, Bicycle Path
- General Transport
- Parking Area
- Petrol Station
- Taxi Rank

Information
- Bank, ATM
- Embassy/Consulate
- Hospital, Medical
- Information
- Internet Facilities
- Police Station
- Post Office, GPO
- Telephone
- Toilets

Geographic
- Lighthouse
- Lookout
- Mountain, Volcano
- National Park
- Pass, Canyon
- River Flow

LONELY PLANET OFFICES

Australia
Head Office
Locked Bag 1, Footscray, Victoria 3011
☎ 03 8379 8000, fax 03 8379 8111
talk2us@lonelyplanet.com.au

USA
150 Linden St, Oakland, CA 94607
☎ 510 893 8555, toll free 800 275 8555
fax 510 893 8572
info@lonelyplanet.com

UK
72–82 Rosebery Ave,
Clerkenwell, London EC1R 4RW
☎ 020 7841 9000, fax 020 7841 9001
go@lonelyplanet.co.uk

Published by Lonely Planet Publications Pty Ltd
ABN 36 005 607 983

© Lonely Planet Publications Pty Ltd 2006

© photographers as indicated 2006

Cover photographs by Lonely Planet Images: Climber atop Summit Tor, Beinn Mheadhoin in the Cairngorms, Graeme Cornwallis (front); Bar at Beluga, Jonathan Smith (back). Many of the images in this guide are available for licensing from Lonely Planet Images: www.lonelyplanetimages.com.

Printed through Colorcraft Ltd, Hong Kong.
Printed in China